MW00580738

Program Authors

Dr. Douglas Fisher
San Diego State University
San Diego, California

Dr. Jan Hasbrouck
Educational Consultant and Researcher
J.H. Consulting
Vancouver, Washington
Gibson Hasbrouck and Associates
Wellesley, Massachusetts

Dr. Timothy Shanahan
University of Illinois at Chicago
Chicago, Illinois

Mc
Graw
Hill
Education

Bothell, WA • Chicago, IL • Columbus, OH • New York, NY

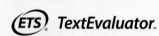

ETS *TextEvaluator*

ETS and the ETS logo are registered trademarks of Educational
Testing Service (ETS). TextEvaluator is a trademark of
Educational Testing Service.

Cover and Title Pages: Nathan Love

www.mheonline.com/readingwonderworks

Send all inquiries to:
McGraw-Hill Education
Two Penn Plaza
New York, New York 10121

ISBN: 978-0-02-129885-3
MHID: 0-02-129885-8

Printed in the United States of America.

1 2 3 4 5 6 7 8 9 RMN 18 17 16 15 14 13   A

Program Authors

Dr. Douglas Fisher

San Diego State University

Co-Director, Center for the Advancement of Reading, California State University

Author of *Language Arts Workshop: Purposeful Reading and Writing Instruction* and *Reading for Information in Elementary School*

Dr. Jan Hasbrouck

J. H. Consulting

Gibson Hasbrouck and Associates

Developed Oral Reading Fluency Norms for Grades 1–8

Author of *The Reading Coach: A How-to Manual for Success* and *Educators as Physicians: Using RTI Assessments for Effective Decision-Making*

Dr. Timothy Shanahan

University of Illinois at Chicago

Professor, Urban Education

Director, UIC Center for Literacy Chair, Department of Curriculum & Instruction

Member, English Language Arts Work Team and Writer of the Common Core State Standards

President, International Reading Association, 2006

Program Reviewers

Kelly Aeppli-Campbell

Escambia County School District
Pensacola, FL

Whitney Augustine

Brevard Public Schools
Melbourne, FL

Shanalee Cannon

Southern Nevada Regional
Professional Development
Program
Las Vegas, NV

Fran Clay

Howard County School District
Ellicott City, MD

Fran Gregory

Metro Nashville Public Schools
Nashville, TN

Elaine M. Grohol, NBCT, Ed.S.

Osceola County School District
Kissimmee, Florida

Randall B. Kincaid

Sevier County Schools
Sevierville, TN

Angela Reese

Bay District Schools
Panama City, FL

Program Components

Interactive Worktext

Apprentice Leveled Readers

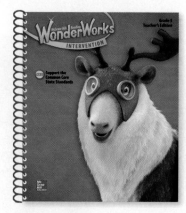
Teacher's Edition

Assessment

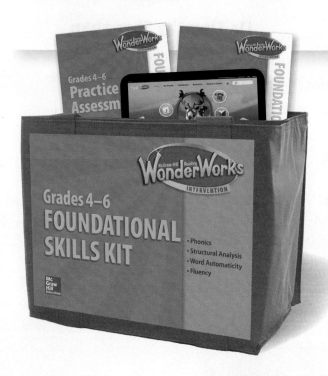

Foundational Skills Kit

Go Digital

For the Teacher

For the Students

 Plan
Customizable Lesson Plans

 Manage and Assign
Student Grouping and Assignments

 Professional Development
Lesson and CCSS Videos

 My To Do List
Assignments Assessments

 Words to Know
Build Vocabulary

 Teach
Instructional Lessons

 Assess
Online Assessments Reports and Scoring

Additional Online Resources
Graphic Organizers

 **Read**
e Books Interactive Texts

 PowerPAL for Reading
Adaptive Learning System

www.connected.mcgraw-hill.com

How *WonderWorks* Supports *Wonders*

Scaffolded Support	Core Grade-Level Instruction

Teach and Model

Interactive Worktext

- Write-in worktext
- Same weekly content and vocabulary as *Reading Wonders*
- Interactive activities to help students develop close reading skills

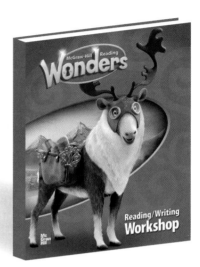

Interactive Worktext

Reading/Writing Workshop

Practice and Apply

Apprentice Leveled Reader

- Same weekly content and vocabulary as *Reading Wonders*
- Two selections in each reader that allow students to apply close reading skills
- Acceleration plan that allows students to level up to the leveled readers in *Reading Wonders*

On Level

Apprentice Level

Approaching Level

Teaching with *WonderWorks*

TEACH AND MODEL

Scaffold Weekly Concept
Grade-Appropriate Topics, including Science and Social Studies

Close Reading
Scaffolded Complex Texts

Respond to Reading

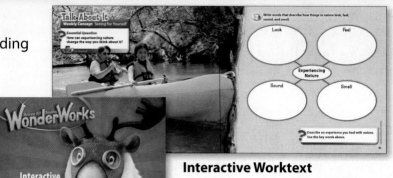

Interactive Worktext

- **Visual Vocabulary Cards**
- **Interactive Graphic Organizers**
- **Interactive Minilessons**
- **e Books**

PRACTICE AND APPLY

Close Reading
Scaffolded Complex Texts

Respond to Reading

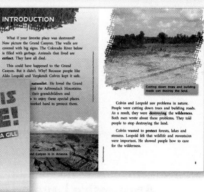

Apprentice Leveled Readers

- **Interactive Graphic Organizers**
- **Interactive Minilessons**
- **e Books**

WRITE AND ASSESS

Review and Reteach
Vocabulary
Comprehension Skills

Write About Reading
Scaffolded Analytical Writing

Assess
Weekly Assessment

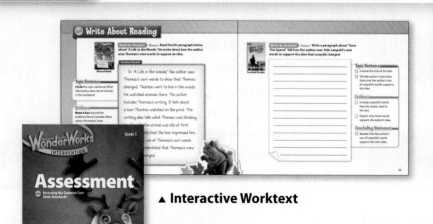

▲ **Interactive Worktext**

◄ **Assessment**

- **e Books**
- **Online Assessment and Reports**

DIFFERENTIATE Foundational Skills

Foundational Skills Kit

- Flexible, explicit instruction for the following strands:
  - Phonics
  - Structural Analysis
  - Word Recognition
  - Fluency
- Ample practice for achieving accuracy and fluency
- Assessment to monitor progress and mastery

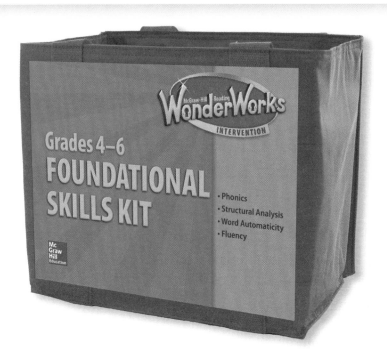

Foundational Skills Lesson Cards

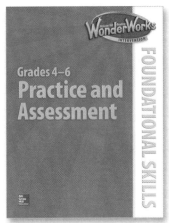

Foundational Skills Practice and Assessment

PowerPAL for Reading Adaptive Learning System

Digital Support
- e Books
- Online Assessments and Reporting

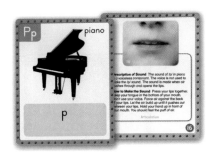

Sound-Spelling Cards

Sound-Spelling WorkBoards

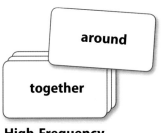

High-Frequency Word Cards

Letter and Word-Building Cards

Assessment in *WonderWorks*

Placement and Diagnostic Assessment

Includes diagnostic assessments for

- Phonics
- Fluency
- Reading Comprehension

Recommendations for placement into
Reading WonderWorks

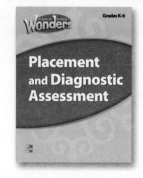

**Wonders
Placement and
Diagnostic Assessment**

Quick Checks

Informal teacher observations based on student
practice within daily lessons

✓ *Quick Check* Can students understand the weekly
vocabulary in context? If not, review vocabulary
using the **Visual Vocabulary Cards** before teaching
Lesson 2.

Weekly Assessment

- Assesses comprehension and vocabulary
- Focused on finding and citing text evidence
- Includes written short responses
- One text per test
- 50% Literature and 50% Informational Text

**WonderWorks
Assessment**

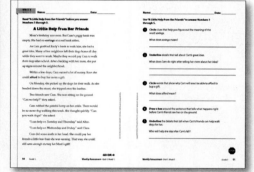

Mid-Unit Assessment

- Assesses text-dependent comprehension
  and vocabulary
- Includes two texts per test with text-dependent
  questions
- 50% Literature and 50% Informational Text

**WonderWorks
Assessment**

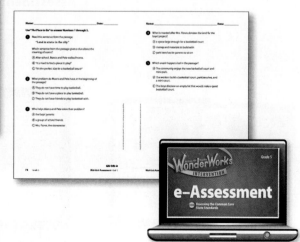

Unit Assessment

Every 6 weeks

- Assesses text-dependent comprehension and vocabulary
- Includes two texts per test with text-dependent questions
- 50% Literature and 50% Informational Text

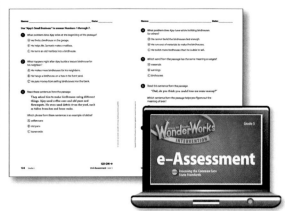

**WonderWorks
Assessment**

Foundational Skills Assessment

Every 6 weeks

- Phonics and Structural Analysis Survey
- Oral Reading Fluency Assessment

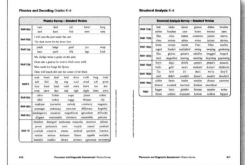

**WonderWorks
Foundational Skills
Practice and Assessment**

Exit Test

- Assesses text-dependent comprehension and vocabulary
- Includes two texts per test with text-dependent questions
- 50% Literature and 50% Informational Text

Exiting Out of *WonderWorks*

Students who score 85% or higher on the *Reading WonderWorks* Unit Assessment participate in "Level Up" instruction during Week 6 of the unit and take the Exit Test.

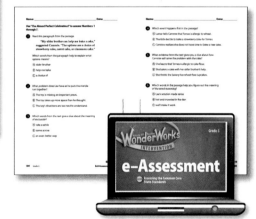

**WonderWorks
Assessment**

If students

- score 85% or higher on the *Reading WonderWorks* Exit Test
- achieve Fluency Assessment goals for the unit
- successfully apply close reading skills with the Approaching Leveled Reader
- score mostly 4–5 on the Level Up Write About Reading prompt
- reach grade-level benchmarks in the Foundational Skills Assessments and *PowerPAL for Reading*

Then consider moving students out of *Reading WonderWorks.*

Contents

Unit 1

Unit 2

Unit 3

(t) Maryn Roos; (b) Stockbyte/Getty Images

Unit 4

(t) Jimmy Holder; (b) Elizabeth Buttler

Unit 5

Unit 6

UNIT 1 PLANNER

EUREKA! I've Got It!

Week 1 Meeting a Need	Week 2 Trial and Error	Week 3 Seeing for Yourself

Week 1 — Meeting a Need

ESSENTIAL QUESTION
How do we get the things we need?

Build Background

CCSS Vocabulary
L.5.4a afford, loan, profit, prosper, risk, savings, scarce, wages

Access Complex Text A C T
Connection of Ideas

CCSS Comprehension
RL.3.3 Skill: Character, Setting, Plot: Sequence
Respond to Reading

CCSS Write About Reading *Analytical Writing*
W.5.9a Inform/Explain: Illustrations

Week 2 — Trial and Error

ESSENTIAL QUESTION
What can lead us to rethink an idea?

Build Background

CCSS Vocabulary
L.5.4a accomplish, anxious, assemble, decipher, distracted, navigate, options, retrace

Access Complex Text A C T
Organization

CCSS Comprehension
RL.4.3 Skill: Character, Setting, Plot: Problem and Solution
Respond to Reading

CCSS Write About Reading *Analytical Writing*
W.5.9a Opinion: Genre

Week 3 — Seeing for Yourself

ESSENTIAL QUESTION
How can experiencing nature change the way you think about it?

Build Background

CCSS Vocabulary
L.5.4a debris, emphasis, encounter, generations, indicated, naturalist, sheer, spectacular

Access Complex Text A C T
Sentence Structure

CCSS Comprehension
RI.5.3 Skill: Text Structure: Cause and Effect
Respond to Reading

CCSS Write About Reading *Analytical Writing*
W.5.9b Inform/Explain: Genre

A S S E S S M E N T

Week 1
✓ *Quick Check*
Vocabulary, Comprehension

✓ **Weekly Assessment**
Assessment Book, pp. 10–11

Week 2
✓ *Quick Check*
Vocabulary, Comprehension

✓ **Weekly Assessment**
Assessment Book, pp. 12–13

Week 3
✓ *Quick Check*
Vocabulary, Comprehension

✓ **Weekly Assessment**
Assessment Book, pp. 14–15

✓ **MID-UNIT ASSESSMENT**
Assessment Book, pp. 72–79

✓ **Fluency Assessment**
Assessment Book, pp. 234–249

Use the Foundational Skills Kit for explicit instruction of phonics, structural analysis, fluency, and word recognition. Includes *PowerPAL for Reading* adaptive learning system.

Week 4 Inventions	Week 5 New Technology	Week 6 ASSESS

<table>
<tr><td>

ESSENTIAL QUESTION
How does technology lead to creative ideas?

Build Background

(ccss) **Vocabulary**
L.5.4a *breakthrough, captivated, claimed, devices, enthusiastically, envisioned, passionate, patents*

Access Complex Text (A)(C)(T)
Connection of Ideas

(ccss) **Comprehension**
RI.5.5 Skill: Text Structure: Sequence
Respond to Reading

(ccss) **Write About Reading**
W.5.9b Inform/Explain: Genre

</td><td>

ESSENTIAL QUESTION
What are the positive and negative effects of new technology?

Build Background

(ccss) **Vocabulary**
L.5.4a *access, advance, analysis, cite, counterpoint, data, drawbacks, reasoning*

Access Complex Text (A)(C)(T)
Connection of Ideas

(ccss) **Comprehension**
RI.5.8
RI.6.6 Skill: Author's Point of View
Respond to Reading

(ccss) **Write About Reading**
W.5.9b Opinion: Point of View

</td><td>

RETEACH   **LEVEL UP**

Reteach
Comprehension Skills

Vocabulary

Write About Reading

Level Up
Read Approaching Leveled Reader

Write About Reading:
Compare Texts

</td></tr>
</table>

A S S E S S M E N T

<table>
<tr><td>

✓ *Quick Check*
Vocabulary, Comprehension

✓ **Weekly Assessment**
Assessment Book, pp. 16–17

</td><td>

✓ *Quick Check*
Vocabulary, Comprehension

✓ **Weekly Assessment**
Assessment Book, pp. 18–19

</td><td>

✓ **Unit Assessment**
Assessment Book, pp. 122–130

✓ **Fluency Assessment**
Assessment Book, pp. 234–249

✓ **EXIT TEST**
Assessment Book, pp. 178–186

</td></tr>
</table>

ABOUT UNIT 1

Unit 1

EUREKA!
I've Got It!

THE **BIG**
Idea
Where can an idea begin?

UNIT 1 OPENER,
pp. 16–17

The Big Idea

Where can an idea begin?

Talk About It

Read aloud the Big Idea on page 16 of the **Interactive Worktext:** *Where can an idea begin?* Have students name inventions, games, or books. Say: *These things exist because someone came up with an idea for them. For example, the inventor William Judson wanted an easier way to lace up boots, so he came up with the idea for a zipper. What other ideas could solve this problem?* (Answers will vary.)

Discuss the photo on pages 16–17. Say: *What do you see in the photograph?* (a Ferris wheel) *What other object do you think this structure looks like?* (a bicycle wheel) Say: *The inventor of the Ferris wheel, Charles Ferris, came up with his idea for a ride by looking at a bicycle wheel.* Have partners discuss how the Ferris wheel is like a bicycle wheel. (Possible answers: both are the shape of a circle; both have a spokes, fork; both move in a circle around a center axis) *How is Charles Ferris's idea different than a bicycle wheel?* (Possible answers: it's bigger, it has seats to carry people) *How would you make this amusement park ride different? Discuss your ideas.* Have partners or small groups discuss and share ideas with the class.

Say: *In this unit, we will be reading ten selections about ways people come up with ideas. In one selection, a girl comes up with an idea to help her family. In another selection, a writer has an idea for a new technology.*

Build Fluency

Each week, use the **Interactive Worktext** Shared Reads and **Apprentice Leveled Readers** for fluency instruction and practice. Keep in mind that reading rates vary with the type of text that students are reading as well as the purpose for reading. For example, comprehension of complex informational texts generally requires slower reading.

Explain/Model Use the Fluency lessons on pages 374–378 to explain the skill. Then model the skill by reading the first page of the week's Shared Read or Leveled Reader.

Practice/Apply Choose a page from the Shared Read or Leveled Reader. Have one group read the top half of the page one sentence at a time. Remind children to apply the skill. Have the second group echo-read the passage. Then have the groups switch roles for the second half of the page. Discuss how each group applied the skill.

> **Weekly Fluency Focus**
>
> **Week 1** Expression and Accuracy
> **Week 2** Intonation
> **Week 3** Expression and Phrasing
> **Week 4** Expression and Phrasing
> **Week 5** Phrasing

Foundational Skills Kit You can also use the **Lesson Cards** and **Practice** pages from the **Foundational Skills Kit** for targeted Fluency instruction and practice.

A C T Access Complex Text

Reader and Task

TEXT COMPLEXITY

Interactive Worktext

	Week 1	Week 2	Week 3	Week 4	Week 5
Quantitative	"A Fresh Idea"	"Whitewater Adventure"	"A Life in the Woods"	"Fantasy Becomes Fact"	"Are Electronic Devices Good for Us?"
	Lexile 540 TextEvaluator™ 24	Lexile 520 TextEvaluator™ 31	Lexile 530 TextEvaluator™ 22	Lexile 530 TextEvaluator™ 35	Lexile 640 TextEvaluator™ 35
Qualitative	• Connection of Ideas • Vocabulary	• Organization • Genre • Sentence Structure • Vocabulary	• Sentence Structure • Vocabulary	• Connection of Ideas • Vocabulary	• Connection of Ideas • Vocabulary

The Weekly Concept lessons will help determine the reader's knowledge and engagement in the weekly concept.

Reader and Task	Weekly Concept: p. 6 Questions and tasks: pp. 8–9	Weekly Concept: p. 16 Questions and tasks: pp. 18–19	Weekly Concept: p. 26 Questions and tasks: pp. 28–29	Weekly Concept: p. 38 Questions and tasks: pp. 40–41	Weekly Concept: p. 48 Questions and tasks: pp. 50–51

Apprentice Leveled Reader

	Week 1	Week 2	Week 3	Week 4	Week 5
Quantitative	"Parker's Plan"	"Dog Gone"	"Save This Space!"	"Snapshot! The Story of George Eastman"	"What About Robots?"
	Lexile 500 TextEvaluator™ 17	Lexile 480 TextEvaluator™ 27	Lexile 490 TextEvaluator™ 23	Lexile 580 TextEvaluator™ 18	Lexile 600 TextEvaluator™ 29
Qualitative	• Connection of Ideas • Genre • Vocabulary	• Organization • Genre • Vocabulary	• Sentence Structure • Connection of Ideas • Genre • Vocabulary	• Connection of Ideas • Genre • Vocabulary	• Connection of Ideas • Genre • Vocabulary

The Weekly Concept lessons will help determine the reader's knowledge and engagement in the weekly concept.

Reader and Task	Weekly Concept: p. 6 Questions and tasks: pp. 10–13	Weekly Concept: p. 16 Questions and tasks: pp. 20–23	Weekly Concept: p. 26 Questions and tasks: pp. 30–33	Weekly Concept: p. 38 Questions and tasks: pp. 42–45	Weekly Concept: p. 48 Questions and tasks: pp. 52–55

See pages 379 for details about Text Complexity measures.

Objectives
- Develop oral language
- Build background about meeting needs
- Understand and use weekly vocabulary
- Read realistic fiction text

Materials
- Interactive Worktext, pp. 18–25
- Visual Vocabulary Cards: 1–8

☞ **Go** Digital
- Interactive eWorktext
- Visual Vocabulary Cards

Scaffolding for **WONDERS** Reading/Writing Workshop

WEEKLY CONCEPT

 5–10 Minutes   SL.5.1b   SL.5.1c   **CCSS**

Talk About It

Essential Question Read aloud the Essential Question on page 18 of the **Interactive Worktext**: *How do we get the things we need?* Explain that we need certain things to help us survive, such as food, water, clothing, and shelter. Say: Meeting a need *means getting what you need to survive. People meet their needs in many different ways.*

- Discuss the photograph on page 18. Ask: *What does this family need: food, water, shelter, or clothing?* (food) *How is this family meeting that need?* (They are picking vegetables from a garden.)

I Do Say: *I am going to think about a time when I did something to meet a need. When I was thirsty, I went to the drinking fountain to get water. I will write this down on page 19 under* Water.

We Do Say: *Let's look at the photo and think about how the family is meeting a need. What is the family doing?* (picking vegetables) *Are they working by themselves or together?* (together) *What is another way the family could get food?* (Possible answers: buy it from a store or market; trade for food) As students describe other ways to get food, work with them to add words to the web under *Food* on page 19. Then have them brainstorm ways people can get water, clothing, and shelter and add those words to the web.

You Do Have partners work together to describe a time when they had to get something they needed (for example, finding shelter when it starts to rain). Have them use words in the web (food, shelter, clothing, water), and answer the questions: *What did you need? What did you do to get it?*

REVIEW VOCABULARY

 10–15 Minutes   L.5.4a   L.5.5c   L.5.6   **CCSS**

Review Weekly Vocabulary Words

- Use the **Visual Vocabulary Cards** to review the weekly vocabulary.

- Read together the directions for the Vocabulary activity on page 20 of the **Interactive Worktext**. Then complete the activity.

1 **prosper** Have partners ask each other questions to help them decide which two words are synonyms for *prosper* (succeed, grow)

2 **savings** Have students complete the sentence starter: *One way I can build my savings is by _____.* (Possible answers: putting money I get for a birthday or from doing chores in the bank; don't spend the money I earn)

3 **afford** Offer an example of something you see in the classroom that you would like to be able to *afford*. Then ask: *What are some things you see that you would like to be able to* afford? (Possible answers: book, backpack, computer)

4 **loan** Have students use the sentence starter: *I might ask a friend for a loan because _____.* (Possible answers: I want to buy a snack and don't have any money.)

5 **risk** Have partners brainstorm a list of sports. Then ask students to identify the sports in which players take a big *risk* and discuss why there is a *risk*. (Possible answers: football, mountain biking, skateboarding)

6 **profit** Have students complete this sentence frame: *I make a profit when I _____.* (make more money than I spend)

7 **scarce** Say: *Look around. What items in the room become scarce?* Have students point to the items. (<u>Possible answers:</u> paper, pencils, chalk) Then have partners discuss what they do when the item is *scarce*. (look for more; ask to borrow some from another classroom)

8 **wages** Have students talk about chores they have done. Ask: *What chore can you do to earn wages?* Have students draw a picture of themselves doing that chore. Then have partners tell what they would do with their *wages*. (Drawings may include washing the dishes; washing the car; walking the dog.)

High-Utility Words

Explain that sequence words, such as *first, second, then, next,* and *finally* tell the order in which events happen. Have students turn to page 21 in the **Interactive Worktext**. Read the first two sentences and discuss the circled sequence word, *First*. Point out that the word is used to tell the first thing Danny did to get the spelling list. Have partners work together to circle the other sequence words in the passage. *(Next, Finally, Then, The next day)* Then have students complete the following sentence frames with events that happened before school. For example, *First, I woke up at _____. Then, I _____. Next, _____. Finally, I _____ to get to school.*

> **ELL ENGLISH LANGUAGE LEARNERS**
>
> Help students complete their sentence frames. Then ask questions using sequence words. *What did you do* first*? What did you do* next*?*

READ COMPLEX TEXT

15–20 Minutes   RL.5.1   RF.5.4c

Read: "A Fresh Idea"

- Have students turn to page 22 in the **Interactive Worktext** and read aloud the Essential Question. Explain that they will read how one girl helps meet a need in her neighborhood. Ask: *What is the title?* ("A Fresh Idea") *The word* fresh *can mean "new or different." Look at the picture. Who do you think will come up with the new or different idea?* (the girl on the swing)

- Read "A Fresh Idea" together. Note that the weekly vocabulary words are highlighted in yellow. Expand vocabulary words are highlighted in blue.

- Have students use the "My Notes" section on page 22 to write questions they have, words they don't understand, and details they want to remember. Model how to use the "My Notes" section. *I can write notes about questions I have as I read. In the second paragraph on page 23, I see the word* lot, *and I'm not sure what it means in this sentence. I will write* lot *with a question mark next to it in the "My Notes" section. I will look for clues to its meaning when I reread. In the last paragraph on page 23, I read that Mali had an idea. I wonder: What is Mali's idea? I will write this question under "My Notes." When we reread the story, I will ask my questions so I better understand what I am reading.*

> **ELL ENGLISH LANGUAGE LEARNERS**
>
> As you read together, have students highlight each part of the story they have a question about. After reading, help them write their questions in the "My Notes" section.

 Quick Check **Can students understand the weekly vocabulary in context? If not, review vocabulary using the Visual Vocabulary Cards before teaching Lesson 2.**

WEEK 1 LESSON 2

Objectives
- Read realistic fiction text
- Understand complex text through close reading
- Recognize and understand sequence
- Respond to the selection, using text evidence to support ideas

Scaffolding for **Wonders** Reading/Writing Workshop

Materials
Interactive Worktext, pp. 22–27

☞ **Go** Digital
- Interactive eWorktext
- Sequence Mini-Lesson

REREAD COMPLEX TEXT

20–25 Minutes   RL.3.3 RL.5.1 RL.5.4 L.5.4a CCSS

Close Reading: "A Fresh Idea"

Reread "A Fresh Idea" with students. As you read together, discuss important passages in the text. Have students respond to text-dependent questions, including those in the **Interactive Worktext**.

🔍 Page 23

Expand Vocabulary Have students locate *stand* in the first paragraph and read the sentence aloud. Ask them to discuss different meanings of the word *stand*. *What details in the first and second paragraph are clues to the meaning of the word* stand? (the tomatoes Mrs. Fair sells; Mrs. Fair set up her stand; close her stand; run it)

Connection of Ideas Ⓐ Ⓒ Ⓣ Read together what Mali says to her Mom in the first and third paragraphs. Have students underline details that show what Mali thinks about Mrs. Fair's tomatoes. (I love the tomatoes Mrs. Fair sells; It's the only place to buy fresh tomatoes.) Read the first two sentences of the fourth paragraph aloud. Ask: *Why does Mali wish she could grow tomatoes?* (Mrs. Fair's stand is closed and she wants a way to have fresh tomatoes.)

Vocabulary Have students locate the word *selfish* in the third paragraph and read the sentence aloud. Say: What does Mali say that shows she wasn't *selfish*? (We all need fruits and vegetables.) *What does* selfish *mean?* (thinking of your own needs)

Sequence Say: *In this story's plot, a sequence of events leads the main character, Mali, to get an idea. Let's figure out the sequence of events. What is the most important event at the beginning of the story?* (Mali finds out that Mrs. Fair's stand will be closed.) Then have students

reread the last paragraph. Let's figure out the order of events that happen in this part of the story. Ask: *What does Mali do after she gets home?* (she went to her backyard) *Who does Mali see?* (she sees Mr. Taylor) *What event happens after?* (Mali gets an idea) *Let's keep reading to find out about Mali's idea.* Have students circle any sequence words. Give examples: *after, next, then.* (After, Just then, Then)

🔍 Page 24

Connection of Ideas Ⓐ Ⓒ Ⓣ Have students review the last paragraph on page 23. Ask: *What does Mali think about growing tomatoes in her yard?* (it's too small) *What does Mr. Taylor's yard look like?* (it has flowers) Then read the first paragraph on page 24 together. *What does Mali tell Mr. Taylor she wants?* (I want to grow tomatoes. I want you to keep your daffodils, though.) *Put these details together. What is Mali's idea?* (She wants to grow tomatoes in Mr. Taylor's yard.)

Vocabulary Have students find the word *invest* in the fourth paragraph. Explain that to *invest* means to pay for something that will give something back in return. *If Mali invests in tomato plants, what do you think she will she get in return*? (tomatoes)

Expand Vocabulary Read the definition of *allowance* together. *What does* allowance *mean?* (money given to you) *Draw a box around clue words and phrases that help you understand the meaning of the word.* (have savings; saving money to buy) *What does Mali decide to do with savings from her* allowance? (She decides to buy some tomato plants)

High-Utility Words Have students locate a sequence word or phrase in the first sentence of the last paragraph. (the next day) Have students discuss how the word helps them understand the order of events. (the word tells when Mali bought the tomatoes.)

Sequence Ask: *What important event happens after Mali tells Mr. Taylor her idea?* (Mr. Taylor loans Mali his land) Have partners reread the last paragraph. *What events happen after Mali buys tomato plants? Number the sentences to show the sequence of events.* (1: Mr. Taylor taught Mali how to prepare the soil and place the plants. 2: After that, Mali put stakes in the ground to hold the thin plant stems up.) *Now write the steps that Mali and Mr. Taylor do last.* (water, pull weeds, and wait) Have students point out sequence words in the last paragraph that helped them understand the order of events. (next, after, then) Then have students turn to their partner and paraphrase the key events in the paragraph.

Page 25
Sequence Have partners reread the first paragraph and label the first two events on Saturday with numbers 1 and 2. (1: Mali and Mr. Taylor filled several crates with ripe tomatoes; 2: They took them to market.) *What happens by the end of the day?* (They had sold all of the tomatoes.)

Expand Vocabulary Have students locate the word *earned* in the second paragraph and reread the sentence. *What does* earned *mean?* (to get money through work) Have students circle clues to the word. (wages; money) Ask: *What work did Mali do to earn money?* Have partners go back through the story to find the work Mali did. Have partners complete the sentence frame: *Mali earned money by _____, _____, and _____.* (Possible answers: planting the tomato plants, watering them, pulling weeds, filling crates, taking tomatoes to the market, and selling them.)

Connection of Ideas ACT Point to the last paragraph. Ask: *How does Mr. Taylor feel at the end of the story? Underline text evidence.* (Possible answers: hopeful, happy; He was already looking forward to next summer.) Have students look back at page 23 and point to text evidence that tells about Mr. Taylor's feelings. (Mali saw he had a sad look on his face.) *How do Mr. Taylor's feelings change from the beginning to the end of the story?* (Mr. Taylor felt sad at the beginning but now feels happy.)

RESPOND TO READING
10–20 Minutes   RL.5.1   RL.5.3   W.5.9a   SL.5.1d   CCSS

Respond to "A Fresh Idea"
Have students summarize "A Fresh Idea" orally to demonstrate comprehension. Then have partners answer the questions on page 26 of the **Interactive Worktext** using the discussion starters. Tell them to use text evidence to support their answers. Have students write the page number(s) on which they found the text evidence for each question.

1. *What does Mali need at the beginning of the story?* (Mali needs a place to get fresh tomatoes. <u>Text Evidence</u>: p. 23)

2. *What does Mr. Taylor need at the beginning of the story?* (Mr. Taylor needs a friend. <u>Text Evidence</u>: p. 23)

3. *What do Mali and Mr. Taylor do to get what they need?* (Mali and Mr. Taylor start a garden. Mr. Taylor offers Mali his land. They both get what they need by working together. Mali gets fresh tomatoes. Mr. Taylor gets a friend. <u>Text Evidence</u>: pp. 24, 25)

After students discuss the questions on page 26, have them write a response to the question on page 27. Tell them to use their partner discussions and notes about "A Fresh Idea" to help them. Circulate and provide guidance.

 Quick Check Do students understand vocabulary in context? If not, review and reteach using the instruction on page 14.

Can students use key details to determine sequence of events? If not, review and reteach using the instruction on page 14 and assign the Unit 1 Week 1 digital mini-lesson.

Can students write a response to "A Fresh Idea"? If not, provide sentence frames to help them organize their ideas.

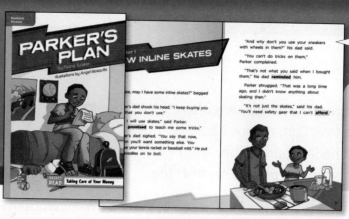

Objectives
- Understand and use new vocabulary words
- Read realistic fiction text
- Recognize and understand sequence
- Understand complex text through close reading

Materials
- "Parker's Plan" Apprentice Leveled Reader, pp. 2–8
- Graphic Organizer: Sequence

☞ **Go** Digital
- Apprentice Leveled Reader eBook
- Downloadable Graphic Organizer
- Sequence Mini-Lesson

BEFORE READING

10–15 Minutes   SL.5.1c   SL.5.1d   L.5.4a   L.5.6

Introduce "Parker's Plan"

- Read the Essential Question on the title page of "Parker's Plan" **Apprentice Leveled Reader**: *How do we get the things we need? We will read about a boy who learns how to get something he needs.*

- Read the title of the main read. Have students look at the cover art and the illustration on page 3. *What do you think this selection will be about?* (a boy who makes a plan to do something) *Why do you think that?* (the title and cover art)

Expand Vocabulary

Display each word below. Say the words and have students repeat them. Then use the Define/Example/Ask routine to introduce each word.

1 expensive (page 8)

Define: costing a lot of money

Example: Ken saved his money to buy an *expensive* computer game.

Ask: Name one thing that is *expensive* to buy.

2 promised (page 2)

Define: told someone that you would definitely do something

Example: I *promised* my sister I would help her with homework.

Ask: What have you *promised* someone recently?

3 reminded (page 3)

Define: caused someone to remember something

Example: Dad *reminded* me to take my lunch.

Ask: What has a family member *reminded* you to do?

DURING READING

20–30 Minutes   RL.3.3   RL.5.1   SL.5.1b   L.5.4a

Close Reading

🔍 **Pages 2–3**

Genre Ⓐ Ⓒ Ⓣ Have students look at the illustration on page 3 and then read pages 2 and 3 aloud. Ask: *How do you know "Parker's Plan" is realistic fiction?* (The illustrations and dialogue show characters who dress, look, and speak like real people.)

Connection of Ideas Ⓐ Ⓒ Ⓣ *Look at the second paragraph. What does Parker's dad say about the skates?* (He says Parker doesn't use the things that his dad buys him.) *In the fourth paragraph, what does Parker's dad say about the skates? How does he feel about the skates?* (He says Parker won't use the skates and will just ask for something else. Parker's dad doesn't want to buy him the skates.)

Character, Setting, Plot: Sequence Point out that characters and setting are introduced in the beginning of the story. *Who are the characters in this story?* (Parker and his dad) *Where does this part of the story take place?* (their home, at dinnertime.) *What is the first thing Parker does?* (beg his dad to buy him inline skates.)

Have students record the characters and setting in their sequence chart. Then have them record events from the beginning of the story. As they continue, they will record events in the middle and the end of the story.

Pages 4–5

Character, Setting, Plot: Sequence Read page 4. *What things does Parker say to convince his dad to buy him skates and safety gear?* (First Parker suggests that they buy the things on sale. Then he promises to use the gear every day.) *Is Parker able to change his dad's mind? How can you tell?* (Parker's dad does not change his mind. He says no.)

STOP AND CHECK *Read the question in the Stop and Check box on page 4.* (His dad is always buying him things that Parker never ends up using very much.)

Connection of Ideas ACT Read the first paragraph on page 5. Ask: *How do you think Parker feels? How can you tell?* (He is angry. He thinks,"It wasn't fair … Why should he miss out?") Reread the second paragraph on page 5. Ask: *How does Parker feel in the second paragraph? How do you know?* (He feels better. The words "Then he grinned" show that Parker is no longer angry.) *Why does his mood change?* (Parker realizes that he can try to get the money on his own.)

Pages 6–7

Vocabulary Ask students to find the word *hopeless* on page 6. Point out the root word *hope* and explain the meaning of the suffix *–less*. (without) Ask students what *hopeless* means. (without hope) Ask students to think of other words with the suffix *–less*. (helpless, useless, fearless, sugarless)

Character, Setting, Plot: Sequence Ask students to read page 7. *Why does Parker suddenly feel excited?* (When Parker gets the idea of earning the money, he gets excited and rushes out to tell his dad.) *What does Parker's dad think of Parker's idea?* (Parker's dad says it is a "great idea.") *Why does he think that?* (His dad thinks that Parker will use the skates if Parker works to buy them.)

Page 8

Character, Setting, Plot: Sequence Ask students to read page 8. *On page 7, dad gives Parker a job mopping the floor. What happens next, on page 8?* (Parker gets a lot of jobs to earn money. Dad says he'd better find Parker even more jobs.)

STOP AND CHECK *Read the question in the Stop and Check box on page 8.* (His dad helps by paying Parker to do jobs around the house. Then he offers to find Parker more jobs.)

Have partners review their Sequence Chart for pages 2–8 and discuss what they learned.

✓ *Quick Check* **Do students understand weekly vocabulary in context? If not, review and reteach using the instruction on page 14.**

Can students determine the sequence of events in a story? If not, review and reteach using the instruction on page 14 and assign the Unit 1 Week 1 digital mini-lesson.

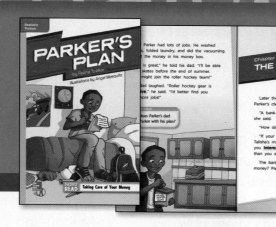

WEEK 1
LESSON

4

Objectives
• Understand and use new vocabulary
• Read realistic fiction text
• Understand sequence in a plot
• Understand complex text through close reading
• Respond to the selection, using text evidence to support ideas

Scaffolding for **Wonders** Approaching Leveled Reader

Materials
"Parker's Plan" Apprentice Leveled Reader, pp. 9–20
• Graphic Organizer: Sequence

☞ **Go** Digital
• Apprentice Leveled Reader eBook
• Downloadable Graphic Organizer
• Sequence Mini-Lesson

BEFORE READING

5–10 Minutes   SL.5.1c   SL.5.1d   L.5.4a   L.5.6

Expand Vocabulary

Display each word below. Say the words and have students repeat them. Then use the Define/Example/Ask routine to introduce each word.

❶ account (page 9)

Define: a place to keep money in a bank

Example: I opened a bank *account* when I got a job.

Ask: Would you prefer to keep your money in a bank account or at home?

❷ employee (page 10)

Define: someone who works at a job

Example: The bus driver is an *employee* of the bus company.

Ask: Who are some *employees* working at this school?

❸ interest (page 9)

Define: the money you earn from saving your money in a bank

Example: I made five dollars *interest* on the money in my savings account.

Ask: *Why is it good to have a bank account that earns interest?*

❹ organized (page 13)

Define: put things in order

Example: I *organized* my closet so that I could easily find my things.

Ask: What is something that you have *organized*?

❺ transfer (page 10)

Define: to move from one place to another

Example: When I moved across town, I had to *transfer* to a new school.

Ask: Why might a person *transfer* money into a savings account?

DURING READING

15–20 Minutes   RL.3.3   RL.5.1   RL.5.4   SL.5.1b

Close Reading

Page 9

Connection of Ideas Ⓐ Ⓒ Ⓣ Point to the second sentence on page 9. Ask: *Which character is speaking?* (Talisha's mom) *How do you know?* (The text says, "Talisha's mom talked to Parker's class about her job in a bank.")

Sequence *What event happens at the beginning of Chapter 3?* (Talisha's mom visits Parker's class and explains about saving money in the bank.)

Pages 10–11

Sequence Have students look at the illustration on pages 10 and 11 and read the text. *What is the first thing that happens on page 10?* (Parker's dad takes him to the bank. Parker opens a bank account.) *What happens next?* (Parker opens a bank account.) *What happens when Parker and his dad get home?* (Parker's dad goes online and puts money into Parker's new account.)

Connection of Ideas Ⓐ Ⓒ Ⓣ *On page 11, why won't Parker's dad let him buy skates after he saves enough money?* (Parker's dad wants Parker to wait until he has the money to buy safety gear too.) Have students add the events to the Sequence Chart.

STOP AND CHECK *Read the question in the Stop and Check box on page 11.* (The bank account will help Parker make more money because the money he has in the account will earn interest.)

 Pages 12–13

Genre Ⓐ Ⓒ Ⓣ Ask: *What do the illustrations on page 13 show? How do you know?* (The illustrations show all the jobs that Parker is doing. The text talks about how he is cleaning and organizing and carrying groceries for his neighbors.)

Connection of Ideas Ⓐ Ⓒ Ⓣ Ask: *What do we learn about Parker from how he acts in this part of chapter 4?* (Parker is someone who can work hard and stick with a plan. He carries groceries, organizes kitchens, and cleans shoes. He looks for more work by putting up posters and giving out fliers.)

Have students add the events to the Sequence Chart.

 Pages 14–15

Vocabulary Ask students to find the idiom *red as a beet* on page 14. Give students support here. They may not know what it means. Explain that this idiom means that Parker's face turned red because he was embarrassed. Ask: *Why did Parker turn as red as a beet?* (He felt embarrassed because he had to tell his dad that he didn't want skates any more.)

Sequence Ask students to turn to a partner and discuss: *What does Parker say and do at the end of the story? How does his dad feel about this?* (Parker says he doesn't want to buy skates. He wants to buy a racing bike. His dad likes this idea. He says, "Go for it!")

Have students add the events to their Sequence Chart. Have partners discuss what they have recorded in their charts for this part of the selection.

STOP AND CHECK *Read the question in the Stop and Check box on page 15.* (Mrs. Goldstein offers Parker work, which gives him and his dad the idea to ask for work from other neighbors they know well.)

AFTER READING

10–15 Minutes   RL.5.1   RL.5.2   RL.5.9   W.5.9a   L.5.4a

Respond to Reading

Compare Texts Have students compare how characters in "A Fresh Idea" and "Parker's Plan" get what they need. Then say: *Why are the events in these stories like real life?*

Summarize Have students turn to page 16 and summarize the selection. (Answers should include details from the selection.)

 Text Evidence

Have partners work together to answer questions on page 16. Remind students to use their Sequence Chart.

Sequence (Parker wants a pair of inline skates; Parker's dad refuses to buy the skates; he tries to figure out how to buy them; Parker decides to earn money to buy skates.)

Vocabulary (Fliers are sheets of paper with ads on them that you can hand out. Parker put up posters and gave out fliers.)

Write About Reading (Talisha's mom comes to Parker's class to talk about her job at the bank. Parker learns that a bank will pay you interest if you have an account. Parker tells his dad and they go to the bank to open an account.)

Independent Reading

Encourage students to read the paired selection "Taking Care of Your Money" on pages 17–19. Have them summarize the selection and compare it to "Parker's Plan." Have partners answer the "Make Connections" questions on page 19.

✓ *Quick Check* **Can students identify Sequence? If not, review and teach using the instruction on page 14 and assign the Unit 1 Week 1 digital mini-lesson.**

Can students respond to the selection using text evidence? If not, provide, sentence frames to help them organize their ideas.

Objectives
• Review weekly vocabulary words
• Review sequence
• Write an analysis of an illustration

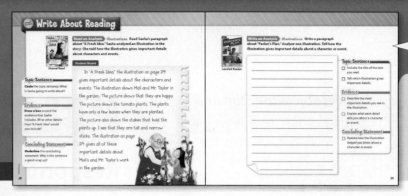

Materials
• Visual Vocabulary Cards: 1–8
• Interactive Worktext, pp. 28–29
• Assessment Book, pp. 10–11

☞ **Go Digital**
• Visual Vocabulary Cards
• Sequence Mini-Lesson
• Interactive eWorktext

REVIEW AND RETEACH

5–10 Minutes RL.3.3 L.5.4a L.5.6

Weekly Vocabulary

Display one **Visual Vocabulary Card** at a time and ask students to use the vocabulary word in a sentence. If students have difficulty, have them find the word in "A Fresh Idea" and use the context clues to define it.

Comprehension: Sequence

I Do Write and say: *Ria lost her backpack. First, she searched her closet. Then she looked under the bed. Finally, she picked up her coat. She found her backpack underneath it.* Circle the first sentence. *This is the most important event at the beginning of the story.* Draw a box around sentences 2-4. Say: *These sentences tell the sequence of events that leads Ria to find her backpack.* Point out sequence words *First, Then, Finally.* Say: *These sequence words help show the order of events that follow.* Number the sentences to show the order.

We Do Display: *Ben decided to adopt a dog. First, he read all about dogs. Next he talked to his friends who have dogs. Finally, he went to the shelter to find a dog.* Say: *What is the most important event at the beginning of the story?* (Ben decided to adopt a dog) *Let's find the sequence of events that follow. I read that first he read all about dogs. What happened next?* (he talked to his friends) *What happened last?* (he went to the shelter)

You Do Write another series of events: *Dana sees that her bike has a flat tire. First, Dana finds the hole in the tire. After that, she patches the hole. Then she puts more air in the tire. Finally, she rides her bike.* Have partners identify the most important event at the beginning of the story. Then have partners number the events in the story and circle sequence words.

WRITE ABOUT READING

25–35 Minutes RL.5.7 W.5.4 W.5.5 W.5.9a

Read an Analysis

• Ask students to look back at "A Fresh Idea" in the **Interactive Worktext**. Have volunteers identify the characters, setting, and events in the illustrations. *How do the illustrations give important details about the characters, setting, and events?*

• Read aloud the introduction on page 28. *Sasha's paragraph is not a summary. She is writing an analysis, or a detailed description, of "A Fresh Idea." When you analyze, you ask yourself "how" and "why" questions.*

• *When you write an analysis, you must include certain elements. The first element is the* topic sentence. *It should be clear, focused, and tell the main idea. Read the beginning of Sasha's paragraph and circle the topic sentence. What important information has she included in this sentence?* (story's title; the page number of the illustration that gives important details)

• *Another element of analysis is* text evidence. *Sasha supports the topic sentence with details from the illustration. Reread the model and draw a box around the text evidence.* (sentences 2 through 7) *Look back at the illustration on page 24. What other details in the illustration might be included as text evidence?* (Mali and Mr. Taylor are both doing work.)

• *The final element of an analysis is the* concluding statement. *A good concluding sentence restates the topic sentence and wraps up the main idea. Underline the concluding statement. How is the concluding statement like the topic sentence?* (Both say that the illustration gives important details.) *How does it wrap up the paragraph? Point to words Sasha uses that wrap up the details.* (all of these important details)

Write an Analysis

Analytical Writing

Guided Writing Read the writing prompt on page 29 together. Have students write about "Parker's Plan" or another text they read this week. Have them select an illustration to write about. Guide students to answer the questions: *What do you learn about the character or event by looking at the details in the illustration? Why are those details important? Use the checklist to help you figure out the right information to include in each section.*

Peer Conference Have students read their analysis to a partner. Listeners should identify the strongest text evidence that supports the topic sentence and discuss any sentences that are unclear.

Teacher Conference Check students' writing for complete sentences and text evidence that supports their topic. Review the concluding statement. *Does this sentence tie all of the elements together?* If necessary, have students revise the concluding statement by restating the topic sentence.

Level Up

▲ **Approaching Leveled Reader**

▲ **Reading/Writing Workshop**

▲ **Apprentice Leveled Reader**

▲ **Interactive Worktext**

IF students read the Apprentice Level Reader fluently and the **Interactive Worktext** Shared Read fluently and answer the Respond to Reading questions

THEN read together the Approaching Level Reader main selection and the **Reading/Writing Workshop** Shared Read from *Reading Wonders*. Have students take notes as they read, using self-stick notes. Then ask and answer questions about their notes.

Writing Rubric

	4	3	2	1
Topic Sentence	There is one clear, focused topic sentence.	Topic sentence is less focused, somewhat clear.	Topic is presented in short phrases.	There is no topic sentence.
Text Evidence	Topic is supported by two or more text details.	Evidence includes only one detail from the text.	Little to no evidence is cited from the text.	No text evidence is included.
Concluding Statement	Clearly restates the topic sentence; wraps up the details.	Restatement is less focused; attempts to wrap up the details.	Vaguely restates the topic. Doesn't correlate well to text evidence.	There is no conclusion.
Writing Style	Writes in complete sentences. Uses correct spelling and grammar.	Uses complete sentences and phrases. Writing has spelling and grammar errors.	Few or no complete sentences. There are many spelling and grammar errors.	Does not write accurately or in complete sentences.

ASSESSMENT

Weekly Assessment

Have students complete the Weekly Assessment using **Assessment** book pages 10–11.

WEEK 2 LESSON

1

Objectives
- Develop oral language
- Build background about rethinking ideas
- Understand and use weekly vocabulary
- Read realistic fiction text

Scaffolding for **McGraw-Hill Reading Wonders** Reading/Writing Workshop

Materials
Interactive Worktext, pp. 30–37
- Visual Vocabulary Cards: 9–16

👉 **Go** Digital
- Interactive eWorktext
- Visual Vocabulary Cards

WEEKLY CONCEPT

5–10 Minutes   SL.5.1b   SL.5.1c   CCSS

Talk About It

Essential Question Read aloud the Essential Question on page 30 of the **Interactive Worktext**: *What can lead us to rethink an idea?* Explain that when you *rethink* an idea, you think about the idea again in a different way. Say: *Sometimes an idea doesn't work. Then you have to rethink the idea to figure out what went wrong and how to make it better.*

- Discuss the photograph on page 30. Ask: *What problem caused these campers to rethink their idea?* (It started raining.)

I Do Say: *I am going to think about a time when I had to rethink an idea. When I was making bread, I measured out the ingredients and mixed them all together. But when I baked the bread, it didn't taste good. Then I saw that I missed a step. Next time, I will be more careful. I will write* Be more careful *in the word web.*

We Do Say: *Let's look at the photo and think about what led these campers to rethink their idea. What were they trying to do?* (go camping) *What went wrong?* (it started to rain) *What could they do differently next time?* (check the weather; be prepared; make a plan) As students describe what the campers could do to rethink their next trip, work with them to add words to the web on page 31. Then have them tell what they would do if they were one of the campers.

You Do Have partners work together to describe a time when they had to rethink the way they did something (for example, ways to find something they lost). Have them use some words in the web, and answer the questions: *What did you do? What made your rethink your idea? What helped you next time?*

REVIEW VOCABULARY

10–15 Minutes   L.5.1   L.5.4a   L.5.5c   L.5.6   CCSS

Review Weekly Vocabulary Words

- Use the **Visual Vocabulary Cards** to review the weekly vocabulary.

- Read together the directions for the Vocabulary activity on page 32 of the **Interactive Worktext**. Then complete the activity.

1 **assemble** Have students tell where they *assemble* with friends. Then have them tell other words that have the same or almost the same meaning. (meet; get together)

2 **decipher** Write your own name on the board neatly; then scribble a signature next to it. Ask: *Which name is difficult to decipher?* Discuss what makes the name hard to read. Have students write their own name so it would be hard to *decipher*. Have partners compare what they wrote and tell what makes the names difficult to *decipher*. (Names should be hard to read, such as written backwards or scribbled.)

3 **navigate** Have partners brainstorm vehicles a person can use to *navigate* on land. (Possible answers: truck, car, train)

4 **distracted** Ask students to complete this sentence starter: *When I'm reading, I can be distracted by the sound of _____.* (Possible answers: a phone ringing, a car alarm, someone talking)

5 **retrace** Point out the prefix *re-*. Explain that *re-* is added to the beginning of a word and means "again" or "back." Have students identify the base word and prefix and then write the meaning. (trace; re; to again). *Show how you would retrace your step*

6 **options** Have students point to each place as they complete the sentence frame: *The two best options for places to hang art are _____ and _____.* (Possible answers: bulletin board, windows, wall)

7 **accomplish** Explain how you felt when you accomplished a goal, such as winning a sports game Ask students to complete the sentence frame: *When I accomplish something, I feel _____.* (Possible answers: good about myself, happy)

8 **anxious** Discuss with students situations or events that have made them feel *anxious. How do you look when you are anxious?* Have students draw a picture of themselves to show how they look. Then have students use other words to describe how they look in their drawings.

High-Utility Words

Have students turn to page 33 in the **Interactive Worktext.** Explain that contractions are a shortened form of two words. Some contractions are made up of a verb, or action word, and the word *not.* Discuss the circled word, *can't,* and point out that the word is a contraction made up of the words *can* and *not.* Point out that the apostrophe takes the place of the missing letters *no.* Have partners work together to circle the other contractions in the passage. (*aren't, shouldn't, don't haven't*) Then have partners tell the two words that make up each contraction.

ELL ENGLISH LANGUAGE LEARNERS

Write these words on note cards: *aren't, don't, haven't, are not, do not, have not.* Have students point to the cards that show contractions and say the contraction aloud. Then have students match the cards *are not, do not, have not* with a contraction.

READ COMPLEX TEXT
15–20 Minutes   RL.5.1   RF.5.4c

Read: "Whitewater Adventure"

- Have students turn to page 34 in the **Interactive Worktext** and read aloud the Essential Question. Explain that they will read a story about a girl who has an adventure with her family. Ask: *What is the title?* ("Whitewater Adventure") *Look at the picture.* Point to the white froth of the waves in the illustration. Whitewater *describes rough waves like these. Where do you think this story takes place?* (on a raft in rough waves)

- Read "Whitewater Adventure" together. Note that the weekly vocabulary words are highlighted in yellow. Expand vocabulary words are highlighted in blue.

- Have students use the "My Notes" section on page 34 to write questions they have, words they don't understand, and details they want to remember. Model how to use the "My Notes" section. *I can write notes about questions I have as I read. In the first paragraph on page 35 I see the phrase* full of herself *and I'm not sure what it means. I will write* full of herself *with a question mark next to it in the "My Notes" section and look for clues to its meaning when I reread. I also read that Nina's sister, Marta, corrects her. I wonder:* Why does Marta correct her? *I will write my question in the "My Notes" section. When we reread the story, I will ask my questions so I better understand what I am reading.*

ELL ENGLISH LANGUAGE LEARNERS

As you read together, have students highlight each part of the story they have a question about. After reading, help them write their questions in the "My Notes" section.

 Quick Check Can students understand the weekly vocabulary in context? If not, review vocabulary using the **Visual Vocabulary Cards** before teaching Lesson 2.

WEEK 2
LESSON

2

Objectives
• Read realistic fiction text
• Understand complex text through close reading
• Recognize and understand problem and solution
• Respond to the selection, using text evidence to support ideas

Scaffolding for **Wonders** Reading/Writing Workshop
McGraw-Hill Reading

Materials
Interactive Worktext, pp. 34–39

☞ **Go** Digital
• Interactive eWorktext
• Problem and Solution Mini-Lesson

REREAD COMPLEX TEXT

20–25 Minutes   RL.4.3 RL.5.1 RL.5.4 L.5.4a L.5.5c CCSS

Close Reading: "Whitewater Adventure"

Reread "Whitewater Adventure" with students. As you read together, discuss important passages in the text. Have students respond to text-dependent questions, including those in the **Interactive Worktext**.

🔍 **Page 35**

High-Utility Words Point to the contraction *don't* in the first sentence. *What words make up this contraction?* (*do not*) Have students use the contraction in a sentence.

Problem and Solution Have students reread the first paragraph. Explain that a narrator is the person telling the story. *The narrator uses "I" to talk about herself. We learn her name when she tells something her sister says to her. Circle the narrator's name.* (Nina) Then model how to identify a problem: *In an adventure story, characters usually face problems. Let's figure out the narrator's problem together. One way to find a problem is to look for what the narrator has to do or change. What is the narrator going to do?* (whitewater rafting with her family.) *What does Nina think about the way she paddles compared to her family?* (She's not as strong as they are.) *What does Nina's sister want her to change?* (the way she paddles) *Put these details together to figure out Nina's problem. What is it?* (She doesn't think she is as good at rafting as her family.) *I wonder how she will solve this problem. Let's keep reading to find out.*

Organization Ⓐ Ⓒ Ⓣ Explain that figuring out the order in which events take place helps you understand how one event leads to another. *Reread the first two paragraphs. Draw a box around words that tell when*

the family's rafting trip begins. ("That morning") *What events happened before that morning?* (The family has been on rafting trips before with guides. Nina's sister has corrected her.) Have students paraphrase the most important events in the first two paragraphs.

Sentence Structure Ⓐ Ⓒ Ⓣ Point out the dashes in the second paragraph, and explain that each dash indicates a pause in the dialogue. *What is Dad reading aloud?* (a checklist) *Why do you think Dad pauses while reading his list?* (to look for the equipment before he checks it off.)

Expand Vocabulary Read aloud the definition of *route*. *Sometimes an author restates a word or uses a similar word in nearby sentences. Which word in the last paragraph has a similar meaning as* route? (way)

🔍 **Page 36**

Expand Vocabulary Point out *halt. What does* halt *mean?* (stop) Have students mark text evidence that shows what caused the raft to come to a halt. ("We're stuck on some rocks!")

Problem and Solution Point to the first paragraph. *What does the narrator say is a problem?* (the raft came to a halt.) *What caused the problem?* (they were distracted and got stuck on some rocks) *Which character tries to solve the problem first?* (Marta) *What does she do?* (She tries shouting for help.) *Does this solve the problem?* (no) *Why not?* (There's no one around to help them.) *What does the family try to do next to solve the problem?* (shift the raft off the rocks) Then have students look for another problem the family faces and point to text evidence. (storm clouds were gathering)

Problem and Solution *Sometimes a narrator tells us how he or she feels about story events. The narrator may or may not say these words in dialogue.* Have students mark the text that shows how the narrator feels about the problem. (beginning to feel anxious) *Does the narrator* *know what the problem is right away? How do you know?* (No; she asks "What's wrong?") *Why would this make her feel anxious?* (she doesn't know what will happen)

Page 37

Vocabulary Read aloud the sentence containing *drizzle* in the first paragraph. *What detail is a clue to what drizzle means?* (the darkening sky)

Expand Vocabulary Have students read the definition of *admit*. Ask: *What doesn't the family want to admit?* (we were running out of options) Prompt students to think about how they would feel if the options, or ways, to solve a problem were not working. *Why do you think no one wanted to admit that they were running out of options?* (it's scary to not know how to solve a problem)

Problem and Solution *Which character comes up with the idea that solves the problem?* (Nina) *Which sentence describes the idea?* ("What if we lift the side of the raft away from the rocks?") Have students look back at page 36 and paraphrase the problem. Then have them review page 37 to paraphrase the solution.

Organization **ACT** Ask students to look back to the first paragraph of the story and point to text evidence that shows what Nina thinks about herself. (I am not as strong as they are.) *How do those thoughts usually make people feel?* (sad or worried) Ask students to reread the last paragraph to find the text evidence that shows how Nina feels at the end. (I felt like I could accomplish anything I wanted.) *How do Nina's feelings change?* (She doesn't feel strong at first. At the end, she feels like she can accomplish anything.)

Genre **ACT** Explain that a realistic adventure story includes events that are suspenseful or exciting and that could happen in real life. *What events in this story are exciting or suspenseful?* (Possible answers: the family goes on a rafting trip; Nina sees a bear; the family gets stuck on a rock; it starts to rain while they are rafting) Have partners discuss whether the events they described could happen in real life.

RESPOND TO READING

10–20 Minutes   RL.5.1   RL.5.3   W.5.9a   SL.5.1d

Respond to "Whitewater Adventure"

Have students summarize "Whitewater Adventure" orally to demonstrate comprehension. Then have partners answer the questions on page 38 of the **Interactive Worktext** using the discussion starters. Tell them to use text evidence to support their answers. Have students write the page number(s) on which they found the text evidence for each question.

1. *How does Dad think the family can move the raft off the rock?* (Dad thinks they can move the raft by moving to the back of the raft. When the family does this nothing happens. Text Evidence: p. 36)

2. *What does Mom think the family should do?* (Mom thinks the family should sway the boat from side to side. When the family does this, the raft still doesn't move. Text Evidence: p. 37)

3. *What happens when the family tries the narrator's idea?* (The narrator thinks they should lift the side of the raft away from the rocks. When the family tries her idea, the raft breaks free. Text Evidence: p. 37)

After students discuss the questions on page 38, have them write a response to the question on page 39. Tell them to use their partner discussions and notes about "Whitewater Adventure" to help them. Circulate and provide guidance.

 Quick Check Do students understand vocabulary in context? If not, review and reteach using the instruction on page 24.

Can students use key details to determine a problem and solution? If not, review and reteach using the instruction on page 24 and assign the Unit 1 Week 2 digital mini-lesson.

Can students write a response to "Whitewater Adventure"? If not, provide sentence frames to help them organize their ideas.

WEEK 2 LESSON 3

Objectives
- Understand and use new vocabulary words
- Read realistic fiction
- Recognize and understand problem and solution
- Understand complex text through close reading

Materials
- "Dog Gone" Apprentice Leveled Reader pp. 2–9
- Graphic Organizer: Problem/Solution

☞ **Go** Digital
- Apprentice Leveled Reader eBook
- Downloadable Graphic Organizer
- Problem and Solution Mini-lesson

Scaffolding for **Wonders** Approaching Leveled Reader

BEFORE READING

10–15 Minutes   SL.5.1c   SL.5.1d   L.5.4a   L.5.6   CCSS

Introduce "Dog Gone"

- Read the Essential Question on the title page of "Dog Gone" **Apprentice Leveled Reader**: *What can lead us to rethink an idea? We will read about a family that must think hard to solve a problem.*

- Read aloud the title of the book. Have students look at the images. *What do you think this story will be about?* (A family loses their dog) *Why do you think so?* (the title, illustrations)

Expand Vocabulary

Display each word below. Say the words and have students repeat them. Then use the Define/Example/Ask routine to introduce each word.

1 borrowed (page 8)

Define: to take and use something that will be returned

Example: I *borrowed* a book from the library.

Ask: What have you *borrowed* from a friend?

2 desperately (page 5)

Define: in a worried way, or very much

Example: I *desperately* looked around for my homework.

Ask: On a very hot day, what have you *desperately* wanted?

3 scrambled (page 3)

Define: moved quickly using hands and feet

Example: I *scrambled* over the log to follow the bug.

Ask: How would you *scramble* over a fence?

4 vanished (page 5)

Define: disappeared completely

Example: The light snow *vanished* in one day.

Ask: Has something that belonged to you ever *vanished*?

DURING READING

20–30 Minutes   RL.4.3   RL.5.1   SL.5.1b   L.5.4a   CCSS

Close Reading

🔍 **Pages 2–3**

Genre Have students look at the illustration on page 2. Then read page 2 aloud. *Is this a made-up story or does it give information about a topic? How do you know?* (It is a made-up story. It has characters. They say and do things real people could say and do.)

Problem and Solution Explain that a problem often happens at the beginning of a story. Identifying the characters and the setting helps us understand the problem. Ask: *Based on what you've read on pages 2 and 3, who are the characters in this story?* (Papa, Eva, Miguel, and Lucho.) *What are they doing? What is the setting in this part of the story?* (They are taking a break on their way to visit Abuelita. They are driving through a place with rocky paths.) *What is the problem they have?* (Lucho runs off on a rocky path on page 3.)

Help students record the characters and setting in their Problem and Solution charts. Then have them record the problem. As they continue, they will record any steps the characters take to solve the problem.

Organization (A C T) Have students find "Just then" on page 3. Help students to understand that the author uses these words to stress that the events happened very quickly, at the same time. Ask: *What caused Lucho to run away?* (Miguel unclips Lucho's leash. At that moment, a small animal runs across the trail, and Lucho runs off.)

🔍 **Pages 4–5**

Problem and Solution Remind students that the characters in a story often have to make several attempts to solve a problem. Ask: *What is the next thing they do to find Lucho?* (Then they go tell Papa.) *What does Papa do?* (He goes with Miguel to where Lucho got lost. He calls for Lucho.)

STOP AND CHECK *Read the question in the Stop and Check box on page 4.* (He didn't want her to get lost.)

🔍 **Pages 6–7**

Organization (A C T) Have students reread the third paragraph on page 6. Explain that the woman gives a hint of what might happen later in the story. Say: *Hints like this in a story are called foreshadowing. What is the woman warning them about?* (steep cliffs) **What do you think might happen, based on this hint?** (Possible answer: Lucho is going to fall down a cliff.)

Vocabulary Ask students to find the word *bluffs* on page 6. Explain that the word *bluffs* has different meanings. *Bluffs* can mean "steep hills." But the verb *bluffs* means "tries to trick someone by pretending you will do something". Ask: *What does* bluffs *mean on page 11? How can you tell?* (The woman warns them about steep bluffs. Bluffs must mean hills.)

Problem and Solution *What problem does the family have on page 6?* (They still can't find Lucho and it is getting late.) *What do they decide to do so that they can solve their problem?* (They stay overnight so they can keep looking.)

STOP AND CHECK *Read the question in the Stop and Check box on page 6.* (Lucho chased an animal off the trail and didn't come back when he was called.)

Problem and Solution Have students read page 7. *How does the woman from the motel try to help them solve the problem?* (She gives them a special map showing the trail and the bluffs in the area.)

Genre (A C T) Ask: *Why do you think Miguel pleads with, or begs, his father to search for Lucho before breakfast?* (Miguel is worried about Lucho so he begs his father to search right away.) *Is this the way that real kids behave?* (yes)

🔍 **Pages 8–9**

Vocabulary Ask students to find the word *grid* on page 8, and read the sentence. *The sentence tells me that the family is using a* grid *to do something. What is the* grid *used for?* (to keep track of where they've looked) *What do you think a* grid *is?* (A grid might be a design that separates areas on a map.)

Problem and Solution Have partners paraphrase Papa and Eva's plan for using the map on pages 8 and 9. (They will draw a grid and shade in spots where they have already looked.) *How does this plan help them to solve the problem?* (They will not look in the same place twice while searching for Lucho.)

Have partners review their graphic organizer for pages 2–9 and discuss what they learned.

✔️ *Quick Check* Do students understand weekly vocabulary in context? If not, review and reteach using the instruction on page 24.

Can students identify problems and solutions? If not, review and reteach using the instruction on page 24 and assign the Unit 1 Week 2 digital mini-lesson.

WEEK 2 LESSON 4

Objectives
- Understand and use new vocabulary
- Read realistic fiction
- Recognize and understand problem and solution
- Understand complex text through close reading
- Respond to the selection, using text evidence to support ideas

Scaffolding for **Wonders** Approaching Leveled Reader

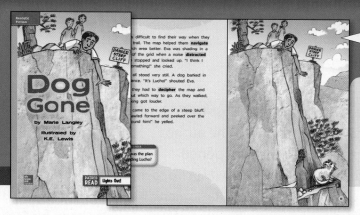

Materials
- "Dog Gone" Apprentice Leveled Reader, pp. 10–20
- Graphic Organizer: Problem/Solution

☞ **Go Digital**
- Apprentice Leveled Reader eBook
- Downloadable Graphic Organizer
- Problem and Solution Mini-Lesson

BEFORE READING

5–10 Minutes   SL.5.1c SL.5.1d L.5.4a L.5.6

Expand Vocabulary

Display each word below. Say the words and have students repeat them. Then use the Define/Example/Ask routine to introduce each word.

1 anchored (page 14)

Define: held firmly in position

Example: The thread *anchored* the button in place on the shirt.

Ask: What could be used to *anchor* bookshelves to the walls?

2 reassured (page 12)

Define: said something to help calm someone's fears

Example: My sister *reassured* me that we would be safe on the Ferris wheel.

Ask: What can you say to *reassure* a teammate who is nervous before a big game?

3 rescue (page 12)

Define: to save from a dangerous situation

Example: Firefighters can *rescue* people from burning houses.

Ask: How could you *rescue* a cat from a tall tree?

DURING READING

15–20 Minutes   RL.4.3 SL.5.1b L.5.4a

Close Reading

🔍 **Pages 10–11**

Problem and Solution Have students read the last paragraph on page 10. Ask: *What important event happens?* (Papa finds Lucho.) *Is the problem now solved? Why or why not?* (It's not. Lucho is stuck on the ledge of a steep hill.)

STOP AND CHECK *Read the question in the Stop and Check box on page 10.* (to search for the dog in each area on the grid)

🔍 **Pages 12–13**

Genre 🅰🅒🆃 Ask students to look at the illustration. *Why do you think the author included this picture?* (It shows the scary situation Lucho is in on the ledge.)

Organization 🅰🅒🆃 Have students reread page 12. *What has happened to Lucho?* (He has fallen down a steep bluff.) *How do the characters find out?* (Papa leans over the cliff and describes what he sees. He can see Lucho below on the ledge.) *What might happen next?* (The family will have to figure out a way to get Lucho up from the bottom of the cliff.)

Problem and Solution Explain that there are still important events in the story that are building to the solution. *What solution does Jodi suggest?* (She offers to climb down and get Lucho herself. "I've climbed here before," she said. "I'll go down.")

Vocabulary Ask students to find the word *rethink* on page 12. Explain that *re-* is a prefix meaning "again." Ask students to use the meaning of the prefix to give the meaning of *rethink*. (to think again)

Pages 14–15

Problem and Solution. *What was the main problem in this story?* (Lucho gets trapped on a ledge and goes missing.) What is the solution at the end? Who helps solve the problem? (Jodi the climber rescues the dog). Have students write the solution on their graphic organizer.

Vocabulary Tell students that *bolt* is a word with more than one meaning. Bolt *can be used as an action verb meaning "to run fast": The runner bolted to the finish line. It can also be a kind of metal fastener: I used a bolt to attach the door to the wall.* Ask students to read the first paragraph on page 14, paying attention to the word *bolt. What is the meaning of* bolt *in this context?* (a metal fastener)

STOP AND CHECK *Read the question in the Stop and Check box on page 15.* (They asked Jodi to climb down and bring Lucho back up.)

AFTER READING

10–15 Minutes   RL.5.1   RL.5.2   RL.5.9   W.5.9a   L.5.4a   CCSS

Respond to Reading

Compare Texts Have students compare how the family in "Dog Gone" solved their problem with the way the family in "Whitewater Adventure" solved a problem. Ask: *What problem have you worked with other people to solve?*

Summarize Have students turn to page 16 and summarize the selection. (Answers should include details about how the family solved their problem.)

Text Evidence

Have partners work together to answer questions on page 16. Remind students to use their Problem and Solution Charts.

Problem and Solution (Problem: The children couldn't find Lucho; Solution: They asked their dad for help; Problem: After finding Lucho, they couldn't reach him; Solution: They asked climbers to help.)

Vocabulary (If Miguel is pointing to bushes and saying "scrub," they have the same meaning.)

Write About Reading (The family tried following the trail and calling Lucho. When that didn't work, they made a grid on the map to keep track of where they searched.)

Independent Reading

Encourage students to read the paired selection "Lights Out!" on pages 17–19. Have them summarize the selection and compare it to "Dog Gone" Have partners answer the "Make Connections" questions on page 19.

 Quick Check **Can students identify Problem and Solution? If not, review and teach using the instruction on page 24 and assign the Unit 1 Week 2 digital mini-lesson.**

Can students respond to the selection using text evidence? If not, provide, sentence frames to help them organize their ideas.

WEEK 2
LESSON
5

Objectives
• Review weekly vocabulary words
• Review problem and solution
• Write an analysis about how well an author creates suspense

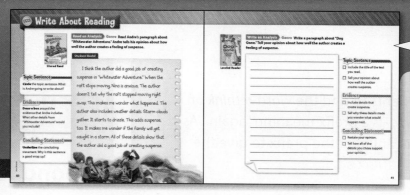

Materials
• Visual Vocabulary Cards: 9–16
• Interactive Worktext, pp. 40–41
• Assessment Book, pp. 12–13

☞ **Go** Digital
• **Visual Vocabulary Cards**
• **Problem and Solution Mini-Lesson**
• **Interactive eWorktext**

Scaffolding for **Wonders** Reading/Writing Workshop

REVIEW AND RETEACH

5–10 Minutes   RL.4.3 RL.5.1 L.5.4a L.5.6

Weekly Vocabulary

Display one **Visual Vocabulary Card** at a time and ask students to use the word in a sentence. If students have difficulty, have them find the word in "Whitewater Adventure" and use the context clues to define it.

Comprehension: Problem/Solution

I Do Write and say: *It started raining as soon as Amy walked outside her house. She knew she would get wet. So Amy went back inside. Then she got her mom's umbrella and her rain boots.* Explain that characters in a story usually have a problem that needs to be solved. *Who had the problem? Amy. What was Amy's problem?* Write *problem* above "started raining." *What was the solution?* Write *solution* above "got her mom's umbrella and her rain boots." Explain that the way the problem is solved is the solution.

We Do Display: *Tina did not make the soccer team last year. She was upset. She started to practice every day after school. This year, she made the team.* Say: We are going to find a problem and solution together. *Who has the problem?* (Tina) *What is the problem?* (She did not make the soccer team) *How does she solve it?* (she started to practice every day)

You Do Write another series of events with a problem and solution: *Jamal's best friend Paul moved to another state. Jamal misses Paul. Jamal and Paul decide to call each other every Saturday. They use a computer and a camera to chat. Jamal still misses Paul, but now he sees him every Saturday.* Have partners find the problem, the steps that lead to a solution, and the solution.

WRITE ABOUT READING

25–35 Minutes   RL.5.1 W.5.4 W.5.5 W.5.9a

Read an Analysis

• Ask students to look back at "Whitewater Adventure" in the **Interactive Worktext**. Have volunteers review events in the story. *How does the author use details to make the adventure story suspenseful or exciting?*

• Read aloud the directions on page 40. *Andre's paragraph is not a summary. It is an analysis, or detailed description, of how the author creates suspense. When you analyze, you ask yourself "how" and "why" questions to think about the way the text is written.*

• Say: *When you write an analysis, you need to include a topic sentence. In opinion writing, a good topic sentence presents a clear opinion. Circle the topic sentence in Andre's analysis. What is his opinion?* (The author did a good job creating suspense.) *What other information has Andre included in this sentence?* (the text's title)

• *Another element of analysis is text evidence. Andre supports his opinion with important details about suspenseful parts of the story. Reread the model and draw a box around the text evidence.* (sentences 2-3; 5-7) *Can you find text evidence to support this analysis? Look back at page 36. What happens when Marta yells?* (All they hear back is an echo.) *How does that build suspense?* (Possible answer: This makes me wonder how the family will get help.)

• *The final element of an analysis is the concluding statement. Underline the concluding statement. How is it like the topic sentence?* (Both sentences say that the author did a good job of creating suspense.) *What words in Andre's concluding statement wrap up the paragraph?* (all of these details)

Write an Analysis

Analytical Writing

Guided Writing Read the writing prompt on page 41 together. Have students write about "Dog Gone" or another text they read this week. Have them look for details that create suspense. Say: *Use the checklist to help you figure out the right information to include in each section.* Guide students to ask "how" and "why" questions, such as: *How well did the author create suspense? Why are some events suspenseful?*

Peer Conference Have students read their analysis to a partner. Listeners should identify the strongest text evidence that supports the opinion and discuss any sentences that are unclear.

Teacher Conference Check students' writing for complete sentences and text evidence that supports their opinion. Review the concluding statement. *Does this sentence tie all of the elements together?* If necessary, have students revise the concluding statement by restating the topic sentence.

Level Up

▲ Apprentice Leveled Reader

▲ Approaching Leveled Reader

▲ Interactive Worktext

▲ Reading/Writing Workshop

IF students read the Apprentice Level Reader fluently and the **Interactive Worktext** Shared Read fluently and answer the Respond to Reading questions

THEN read together the Approaching Level Reader main selection and the **Reading/Writing Workshop** Shared Read from *Reading Wonders*. Have students take notes as they read, using self-stick notes. Then ask and answer questions about their notes.

Writing Rubric

	4	3	2	1
Topic Sentence	Topic sentence presents a clear opinion.	Topic sentence presents an opinion somewhat clearly.	Topic is presented in short phrases; opinion is unclear.	There is no topic sentence; no opinion is presented.
Text Evidence	Opinion is supported by two or more details.	Opinion is only supported by one detail from the text.	Little to no evidence from text supports opinion.	No text evidence is included; does not support opinion.
Concluding Statement	Clearly restates an opinion; wraps up the details.	Restatement is less focused; attempts to wrap up the details.	Vaguely restates opinion. Doesn't correlate well to text evidence.	There is no conclusion.
Writing Style	Writes in complete sentences. Uses correct spelling and grammar.	Uses complete sentences and phrases. Writing has spelling and grammar errors.	Few or no complete sentences. There are many spelling and grammar errors.	Does not write accurately or in complete sentences.

ASSESSMENT

Weekly Assessment

Have students complete the Weekly Assessment using **Assessment** book pages 12–13.

WEEK 3 LESSON 1

Objectives
- Develop oral language
- Build background about nature
- Understand and use weekly vocabulary
- Read narrative nonfiction text

Scaffolding for **McGraw-Hill Reading Wonders** Reading/Writing Workshop

Materials
Interactive Worktext, pp. 42–49
• Visual Vocabulary Cards: 17–24

☞ **Go** Digital
• **Interactive eWorktext**
• **Visual Vocabulary Cards**

WEEKLY CONCEPT

5–10 Minutes   SL.5.1b   SL.5.1c   CCSS

Talk About It

Essential Question Read aloud the Essential Question on page 42 of the **Interactive Worktext:** *How can experiencing nature change the way you think about it?* Explain that nature includes things in the world that are not made by people, such as mountains, forests, rivers, lakes, and oceans. Say: *We learn about nature by experiencing it. A person who studies nature is a naturalist.*

• Discuss the photograph on page 42. Ask: *How are the two naturalists in the photo experiencing nature?* (canoeing on a stream in the woods) Ask which senses—seeing, hearing, smelling, touching—the people in the photo are probably using. (all of them)

I Do Say: *I am going to imagine that I am in the canoe experiencing nature. I am listening. What can I hear? I hear the water rushing by the canoe. I hear my paddle splashing in the water. I hear birds in the trees chirping. I will write these sounds in the web on page 43 under* Sound.

We Do Say: *Let's look at the photo and think about another way the people experience nature. What do they see?* (green and brown trees; tan water) As students describe what they see, work with them to complete their webs on page 43. Then have them tell what they might smell or feel and add those words.

You Do Have partners work together to describe an experience they each had in nature (for example, in a city park or on a hike in the woods). Have them use the key words in the web (look, sound, feel, smell) and answer the questions: *What did you do? What did you see? What did you hear? What did you smell? What did you touch and how did it feel?*

REVIEW VOCABULARY

10–15 Minutes   L.5.1a   L.5.1c   L.5.4a   L.5.5c   L.5.6   CCSS

Review Weekly Vocabulary Words

• Use the **Visual Vocabulary Cards** to review the weekly vocabulary.

• Read together the directions for the Vocabulary activity on page 44 of the **Interactive Worktext**. Then complete the activity.

1 **debris** Have students use the sentence starter: *In a pile of debris, you might see _____.* (Possible answers: dirt, leaves, branches)

2 **indicated** Have students use the following sentence frame: *_____ and _____ indicate time.* (clock, computer, calendar) Ask students to form the past tense of *indicate*.

3 **emphasis** Ask students to name a place or describe a time when they felt cold. *How do you use your voice, hands, and face to add emphasis?* (Students can rub and blow into their hands to demonstrate feeling cold.) *What are other ways you can add emphasis to something you say?* (Actions will vary.)

4 **sheer** Have students complete sentence frames: *_____ and _____ have sheer sides.* (Possible answers: desk side, wall, door) *It feels _____.* (Possible answers: steep, straight; smooth) Discuss multiple meanings for *sheer*, including the target meaning for the activity.

5 **generations** Have students complete the sentence: *_____ is from another generation.* (Possible answers: name of a grandparent, great aunt or uncle) Ask students to form the plural of *generation*.

6 **naturalist** Point out the suffix *-ist*. Explain to students that *-ist* is added to the end of a word to describe a person that does, studies, or makes something. (nature; *-ist*; someone who studies nature)

7 **spectacular** Ask students to tell how they feel when they see something *spectacular*. Then have them tell other words that have the same meaning as *spectacular*. (Possible answers: exciting, incredible, awesome)

8 **encounter** Ask students if they have been to or seen a beach. Show pictures as necessary. Ask students to describe their drawing by using the sentence frame: *I might have an encounter with _____ at the beach.* (Drawings may include seashells, crabs, birds, sand castles)

High-Utility Words

Explain that prepositions, such as *to, at, on, up, down, against, around, under, over,* and *in*, are connecting words that link one word to another. Prepositions show a direction or a location of something. Have students turn to page 45 in the **Interactive Worktext**. Have partners circle prepositions in the passage. (in, against, under, up, down, to, at, around) Write the sentence frame: *I went _____ the mountain.* Have students use different prepositions in the sentence and tell how each changes the meaning. Then have students partner read the passage.

> **ELL ENGLISH LANGUAGE LEARNERS**
>
> Display the prepositions *in, under, up, down, on, against, around*. Point to and say each preposition. Have students repeat it and show the direction it indicates with their hand or body.

READ COMPLEX TEXT

15–20 Minutes RI.5.1 RF.5.4c

Read "A Life in the Woods"

- Have students turn to page 46 in the **Interactive Worktext** and read aloud the Essential Question. Explain that Henry David Thoreau was an American writer and *naturalist* who lived in the 1800s. Ask: *What is the title?* ("A Life in the Woods") *What does the photo show?* (trees, woods) *Use these clues. Where do you think Thoreau experiences nature?* (in the woods)

- Read the selection together. Note that the weekly vocabulary words are highlighted in yellow. Expand vocabulary words are highlighted in blue.

- Have student use the "My Notes" section on page 46 to write questions they have, words they don't understand, and things they want to remember. Model how to use the "My Notes" section. *I can write notes about questions I have as I read. In the first paragraph on page 47, I am not sure what the word* chatter *means. I will write* chatter *with a question mark beside it in the "My Notes" section. As I continue to read this paragraph, I am not sure why Thoreau was upset so I will write a question in the "My Notes" section:* Why was Thoreau upset? *When we reread the story, I will ask my questions so I better understand what I am reading.*

> **ELL ENGLISH LANGUAGE LEARNERS**
>
> As you read together, have students highlight parts of the text they have questions about. After reading, help them write their questions in the "My Notes" section.

 Quick Check Can students understand the weekly vocabulary in context? If not, review vocabulary using the **Visual Vocabulary Cards** before teaching Lesson 2.

WEEK 3 LESSON 2

Objectives
- Read narrative nonfiction text
- Understand complex text through close reading
- Recognize and understand cause-and-effect relationships
- Respond to the selection, using text evidence to support ideas

Scaffolding for **WONDERS** Reading/Writing Workshop
McGraw-Hill Reading

Materials
Interactive Worktext, pp. 46–51

☞ **Go** Digital
- Interactive eWorktext
- Cause and Effect Mini-Lesson

REREAD COMPLEX TEXT

20–25 Minutes   RI.5.1 RI.5.3 RI.5.4 L.5.2 L.5.4a CCSS

Close Reading: "A Life in the Woods"

Reread "A Life in the Woods" with students. As you read together, discuss important passages in the text. Have students respond to text-dependent questions, including those in the **Interactive Worktext**.

 Page 47

Vocabulary Have a student locate the word *chatter* and read the sentence aloud. *What does* chatter *mean? What clues help you understand the meaning of chatter?* (noisy talk; guests; filled his ears; noise in his family's house)

Expand Vocabulary Have students point to *stared*. Demonstrate staring at an object. *What did Thoreau stare at?* (the page) *Why did he stare?* (He wasn't able to write.)

Sentence Structure **A C T** Have students draw a box around *"Concord, MA, 1841." What do the quotation marks show?* (someone is speaking or writing) *Do these quotation marks indicate speaking or writing?* (writing) *Who is writing?* (Thoreau)

Cause and Effect Say: *The author used causes and effects to show what happened to Thoreau and why it happened.* Model using text evidence to find a cause and effect in the first paragraph on page 47. *I read, "There was so much noise in his family's house. So Thoreau headed outside."* So much noise *is the cause.* So *is the signal word.* Have students look for another cause and effect. Have them circle the cause and underline the effect. If there is a signal word, have them put a star next to it. Give examples of signal words: *as a result, because,* and *so.* (Signal word: because Cause: because he was upset; Effect: He shut the front door hard with emphasis.)

 Page 48

High-Utility Words Point to the prepositions *to, up, down, in,* and *under* in the first paragraph on page 48. Have students use their hands to show which direction each preposition indicates.

Vocabulary Point out the word *loon* in the "On Walden Pond" section. Ask: *What is a loon? What clues help you understand the meaning of* loon? (*bird* in the next sentence; photo and caption on page 49)

Expand Vocabulary Discuss the word *habits. What are some details that help you understand the habits of a loon?* (dove quickly, swam, call, howling laugh)

Sentence Structure **A C T** Say: *Punctuation affects the meaning of a sentence.* Point out the sentence: *"The loon came up somewhere else!"* Ask: *What punctuation mark is at the end of this sentence?* (exclamation point) *What does an exclamation mark show?* (surprise or excitement) *What feeling does the author express about where the loon comes up?* (surprise) Prompt students to look for another exclamation point on page 48 and tell why the author used it. (first paragraph: *Writing was easy because this place was so beautiful!*; to show excitement.)

Cause and Effect Reread Thoreau's journal entry together aloud. Explain the meaning of the words *uttered* and *prolonged*. Point out the pronoun *he* and ask: *What is Thoreau describing?* (the loon) *What did the loon do?* (howled) *What happened after the loon howled?* (a wind came, rippled the water, and filled the air with mist) *What did this cause Thoreau to feel?* (impressed) Help students find and mark the cause and effect that Thoreau describes. Point out that there is not a signal word. (Cause: there came a wind from the east and rippled the surface, and filled the whole air with misty rain; Effect: I was impressed) Then help students paraphrase the journal entry.

Page 49

Vocabulary *Reread the first sentence. What makes the scene* spectacular? (The loon's howling; the wind and the rain were very beautiful and amazing.)

Expand Vocabulary Have students locate and point out the word *awe*. The text says that Thoreau "watched the moles outside in awe." This means he was amazed by them. Which sentences help you understand why he watched in awe? (In winter, he warmed his cabin by fire and watched the moles outside in awe. They warmed their nest with their own body heat.)

Sentence Structure **A**C**T** Have students reread the first sentence in "Back to Concord." Point out the words "Like the geese" before the comma. Now look at the rest of the sentence. *Who is like the geese?* (Thoreau) *What word tells us that the author is comparing the geese to Thoreau?* (like) *How is Thoreau like the geese?* (He also leaves Walden Pond at the end of the season.)

Cause and Effect Have students reread the page and find examples of causes and their effects on page 49. (Cause: moles warmed their nest with their own body heat; Effect: Thoreau watched them in awe.) *Now find the cause and effect in the first two sentences in "Back to Concord."* (Cause: He had done what he had set out to do. Effect: Thoreau left Walden Pond) Point out that there is no signal word in this cause and effect. If students have difficulty finding the cause and effect, ask these questions: *What did Thoreau do at season's end? Why did he do it?*

RESPOND TO READING

10–20 Minutes   RI.5.1   RI.5.2   RI.5.3   W.5.9b   SL.5.1d   CCSS

Respond to "A Life in the Woods"

Have students summarize "A Life in the Woods" orally to demonstrate comprehension. Then have partners answer the questions on page 50 of the **Interactive Worktext** using the discussion starters. Tell them to use text evidence to support their answers. Have students write the page number(s) on which they found the text evidence for each question.

1. *What did Thoreau think about nature at first?* (Possible answer: Thoreau thought nature was a place he could be alone and write his book; Text Evidence: p. 47)

2. *What did Thoreau think about nature after living in the woods?* (Possible answer: He thought it was amazing and understood it better; Text Evidence: pp. 48, 49)

3. *What caused Thoreau to change the way he thought about nature?* (Possible answer: He saw how animals lived and had amazing encounters with them; Text Evidence: pp. 48, 49)

After students discuss the questions on page 50, have them write a response to the question on page 51. Tell them to use their partner discussions and notes about "A Life in the Woods" to help them. Circulate and provide guidance.

 Quick Check Do students understand vocabulary in context? If not, review and reteach using the instruction on page 34.

Can students use key details to determine a cause and an effect? If not, review and reteach using the instruction on page 34 and assign the Unit 1 Week 3 digital mini-lesson

Can students write a response to "A Life in the Woods"? If not, provide sentence frames to help them organize their ideas.

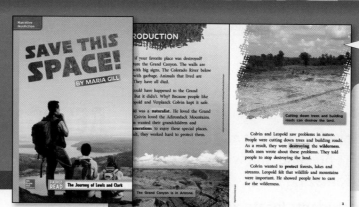

WEEK 3 LESSON

3

Objectives
- Understand and use new vocabulary words
- Read narrative nonfiction text
- Recognize and understand cause and effect
- Understand complex text through close reading

Materials
"Save This Space!" Apprentice Leveled Reader, pp. 2–9
- Graphic Organizer: Cause/Effect

☞ **Go** Digital
- Apprentice Leveled Reader eBook
- Downloadable Graphic Organizer
- Cause and Effect Mini-Lesson

Scaffolding for **Wonders** Approaching Leveled Reader

BEFORE READING

10–15 Minutes   SL.5.1c SL.5.1d L.5.4a L.5.6

Introduce "Save This Space!"

- Read the Essential Question on the title page of the "Save This Space!" **Apprentice Leveled Reader**: *How can experiencing nature change the way you think about it? We will read about experiences that changed how two men thought about nature.*

- Read the title of the main read. Have students look at the images. *Is this a fiction or a nonfiction book?* (nonfiction) *How do you know?* (gives information; includes photos, captions, and a map) *What do most of the photographs show?* (pictures from nature)

Expand Vocabulary

Display each word below. Say the word and have students repeat it. Then use the Define/Example/Ask routine to introduce each word.

1 damage (page 5)

Define: harm that is done to something

Example: The *damage* to the car from the crash will cost a lot to fix.

Ask: What kind of *damage* from a storm have you seen?

2 dangerous (page 7)

Define: likely to cause something bad to happen

Example: Wild animals can be *dangerous*.

Ask: What is the most *dangerous* sport to play?

3 decided (page 4)

Define: made a choice

Example: Eric *decided* to have pizza for lunch.

Ask: What have you *decided* to do this weekend?

4 destroying (page 3)

Define: wrecking or ruining completely

Example: Wild deer are *destroying* our garden.

Ask: What could *destroy* a forest?

DURING READING

20–30 Minutes   RI.5.3 RI.5.4 SL.5.1b L.5.4a

Close Reading

🔍 **Pages 2–3**

Sentence Structure Ⓐ Ⓒ Ⓣ Read the first paragraph. Point out the question mark. *An author sometimes uses questions at the beginning of articles to catch the reader's interest. Why is this author asking a question?* (to get the reader's interest)

Cause and Effect Read the last two sentences on page 2. Point out the signal words *as a result. I know the signal words* as a result *always come before an effect, so the effect is:* the men decided to keep these places safe. *What caused them to keep them safe? They wanted their grandchildren to enjoy these places. This tells the cause.* Have students record the causes and effects they identify on their Cause and Effect Chart as they read the selection.

Cause and Effect Have a student reread the first three sentences on page 3. *Are there any signal words?* (as a result) *What was happening to the wilderness?* (People were destroying it.) *Why was the wilderness being destroyed?* (People were cutting down trees and building roads.) *What is the cause?* (Cause: People were cutting down trees and making roads.) *What is the effect?* (Effect: They were destroying the wilderness.)

Pages 4–5

Vocabulary *Read the first paragraph on page 5. What clue helps you understand the word* loggers? (the words "cut down the trees")

Genre **ACT** *Look at the map on page 5. Read the title. What does the map show?* (where the Adirondacks are located in New York state) Have students point out the mountains, rivers, and streams.

Cause and Effect *What did people do to the forest?* (cut down the trees) *What was the effect in the spring?* (the snow melted quickly) *What is the cause?* (Cause: cutting down the forests) *What is the effect?* (Effect: the snow melts quickly) *What happened when water and debris filled up streams and rivers?* (Effect: they caused floods) *What is the cause and the effect?* (Cause: water and debris filled up streams; Effect: they caused floods)

Pages 6–7

Connection of Ideas **ACT** *Read the sentence on page 6 with the word* emphasis. *Why do you say something with* emphasis? (to bring attention to it or to show a strong feeling) *What did Colvin do for emphasis?* (placed river ice in the glasses of the people at a meeting) *Why did he do that?* (show the importance of keeping the water clean enough to drink)

Cause and Effect *Look at the first paragraph on page 6. Is there a signal word?* (so) *What is the cause and its effect?* (Cause: Colvin wanted the government to protect the water. Effect: He made a plan.) *What did Colvin do with the ice? What happened? Tell the cause and the effect.* (Cause: Colvin put ice from the river into everyone's glasses. Effect: Everyone saw that water was important.)

STOP AND CHECK *Read the question in the Stop and Check box on page 7.* (The land was rough and the team had to climb over tall, steep mountains. There were also dangerous wild animals.)

Pages 8–9

Sentence Structure **ACT** *Read the text in the blue box on page 8. Point out the word* desolate *and explain its meaning, "deserted, without people." What do the quotation marks mean?* (These are Colvin's exact words.) *Why do you think the author included this quote?* (He wanted the reader to see the mountains as Colvin saw them.) Help students paraphrase the quote. (This is a wild place without any people. When we first see it, it is dark and raining.)

Cause and Effect *Reread the first paragraph on page 9. Is there a signal word?* (no) *What did the government do?* (The government made the Adirondacks a protected national park.) *Why did they do it?* (Colvin told them to protect the Adirondacks.) *Tell the cause and effect* (Cause: Colvin told the government they should protect the wilderness. Effect: They made the Adirondacks into a national park.)

STOP AND CHECK *Read the question in the Stop and Check box on page 9.* (He loved the Adirondacks. He felt it was important to protect forests and to keep the water clean.)

Have partners review their Cause and Effect Charts for pages 2–9 and discuss what they learned.

 Quick Check **Do students understand weekly vocabulary in context? If not, review and reteach using the instruction on page 34.**

Can students use details to determine a cause and its effect? If not, review and reteach using the instruction on page 34 and assign the Unit 1 Week 3 digital mini-lesson.

Objectives
- Understand and use new vocabulary
- Read narrative nonfiction text
- Understand complex text through close reading
- Understand cause and effect
- Respond to the selection, using text evidence to support ideas

Scaffolding for **Wonders** Approaching Leveled Reader

Materials
"Save This Space!" Apprentice Leveled Reader, pp. 10–20
- Graphic Organizer: Cause/Effect

☞ **Go** Digital
- Apprentice Leveled Reader eBook
- Downloadable Graphic Organizer
- Cause and Effect Mini-Lesson

BEFORE READING

5–10 Minutes   SL.5.1c   SL.5.1d   L.5.4a   L.5.6   CCSS

Expand Vocabulary

Display each word below. Say the word and have students repeat it. Then use the Define/Example/Ask routine to introduce each word.

① balance (page 12)

Define: when opposite forces are equal

Example: Ken eats many different kinds of foods for a healthy *balance* in his diet.

Ask: How do you keep a seesaw in *balance*?

② encouraged (page 13)

Define: tried to get someone to do something

Example: The mayor *encouraged* people to vote for her again.

Ask: Which movies have you *encouraged* your friends to see?

③ environment (page 17)

Define: the air, the water, and the land around us

Example: Lakes and rivers are an important part of our *environment*.

Ask: Why is it important to protect the *environment*?

④ waste (page 17)

Define: when something has been used in a careless way

Example: A leaky faucet causes a *waste* of water.

Ask: What can we do to stop our *waste* of electricity?

DURING READING

15–20 Minutes   RI.5.3   RI.5.4   SL.5.b   L.5.6   CCSS

Close Reading

🔍 **Pages 10–11**

Key Details *Who is Chapter 2 about?* (Aldo Leopold) *Where did he work?* (Apache National Forest in Arizona)

Sentence Structure   *Why does the author use Aldo Leopold's first and last name in the first sentence but only his last name in the other sentences on this page?* (In informational text, authors usually use a person's first and last name once.)

Cause and Effect Review the cause-and-effect text structure and signal words. Have students reread the first paragraph on page 11. Point out the third and fourth sentences and the signal words, *as a result.* Ask: *Why should people count game animals?* (so they know which ones were low in numbers) *The cause is: People should count game animals. The effect is: That way they would know which animals were low in numbers.* Have students record each cause and effect that they identify on their Cause-and-Effect Chart as they read the selection.

Cause and Effect Read the first two sentences in the second paragraph. *Is there a signal word in these sentences?* (no) *What is the cause?* (Leopold felt game animals should be protected from predators) *What is the effect?* (He was in favor of shooting predators.)

🔍 **Pages 12–13**

Vocabulary *Read pages 12–13. What does "upset the balance" mean?* (having too many of one plant or animal and not enough of another) *What clues in the text help you?* (the first paragraph on page 13 gives an example: Most of the wolves and mountain lions had been killed.)

Cause and Effect *Read the first paragraph on page 13. Why did the number of deer grow quickly? What is the cause? What is the effect?* (Cause: Most of the wolves and mountain lions had been killed. Effect: The number of deer grew quickly.) *What happened when there were too many deer?* (They ate lots of plants and damaged the plant life.) Have students write these causes and effects on their charts.

Vocabulary Discuss the quotation in the blue box and the meaning of *organism*: "a living thing." Then ask students what Aldo Leopold meant. (He is comparing the forest/land to a living thing. Both game and predators are part of this living thing. The forest/land needs both of them to live.)

Pages 14–15

Cause and Effect *What happened after Leopold wrote a plan? What is the cause? What is the effect?* Cause: Leopold wrote a plan to save the Grand Canyon. Effect: The plan saved the land and animals; the Grand Canyon became a national park in 1919.)

STOP AND CHECK *Read the Stop and Check box on page 15.* (Leopold wanted to protect the Grand Canyon after seeing new roads, hotels and stores on the land, dirty water in the rivers, and garbage on the ground.)

Pages 16–17

Genre **A C T** *Read the caption on page 16 and look at the photos. Why do you think the author included these images?* (to show what might happen to other animals if we do not do anything to protect the wildlife)

Connection of Ideas **A C T** *Reread the first paragraph on page 2 and the last two paragraphs on page 17. How are these connected?* (Page 2 states what might happen if we don't take care of the land. Page 17 suggests ways we can help to protect the land.)

AFTER READING

10–15 Minutes   RI.5.1   RI.5.2   RI.5.5   RI.5.9   W.5.9b

Respond to Reading

Compare Texts Have students compare experiences that Thoreau had in nature with those of Leopold and Colvin. Then ask: *Have you had similar experiences?*

Summarize Have students turn to page 18 and summarize the selection. (Answers include details from the selection that show how Colvin and Leopold helped create laws that protected the wilderness.)

Text Evidence

Have partners work together to answer questions on page 18. Remind students to use their Cause and Effect Charts.

Cause and Effect (He wanted to be sure there was enough game to hunt.)

Vocabulary (wild animals that are hunted; hunting, Deer and ducks are game.)

Write About Reading (Possible answers: Leopold went on a hunting trip to Mexico. He saw that the forest was healthy and it still had predators. This made him realize that predators are an important part of a balanced ecosystem.)

Independent Reading

Encourage students to read the paired selection "The Journey of Lewis and Clark" on pages 19–21. Have them summarize the selection and compare it to "Save This Space!" Have them work with a partner to answer the "Make Connections" questions on page 21.

✓ *Quick Check* **Can students identify a cause and its effect? If not, review and reteach using the instruction on page 34 and assign the Unit 1 Week 3 digital mini-lesson.**

Can students respond to the selection using text evidence? If not, provide sentence frames to help them organize their ideas.

WRITE & ASSESS

Objectives
- Review weekly vocabulary words
- Review cause and effect
- Write an analysis about an author's use of primary sources to support an idea

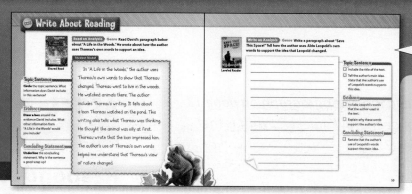

Materials
- Visual Vocabulary Cards: 17–24
- Interactive Worktext, pp. 52–53
- Assessment Book, pp. 14–15

👉 **Go** Digital
- Visual Vocabulary Cards
- Cause and Effect Mini-Lesson
- Interactive eWorktext

Scaffolding for **Wonders** McGraw-Hill Reading Reading/Writing Workshop

---

REVIEW AND RETEACH

5–10 Minutes   RI.5.3   L.5.4a   L.5.6

Weekly Vocabulary

Display one **Visual Vocabulary Card** at a time and ask students to use the vocabulary word in a sentence. If students have difficulty creating a sentence, have them find the word in "A Life in the Woods" and use the context clues in the passage to define the vocabulary word.

Comprehension: Cause and Effect

I Do Write and say: *Sue's friends were talking, so she did not hear the phone ring.* Say: *Why didn't Sue hear the phone ring? Her friends were talking.* Write *cause* above the first part of the sentence and *effect* above the second part. Circle the word *so*. Say: *This sentence shows a cause and its effect. Authors organize ideas using causes and effects. They often use signal words, such as* because, so, as a result, *or* therefore *to show a cause and its effect.* Display: *I got a new bike. I felt happy.* Point out that there is a cause (got a new bike) and effect (felt happy) but no signal words.

We Do Display: *Ed was hungry. As a result, he ate lunch.* Say: *We are going to find a cause and effect together. How does Ed feel?* (hungry) *What does he do because he is hungry?* (eat lunch) *What is the cause?* (Ed is hungry) *What is the effect?* (Ed eats lunch) *What are the signal words?* (as a result)

You Do Display: *Leah gave her dog a bath. Because her hands were wet, she couldn't hold onto the soap. It dropped onto the floor and spilled. The floor became covered in soap. So Leah had to clean up the floor when she was done giving her dog a bath.* Have partners identify causes, effects, and any signal words.

WRITE ABOUT READING

25–35 Minutes   W.5.4   W.5.5   W.5.9b

Read an Analysis

- Ask students to look back at "A Life in the Woods" in the **Interactive Worktext**. Have volunteers review their notes. *How did the author's use of Thoreau's own words help you understand the main idea of the text?*

- Read aloud the directions on page 52. Read aloud the student model. *David's writing is not a summary. The student is writing an analysis, or a detailed description, of how the author of "A Life in the Woods" used Thoreau's own words to support an idea.*

- Say: *When you write an analysis, you need to include certain elements. The first element is the topic sentence. It should be clear and focused. Read the beginning of the paragraph and circle the topic sentence. What important pieces of information has David included in this sentence?* (text's title; author's use of Thoreau's own words; author's idea that Thoreau changed)

- *Another element of analysis is text evidence. David supports the topic sentence with details from the text that show how the author used Thoreau's words. Reread the model and draw a box around the text evidence.* (sentences 2–8) *Look back at "A Life in the Woods." What other details might be included as text evidence?* (The author included Thoreau's thoughts on page 47 to show that he wanted to stay in the woods.)

- *The final element is the concluding statement. Underline the concluding statement. How is the concluding statement like the topic sentence?* (both say that the author used Thoreau's words; both say that Thoreau changed.) *Why is the sentence a good wrap up?* (It restates the topic sentence.)

Write an Analysis

Guided Writing Read the writing prompt on page 53 together. Have students write about "Save This Space!" or another text they read this week. Have them review their notes. *Use the checklist to help you figure out the right information to include in each section.* Guide students to ask "how" and "why" questions, such as: *How does the author use Leopold's words to support the main idea?*

Peer Conference Have students read their analysis to a partner. Listeners should identify the strongest text evidence that supports the topic sentence and discuss any sentences that are unclear.

Teacher Conference Check students' writing for complete sentences and text evidence that supports their topic. Review the concluding statement: *Does this sentence tie all of the elements together?* If necessary, have the student revise the concluding statement by restating the topic sentence orally and then in writing.

Level Up

▲ **Approaching Leveled Reader**

▲ **Reading/Writing Workshop**

▲ **Apprentice Leveled Reader**

▲ **Interactive Worktext**

IF students read the Apprentice Level Reader fluently and the **Interactive Worktext** Shared Read fluently and answer the Respond to Reading questions

THEN read together the Approaching Level Reader main selection and the **Reading/Writing Workshop** Shared Read from *Reading Wonders*. Have students take notes as they read, using self-stick notes. Then ask and answer questions about their notes.

Writing Rubric

	4	3	2	1
Topic Sentence	There is one clear, focused topic sentence.	Topic sentence is less focused, somewhat clear.	Topic is presented in short phrases.	There is no topic sentence.
Text Evidence	Topic is supported by two or more text details.	Evidence includes only one detail from the text.	Little to no evidence is cited from the text.	No text evidence is included.
Concluding Statement	Restates the topic sentence; wraps up the details.	Restatement is less focused; attempts to wrap up the details.	Vaguely restates topic. Doesn't correlate well to text evidence.	There is no conclusion.
Writing Style	Writes in complete sentences. Uses correct spelling and grammar.	Uses complete sentences and phrases. Writing has spelling and grammar errors.	Few or no complete sentences. There are many spelling and grammar errors.	Does not write accurately or in complete sentences.

ASSESSMENT

Weekly Assessment

Have students complete the Weekly Assessment using **Assessment** book pages 14–15.

WEEK 3

▶ **Mid-Unit Assessment,** pages 72–79

▶ **Fluency Assessment,** pages 234–239

Unit 1 Mid-Unit Assessment

CCSS TESTED SKILLS

✓ COMPREHENSION	✓ VOCABULARY
• Character, Setting, Plot: Sequence **RL.3.3** • Character, Setting, Plot: Problem and Solution **RL.4.3** • Cause and Effect **RI.5.3**	• Context Clues **L.5.4a**

Using Assessment and Writing Scores

RETEACH	IF ...	THEN ...
COMPREHENSION	Students answer 0–5 multiple-choice items correctly ...	... reteach tested skills using instruction on pages 364–371.
VOCABULARY	Students answer 0–2 multiple-choice items correctly ...	... reteach tested skills using instruction on page 364.
WRITING	Students score mostly 1–2 on weekly writing rubrics throughout the unit...	... reteach writing using instruction on pages 372–373.

Fluency Assessment

Conduct assessments individually using the differentiated fluency passages in Assessment. Students' expected fluency goal for this Unit is 100–120 WCPM with an accuracy rate of 95% or higher.

Weeks 4 and 5

Monitor students' progress on the following to inform how to adjust instruction for the remainder of the unit.

ADJUST INSTRUCTION	
ACCESS COMPLEX TEXT	If students need more support for accessing complex text, provide additional modeling of prompts in Lesson 2 of Week 4, pages 40–41, and Week 5, pages 50–51. After you model how to identify the text evidence, guide students to find text evidence in Lessons 3 and 4 in Week 4, pages 42–45, and Week 5, pages 52–55.
FLUENCY	For those students who need more support with Fluency, focus on the Fluency lessons in the Foundational Skills Kit.
WRITING	If students need more support incorporating text evidence in their writing, conduct the Write About Reading activities in Lessons 4 and 5 as group writing activities.
FOUNDATIONAL SKILLS	Review students' individualized progress in *PowerPAL for Reading* to determine which foundational skills to incorporate into your lessons for the remainder of the unit.

Teach and Model WORKTEXT

Objectives
- Develop oral language
- Build background about technology
- Understand and use weekly vocabulary
- Read a biography

Materials
- Interactive Worktext, pp. 54–61
- Visual Vocabulary Cards: 25–32

☞ **Go Digital**
- Interactive eWorktext
- Visual Vocabulary Cards

Scaffolding for **WONDERS** Reading/Writing Workshop

WEEKLY CONCEPT

5–10 Minutes   SL.5.1b   SL.5.1c   **CCSS**

Talk About It

Essential Question Read aloud the Essential Question on page 54 of the **Interactive Worktext:** *How does technology lead to creative ideas?* Explain that technology includes machines, tools, and devices. Give examples of technology, such as computers, cell phones, MP3 players, and tablets. Say: *Technology we use today can lead to new ideas and inventions in the future.*

- Discuss the photograph on page 54. Ask: *How is the girl in the photograph using technology?* (She is using a guitar and a tablet to play music)

I Do Say: *I am going to look closely at the photograph and think about how each invention can help the girl create something new. I see a guitar. The girl can use the guitar to play a new song or come up with a new type of music. On page 55, I will write "guitar" in an oval and write how this technology helps the girl "play a new song" and "create a new type of music."*

We Do Say: *Let's look at the photo and think about another invention in the photograph. What other technology do you see?* (a tablet) *What does this invention help the girl do?* (Possible answers: it helps her read, write, record, or share music) Have students brainstorm different ways the girl could be using each invention in the photograph. Work with them to add their ideas to their webs.

You Do Have partners describe a favorite technology and tell what it allows them to do. Have them use some of the words in their webs to answer the questions: *What technology do you use? What does it let you do? How could it help you create new things?*

REVIEW VOCABULARY

10–15 Minutes   L.5.1a   L.5.4a   L.5.5c   L.5.6   **CCSS**

Review Weekly Vocabulary Words

- Use the **Visual Vocabulary Cards** to review the weekly vocabulary.

- Read together the directions for the Vocabulary activity on page 56 of the **Interactive Worktext.** Then complete the activity.

❶ envisioned Have students use the following sentence starter: *When I grow up, I envision being a(n) _____.* (Possible answers: teacher, baseball player, actress) Ask students to form the past tense of *envision.*

❷ passionate Have students use the sentence frame: *I am passionate about _____ and _____.* (Possible answers: soccer, playing piano, drawing)

❸ enthusiastically Ask students to describe how they would feel if they scored a goal. (Possible answers: good, happy, excited) Then have students read the sentence and ask: *How would you use your voice to say it enthusiastically? How would you use your hands and face?* (Actions will vary, such as smiling, raising arms, saying the sentence quickly or loudly)

❹ claimed Model naming something in the classroom that you have *claimed* as your own. Then have students use this sentence starter: *In this classroom, I have claimed _____.* (Possible answers: a desk, a book, a notebook)

❺ patents Have students read their sentences aloud. (Possible answers: they keep others from claiming their ideas) Then have partners discuss inventions that they think should have *patents.*

6 **captivated** Say: *Show me how you would look if you were captivated by something.* (Actions will vary, but students should show an expression of awe, amazement, or be focused on one thing) Then have partners ask each other questions to help them decide which of the words are synonyms for *captivated.* (amazed, interested)

7 **breakthrough** Have partners discuss a time when they had a *breakthrough.* Then provide this sentence starter: *If I had a breakthrough, I would say, "_____!"* (Possible answers: Yes! I got it! Eureka! That's it! Students' voices should reflect excitement.)

8 **devices** Work with students to brainstorm a list of *devices.* Then have them choose one to draw. (Drawings may include a computer, a television, an MP3 player, a toaster, a cell phone.) Have students use these sentence frames to create a caption: _____ *is a device. I use this device to _____.*

High-Utility Words

Have students turn to page 57 of the **Interactive Worktext.** Explain that some words such as *and, but,* and *or* are connecting words. They join words or ideas. Say: And *shows that two ideas are related.* But *shows that two ideas are different.* Or *shows that there is a choice between two ideas.* Have partners circle connecting words in the passage. (or, but, and) Have students take turns reading the sentences. Then have students tell two things they can do using one of the connecting words they circled.

> **ELL ENGLISH LANGUAGE LEARNERS**
>
> Help students use connecting words to tell about things they can do. Model: *Can you sing or dance? I can sing and dance.* Have them complete the sentence frames: *I can _____ and _____.*

READ COMPLEX TEXT

15–20 Minutes   RI.5.1   RF.5.4c

Read: "Fantasy Becomes Fact"

- Have students turn to page 58 in the **Interactive Worktext** and read aloud the Essential Question. Explain that Arthur C. Clarke was a writer and an inventor. Ask: *What is the title?* ("Fantasy Becomes Fact") *What does the photograph show?* (an object in space) *Let's use these clues. What do you think Arthur C. Clarke wrote about?* (Possible answer: made-up stories about space; science fiction; stories with inventions)

- Read "Fantasy Becomes Fact" together. Note that the weekly vocabulary words are highlighted in yellow. Expand vocabulary words are highlighted in blue.

- Have students use the "My Notes" section on page 58 to write questions they have, words they don't understand, and details they want to remember. Model how to use it: *I can write notes and questions I have as I read. In the first paragraph on page 59, I am not sure what* science fiction *means. I will write* Science fiction? *in the "My Notes" section. As I continue to read, I wonder what things Arthur imagined that became real inventions. I will write a question in the "My Notes" section:* Which inventions that Arthur imagined became real? *When we reread the passage, I will ask my questions so I better understand what I am reading.*

> **ELL ENGLISH LANGUAGE LEARNERS**
>
> As you read together, have students highlight parts of the text they have questions about. After reading, help them write their questions in the "My Notes" section.

 Quick Check Can students understand the weekly vocabulary in context? If not, review vocabulary using the **Visual Vocabulary Cards** before teaching Lesson 2.

WEEK 4 LESSON

2

Objectives
- Read a biography
- Understand complex text through close reading
- Recognize and understand sequence
- Respond to the selection, using text evidence to support ideas

Materials
Interactive Worktext, pp. 58–63

👉 **Go** Digital
- Interactive eWorktext
- Sequence Mini-Lesson

Scaffolding for **WONDERS** Reading/Writing Workshop

REREAD COMPLEX TEXT

20–25 Minutes   RI.5.1   RI.5.3   RI.5.4   L.5.4a   L.5.5c   (CCSS)

Close Reading: "Fantasy Becomes Fact"

Reread "Fantasy Becomes Fact" with students. As you read together, discuss important passages in the text. Have students respond to text-dependent questions, including those in the **Interactive Worktext.**

🔍 Page 59

Connection of Ideas 🅐🅒🅣 Read the first sentence of the second paragraph and say: *Arthur wrote about technologies that had not yet been invented.* Have students draw a box around this detail in the text. Ask: *What are some other things that Arthur wrote about?* Have students read the rest of the paragraph and draw a box around other details that tell what Arthur wrote about. (advanced computers, spaceships) Say: *What do these details have in common?* (they are about science; they are about things that hadn't been invented) Say: *Turn to a partner. Talk about what these details tell us about Arthur.* (Possible answers: He had a good imagination; he was very creative; he liked science.)

Expand Vocabulary Read the definition together. Say: *Sometimes an author restates a word or uses a word with a similar meaning in the same paragraph. Which word in the second paragraph has the same meaning as* developed? (Possible answers: invented, wrote)

Sequence Model for students how to identify sequence in a biography. *As I read, I see words about time and Arthur's age. For example, "as a child" tells me about a certain time in Arthur's life.* Have students reread the text under "Science at an Early Age" and underline phrases that signal time order. (as a child, born in

England in 1917, school years, just 13, when Arthur was a teenager, 19 years old) Say: *These words help us know when key events happened in Arthur's life.* Have students paraphrase the key events that happened before Arthur was 19 years old. (he became interested in astronomy; he wrote science fiction stories; his father died) *What key events happened next?* (He moved to London and got a job.)

🔍 Page 60

Connection of Ideas 🅐🅒🅣 Point to and read aloud *"This technology gave him ideas."* in the first paragraph. Ask: *What technology gave Arthur ideas?* (radar) *What did Arthur imagine? Point to the text evidence.* (a breakthrough in communication systems) *Draw a box around the description of this system.* (He pictured a wireless system. It would use satellites. Rockets would carry satellites into space. The satellites would send signals around the Earth.) Then use the sentence frame: _____ and _____ *gave Arthur ideas for a communication system.* (radar, rockets)

Vocabulary Remind students that a *breakthrough* is an "important advance." Ask: *Why was Arthur's idea for a wireless system a breakthrough?* (Possible answer: it did not exist at the time)

Vocabulary Have students study the illustration on this page. Ask: *What is a satellite?* (an object in space that moves around a larger object in space) *What clues help you understand the meaning of* satellite? (wireless; rockets would carry satellites into space; around the Earth; picture and caption on page 60.)

Expand Vocabulary Have students locate the word *exist*. Read the definition together. Say: *Let's list technologies we read about that existed before Arthur imagined a wireless communications system.* (radar, planes, radio signals, rockets) *Now, let's draw a circle*

around the technology that did not exist *when Arthur imagined a wireless communication system.* (satellites)

Sequence Have partners point to words that signal time in the second paragraph. (In 1957; first; In the 1960s, before, Years later) Ask: *When was a satellite communications system created?* (In the 1960s, a satellite communications system was created.) *What technology became possible years later?* (cell phone communication) Have students turn to a partner and paraphrase events in the paragraph, using correct sequence.

 Page 61

Connection of Ideas Ⓐ Ⓒ Ⓣ Help students mark details that tell what HAL can do and what computers today can do. (HAL: controls almost everything, thinks for itself, recognizes human voices, speaks; Computers: control devices in homes, cars, planes, and spacecraft; recognize human voices; speak) Have partners discuss which details they marked are similar. (both control devices, recognize human voices, and speak.) Then have partners discuss what HAL can do that computers today can't do. (HAL controls almost everything and thinks for itself.)

Expand Vocabulary Review the definition of *common. What word in the sentence is a clue to the meaning of* common? (many) Have partners pointing to something they see that is common in a classroom.

Connection of Ideas Ⓐ Ⓒ Ⓣ *Besides HAL, what other technologies did Arthur write about in* 2001: A Space Odyssey? (space stations, missions to far-off planets, news on electronic screens) *Which of these technologies became real inventions? Give two examples.*

High-Utility Words Point to the sentence and have students read aloud: "Arthur's novel also predicted space stations and missions to far-off planets." *What connecting word do you see in this sentence?* (and) Have students find examples of other connecting words in the last paragraph. (and, but)

RESPOND TO READING

10–20 Minutes RI.5.1 RI.5.2 RI.5.3 W.5.9b SL.5.1d

Respond to "Fantasy Becomes Fact"

Have students summarize "Fantasy Becomes Fact" orally to demonstrate comprehension. Then have partners answer the questions on page 62 of the **Interactive Worktext** using the discussion starters. Tell them to use text evidence to support their answers. Have students write the page number(s) on which they found the text evidence for each question.

1. *What technology did Arthur learn to use in the Royal Air Force?* (radar, which can send and receive signals to track objects.) Text Evidence: p. 60)

2. *What other technology existed when Arthur thought of a communications system?* (rockets are another technology that existed when Arthur thought of a communications system. Text Evidence: p. 60)

3. *How was Arthur's idea for a communications system different than existing technology?* (Arthur thought rockets could go into space, radar signals could be sent by satellites from space. Text Evidence: p. 60)

After students discuss the questions on page 62, have them write a response to the question on page 63. Tell them to use their partner discussions and notes about "Fantasy Becomes Fact" to help them. Circulate and provide guidance.

✓ *Quick Check* **Do students understand vocabulary in context? If not, review and reteach using the instruction on page 46.**

Can students use key details to determine sequence? If not, review and reteach using the instruction on page 46 and assign the Unit 1 Week 4 digital mini-lesson.

Can students write a response to "Fantasy Becomes Fact"? If not, provide sentence frames to help them organize their ideas.

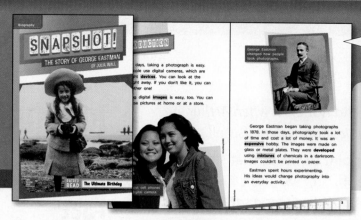

Objectives
- Understand and use new vocabulary words
- Read biographical text
- Recognize and understand sequence
- Understand complex text through close reading

Materials
- "Snapshot! The Story of George Eastman" Apprentice Leveled Reader, pp. 2–7
- Graphic Organizer: Sequence

☞ **Go** Digital
- Apprentice Leveled Reader eBook
- Downloadable Graphic Organizer
- Sequence Mini-Lesson

BEFORE READING

10–15 Minutes   SL.5.1c   SL.5.1d   L.5.4a   L.5.6   **CCSS**

Introduce "Snapshot! The Story of George Eastman"

- Read the Essential Question on the title page of "Snapshot! The Story of George Eastman" **Apprentice Leveled Reader:** *How does technology lead to creative ideas? We'll read about someone who used technology to help change the way people take photographs.*

- Read the title of the main read. Have students look at the images. Ask: *What are the photographs mainly about?* (There are photos of cameras. There is a portrait of George Eastman.)

Expand Vocabulary

Display each word below. Say the words and have students repeat them. Then use the Define/Example/Ask routine to introduce each word.

1 **expensive** (page 3)

Define: something that costs lot of money

Example: The *expensive* digital camera cost $800.

Ask: What other things are *expensive* to buy?

2 **images** (page 2)

Define: pictures of people, places, or things

Example: The photographer is famous for his *images* of wild animals.

Ask: What *images* would you like to photograph?

3 **mixtures** (page 3)

Define: combinations of ingredients

Example: The artist made *mixtures* of paint to create new colors.

Ask: What foods could you combine to make a *mixture* that is good to eat?

DURING READING

20–30 Minutes   RI.5.1   RI.5.5   SL.5.1b   SL.5.1c   L.5.4a   **CCSS**

Close Reading

🔍 **Pages 2–3**

Genre **A C T** Explain that a biography is the true story of a person's life written by another person. *How do you know that this is a biography?* (there is a photograph of George Eastman on page 3. The author gives facts about George Eastman and his important ideas.)

Connection of ideas **A C T** Have students read pages 2 and 3, look at the photographs, and read the captions. Ask: *On page 2, what are digital cameras like today?* (they are small, light cameras; you can see photos right away) *What were cameras like for George Eastman in 1878?* (Photography took a lot of time and cost a lot of money. Images were made on glass or metal plates in a darkroom.)

Pages 4–5

Sequence Remind students that authors usually tell the events in a person's life in the order in which they happened. *What important events does the author tell about in the first paragraph?* (George was born in 1854. His father died when he was 7 and he left school to get a job at 14.) *What important event happened when George was 24?* (He bought his first camera.)

Have students record the important events on their Sequence Chart as they continue reading.

Vocabulary Have students locate the phrase "pack-horse load" on page 5. Explain that a pack horse is used to carry goods on its back and in bags on its side. *Why do you think Eastman compared carrying a lot of equipment to a "pack-horse load"?* (people used pack horses to carry a lot of things, just like Eastman had to carry a lot of equipment to take photographs)

Vocabulary Have students find the word *tripod* on page 5 and look at the photograph on page 4. Say: *Tri means "three," and* pod *means "foot." Why is this piece of equipment called a tripod?* (It has three "feet.") *What is the purpose of a tripod?* (It holds a camera steady.)

Sentence Structure A C T Read aloud the final sentence on page 5. *What did Eastman need to develop photographs?* (glass plates, tanks, chemicals, and water) *How are these items listed in the sentence?* (a comma separates each item; the connecting word *and* appears between the two items listed at the end of the sentence.)

STOP AND CHECK *Read the question in the Stop and Check box on page 5.* (Eastman's camera was big and he needed a tripod, heavy canvas tent, glass plates, tanks, chemicals, and water to use it.)

Pages 6–7

Vocabulary Have students find the multiple-meaning word *develop* in the second paragraph on page 6. *What does* develop *mean in this sentence?* (to turn a wet plate into a photograph) *What clue helps you figure it out?* (The words *the photo would be ruined* tell me that when Eastman develops a wet plate it turns into a photo.)

Genre A C T *What can we learn from the Wet-Plate Process sidebar?* (It shows what a photographer had to do to take a photo using wet plate technology.) *What do the numbers mean?* (The numbers show the order of the steps in the process.)

Connection of Ideas A C T Read page 7 aloud. Say: *Remember that the Introduction told us that Eastman's ideas changed photography.* Ask: *How did Eastman's dry plate change photography?* (made it faster, less messy)

Sequence Direct students to the last paragraph on page 7. *What sequence words help you understand the steps Eastman took to begin selling the dry plate?* (After more than two years, Then, In 1880) Have students turn to a partner and use the sequence words to explain what Eastman did. Have students record the key events in their Sequence chart.

STOP AND CHECK *Read the question in the Stop and Check box on page 7.* (Dry plates were easier to use. A wet plate had to be prepared before taking each photograph and developed quickly afterward.)

Have partners review their Sequence Charts for pages 2–7 and discuss what they learned.

 Quick Check Do students understand weekly vocabulary in context? If not, review and reteach using the instruction on page 46.

Can students use details to determine the sequence of events? If not, review and reteach using the instruction on page 46 and assign the Unit 1 Week 4 Sequence digital mini-lesson.

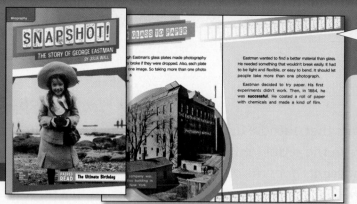

Objectives
- Understand and use new vocabulary
- Read biographical text
- Understand sequence
- Understand complex text through close reading
- Respond to the selection, using text evidence to support ideas

Materials
"Snapshot! The Story of George Eastman" Apprentice Leveled Reader, pp. 8–20
- Graphic Organizer: Sequence

☞ **Go** Digital
- Apprentice Leveled Reader eBook
- Downloadable Graphic Organizer
- Sequence Mini-Lesson

Scaffolding for **Wonders** Approaching Leveled Reader

BEFORE READING

5–10 Minutes   SL.5.1c   SL.5.1d   L.5.4a   L.5.6   **CCSS**

Expand Vocabulary

Display each word below. Say the words and have students repeat them. Then use the Define/Example/Ask routine to introduce each word.

1 instant (page 14)

Define: happening right away

Example: I poured hot water into the cup of *instant* soup.

Ask: What kinds of *instant* foods and drinks have you had? Why are they called "instant"?

2 modern (page 14)

Define: going on now, not in the past

Example: *Modern* people use their cell phones to take pictures.

Ask: What are some other *modern* technologies?

3 successful (page 9)

Define: when you reach a goal

Example: The baseball team was *successful* when a player hit a home run.

Ask: What is something that you have been *successful* in doing?

DURING READING

15–20 Minutes   RI.5.1   RI.5.5   SL.5.1b   SL.5.1c   L.5.4a   **CCSS**

Close Reading

 Pages 8–9

Connection of Ideas **A C T** Read page 8. Ask: *Is there a signal word in the first sentence?* (Although) Explain that *Although* signals a contrast between a good feature of glass plates and a problem. Ask: *What is the signal word in the next sentence? What does it tell the reader?* (*Also* in the next sentence signals another problem with glass plates.)

Key Details *What were some of the problems Eastman had with the glass plates?* (They broke easily, and they let a photographer take only one picture at a time.) *What kind of material was Eastman looking for?* (He needed something that wouldn't break as easily as glass, was light, and flexible so it could bend) *How did Eastman solve the problem?* (He coated a roll of paper with chemicals and made a kind of film)

Sequence Ask: *What time order signal words do you notice in the second paragraph on page 9?* (Then, in 1884,) *What important event happened that year?* (He found a way to use paper to make a kind of film.) Have students add this event to their Sequence Charts.

Genre **A C T** Discuss the photograph on page 8. Have students read the caption. *What does the photo show?* (Eastman's company building in New York) Explain that authors of biographies include photos to give more information about the person, and the time when the person lived.

Pages 10–11

Sequence *What did Eastman do after he invented paper film?* (he worked on a way to put a roll of film into a camera) *Who helped him?* (an engineer, William Walker) *What problem would that solve?* (you could take more than one picture) *How did their solution work?* (paper moved from one spool to another)

Genre **A C T** *How does the image on page 10 help you understand the text in the second paragraph?* (Instead of imagining what the two spools look like, I can see what they look like.)

Connection of Ideas **A C T** Read the first paragraph on page 11. *Why weren't professional photographers interested in paper film?* (Photos were not as clear as those from glass plates.) *What did Eastman invent?* (a smaller lighter camera that was hand-held) *How did this change photography?* (more people could take photos)

STOP AND CHECK *Read the question in the Stop and Check box on page 11.* (Eastman's camera was small and light, and it could be held by hand.)

Pages 12–13

Vocabulary *What clues in the second paragraph on page 12 help you understand the phrase "Word spread"?* (The text says that people tried the cameras. Then sales grew. People must have told other people about the cameras; or spread the word.)

Sequence *What two important events did you read about on pages 12 and 13?* (Eastman's camera went on sale; Eastmans's children's camera went on sale) *What signal words help you understand when the events happened?* (in 1888; in 1900) Have students add the key events to their Sequence Charts.

STOP AND CHECK *Read the question in the Stop and Check box on page 13.* (The children's camera was affordable and very easy to use.)

Page 14

Sequence *Read the second to last sentence on page 14. What are the signal words?* (since then) *How did photography change since Eastman's death?* (color film was invented; instant cameras, and digital cameras)

AFTER READING

10–15 Minutes   RI.5.2   RI.5.5   RI.5.9   W 5.9b   L.5.4a   **CCSS**

Respond to Reading

Compare Texts Have students compare how Clarke in "Fantasy Becomes Fact" and Eastman in "Snapshot! The Story of George Eastman" used technology for creative ideas. Ask: *How did technology lead to creative ideas?*

Summarize Have students turn to page 15 and summarize the selection. (Answers should show the important events in Eastman's life in order.)

Text Evidence

Have partners work together to answer questions on page 15. Remind students to use their Sequence Charts.

Sequence (He experimented with chemical formulas, invented a way to coat glass plates with chemicals, and baked the glass plates in an oven.)

Vocabulary (the clue "easy to bend")

Write About Reading (Eastman wanted a material that was easier to use than glass. He experimented with paper and chemical formulas and finally made paper film. With William Walker he made a spooled film holder.)

Independent Reading

Encourage students to read the paired selection "The Ultimate Birthday" on pages 16–18. Have them summarize the selection and compare it to "Snapshot! The Story of George Eastman." Have them work with partners to answer the "Make Connections" questions on page 18.

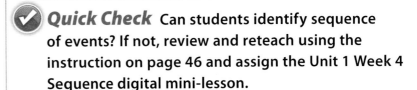 **Quick Check** Can students identify sequence of events? If not, review and reteach using the instruction on page 46 and assign the Unit 1 Week 4 Sequence digital mini-lesson.

Can students respond to the selection using text evidence? If not, provide sentence frames to help them organize their ideas.

**WEEK 4
LESSON**

5

Objectives
- Review weekly vocabulary words
- Review sequence
- Write an analysis about how photographs give important details about a subject

Materials
- **Visual Vocabulary Cards: 25–32**
- **Interactive Worktext, pp. 64–65**
- **Assessment Book, pp. 16–17**

☞ **Go Digital**
- **Visual Vocabulary Cards**
- **Sequence Mini-Lesson**
- **Interactive eWorktext**

Scaffolding for **Wonders** Reading/Writing Workshop

REVIEW AND RETEACH

5–10 Minutes   RI.5.3   L.5.4a   L.5.6   CCSS

Weekly Vocabulary

Display one **Visual Vocabulary Card** at a time and ask students to use the vocabulary word in a sentence. If students have difficulty, have them find the word in "Fantasy Becomes Fact" and use context clues in the passage to define the vocabulary word.

Comprehension: Sequence

I Do Write and say: *Thomas Edison was born in Ohio in 1847.* Ask: *When was Thomas Edison born? He was born in 1847.* Circle *1847.* Say: *This sentence tells me when an event took place. Authors organize events using sequence. They often use signal words that indicate time such as numbers, dates, and words such as* before, after, *or* then. Display: *His family moved to Michigan. Thomas started school.* Point out that there is also a sequence of events in these sentences, but no signal words.

We Do Display: *In 1859, Thomas started selling newspapers on a train. Soon, he began doing science experiments in one of the train cars.* Say: *Let's find the sequence of events together. What did Thomas do first?* (he started selling newspapers on a train) *What happened after that?* (he set up science experiments in one of the cars) *What are the signal words?* (In 1859, Soon)

You Do Display: *Thomas moved to Boston in 1868. He got a job in an office. In 1869, he left his job to work on his inventions. Later that year, he moved to New York. He got a job fixing and improving printers.* Have partners identify the sequence of the key events and identify the signal words.

WRITE ABOUT READING

25–35 Minutes   W.5.4   W.5.5   W.5.9b   CCSS

Read an Analysis

- Ask students to look back at "Fantasy Becomes Fact" in the **Interactive Worktext**. Have volunteers review the photographs and illustrations. Ask: *How did the author use photographs and illustrations to convey information?*

- Read aloud the introduction on page 64. *Ian's paragraph is not a summary. It is an analysis, or a detailed description.* Read aloud the student model. *Ian analyzed how the author used photographs to give important details about Arthur C. Clarke.*

- Say: *When you write an analysis, you need to include certain elements. The first element is a* topic sentence. *It should be clear and focused. Read Ian's paragraph and circle the topic sentence. What important pieces of information has Ian included in this sentence?* (text's title; the author used photographs to give important details about Arthur C. Clarke)

- *Another element is* text evidence. *Ian supports his topic sentence by describing details he sees in a photograph that give him important information about Arthur C. Clarke. Reread the paragraph and draw a box around the text evidence.* (sentences 2-6) *What other details in the photograph do you see that could be included as evidence?* (Arthur is looking closely at the tool) *What do these details tell about Arthur?* (he is focused)

- *The final element is the* concluding statement. *Underline the concluding statement. How is this sentence similar to Ian's topic sentence?* (It restates that the author used photographs to tell about Arthur.) *Which words does Ian use to wrap up all the details in the paragraph?* (a lot)

Analytical Writing

Write an Analysis

Guided Writing Read the writing prompt on page 65 together. Have students write about "Snapshot! The Story of George Eastman" or another text they read this week. Have them choose a photograph or illustration. To analyze, ask: *How does the photograph give important details? Why is it important? Use the checklist to help you figure out the right information to include in each section.*

Peer Conference Have students read their analysis to a partner. Listeners should identify the strongest text evidence that supports the topic sentence and discuss any sentences that are unclear.

Teacher Conference Check students' writing for complete sentences and text evidence that supports their topics. Review the concluding statements. *Does this sentence tie all of the elements together?* If necessary, have students revise their concluding statements by restating their topic sentences.

Level Up

▲ Apprentice Leveled Reader

▲ Approaching Leveled Reader

▲ Interactive Worktext

▲ Reading/Writing Workshop

IF students read the Apprentice Level Reader fluently and the **Interactive Worktext** Shared Read fluently and answer the Respond to Reading questions

THEN read together the Approaching Level Reader main selection and the **Reading/Writing Workshop** Shared Read from *Reading Wonders.* Have students take notes as they read, using self-stick notes. Then ask and answer questions about their notes.

Writing Rubric

	4	3	2	1
Topic Sentence	There is one clear, focused topic sentence.	Topic sentence is less focused, somewhat clear.	Topic is presented in short phrases.	There is no topic sentence.
Text Evidence	Topic is supported by two or more text details.	Evidence includes only one detail from the text.	Little to no evidence is cited from the text.	No text evidence is included.
Concluding Statement	Clearly restates the topic sentence; wraps up the details.	Restatement is less focused; attempts to wrap up the details.	Vaguely restates the topic. Doesn't correlate well to text evidence.	There is no conclusion.
Writing Style	Writes in complete sentences. Uses correct spelling and grammar.	Uses complete sentences and phrases. Writing has spelling and grammar errors.	Few or no complete sentences. There are many spelling and grammar errors.	Does not write accurately or in complete sentences.

ASSESSMENT

Weekly Assessment

Have students complete the Weekly Assessment using **Assessment** book pages 16–17.

Objectives
- Develop oral language
- Build background about the positive and negative effects of new technology
- Understand and use weekly vocabulary
- Read persuasive text

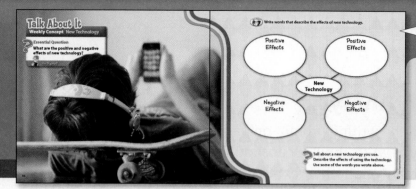

Materials
• Interactive Worktext, pp. 66–73
• Visual Vocabulary Cards: 33–40

☞ **Go** Digital
• Interactive eWorktext
• Visual Vocabulary Cards

Scaffolding for **Wonders** Reading/Writing Workshop

WEEKLY CONCEPT

5–10 Minutes   SL.5.1b   SL.5.1c

Talk About It

Essential Question Read aloud the Essential Question on page 66 of the **Interactive Worktext**: *What are the positive and negative effects of new technology?* Explain that a *positive effect* is a good result and a *negative effect* is a bad result. Say: *Using technology can have good and bad effects.*

- Discuss the photograph on page 66. Ask: *What new technology is this boy using?* (headphones, smart phone, or mp3 player)

I Do Say: *I am going to look at the photograph and think of one negative effect of using technology. I see that the boy is using a phone or mp3 player. He is resting his head on his skateboard instead of being active and using his skateboard. I think this is one negative effect of using technology. I will write "not being physically active" under "Negative Effects" in the web on page 67.*

We Do Say: *Let's look at the photo and think about a positive effect of using technology. Point to the headphones. What do headphones let you do?* (listen to music without bothering others) *Is this a positive or negative effect of using technology?* (positive) Have students brainstorm other effects and work with them to add words to the web on page 67. Then have them tell another positive and negative effect of using the technologies they see in the photograph.

You Do Have partners describe technologies they use. (for example, computers, video games, cell phones) and tell their positive and negative effects. Have answer the questions, using some words from the web: *What technology do you use? What is a positive effect of using the technology? What is a negative effect?*

REVIEW VOCABULARY

10–15 Minutes   L.5.4a   L.5.5c   L.5.6

Review Weekly Vocabulary Words

- Use the **Visual Vocabulary Cards** to review the weekly vocabulary.

- Read together the directions for the Vocabulary activity on page 68 of the **Interactive Worktext**. Then complete the activity.

1 **advance** Explain that a synonym is a word with the same or almost the same meaning as another word. Have partners discuss the options to decide which word or phrase is a synonym for *advance*. (move ahead)

2 **data** Have students read the sentences aloud. Ask: *Which sentences include data about a dog?* (My dog weighs 12 pounds. The dog's tail is 4 inches long.) Then have students give an example of data about a pet or animal they know about.

3 **access** Have students complete the following sentence frame: *I need a _____ to access a locker.* (Possible answers: key, number code)

4 **cite** Ask: *What do you do when you* cite *information?* (tell where you got it from) Have students use the sentence frame: *For a report on the president, I would* cite *information from a _____.* (biography)

5 **counterpoint** Offer an example of counterpoints. Say: *The soup was yummy. The soup was gross. The second statement is a counterpoint to the first. What would be a counterpoint to: The movie was exciting?* (Possible answer: The movie was boring.)

6 **reasoning** Have partners discuss the meaning of *reasoning*. Then ask: *Does doing a math problem* *require reasoning?* (yes) Have partners ask each other similar questions to decide which activities require *reasoning.* (solving a jigsaw puzzle; fixing a bicycle)

7 **drawbacks** Have students complete this sentence frame: *I like staying up late, but there is one drawback. The next day, I _____.* (Possible answer: feel tired) Then ask students to form the plural.

8 **analysis** Ask students to list tools people use to make an analysis of an object. Record students' responses. (Possible answers: microscope, lens, camera, ruler, telescope) Have each student choose one object from the list to draw. Then, have students complete this sentence frame to write captions for their drawings: *A _____ helps you make an analysis of a _____.*

High-Utility Words

Explain that a suffix is a word part added to the end of a word that changes the word's meaning. Have students look at the High-Utility Words activity on page 69 in the **Interactive Worktext**. Discuss the meaning of the suffix *-er.* Have partners circle words that end in *-er* in the passage. (teacher, composers, leader, player, singer, listeners, performers) Have students use the meaning of the suffix to suggest meanings for each word. Then have partners read the passage.

ELL ENGLISH LANGUAGE LEARNERS

Write the words *listen, sing, play, teach,* and the suffix *er* on index cards. Display together *listen* and *er* and say *listener.* Have students repeat. Display the remaining words with the suffix and prompt students to say the word parts together.

Read: "Are Electronic Devices Good for Us?"

- Have students turn to page 70 in the **Interactive Worktext** and read aloud the Essential Question. Explain that the selection includes two articles that present different viewpoints. Ask: *What is the title?* ("Are Electronic Devices Good for Us?") *Look at the photographs and titles of each article. Which article do you think is for using electronic devices?* ("Plugged In") *Which article do you think is against using electronic devices?* ("Tuned Out")

- Read "Are Electronic Devices Good for Us?" together. Note that weekly vocabulary words are highlighted in yellow. Expand Vocabulary words are in blue.

- Have students use the "My Notes" section on page 70 to write questions they have, words they don't understand, and details they want to remember. Model how to use the "My Notes" section. *I can write notes about questions I have as I read. As I read the first paragraph, I wonder how electronic devices help kids. I'll write a question in the "My Notes" section and ask my questions as I reread. In the second paragraph, I'm not sure what the word* critics *means. I'll write* critics *with a question mark beside it in the "My Notes" section.*

ELL ENGLISH LANGUAGE LEARNERS

As you read together, have students highlight parts of the selection that they have questions about. After reading, help them write their questions under "My Notes."

 Quick Check Can students understand the weekly vocabulary in context? If not, review vocabulary using the **Visual Vocabulary Cards** before teaching Lesson 2.

WEEK 5 LESSON 2

Objectives
- Read persuasive text
- Understand complex text through close reading
- Recognize and understand author's point of view
- Respond to the selection using text evidence to support ideas

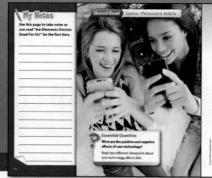

Materials
Interactive Worktext, pp. 70–75

☞ **Go** Digital
- Interactive eWorktext
- Author's Point of View Mini-Lesson

Scaffolding for **WONDERS** Reading/Writing Workshop

REREAD COMPLEX TEXT

20–25 Minutes   RI.5.1 RI.5.6 RI.5.8 RI.6.6 L.5.4a CCSS

Close Reading: "Are Electronic Devices Good for Us?"

Reread "Are Electronic Devices Good for Us?" with students. As you read together, discuss important passages in the text. Have students respond to text-dependent questions, including those in the **Interactive Worktext**.

Page 71

Expand Vocabulary Have students locate the word *media*. Note that media can be print or electronic. *What kind of media is the author talking about?* (electronic) Have partners review the first paragraph and look for examples of electronic media. (Possible answers: Internet, video games, cell phones, computers, smart phones)

Author's Point of View Say: *An author's choice of words and use of facts are clues to the author's point of view, or position. Let's look for clues to the author's point of view together.* Reread the title of the article and first sentence, and have students echo. Say: *The idiom* plugged in *suggests being connected to technology. The sentence below the title states that electronic devices help kids.* Ask: *Is* help *a positive or negative word?* (positive) *Use these clues. Does the author think electronic devices are good or bad for kids?* (Electronic devices are good for kids.) *Now let's look for details that support this position. In the second paragraph, I read that "Heavy media users were more physically active." This detail shows that electronic media helps kids. Underline this detail. Now look for another detail that supports this position.* (Possible answers: Video games may increase visual attention; kids learn to switch

tasks easily; learning to use the Web responsibly can sharpen kids' reasoning skills.)

Connection of Ideas Ⓐ Ⓒ Ⓣ Have students reread the third paragraph and list key details. (Kids can learn to switch tasks easily. Video games increase visual attention. Kids use the Web to access information. Learning to use the Web responsibly can sharpen kids' reasoning skills.) Then read aloud the graph's title and caption. Ask: *How many teens age 12 to 17 get their news online?* (62 percent) *How is this information similar to information in the third paragraph? Which detail does it support?* (Kids also use the Web to access information.)

Page 72

Author's Point of View Have students review the title of the selection and the title of this article. Ask: *What do you think "Tuned Out" means? Look for clues in the photograph.* (Possible answer: not listening) *Is this a good thing or bad thing?* (bad) *Now reread the sentence below the article title. Is the word* harm *positive or negative?* (negative) *Use these clues. What do you think the author's position is?* (Electronic devices are bad for kids.) *What other words are clues to the author's position?* (alarming, disadvantages) If students have difficulty, ask: *Which words are strong words? Are these words positive or negative?* Then have students look for facts that support the author's position. Remind students that facts can be proven. (Possible answers: media use does not actually bring good grades, pie graphs showing that good grades increase as media use goes down)

Expand Vocabulary Have students locate *report*. Read aloud the sentence. Ask: *Which word helps you know that a report is the written results of a study?* (says)

High-Utility Words Have students underline *users* in the diagram. Ask: *What is the base word?* (use) *What is the suffix?* (-er) *What does* user *mean?* (one who uses)

Connection of Ideas Read aloud the second paragraph. Then draw students' attention to the pie graphs. Say: *In this study, students were divided into categories: heavy media users, moderate media users, and light media users. Which group uses media the most?* (heavy users) *Review the percentages of good grades students reported. Which group had the lowest percentage of good grades?* (heavy media users) *How is this information similar to information in the second paragraph? Which sentence in the text does this information support?* (To cite one report, more media use does not mean better grades.)

Page 73

Author's Point of View Have students reread the first paragraph. Ask: *Does the author agree or disagree with people who claim that using technology helps kids make friends?* (disagree) *What facts support the author's position?* (Teens stay in touch with friends they already have. They do not use online social networks to make new friends.)

Author's Point of View Have partners reread the last paragraph aloud. Ask: *Which sentence tells the author's point of view?* (Kids should be careful about using too much technology.) If students have difficulty, explain the meanings of idiomatic expressions, and ask: *Which sentence includes strong words? What does the author think kids should do?*

Connection of Ideas Draw a Venn diagram on the board, and label the circles *Author 1* and *Author 2*. Read aloud the first paragraph of each article. Ask: *Which two sentences give similar information?* (Plugged In: fifth sentence; Tuned Out: third sentence) *What do the authors agree on?* (Kids spend a lot of time using electronic devices.) Write this where the circles overlap. Read aloud the last paragraph of each article. *How are the authors' opinions about kids using technology different?* (One author thinks using technology helps kids; the other author thinks using too much technology can harm kids.) Write these opinions in the appropriate outer circles.

RESPOND TO READING

10–20 Minutes   RI.5.1   RI.5.2   RI.5.3   W.5.9b   SL.5.1d   **CCSS**

Respond to "Are Electronic Devices Good for Us?"

Have students summarize "Are Electronic Devices Good for Us?" orally to demonstrate comprehension. Then have partners answer the questions on page 74 of the **Interactive Worktext** using the discussion starters. Tell them to use text evidence to support their answers. Have students write the page number(s) on which they found the text evidence for each question.

1. *What are positive effects of kids using the Web?* (The Web helps kids access information. It can improve their reasoning skills. Text Evidence: p. 71)

2. *What are negative effects of kids using the Web?* (It may not help kids get better grades or make new friends. It can be dangerous to meet new people through the Web. Text Evidence: pp. 72–73)

3. *What are the positive and negative effects of using devices to multitask?* (Kids' thinking can improve when they multitask. A negative effect is that they may not be able to do each task well. Evidence: p. 73)

After students discuss the questions on page 74, have them write a response to the question on page 75. Tell them to use their partner discussions and notes about "Are Electronic Devices Good for Us?" to help them. Circulate and provide guidance.

 Quick Check **Do students understand vocabulary in context? If not, review and reteach using the instruction on page 56.**

Can students use word choice, facts, and key details to determine author's point of view? If not, review and reteach using the instruction on page 56 and assign the Unit 1 Week 5 digital mini-lesson.

Can students write a response to "Are Electronic Devices Good for Us?" If not, provide sentence frames to help them organize their ideas.

WEEK 5 LESSON 3

Objectives
- Understand and use new vocabulary
- Read expository text
- Recognize and understand the author's point of view
- Understand complex text through close reading

Materials
- "What About Robots?" Apprentice Leveled Reader: pp. 2–9
- Graphic Organizer: Author's Point of View

☞ **Go Digital**
- Apprentice Leveled Reader eBook
- Downloadable Graphic Organizer
- Author's Point of View Mini-Lesson

Scaffolding for **Wonders** Approaching Leveled Reader

BEFORE READING

10–15 Minutes   SL.5.1c SL.5.1d L.5.4a L.5.6 CCSS

Introduce "What About Robots?"

- Read the Essential Question on the title page of "What About Robots?" **Apprentice Leveled Reader**: *What are the positive and negative effects of new technology?* Say: *We will read about the positive and negative effects of robots so that you can form your own opinions about their usefulness.*

- Read the title of the main read. Have students look at the chapter titles, images, and sidebars. *What do you think you will learn about?* (robots and how they are used) *Why do you think that?* (The images show different kinds of robots and how they are used.)

Expand Vocabulary

Display each word below. Say the words and have students repeat them. Then use the Define/Example/Ask routine to introduce each word.

① avoid (page 7)

Define: to stay away from

Example: The quarterback was able to *avoid* the tackle.

Ask: What other things do athletes try to *avoid?*

② interacts (page 5)

Define: to act on or influence each other

Example: Friends *interact* with each other when they talk and share ideas.

Ask: How have you *interacted* with people today?

③ mechanical (page 5)

Define: having to do with machines

Example: Airplanes are made of *mechanical* parts.

Ask: What other objects have *mechanical* parts?

④ technology (page 2)

Define: machines based on practical science

Example: Washing machines are a time-saving *technology*.

Ask: What forms of *technology* do you use each day?

DURING READING

20–30 Minutes   RI.5.1 RI.5.8 RI.6.6 SL.5.1b L.5.4b CCSS

Close Reading

🔍 **Pages 2–3**

Author's Point of View Explain that an author may express an opinion, or point of view, in an article. Readers must pay attention to how opinions and facts are presented. Then we can identify the author's point of view. Read the first paragraph on page 2 aloud. Ask: *What words give us a clue about how the author feels about technology?* (Life would be hard without technology.) Help students record details in their Author's Point of View charts as they read.

Vocabulary Help students to understand challenging domain-specific vocabulary as they read the selection. For example, say: *The author says the machines we use every day are examples of* technology. *On page 2, what machines are mentioned in the first paragraph?* (washing machines, refrigerators; cars, computers, cell phones) On page 3, explain that bold type shows that *robotics* is defined in the glossary at the back.

Author's Point of View Read the first paragraph on page 3 aloud. Ask: *What are the two points of view the author presents?* (Some people think robots are useful; others worry that we will become dependent on robots.) *Whose point of view does the author present in the second paragraph?* (her own) *What is her point of view?* (Readers should look at the facts before making a decision.)

Pages 4–5

Connection of Ideas **ACT** Have students find and read the definition of *robot* on page 4. Then have them read the first paragraph on page 5. Ask: *Why does the author reject the definition of* robot *from page 4?* (It also describes a washing machine, which isn't a robot.) Have students read on. Ask: *What definition does the author like?* (a machine that uses information around it to decide what to do)

Author's Point of View *What phrase on page 5 signals that the author is stating her opinion of the best definition of a robot?* (the phrase *better definition*)

Pages 6–7

Connection of Ideas **ACT** Help students connect the author's definition of a robot with the discussion on pages 6 and 7. Ask: *Do automatons fit the author's definition of a robot?* (no) *Does Elsie the Tortoise fit the definition?* (yes) *Why do you say this?* (Automatons do not interact with their environments. Elsie the Tortoise did.)

Author's Point of View Have students read the sidebar on page 7. *What are the two points of view about robots that are presented?* (robots as evil or robots as friends)

Vocabulary On page 6, point out that *automaton* is defined in the glossary. Also explain that the Greek root *auto,* which means "self," gives a clue to its meaning. An *automaton* is a machine that works by itself.

STOP AND CHECK Read the question in the Stop and Check box on page 7. (Automatons do not process information about their environment.)

Pages 8–9

Author's Point of View Ask: *What text evidence on page 8 shows that the author has a positive view of the use of robots in factories?* (She states that robots can save a company a lot of money because they are faster than humans, don't get tired and make mistakes, and don't get bored.)

Genre **ACT** Point out that expository text often includes text features like the pie graph on page 9. Ask: *What does the pie graph show?* (where in the world industrial robots are located) *Which area of the world has the largest percentage of industrial robots?* (Asia)

Connection of Ideas **ACT** Point out the sidebar on page 9. Ask: *What information does the author present in the sidebar?* (two opposing views of using robots in the workplace) *What does the author ask the reader to think about?* (whether it is a good idea to have robots at work)

STOP AND CHECK Read the question in the Stop and Check box on page 9. (They worried that workers would lose their jobs because robots would replace them. They also worried about safety.)

Have partners review their Author's Point of View charts for pages 2–9 and discuss what they learned.

 Quick Check Do students understand weekly vocabulary in context? If not, review and reteach using the instruction on page 56.

Can students identify an author's point of view? If not, review and reteach using the instruction on page 56 and assign the Unit 1 Week 5 digital mini-lesson.

WEEK 5 LESSON

4

Objectives
- Understand and use new vocabulary
- Read expository text
- Recognize and understand the author's point of view
- Understand complex text through close reading
- Respond to the selection using text evidence to support ideas

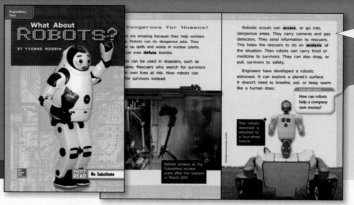

Materials
- "What About Robots?" Apprentice Leveled Reader: pp. 10–18
- Graphic Organizer: Author's Point of View

☞ **Go** Digital
- Apprentice Leveled Reader eBook
- Downloadable Graphic Organizer
- Author's Point of View Mini-Lesson

Scaffolding for **Wonders** Approaching Leveled Reader

BEFORE READING

5–10 Minutes   SL.5.1c   SL.5.1d   L.5.4a   L.5.6   **CCSS**

Expand Vocabulary

Display each word below. Say the words and have students repeat them. Then use the Define/Example/Ask routine to introduce each word.

❶ errors (page 12)

Define: mistakes

Example: We made *errors* when we measured the ingredients for the cookies.

Ask: What is another example of an activity in which you could make *errors*?

❷ filtering (page 15)

Define: separating out

Example: I use a strainer for *filtering* out pebbles from soil.

Ask: What other items might need *filtering*?

❸ opinions (page 17)

Define: what one thinks, believes, or feels about something

Example: Mario had a negative *opinion* of the movie, but his brother liked it.

Ask: In your *opinion*, what is the best show on television?

❹ sort (page 17)

Define: to put things in groups according to type

Example: We *sorted* the socks by color and size.

Ask: How could you *sort* a pile of books?

DURING READING

15–20 Minutes   RI.5.1   RI.5.8   RI.6.6   SL.5.1b   L.5.6   **CCSS**

Close Reading

🔍 **Pages 10–11**

Author's Point of View Read the first paragraph on page 10 aloud. Ask: *What words help you identify the author's point of view about robots?* (Robots are amazing because they help workers stay safe.) *What is the author's opinion about robots?* (Robots are amazing and helpful.)

Author's Point of View Draw students' attention to the references to dangerous work on pages 10 and 11. Ask: *What evidence does the author provide to support the point of view that robots can do dangerous jobs?* (clean up spills and waste at nuclear plants; defuse bombs; search for survivors and provide assistance during natural disasters; explore space)

Connection of Ideas **A C T** Read aloud the last paragraph on page 11. Ask: *What is the author comparing?* (robotic and human astronauts) *Why do you think the author makes the comparison?* (to show that there are advantages to using robotic astronauts)

STOP AND CHECK Read the question in the Stop and Check box on page 11. (Robots can work faster than humans; they don't get tired and make mistakes.)

🔍 **Pages 12–13**

Author's Point of View Have students read the last paragraph on page 12. Ask: *Which sentence states the author's point of view?* (first) *What is the point of view?* (There are drawbacks to using robots in hospitals.) *What evidence does the author provide to support her position?* (Some people are frightened of robots; other worry about errors; many patients like to see another human.)

Genre ⒶⒸⓉ Draw students' attention to the bar graph on page 13. Ask: *What does the graph show?* (number of operations where robots are used) *Did the use of surgical robots increase or decrease between 2005 and 2010?* (increase)

Pages 14–15

Connection of Ideas ⒶⒸⓉ Read aloud the points of view presented in the sidebar on page 14. Ask: *What details in the text on pages 14 and 15 support the first point of view?* (Robots can help the environment by cleaning up pollutants; robots can be powered by solar panels; robots can sort plastics for recycling or filter out pollutants.) *What details in the text support the second point of view?* (Robots are made from mined materials; robot factories use up resources; throwing away old parts can harm the environment.)

Vocabulary Have students locate the word *foe* in the sidebar on page 14. Explain that *foe* is the opposite of *friend*. Ask: *Which quote in the sidebar expresses the opinion that robots are* foes? (the second one)

Author's Point of View Read page 15. Ask: *What sentence gives a clue to the author's point of view about robots?* (Robots can help save the planet!) Ask: *Is the author for or against robots?* (for them)

Vocabulary Have students locate the word *solar* on page 15. Ask: *What clue in the next sentence helps you understand what* solar *means?* (energy from the sun)

Pages 16–17

Vocabulary Have students locate *intelligence* on page 16. *What are two definitions of* intelligence? (being good at analyzing information; getting information from the environment to make a decision) Point out that the author gives two definitions to suggest that robots have intelligence.

Author's Point of View Read paragraph one on page 17. *What sentence shows the author's point of view about robots?* (In the future, robots will do even more good things.) *Is the author for or against robots?* (for them)

AFTER READING

10–15 Minutes   RI.5.1   RI.5.2   RI.5.9   W.5.9b   L.5.4a

Respond to Reading

Compare Texts Have students compare and contrast the advantages and disadvantages of technology as presented in "Are Electronic Devices Good for Us?" and "What About Robots?" Ask: *In your opinion, is technology a good thing? Support your opinion with reasons/evidence.*

Summarize Have students turn to page 18 and summarize the selection. (Answers should include details from the selection.)

Text Evidence

Have partners work together to answer questions on page 18 using their Author's Point of View charts.

Author's Point of View (The author has a positive point of view about new uses for robots. The author states problems, then advantages. She ends by saying that robots will do even more good things in the future.)

Vocabulary ("hard work;" the text says that *robot* comes from a Czech word for labor or hard work)

Write About Reading (The author is for robots and calls them "amazing." On page 15, the author says robots will help save the planet.)

Independent Reading

Encourage students to read the paired selection "No Substitute" on pages 19–21. Have them summarize it and compare it to "What About Robots?" Have partners answer the "Make Connections" questions on page 21.

 Quick Check **Do students understand weekly vocabulary in context? If not, review and reteach using the instruction on page 56.**

Can students identify an author's point of view? If not, review and reteach using the instruction on page 56 and assign the Unit 1 Week 5 digital mini-lesson.

WRITE & ASSESS

Objectives
- Review weekly vocabulary words
- Review author's point of view
- Write an analysis about how well an author supports his or her opinion

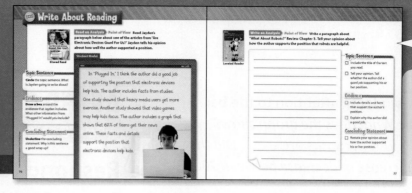

Materials
- Visual Vocabulary Cards: 33–40
- Interactive Worktext, pp. 76–77
- Assessment Book, pp. 18–19

☞ **Go** Digital
- Visual Vocabulary Cards
- Author's Point of View Mini-Lesson
- Interactive eWorktext

Scaffolding for **McGraw-Hill Reading WONDERS** Reading/Writing Workshop

---

REVIEW AND RETEACH

5–10 Minutes   RI.6.6   L.5.4a   L.5.6

Weekly Vocabulary

Display one **Visual Vocabulary Card** at a time and ask students to use the vocabulary word in a sentence. If students have difficulty, have them find the word in "Are Electronic Devices Good for Us?" and use the context clues to define it.

Comprehension: Author's Point of View

I Do   Write and say: *Smart phones are the best way to communicate. Smart phones help people easily access information. Smart phones help people connect to the Web anywhere. Underline best, help, and easily. These words express a positive feeling.* Circle the last two sentences. *These details tell ways smart phones are helpful. From these clues, I know the author's point of view: Smart phones are good.*

We Do   Display: *Smart phones can be harmful. They cause people to be distracted. When people use them in the car, it can cause accidents.* Ask: *Which words express feeling?* (harmful; distracted, accidents) *Is the feeling expressed positive or negative?* (negative) *What details does the author include?* (They cause people to be distracted. When people use them in the car, it can cause accidents.) *What is the author's point of view?* (Smart phones are not good.)

You Do   Display: *Tablets are an important technology. They are lighter than computers. They allow people to easily take information with them.* Have partners identify the opinion words, details that support the author's position, and the author's point of view.

WRITE ABOUT READING

25–35 Minutes   W.5.1   W.5.4   W.5.5   W.5.9b

Read an Analysis

- Ask students to look back at "Are Electronic Devices Good for Us?" in the **Interactive Worktext**. Have volunteers review their notes. *How well did the authors of the articles support their points of view?*

- Read aloud the directions on page 76. Say: *When you analyze, you ask yourself "how" and "why" questions.* Read aloud the student model. Say: *Jayden's writing is not a summary. Jayden is writing an analysis, or a detailed description. Jayden writes his opinion about how well the author of the article "Plugged In" supported his or her position.*

- *An analysis always includes certain elements. Circle the topic sentence. What important information is included in this sentence?* (text's title; Jayden's opinion that the author did a good job of supporting the position; the author's position on the topic)

- *Another element of an analysis is text evidence. The student supports the topic sentence with facts and details from the text. Reread the model and draw a box around the text evidence.* (sentences 2–5) *Look back at your notes about "Plugged In." What other details might be included as text evidence in the model?* (Possible answer: Learning to use the Web responsibly can improve kids' reasoning skills.)

- *The final element is the concluding statement. Underline the concluding statement. How is the concluding statement like the topic sentence?* (Both state the author's position that electronic media helps kids.) *Which words does Jayden use to wrap up the text evidence?* ("These facts and details")

Write an Analysis

Analytical Writing

Guided Writing Read the writing prompt on page 77 together. Have students write about "What About Robots?" or another text they read this week. Have them review their notes. *Use the checklist to help you figure out the right information to include in each section.* Guide students to ask "how" and "why" questions to analyze text evidence, such as *Why are these details important?*

Peer Conference Have students read their analysis to partners. Listeners should identify the strongest text evidence that supports the topic sentence and discuss any sentences that are unclear.

Teacher Conference Check students' writing for complete sentences and text evidence that supports their opinion. Review the concluding statement. *Does this sentence tie all of the elements together?* If necessary, have students revise their concluding statement by restating their topic sentence.

Level Up

▲ Apprentice Leveled Reader

▲ Approaching Leveled Reader

▲ Interactive Worktext

▲ Reading/Writing Workshop

IF students read the Apprentice Level Reader fluently and the **Interactive Worktext** Shared Read fluently and answer the Respond to Reading questions,

THEN read together the Approaching Level Reader main selection and the **Reading/Writing Workshop** Shared Read from *Reading Wonders*. Have students take notes as they read, using self-stick notes. Then ask and answer questions about their notes.

Writing Rubric

	4	3	2	1
Topic Sentence	Topic sentence presents a clear opinion.	Topic sentence presents an opinion, somewhat clearly.	Topic is presented in short phrases; opinion is unclear.	There is no topic sentence; no opinion is presented.
Text Evidence	Opinion is supported by two or more text details.	Opinion is only supported by one detail from the text.	Little to no evidence from the text supports opinion.	No text evidence is included; does not support opinion.
Concluding Statement	Clearly restates an opinion; wraps up all the details.	Restatement is less focused; attempts to wrap up the details.	Vaguely restates opinion. Doesn't correlate well to text evidence.	There is no conclusion.
Writing Style	Writes in complete sentences. Uses correct spelling and grammar.	Uses some complete sentences. Writing has spelling and grammar errors.	Few or no complete sentences. There are many spelling and grammar errors.	Does not write accurately or in complete sentences.

ASSESSMENT

Weekly Assessment

Have students complete the Weekly Assessment using **Assessment** book pages 18–19.

WEEK 6

▶ **Unit Assessment,**
pages 122–130

▶ **Fluency Assessment,**
pages 234–239

▶ **Exit Test,**
pages 178–186

Unit 1 Assessment

CCSS TESTED SKILLS

✓ COMPREHENSION	✓ VOCABULARY
• Character, Setting, Plot: Sequence RL.3.3 • Character, Setting, Plot: Problem and Solution RL.4.3 • Cause and Effect RI.5.3 • Sequence RI.5.5 • Author's Point of View RI.5.8, RI.6.6	• Context Clues L.5.4a

Using Assessment and Writing Scores

🔄 RETEACH	IF ...	THEN ...
COMPREHENSION	Students answer 0–7 multiple-choice items correctly ...	... reteach tested skills using instruction on pages 364–371.
VOCABULARY	Students answer 0–3 multiple-choice items correctly ...	... reteach tested skills using instruction on page 364.
WRITING	Students score mostly 1–2 on weekly Write About Reading rubrics throughout the unit...	... reteach writing using instruction on pages 372–373.

🔼 LEVEL UP	IF ...	THEN ...
COMPREHENSION	Students answer 8–10 multiple-choice items correctly ...	... have students read the *Save This Space!* Approaching Leveled Reader. Use the Level Up lesson on page 60.
WRITING	Students score mostly 3–4 on weekly Write About Reading rubrics throughout the unit...	... use the Level Up Write About Reading lesson on page 61 to have students compare two selections from the unit.

Fluency Assessment

Conduct assessments individually using the differentiated fluency passages in **Assessment**. Students' expected fluency goal for this Unit is 100–120 WCPM with an accuracy rate of 95% or higher.

Exit Test

If a student answers 13–15 multiple-choice items correctly on the Unit Assessment, administer the Unit 1 Exit Test at the end of Week 6.

Time to Exit WonderWorks

Exit Test

If...
Students answer 13–15 multiple choice items correctly...

Fluency Assessment

If...
Students achieve their Fluency Assessment goal for the unit...

Level Up Lessons

If...
Students are successful applying close reading skills with the Approaching Leveled Reader in Week 6...

If...
Students score mostly 4–5 on the Level Up Write About Reading assignment...

Foundational Skills Kit

If...
Students have mastered the Unit 1 benchmark skills in the Foundational Skills Kit and *PowerPAL for Reading* adaptive learning system...

Then...
... consider exiting the student from *Reading WonderWorks* materials into the Approaching Level of *Reading Wonders*.

WEEK 6

▶ **Read Approaching Leveled Reader**

Approaching Leveled Reader

Apprentice Leveled Reader

▶ **Write About Reading**

Interactive Worktext Shared Read

Apprentice Leveled Reader

Read Approaching Leveled Reader

RI.5.10

Save This Space!

Before Reading

Preview Discuss what students remember about Verplanck Colvin and Aldo Leopold and their work to protect special places from development. Tell them they will be reading a more challenging version of *Save This Space!*

Vocabulary Use routines on the **Visual Vocabulary Cards** to review the Weekly Vocabulary words. Use pages 30 and 32 to review the Expand Vocabulary words.

A C T During Reading

▶ **Vocabulary** Provide definitions for challenging words that are new to this level, such as: *imagine* (page 2), *development* (page 2), *journals* (page 3), *terrible* (page 5), *evaporating* (page 5).

▶ **Genre** Help students to understand the new text feature "How to Measure a Mountain" at the bottom of pages 8 and 9. Guide students to find *triangulation* in the glossary. Ask students to look at the diagram and point out where Colvin stood to measure the mountain. Discuss with students how the diagram helps to explain the text, and how the text feature gives more information about Colvin's work.

▶ **Sentence Structure** Students may need help understanding longer complex sentences containing more than one idea. Read aloud the second sentence in the second paragraph on page 4. Break it down into two simpler sentences that show the relationship between the ideas: *The descriptions of the lakes, rivers, and pine forests caught Colvin's imagination. As a result, Colvin began to explore the Adirondacks.* After students read the simple sentences, have them read the complex sentence aloud.

After Reading

Ask students to complete the Respond to Reading questions on page 18 after they have finished reading. Provide additional support as needed to help students use the weekly vocabulary strategy to answer question 3.

Write About Reading

W.5.1   W.5.9b

Read an Analysis

- Distribute the Unit 1 Downloadable Model and Practice that compares two related texts, the **Interactive Worktext** Shared Read "Fantasy Becomes Fact" and the **Apprentice Leveled Reader** "Snapshot! The Story of George Eastman." Read the model aloud.

- Point out the signal word *both* in the topic sentence, which tells readers how the two texts are alike and the word *but* which signals a difference. Have students reread the topic sentence. Ask: *How do you know Quentin is telling his opinion?* (he writes "I think") *What other information does Quentin include in his topic sentence?* (titles of both texts)

- Ask: *What details does Quentin include from "Snapshot! The Story of George Eastman" that support his opinion?* (sentences 2–4) *What details does Quentin include from "Fantasy Becomes Fact" that support his opinion?* (the fifth sentence) *Why is the concluding statement a good wrap up?* (Quentin restates his opinion.)

Write an Analysis

Analytical Writing

Guided Practice Display: *Write a paragraph that compares one article from "Are Electronic Devices Good for Us?" to "What About Robots?" Tell your opinion about which author was more persuasive.*

- Alternatively, let students select two texts to compare.

- Use the Unit 1 Downloadable Model and Practice to guide students' writing.

- Tell them to begin with a topic sentence and include details from both texts to support their opinion.

- Remind students that the concluding statement should restate their opinion and wrap up the details.

Teacher Conference Check students' writing for complete sentences. Did they include a topic sentence that tells an opinion? Did they cite text evidence? Did they restate their opinion in the last sentence?

Writing Rubric

	4	3	2	1
Topic Sentence	Topic sentence presents a clear opinion.	Topic sentence presents an opinion, somewhat clearly.	Topic is presented in short phrases; opinion is unclear	There is no topic sentence; no opinion is presented.
Text Evidence	Opinion is supported by two or more text details.	Opinion is only supported by one detail from the text.	Little to no evidence from the text supports opinion.	No text evidence is included; does not support opinion.
Concluding Statement	Clearly restates an opinion; wraps up all the details.	Restatement is less focused; attempts to wraps up the details.	Vaguely restates opinion. Doesn't correlate well to text evidence.	There is no conclusion.
Writing Style	Writes in complete sentences. Uses correct spelling and grammar.	Uses complete sentences and phrases. Writing has spelling and grammar errors.	Has few or no complete sentences. There are many spelling and grammar errors.	Does not write accurately or in complete sentences.

UNIT 2 PLANNER
Taking the Next Step

Week 1 Reaching a Compromise	Week 2 Seeking the Answer	Week 3 Investigations

ESSENTIAL QUESTION *What do good problem solvers do?*	**ESSENTIAL QUESTION** *What can you do to get the information you need?*	**ESSENTIAL QUESTION** *How do we investigate questions about nature?*
Build Background	**Build Background**	**Build Background**
CCSS 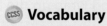 **Vocabulary** L.5.4a *committees, convention, debate, proposal, representatives, resolve, situation, union*	**CCSS** **Vocabulary** L.5.4a *circumstances, consideration, consults, destiny, expectations, presence, reveal, unsure*	**CCSS** **Vocabulary** L.5.4a *behaviors, disappearance, energetic, flurry, migrate, observation, theory, transformed*
Access Complex Text A C T Connection of Ideas	**Access Complex Text** A C T Sentence Structure	**Access Complex Text** A C T Purpose
CCSS **Comprehension** RI.5.3 Skill: Text Structure: Problem and Solution Respond to Reading	**CCSS** **Comprehension** RL.5.3 Skill: Character, Setting, Plot: Compare and Contrast Respond to Reading	**CCSS** **Comprehension** RL.5.5 Skill: Text Structure: Sequence Respond to Reading
CCSS **Write About Reading** *Analytical Writing* W.5.9b Inform/Explain: Text Structure	**CCSS** **Write About Reading** *Analytical Writing* W.5.9a Inform/Explain: Illustrations	**CCSS** **Write About Reading** *Analytical Writing* W.5.9b Opinion: Text Structure

A S S E S S M E N T

✓ *Quick Check* Vocabulary, Comprehension	✓ *Quick Check* Vocabulary, Comprehension	✓ *Quick Check* Vocabulary, Comprehension
✓ **Weekly Assessment** Assessment Book, pp. 20–21	✓ **Weekly Assessment** Assessment Book, pp. 22–23	✓ **Weekly Assessment** Assessment Book, pp. 24–25

✓ **MID-UNIT ASSESSMENT**
Assessment Book, pp. 80–87

✓ **Fluency Assessment**
Assessment Book, pp. 234–249

Use the Foundational Skills Kit for explicit instruction of phonics, structural analysis, fluency, and word recognition. Includes _PowerPAL for Reading_ adaptive learning system.

Week 4
A Plan of Action

ESSENTIAL QUESTION
When has a plan helped you accomplish a task?

Build Background

CCSS **Vocabulary**
L.5.4a _assuring, detected, emerging, gratitude, guidance, outcome, previous, pursuit_

Access Complex Text
Organization

CCSS **Comprehension**
RL.5.2 Skill: Theme
Respond to Reading

CCSS **Write About Reading**
W.5.9a Inform/Explain: Theme

Week 5
Making It Happen

ESSENTIAL QUESTION
What motivates you to accomplish a goal?

Build Background

CCSS **Vocabulary**
L.5.4a _ambitious, memorized, satisfaction, shuddered_

Poetry Terms
free verse, narrative, repetition, rhyme

Access Complex Text
Genre

CCSS **Comprehension**
RL.5.2 Skill: Theme
Respond to Reading

CCSS **Write About Reading** _Analytical Writing_
W.5.9a Opinion: Genre

Week 6
ASSESS

RETEACH   **LEVEL UP**

Reteach
Comprehension Skills

Vocabulary

Write About Reading

Level Up
Read Approaching Leveled Reader

Write About Reading:
Compare Texts

A S S E S S M E N T

✔ _**Quick Check**_
Vocabulary, Comprehension

✔ **Weekly Assessment**
Assessment Book, pp. 26–27

✔ _**Quick Check**_
Vocabulary, Comprehension

✔ **Weekly Assessment**
Assessment Book, pp. 28–29

✔ **Unit Assessment**
Assessment Book, pp. 131–139

✔ **Fluency Assessment**
Assessment Book, pp. 234–249

✔ **EXIT TEST**
Assessment Book, pp. 187–195

ABOUT UNIT 2

Unit 2

Taking the Next Step

The Big Idea
What does it take to put a plan into action?

UNIT 2 OPENER,
pp. 78–79

The Big Idea
What does it take to put a plan into action?

Talk About It

Read aloud the Big Idea on page 78 of the **Interactive Worktext:** *What does it take to put a plan into action?* Have students think about plans they have made. Say: *When we make a plan, we think about the steps we need to take to complete a task. Then we follow the steps in order. For example, when I plan to see a movie at the movie theater, I first find out the show time. Then I figure out what time I need to leave to get there on time. What steps do you take to go to a movie or visit a friend?* (Answers will vary.)

Discuss the photo on pages 78–79. Say: *What are the people in the photograph doing?* (building a model of a city) *How will making a model help them build the city?* (Possible answer: It helps them plan where things go.) *What step do you think the people had to do first before they put the pieces on the model?* (Possible answers: made drawings, colored the base, cut out pieces for the buildings) *When has a plan helped you complete a task?* Have partners or small groups discuss this question and share their ideas with the class.

Tell students that even simple tasks require a plan. Say: *In this unit, we will be reading ten selections. Each selection is about putting a plan into action. In one selection, colonists plan for a new nation. In another selection, a young man makes a plan to find an important object.*

Build Fluency

Each week, use the **Interactive Worktext** Shared Reads and **Apprentice Leveled Readers** for fluency instruction and practice. Keep in mind that reading rates vary with the type of text that students are reading as well as the purpose for reading. For example, comprehension of complex informational texts generally requires slower reading.

Explain/Model Use the Fluency lessons on pages 374–378 to explain the skill. Then model the skill by reading the first page of the week's Shared Read or Leveled Reader.

Practice/Apply Choose a page from the Shared Read or Leveled Reader. Have one group read the top half of the page one sentence at a time. Remind children to apply the skill. Have the second group echo-read the passage. Then have the groups switch roles for the second half of the page. Discuss how each group applied the skill.

> **Weekly Fluency Focus**
> **Week 1** Rate and Accuracy
> **Week 2** Expression and Accuracy
> **Week 3** Expression and Phrasing
> **Week 4** Rate
> **Week 5** Expression and Phrasing

You can also use the **Lesson Cards** and **Practice** pages from the **Foundational Skills Kit** for targeted Fluency instruction and practice.

 **Access Complex Text**

Qualitative Quantitative
Reader and Task
TEXT COMPLEXITY

Interactive Worktext

	Week 1	Week 2	Week 3	Week 4	Week 5
	"Creating a Nation"	"A Modern Cinderella"	"Growing in Place: The Story of E. Lucy Braun"	"The Magical Lost Brocade"	"A Simple Plan"
Quantitative	Lexile 520 TextEvaluator™ 30	Lexile 540 TextEvaluator™ 31	Lexile 530 TextEvaluator™ 25	Lexile 590 TextEvaluator™ 22	Lexile N/A TextEvaluator™ N/A
Qualitative	• Connection of Ideas • Genre • Vocabulary	• Sentence Structure • Prior Knowledge • Vocabulary	• Purpose • Connection of Ideas • Vocabulary	• Organization • Genre • Vocabulary	• Genre • Connection of Ideas • Vocabulary
Reader and Task	The Weekly Concept lessons will help determine the reader's knowledge and engagement in the weekly concept.				
	Weekly Concept: p. 66 Questions and tasks: pp. 68–69	Weekly Concept: p. 76 Questions and tasks: pp. 78–79	Weekly Concept: p. 86 Questions and tasks: pp. 88–89	Weekly Concept: p. 98 Questions and tasks: pp. 100–101	Weekly Concept: p. 108 Questions and tasks: pp. 110–111

Apprentice Leveled Reader

	Week 1	Week 2	Week 3	Week 4	Week 5
	"The Bill of Rights"	"The Bird of Truth"	"Norman Borlaug and the Green Revolution"	"The Lion's Whiskers"	"Clearing the Jungle"
Quantitative	Lexile 600 TextEvaluator™ 31	Lexile 580 TextEvaluator™ 28	Lexile 580 TextEvaluator™ 27	Lexile 590 TextEvaluator™ 16	Lexile 500 TextEvaluator™ 20
Qualitative	• Connection of Ideas • Genre • Sentence Structure • Vocabulary	• Sentence Structure • Connection of Ideas • Genre • Vocabulary	• Purpose • Genre • Connection of Ideas • Vocabulary	• Organization • Genre • Sentence Structure • Connection of Ideas • Vocabulary	• Genre • Connection of Ideas • Vocabulary
Reader and Task	The Weekly Concept lessons will help determine the reader's knowledge and engagement in the weekly concept.				
	Weekly Concept: p. 66 Questions and tasks: pp. 70–73	Weekly Concept: p. 76 Questions and tasks: pp. 80–83	Weekly Concept: p. 86 Questions and tasks: pp. 90–93	Weekly Concept: p. 98 Questions and tasks: pp. 102–105	Weekly Concept: p. 108 Questions and tasks: pp. 112–115

See pages 379 for details about Text Complexity measures.

WEEK 1 LESSON 1

Objectives
- Develop oral language
- Build background about how people solve problems
- Understand and use weekly vocabulary
- Read expository text

Materials
Interactive Worktext, pp. 80–87
- Visual Vocabulary Cards: 41–48

☞ **Go** Digital
- Interactive eWorktext
- Visual Vocabulary Cards

Scaffolding for **Wonders** Reading/Writing Workshop

WEEKLY CONCEPT

5–10 Minutes SL.5.1b SL.5.1c

Talk About It

Essential Question Read aloud the Essential Question on page 80 of the **Interactive Worktext**: *What do good problem solvers do?* Say: *Sometimes people work with others to solve problems. Each person in a group may have a different plan to solve the problem. Good problem solvers sometimes compromise. This means giving up part of a plan to agree on a solution.*

- Discuss the photograph on page 80. Ask: *What are these boys doing?* (looking at a map) *What problem do they need to solve?* (how to get somewhere)

I Do Say: *I am going to imagine I am in this situation. What would I do? I probably would discuss ideas about what to do with my friends. This is a good way to solve a problem. I will write "discuss ideas" on page 80.*

We Do Say: *Let's look at the photo and think about how the boys can solve the problem. Are they working by themselves or together?* (together) *How can working together help them solve the problem?* (Possible answer: they can think of different ways to get where they want to go.) *If the boy pointing to the map has a different plan than the others, what would be a good way to solve the problem?* (Possible answers: compromise; agree on the best solution) As students describe ways to solve problems, work with them to complete their web on page 81. Then have them tell what they would do if they were in that situation.

You Do Have partners describe a time when they worked in a group to solve a problem. Have them answer the questions: *What was the problem? How did you work together? How did you solve the problem?*

REVIEW VOCABULARY

10–15 Minutes L.5.4a L.5.5c L.5.6

Review Weekly Vocabulary Words

- Use the **Visual Vocabulary Cards** to review the weekly vocabulary.

- Read together the directions for the Vocabulary activity on page 82 of the **Interactive Worktext.** Then complete the activity.

1 committees Have students use the sentence frame: _____ and _____ are two committees I could join. (Answers will vary but should include two committees in the class or school.)

2 convention Have partners discuss which things might be at a convention for football players. (coaches, sports equipment) Ask: *Why would football players want these things at a convention?* (Possible answers: they would want to talk to the coaches; they would want to try out the equipment)

3 representatives Have students use the sentence frame: *I think _____ and _____ would be good representatives because _____.* (Answers will vary; explanations should include qualities of good representatives)

4 resolve Have partners take turns asking each other the following question and writing their answer: *What would you do to resolve a problem with a friend?* (Possible answers: talk to your friend, ask someone else for help.)

5 debate Say: *Synonyms are words that have the same or almost the same meaning. Debate and argue are synonyms. What is another word that means almost the same as debate?* (Possible answer: talk about, discuss)

6 **union** Ask: *What is a union?* (a group of people joined together) Have students complete the sentence frame: *People on a soccer team are a union because _____.* (they are joined together to play against other teams.)

7 **proposal** Have students use this sentence starter as they meet with partners: *My proposal for improving our school is to _____.* (Possible answers: clean up the school, get new computers)

8 **situation** Ask: *Why are helmets important?* (They protect you from hurting your head.) Ask students to draw and share a picture of a person in a *situation* when they would need a helmet. (Drawings may show a person biking, skateboarding, playing football.)

High-Utility Words

Explain that time and sequence words tell the order of events. Give examples such as *last week, finally, first, then,* and *later.* Remind students that dates and years are also used in text to show when events happened. Have students look at the High Utility Words activity on page 83 in the **Interactive Worktext.** Have partners work together to circle the time and sequence words in the passage. *(First, The next day, after a week, Finally)* Then have students complete this sentence frame with time and sequence words to tell about events in the school year: *Last year, _____. This year, _____. Today, _____.*

> **ELL ENGLISH LANGUAGE LEARNERS**
>
> Ask questions to help students complete their sentence frames, such as *What grade were you in last year? What grade are you in this year? What did you do today?*

READ COMPLEX TEXT
15–20 Minutes   RI.5.1   RF.5.4c

Read "Creating a Nation"

- Have students turn to page 84 in the **Interactive Worktext** and read aloud the Essential Question. Explain that they will read about how the United States became a nation. Ask: *What is the title?* ("Creating a Nation") *What does the picture show?* (men watching a man sign a paper) *Do you think the text will be about events that take place today or in the past? Why?* (in the past; people are wearing old-fashioned clothes; the man is using a quill pen)

- Read "Creating a Nation" together. Note that the weekly vocabulary words are highlighted in yellow. Expand vocabulary words are in blue.

- Have students use the "My Notes" section on page 84 to write questions they have, words they don't understand, and details they want to remember. Model how to use the "My Notes" section. *I can write notes about questions I have as I read. In the first paragraph on page 85, I see the word* colonists, *and I'm not sure what it means. I will write* colonists *with a question mark next to it in the "My Notes" section. As I keep reading, I'm not sure why King George punished the colonies. I'll write* Why did King George punish the colonies? *When we reread, I will look for answers to my questions.*

> **ELL ENGLISH LANGUAGE LEARNERS**
>
> As you read together, have students highlight parts of the text they have questions about. After reading, help them write their questions in the "My Notes" section. Then help them locate answers to their questions in the text.

 Quick Check Can students understand the weekly vocabulary in context? If not, review vocabulary using the **Visual Vocabulary Cards** before teaching Lesson 2.

WEEK 1 LESSON

2

Objectives
- Read expository text
- Understand complex text through close reading
- Recognize and understand problem and solution in a text
- Respond to the selection, using text evidence to support ideas

Materials
Interactive Worktext, pp. 84–89

☞ **Go** Digital
- Interactive eWorktext
- Problem and Solution Mini-Lesson

Scaffolding for **Wonders** Reading/Writing Workshop

REREAD COMPLEX TEXT

20–25 Minutes   RI.5.1   RI.5.4   RI.5.3   L.5.4a   **CCSS**

Close Reading: "Creating a Nation"

Reread "Creating a Nation" with students. As you read together, discuss important passages in the text. Have students respond to text-dependent questions, including those in the **Interactive Worktext.**

🔍 **Page 85**

High Utility Words Reread the first sentence. Ask: *What does "In 1765" tell you?* (the year) Have partners identify other time and sequence words on the page. (In 1770; By 1773; One night)

Connection of Ideas Ⓐ Ⓒ Ⓣ Reread the first two paragraphs aloud. *What was the Stamp Act?* (a law) *What did it force colonists to do?* Guide students draw a circle around "pay a tax for the paper." Then ask: *What could British people do that colonists could not do?* (choose representatives) *Think about what colonists were forced to do and what they could not do after the Stamp Act. Why did they think the Stamp Act was unfair?* (They had to pay a tax but could not choose representatives to speak for them in government.)

Expand Vocabulary Read the definition of *protests* together. *What did women do to protest against a tax on cloth?* (wove their own cloth) Have partners identify other *protests* colonists held.

Problem and Solution Say: *The author presents the problems colonists faced and then the steps they took to solve the problems.* Model using text evidence to find a problem and a step to a solution. *In the second paragraph, I read "Most colonists thought the Stamp Act was unfair." The word "unfair" tells me the Stamp Act is the problem. As I read, I will look for actions the colonists take*

to solve it, such as "Many colonists held protests." The signal word "Consequently" in the third paragraph tells me there is a solution: it was repealed, or canceled. Give examples of other words that signal a solution: *as a result, therefore, so.* Then have students look for a problem colonists faced in 1773. (there was still a tax on tea) Ask: *What steps did the colonists take to solve the problem? Mark text evidence.* (Colonists held a protest. One night, they slipped onto British ships in Boston Harbor. They tossed the ships' cargo—tea—overboard.) *Let's keep reading to find out if these steps solved the problem.*

🔍 **Page 86**

Expand Vocabulary *What does* banned *mean?* (not allowed) Have students discuss clues to the meaning of *banned.* (punished, closed the port) Then have students circle what King George *banned.* (town meetings)

Problem and Solution Reread the first two paragraphs. Point out that *patriots* and *loyalists* were two groups of colonists. Have students locate the text that describes the patriots and loyalists and mark what each group wanted to do. (Patriots wanted to fight for independence. Loyalists wanted peace with the king.) Have partners discuss how the colonists decided what to do. (Colonists sent representatives to meet and discuss what to do.)

Vocabulary Point out the word *delegates* in the second paragraph. Explain that *delegates* are people chosen to speak or act for others. *What other word in this paragraph means the same as delegates?* (representatives)

Connection of Ideas Ⓐ Ⓒ Ⓣ Guide students to locate and mark the actions of the First Continental Congress. (The delegates decided to send a plan, or proposal, for peace to King George.) Then have students reread the second to last paragraph and mark the actions of the Second Continental Congress. (They made George

Washington head of the new army. They also sent another peace proposal to King George.) *Say: Let's compare and contrast. How were the actions of each Congress similar?* (At both meetings, delegates tried to make peace with King George.) *How were they different?* (At the Second Continental Congress, the delegates made George Washington the head of the army.)

Page 87

Vocabulary Explain that *rights* are freedoms. *What examples of rights does the author include in the text?* (life, liberty, and the pursuit of happiness) Explain the meanings of *liberty* and *the pursuit of happiness*. Explain that these words appear in the Declaration of Independence.

Problem and Solution Have partners reread the first paragraph and mark the problem King George caused. (King George had taken away colonists' rights.) *What did Jefferson think was the solution?* Have them underline any signal words they see. (The colonies had to separate from Britain; therefore)

Expand Vocabulary Discuss the meaning of *approve* and have students look for a clue to the meaning of the word in the sentence. (agreed) *Ask: What document did Congress approve in 1776?* (Declaration of Independence) *What document did Congress approve in 1781?* (Articles of Confederation)

Problem and Solution Have students reread the last two paragraphs. *Ask: Which sentence tells you that the new nation has a problem? Circle this sentence.* (However, the new nation's government wasn't working very well.) *What is the nation's problem?* (The states often disagreed.)

Genre Have students point to each year in the time line and read the events below. *Ask: What events are shown on the time line?* (events of the American Revolution) *What events happened in 1775?* (the Battle of Lexington and Concord; Second Continental Congress begins) *Did Congress sign the Declaration of Independence before or after these events?* (after)

RESPOND TO READING

10–20 Minutes   RI.5.1   RI.5.2   RI.5.3   W.5.9b   SL.5.1d

Respond to "Creating a Nation"

Have students summarize "Creating a Nation" orally to demonstrate comprehension. Then have partners answer the questions on page 88 of the **Interactive Worktext** using the discussion starters. Tell them to use text evidence to support their answers. Have students write the page number(s) on which they found the text evidence for each question.

1. *What did colonists do to solve the problem of the Stamp Act and other taxes?* (Possible answers: They held protests, including making their own cloth. They dumped tea into the harbor. Text Evidence: p. 85)

2. *How did colonists decide what to do to solve the problem of the "Intolerable Acts"?* (They sent representatives to a convention to discuss what to do. Text Evidence: p. 86)

3. *What did Congress do to try to solve problems with Great Britain?* (Possible answer: They discussed what to do; sent peace proposals to King George; formed a committee to write a declaration of independence. Text Evidence: p. 86)

After students discuss the questions on page 88, have them write a response to the question on page 89. Tell them to use their partner discussions and notes about "Creating a Nation" to help them. Circulate and provide guidance.

✓ Quick Check Do students understand vocabulary in context? If not, review and reteach using the instruction on page 74.

Can students use key details to determine problems and solutions? If not, review and reteach using the instruction on page 74 and assign the Unit 2 Week 1 digital mini-lesson.

Can students write a response to "Creating a Nation"? If not, provide sentence frames to help them organize their ideas.

Objectives
- Understand and use new vocabulary words
- Read expository text
- Recognize and understand problem and solution
- Understand complex text through close reading

Materials
- "The Bill of Rights" Apprentice Leveled Reader: pp. 2–10
- Graphic Organizer: Problem and Solution

- **Go Digital**
- Apprentice Leveled Reader eBook
- Downloadable Graphic Organizer
- Problem and Solution Mini-Lesson

Scaffolding for **Wonders** Approaching Leveled Reader

BEFORE READING

10–15 Minutes   SL.5.1c   SL.5.1d   L.5.4a   L.5.6   **CCSS**

Introduce "The Bill of Rights"

- Read the Essential Question on the title page of "The Bill of Rights" **Apprentice Leveled Reader**: *What do good problem solvers do? We will read about how American leaders worked together to solve problems when the country was very new.*

- Read the title of the main read. Have students look at the images. *Is this selection fiction, or does it give information about a topic?* (gives information) *How can you tell?* (The title sounds like it will contain facts, not a made-up story.) *What do most of the illustrations show?* (maps, historical portraits, old documents)

Expand Vocabulary

Display each word below. Say the words and have students repeat them. Then use the Define/Example/Ask routine to introduce each word.

1 insisted (page 6)

Define: asked for something very firmly; demanded

Example: I *insisted* on telling my side of the story.

Ask: When have you *insisted* on getting something you wanted or needed?

2 unfairly (page 9)

Define: in a way that is not fair or right

Example: Cinderella was treated *unfairly* by her wicked stepmother and stepsisters.

Ask: What other stories have you read in which a character is treated *unfairly*? Explain.

3 valued (page 5)

Define: felt that something was important

Example: I *valued* my new bike and took care of it.

Ask: What is something you have *valued* highly?

DURING READING

20–30 Minutes   RI 5.1   RI.5.3   SL.5.1b   SL.5.1d   L.5.4b   **CCSS**

Close Reading

Pages 2–3

Genre   Point out the illustration on page 2. Ask: *What does the map show?* (original thirteen states) Have students point to Pennsylvania, the state where the Convention was held, on the map.

Problem and Solution Explain that looking for signal words can help readers spot problem and solution structures. Have students read the second paragraph on page 2. Ask: *Is there a signal word?* (However) *What problem did the colonists have?* (They had decisions to make.) Explain that there may not be a word signaling the problem and solution, as on page 3. *What did the colonists do on page 3?* (held a meeting) *How did this solve the problem?* (Delegates met to make a plan for the government.) Have students record information in their Problem and Solution Chart, and continue as they read.

Specific Vocabulary Help students to figure out challenging domain-specific vocabulary throughout this selection by using context, word parts, and the glossary.

Pages 4–5

Vocabulary Point out the term *Anti-Federalists* on page 5. Explain that the prefix *anti-* means "against or opposed to." Ask: *How do you think Anti-Federalists got their name?* (They were against the ideas of the Federalists.)

STOP AND CHECK *Read the question in the Stop and Check box on page 5.* (Federalists wanted a strong government. Anti-Federalists wanted more freedom and stronger state governments.)

Pages 6–7

Sequence Remind students that signal words can show that events happen in a particular order. Have partners identify two signal words in the first paragraph on page 6. (first, then) Which state was first to approve the Constitution? (Delaware) Which states approved it next? (New Jersey and Georgia)

Problem and Solution Have students read the third paragraph on page 6. Explain that the differing views of the Federalists and the Anti-Federalists was a problem for America's leaders. Ask: *What did Anti-Federalist Patrick Henry demand?* (a bill of rights as part of the Constitution) *What solution did James Madison suggest?* (If he were elected to Congress, he would work to add a bill of rights.) Have students add this information to their charts.

Connection of Ideas **ACT** Remind students that connecting ideas while reading can help readers understand a text. Read page 7. Ask: *Why was it important how many states voted to approve the Constitution? Look back at the last paragraph of page 3 to find the answer.* (The new government could not begin unless 9 of the 13 states approved the Constitution.)

STOP AND CHECK *Read the question in the Stop and Check box on page 7.* (Some states wanted greater freedom to make their own decisions. They thought the Constitution would give too much power to the government.)

Pages 8–9

Problem and Solution Read page 8. Then ask: *What problem did Madison have as he worked on a bill of rights?* (Many people thought the bill wasn't needed.) *How did he solve that problem?* (He spent three months getting people to talk about his plan.) Have students add this information to their charts.

Connection of Ideas **ACT** Read the text in the dark box on page 8 aloud. Ask: *What do you learn from the text in this box?* (The box explains the process for changing the Constitution.) Then ask students to read page 9. Help them to understand that the process described in the box on page 8 had to be followed to add the Bill of Rights. Ask: *What happened after Congress approved twelve amendments to the Constitution?* (The states also had to vote to approve the amendments. Only ten were approved by the states.)

Page 10

Genre **ACT** Read the timeline on page 10. Ask: *What events are shown on this timeline? How are the events organized?* (The events that led to the Bill of Rights being added to the Constitution are shown in the order they occurred, with the earliest events at the top.) *What event happened first? When did it happen?* (Madison introduced the Bill of Rights on April 1789.) *What happened last?* (Virginia voted yes on December 1791.) *What was happening in between these dates?* (Each state had to vote on the Bill of Rights.)

STOP AND CHECK *Read the question in the Stop and Check box on page 10.* (He organized a group in Congress to make sure that a Bill of Rights got written and then voted on.)

Have partners review their Problem and Solution Charts for pages 2–10 and discuss what they learned.

 Quick Check Do students understand weekly vocabulary in context? If not, review and reteach using the instruction on page 74.

Can students understand problem and solution? If not, review and reteach using the instruction on page 74 and assign the Unit 2 Week 1 digital mini-lesson.

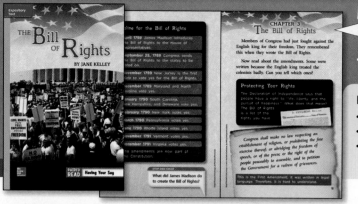

WEEK 1
LESSON

4

Objectives
- Understand and use new vocabulary
- Read expository text
- Understand problem and solution
- Understand complex text through close reading
- Repond to the selection, using text evidence to support ideas

McGraw-Hill Reading **Wonders**
Scaffolding for Approaching Leveled Reader

Materials
- "The Bill of Rights" Apprentice Leveled Reader: pp. 11–24
- Graphic Organizer: Problem and Solution

☞ **Go** Digital
- Apprentice Leveled Reader eBook
- Downloadable Graphic Organizer
- Problem and Solution Mini-Lesson

BEFORE READING

5–10 Minutes SL.5.1c SL.5.1d L.5.4a L.5.6

Expand Vocabulary

Display each word below. Say the words and have students repeat them. Then use the Define/Example/Ask routine to introduce each word.

1 accused (page 14)

Define: blamed for doing something wrong

Example: My sister *accused* me of eating all the cookies.

Ask: What stories can you think of in which the hero is *accused* of doing something wrong?

2 defend (page 14)

Define: protect or speak up for something

Example: In a war, soldiers *defend* our country.

Ask: How does a soccer goalie *defend* the goal?

3 mistreating (page 15)

Define: doing bad things to someone or something

Example: Cory was *mistreating* his new phone when he left it in his pocket and sat on it.

Ask: In what ways could someone *mistreat* a library book?

4 permission (page 12)

Define: agreement or approval

Example: Mom gave me *permission* to go to the party.

Ask: Why do you need *permission* to go on a class trip?

DURING READING

15–20 Minutes RI.5.3 SL.5.1b SL.5.1d L.5.4b

Close Reading

🔍 **Page 11**

Vocabulary *In the box on page 11, it says the Declaration of Independence talks about a right to "the pursuit of happiness." The word* pursuit *means "when someone tries to get or achieve something." How do people "pursue happiness"?* (try to do something that makes us happy)

Connection of Ideas Ⓐ Ⓒ Ⓣ *Reread paragraphs one and two on page 11. Ask students to find the signal word in paragraph 2.* (because) *Ask: What recent events were on the mind of the people who wrote the Bill of Rights? What did they do because of their experiences?* (Members of Congress had been fighting against the king of England. They added amendments to the Bill of Rights as a result.)

🔍 **Pages 12–13**

Vocabulary Have students look at the caption on page 12. Ask: *What does it mean to* meet peacefully? (to meet without causing a problem) *What is another word for* peacefully? (quietly)

Problem and Solution Read page 13. Then ask: *What problem did the Fourth Amendment solve?* (People could not be searched or arrested for no reason.) Have students add this information to their Problem and Solution Chart.

Organization Ⓐ Ⓒ Ⓣ Ask: *What do the headings in this chapter have in common?* (They are all amendment numbers from the Bill of Rights.) *Read the heading at the top of page 13.* (The Fourth Amendment) *What do you think the next section in this chapter will be about?* (the Fifth Amendment)

Pages 14–15

Genre (A)(C)(T) Have students read page 15. Ask them to look at the illustration and read the caption aloud. Ask: *What does the illustration on page 15 show? Why do you think the author included it?* (The picture shows a person being punished in a harsh way in the 1700s. By seeing the picture, I can understand more about why the Eighth Amendment was needed.)

Sentence Structure (A)(C)(T) Read aloud paragraph two on page 15. *What two ideas are included in this sentence?* (A person has rights—even if he or she committed a crime.)

Pages 16–17

Problem and Solution Read page 16. Then ask: *What problem do the Ninth and Tenth Amendments solve?* (the problem of trying to list every possible right in the Bill of Rights) *What is the solution?* (All rights not listed in the Constitution as belonging to Congress are said to belong to the states or to the people.)

STOP AND CHECK *Read the question in the Stop and Check box on page 16.* (Some rights include freedom of religion and speech, the right to own guns, and the right to a trial by jury.)

Connection of Ideas (A)(C)(T) Read the second paragraph on page 17. Explain that the paragraph says that the process that was used to develop the Bill of Rights still works today. Then ask: *What process are people using today that still works?* (People today work together to solve problems just as the people who wrote the Bill of Rights did.)

Genre (A)(C)(T) Ask students to look at the photograph on page 17 and read the caption aloud. Ask: *What does the photo on page 17 show? Why do you think the author included it?* (The picture shows women in Iraq who have voted. This photograph shows that women's right to vote is important all over the world.)

AFTER READING
10–15 Minutes   RI.5.1   RI.5.2   RI.5.9   W.5.9b   L.5.4a   CCSS

Respond to Reading

Compare Texts Have students compare how colonists solved problems in "Creating a Nation" with how the new American states solved problems in "The Bill of Rights." Ask: *What problem have you solved as part of a group?*

Summarize Have students turn to page 18 and summarize the selection. (Answers should include details from the selection about problems leaders faced in forming a nation and how they tried to solve them.)

Text Evidence

Have partners work together to answer questions on page 18. Remind students to use their Problem and Solution Chart.

Problem and Solution (It took months to agree about Madison's plan for a bill of rights. They had to decide which rights to include and compromise.)

Vocabulary (to strongly complain about something)

Write About Reading (Anti-Federalists in Virginia would not ratify the Constitution without a bill of rights. Madison promised to work to add it after approval.)

Independent Reading

Encourage students to read the paired selection "Having Your Say" on pages 19–21. Have them summarize the selection and compare it to "The Bill of Rights." Have them work with a partner to answer the "Make Connections" questions on page 21.

 Quick Check **Can students identify Problem and Solution? If not, review and teach using the instruction on page 74 and assign the Unit 2 Week 1 digital mini-lesson.**

Can students respond to the selection using text evidence? If not, provide, sentence frames to help them organize their ideas.

Objectives
- Review weekly vocabulary words
- Review problem and solution
- Write an analysis of how an author uses headings to organize events

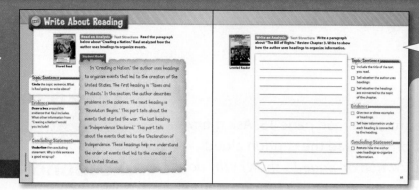

Materials
- Visual Vocabulary Cards: 41–48
- Interactive Worktext, pp. 90–91
- Assessment Book, pp. 20–21

☞ **Go** Digital
- Visual Vocabulary Cards
- Problem/Solution Mini-Lesson
- Interactive eWorktext

Scaffolding for **WONDERS** Reading/Writing Workshop

REVIEW AND RETEACH

5–10 Minutes   RI.5.3 L.5.4a L.5.6

Weekly Vocabulary

Display one **Visual Vocabulary Card** at a time and ask students to use the vocabulary word in a sentence. If students have difficulty, have them find the word in "Creating a Nation" and use the context clues to define it.

Comprehension: Problem/Solution

I Do Write and say: *The mayor noticed that car traffic on Main Street was very busy. People walking could not cross the street. So she decided to add a stop sign and a crossing guard. Now people can cross Main Street.* These sentences show a problem and solution. Ask: *What is the problem? People walking could not cross the street.* Write *problem* above this sentence. *What is the solution? She decided to add a stop sign and a crossing guard.* Write *solution* above the second sentence. Circle *So.* Say: Sometimes authors use signal words like *so, as a result,* and *therefore* to show a solution to a problem.

We Do Display: *Mayor Russo was nervous he would forget his speech. He wrote notes to remind him what to say. His speech was a success.* Say: *What was Mayor Russo's problem?* (he was nervous he would forget his speech) *What was the solution?* (he wrote notes) Point out that there are no signal words.

You Do Write another text containing a problem and a solution: *The library needed new computers, but did not have much money. The librarian asked for donations. People in the community raised money. As a result, the library got new computers.* Have partners identify the problem, steps to the solution, the solution, and any signal words.

WRITE ABOUT READING

25–35 Minutes   W.5.4 W.5.5 W.5.9b

Read an Analysis

- Ask students to look back at "Creating a Nation" in the **Interactive Worktext.** Have volunteers review the headings on pages 85–87. *How did the author's use of headings help you understand the order of events?*

- Read aloud the directions on page 90. *Raul's paragraph is not a summary. He is writing an* analysis, *or a detailed description, of "Creating a Nation." When you analyze, ask yourself "how" and "why" questions. Raul has asked himself these kinds of questions to think about how the author's use of headings helped him understand information in the text.*

- Say: *When you write an analysis, you need to include certain elements. The first element is the topic sentence. Read Raul's paragraph and circle the topic sentence.* (the first sentence) *What important information has Raul included in it?* (text's title; how the author uses headings)

- *Another element is text evidence. Raul supports the topic sentence with examples of headings the author used and information the author includes under each heading. Reread Raul's paragraph. Then draw a box around the text evidence.* (sentences 2 through 7)

- *The final element of the analysis is the concluding statement.* Have students underline the concluding statement. *How is Raul's concluding statement like his topic sentence?* (Both sentences say that the headings organize or order the events.) *Which words does Raul include to wrap up all the evidence?* ("These headings")

Analytical Writing
Write an Analysis

Guided Writing Read the writing prompt on page 91 together. Have students write about "The Bill of Rights" or another text they read this week. Have them review their notes. *Use the checklist to help you know what information to include in each section.* Guide students to ask "how" and "why" questions, such as *How do the headings connect to the main idea of a chapter?*

Peer Conference Have students read their analysis to a partner. Listeners should identify the strongest text evidence that supports the topic sentence and discuss any sentences that are unclear.

Teacher Conference Check students' writing for complete sentences and text evidence that supports their topic. Review the concluding statement. *Does this sentence tie all of the elements together?* If necessary, have students revise the concluding statement by restating the topic sentence.

Level Up

▲ Apprentice Leveled Reader

▲ Approaching Leveled Reader

▲ Interactive Worktext

▲ Reading/Writing Workshop

IF students read the Apprentice Level Reader fluently and the **Interactive Worktext** Shared Read fluently and answer the Respond to Reading questions

THEN read together the Approaching Level Reader main selection and the **Reading/Writing Workshop** Shared Read from *Reading Wonders*. Have students take notes as they read, using self-stick notes. Then ask and answer questions about their notes.

Writing Rubric

	4	3	2	1
Topic Sentence	There is one clear, focused topic sentence.	Topic sentence is less focused, somewhat clear.	Topic is presented in short phrases.	There is no topic sentence.
Text Evidence	Topic is supported by two or more text details.	Evidence includes only one detail from the text.	Little to no evidence is cited from the text.	No text evidence is included.
Concluding Statement	Clearly restates the topic sentence; wraps up all the details.	Restatement is less focused; attempts to wrap up the details.	Vaguely restates the topic. Doesn't correlate well to text evidence.	There is no conclusion.
Writing Style	Writes in complete sentences. Uses correct spelling and grammar.	Uses complete sentences and phrases. Writing has spelling and grammar errors.	Few or no complete sentences. There are many spelling and grammar errors.	Does not write accurately or in complete sentences.

ASSESSMENT

Weekly Assessment

Have students complete the Weekly Assessment using **Assessment** book pages 20–21.

WEEK 2 LESSON

1

Objectives
- Develop oral language
- Build background about ways to get information
- Understand and use weekly vocabulary
- Read a fairy tale

Scaffolding for **Wonders** Reading/Writing Workshop

Materials
- Interactive Worktext, pp. 92–99
- Visual Vocabulary Cards: 49–56

☞ **Go** Digital
- Interactive eWorktext
- Visual Vocabulary Cards

WEEKLY CONCEPT

5–10 Minutes   SL.5.1b SL.5.1c CCSS

Talk About It

Essential Question Read aloud the Essential Question on page 92 of the **Interactive Worktext**: *What can you do to get the information you need?* Say: *Sometimes you have to look for information to answer a question.*

- Discuss the photograph on page 92. Ask: *What are these people doing?* (looking at the night sky) *What information do you think they are looking for?* (<u>Possible answers:</u> information about the stars, moon, planets)

I Do Say: *I am going to look at the photograph and look for one way the people are getting information. I see that the boy is pointing. I wonder if he is asking a question about what he sees. I know that one way to get information is ask an expert, or someone who knows a lot about the subject. I will write "ask an expert" in the web on page 93.*

We Do Say: *Let's look at the photo together and look for other ways these people are getting information. What tool do you see in the photograph?* (<u>Possible answer:</u> a telescope) *How could this help the people get information?* (they can look more closely at things in the sky.) Guide students to add "use a tool" and "look more closely" to their word webs. Have them look for other ways the people are getting information and work with them to add words and phrases to the web on page 93. Then have them tell how they would get information about the night sky.

You Do Have partners describe a time when they needed information. Have them answer the questions: *What information did you need? What did you do? Where did you find the information you needed?*

REVIEW VOCABULARY

10–15 Minutes   L.5.1 L.5.4a L.5.6 CCSS

Review Weekly Vocabulary Words

- Use the **Visual Vocabulary Cards** to review the weekly vocabulary.

- Read together the directions for the Vocabulary activity on page 94 of the **Interactive Worktext**. Then complete the activity.

① **circumstances** Have students use this sentence frame: *Two circumstances that would cause me to close a window would be if it was _____ or if there was _____.* (raining, snowing, wind blowing, noise outside)

② **consults** Have partners discuss the question and decide which of the three options is the best person to consult to find a book. (a librarian) Then have students complete the sentence frame: *A librarian would be a good person to consult to find a book because _____.*

③ **consideration** With students, brainstorm a list of things to pack for a trip to the beach. Discuss what you would take into *consideration* such as *What if it rains?* and *What if I get cold?* Have partners share their responses to the sentence frame. (<u>Possible answers:</u> where I am going; the weather; how long I'll be away; what I'll be doing on the trip)

④ **presence** Have students look around to see who is sitting near them. Then have them use the sentence frame: *_____, _____, and _____ are in my presence.* (Answers will vary.)

⑤ **destiny** Say: *I've always liked helping young people learn. Today, I'm a teacher! It was my* destiny. Then ask students to predict the *destiny* for someone who likes to dance today. (Possible answers: dancer, dance teacher, choreographer)

6 **expectations** Have partners complete the sentence frames: *One of my expectations for this year is that I will _____. Another expectation is that I will _____.* (Possible answers: make new friends, learn something new, get good grades)

7 **unsure** Point out the prefix *un-*. Explain that *un-* is added to the beginning of a word and often means *not*. Have students mark the base word (sure) and prefix (un) and then define *unsure.* (not sure)

8 **reveal** Have students describe tricks that they have seen magicians do. Ask students to complete this sentence frame: *A magician might reveal a _____ from a hat.* Then have students draw a picture to go with their sentence. (Drawings should reflect a magician revealing something from a hat, such as a bunny, birds, scarves.)

High-Utility Words

Explain that two words can be joined together to form a contraction. Have students look at the High Utility Words activity on page 95 of the **Interactive Worktext**. Point out that the circled contraction, *I'm*, is made up of the words *I* and *am*. The apostrophe takes the place of the *a* in *am*. Give other examples, such as *he's* and *we'll*. Then have partners circle the other contractions in the passage. (It's, She's, They're, you'll, it's, I'll, you're) Then have partners tell the two words make up each contraction they circled.

> **ELL ENGLISH LANGUAGE LEARNERS**
>
> Write these words on note cards: *I'm, you're, it's, they're, I am, you are, it is, they are.* Have students point to the cards that show a contraction and say the contraction out loud. Then have partners match the cards *I am, you are, it is,* and *they are* with a contraction.

READ COMPLEX TEXT

15–20 Minutes   RL.5.1   RF.5.4c

Read "A Modern Cinderella"

- Have students turn to page 96 in the **Interactive Worktext** and read aloud the Essential Question. Explain that they will read a new version of the fairy tale "Cinderella." Ask: *What is the title?* ("A Modern Cinderella") Say: Modern *means "happening in today's world." Look at the picture and think about other Cinderella stories you have read. How does this Cinderella look different?* (Possible answer: This Cinderella looks like a regular girl.)

- Read "A Modern Cinderella" together. Note that the weekly vocabulary words are highlighted in yellow. Expand vocabulary words are highlighted in blue.

- Have students use the "My Notes" section on page 96 to write questions they have, words they don't understand, and details they want to remember. Model how to use the "My Notes" section. *I can write notes about questions I have as I read. In the first paragraph, I read that the Prince "felt as if he were floating on a cloud" and I'm not sure what that means. I will write* floating on a cloud *with a question mark next to it in the "My Notes" section. As I continue to read, I'll write questions I have about the characters and events. When we reread the story, I will ask my questions.*

> **ELL ENGLISH LANGUAGE LEARNERS**
>
> As you read together, have students pause to mark anything about the story that they find confusing or unclear. Guide them to write questions in the "My Notes" section.

 Quick Check Can students understand the weekly vocabulary in context? If not, review vocabulary using the **Visual Vocabulary Cards** before teaching Lesson 2.

Objectives
- Read a fairy tale
- Understand complex text through close reading
- Recognize and understand how to compare and contrast plot events
- Respond to the selection, using text evidence to support ideas

Materials
Interactive Worktext, pp. 96–101

☞ **Go** Digital
- Interactive eWorktext
- Compare and Contrast Mini-Lesson

Scaffolding for **WONDERS** Reading/Writing Workshop

REREAD COMPLEX TEXT

20–25 Minutes   RL.5.3   RL.5.9   RL.5.4   L.5.4a   CCSS

Close Reading: "A Modern Cinderella"

Reread "A Modern Cinderella" with students. As you read together, discuss important passages in the text. Have students respond to text-dependent questions, including those in the **Interactive Worktext**.

Page 97

Prior Knowledge Briefly summarize the traditional Cinderella story or have students discuss the characters and events from Cinderella stories they have read. Then reread the first two paragraphs and ask: *What is different about this Cinderella story?* (Possible answers: the Prince is dancing for a TV show, not a ball; the girl's cell phone rings at midnight instead of a clock chiming; she leaves behind a purple sneaker, not a glass slipper)

Sentence Structure A C T Reread the first sentence aloud together, pausing at the dashes. Have students draw a box around the text between the two dashes. Ask: *Does the detail between the dashes tell about characters, setting, or an event?* (setting) *Why is this detail important?* (Possible answer: it tells when the events take place)

Expand Vocabulary Read the definition of *sources* together. Ask: *What sources did the Prince use to get information? Circle the first two sources he used.* (everyone who was at the show; the Internet)

Compare and Contrast Say: *Comparing and contrasting events and details can help readers remember the order of events and understand how characters change. Let's compare and contrast the story events and characters so far. What important events happened on this page?* (the

Prince dances with a young woman; at midnight the young woman leaves; the Prince tries to use the sneaker she left behind to find her) *How does the Prince feel before midnight? Look for words that describe his feelings.* (the Prince was very happy; he felt as if he were floating on a cloud.) *How does the Prince feel after midnight? Look for actions or words that show the Prince's feelings.* (the Prince cried; The Queen saw the Prince's tears.) *How did the Prince's feelings change?* (His feelings changed from being happy to being sad.)

Page 98

Expand Vocabulary Point to the word *quest* in the first paragraph on page 98. Ask: *What clues in this paragraph help you understand what* quest *means?* (*search*) *What does the Prince want to find on his* quest? (the dancer)

Compare and Contrast Say: *The prince took the sneaker to different houses.* Have students reread the third and fourth paragraphs and compare events. *Underline details that show how events are similar.* (another woman eagerly tried on the sneaker; three sisters stood in front, ready to try on the shoe; not one foot met his expectations; The shoe fit none of them) *Circle details in the third paragraph that are clues to the Prince's feelings. Circle details in the fourth paragraph that are clues to the Prince's feelings. How do his feelings change?* (The Prince was full of hope; The Prince became sad.)

Sentence Structure A C T Have students draw a box around the text in parentheses. (They'd been following the news all over the kingdom.) *Point to* They'd *and ask: Who does "they" refer to?* (the three sisters) *What does the sentence in parentheses explain? Reread the paragraph to help you.* (the sentence explains why the sisters were ready to try on the shoe when the Prince arrived)

Vocabulary Point out the words *their eyes became narrow slits* in the last paragraph. Explain the meaning of *slits.* Say: *Sometimes an author uses a metaphor to help us create a picture in our minds. A metaphor compares two unlike things. What two things are being compared?* (the sisters' eyes and narrow slits) *Show me what the sisters' eyes looked like.* (Students should narrow their eyes.) *What other word helped you picture how the sisters looked?* (frowned) *How do you think they felt?* (angry, upset)

Connection of Ideas (A C T) Point to the last paragraph. *What does the young woman hand to her sister?* (a cell phone) *What other character in this story had a cell phone?* (the young woman who danced with the Prince) *Who is this young woman?* (the missing dancer)

Page 99

Expand Vocabulary Ask: *When you* request *something, what do you do?* (ask for it) *What does the Prince first* request? (Please try this on.) *Have partners discuss other things the Prince* requested. (Possible answers: he requested the woman to become his dance partner; he requested her to say yes; he requested her name)

High-Utility Words Ask: *What contraction is in the third paragraph?* (You're) *What two words are combined?* (*You* and *are.*) Have partners draw a box around each contraction on the page and discuss their meanings.

Compare and Contrast Have students reread the first four paragraphs. *What does the Prince hope the woman will become?* (my dance partner forever) *What does the woman plan to do tomorrow?* (dance) *What else does she plan to do?* (travel) Explain that something a person wants to happen is a goal. *Compare their goals. How are their goals alike?* (They both want to dance.) *How are their goals different?* (The Prince wants the woman to be his dance partner forever; the woman wants to travel.)

Expand Vocabulary *What does Cinderella tell the Prince right before he looked puzzled?* (TTYLP) *Why is the Prince puzzled?* (He doesn't understand what TTYLP means.)

RESPOND TO READING

10–20 Minutes RL.5.1 W.5.9a SL.5.1d

Respond to "A Modern Cinderella"

Have students summarize "A Modern Cinderella" orally to demonstrate comprehension. Then have partners answer the questions on page 100 of the **Interactive Worktext** using the discussion starters. Tell them to use text evidence to support their answers. Have students write the page number(s) on which they found the text evidence for each question.

1. *At the beginning of the story, what does the Prince do to find the young woman?* (Possible answer: He talks to people who had been at the show. He searches on the Internet. He puts up posters. Text Evidence: p. 97)

2. *How does the Prince search the kingdom for the young woman?* (Possible answer: He goes to every house. He looks for the young woman by having each woman try on the shoe. Text Evidence: p. 98)

3. *How does the Prince find out the name of the young woman?* (Possible answer: He finds the young woman whose foot fits in the shoe. Then he asks her to reveal her name. Text Evidence: p. 99)

After students discuss the questions on page 100, have them write a response to the question on page 101. Tell them to use their partner discussions and notes about "A Modern Cinderella" to help them. Circulate and provide guidance.

✓ *Quick Check* **Do students understand vocabulary in context? If not, review and reteach using the instruction on page 84.**

Can students use key details to compare and contrast events? If not, review and reteach using the instruction on page 84 and assign the Unit 2 Week 2 digital mini-lesson.

Can students write a response to "A Modern Cinderella"? If not, provide sentence frames to help them organize their ideas.

Objectives
- Understand and use new vocabulary words
- Read a fairy tale
- Compare and contrast story events, characters, and settings
- Understand complex text through close reading

Materials
- "The Bird of Truth" Apprentice Leveled Reader: pp. 2–7
- Graphic Organizer: Compare and Contrast

☞ **Go Digital**
- Apprentice Leveled Reader eBook
- Downloadable Graphic Organizer
- Compare and Contrast Mini-Lesson

Scaffolding for **Wonders** Approaching Leveled Reader

BEFORE READING

10–15 Minutes   SL.5.1c   SL.5.1d   L.5.4a   L.5.6

Introduce "The Bird of Truth"

- Read the Essential Question on the title page of "The Bird of Truth" **Apprentice Leveled Reader**: *What can you do to get information? We will read about a brother and a sister who search for information about themselves.*

- Read the title of the main read. Have students look at the images. *What do you think this story will be about?* (a boy and a girl who are friends with birds) *Why do you think so?* (the title and the picture on page 3)

Expand Vocabulary

Display each word below. Say the words and have students repeat them. Then use the Define/Example/Ask routine to introduce each word.

❶ despair (page 2)

Define: a feeling that there is no hope

Example: I was in *despair* after my eyeglasses broke.

Ask: What might cause you to be in *despair*?

❷ insult (page 4)

Define: cruel or disrespectful words

Example: The *insult* about my haircut hurt my feelings.

Ask: How should you respond to an *insult*?

❸ perched (page 5)

Define: rested on something (for birds)

Example: The birds *perched* on the tree branch.

Ask: Where else have you seen birds *perching*?

DURING READING

20–30 Minutes   RL.5.1   RL.5.3   SL.5.1b   L.5.4a

Close Reading

🔍 **Pages 2–3**

Sentence Structure Ⓐ Ⓒ Ⓣ Read aloud the third paragraph on page 2. Then say: *The commas and the word* but *tell me that there are several things happening in this sentence. One event begins the sentence: The man brought the babies to his wife.* Have partners identify the other two things that happen in the sentence. (The wife saw the babies; the wife became very upset.)

Compare and Contrast Read page 3. Ask: *How does the wife feel when she sees the twins? Compare her reaction to her husband's.* (She is upset because they already have eight children. Her husband says he had to save them from drifting out to sea.)

Compare and Contrast Ask: *Find the sentence on page 3 that tells how the adoptive parents feel about the twins.* (They came to love them even more than their own children.) *How do the other children feel about the twins?* (They were jealous and picked on the twins.) *What is different about how the parents and the other children treated the twins?* (The parents loved the twins; the children were jealous and teased them.)

Genre Ⓐ Ⓒ Ⓣ Have children look at the illustration on page 3 and reread the last paragraph. Ask: *What does the illustration show?* (The twins are feeding the birds by the river.) *What do the birds do to thank the children for their kindness?* (teach the twins to speak the language of birds.) *Could this happen in real life?* (no)

Have students continue to record events and their outcomes on their graphic organizers.

Pages 4–5

Vocabulary Have students identify the word *taunt* in the first paragraph on page 4. Ask: *What clues help you to figure out what* taunt *means? What do you think it means?* (The word *tease* makes me think that *taunt* means to tease or insult someone.)

STOP AND CHECK *Read the question in the Stop and Check box on page 5.* (The fisherman found the twins floating in a cradle. He took them home, and he and his wife adopted them.)

Compare and Contrast Ask students to read page 5. Ask: *How did the children feel when they saw a house at the end of the day?* (They were happy because they thought they could have a hot meal and sleep in a warm bed.) *What did they find inside the house? How do you think that make them feel?* (The house was dark and deserted. The children must have been disappointed.) Point out that the children say cheerful things and smile, even though they are not happy. They are trying to be brave.

Vocabulary Have students find the word *unaware* in the first paragraph on page 4. Ask: *How does the prefix "un-" help you to figure out what* unaware *means?* (It means "not" so "unaware" means "not aware.")

Pages 6–7

Sentence Structure **A** **C** **T** Say: *The text on pages 6 and 7 shows the birds speaking to each other. What dialogue does the palace swallow say on page 6? Point to it.* (paragraphs 1 and 4) *What clues help you identify which bird is speaking?* (In the first paragraph, a swallow talks about how it is good to be back. In paragraph 4, the words, "said the palace swallow" show who is speaking.)

Connection of Ideas **A** **C** **T** Have students read the stories that the palace swallow tells on page 7. *The palace swallow tells two stories on page 7. What is the difference between them?* (The first story is the false story told by nobles to the king. The second story is what really happened.) *How do you know which story is true?* (A country swallow asks if the story is true and the palace swallow says, "Of course not!" and then tells what really happened.)

Compare and Contrast Say: *Find the sentence in the first paragraph of dialogue on page 7 that tells why the nobles wanted to stop the king's marriage.* (They wanted him to marry one of their daughters.) *What did the king do instead?* (He married the tailor's daughter.)

STOP AND CHECK *Read the question in the Stop and Check box on page 7.* (They learn that the king doesn't know he has twin children who were taken away, put in a crystal cradle, and found by a fisherman.)

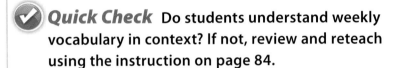 **Quick Check** Do students understand weekly vocabulary in context? If not, review and reteach using the instruction on page 84.

Can students compare and contrast events in a story? If not, review and reteach using the instruction on page 84 and assign the Unit 2 Week 2 digital mini-lesson.

Objectives
- Understand and use new vocabulary words
- Read a fairy tale
- Compare and contrast story events, character, and setting
- Understand complex text through close reading

Scaffolding for **Wonders** Approaching Leveled Reader

Materials
- "The Bird of Truth" Apprentice Leveled Reader: pp. 8–20
- Graphic Organizer: Compare and Contrast

☞ **Go** Digital
- Apprentice Leveled Reader eBook
- Downloadable Graphic Organizer
- Compare and Contrast Mini-Lesson

BEFORE READING

5–10 Minutes   SL.5.1c   SL.5.1d   L.5.4a   L.5.6

Expand Vocabulary

Display each word below. Say the words and have students repeat them. Then use the Define/Example/Ask routine to introduce each word.

① reunited (page 15)

Define: brought together after being apart

Example: My cousin and I are *reunited* every summer.

Ask: If you were *reunited* with a good friend after a year, what would you say?

② terrified (page 12)

Define: very frightened

Example: The ghost story made the children feel *terrified*.

Ask: What kinds of movies or stories could make you feel *terrified?*

③ uproar (page 10)

Define: a noisy disturbance

Example: The audience made an *uproar* when the concert was canceled.

Ask: What could cause an *uproar* at a baseball game?

DURING READING

15–20 Minutes   RL.5.1   RL.5.3   SL.5.1c   L.5.4a

Close Reading

🔍 **Pages 8–9**

Compare and Contrast Say: *Find what the girl says at the beginning of Chapter 3 when she learns they are the royal children.* ("They're talking about us!") *How do the twins react when they learn the Bird of Truth can help them prove who they are?* (They knew what they had to do.) *How are these reactions different?* (At first they are surprised. Then, they are determined to find the Bird of Truth.)

Genre Ⓐ Ⓒ Ⓣ Say: *Find the sentence on page 9 that tells what the dove told the twins to do.* ("Follow the wind," said the dove.) *Is this something that could really happen or something that just happens in fairy tales?* (in fairy tales)

🔍 **Pages 10–12**

Vocabulary Have students locate the word *aviary* in the fourth paragraph on page 10. Ask: *What will the twins see in the* aviary? (many brightly colored birds) *What do you think an* aviary *is?* (a place where many birds live)

Sentence Structure Ⓐ Ⓒ Ⓣ Have students take a closer look at the fourth paragraph on page 10. Ask: *Does the owl speak in short sentences, or in long sentences?* (short sentences) *Why might short sentences be important at this moment in the story?* (The owl is giving quick instructions to the twins. They have to act fast while the giant is asleep.)

Compare and Contrast Ask: *On page 10, what is different about how the twins treat the Birds of Bad Faith and the Bird of Truth?* (The twins ignore the Birds of Bad Faith, but they help the Bird of Truth.)

STOP AND CHECK *Read the question in the Stop and Check box on page 12.* (The turtledove told the twins how to find the castle, and the owl told them how to identify the Bird of Truth.)

Pages 13–15

Character, Setting, Plot: Sequence Ask: *What does the king do after the Bird of Truth tells him the twins are at the palace?* (He has the children brought in.) *What happens to the twins?* (The king takes them to the queen. Everyone hugs.) *How was life for the twins the same and different from the beginning of the story?* (Same: They were with parents who loved them. Different: At first they were with a fisherman and his large family. At the end they were with a king and queen.)

Connection of Ideas **A C T** Say: *To make sense of a story, we should look for connections between events. Here, at the end of the story, what do the nobles do?* (flee the kingdom) *Think back. Years earlier, what did the nobles do to the king's family?* (They tried to kill the king's children. They imprisoned the queen. They lied to the king.) *Why do you think that the nobles flee the kingdom now?* (Now that the king knows the truth, he will want to punish them. The nobles flee the kingdom to escape punishment.)

Sentence Structure **A C T** Have students read the dialogue on page 14 aloud. Ask: *What do the king and the queen find out by speaking to each other?* (The queen learns that the king did not get her letters. The king learns that the nobles lied to him.)

Genre **A C T** Explain that most fairy tales have a bad person or villain. *Find the word on page 15 used to describe the nobles.* (wicked) *Who were the villains in this story?* (the nobles) *What words do you find at the end of this story that appear at the end of many fairy tales?* (lived happily ever after)

STOP AND CHECK *Read the question in the Stop and Check box on page 15.* (The twins bring the Bird of Truth to the king. She tells the king that these are his children. The king and twins free the queen.)

AFTER READING
10–15 Minutes   RL.5.1   RL.5.2   RL.5.9   W.5.9a   L.5.4a (CCSS)

Respond to Reading

Compare Texts Have students compare how characters in "A Modern Cinderella" and "The Bird of Truth" got the information they needed. Then ask: *Think of a time when you needed information. How did you get the information?*

Summarize Have students turn to page 16 and summarize the selection. (Answers should include important details from the selection.)

Text Evidence

Have partners work together to answer questions on page 16. Remind students to use their Compare and Contrast Chart.

Compare and Contrast (The twins learn different things, but they use the birds' language both times.)

Vocabulary (the word *relax* in the next sentence helps me figure out that *comforting* means calming)

Write About Reading (The twins are adopted by a fisherman's family. Bad treatment in their adoptive family made them leave. They find out they are the king's children. They find a loving family at the end.)

Independent Reading

Encourage students to read the paired selection "The Singers of Bremen" on pages 17–19. Have them summarize the selection and compare it to "The Bird of Truth." Have them work with a partner to answer the "Make Connections" questions on page 19.

✓ *Quick Check* **Can students compare and contrast story events? If not, review and teach using the instruction on page 84 and assign the Unit 2 Week 2 digital mini-lesson.**

Can students respond to the selection using text evidence? If not, provide sentence frames to help them organize their ideas.

WRITE & ASSESS

WEEK 2 LESSON

5

Objectives
- Review weekly vocabulary words
- Review character, setting, plot: compare and contrast
- Write an analysis about an illustration

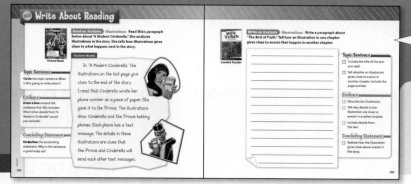

Materials
- Visual Vocabulary Cards: 49–56
- Interactive Worktext, pp. 102–103
- Assessment Book, pp. 22–23

☞ **Go** Digital
- Visual Vocabulary Cards
- Compare/Contrast Mini-Lesson
- Interactive eWorktext

Scaffolding for **Wonders** Reading/Writing Workshop

REVIEW AND RETEACH

5–10 Minutes   RL.5.3 L.5.4a L.5.6   CCSS

Weekly Vocabulary

Display one **Visual Vocabulary Card** at a time and ask students to use each word in a sentence. If students have difficulty, have them find the word in "A Modern Cinderella" and use the context clues to define it.

Comprehension: Compare/Contrast

 I Do Write and say: *Last year, Kylie tried out for the school play, but she couldn't remember her lines. She didn't get a part. This year, she practiced her lines and tried out for the play again. She got the part she wanted.* Underline words that show how the events are similar (tried out for the school play, tried out for the play again). Circle words that show how the events are different (she couldn't remember her lines; she didn't get a part; she practiced her lines; she got the part she wanted) *By comparing and contrasting the events this year and last year, I can better understand the order of events and how Kylie changed.*

We Do Display: *Gabe was new at school. When he first went to lunch, he felt shy and sat by himself. One day, he talked to Jo and Rob in line. Now when he goes to lunch, he sits with them.* Then ask: *Which events are similar?* (Gabe goes to lunch at school.) *How are the events and outcomes different?* (first he is shy and sits by himself; later he talks to Jo and Rob and sits with them)

You Do Write: *A few years ago, Sam wanted to learn how to ride a bike. His uncle showed him what to do. Now Sam's little brother wants to learn how to ride a bike. Sam can now show his brother what to do.* Have students compare and contrast the events.

WRITE ABOUT READING

25–35 Minutes   RL.5.7 W.5.4 W.5.5 W.5.9a   CCSS

Read an Analysis

- Ask students to look back at "A Modern Cinderella" in the **Interactive Worktext**. Have them review the story events and illustrations. *How did the illustrations help you understand story events? Did any illustrations help you predict events that happened later?*

- Read aloud the directions on page 102 and the student model. *Mia is writing an analysis, or a detailed description, of "A Modern Cinderella." She asked herself "how" and "why" questions, such as* Why is an illustration important? *and* How does an illustration give clues about what happens next in the story? *These questions can help you analyze a text, too.*

- Say: *An analysis includes certain elements. The first element is the topic sentence. Reread Mia's paragraph and circle the topic sentence. What information has Mia included in this sentence?* (text's title; which illustration she is analyzing; her main idea about the illustration)

- *Another element of analysis is text evidence. Mia supports her topic sentence with details from the illustration. Reread the model and then draw a box around the text evidence.* (Sentences 2 through 5) *Let's look back at the illustration on page 99. What other details in the illustration support Mia's idea?* (Possible answer: Both the Prince and Cinderella are smiling, so I think they'll be happy.)

- *The final element of the analysis is the concluding sentence. How is the concluding statement like the topic sentence?* (Both say that the illustration gives clues.) *Which words wrap up the text evidence?* (the details in these illustrations)

Analytical Writing

Write an Analysis

Guided Writing Read the writing prompt on page 103 together. Have students write about "The Bird of Truth" or another text they read this week. Have them review the illustrations. *Use the checklist to figure out the information to include in each section.* Guide students to ask "how" and "why" questions, such as *How are details in an illustration connected to events in another chapter?*

Peer Conference Have students read their analysis to a partner. Listeners should identify the strongest text evidence that supports the topic sentence and discuss any sentences that are unclear.

Teacher Conference Check students' writing for complete sentences and text evidence that supports their topic. Review the concluding statement. *Does this sentence tie all of the elements together?* If necessary, have students revise the concluding statement by restating the topic sentence.

Level Up

▲ **Apprentice Leveled Reader**

▲ **Approaching Leveled Reader**

▲ **Interactive Worktext**

▲ **Reading/Writing Workshop**

IF students read the **Apprentice Level** Reader fluently and the **Interactive Worktext** Shared Read fluently and answer the Respond to Reading questions

THEN read together the **Approaching Level** Reader main selection and the **Reading/Writing Workshop** Shared Read from *Reading Wonders.* Have students take notes as they read, using self-stick notes. Then ask and answer questions about their notes.

Writing Rubric

	4	3	2	1
Topic Sentence	There is one clear, focused topic sentence.	Topic sentence is less focused, somewhat clear.	Topic is presented in short phrases.	There is no topic sentence.
Text Evidence	Topic is supported by two or more text details.	Evidence includes only one detail from the text.	Little to no evidence is cited from the text.	No text evidence is included.
Concluding Statement	Clearly restates the topic sentence; wraps up all the details.	Restatement is less focused; attempts to wrap up the details.	Vaguely restates the topic. Doesn't correlate well to text evidence.	There is no conclusion.
Writing Style	Writes in complete sentences. Uses correct spelling and grammar.	Uses complete sentences and phrases. Writing has spelling and grammar errors.	Few or no complete sentences. There are many spelling and grammar errors.	Does not write accurately or in complete sentences.

ASSESSMENT

Weekly Assessment

Have students complete the Weekly Assessment using **Assessment** book pages 22–23.

WEEK 3 LESSON 1

Objectives
- Develop oral language
- Build background about investigating nature
- Understand and use weekly vocabulary
- Read a biography

Materials
- Interactive Worktext, pp. 104–111
- Visual Vocabulary Cards: 57–64

☞ **Go** Digital
- Interactive eWorktext
- Visual Vocabulary Cards

Scaffolding for **Wonders** Reading/Writing Workshop

WEEKLY CONCEPT

5–10 Minutes   SL.5.1b   SL.5.1c

Talk About It

Essential Question Read aloud the Essential Question on page 104 of the **Interactive Worktext**: *How do we investigate questions about nature?* Remind students that nature includes things in the world like mountains, forest, rivers, lakes, and oceans. Say: *We can learn about nature by investigating, or studying, the world around us.*

- Discuss the photograph on page 104. Ask: *What are these people doing?* (looking at fish) *What questions do you think they have about the fish?* (Possible answer: what kind of fish they are)

I Do Say: *One time I had a question about a bird I saw. I wondered what kind of bird it was. So I listened to the bird's call. I also took notes about its color and size. I used this information and looked in a book to help me identify the bird. I will write "listen closely," "take notes," and "look in a book" in the web on page 105.*

We Do Say: *Let's look at the photo and look for other ways people investigate nature. Where are these people?* (at an aquarium) *Why would they go there?* (to learn about animals that live in the water) *Going to an aquarium or museum is one way to investigate a question about nature. Let's add this to the web.* Then have them discuss the tools and senses people are using to investigate nature and add words to the web.

You Do Have partners describe a time when they investigated a question about something in nature. Have them answer the questions, using some words they wrote in the web, as appropriate: *What question did you have about nature? What did you do to answer your question? What senses and tools did you use?*

REVIEW VOCABULARY

10–15 Minutes   L.5.1a   L.5.4a   L.5.5c   L.5.6

Review Weekly Vocabulary Words

- Use the **Visual Vocabulary Cards** to review the weekly vocabulary.

- Read together the directions for the Vocabulary activity on page 106 of the **Interactive Worktext.** Then complete the activity.

1 **energetic** Have students describe what they like to do when they feel energetic. (Possible answers: run, play, jump) Have volunteers model an *energetic* walk. (Students should demonstrate walking fast or with a bounce in their step.)

2 **observation** Ask: *Do we make an observation with our eyes, our ears, or our mouths?* (our eyes) Have partners complete the sentence starter: *To make an observation of stars, I would _____.* (Possible answers: go outside, look up, use a telescope, or make notes of what I saw)

3 **theory** Have partners discuss the options and tell which option would be a good *theory* to explain why a puddle is on the floor. (a glass of water spilled)

4 **flurry** Provide this sentence frame: *I see a flurry of leaves fall from trees during _____.* (Possible answers: a storm; autumn)

5 **behaviors** Have partners discuss classroom rules and then use the sentence frame: *_____, _____, and _____ are good behaviors.* (Possible answers: raising your hand to talk; listening when others are talking; sitting at desk)

6 **migrate** Have partners ask each other questions to determine which words are synonyms for *migrate.* (move; journey)

7 **disappearance** Have students mark the word parts. Then have them use the sentence starter: *When there is a* disappearance, _____. (Possible answers: something goes away; something is no longer able to be seen)

8 **transformed** Have students describe what a plant that needs water looks like. (brown, wilted) Then ask: *How does a plant look after it has been watered?* (better, stronger, green) After students make their drawing, have them write a caption using the word *transformed*. (Drawings will vary, but should show two plants: one wilted and one strong, and should include a caption using the word *transformed*.)

High-Utility Words

Have students turn to page 107 of the **Interactive Worktext**. Explain that prepositions tell the direction or location of something. Give examples: *on, around, by, through, between, toward.* Then have partners identify the prepositions in the passage. (between, in, around, near, by) Write this sentence frame: *I am walking _____ the door.* Have students add a preposition and tell how each changes the meaning of the sentence.

> **ELL ENGLISH LANGUAGE LEARNERS**
>
> Display the prepositions: *through, by, toward, into.* Say each word aloud and have students repeat. Then guide students to complete the sentence frame using each preposition and demonstrate the action.

READ COMPLEX TEXT
15–20 Minutes   RI.5.1   RF.5.4c

Read: "Growing in Place"

- Have students turn to page 108 in the **Interactive Worktext** and read aloud the Essential Question. Explain that Lucy Braun studied living things in their natural settings. Ask: *What is the title?* ("Growing in Place") *What do the illustrations show?* (plants) *What kinds of living things do you think Lucy Braun was interested in?* (plants)

- Read the selection together. Note that the weekly vocabulary words are highlighted in yellow. Expand Vocabulary words are highlighted in blue.

- Have students use the "My Notes" section on page 108 to write words they don't understand, and details they want to remember. Model how to use the "My Notes" section. *I can write notes about questions I have as I read. In the first paragraph on page 109, I'm not sure what* basis *means. I will write* basis? *in the "My Notes" section. As I continue to read, I wonder why Lucy thought naming was important. I will write a question in the "My Notes" section:* Why were correct names important to Lucy? *When we reread, I will ask my questions so I better understand what I am reading.*

> **ELL ENGLISH LANGUAGE LEARNERS**
>
> As you read together, have students mark parts of the text they have questions about. After reading, help them write questions in the "My Notes" section. Then help them locate the answers to their questions in the text.

 Quick Check Can students understand the weekly vocabulary in context? If not, review vocabulary using the **Visual Vocabulary Cards** before teaching Lesson 2.

Objectives
- Read a biography
- Understand complex text through close reading
- Recognize and understand sequence
- Respond to the selection, using text evidence to support ideas

Scaffolding for **WONDERS** Reading/Writing Workshop

Materials
Interactive Worktext, pp. 108–113

☞ **Go Digital**
- Interactive eWorktext
- Sequence Mini-Lesson

REREAD COMPLEX TEXT

20–25 Minutes   RI.5.1   RI.5.3   L.5.1.a   L.5.6   (CCSS)

Close Reading: "Growing in Place"

Reread "Growing in Place" with students. As you read together, discuss important passages in the text. Have students respond to text-dependent questions, including those in the **Interactive Worktext.**

🔍 Page 109

Purpose Ⓐ Ⓒ Ⓣ Say: *A biography tells about a real person's life. Let's reread the first paragraph together and find the sentence that tells who this biography is about.* (first sentence: Emma Lucy Braun) *Now let's find the sentence that tells what she was interested in.* (last sentence: plants)

High-Utility Words Point to the preposition *through* in the second paragraph. Have students describe or show the direction the word indicates. The have partners do a search for other prepositions on the page.

Expand Vocabulary Model how to use text evidence to answer the question by rereading the third paragraph and asking after each sentence: *Is there a fact or detail here that Lucy would have written down?* Guide students to box those details. (the number of leaves on a stem; the shapes of leaves)

Vocabulary Point out the domain-specific words *herbarium* and *botany* in the last paragraph. Say: *Authors sometimes give definitions for words in the text.* Have partners look for clues to the meanings of these words in the paragraph. Then ask: *What is an* herbarium? *Point to the text evidence.* (a collection of dried plants) *What does* botany *mean? Point to the text evidence.* (the study of plants)

Sequence *In a biography, an author often organizes events in the order events in sequence.* Model identifying sequence in a biography. *As I read, I will look for signal words that help me understand the order of events in Lucy's life. Read aloud the first sentence in the second paragraph. Underline the phrase "As a child." This phrase tells the time in Lucy's life when she became interested in plants. Let's write "1" next to this sentence. Next, find the paragraph that tells about Lucy's herbarium.* (paragraph 4) *Who did Lucy make an herbarium with at first?* (her mother) *Let's write "2" next to the sentence that tells when Lucy created her own herbarium.* (In high school, Lucy created her own herbarium) *Then underline any time or sequence words that helped you.* (In high school)

🔍 Page 110

Expand Vocabulary Discuss the definition of *believe. What did Lucy believe?* Use the sentence starter: *Lucy believed that _____.* (plant life could migrate over time.)

Sequence Say: *In a biography, years and other dates can be clues to the sequence of events in the subject's life.* Have partners locate years, dates, and other sequence words in the text. *In what year did Lucy begin to teach botany?* (1917) *What did Lucy do before she became a teacher?* (studied) *Botany is a subject people study in school. What other subjects did Lucy study?* (geology and ecology)

Expand Vocabulary Have students read the definition of *tend* aloud. Then ask students to form the past tense of the word *tend. What words in the text are clues to the meaning of the word?* (took care of) Then have students complete the sentence frame: *Lucy tended _____.* (indoor and outdoor gardens) Have partners discuss some ways that someone might tend to a garden.

Connection of Ideas Ⓐ Ⓒ Ⓣ Work with students to make a list of things that Lucy is interested in. Then make a list of things that Annette is interested in. Ask: *How* *are the sisters alike?* (They are both interested in nature.) *How are they different?* (Lucy is interested in plants, rocks, and how living things behave in their natural settings. Annette is interested in insects.)

Page 111

Sequence Have students reread the page and tell any time and sequence words they see. Then ask: *Which sentence tells what Lucy did later in her life?* (Later in her life, Lucy wrote field guides.) Have partners locate the sentence that tells what Lucy did in 1950. (In 1950, she published an important guide.) Ask: *Why is this event important to ecologists today?* If students have difficulty, tell the meaning of *ecologists* and guide them to reread the last two sentences of the first paragraph to help them answer the question. (The guide helps ecologists study changes in the forests.)

Expand Vocabulary Ask: *What did Lucy publish? Which sentences describe what she published?* (In 1950, she published an important guide. It describes forest plants in the eastern United states.) *What clues in the paragraph help you understand the meaning of the word* publish? Have students point to the text evidence. (Possible answers: wrote; books)

Vocabulary Have students point out the phrase *become extinct,* in the second paragraph. Ask: *What words nearby help you know the meaning of the phrase* become extinct? (or disappear) *If the snakeroot becomes extinct, what happens to it?* (It goes away.)

Purpose **ACT** Have students read the title and direction line in the box. Then use the sentence starter: *The steps tell how you can _____.* (identify plants in your area) *What else have you read about on this page that would help someone identify plants?* (Possible answers: field guides, the herbarium at the Smithsonian Institution.) *Why do you think the author included a box on plant identification in Lucy Braun's biography?* (Possible answer: Lucy was interested in identifying plants.)

RESPOND TO READING

10–20 Minutes   RI.5.1   RI.5.3   W.5.9b   SL.5.1d   (CCSS)

Respond to "Growing in Place"

Have students summarize "Growing in Place" orally to demonstrate comprehension. Then have partners answer the questions on page 112 of the **Interactive Worktext** using the discussion starters. Tell them to use text evidence to support their answers. Have students write the page number(s) on which they found the text evidence for each question.

1. *What did Lucy's mother teach Lucy to do to tell plants apart?* (Possible answer: Lucy's mother taught Lucy to use her powers of observation, to look at parts of plants, and to collect and preserve parts of plants. Text Evidence: p. 109)

2. *What did Lucy do when she was a teacher that helped her study plants?* (Possible answer: She collected plants from around the country and took photographs of them. Text Evidence: p. 110)

3. *What did Lucy do that helped other people tell plants apart?* (Possible answer: Lucy wrote field guides. She collected plants that are now part of a collection that people can use to study plants. Text Evidence: p. 111)

After students discuss the questions on page 112, have them write a response to the question on page 113. Tell them to use their discussions and notes about "Growing in Place" to help them. Circulate and provide guidance.

 Quick Check **Do students understand vocabulary in context? If not, review and reteach using the instruction on page 94.**

Can students use signal words and key events to identify sequence? If not, review and reteach using the instruction on page 94 and assign the Unit 2 Week 3 digital mini-lesson.

Can students write a response to "Growing in Place"? If not, provide sentence frames to help them organize their ideas.

WEEK 3 LESSON 3

Objectives
• Understand and use new vocabulary words
• Read a biography
• Recognize and understand sequence
• Understand complex text through close reading

Materials
"Norman Borlaug and the Green Revolution" Apprentice Leveled Reader: pp. 2–7
• Graphic Organizer: Sequence

☞ **Go** Digital
• Apprentice Leveled Reader eBook
• Downloadable Graphic Organizer
• Sequence Mini-Lesson

Scaffolding for **Wonders** Approaching Leveled Reader

BEFORE READING

10–15 Minutes   SL.5.1c   SL.5.1d   L.5.4a   L.5.6

Introduce "Norman Borlaug and the Green Revolution"

• Read the Essential Question on the title page of "Norman Borlaug and the Green Revolution" **Apprentice Leveled Reader:** *How do we investigate questions about nature? We'll read about someone who used science to grow more wheat to feed people.*

• Read the title of the main read. Have students look at the images. Ask: *What do you think this selection is about?* (the life of Norman Borlaug)

Expand Vocabulary

Display each word below. Say the words and have students repeat them. Then use the Define/Example/Ask routine to introduce each word.

1 exhausted (page 2)

Define: very weak or tired

Example: We felt *exhausted* after our long hike.

Ask: When might you feel *exhausted*?

2 prevent (page 4)

Define: stop something from happening

Example: Traffic lights *prevent* accidents.

Ask: How can you *prevent* getting cavities?

3 process (page 6)

Define: the steps taken to make something happen

Example: The *process* of making bread is simple but it takes time.

4 ruined (page 6)

Define: The rain *ruined* our picnic.

Example: How could a meal get *ruined*?

Ask: How would you feel if your favorite sweater got *ruined* in the wash?

DURING READING

20–30 Minutes   RI.5.1   RI.5.5   SL.5.1b   SL.5.1d   L.5.6

Close Reading

🔍 **Pages 2–3**

Purpose Ⓐ Ⓒ Ⓣ Explain that authors often do not state directly why they wrote an article, or how they feel about the people being described. Read page 2 aloud. Say: *This selection begins with a dramatic event. What happened?* (Norman was caught in a blizzard. He almost died.) *Did this really happen?* (yes) *Why do you think that the author began the biography with this event?* (It makes the reader interested in Borlaug. It shows that Borlaug learned how to be tough when he was young.)

Vocabulary Have students find the word *inspired* on page 2. *In the very next sentence, Norman said that Sina made him keep going. Using context clues, what do you think* inspired *means?* (*Inspired* means encouraged to go on.)

Sequence *Find the signal words that tell about how old Norman was when he worked on the family farm.* (From a young age) *What words tell when Norman wrestled?* (in high school) *Which event came first?* (working on the farm) Help students record these events on their Sequence Charts.

Vocabulary Read the box on page 3 aloud. Say: *One hundred percent means all of something. What did Norman's coach mean when he encouraged Norman to "give 105%"?* (He was encouraging Norman to try really hard, to really push himself.)

Pages 4–5

Problem and Solution Read page 4. Then ask: *What problem did Norman hear Dr. Stakman talk about?* (How rust fungus was destroying crops.) *Find the sentence in the second paragraph that shows that Norman wants to help find a solution to this problem.* (Norman wanted to help stop rust.)

STOP AND CHECK *Read the question in the Stop and Check box on page 4.* (Dr. Stakman, a scientist who talked about a fungus that destroys crops)

Sequence *Find a phrase that gives a clue about when the events in Chapter 2 happen.* (After college) *When was the food shortage in Mexico happening?* (1944) Remind students to record these events in their Sequence Charts.

Purpose Have students point to the diagram of wheat and the boxed explanation of the word *yield*. Ask: *Do the diagram and the text box give us information about Norman's life?* (no) *Why do you think the author wanted to include this information?* (She wanted readers to have more information about something that was very important to Norman Borlaug.)

Pages 6–7

Connection of Ideas Have students look back at the last paragraph on page 4. Then read the first paragraph on page 6 aloud. *What problem was happening in Mexico? How does that relate to what Norman studied in college?* (Mexico's wheat was being ruined by rust fungus. Norman learned about rust fungus in college from Dr. Stakman.)

Problem and Solution Have students read the last paragraph on page 7 carefully. Ask: *What did Norman have to do in order to solve Mexico's food problems?* (find a new place to grow wheat in summer) *How would growing plants all year help solve the problem?* (He thought he could create a new type of wheat faster.)

Vocabulary Read the caption on page 7 aloud. Explain that a *revolution* is a complete change in the way something is done. Ask: *What do you think the phrase "green revolution" means? Use the photograph to help you figure it out.* (The photo on pages 6 and 7 shows Borlaug in a green field. By changing how people grew wheat, he created a revolution of growing green plants.)

STOP AND CHECK *Read the question in the Stop and Check box on page 7.* (He worked on breeding wheat that could resist rust and have a higher yield.)

Have partners review their Sequence Charts for pages 2–7 and discuss what they learned.

Quick Check Do students understand weekly vocabulary in context? If not, review and reteach using the instruction on page 94.

Can students use details to determine the sequence of events? If not, review and reteach using the instruction on page 94 and assign the Unit 2 Week 3 digital mini-lesson.

WEEK 3 LESSON 4

Objectives
- Understand and use new vocabulary
- Read a biography
- Understand sequence
- Understand complex text through close reading
- Respond to the selection, using text evidence to support ideas

Scaffolding for **Wonders** Approaching Leveled Reader

Materials
- "Norman Borlaug and the Green Revolution" Apprentice Leveled Reader: pp. 8–20
- Graphic Organizer: Sequence

☞ **Go** Digital
- Apprentice Leveled Reader eBook
- Downloadable Graphic Organizer
- Sequence Mini-Lesson

BEFORE READING

5–10 Minutes   SL.5.1c   SL.5.1d   L.5.4a   L.5.6

Expand Vocabulary

Display each word below. Say the words and have students repeat them. Then use the Define/Example/Ask routine to introduce each word.

1 benefit (page 11)

Define: anything that helps someone

Example: Exercise has many *benefits* for my health.

Ask: What else has a *benefit* for your health?

2 increased (page 13)

Define: made something bigger or better

Example: I *increased* my grade by doing extra credit.

Ask: What other habits *increase* grades?

3 local (page 9)

Define: near where you live

Example: We buy most of our food at a *local* supermarket.

Ask: What other stores are *local* to our community?

4 resisted (page 10)

Define: was not hurt by or was not affected by

Example: Last winter, I *resisted* the flu and did not get sick.

Ask: Why would you need a jacket that *resists* water?

DURING READING

15–20 Minutes   RI.5.1   RI.5.5   SL.5.1b   SL.5.1d   L.5.6

Close Reading

🔍 **Pages 8–9**

Purpose Ⓐ Ⓒ Ⓣ Discuss the map on page 8. *What is the title of the map?* (Wheat-breeding Sites in Mexico) Have students point to Toluca Valley and Chapingo, which are mentioned in the text above the map. Discuss why the author also included the Yaqui Valley. (Yaqui Valley is where Borlaug did research, so it is important to the story.) Point out that Mexico City is Mexico's capital.

Sequence *In paragraph 1 on page 9, what process is being described?* (Borlaug is crossbreeding different kinds of wheat in the Yaqui Valley.) *Find a sequence word in paragraph 1. What step does that word signal?* (Then; the best plants were crossed with other plants to create new types of wheat.) *What was the final result of growing wheat all year?* (the breeding rate of the wheat was doubled.)

🔍 **Pages 10–11**

Compare and Contrast *What did Borlaug's team do?* (crossed dwarf plants with taller plants) *How was the new kind of wheat similar to the dwarf wheat?* (Both kinds had a strong stem.) *How was it similar to the taller kind of wheat?* (Both kinds resisted rust.)

Purpose Ⓐ Ⓒ Ⓣ *Look at the diagram and caption on page 11. Ask: What information does this diagram show?* (It compares wheat yield in 1945 with the yield in 1965.) *Point to the part that shows more wheat being produced. Why do you think the author included this information?* (The box on the right shows the wheat yield in 1965. It is ten times more than in 1945. This information shows how Borlaug's work helped people grow more wheat.)

STOP AND CHECK *Read the question in the Stop and Check box on page 11.* (He traveled around Mexico to find places with different climates. Then he grew plants in one place in the winter, and other places in the summer.)

Pages 12–13

Sequence *Find the sequence words that begin Chapter 4.* (In the 1960s) *What important event happened in those years?* (a food shortage in India and Pakistan) *What two things did Borlaug do to help?* (He sent new wheat seeds and told the people how to grow the wheat.)

Purpose **ACT** *What can we learn from the map on page 12? Why do you think the author included it?* (It shows where Mexico, India, and Pakistan are. The author wants to show how far Borlaug sent his wheat seeds.)

Vocabulary Have students point to the term *nutrients* on page 13. Read page 13 and ask: *What clues help you figure out what* nutrients *means?* (It must be food, because it is something that plants need, along with water, to grow.) *Plants get* nutrients *from the soil and they get more* nutrients *when fertilizer is used. How do you get nutrients?* (by eating food, taking vitamins)

Page 14

Genre **ACT** Explain that most biographies include the person's greatest achievements. Have partners review page 14 and then respond to this question: *What did Norman achieve during his life?* (won the Nobel Peace Prize; saved millions of lives; showed that science and technology could transform farming; helped to build a worldwide community of scientists)

STOP AND CHECK *Read the question in the Stop and Check box on page 14.* (It improved how people farmed so they could grow a lot more food on the same amount of land. It also encouraged scientists from all over to work together.)

AFTER READING

10–15 Minutes   RI.5.1   RI.5.2   RI.5.9   W.5.9b   L.5.4a   **CCSS**

Respond to Reading

Compare Texts Have students compare and contrast how Lucy Braun and Norman Borlaug investigated questions about nature. Then, ask: *What questions do you have about nature? How would you investigate them?*

Summarize Have students turn to page 15 and summarize the selection. (Answers should include details about the progression of events in Borlaug's life.)

Text Evidence

Have partners work together to answer questions on page 15. Remind students to use their Sequence Charts.

Sequence (Borlaug grew up on a farm. After he graduated, he went to college. There, a talk from Dr. Stakman got him interested in becoming a plant scientist so that he could help end world hunger.)

Vocabulary (A *community* is a group of people who work together or live together.)

Write About Reading (India and Pakistan had millions of people that could starve; Borlaug shipped the new wheat seeds there and explained how to grow them; scientists began working together to breed more plants.)

Independent Reading

Encourage students to read the paired selection "Golden Apples" on pages 16–18. Have them summarize the selection and compare it to Norman Borlaug's biography. Have partners answer the "Make Connections" questions on page 18.

 Quick Check **Can students identify sequence? If not, review and reteach using the instruction on page 94 and assign the Unit 2 Week 3 digital mini-lesson.**

Can students respond to the selection using text evidence? If not, provide sentence frames to help them organize their ideas.

WEEK 3 LESSON 5

Objectives
- Review weekly vocabulary words
- Review sequence
- Write an analysis to share an opinion about how an author organizes events in a biography

Scaffolding for **Wonders** McGraw-Hill Reading Reading/Writing Workshop

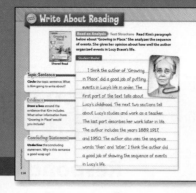

Materials
- Visual Vocabulary Cards: 57–64
- Interactive Worktext, pp. 114–115
- Assessment Book, pp. 24–25

👉 **Go** Digital
- Visual Vocabulary Cards
- Sequence Mini-Lesson
- Interactive eWorktext

REVIEW AND RETEACH

5–10 Minutes   RI.5.3   L.5.4a   L.5.6

Weekly Vocabulary

Display one **Visual Vocabulary Card** at a time and ask students to use the vocabulary word in a sentence. If students have difficulty, have them find the word in "Growing in Place" and use the context clues to define it.

Comprehension: Sequence

I Do   Write and say: *As a child, Lucy enjoyed looking at plants and flowers. In high school, Lucy began to study plants. Later, Lucy wrote a book about plants.* Circle the sequence words *As a child, In high school,* and *Later. These signal words help me understand the sequence of events that led Lucy to write a book about plants. The events are organized in the order in which they happen.* Display: *Lucy walked to the woods with her parents. They enjoyed looking at the wildflowers there.* Point out that these sentences also give a sequence of events but do not include signal words.

We Do   Display: *George first learned how to use a camera in 1982. Years later, he published his photographs in a magazine. After his death, George's photographs were displayed in a museum.* Say: *Which event happened first?* (George learned to use a camera) *What event happened next?* (he published his photographs) *What event happened last?* (his photographs were displayed in a museum) *What time and sequence words helped you?* (1982, Years later, After his death)

You Do   Display another short passage from a biography. Have partners tell the order of the events and identify any time and sequence words.

WRITE ABOUT READING

25–35 Minutes   W.5.1a   W.5.1b   W.5.1d   W.5.5   W.5.9.b

Read an Analysis

- Ask students to look back at "Growing in Place" in the **Interactive Worktext**. Have volunteers review important events. Ask: *How did the author's use of sequence help you understand the important events in Lucy's life?*

- Read aloud the directions on page 114. *Kim's paragraph is not a summary. It is an analysis, or detailed description. Kim wrote it to explain her opinion about how the author sequenced the events in the biography of Lucy Braun.*

- Say: *When you write an analysis, you need to include certain elements. The first element is a* topic sentence. *Read Kim's paragraph and circle the topic sentence. What important information is in this sentence?* (text's title; Kim's opinion about how the author put events in order)

- *Another element is* text evidence. *Kim supports her opinion with details from the text. Box the text evidence.* (sentences 2–6) *What specific information from the text does Kim include?* (parts of the text, years and time order words the author includes) *What other information from the text would you include?* (Possible answer: the author uses the sequence words *As a child* and *In high school*)

- *The final element is the* concluding statement. *Underline the concluding statement. How is the concluding statement like the topic sentence?* (Both say that the author did a good job of showing the order of events in Lucy's life) *Why is it a good wrap up?* (it restates Kim's opinion)

✏️ **Analytical Writing** Write an Analysis

Guided Writing Read the writing prompt on page 115 together. Have students write about "Norman Borlaug and the Green Revolution" or another text they read this week. Have them review their Sequence Charts. *Use the checklist to help you figure out the right information to include in each section.* Guide students to ask "why" and "how" questions when they analyze text evidence.

Peer Conference Have students read their analysis to a partner. Listeners should identify the strongest text evidence that supports the topic sentence and discuss any sentences that are unclear.

Teacher Conference Check students' writing for complete sentences and text evidence that supports their topics. Review the concluding statements. *Does this sentence tie all of the elements together?* If necessary, have students revise their concluding statements by restating their topic sentences.

Level Up

▲ Approaching Leveled Reader

▲ Reading/Writing Workshop

▲ Apprentice Leveled Reader

▲ Interactive Worktext

IF students read the `Apprentice Level` Reader fluently and the **Interactive Worktext** Shared Read fluently and answer the Respond to Reading questions

THEN read together the `Approaching Level` Reader main selection and the **Reading/Writing Workshop** Shared Read from *Reading Wonders*. Have students take notes as they read, using self-stick notes. Then ask and answer questions about their notes.

Writing Rubric

	4	3	2	1
Topic Sentence	Topic sentence presents a clear opinion.	Topic sentence presents an opinion, somewhat clearly.	Topic is presented in short phrases; opinion is unclear.	There is no topic sentence; no opinion is presented.
Text Evidence	Opinion is supported by two or more text details.	Opinion is only supported by one detail from the text.	Little to no evidence from the text supports opinion.	No text evidence is included; does not support opinion.
Concluding Statement	Clearly restates an opinion; wraps up all the details.	Restatement is less focused; attempts to wrap up the details.	Vaguely restates opinion. Doesn't correlate well to text evidence.	There is no conclusion.
Writing Style	Writes in complete sentences. Uses correct spelling and grammar.	Uses complete sentences and phrases. Writing has spelling and grammar errors.	Few or no complete sentences. There are many spelling and grammar errors.	Does not write accurately or in complete sentences.

ASSESSMENT

Weekly Assessment

Have students complete the Weekly Assessment using **Assessment** book pages 24–25.

WEEK 3

▶ **Mid-Unit Assessment,** pages 80–87

▶ **Fluency Assessment,** pages 234–239

Unit 2 Mid-Unit Assessment

CCSS TESTED SKILLS

✔ COMPREHENSION	✔ VOCABULARY
• Problem and Solution RI.5.3	• Context Clues L.5.4a
• Compare and Contrast RL.5.3	
• Sequence RI.5.5	

Using Assessment and Writing Scores

↻ RETEACH	IF ...	THEN ...
COMPREHENSION	Students answer 0–5 multiple-choice items correctly ...	... reteach tested skills using instruction on pages 364–371.
VOCABULARY	Students answer 0–2 multiple-choice items correctly ...	... reteach tested skills using instruction on page 364.
WRITING	Students score mostly 1–2 on weekly writing rubrics throughout the unit...	... reteach writing using instruction on pages 372–373.

Fluency Assessment

Conduct assessments individually using the differentiated fluency passages in Assessment. Students' expected fluency goal for this Unit is 100–120 WCPM with an accuracy rate of 95% or higher.

Weeks 4 and 5

Monitor students' progress on the following to inform how to adjust instruction for the remainder of the unit.

ADJUST INSTRUCTION	
ACCESS COMPLEX TEXT	If students need more support for accessing complex text, provide additional modeling of prompts in Lesson 2 of Week 4, pages 100–101, and Week 5, pages 110–111. After you model how to identify the text evidence, guide students to find text evidence in Lessons 3 and 4 in Week 4, pages 102–105, and Week 5, pages 112–115.
FLUENCY	For those students who need more support with Fluency, focus on the Fluency lessons in the Foundational Skills Kit.
WRITING	If students need more support incorporating text evidence in their writing, conduct the Write About Reading activities in Lessons 4 and 5 as group writing activities.
FOUNDATIONAL SKILLS	Review student's individualized progress in *PowerPAL for Reading* to determine which foundational skills to incorporate into your lessons for the remainder of the unit.

WEEK 4 LESSON 1

Objectives
- Develop oral language
- Build background about how a plan helps accomplish a task
- Understand and use weekly vocabulary
- Read a folktale

Materials
- Interactive Worktext, pp. 116–123
- Visual Vocabulary Cards: 65–72

☞ **Go** Digital
- Interactive eWorktext
- Visual Vocabulary Cards

Scaffolding for **Wonders** Reading/Writing Workshop

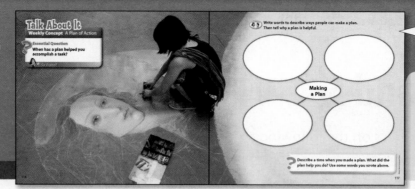

WEEKLY CONCEPT

5–10 Minutes   SL.5.1b   SL.5.1c   CCSS

Talk About It

Essential Question Read aloud the Essential Question on page 116 of the **Interactive Worktext:** *When has a plan helped you accomplish a task?* Explain that a task is work that is to be completed. Say: *Thinking of a plan before you begin a task helps you know what to do.*

- Discuss the photograph on page 116. Ask: *What task is this girl doing?* (she is coloring a drawing) *What tells you the girl has a plan?* (there is an outline)

I Do Say: *I am going to think of a time when I made a plan to accomplish a task. One time, I wanted to make soup. I followed a recipe. First I had to make sure I had all the ingredients. Then I had to follow steps to wash and chop the ingredients before adding them to the soup. I did the steps in order. This plan helped me make soup. I will add "get ingredients" and "follow steps" to the word web on page 117.*

We Do Say: *Let's look at the photo. Did the girl have a plan before she colored her drawing? How do you know?* (yes, I see an outline) *What tools did she have to have before she started drawing?* (colored chalk) Guide students to add *make an outline* and *get tools* to the web. Have students brainstorm other ways the girl made a plan before she began drawing. Work with them to add their ideas to their webs.

You Do Have partners describe a time when they made a plan to do something. Have them review some of the words or ideas in their webs before they answer the questions: *What did you plan to do? What did you do before you started? How did a plan help you?* Have partners discuss why a plan is helpful.

REVIEW VOCABULARY

10–15 Minutes   L.5.4a   L.5.5c   L.5.6   CCSS

Review Weekly Vocabulary Words

- Use the **Visual Vocabulary Cards** to review the weekly vocabulary.
- Read together the directions for the Vocabulary activity on page 118 of the **Interactive Worktext.** Then complete the activity.

1 **pursuit** Have students use the following sentence frame: *A _____ might be in pursuit of a mouse.* (Possible answers: cat, dog, owl, hawk)

2 **assuring** Read the sentence aloud with an *assuring* tone and have students echo your reading. Then have partners tell what they would say when assuring a classmate. (Possible answers: You will do great. You will do better next time.)

3 **gratitude** Have partners discuss nice things that people have done for them. Ask: *How did you show your gratitude?* (Possible answers: sent a note; did something nice for them in return) Then have partners read aloud the choices and decide which options are examples of showing gratitude. (Give someone a small gift. Thank someone for helping you.)

4 **outcome** Have students discuss what happens when people take swimming lessons. Then have them complete the sentence frame: *One outcome I would expect from taking swimming lessons is _____.* (Possible answers: I would know how to swim; I would be a better/faster swimmer)

5 **guidance** Have the partners take turns guiding each other around the room. Tell the leaders to give specific directions, such as "Move three steps forward."

(Demonstrations will vary.) **Then ask:** *How did you give guidance to your partner?* (Possible answers: told him/her how many steps to take; direction words such as *left* and *right*)

6 **detected** **Ask:** *Which words are synonyms for detected?* (sensed, saw) *Which of the three words has the opposite meaning as detected?* (missed)

7 **previous** Have students use the sentence starter: *This year, I am different from the previous year because _____.* (Possible answers: I am taller; I am better at math; I began playing sports)

8 **emerging** Have partners brainstorm a list of creatures and their homes, such as snail/shell and rabbit/hole. Then have students choose one to draw. (Drawings will vary.) Have students use the word *emerging* to write a caption for their drawing.

High-Utility Words

Have students look at the High Utility Words activity on page 119 of the **Interactive Worktext.** Discuss the definition of *homographs*. Read the first two sentences. Have students tell the meaning of the word *present* in each sentence. Then have partners take turns reading the rest of the sentences. Have partners circle homographs. (change, can, store) Then have them discuss the meanings of the words they circled.

> **ELL ENGLISH LANGUAGE LEARNERS**
>
> Reread the passage. After every two sentences, stop and help them identify homographs in the passage, such as: *Which two words look the same? Now point to the word that means "to show."* Have students point to and say each homograph aloud.

READ COMPLEX TEXT

15–20 Minutes   RL.5.1   RF.5.4c

Read: "The Magical Lost Brocade"

- Have students turn to page 120 in the **Interactive Worktext** and read aloud the Essential Question. **Ask:** *What is the title?* ("The Magical Lost Brocade") Explain that a *brocade* is a cloth that has a raised pattern. Then ask: *Is the story made up or true?* (made up) *What clues in the title and picture tell you it is made up?* (*magical* in the title; illustrations rather than photographs)

- Read "The Magical Lost Brocade" together. Note that the weekly vocabulary words are highlighted in yellow. Expand Vocabulary words are in blue.

- Have students use the "My Notes" section on page 120 to write questions they have, words they don't understand, and details they want to remember. Model how to use the "My Notes" section. *I can write notes about questions I have as I read. In the first paragraph on page 121, I'm not sure what heartbroken means. I will write heartbroken? in the "My Notes" section. As I continue to read this paragraph, I am not sure why Ping went off in pursuit of the brocade. I will write a question in the "My Notes" section: Why does Ping leave? When we reread the story, I will ask my questions so I better understand what I am reading.*

> **ELL ENGLISH LANGUAGE LEARNERS**
>
> As you read together, have students mark parts of the text they have questions about. After reading, help them write their questions in the "My Notes" section. Then help them locate answers to their questions in the text.

 Quick Check Can students understand the weekly vocabulary in context? If not, review vocabulary using the **Visual Vocabulary Cards** before teaching Lesson 2.

WEEK 4 LESSON

2

Objectives
- Read a folktale
- Understand complex text through close reading
- Recognize and understand theme
- Respond to the selection, using text evidence to support ideas

Scaffolding for **WONDERS** Reading/Writing Workshop

Materials
Interactive Worktext, pp. 120–125

☞ **Go Digital**
- Interactive eWorktext
- Theme Mini-Lesson

REREAD COMPLEX TEXT

20–25 Minutes RL.5.1 RL.5.2 RL.5.9 L.5.4a L.5.6 CCSS

Close Reading: "The Magical Lost Brocade"

Reread "The Magical Lost Brocade" with students. As you read together, discuss important passages in the text. Have students respond to text-dependent questions, including those in the **Interactive Worktext.**

Page 121

Expand Vocabulary Have students locate the word *impossible* in the first paragraph and read the sentence. Ask: *What is* impossible *for the woman to do?* (give Ping a better home) *Why is it impossible?* Guide students to look for details in the text. (She did not make much money.)

Theme *To figure out the story's theme, I'm going look for clues in what the characters do and say. In the first paragraph, I read that the woman was heartbroken, or upset, when the wind took the brocade away. What did Ping say or do when this happened?* (He went off in pursuit of the cloth, assuring his mother as he left and promising to return with the brocade.) *What does this detail tell you about Ping?* (Possible answers: he is caring) If students have difficulty making an inference about Ping, ask: *Are Ping's actions caring or selfish? How do you know?* (Possible answers: caring; he promises to get the brocade back)

Organization Ⓐ Ⓒ Ⓣ Say: *The bearded man gives clues about what Ping will do next.* Have students reread the last paragraph and look for clues to where Ping will go. *Where does the bearded man say Ping will go first?* (Fire Valley) *Where does the man say Ping will go next?* (Ice Ocean) *What is the name of the last place Ping will travel to?* (the Mountain of the Sun) *Do you think Ping's trip*

will be easy or difficult? What text evidence tells you this? Point to clues in the text. (Difficult; cross through Fire Valley without saying a word; ride through the icy waters without shivering; on top of this steep peak)

Page 122

Expand Vocabulary Have students reread the first paragraph and locate the word *journey. What is a journey?* (a long trip) *Which words in the text are clues to the meaning of journey?* (Possible answers: traveled for three days; reached; crossed) *How long was Ping's journey to Fire Valley?* (three days)

High-Utility Words Point to the word *tears* in the first paragraph. Ask: *What is the meaning of* tears *in this sentence?* (what happens when you cry) *What clues in the text helped you figure out the meaning?* (Ping's eyes) *What is another meaning for this word?* (to rip paper) Then have partners look for other homographs in the last two paragraphs and discuss their meanings. (just, wind)

Theme Have students look for a promise Ping makes in the first paragraph. *What does Ping say he will do?* (I'll do my best) Discuss with students what it means to *do your best.* Then have partners underline sentences in the text that show Ping met his promise. (The intense heat brought tears to his eyes, but he said nothing. They rode through the chilly waves, but Ping did not shiver. He rode up a steep trail, grasping the reins)

Organization Ⓐ Ⓒ Ⓣ Have students review and retell the events the bearded man told Ping would happen on his trip. *Ask: What did the bearded man say Ping would find at the palace?* (the brocade) *Did Ping find it? Draw a box around the paragraph that tells you this.* (Yes; the last paragraph) *What happens that was not a part of the bearded man's plan? Who did Ping meet?* (he meets Princess Ling)

Page 123

Organization A C T Say: *Writers sometimes give hints about events that happen later in a story.* Have students reread the page and discuss the story events. *Ask: Who does Ping find when he unrolls the brocade?* (Princess Ling) *Now look in the first paragraph for clues that this event would happen.* (He detected a knowing smile on her face as they said goodbye.)

Expand Vocabulary Read the definition of *announce* together. Have students circle the words Ping *announced* when he returned home. ("Here is your brocade, Mother!") Then have students demonstrate how he would say these words.

Theme Reread the last paragraph aloud and say: *Ping had done his best and fulfilled his promise. What promise did he fulfill?* (He brings back his mother's brocade.) If students have difficulty, have them review details about Ping they marked in the story or wrote in their notes. Then ask: *What happens to Ping after he fulfills his promise?* (Their hut became a magnificent house with gardens. Ping and the princess got married; they all lived happily in their beautiful home and gardens!) *Is this a good or bad thing?* (good) *Now put all these details together to figure out the big idea, or theme of the story.* (Possible answer: When you keep a promise and work hard, you will be rewarded.)

Genre A C T Reread the last sentence aloud. Ask: *What words or phrases in this sentence have you heard at the end of other fairy tales or folk tales?* (they all lived happily) Have partners name another fairy tale or folktale that has a similar ending. Then have them discuss how this folktale is similar and different from that tale.

RESPOND TO READING

10–20 Minutes   RL.5.1   W.5.9a   SL.5.1d

Respond to "The Magical Lost Brocade"

Have students summarize "The Magical Lost Brocade" orally to demonstrate comprehension. Then have partners answer the questions on page 124 of the **Interactive Worktext** using the discussion starters. Tell them to use text evidence to support their answers. Have students write the page number(s) on which they found the text evidence for each question.

1. *What was Ping's plan when he left home?* (to bring back his mother's brocade; Text Evidence: p. 121)

2. *How did the bearded man's plan help Ping get the brocade?* (He told Ping where the brocade was and how to get there. He warned him about dangers. He also lent Ping a horse. Text Evidence: pp. 121–122)

3. *How did Ping accomplish getting the brocade and bringing it back home?* (Possible answer: He followed the bearded man's plan to get the brocade; he followed the same directions to bring back the brocade; he did his best. Text Evidence: pp. 122–123)

After students discuss the questions on page 124, have them write a response to the question on page 125. Tell them to use their partner discussions and notes about "The Magical Lost Brocade" to help them. Circulate and provide guidance.

 Quick Check Do students understand vocabulary in context? If not, review and reteach using the instruction on page 106.

Can students use key details to determine the theme? If not, review and reteach using the instruction on page 106 and assign the Unit 2 Week 4 digital mini-lesson.

Can students write a response to "The Magical Lost Brocade"? If not, provide sentence frames to help them organize their ideas.

Objectives
- Understand and use new vocabulary words
- Read a folktale
- Recognize and understand theme
- Understand complex text through close reading

Materials
- "The Lion's Whiskers" Apprentice Leveled Reader: pp. 2–9
- Graphic Organizer: Theme

☞ **Go** Digital
- Apprentice Leveled Reader eBook
- Graphic Organizer
- Theme Mini-Lesson

Scaffolding for Wonders **Approaching Leveled Reader**

BEFORE READING

10–15 Minutes　　SL.5.1c　SL.5.1d　L.5.4a　L.5.6　CCSS

Introduce "The Lion's Whiskers"

- Read the Essential Question on the title page of "The Lion's Whiskers" **Apprentice Leveled Reader:** *When has a plan helped you accomplish a task? We will read about a woman who made a plan to accomplish a difficult task.*

- Read the title of the main read. Have students look at the images. *Where do you think the characters live?* (in a village in the country, maybe somewhere in Africa) *How do you know?* (The illustrations show a hut, grass and plants, and a lion.)

Expand Vocabulary

Display each word below. Say the words and have students repeat them. Then use the Define/Example/Ask routine to introduce each word.

①　determined (page 6)

Define: firm in sticking to a purpose

Example: I was *determined* to get an A in math.

Ask: What is a goal you were *determined* to meet?

②　fled (page 9)

Define: ran away or escaped

Example: The cat *fled* from the barking dog.

Ask: When have you *fled* from something?

③　hardworking (page 2)

Define: willing to make a big effort to get a job done

Example: The *hardworking* student finished her essay.

Ask: How can you tell that a student is *hardworking*?

④　loneliness (page 3)

Define: sadness that comes from feeling alone

Example: When Sue's sister went away to college, Sue suffered from *loneliness*.

Ask: What stories have you read about a character who experiences *loneliness*?

DURING READING

20–30 Minutes　　RL.5.1　RL.5.2　SL.5.1b　L.5.4a　CCSS

Close Reading

🔍 **Pages 2–3**

Genre Ⓐ Ⓒ Ⓣ　Have students read page 2. Point out that the words *There once was a woman* at the beginning of this story are a clue that this is a folktale. It shows that this is an old story from long ago. Ask: *Who is the main character in this story?* (Alitash) *Where does the story take place?* (the mountains of Ethiopia)

Sequence　Ask: *What events led to Alitash coming to live with Dawit as his stepmother?* (Alitash married a man named Tesfa. Tesfa was married but his wife died. He has a young son named Dawit. Alitash became Dawit's stepmother when she married Tesfa.)

Character, Setting, Plot　Ask: *How does Alitash feel about Dawit?* (Alitash is happy to have Dawit as her stepson.) *What is Alitash's problem?* (Dawit is not happy. He still missed his real mother.) *What is Alitash's goal?* (She wants Dawit to grow to love her.)

STOP AND CHECK　*Read the question in the Stop and Check box on page 3.* (He misses his mother who died.)

Pages 4–5

Theme Explain that the theme of a story is usually not stated directly. To find the theme, we must look at what the characters say and do. Ask students to locate the sentence on page 4 that tells about an important event. (In the first sentence, it says that Alitash visits a wise woman.) *Why does Alitash go to see the wise woman?* (Alitash wants the wise woman to make a potion so that Dawit will love her.)

Help students record what Alitash says and does in their Theme charts. As students continue to read, have them record important details in their charts.

Genre A C T Explain that in folktales, the main character is often given a difficult task to do in order to get what he or she wants. Ask: *What task does the wise woman tell Alitash she must do?* (Alitash must go alone into the desert and get three whiskers from a living lion.)

Vocabulary Have students find the word *gasped* at the end of page 5. Explain that to *gasp* means *to breathe in, in a way that can be heard.* You *gasp* when you're surprised or scared or hurt. Model a gasp and have students repeat. Ask: *Why does Alitash gasp when the wise woman tells her to get three lion whiskers?* ("She knew this was very dangerous." She is surprised and shocked at the thought of this task.)

STOP AND CHECK *Read the question in the Stop and Check box on page 5.* (The wise woman wants Alitash to bring her three whiskers from a lion.)

Pages 6–7

Sentence Structure A C T Read aloud the many questions on page 6. Ask: *Who is asking the questions?* (Alitash) *Who is Alitash asking?* (herself) *What is Alitash trying to do as she asks the questions?* (She is trying to figure out a plan for getting the lion's whiskers.)

Vocabulary Have students point to the word *clever* on page 6. Ask: *What does* clever *mean? What clue helps you understand what it means?* (smart or wise; she thinks of a plan) Then say: *As we keep reading, let's see how Alitash shows that she is* clever.

Sequence Have students read page 7. Explain that this is where Alitash starts to put her plan in action. *What did Alitash do first?* (She carried a piece of meat into the desert.) *What did she do next?* (She walked to Lion Canyon.) *What did Alitash do last?* (She walked toward the lion and stared at him.) *What did the lion do then?* (He stared back at her.)

Pages 8–9

Theme Have students read page 9. Ask: *How does the lion react to Alitash the first time they meet?* (He stands and roars.) *How does Alitash react to the lion?* (She drops the meat, runs away, and doesn't look back.) *What does Alitash do the next day?* (She goes back into the desert.) *What does this show about the kind of person Alitash is?* (It shows she has courage. It also shows she doesn't give up.)

Organization A C T *In many folktales, characters must keep trying to reach their goal. Do you think that Alitash will go back to the desert? Why or why not?* (Yes, because she already went back once. She still needs to get the lion's whiskers.)

Have partners review the Theme Graphic Organizers for pages 2–9 and discuss what they learned.

✓ **Quick Check** Do students understand weekly vocabulary in context? If not, review and reteach using the instruction on page 106.

Can students identify the theme? If not, review and reteach using the instruction on page 106 and assign the Unit 2 Week 4 digital mini-lesson.

WEEK 4
LESSON

4

Objectives
• Understand and use new vocabulary
• Read a folktale
• Understand theme
• Understand complex text through close reading
• Respond to the selection, using text evidence to support ideas

Materials
• "The Lion's Whiskers" Apprentice Leveled Reader: pp. 10–20
• Graphic Organizer: Theme

☞ **Go** Digital
• Apprentice Leveled Reader eBook
• Downloadable Graphic Organizer
• Theme Mini-Lesson

Scaffolding for **Wonders** Approaching Leveled Reader

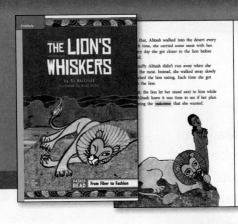

BEFORE READING

5–10 Minutes   SL.5.1c   SL.5.1d   L.5.4a   L.5.6   CCSS

Expand Vocabulary

Display each word below. Say the words and have students repeat them. Then use the Define/Example/Ask routine to introduce each word.

1 goal (page 14)

Define: something that someone works to get or to do

Example: The runner's *goal* was to win the race.

Ask: What is a *goal* that you have for yourself?

2 patience (page 14)

Define: being able to wait or to face a problem without getting upset

Example: The father showed great *patience* toward his crying baby.

Ask: What is another situation that requires *patience?*

3 snarled (page 11)

Define: growled in a threatening way by showing teeth

Example: The dog *snarled* when the cat came near its bowl.

Ask: What do you think would cause an animal to *snarl?*

DURING READING

15–20 Minutes   RL.5.1   RL.5.2   SL.5.1b   L.5.4a   CCSS

Close Reading

🔍 **Pages 10–11**

Organization **A C T** Have students read page 10. Ask: *What does Alitash do that is different every time she goes to the lion?* (Every day Alitash gets closer and closer to the lion. She starts walking away instead of running.) *Look at the first paragraph. What does the lion do that is different?* (Eventually, he lets Alitash stand next to him while he eats.)

Vocabulary Have students find the word *eventually* on page 10. Discuss clues that help the students understand the meaning of the word, "after a long time." Ask: *Did Alitash stop running away from the lion right away or did it take time?* (It took her many trips to get over her fear.)

Genre **A C T** Explain that most folktales contain imagery, or words and phrases that help create pictures in the reader's mind. Read aloud the first two sentences on page 11. Then ask: *Why is Alitash's heart pounding?* (She is afraid of the lion.) *How do these words create a picture in your mind?* (They help me understand how Alitash is feeling as she gets closer to the lion.)

Organization **A C T** Have students read the rest of page 11. Ask: *What is the final thing that Alitash does differently from the other times when she goes to the lion?* (She brings a knife into the desert. She cuts off some of the lion's whiskers while he is eating.)

Theme Reread the last paragraph on page 11. Ask: *Why does Alitash thank the lion?* (He allowed her to take the whiskers for the potion that will make Dawit love her.) Have students record this information on their graphic organizers.

STOP AND CHECK *Read the Stop and Check box on page 11.* (She took meat to a lion in the desert, getting a little closer to him every day.)

Pages 12–13

Sentence Structure (A)(C)(T) Read aloud the second sentence on page 12. Then say: *Let's take apart and paraphase this sentence. What three things happen here?* (Alitash gives Dawit his dinner. He smiles a little. Alitash sees it.) *Why are these things important?* (They make Alitash think her plan is working.)

Theme Have students find the word *amazed* on page 13. Ask: *Why do you think the woman is amazed to see the whiskers?* (She didn't think Alitash could do something so dangerous.) *What are some words that mean the same thing as amazed?* (surprised, shocked)

Connection of Ideas (A)(C)(T) *At the top of page 13, what does Alitash think the woman will do when she gives her the lion's whiskers?* (make a love potion) *What does the wise woman actually do?* (She throws the whiskers into the fire.) *What does the wise woman say about the potion?* ("You do not need a potion.")

Pages 14–15

Connection of Ideas (A)(C)(T) Read aloud the questions and answers on page 14. Then ask: *How did Alitash treat the lion?* (with patience and respect) *What happened because of the way Alitash treated the lion?* (She got what she wanted: the whiskers.) *Find the text that tells what the wise woman said Alitash must do to win Dawit's love.* (Treat him with patience and respect like you did with the lion.)

Theme *Why did Alitash reach her goal of getting the whiskers?* (Her plan worked because she followed the plan, was patient, and focused on her goal.)

STOP AND CHECK *Read the Stop and Check box on page 15.* (She threw them into the fire and told Alitash that she didn't need a potion. She should treat Dawit the same way she treated the lion: go slowly, have patience, and focus on her goal.)

AFTER READING
10–15 Minutes   RL.5.1   RL5.2   RL.5.9   W.5.9a   L.5.4a   CCSS

Respond to Reading

Compare Texts Have students compare and contrast how Ping and Alitash use plans to accomplish tasks. Then ask: *How have you used a plan to accomplish a task?*

Summarize Have students turn to page 16 and summarize the selection. (Answers should include details from the selection suggesting the importance of planning and working patiently to meet a goal.)

Text Evidence

Have partners work together to answer questions on page 16. Remind students to use their Theme Charts.

Theme (If you do not give up, you can reach your goal. Alitash shows patience and determination to get the lion's whiskers and to win her stepson's love.)

Vocabulary (*Paused* means "stopped for a short time." Alitash had to stop running to look over her shoulder.)

Write About Reading (At the end of the story, Alitash gives her relationship with Dawit time to grow. Alitash and Dawit begin to grow closer.)

Independent Reading

Encourage students to read the paired selection "From Fiber to Fashion" on pages 17–19. Have them summarize the selection and compare it to "The Lion's Whiskers." Have them work with partners to answer the "Make Connections" questions on page 19.

 Quick Check **Can students identify a theme? If not, review and reteach using the instruction on page 106 and assign the Unit 2 Week 4 digital mini-lesson.**

Can students respond to the selection using text evidence? If not, provide, sentence frames to help them organize their ideas.

Objectives
- Review weekly vocabulary words
- Review theme
- Write an analysis of an author's use of repetition to convey a theme

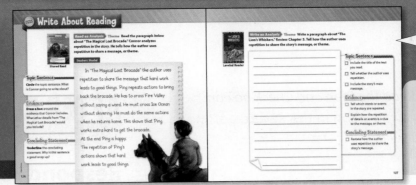

Materials
- Visual Vocabulary Cards: 65–72
- Interactive Worktext, pp. 126–127
- Assessment Book, pp. 26–27

☞ **Go Digital**
- Visual Vocabulary Cards
- Theme Mini-Lesson
- Interactive eWorktext

Scaffolding for **Wonders** Reading/Writing Workshop

REVIEW AND RETEACH

5–10 Minutes   RL.5.2 L.5.4a L.5.6

Weekly Vocabulary

Display one **Visual Vocabulary Card** at a time and ask students to use the word in a sentence. If students have difficulty, have them find the word in "The Magical Lost Brocade" and use the context clues to define it.

Comprehension: Theme

I Do Display: *Crow challenged Cat to a race. "I'll be sure to win," Crow said. "A cat can't run faster than a crow can fly. I won't even need to practice." But Cat practiced running the course every day before the race. When the day of the race came, Cat crossed the finish line first.* Underline what the crow says. *What happens to Crow? He loses the race.* Circle what Cat does. *What happens to Cat? She wins the race. These are clues to the theme: Practice leads to success.*

We Do Display: *Lion captured Mouse. Mouse told Lion that if he let him go, he could help him. Lion laughed, "You are too little to help me." But he let him go. Days later, Lion got trapped in a net. Mouse nibbled the net and set Lion free. Mouse said, "I may be small, but I can help you."* Say: *Let's find a theme together. What does Lion say?* ("You are too little to help me.") *What happens to Lion?* (He gets trapped in a net; mouse sets him free.) *What does the story tell you about judging others?* (don't judge others by the way they look)

You Do Display a passage from a folktale or fairy tale, such as Fox and the Crow. Have partners discuss what crow and fox do and say. Guide students to discuss what happens to the crow in the end to help them determine the theme.

WRITE ABOUT READING

25–35 Minutes   RL.5.2 W.5.4 W.5.5 W.5.9a

Read an Analysis

- Ask students to look back at "The Magical Lost Brocade" in the **Interactive Worktext**. Have volunteers review their notes. Ask: *What does the main character do and say that helps you understand the theme?*

- Read aloud the directions on page 126. *Connor's paragraph is not a summary. It is an analysis. When you analyze, ask yourself "how" and "why" questions. Connor has asked himself why the author used repetition and how this repetition shares the story's message, or theme.*

- Say: *An analysis always includes certain elements. The first element is a* topic sentence. *Read Connor's paragraph and circle the topic sentence. What important information is in this sentence?* (text's title; the author uses repetition to share the theme; the story's theme)

- *Another element of analysis is* text evidence. *Connor supports the topic sentence with details from the text.* Have students box the text evidence. (sentences 2–6) *What other text evidence might be included in the model?* (Ping rode up and down the mountain.)

- *The final element is the* concluding statement. *A good concluding statement restates the topic sentence and wraps up the main idea.* Have students underline the concluding statement. *How is the concluding statement like the topic sentence?* (Both sentences say that repetition shows the story's theme; both include the story's theme) *Which words in the concluding statement wrap up the evidence?* (the repetition of Ping's actions)

Write an Analysis
Analytical Writing

Guided Writing Read the writing prompt on page 127 together. Have students write about "The Lion's Whiskers" or another text they read this week. Have them review Chapter 3 and their notes. *Use the checklist to help you figure out the information to include in each section.* Guide students to ask questions, such as *How does the author share the theme?* and *Why is repetition in the story important?*

Peer Conference Have students read their analyses to partners. Listeners should identify the strongest text evidence that supports the topic sentences and discuss any sentences that are unclear.

Teacher Conference Check students' writing for complete sentences and text evidence that supports their topic. Review the concluding statement. Ask: *Does this sentence tie all of the elements together?* If necessary, have students revise the concluding statement by restating the topic sentence.

Level Up

▲ Approaching Leveled Reader

▲ Reading/Writing Workshop

Apprentice Leveled Reader

▲ Interactive Worktext

IF students read the Apprentice Level Reader fluently and the **Interactive Worktext** Shared Read fluently and answer the Respond to Reading questions

THEN read together the Approaching Level Reader main selection and the **Reading/Writing Workshop** Shared Read from *Reading Wonders*. Have students take notes as they read, using self-stick notes. Then ask and answer questions about their notes.

Writing Rubric

	4	3	2	1
Topic Sentence	There is one clear, focused topic sentence.	Topic sentence is less focused, somewhat clear.	Topic is presented in short phrases.	There is no topic sentence.
Text Evidence	Topic is supported by two or more text details.	Evidence includes only one detail from the text.	Little to no evidence is cited from the text.	No text evidence is included.
Concluding Statement	Clearly restates the topic sentence; wraps up all the details.	Restatement is less focused; attempts to wrap up the details.	Vaguely restates the topic. Doesn't correlate well to text evidence.	There is no conclusion.
Writing Style	Writes in complete sentences. Uses correct spelling and grammar.	Uses complete sentences and phrases. Writing has spelling and grammar errors.	Few or no complete sentences. There are many spelling and grammar errors.	Does not write accurately or in complete sentences.

ASSESSMENT

Weekly Assessment

Have students complete the Weekly Assessment using **Assessment** book pages 26–27.

WEEK 5
LESSON

1

Objectives
- Develop oral language
- Build background about accomplishing goals
- Understand and use weekly vocabulary
- Read poetry

Materials
- Interactive Worktext, pp. 128–135
- Visual Vocabulary Cards: 73–76

☞ **Go** Digital
- Interactive eWorktext
- Visual Vocabulary Cards

Scaffolding for **WONDERS** Reading/Writing Workshop

WEEKLY CONCEPT

5–10 Minutes   SL.5.1b   SL.5.1c   CCSS

Talk About It

Essential Question Read aloud the Essential Question on page 128 of the **Interactive Worktext**: *What motivates you to accomplish a goal?* Explain the meaning of *motivate* and *accomplish*. Say: *Sometimes you have to work hard to accomplish a goal. When you are motivated to accomplish a goal, you work extra hard.*

- Discuss the photograph on page 128. Ask: *What is the girl in the photograph doing?* (running) *What do you think is her goal?* (Possible answers: to win the race; to finish the race) *Do you think she is motivated to accomplish it? How can you tell?* (Yes; she is smiling.)

I Do Say: *One time, my sister took lessons and learned how to swim. When I saw her swim, it looked like fun! I was inspired to learn to swim, too. This motivated me to take swimming lessons, and soon I accomplished my goal. I will write "inspired by others" on page 129.*

We Do Say: *Let's look at the photo and think about what motivates the girl to run. What do you see around the girl that could motivate the girl to keep running?* (other people running; a person giving her a high-five; a finish line) Guide students to add words to the web on page 129. Have them brainstorm other reasons the girl might be motivated to keep running.

You Do Have partners describe a goal they accomplished that gave them satisfaction. Have them tell their partners why they were motivated. Have them answer the questions: *What was your goal? What did you do to help you accomplish your goal? What motivated you to accomplish the goal? How did you feel about yourself after?*

REVIEW VOCABULARY

10–15 Minutes   L.5.4a   L.5.5c   L.5.6   CCSS

Review Weekly Vocabulary Words

- Use the **Visual Vocabulary Cards** to review the weekly vocabulary.

- Read together the directions for the Vocabulary activity on page 130 of the **Interactive Worktext**. Then complete the activity.

1 **ambitious** Have students describe how an *ambitious* person would work. (Possible answers: work hard, practice) Then have partners decide which of the three words means the opposite of *ambitious*. (lazy)

2 **shuddered** Have partners demonstrate *shudder* to partners. Have students describe their partner's actions. Then have them complete the sentence starter: *One time, I shuddered when _____.* (Answers will vary, but students may describe a time when they were cold or scared.)

3 **memorized** Ask: *What phone number or date have you memorized?* (Answers will vary, but may include a home phone number or a date of birth.) *Why have you memorized this number or date?* (Possible answers: it is my home number, my birthday)

4 **satisfaction** Have students describe a time when they felt satisfaction. Offer an example, such as *I felt satisfaction when I finished my art project.* Then ask: *How do you look when you feel satisfaction? Draw a face to show what you look like when you feel satisfaction.* (Drawings will vary, but should show a face with a smile.)

Poetry Terms

Have students look at the Poetry Terms activity on page 131 of the **Interactive Worktext**. Read together the directions for the Poetry Terms activity. Read the poem aloud. Discuss the definitions of the poetry terms and give examples, as appropriate. Then have partners use the poem to complete each activity.

5 **narrative** Read aloud the definition of a *narrative* poem. *Who are the characters in this poem?* (Sara and a pitcher) Reread the poem aloud and pause after each stanza to ask: *What important event happens in this part of the poem?* (Sara walks up to bat; Sara holds the bat; Sara strikes the ball and sprints for a home run.)

6 **repetition** Say: *As I read, listen for the repetition of words or phrases.* Reread the first two stanzas aloud. Then ask: *Which phrase did you hear more than once?* (Then she focused)

7 **rhyme** Provide examples of rhyming words. Then have partners read aloud the second stanza of "Up to Bat." Ask: *Which pair of words rhyme?* (clasp, grasp)

8 **free verse** Say a nursery rhyme and clap to show that it has a pattern of rhyming words and beats. Then discuss the definition of a free verse poem. Read the last stanza of "Up to Bat." Ask: *Does this poem sound like a nursery rhyme or a free verse poem?* (free verse poem) Have partners explain their answers. (It does not have a pattern of beats or rhyming words.)

> **ELL ENGLISH LANGUAGE LEARNERS**
>
> For *narrative*, use the sentence frame: *In this narrative poem, _____ is playing _____.* For *free verse*, read aloud the definition and ask: *Does a free verse poem have a pattern of beats?* When teaching *repetition* and *rhyme*, lead students to echo multiple examples.

READ COMPLEX TEXT
15–20 Minutes   RL.5.1   RF.5.4c

Read: "A Simple Plan" and "Rescue"

- Have students turn to page 132 in the **Interactive Worktext** and read aloud the Essential Question. Explain that they will read two poems that illustrate what can motivate people to work toward a goal. Ask: *What is the title of the first poem?* ("A Simple Plan") *What do the photographs show?* (a boy smiling and running with a dog; a boy smiling) *Use these clues. Do you think the character or characters in the first poem will accomplish a goal?* (yes) *How can you tell?* (Both boys are smiling.) Then have partners review the title and photograph of "Rescue." Ask: *What do you think is the speaker's goal in this poem?* (Possible answer: rescuing a bird)

- Read "A Simple Plan" and "Rescue" together. Note that the weekly vocabulary words are not highlighted.

- Have students use the "My Notes" section on page 132 to write questions they have, words they don't understand, and details they want to remember. Model how to use the "My Notes" section. *If I have a question about one of the poems or I am confused about something, I can write a note in the "My Notes" section. For example, in "A Simple Plan," I'm not sure what the line "He schemes a simple plot" means. So I'll write this line with a question mark in the "My Notes" section.*

> **ELL ENGLISH LANGUAGE LEARNERS**
>
> As you read together, have students highlight the words, phrases, and lines of the poem that are confusing. After reading, help them write notes and questions in the "My Notes" section.

 Quick Check Can students understand the weekly vocabulary in context? If not, review vocabulary using the **Visual Vocabulary Cards** before teaching Lesson 2.

WEEK 5 LESSON 2

Objectives
- Read poetry
- Understand complex text through close reading
- Recognize and understand theme
- Respond to the selection, using text evidence to support ideas

Materials
Interactive Worktext, pp. 132–137

☞ **Go Digital**
- Interactive eWorktext
- Theme Digital Mini-Lesson

Scaffolding for **WONDERS** Reading/Writing Workshop

REREAD COMPLEX TEXT

20–25 Minutes   RL.5.2   RL.5.4   L.5.5a   L.5.6   (CCSS)

Close Reading: "A Simple Plan" and "Rescue"

Reread the poems "A Simple Plan" and "Rescue" with students. As you read together, discuss important lines in the poems. Have students respond to text-dependent questions, including those in the **Interactive Worktext**.

🔍 Page 133

Vocabulary Have students find the word *schemes* in the second line on page 132. Explain that *schemes* means "makes a secret plan." *What clues in the nearby lines help you understand the meaning of the word* schemes? ("I think I'll change the world.")

Genre Explain to students that "A Simple Plan" is a narrative poem. Say: *A narrative poem tells a story. It includes characters and may include dialogue.* As you reread page 132, have students circle the names of the characters. (Jack, John) Say: *Quotation marks show that a character is speaking. Sometimes a character's words continue over more than one line. On page 132, I see the words* "I think I'll change the world,"; "A little, not a lot." *in quotation marks. Let's draw a box around these lines. Who says these words?* (Jack) Then have partners reread the first six lines on page 133 and draw a box around the first speaker's words. ("Who wants to do another's chores?"/ John asked. "What does it mean, 'I'll change the world?' You're wasting time. What changes have you seen?") Ask: *Who is speaking?* (John)

Theme Say: *In this narrative poem, I will look for key details about the characters to figure out clues to the theme or lesson of the poem. Read aloud the first seven lines on page 133. I read that Jack "used to think" like John.*

He thought "Why bother?" and "Who cares?" These details tell me that Jack doesn't think that way anymore. I think these are clues to the theme. Let's underline these details and keep reading to find out what happened to Jack that caused him to change. Reread the rest of Jack's words. *What did Jack see?* (grass not mowed; kids not getting along; in the park no games to play) *What did this cause Jack to wonder?* (what was wrong) *What did Jack say he had to do next?* (ask himself, What was I waiting for?) *What lesson does Jack learn about making a change in the world? Underline text evidence.* (we all have the power to change the world; the change can start with me) Have students read the rest of the poem. Ask: *Who else learns this lesson?* (John) *How do you know?* (he says "I think I'll change the world; if I can't , then who can?")

Rhyme Reread aloud the last four lines of the poem with students. Have them listen for rhyming words at the end of each line. *Which two words rhyme?* (plan, can)

🔍 Page 134

Repetition Say: *Poets sometimes use repetition to emphasize an important detail.* Reread the first two lines of the poem "Rescue" with students. *What word do you hear repeated?* (spill) Have students review the photograph and, if necessary, point out that the structure is an oil rig. Ask: *What kind of spill is the speaker talking about?* (an oil spill) *Why do you think the speaker repeats this word?* (because the speaker wants to show that an oil spill is important)

Theme Read aloud the stanza on page 134. Explain the meanings of *sodden* and *bogged down*. Say: *To figure out the theme, we can look for key details and words that express a strong feeling. What are some key details about the sea birds? Draw a box around this text.* (the sodden sea birds, bogged down in waves of oil, a coating so heavy no wing could lift) *Think about the speaker's choice of* words "sodden," "bogged down," and "so heavy no wing could lift." Do these words express a positive or negative feeling? (negative) Do you think the speaker feels hopeful or hopeless about the sea birds? (hopeless)

Connection of Ideas 🅰🅒🅣 Read aloud the last seven lines on page 134. Explain the meaning of *downy*. Ask: *What did the speaker's neighbors look for after the spill?* (sea birds, bogged down in waves of oil) *What does the speaker glimpse?* (a head once downy, but not drowned) *Put these clues together. What do you think the speaker found?* (a sea bird coated in oil)

Genre 🅰🅒🅣 Have students reread the last three lines on page 134. Say: *Punctuation affects the meaning of a poem. Which of these lines includes a dash?* (once downy, but not drowned—) *What does the dash show?* (a pause in the speaker's thoughts) *What causes the speaker to pause?* (the speaker glimpses a head) *What feeling does the speaker express after the dash?* (hope)

🔍 Page 135

Theme Read aloud the stanza and explain the meaning of the idiom "*bring back life*." Say: *Circle details that tell about the speaker's actions.* (Reach, lift, and up; I hold the sickened seagull; bring back life.) *What do these actions tell about the speaker?* (The speaker is helpful.)

Genre 🅰🅒🅣 Read aloud the first two lines on page 135. Ask: *What punctuation mark do you see at the end of the second line?* (an exclamation point) *What does an exclamation mark show?* (excitement or surprise) *What feeling does the speaker express when he or she hears the bird's heart beat?* (Possible answers: excitement, surprise)

Theme Have students reread the last three lines. Ask: *What does the speaker want people to know? Draw a box around the speaker's message.* (Just as one spill can spell disaster,/One boat can bring back life) *Restate this message in your own words.* (Possible answer: One person can make a difference.)

RESPOND TO READING

10–20 Minutes   RL.5.1 W.5.9a SL.5.1d

Respond to "A Simple Plan" and "Rescue"

Have students summarize "A Simple Plan" and "Rescue" orally to demonstrate comprehension. Then have partners answer the questions on page 136 of the **Interactive Worktext** using the discussion starters. Tell them to use text evidence to support their answers. Have students write the page number(s) on which they found the text evidence for each question.

1. *In "A Simple Plan," what makes Jack want to change the world?* (He sees people that need help; he sees changes he wants to make. Text Evidence: p. 133)

2. *In "A Simple Plan," what makes John want to change the world?* (He talks to his brother and learns that he is changing the world. His brother makes John think about what he can do. Text Evidence: p. 133)

3. *In "Rescue," what makes the speaker want to help after the oil spill?* (The speaker sees that the birds are hurt by the oil spill; her neighbors are also helping to find the birds. Text Evidence: p. 134)

After students discuss the questions on page 136, have them write a response to the question on page 137. Tell them to use their partner discussions and notes about "A Simple Plan" and "Rescue" to help them. Circulate and provide guidance.

 Quick Check Do students understand vocabulary in context? If not, review and reteach using the instruction on page 116.

Can students use key details to determine theme? If not, review and reteach using the instruction on page 116 and assign the Unit 2 Week 5 digital mini-lesson.

Can students write a response to "A Simple Plan" and "Rescue"? If not, provide sentence frames to help them organize their ideas.

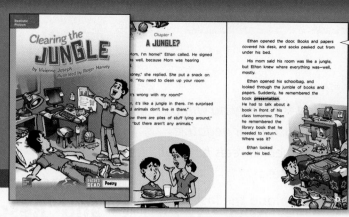

WEEK 5
LESSON

3

Objectives
• Understand and use new vocabulary
• Read realistic fiction
• Recognize and understand theme
• Understand complex text through close reading

Scaffolding for **McGraw-Hill Reading Wonders** Approaching Leveled Reader

Materials
• "Clearing the Jungle" Apprentice Leveled Reader: pp. 2–8
• Graphic Organizer: Theme

Go Digital
• Apprentice Leveled Reader eBook
• Downloadable Graphic Organizer
• Theme Mini-Lesson

BEFORE READING

10–15 Minutes   SL.5.1c   SL.5.1d   L.5.4a   L.5.6   (CCSS)

Introduce "Clearing the Jungle"

• Read the Essential Question on the title page of "Clearing the Jungle" **Apprentice Leveled Reader**: *What are some reasons that would help you work toward a goal? We will read about a boy who is motivated to accomplish a goal that will make his life much better.*

• Read the title of the main read. Have students look through the pages. *Is this selection fiction or nonfiction?* (fiction) *How do you know?* (It has illustrations and dialogue.) *What do you think the main read will be about?* (A boy has a messy room.)

Expand Vocabulary

Display each word below. Say the words and have students repeat them. Then use the Define/Example/Ask routine to introduce each word.

1 **overdue** (page 4)

Define: describes something as late or delayed

Example: Jeremy stood at the bus stop for a long time waiting for the bus that was *overdue*.

Ask: What happens when you return an *overdue* library book?

2 **presentation** (page 3)

Define: when you talk about an idea or give a report in front of an audience

Example: Lila gave a *presentation* on what the new park would look like.

Ask: Why is it important to plan a *presentation*?

3 **responsibility** (page 5)

Define: a job or duty that someone is expected to take care of

Example: Setting the table for dinner is my *responsibility*.

Ask: What is a *responsibility* you might have in the classroom?

4 **trudged** (page 8)

Define: walked with heavy, slow steps

Example: Ian was so tired after the game that he *trudged* slowly home.

Ask: How would people walk as they *trudge* along a snowy path?

DURING READING

20–30 Minutes   RL.5.1   RL.5.2   SL.5.1b   L.5.4a

Close Reading

🔍 **Pages 2–3**

Genre (A)(C)(T) Have students read pages 2 and 3. Recall with students that in realistic fiction, the characters talk and act like real people. The events could really happen. *Who are the characters you meet on page 2?* (Ethan and his mom) *What are they talking about?* (the mess in Ethan's room) *Is this a conversation that a real parent and child could have?* (yes) Read aloud the sentence, *"What's wrong with my room?"* Point out that in this part of the dialogue, the speaker is not identified with a phrase including "said...". *Who is saying this?* (Ethan) *How do you know?* (The next line starts with his mom saying his name, "Ethan.")

Theme. *On page 2, what does Ethan's mom think of his room?* (She thinks it's a mess, like a jungle.) Have students read the second paragraph on page 3. *Do you see a signal word?* (but) Explain that this word signals that Ethan has a different opinion. *What does Ethan think about his room?* (He thinks that he knows where everything is – mostly.) As students read the selection, have them record key details on their Theme charts.

Vocabulary Have students read page 3 and locate the word *jumble* in the third paragraph. Explain that it means a lot of different things mixed together in a messy way. Ask: *What does Ethan see when he looks in his schoolbag?* (a messy bunch of books and papers mixed up together, or jumbled together)

Page 4

Theme *What is Ethan looking for on page 4?* (his library book) *Why does he need this book?* (to make a presentation in school) *What happens when he opens the closet?* (A stack of board games crashes down.) *How does Ethan feel when he finds the book?* (At first he is happy but then he sees that it is overdue.)

STOP AND CHECK Have students answer the question in the Stop and Check box on page 4. (There is stuff everywhere, as there would be in a dense jungle.)

Page 5

Genre A C T *What is happening in the section at the top of page 5? When and where does this scene take place?* (Ethan is talking to his mom at home the next morning.) Point out the line marking a section break on page 5. Explain that this indicates a change of time and setting. *What is happening in the part at the bottom of the page? When and where does this scene take place?* (After Ethan gets to school, he talks to his classmates.)

Pages 6–7

Theme Have a pair of students read aloud the dialogue at the top of page 6. *Why do you think Ethan tells Blake that he should have texted him?* (He was relying on Blake to remind him about the project.) *What does Mr. Wong tell Ethan he must do?* (get organized)

Vocabulary Have students find the word *blush* on page 6. Explain that a person's face turns red when he or she blushes. *What makes Ethan blush?* (He is embarrassed because his part of the science project is late.)

Genre A C T Read the dialogue in the second to last paragraph on page 7 aloud. Ask: *Who is saying this? How can you tell?* (Mr. Wong is saying these words. The sentence "Mr. Wong looked angry" is the clue.)

Page 8

Genre A C T Read the last two paragraphs of page 8. *Why does does Blake ask Ethan about his planner?* (to remind Ethan about the practice session the next day) *How does Ethan answer Blake?* (He nods yes.) *Is Ethan answering truthfully? How can you tell?* (No; he nods yes but "has no idea where his planner is.") *What does this tell you about how Ethan feels?* (He is too embarrassed to admit his problem.)

Theme Explain that a lesson that a character learns in a story may be a theme of the story. Have partners discuss Ethan's problems so far in the story. *What lesson do you think Ethan might learn?* (Ethan is not doing well at school, and disappointing his friends, because he is so disorganized. He might learn the lesson that he needs to take responsibility and get organized.)

STOP AND CHECK Have students answer the Stop and Check question on page 8. (His library book is overdue. He forgot about his science project; did a book presentation instead by mistake; lost a permission slip; forgot about practice; lost his planner.)

Have partners review their Theme charts for pages 2–8 and discuss what they learned.

 Quick Check Do students understand weekly vocabulary in context? If not, review and reteach using the instruction on page 116.

Can students determine the theme? If not, review and reteach using the instruction on page 116 and assign the Unit 2 Week 5 digital mini-lesson.

WEEK 5
LESSON

4

Objectives
- Understand and use new vocabulary
- Read realistic fiction
- Recognize and understand theme
- Understand complex text through close reading
- Respond to the selection using text evidence to support ideas

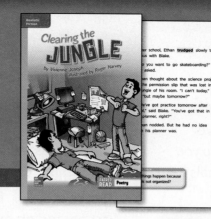

Materials
- "Clearing the Jungle" Apprentice Leveled Reader: pp. 9–20
- Graphic Organizer: Theme

☞ **Go Digital**
- Apprentice Leveled Reader eBook
- Downloadable Graphic Organizer
- Theme Mini-Lesson

Scaffolding for **Wonders** Approaching Leveled Reader

BEFORE READING

5–10 Minutes   SL.5.1c   SL.5.1d   L.5.4a   L.5.6   CCSS

Expand Vocabulary

Display each word below. Say the words and have students repeat them. Then use the Define/Example/Ask routine to introduce each word.

1 brainstorm (page 13)

Define: to think quickly and creatively, especially in a group

Example: The group was able to *brainstorm* a list of great topics in just a few minutes.

Ask: Why is a group helpful to *brainstorm* ideas?

2 clutter (page 10)

Define: a messy collection of things

Example: Toby could not find her pen in the *clutter* on the desk.

Ask: What kinds of things could create *clutter* on a desk?

3 massive (page 9)

Define: large in amount or size

Example: There was a *massive* number of people at the concert.

Ask: What would be a *massive* amount of money?

4 worthwhile (page 12)

Define: rewarding or important enough to take the time to do

Example: Luke felt that the extra study time was *worthwhile* since he got a high grade on the test.

Ask: What is a *worthwhile* activity to do in school?

DURING READING

15–20 Minutes   RL.5.1   RL.5.2   SL.5.1b   L.5.4a   CCSS

Close Reading

🔍 **Page 9**

Genre Ⓐ Ⓒ Ⓣ   Read page 9. Point out that in realistic fiction, what characters say may not reflect what they are really thinking. Readers must look for clues in the text to understand what characters really mean. Say: *Ethan's mom says he can pay the library fine from his allowance. What does Ethan say?* (Okay.) *What is Ethan really thinking when he says this? How can you tell?* (He's not okay. Text clue: "But nothing was okay.")

STOP AND CHECK Have students answer the Stop and Check question on page 9. (He doesn't want to admit he made a mistake: the book presentation is next week.)

🔍 **Pages 10–11**

Connection of Ideas Ⓐ Ⓒ Ⓣ   Read page 10. Explain to students that Tarzan is a story character who grew up in a jungle with apes. Apes beat their chests when they want to look tough and strong. Joe imitates Tarzan because Ethan says that a jungle is ruining his life. *What is Joe ready to do?* (help Ethan get organized)

Theme Have students read pages 10 and 11. Discuss with students how Ethan reaches a turning point in this part of the story. *At the beginning of page 10, how does Ethan feel? How can you tell?* (He feels overwhelmed. "It's too hard," he thinks.) *On page 11, how does Ethan motivate himself to start getting organized?* (He thinks about explorers in real jungles. He realizes he can do it.)

STOP AND CHECK Have students answer the question in the Stop and Check box on page 11. (Joe wrote out a goal with steps that will help Ethan get organized.)

Pages 12–13

Genre (A)(C)(T) Read the chapter title and text on page 12. Explain that in realistic fiction, chapter breaks can signal a change in the story, and give clues about what will happen next in the story. *When does this part of the story begin?* (the next morning) *Based on the title, what do you think will happen?* (Ethan will succeed.)

Theme *On page 12, what has changed?* (Ethan's room is no longer a jungle. He knows where things are. He feels satisfied.) *What has Ethan done to change his room?* (He has cleaned it up and organized things.) *What is he now using to help him be organized that he wasn't using before?* (He has found his planner and written dates in it; he has a calendar pinned to his bulletin board.)

Vocabulary Have students find the word *tame* at the bottom of page 12. Explain that *tame* means to reduce the power of something so it does not cause a problem. It can also mean to make a wild animal obey you. *In what way has Ethan tamed a jungle?* (He cleaned up his mess.)

Connection of Ideas (A)(C)(T) Have students review what Ethan thought about explorers on page 11. (They make their way through dangerous places.) *How did this thought help him?* (It helped him imagine that he could get through his messy room.) *On page 13, when does he think about explorers again?* (when Mr. Wong asks for ideas) *How does this thought help him again?* (He thinks about how he has been a brave explorer in his room. This helps him raise his hand to give an idea.)

Page 14

Vocabulary Read the fourth paragraph on page 14 aloud. Discuss the imagery. Explain that *stalking* describes the way an animal quietly follows an animal it wants to attack. *What is the sound of the wind in the leaves compared to?* (an animal, like a tiger, following an animal it wants to attack)

STOP AND CHECK Have students answer the Stop and Check question on page 14. (He can find things easily; he remembers his permission slip; he thinks of ideas for the project; he is ready to tackle the imaginary tiger and jungle around his tree house.)

AFTER READING
10–15 Minutes   RL.5.1   RL5.2   RL.5.9   W.5.9a   L.5.4a   (CCSS)

Respond to Reading

Compare Texts Have students compare motivations in the poems "A Simple Plan" and "Rescue" with Ethan's motivation in "Clearing the Jungle". Then say: *Talk about a time you accomplished a goal. What motivated you?*

Summarize Have students turn to page 16 and summarize the selection. (Include details that show how Ethan's disorganization caused him problems and how organizing his life helped him solve problems.)

Text Evidence

Have partners work together to answer questions on page 16. Remind students to use their Theme charts.

Theme (It is important to set a goal and then work to meet it. Accomplishing a goal makes you feel confident.)

Vocabulary (*Slip* means "a piece of paper." It can also mean to slide on something and fall or almost fall.)

Write About Reading (Blake expected Ethan to forget the permission slip but Ethan has it. Mr. Wong is pleased with Ethan. These details show that Ethan's hard work towards his goal has made his life better.)

Independent Reading

Encourage students to read the paired selection "Just for Once" on pages 17–19. Have them identify literary elements in this poem, such as rhyme and repetition, and then summarize the poem. Have partners answer the "Make Connections" questions on page 19.

✓ *Quick Check* **Can students determine the theme? If not, review and teach using the instruction on page 116 and assign the Unit 2 Week 5 digital mini-lesson.**

Can students respond to the selection using text evidence? If not, provide sentence frames to help them organize their ideas.

WEEK 5 LESSON 5

Objectives
- Review weekly vocabulary words
- Review theme
- Write an analysis about how an author uses precise language

Scaffolding for McGraw-Hill Reading **Wonders** Reading/Writing Workshop

Materials
- Visual Vocabulary Cards: 73–76
- Interactive Worktext, pp. 138–139
- Assessment Book, pp. 28–29

👉 **Go** Digital
- **Visual Vocabulary Cards**
- **Theme Mini-Lesson**
- **Interactive eWorktext**

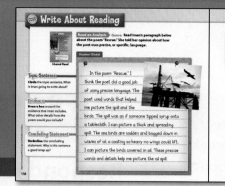

REVIEW AND RETEACH

5–10 Minutes   RL.5.2   L.5.4a   L.5.6   CCSS

Weekly Vocabulary

Display one **Visual Vocabulary Card** at a time and ask students to use the vocabulary word in a sentence. If students have difficulty, have them find the word in "Clearing the Jungle" and use the context clues to define it.

Comprehension: Theme

I Do   Write and read aloud these lines: *A wise old person once said,/ "An idea must begin in your head./ It may come as you sit/ Or while strolling a bit,/ Or even while lying in bed!"* Circle *wise*. Say: *"Wise" tells me the speaker agrees with the person's words.* Underline the last four lines. Say: *All these details tell about places where an idea can begin. I can use these clues to figure out the poem's message: Ideas can begin anywhere.*

We Do   Write and read aloud: *High up on a leafy branch, a bird builds a nest,/ Down below, wrinkly worms wind their way among the roots./ Inside a hole, a squirrels greedily nibbles a nut./ But I see a quiet trunk,/ To rest against and wonder/ About hidden worlds.* Ask: *What are the key details?* (a bird builds a nest; worms wind their way among the roots; inside a hole, a squirrel greedily nibbles a nut) *What do all these details describe?* (They all tell about things animals are doing around the tree.) *What does the speaker see?* (a quiet trunk to rest against) *What is the speaker going to do?* (wonder about hidden worlds) *What is the main message?* (The world is busier than it appears.)

You Do   Have students turn to page 131 of the **Interactive Worktext**. Have partners look for key details to help them identify the message or theme.

WRITE ABOUT READING

25–35 Minutes   W.5.1a   W.5.1d   W.5.4   W.5.5   W.5.9a   CCSS

Read an Analysis

- Ask students to look back at "Rescue" in the **Interactive Worktext**. Have volunteers review their notes. Ask: *How did the poet's use of precise language help you picture the birds and the speaker's actions?*

- Read aloud the directions on page 138. Say: *Iman's paragraph is an analysis, or detailed description, of the poem "Rescue." In her analysis, Iman tells her opinion about how well the poet uses precise language in the poem.* Read aloud the student model.

- Say: *An analysis includes certain elements. The first element is the* topic sentence. Have students circle the topic sentence in the student model. Ask: *What information does Iman include in her topic sentence?* (poem's title; her opinion that the poet did a good job of using precise language)

- *Another element of an analysis is* text evidence. *Iman supports her opinion with details from the poem.* Reread the model and have students draw a box around the text evidence. (sentences 2–5) *What other words or details from the poem would support Iman's opinion?* (Possible answer: I glimpse a head once downy.)

- *The final element of an analysis is the* concluding statement. Have students underline the concluding statement. Ask: *Why is Iman's concluding statement a good wrap up?* (Her concluding statement says that the words and details are precise and that they helped her picture the oil spill.) *Which words in the concluding statement wrap up the text evidence?* ("these precise words and details")

✎ **Analytical Writing** Write an Analysis

Guided Writing Read the writing prompt on page 139 together. Have students write about "Clearing the Jungle" or another text they read this week. Have them review their notes. Say: *Use the checklist to help you figure out the right information to include in each section.* Guide students to ask "how" and "why" questions as they analyze text evidence.

Peer Conference Have students read their analysis to a partner. Listeners should identify the strongest text evidence that supports the topic sentence and discuss any sentences that are unclear.

Teacher Conference Check students' writing for complete sentences and text evidence that supports their opinion. Review the concluding statement. *Does this sentence tie all of the elements together?* If necessary, have students revise the concluding statement by restating the topic sentence.

Level Up

▲ Apprentice Leveled Reader   ▲ Approaching Leveled Reader   ▲ Interactive Worktext   ▲ Reading/Writing Workshop

IF students read the Apprentice Level Reader fluently and the **Interactive Worktext** Shared Read fluently and answer the Respond to Reading questions

THEN read together the Approaching Level Reader main selection and the **Reading/Writing Workshop** Shared Read from *Reading Wonders*. Have students take notes as they read, using self-stick notes. Then ask and answer questions about their notes.

Writing Rubric

	4	3	2	1
Topic Sentence	Topic sentence presents a clear opinion.	Topic sentence presents an opinion somewhat clearly.	Topic is presented in short phrases; opinion is unclear.	There is no topic sentence; no opinion is presented.
Text Evidence	Opinion is supported by two or more details.	Opinion is only supported by one detail from the text.	Little to no text evidence supports opinion.	No text evidence is included; does not support opinion.
Concluding Statement	Clearly restates an opinion; wraps up the details.	Restatement is less focused; attempts to wrap up the details.	Vaguely restates opinion. Doesn't correlate well to text evidence.	There is no conclusion.
Writing Style	Writes in complete sentences. Uses correct spelling and grammar.	Uses complete sentences and phrases. Writing has spelling and grammar errors.	Few or no complete sentences. There are many spelling and grammar errors.	Does not write accurately or in complete sentences.

ASSESSMENT

Weekly Assessment

Have students complete the Weekly Assessment using **Assessment** book pages 28–29.

WEEK 6

▶ **Unit Assessment,**
pages 131–139

▶ **Fluency Assessment,**
pages 234–239

▶ **Exit Test,**
pages 187–195

Unit 2 Assessment

CCSS TESTED SKILLS

✓ COMPREHENSION	✓ VOCABULARY
• Problem and Solution RI.5.3	• Context Clues L.5.4a
• Compare and Contrast RL.5.3	
• Sequence RI.5.5	
• Theme RL.5.2	
• Theme RL.5.2	

Using Assessment and Writing Scores

⟳ RETEACH	IF ...	THEN ...
COMPREHENSION	Students answer 0–7 multiple-choice items correctly ...	... reteach tested skills using instruction on pages 364–371.
VOCABULARY	Students answer 0–3 multiple-choice items correctly ...	... reteach tested skills using instruction on page 364.
WRITING	Students score mostly 1–2 on weekly Write About Reading rubrics throughout the unit...	... reteach writing using instruction on pages 372–373.

LEVEL UP	IF ...	THEN ...
COMPREHENSION	Students answer 8–10 multiple-choice items correctly ...	... have students read *The Bill of Rights* Approaching Leveled Reader. Use the Level Up lesson on page 120.
WRITING	Students score mostly 3–4 on weekly Write About Reading rubrics throughout the unit...	... use the Level Up Write About Reading lesson on page 121 to have students compare two selections from the unit.

Fluency Assessment

Conduct assessments individually using the differentiated fluency passages in **Assessment**. Students' expected fluency goal for this Unit is 100–120 WCPM with an accuracy rate of 95% or higher.

Exit Test

If a student answers 13–15 multiple-choice items correctly on the Unit Assessment, administer the Unit 2 Exit Test at the end of Week 6.

Time to Exit WonderWorks

Exit Test

If...

Students answer 13–15 multiple choice items correctly...

Fluency Assessment

If...

Students achieve their Fluency Assessment goal for the unit...

Level Up Lessons

If...

Students are successful applying close reading skills with the Approaching Leveled Reader in Week 6...

If...

Students score mostly 4–5 on the Level Up Write About Reading assignment...

Foundational Skills Kit

If...

Students have mastered the Unit 2 benchmark skills in the Foundational Skills Kit and *PowerPAL for Reading* adaptive learning system...

Then...

... consider exiting the student from *Reading WonderWorks* materials into the Approaching Level of *Reading Wonders*.

▶ **Read Approaching Leveled Reader**

Approaching Leveled Reader

Apprentice Leveled Reader

Read Approaching Leveled Reader

RI.5.10

The Bill of Rights

Before Reading

Preview Discuss what students remember about the Bill of Rights. Tell them that they will be reading a more challenging version of *The Bill of Rights*.

Vocabulary Use routines on the **Visual Vocabulary Cards** to review the Weekly Vocabulary words. Use pages 70 and 72 to review the Expand Vocabulary words.

A C T During Reading

▶ **Specific Vocabulary** Provide definitions for the following difficult or domain-specific social studies words that are new to this level: *challenging* (page 3), *hard-won* (page 3), *central government* (page 4), *federal government* (page 4), and *grand jury* (page 14).

▶ **Connection of Ideas** Students may need help understanding that the Constitution and its amendments established laws and assured the people of the United States freedoms. These laws are still in effect today. After reading page 8, discuss the text feature "Amending the Constitution" with students. Explain that the Constitution can be changed if a majority of the people feel that change is necessary. Point out that many laws, such as the laws governing civil rights, were added to the Constitution over time.

▶ **Sentence Structure** Students may need help understanding complex sentences. Look at page 11. Echo-read the first sentence on the page. Help students find pauses by chunking the text as they read long sentences.

After Reading

Ask students to complete the Respond to Reading questions on page 18 after they have finished reading. Provide additional support as needed to help students use the weekly vocabulary strategy to answer question 3.

▶ **Write About Reading**

Interactive Worktext Shared Read

Apprentice Leveled Reader

Write About Reading

W.5.2   W.5.9a   CCSS

Read an Analysis

- Distribute the Unit 2 Downloadable Model and Practice that compares two related texts, the **Interactive Worktext** Shared Read "A Modern Cinderella" and the **Apprentice Leveled Reader** "The Bird of Truth." Read the model aloud.

- Point out the signal word *both* in the topic sentence, which tells readers how the two texts are alike. Have students circle and reread the topic sentence. Ask: *What other information does Elena include in her topic sentence?* (titles of both texts)

- Have students mark text evidence and ask: *What details does Elena include from "Bird of Truth" that shows it is different from "A Modern Cinderella"?* (sentences 2–4) *What details does Elena include from "A Modern Cinderella" that shows it is different from "Bird of Truth"?* (sentences 5–6) *Why is the concluding statement a good wrap up?* (Elena restates how the texts are alike and different.)

Write an Analysis
Analytical Writing

Guided Practice Display this prompt: *Write a paragraph that compares "The Magical Lost Brocade" to "The Lion's Whiskers." Tell how characters achieve goals in each story.*

- Alternatively, let students select two texts to compare.

- Use the Unit 2 Downloadable Model and Practice to guide students' writing.

- Tell them to begin with a topic sentence and include details from each text that shows how the characters are alike and different.

- For the concluding statement, remind students to restate the topic sentence and wrap up the details.

Teacher Conference Check students' writing for complete sentences. Did they begin with a topic sentence? Did they cite text evidence? Did they restate the topic sentence in the last sentence?

Writing Rubric

	4	3	2	1
Topic Sentence	There is one clear, focused topic sentence.	Topic sentence is less focused, somewhat clear.	Topic is presented in short phrases.	There is no topic sentence.
Text Evidence	Topic is supported by two or more text details.	Evidence includes only one detail from the text.	Little to no evidence is cited from the text.	No text evidence is included.
Concluding Statement	Clearly restates the topic sentence; wraps up all the details.	Restatement is less focused; attempts to wrap up the details.	Vaguely restates the topic. Doesn't correlate well to text evidence.	There is no conclusion.
Writing Style	Writes in complete sentences. Uses correct spelling and grammar.	Uses complete sentences and phrases. Writing has spelling and grammar errors.	Has few or no complete sentences. There are many spelling and grammar errors.	Does not write accurately or in complete sentences.

UNIT 3 PLANNER
Getting from Here to There

Week 1 Cultural Exchange	Week 2 Being Resourceful	Week 3 Patterns

ESSENTIAL QUESTION
What can learning about different cultures teach us?

Build Background

 Vocabulary
L.5.4a *appreciation, blurted, complimenting, congratulate, contradicted, critical, cultural, misunderstanding*

Access Complex Text
Sentence Structure

Comprehension
RL.5.2 Skill: Theme
Respond to Reading

Write About Reading *Analytical Writing*
W.5.9a Opinion: Genre

ESSENTIAL QUESTION
How can learning about nature be useful?

Build Background

 Vocabulary
L.5.4a *civilization, complex, cultivate, devise, fashioned, resourceful, shortage, tormentors*

Access Complex Text
Genre

Comprehension
RL5.2 Skill: Theme
Respond to Reading

Write About Reading *Analytical Writing*
W.5.9a Opinion: Plot

ESSENTIAL QUESTION
Where can you find patterns in nature

Build Background

 Vocabulary
L.5.4a *contact, erode, formation, moisture, particles, repetition, structure, visible*

Access Complex Text
Organization

Comprehension
RI.5.2 Skill: Main Idea and Key Details
Respond to Reading

Write About Reading *Analytical Writing*
W.5.9b Inform/Explain: Main Idea and Key Details

A S S E S S M E N T

✓ Quick Check
Vocabulary, Comprehension
✓ Weekly Assessment
Assessment Book, pp. 30–31

✓ Quick Check
Vocabulary, Comprehension
✓ Weekly Assessment
Assessment Book, pp. 32–33

✓ Quick Check
Vocabulary, Comprehension
✓ Weekly Assessment
Assessment Book, pp. 34–35

✓ MID-UNIT ASSESSMENT
Assessment Book, pp. 88–95
✓ Fluency Assessment
Assessment Book, pp. 250–265

Use the Foundational Skills Kit for explicit instruction of phonics, structural analysis, fluency, and word recognition. Includes *PowerPAL for Reading* adaptive learning system.

Week 4 Teamwork	Week 5 Into the Past	Week 6 ASSESS

Week 6 — ASSESS

RETEACH → ← LEVEL UP

Week 4 — Teamwork

ESSENTIAL QUESTION
What benefits come from people working as a group?

Build Background

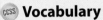 **Vocabulary**

L.5.4a *artificial, collaborate, dedicated, flexible, function, mimic, obstacle, techniques*

Access Complex Text
Connection of Ideas

Comprehension
RI.5.2 Skill: Main Idea and Key Details
Respond to Reading

Write About Reading *Analytical Writing*
W.5.9b Inform/Explain: Main Idea and Key Details

Week 5 — Into the Past

ESSENTIAL QUESTION
How do we explain what happened in the past?

Build Background

 Vocabulary

L.5.4a *archaeologist, era, fragments, historian, intact, preserved, reconstruct, remnants*

Access Complex Text (A C T)
Sentence Structure

Comprehension
RI.5.8 Skill: Author's Point of View
RI.6.6 Respond to Reading

Write About Reading *Analytical Writing*
W.5.9b Opinion: Point of View

Week 6

Reteach
Comprehension Skills

Vocabulary

Write About Reading

Level Up
Read Approaching Leveled Reader

Write About Reading:
Compare Texts

A S S E S S M E N T

✓ Quick Check
Vocabulary, Comprehension

✓ Weekly Assessment
Assessment Book, pp. 36–37

✓ Quick Check
Vocabulary, Comprehension

✓ Weekly Assessment
Assessment Book, pp. 38–39

✓ Unit Assessment
Assessment Book, pp. 140–148

✓ Fluency Assessment
Assessment Book, pp. 250–265

✓ EXIT TEST
Assessment Book, pp. 196–204

ABOUT UNIT 3

UNIT 3 OPENER, pp. 140–141

The Big Idea

What kinds of experiences can lead to new discoveries?

Talk About It

Read aloud the Big Idea on page 141 of the **Interactive Worktext:** *What kinds of experiences can lead to new discoveries?* Have students think about an important experience they had. Say: *We can learn about ourselves and about the world through our experiences. One time I took a ballet class. I discovered how difficult it is to dance ballet. But I also discovered that I liked to dance. What have you discovered by trying a new activity or visiting a new place?* (Answers will vary.)

Discuss the photo on pages 140–141. Ask: *Where can a hot-air balloon take you?* (Possible answers: way up high, over the mountains) *Let's imagine that we are in the hot-air balloon. What could you discover about the world by seeing it from way up high?* (Possible answers: the shapes and colors of the landscape; how high birds fly) *What other experiences can lead to discoveries about the world?* Have partners or small groups discuss this question and share their ideas with the class.

Tell students that even everyday experiences can lead to a discovery. Say: *In this unit, we will be reading ten selections. Each selection is about making a discovery. In one selection, a boy experiences a different culture and makes a discovery about himself. In another selection, historians make discoveries about an ancient civilization.*

Build Fluency

Each week, use the **Interactive Worktext** Shared Reads and **Apprentice Leveled Readers** for fluency instruction and practice. Keep in mind that reading rates vary with the type of text that students are reading as well as the purpose for reading. For example, comprehension of complex informational texts generally requires slower reading.

Explain/Model Use the Fluency lessons on pages 374–378 to explain the skill. Then model the skill by reading the first page of the week's Shared Read or Leveled Reader.

Practice/Apply Choose a page from the Shared Read or Leveled Reader. Have one group read the top half of the page one sentence at a time. Remind children to apply the skill. Have the second group echo-read the passage. Then have the groups switch roles for the second half of the page. Discuss how each group applied the skill.

> ### Weekly Fluency Focus
> **Week 1** Intonation
> **Week 2** Expression and Phrasing
> **Week 3** Rate and Accuracy
> **Week 4** Rate
> **Week 5** Expression and Phrasing

You can also use the **Lesson Cards** and **Practice** pages from the **Foundational Skills Kit** for targeted Fluency instruction and practice.

Access Complex Text

Reader and Task

TEXT COMPLEXITY

Interactive Worktext

	Week 1	Week 2	Week 3	Week 4	Week 5
	"A Reluctant Traveler"	"Survivaland"	"Patterns of Change"	"Gulf Spill Superheroes"	"What Was the Purpose of the Incas' Strange Strings?"
Quantitative	Lexile 610 TextEvaluator™ 29	Lexile 620 TextEvaluator™ 33	Lexile 690 TextEvaluator™ 16	Lexile 690 TextEvaluator™ 35	Lexile 740 TextEvaluator™ 35
Qualitative	• Sentence Structure • Vocabulary	• Genre • Vocabulary	• Organization • Connection of Ideas • Vocabulary	• Connection of Ideas • Prior Knowledge • Vocabulary	• Sentence Structure • Organization • Genre • Vocabulary
Reader and Task	The Weekly Concept lessons will help determine the reader's knowledge and engagement in the weekly concept.				
	Weekly Concept: p. 126 Questions and tasks: pp. 128–129	Weekly Concept: p. 136 Questions and tasks: pp. 138–139	Weekly Concept: p. 146 Questions and tasks: pp. 148–149	Weekly Concept: p. 158 Questions and tasks: pp. 160–161	Weekly Concept: p. 168 Questions and tasks: pp. 170–171

Apprentice Leveled Reader

	Week 1	Week 2	Week 3	Week 4	Week 5
	"All the Way from Europe"	"Over the Top"	"Weather Patterns"	"The Power of a Team"	"The Anasazi"
Quantitative	Lexile 600 TextEvaluator™ 29	Lexile 560 TextEvaluator™ 29	Lexile 660 TextEvaluator™ 19	Lexile 670 TextEvaluator™ 33	Lexile 740 TextEvaluator™ 34
Qualitative	• Sentence Structure • Connection of Ideas • Organization • Vocabulary	• Genre • Vocabulary	• Organization • Sentence Structure • Genre • Connection of Ideas • Vocabulary	• Connection of Ideas • Organization • Genre • Vocabulary	• Sentence Structure • Prior Knowledge • Genre • Vocabulary
Reader and Task	The Weekly Concept lessons will help determine the reader's knowledge and engagement in the weekly concept.				
	Weekly Concept: p. 126 Questions and tasks: pp. 130–133	Weekly Concept: p. 136 Questions and tasks: pp. 140–143	Weekly Concept: p. 146 Questions and tasks: pp. 150–153	Weekly Concept: p. 158 Questions and tasks: pp. 162–165	Weekly Concept: p. 168 Questions and tasks: pp. 172–175

See pages 379 for details about Text Complexity measures.

Objectives
- Develop oral language
- Build background about learning about different cultures
- Understand and use weekly vocabulary
- Read realistic fiction text

Materials
- Interactive Worktext, pp. 142–149
- Visual Vocabulary Cards: 77–84

☞ **Go** Digital
- Interactive eWorktext
- Visual Vocabulary Cards

Scaffolding for **Wonders** Reading/Writing Workshop

WEEKLY CONCEPT

5–10 Minutes   SL.5.1b SL.5.1c CCSS

Talk About It

Essential Question Read aloud the Essential Question on page 142 of the **Interactive Worktext**: *What can learning about different cultures teach us?* Explain that a culture is the arts, beliefs, and behaviors of a group of people. Say: *We can learn about other cultures by watching or joining in their activities. A cultural exchange is when you learn about another culture and teach others about your own.*

- Discuss the photograph on page 142. Ask: *What kind of activity is shown in this photograph?* (a parade) *What are some things that might be important to this culture? Look at the colors and the costumes.* (dragons, the color red)

I Do Say: *One time, I went to a music festival and heard music from a culture in Africa. I listened to the music and heard a strong rhythm. I got to play one of the drums and heard what it sounded like. I will write "listen" and "play instrument" under "Music" on page 143.*

We Do Say: *Let's look at the photo and think about the ways people in this photograph are having a cultural exchange. What activity are the people doing to show the culture?* (wearing costumes, walking in a parade) Point to the audience. *How are these people learning about the culture? What are they doing?* (watching, taking pictures) Guide students to add words under "Activities" on the web. Have them brainstorm other ways people can learn about food, music, art, and activities of other cultures and add words to the web.

You Do Have partners describe a time when they learned about another culture. Have them answer the questions: *What culture did you learn about? What did you do? What is something new that you learned?*

REVIEW VOCABULARY

10–15 Minutes   L.5.4 L.5.6 CCSS

Review Weekly Vocabulary Words

- Use the **Visual Vocabulary Cards** to review the weekly vocabulary.

- Read together the directions for the Vocabulary activity on page 144 of the **Interactive Worktext**. Then complete the activity.

1 **appreciation** Have students complete the following sentence frame: *I show* appreciation *for a gift by _____.* (Possible answers: saying "thank you," sending a thank-you card)

2 **blurted** Ask: *How do you act right after you* blurt *out an answer? Show what you do using your face and hands.* (Students may cover their mouths with their hands or open their eyes wide.) Have partners complete the sentence frame to describe their actions: *After I blurted out an answer, I _____ because _____.* (Possible answers: am embarrassed, sorry)

3 **complimenting** Have partners *compliment* each other. Have students name their partner, using the sentence starters: *_____ is complimenting me.* (Answers will vary.) *A compliment makes me feel _____. (Possible answers: good inside, happy, pleased)*

4 **contradicted** Ask: *Do you agree with the opinion: Everyone likes peanut butter? What would you say to* contradict *this opinion?* (Possible answers: Not everyone likes peanut butter. Some people don't like peanut butter.) Then ask students to form the past tense of *contradict.*

5 **critical** Point to each option. Ask: *Is this something a critical person would say?* (The ending was boring.)

6 **congratulate** Have partners brainstorm situations in which they would congratulate someone. (Someone wins a game, graduates, receives a trophy, or completes a difficult task.) Ask: *What do you say to* congratulate *someone?* (Possible answers: Congratulations! You did it! Great job!) Ask: *How do you feel when you* congratulate *someone?* (excited and happy)

7 **misunderstanding** Ask: *How do you feel when you have a* misunderstanding *with a friend?* Have partners ask each other questions about the options, such as *"Do you feel certain?"* to help them decide. (confused)

8 **cultural** Ask students to give examples of cultures they are familiar with from their own families or neighborhoods. Have partners ask questions about each other's drawings. Have them write a caption for their drawing using the following sentence frame: _____ *is a cultural food/activity.* (Drawings will vary.)

High-Utility Words

Explain that a contraction is a short way of saying or writing a word. Have students turn to page 145 in the **Interactive Worktext**. Discuss how the circled word *can't* is a contraction for the words *can* and *not*. Point out that the apostrophe takes the place of the missing letter *o*. Ask partners to circle other contractions in the passage. (aren't, didn't, haven't, don't, isn't) Have partners take turns reading the dialogue and tell the two words that make up each contraction they circled. (are/not, did/not, have/not, do/not, is/not)

> **ELL ENGLISH LANGUAGE LEARNERS**
> Write the following contractions and phrases on note cards: *can't, cannot, don't, do not, isn't, is not.* Display and read each card aloud. Have students identify and say each contraction. Then have partners match the contraction to the card that shows the words that make it up.

READ COMPLEX TEXT
15–20 Minutes   RL.5.1 RF.5.4c

Read: "A Reluctant Traveler"

- Have students turn to page 146 in the **Interactive Worktext** and read aloud the Essential Question. Explain that they will read about a boy who takes a trip somewhere new. Ask: *What is the title?* ("A Reluctant Traveler") Reluctant *means unwilling or not excited about doing something.* Have students look at the map. *Where is the boy going to go?* (Buenos Aires) *Think about the title. How do you think the boy is going to feel about going there?* (Possible answer: unhappy)

- Read the selection together. Note that the weekly vocabulary words are highlighted in yellow. Expand vocabulary words are highlighted in blue.

- Have students use the "My Notes" section on page 146 to write questions they have, words they don't understand, and details they want to remember. Model how to use the "My Notes" section. *I can write notes about questions I have as I read. In the first paragraph on page 147, I'm not sure where Paul lives. I will write a question in the "My Notes" section:* Where does Paul live? *As I continue to read, I will also write notes about words I don't understand and events I think are important in the story.*

> **ELL ENGLISH LANGUAGE LEARNERS**
> Have students highlight story details they have questions about as you read together. After reading, ask: *What questions did you have about that part of the story?* Help students write notes in the "My Notes" column.

 Quick Check Can students understand the weekly vocabulary in context? If not, review vocabulary using the **Visual Vocabulary Cards** before teaching Lesson 2.

WEEK 1 LESSON 2

Objectives
- Read realistic fiction text
- Understand complex text through close reading
- Recognize and understand theme
- Respond to the selection using text evidence to support ideas

Materials
Interactive Worktext, pp. 146–151

☞ **Go Digital**
- Interactive eWorktext
- Theme Digital Mini-Lesson

Scaffolding for **WONDERS** McGraw-Hill Reading Reading/Writing Workshop

REREAD COMPLEX TEXT

20–25 Minutes   RL.5.1   RL.5.2   L.5.2   L.5.4a   L.5.6   CCSS

Close Reading: "A Reluctant Traveler"

Reread "A Reluctant Traveler" with students. As you read together, discuss important passages in the text. Have students respond to text-dependent questions, including those in the **Interactive Worktext**.

Page 147

Sentence Structure Ⓐ Ⓒ Ⓣ Say: Have students draw a box around *"It's not weird, honey. Argentina's in the Southern Hemisphere. We're in the Northern Hemisphere. So the seasons are opposite."* Ask: *Who is speaking?* (Paul's mom) *Who is she speaking to?* (Paul) Then have students review the page and draw a box around other words characters say. Have them name each speaker. (Paul: "I think packing winter clothes in August is weird." Paul's dad: "Look down there!")

Expand Vocabulary Have students locate *chance*. Read the first four sentences of the third paragraph aloud. Ask: *What did Paul's parents not have a chance to do?* (travel much) *What do Paul's parents now have a chance to do?* (travel to Argentina) *What happened that gave them the chance to do that? Point to text evidence.* (Aunt Lila and Uncle Art moved to Argentina.)

Theme Say: *We can figure out the theme of the story by thinking about what Paul says and thinks, and his actions.* Model using text evidence to find details about the theme. Ask: *In the first paragraph, Paul says: "I think packing winter clothes in August is weird." I also read "This wasn't going to be a fun vacation. He was sure of it." The words "weird" and "wasn't going to be fun" are clues to Paul's opinion about his family's vacation.* Have students

underline these details. Ask: *What does he think?* (it won't be fun.) Have students reread the next two paragraphs and underline other clues that show Paul's thoughts about the trip. (Paul wanted to spend the rest of his summer break hanging out with his friends. He wanted to sleep late and play soccer. They lived in a city already. Why were they going to Buenos Aires?) Say: *I wonder if Paul will think the same thing once he gets to Buenos Aires. Let's keep reading to find out.*

High-Utility Words Have students find a contraction in the first paragraph. (wasn't) Ask: *What two words make up this contraction?* (was not). Have partners look for other contractions on the page. (It's, We're, didn't)

Page 148

Sentence Structure Ⓐ Ⓒ Ⓣ Have students locate the colon in the first paragraph. Ask: *What follows a colon?* (a list of items) Have students draw a box around the list. *What is this a list of?* (food that Uncle Art ordered) Point to the words in italics and explain that these are Spanish words. Explain that the words in parentheses tell the meaning of each word. Ask: *What is the first item in the list?* (*empanadas*) *What does the word mean?* (small meat pies)

Theme Ask: *What does Paul think about the food when it first arrives?* (He doesn't like it.) *What details in the text tell you this?* (Paul made a face) *What does Paul's mom tell him?* ("Don't be so critical, Paul." "Just take a taste.") *What does Paul do?* (He tastes the food.) *What does Paul notice about the food?* (It tasted like other food he has had before.)

Expand Vocabulary Reread the third paragraph aloud. Read the definition of *mood* aloud. Ask: *Is Paul in a good mood or bad mood?* (good) *What does Paul say that is a clue to his mood?* ("This is really good.")

Vocabulary Have students locate the word *multlingual* in the fourth paragraph. Explain that multilingual means to be able to speak many languages. Ask: *What clues in the paragraph help you know the meaning of the word multilingual?* (people from all over the world, speak Spanish)

Page 149

Sentence Structure Say: *Authors use italics in dialogue to show when a speaker is emphasizing a word.* Point out the first sentence. Ask: *What word does Paul emphasize?* (is) Have students read the sentence aloud, adding emphasis to the word in italics. (Students should place more stress on *is*.) *How do you think Paul feels when he says these words?* (Possible answers: impressed, surprised)

Expand Vocabulary Read the definition of *unusual*. Point out the prefix *un-*. Explain that the prefix *un-* means *not. What does* unusual *mean?* (not usual) Reread the second paragraph aloud. Ask: *What is unusual about the neighborhood?* (The buildings were yellow and blue.) *Why is it unusual?* (Most buildings are not painted yellow and blue.)

Theme Have students review their notes about Paul at the beginning and middle of the story. *What did Paul think about Buenos Aires at the beginning of the story?* (He didn't think it would be fun.) Then have partners look for details on page 149 that show Paul's thoughts and feelings. ("That *is* pretty cool." Paul couldn't believe it. "That's a great idea!" Paul smiled, too.) Ask: *What does Paul think about Buenos Aires now?* (He thinks it's great.) Have partners discuss some of the things Paul did on his trip that caused him to change. (He tried new foods. He visited new places. He learned about different activities people did in Buenos Aires.) *What lesson does Paul learn?* (Be open to new experiences.) If students have difficulty, have them reread the last paragraph, and ask: *Why does Paul's mom congratulate him? What does she say their trip is all about?*

RESPOND TO READING

10–20 Minutes   RL.5.1 RL.5.2 W.5.9a SL.5.1d **CCSS**

Respond to "A Reluctant Traveler"

Have students summarize "A Reluctant Traveler" orally to demonstrate comprehension. Then have partners answer the questions on page 150 of the **Interactive Worktext** using the discussion starters. Tell them to use text evidence to support their answers. Have students write the page number(s) on which they found the text evidence for each question.

1. *What did Paul learn about the food in Argentina?* (Possible answer: He learned that people eat different food than he eats at home, but he noticed they had familiar flavors. Text Evidence: p. 148)

2. *What did Paul learn about the people who live in Buenos Aires?* (Possible answer: He learned that they come from all over the world. Many like to watch soccer. Some dance the tango. Text Evidence: pp. 148, 149)

3. *What did Paul learn about himself from his trip?* (Possible answer: He liked Argentinian food and the way people painted buildings for their soccer team. He also learned that he is a good traveler. Text Evidence: pp. 148, 149)

After students discuss the questions on page 150, have them write a response to the questions on page 151. Tell them to use their partner discussions and notes to help them. Circulate and provide guidance.

 Quick Check Do students understand vocabulary in context? If not, review and reteach using the instruction on page 134.

Can students use key details to determine theme? If not, review and reteach using the instruction on page 134 and assign the Unit 3 Week 1 digital mini-lesson.

Can students write a response to "A Reluctant Traveler"? If not, provide sentence frames to help them organize their ideas.

WEEK 1 LESSON 3

Objectives
- Understand and use new vocabulary words
- Read realistic fiction
- Recognize and understand theme
- Understand complex text through close reading

Materials
- "All the Way from Europe" Apprentice Leveled Reader: pp. 2–7
- Graphic Organizer: Theme

Go Digital
- Apprentice Leveled Reader eBook
- Downloadable Graphic Organizer
- Theme Mini-Lesson

Scaffolding for **Wonders** Approaching Leveled Reader

BEFORE READING

10–15 Minutes   SL.5.1c   SL.5.1d   L.5.4a   L.5.6   CCSS

Introduce "All the Way from Europe"

- Read the Essential Question on the title page of "All the Way from Europe" **Apprentice Leveled Reader**: *What can learning about different cultures teach us? We will read about a girl who experiences new cultures.*

- Read the title of the main read. Have students look at the images. *What do you think this book will be about?* (a girl who travels) *Why do you think that?* (illustrations show foreign-looking cities, road signs, a map)

Expand Vocabulary

Display each word below. Say the words and have students repeat them. Then use the Define/Example/Ask routine to introduce each word.

1 communication (page 7)

Define: the sharing of ideas and information

Example: The telephone made *communication* easier.

Ask: How is *communication* important and also fun?

2 glum (page 3)

Define: sad

Example: I felt *glum* when my friends left without me.

Ask: What do people look like when they are *glum*?

3 research (page 3)

Define: to use materials to find out about something

Example: I will *research* the best recipe for chili.

Ask: What would you like to *research* most?

DURING READING

20–30 Minutes   RL.5.1   RL.5.2   SL.5.1b   L.5.4a   CCSS

Close Reading

Pages 2–3

Genre (ACT) Read aloud the first two paragraphs. *Who is the main character?* (Sarah) *Who is telling the story, Sarah (first-person narrator) or a third-person narrator?* (third-person) *How do you know?* (Sarah is named. The text says *she said*, not *I said*.) *What details tell you the story is realistic fiction?* (The dialogue is realistic, the characters are in a real place, and there's a TV.)

Sentence Structure (ACT) Read the first sentence on page 3. *The word* however *shows that this sentence will contrast with an earlier idea. How does Sarah feel after two days in Paris?* (bored) *How is that feeling different from how Sarah felt before she came to Paris?* (She had been excited.) *What does the word* however *tell you about how Sarah is feeling?* (Her feelings have changed.)

Theme Say: *What the characters do, say, and think, and what happens to them, helps me understand the theme of the story. On pages 2 and 3, I read that Sarah is traveling with her mom. Sarah is in Paris. What clues can we find that tell us how she is feeling?* (not happy, turns off the TV and sighs, is getting bored with old buildings, wishes she had her saxophone)

Guide students to record details in their Theme Charts.

Vocabulary Have students locate the multiple-meaning word *deal* at the bottom of page 3. Explain that it means an agreement. Ask: *What helps you understand the meaning of* deal *in this paragraph?* (Sarah's mom is offering a new plan to Sarah. She is asking her to agree.)

Organization **ACT** Explain that the setting changes in this story as Sarah and her mom travel in Europe. Readers must look for details that identify where the characters are. On page 2, the words "They're speaking French!" show that they are in a different country. The illustration of the Eiffel Tower is a clue that they're in Paris. Have students find the place in the first paragraph on page 3 that tells what the setting is. (after these first two days in Paris ...) *Point to the place on page 3 that tells where they went next.* (they drove to Brussels, a city in Belgium)

STOP AND CHECK *Read the question in the Stop and Check box on page 3.* (Her trip to Europe isn't turning out to be as much fun as Sarah thought it would be.)

Pages 4–5

Connection of Ideas **ACT** Read the first paragraph on page 4. *What is Sarah thinking about?* (Sarah is thinking about her mom's idea to change their travel plan.) *What is the new plan?* (Each morning, Sarah's mom will work. In the afternoons, they will go out and do things that Sarah researched and wants to do.) *What does Sarah think about the new plan?* (a great idea)

Vocabulary Discuss Sarah makes a pun by mixing up the vegetable Brussels sprouts with the city of Brussels. The author includes word play like this to make the story fun to read. Tell students they will look for another pun in Chapter 3.

STOP AND CHECK *Read the question in the Stop and Check box on page 4.* (Sarah's mother sees that Sarah isn't interested in the things she took her to see.)

Theme *How are Sarah's feelings about the trip changing on page 5? How can you tell?* (She says "two of my favorite things come from here," and teases her mom with her knowledge of Brussels sprouts.) *What happens on pages 5 and 6 that help change Sarah's feelings?* (Sarah's mom asks Sarah what she'd like to do. Sarah's research uncovers things that interest her.)

Pages 6–7

Vocabulary Have students locate the word *museum* at the top of page 6. Ask: *What clues help you understand the meaning of* museum? (collection, stuff to do)

Sentence Structure **ACT** *An ellipsis is a series of three dots. It shows a pause in speaking or an incomplete thought. Find the paragraph on page 6 with an ellipsis.* Read the paragraph aloud. *Who is speaking?* (Sarah's mom) *How does she feel about Sarah's plan for the day?* (disappointed) *What does she say?* (That sounds good.) *Why does she pause?* (She's trying to find a way to tell Sarah how she really feels.) *Complete her sentence.* (But I was hoping we could include Belgian chocolate.)

Organization **ACT** Read the first sentence on page 7. *Where did Sarah and her mother travel to next?* (Frankfurt, Germany) *Where were they the day before?* (Brussels, Belgium) *Where did their trip begin?* (Paris, France)

Connection of Ideas **ACT** *On page 7, what does Sarah's mom first say about having hot dogs?* (Shouldn't we try some German food?) *Why does she change her mind?* (Sarah explains frankfurters are German.) *Why did Sarah's mom oppose her idea at first?* (She wants them to experience other cultures.)

STOP AND CHECK *Read the question in the Stop and Check box on page 7.* (Brussels sprouts, Tintin stories, and saxophones are from Brussels; hotdogs from Frankfurt.)

Have partners review their Theme charts for pages 2–7 and discuss what they learned.

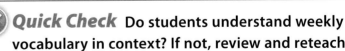 *Quick Check* Do students understand weekly vocabulary in context? If not, review and reteach using the instruction on page 134.

Can students find elements of theme? If not, review and reteach using the instruction on page 134 and assign the Unit 3 Week 1 digital mini-lesson.

**WEEK 1
LESSON**

4

Objectives
- Understand and use new vocabulary
- Read realistic fiction
- Understand theme
- Understand complex text through close reading
- Respond to the selection using text evidence to support ideas

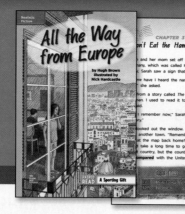

Materials
- "All the Way from Europe" Apprentice Leveled Reader: pp. 8–20
- Graphic Organizer: Theme

☞ **Go** Digital
- Apprentice Leveled Reader eBook
- Downloadable Graphic Organizer
- Theme Digital Mini-Lesson

Scaffolding for **Wonders** Approaching Leveled Reader

BEFORE READING

5–10 Minutes   SL.5.1c   SL.5.1d   L.5.4a   L.5.6

Expand Vocabulary

Display each word below. Say the words and have students repeat them. Then use the Define/Example/Ask routine to introduce each word.

1 commented (page 9)

Define: expressed an idea or opinion

Example: My dad *commented* that I was late.

Ask: Have you ever *commented* on a friend's talents?

2 compared (page 8)

Define: pointed out what is the same or different

Example: My younger sister is tiny *compared* to me.

Ask: What do you do well, *compared* to other people?

3 delicious (page 14)

Define: wonderful to taste

Example: This new flavor of sauce is *delicious*.

Ask: What food do you find *delicious*?

4 interrupted (page 14)

Define: stopped from continuing

Example: The rain *interrupted* our soccer game.

Ask: When were you recently *interrupted*?

5 relieved (page 10)

Define: stopped feeling anxious or upset

Example: I was *relieved* when the storm finally ended.

Ask: What might you say when you feel *relieved* about something?

DURING READING

15–20 Minutes   RL.5.1   RL.5.2   SL.5.1c   L.5.4a

Close Reading

🔍 **Pages 8–9**

Sentence Structure Ⓐ Ⓒ Ⓣ *When words are in italics, they are sloped to the right. Point to the words in italics on page 8. Why does the author use italics there?* (*The Musicians of Bremen* is the title of a book. Titles named in a text are in italics.)

Theme Have students read the last paragraph on page 8 and the first paragraph on page 9. Ask: *What has Sarah learned by comparing the U.S. to Europe?* (Europe's countries are small compared to the U.S.) *Why does Sarah's mom say the U.S. is similar to Europe?* (Europe's different countries are like the different states in the U.S.)

🔍 **Pages 10–11**

Connection of Ideas Ⓐ Ⓒ Ⓣ *Read how Sarah explains hamburgers to her mother on page 10. How is this like her explanation of frankfurters on page 7?* (Both foods were brought by Germans to the U.S. and named for their cities. They are now American foods.)

STOP AND CHECK *Read the question in the Stop and Check box on page 10.* (Sarah has been doing research about each city they visit on their trip.)

Theme Have students read page 11. *What does Sarah do at the hotel in Italy?* (starts researching Naples) *How does Sarah's research change her?* (It makes her want to do research about her home in the U.S.) *What does Sarah's mom think about how Sarah has changed?* (The trip has given her a new appreciation of home.) Have students add details to their Theme charts as they continue to read the selection.

Vocabulary Discuss the pun involving *Hamburgers* on page 10. *Why does Sarah say that they can't eat hamburgers?* (The people of Hamburg, Hamburgers with a capital *h*, are confused with the hamburgers we eat.) Explain that this is another example of word play, like the pun about Brussels sprouts in Chapter 1.

Pages 12–13

Sentence Structure **A C T** Point out the quotation marks in the third paragraph on page 13. Explain that single quotation marks are used to show a quote within a character's dialogue. Ask: *Why is* 'from Naples' *in single quotation marks?* (Sarah is quoting the definition of *Neapolitan* within her speech.)

Character, Setting, Plot Have students read the last paragraph on page 13. Ask: *How do you think Sarah feels when she sees the kids playing soccer?* (She wants to go over and join their game.)

Vocabulary Have students find the word *pizzeria* on page 13. *What clues tell you what* pizzeria *means?* (ordered a pizza)

Pages 14–15

Sentence Structure **A C T** *Read the last three sentences on page 14. Why is* "Grazie!" *in italics and quotation marks?* (It is a foreign word and it is also the word the boy spoke.)

Theme *What does Sarah say on page 15 that shows what she's learned on this trip?* (Soccer, the saxophone, hotdogs, and pizza were all brought to America, and then we got to like them.) *What did Sarah do on this trip that helped her learn those things?* (She researched and followed her interests.) *Think about what Sarah discovers. What is the author's message, or the theme of the story?* (Learning about other cultures can make a person more curious about their own.)

STOP AND CHECK *Read the question in the Stop and Check box on page 15.* (She enjoys finding out about new places. Naples is famous for pizza. She can make friends in Italy.)

AFTER READING
10–15 Minutes   RL.5.1   RL5.2   RL.5.9   W.5.9a   L.5.4

Respond to Reading

Compare Texts Have students compare what Sarah discovers as she learns about a different culture with what Paul discovers in "A Reluctant Traveler." Ask: *What have you discovered by learning about another culture?*

Summarize Have students turn to page 16 and summarize the selection. (Answers should include details from the selection that show how Sarah came to appreciate foreign cultures and her own.)

Text Evidence

Have partners work together to answer questions on page 16. Remind students to use their Theme charts.

Theme (Many things came from Europe: Brussels sprouts, saxophones, hamburgers, etc. Learning about other countries can also teach us about our own.)

Vocabulary (*Sightseeing* means visiting a new place and seeing interesting things.)

Write About Reading (Sarah was bored in Paris. She started to have fun by researching different places. She learned that many of her favorite things came from Europe.)

Independent Reading

Encourage students to read the paired selection "A Sporting Gift" on pages 17–19. Have them summarize the selection and compare it to "All the Way from Europe." Have them work with a partner to answer the "Make Connections" questions on page 19.

✓ *Quick Check* Can students identify the theme in a story? If not, review and reteach using the instruction on page 134 and assign the Unit 3 Week 1 digital mini-lesson.

Can students respond to the selection using text evidence? If not, provide, sentence frames to help them organize their ideas.

Objectives
- Review weekly vocabulary words
- Review theme
- Write an analysis about how an author creates realistic characters

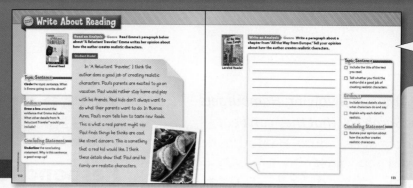

Materials
- Visual Vocabulary Cards: 77–84
- Interactive Worktext, pp. 152–153
- Assessment Book, pp. 30–31

☞ **Go Digital**
- Visual Vocabulary Cards
- Theme Mini-Lesson
- Interactive eWorktext

Scaffolding for **Wonders** McGraw-Hill Reading Reading/Writing Workshop

---

REVIEW AND RETEACH

5–10 Minutes   RL.5.1   RL.5.2   L.5.4a   L.5.6

Weekly Vocabulary

Display one **Visual Vocabulary Card** at a time and ask students to use the vocabulary word in a sentence. If students have difficulty, have them find the word in "A Reluctant Traveler" and use context clues to define it.

Comprehension: Theme

I Do Read aloud the last paragraph of page 148 and the first paragraph of page 149 of the **Interactive Worktext**. Say: *I am going to look closely again at what Paul says and does to find clues to the theme.* Underline: *Paul saw people dancing to music he'd never heard.* and *"That is pretty cool," Paul admitted.* Say: *Paul has a new experience. From what he says, I can tell he thinks it is cool. I can put these details together to figure out a message. I think the message is: It's good to have new experiences.*

We Do Display: *Micah is nervous before a soccer game. His coach says, "Don't worry. Just do your best!" Micah works hard. He helps his team win.* Say: *Let's find the theme together. How does Micah feel before the game?* (He is nervous.) *What does Micah's coach say?* (Don't worry. Just do your best!) *What happens to Micah?* (He works hard. He helps his team win.) *Put these details together. What lesson does Micah learn?* (Doing your best can lead to success.)

You Do Display: *Ali left her backpack on the bus. She didn't have her books for class. "That's okay," her friend Mya said. "We can share my books today." Ali was happy to have such a good friend.* Have partners identify what the characters do and say to figure out the theme.

WRITE ABOUT READING

25–35 Minutes   W.5.1a   W.5.1d   W.5.4   W.5.5   W.5.9a

Read an Analysis

- Ask students to look back at "A Reluctant Traveler" in the **Interactive Worktext**. Have volunteers review their notes about Paul from the story. *How did the author use details to create realistic characters?*

- Read aloud the directions on page 152. Read aloud the student model. *Emma's writing is not a summary. She is writing an analysis, or a detailed description, of how the author creates realistic characters in "A Reluctant Traveler." In this analysis, Emma is sharing her opinion.*

- Say: *When you write an analysis, you need to include certain elements. Circle the topic sentence. What information is included in that sentence?* (text's title, Emma's opinion) *Which words tell you that Emma is sharing her opinion?* (I think, good job)

- *Another element of analysis is text evidence. Emma supports her opinion with details from the text that show how the characters are realistic. Reread the model and draw a box around the text evidence.* (sentences 2, 3, 5, 7) *Look back at your notes about "A Reluctant Traveler." What other details could Emma have included?* (Possible response: Paul says he wants to paint his room in soccer colors.)

- *The final element is the concluding statement.* Have students underline the concluding statement. *How is the concluding sentence like the topic sentence?* (Both say that the characters realistic. Both include the words "I think") *Which words does Emma use to tie all of the elements together?* ("these details")

Analytical Writing ## Write an Analysis

Guided Writing Read the writing prompt on page 153 together. Have students write about "All the Way from Europe." *Use the checklist to help you figure out what information to include in each section.* Guide students to ask "how" and "why" questions, such as *How is the character like a person in real life?*

Peer Conference Have students read their analysis to a partner. Listeners should identify the strongest text evidence that supports the topic sentence and discuss any sentences that are unclear.

Teacher Conference Check students' writing for complete sentences and text evidence that supports their opinion. Review the concluding statement. Ask: *Does this sentence tie all of the elements together?* If necessary, have students revise the concluding statement by restating the topic sentence.

Level Up

▲ Approaching Leveled Reader

▲ Reading/Writing Workshop

▲ Apprentice Leveled Reader

▲ Interactive Worktext

IF students read the **Apprentice Level** Reader fluently and the **Interactive Worktext** Shared Read fluently and answer the Respond to Reading questions

THEN read together the **Approaching Level** Reader main selection and the **Reading/Writing Workshop** Shared Read from *Reading Wonders*. Have students take notes as they read, using self-stick notes. Then ask and answer questions about their notes.

Writing Rubric

	4	3	2	1
Topic Sentence	Topic sentence presents a clear opinion.	Topic sentence presents an opinion, somewhat clearly.	Topic is presented in short phrases; opinion is unclear	There is no topic sentence; no opinion is presented.
Text Evidence	Opinion is supported by two or more text details.	Opinion is only supported by one detail from the text.	Little to no evidence from the text supports opinion.	No text evidence is included; does not support opinion.
Concluding Statement	Clearly restates an opinion; wraps up all the details.	Restatement is less focused; attempts to wrap up the details.	Vaguely restates opinion. Doesn't correlate well to text evidence.	There is no conclusion.
Writing Style	Writes in complete sentences. Uses correct spelling and grammar.	Uses complete sentences and phrases. Writing has spelling and grammar errors.	Few or no complete sentences. There are many spelling and grammar errors.	Does not write accurately or in complete sentences.

ASSESSMENT

Weekly Assessment

Have students complete the Weekly Assessment using **Assessment** book pages 30–31.

WEEK 2 LESSON 1

Objectives
- Develop oral language
- Build background about learning about nature
- Understand and use weekly vocabulary
- Read a fantasy

Materials
- Interactive Worktext, pp. 154–161
- Visual Vocabulary Cards: 85–92

☞ **Go** Digital
- Interactive eWorktext
- Visual Vocabulary Cards

Scaffolding for **Wonders** Reading/Writing Workshop

WEEKLY CONCEPT

5–10 Minutes   SL.5.1b SL.5.1c CCSS

Talk About It

Essential Question Read aloud the Essential Question on page 154 of the **Interactive Worktext**: *How can learning about nature be useful?* Explain that nature includes things in the world that are not made by people, such as oceans, mountains, trees, animals, and weather. Say: *We can use what we learn about nature to get things we need, such as food, clothing, and shelter.*

- Discuss the photograph on page 154. Ask: *What is this person doing?* (building an igloo) *How is this person using something in nature?* (He or she is using snow to build.)

I Do Say: *I am going to think about a time when I used what I learned about nature. One time I planted a vegetable plant in my yard. But its leaves turned brown. Then I learned that it needs lots of sunlight. I moved the plant to a sunny spot. The plant survived and produced lots of vegetables. Learning about nature helped me grow vegetables. I will write this in the web on page 155.*

We Do Say: *Let's look at the photo and think about another way learning about nature can be useful. What is this person using to build the igloo?* (snow) *What do you think this person learned about the snow first?* (that it sticks together) *What do you think the person will use the igloo for?* (shelter) Guide students to add their answers to the word web. Then have partners discuss what they know about snow and brainstorm ways people could use snow (get water, keep things cold).

You Do Have partners describe a time when they used something in nature. Have them answer the questions: *What did you use from nature? What did you learn about it? How did it help you do or get something?*

REVIEW VOCABULARY

10–15 Minutes   L.5.4a L.5.5c CCSS

Review Weekly Vocabulary Words

- Use the **Visual Vocabulary Cards** to review the weekly vocabulary.

- Read together the directions for the Vocabulary activity on page 156 of the **Interactive Worktext**. Then complete the activity.

1 **devise** Have students talk about what a person does before he or she begins to cook. (Possible answers: get a recipe; gather ingredients and tools) Have students use this sentence frame: *It is helpful for a cook to devise a plan because _____.* (Possible answer: He or she needs to have the right ingredients or tools. He or she will know what order to cook things.)

2 **shortage** Ask: *What do plants need to live?* (water, sunlight) *Picture what a plant looks like when there is a shortage of water. Describe what you picture.* (Possible answer: The plant is dry, brown or yellow. It has lost leaves.)

3 **fashioned** Have students point to things in the classroom that are fashioned out of plastic. Have them complete the sentence frame: *A _____ is fashioned out of plastic.* (Possible answers: chair, desk, pen)

4 **tormentors** Point out the suffix *-or.* Explain that *-or* means "someone who." Have partners discuss which of the actions a tormentor would do. (tease, annoy) Then have them define the word. *What does* tormentor *mean?* (someone who teases or annoys)

5 **resourceful** Have students explain what they use a stapler for. (to hold together pieces of paper) *Suppose you ran out of staples. What would you do? How could* *you be* resourceful? (Possible answers: use glue, tape, paper clips)

6 **civilization** Say: *Phone calls are one way people in our civilization communicate. What other ways do people in our civilization communicate?* (letter, e-mail)

7 **complex** Ask: *Name a complex or difficult task.* (Possible answers: putting a bicycle together, writing a research report) *What makes the task* complex? (It is hard to do. It has many steps.) Have partners ask each other questions to identify a synonym and antonym for *complex.* (synonym: puzzling; antonym: simple)

8 **cultivate** Have students discuss ways a person can *cultivate* a tree. Ask students to use this sentence frame to describe their pictures: *One way to cultivate a tree is to _____.* (Possible answers: water it, add soil or fertilizer, give it lots of sun) Ask: *What happens to a tree when you cultivate it?* (Possible answers: It grows. The branches get longer. Their leaves get bigger.)

High-Utility Words

Explain that homophones are words that sounds the same but have different meanings. Write and say: *ate, eight.* Use each word in a sentence. Then have students turn to page 157 of the **Interactive Worktext**. Have students read the first paragraph aloud. Ask partners to circle pairs of homophones in the passage. (their/there, hear/here, no/know, it's/its, whole/hole, buy/by) Have partners choose a pair of homophone from the passage and use each word in a sentence.

> **ELL ENGLISH LANGUAGE LEARNERS**
>
> Display pairs of homophones: *their, there; it's its; here, hear; buy, by.* Say a sentence for each of the two homophones. Have students point to the correct word.

READ COMPLEX TEXT

15–20 Minutes   RL.5.1   RF.5.4c

Read: "Survivaland"

- Have students turn to page 158 in the **Interactive Worktext** and read aloud the Essential Question. Explain that they will read how four friends use what they have learned about nature. Ask: *What is the title?* ("Survivaland") *What does the picture show?* (four children in front of a video game) *Use these clues. What do you think the story will be about?* (Possible Answer: A video game in which the players will have to know about nature to survive.)

- Read "Survivaland" together. Note that the weekly vocabulary words are highlighted in yellow. Expand vocabulary words are highlighted in blue.

- Have students use the "My Notes" section on page 158 to write questions they have, words they don't understand, and details they want to remember. Model how to use the section: *As I read, I can write notes about questions I have. On this page, I want to know about the* Survivaland *game. I will write a note in the "My Notes" section:* How do you play *Survivaland? When we reread the story, I will ask my question so that I will better understand what I am reading. On page 159, I am not sure what it means to be "inside the game." I will write this phrase in the "My Notes" section.*

> **ELL ENGLISH LANGUAGE LEARNERS**
>
> As you read together, have students mark parts of the story they find confusing. After reading, help them write questions in the "My Notes" section.

 Quick Check Can students understand the weekly vocabulary in context? If not, review vocabulary using the **Visual Vocabulary Cards** before teaching Lesson 2.

WEEK 2 LESSON

2

Objectives
- Read a fantasy
- Understand complex text through close reading
- Recognize and understand theme
- Respond to the selection using text evidence to support ideas

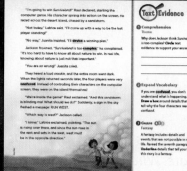

Materials
Interactive Worktext, pp. 158–163

☞ **Go** Digital
- Interactive eWorktext
- Theme Digital Mini-Lesson

Scaffolding for **Wonders** Reading/Writing Workshop McGraw-Hill Reading

REREAD COMPLEX TEXT

20–25 Minutes   RL.5.1   RL.5.2   RL.5.4   L.5.4a   L.5.6   CCSS

Close Reading: "Survivaland"

Reread "Survivaland" with students. As you read together, discuss important passages in the text. Have students respond to text-dependent questions, including those in the **Interactive Worktext**.

 Page 159

Theme Say: *As you read, look at what the characters do and say for clues to the story's theme. I read that Raul, Latrice, Juanita, and Jackson are playing a computer game called* Survivaland. *I read that Jackson says, "Survivaland is too complex." What does Jackson say to explain his opinion about the game?* (It's too hard to have to know all about nature to win.) *What does Jackson think about nature? Point to text evidence.* (knowing about it is just not that important) *Does everyone agree with him?* (no) *How do you know?* (Juanita says "You are so wrong!") *A character's opinion can change in a story. This can be a clue to the theme. Let's keep reading to find out if Jackson's opinion changes.*

Expand Vocabulary Have students point to the word *confused* and reread the paragraph. Say: *What happened that caused the characters to be confused? Draw a box around these details.* (Instead of controlling their characters on the computer screen, they were on the island themselves!)

Genre ⒶⒸⓉ Say: *A fantasy is a made-up story. It can include characters, settings, or events that are not possible in real life. Lets look for details that tell us this story is a fantasy.* Point to the seventh paragraph and read each sentence aloud. After each sentence ask: *Could this happen in real life?* Have students underline details in

the paragraph that could not happen in real life. (We're inside the game! Suddenly, a sign in the sky flashed a message: RUN WEST.)

 Page 160

Expand Vocabulary Have students reread the second paragraph. Then read the definition of *gigantic* aloud. Ask: *What word in this paragraph is a clue to the meaning of gigantic?* (monster-sized) *Name another animal the characters meet.* (crow) *Is this animal gigantic? Point to text evidence that supports your answer.* (yes, huge crow, very large bird)

Vocabulary Have students locate the word *shrieked* in the third paragraph and read the paragraph. Ask: *What do you think* shrieked *means?* (screamed in fear) *What clues in the paragraph helped you know the meaning of the word?* (feared, screaming)

Theme Say: *Let's look at what happens to the characters for clues to the story's theme. After the sandstorm, what problem do the characters face?* (a gigantic butterfly) *What does Raul tell his friends to do?* (rub onion on themselves) *What does Raul know about butterflies? Circle three details.* (They like sweet flowers. They taste with their feet. The taste of a bitter onion would make the butterfly go away.) *How does Raul's knowledge about butterflies help the characters?* (They rub onion on themselves, and the butterfly goes away.) *What does Jackson think about Raul's idea? Point to text evidence.* (He thinks it's a good idea. He says "Raul, I'm glad you're here to help us.")

Genre ⒶⒸⓉ Have students reread the last paragraph. Ask: *Which sentences tells about an event that could not happen in real life?* (Then a huge crow flew down and announced, "I'm hungry!") *Why is it not possible in real life?* (Crows cannot talk.)

Page 161

High-Utility Words Point to the word *knew* in the second paragraph. Have students read it aloud. Say: *Find a homophone for* knew *in the second to last paragraph.* (new) Discuss the meanings of *knew* and *new*.

Genre Ⓐ Ⓒ Ⓣ Have partners reread the fourth paragraph and ask each other questions to identify an event that could not happen in real life. (When they wiped the mud away and opened their eyes, they were back in Raul's house.) If students have difficulty, read each sentence and ask: *Could this event happen in real life?* Then ask: *Why is this event important to the story?* (It tells how the friends return home.)

Expand Vocabulary Have students locate and point to the word *normal. The text says the friends returned to "normal civilization." What is normal about Raul's game room? Look for details in the paragraph that came before. Underline the text evidence.* (It has four walls. The electric sky had become the four white walls of Raul's game room.)

Theme Have partners discuss what Jackson says about nature at the beginning of the story. Ask: *What does Jackson say about nature at the end of the story? Circle these words.* (you've helped me cultivate a new appreciation for nature. And I want to keep on learning more.) *What lesson did he learn?* (Knowing about nature is important.)

RESPOND TO READING

10–20 Minutes   RL.5.1 RL.5.3 W.5.9a SL.5.1d

Respond to "Survivaland"

Have students summarize "Survivaland" orally to demonstrate comprehension. Then have partners answer the questions on pages 162 of the **Interactive Worktext** using the discussion starters. Tell them to use text evidence to support their answers. Have students write the page number(s) on which they found the text evidence for each question.

1. *How does Latrice help her friends get away from the sandstorm?* (She tells them to run west in the opposite direction of the rising sun. <u>Text Evidence</u>: pp. 159, 160)

2. *How does Raul's knowledge about butterflies help his friends?* (Raul tells his friends to rub the onion on themselves because he knows the butterfly will not like the bitter taste. They do and the butterfly goes away. <u>Text Evidence</u>: p. 160)

3. *How does Juanita help her friends get away from the hungry crow?* (Juanita knows that crows are attracted to shiny objects. She throws her shiny jewelry. The crow goes after it. <u>Text Evidence</u>: pp. 160, 161)

After students discuss the questions on page 162, have them write a response to the question on page 163. Tell them to use their discussions and notes to help them. Circulate and provide guidance.

 Quick Check **Do students understand vocabulary in context? If not, review and reteach using the instruction on page 144.**

Can students use key details to determine the theme? If not, review and reteach using the instruction on page 144 and assign the Unit 3 Week 2 digital mini-lesson.

Can students write a response to "Survivaland"? If not, provide sentence frames to help them organize their ideas.

Objectives
- Understand and use new vocabulary words
- Read a fantasy
- Recognize and understand theme
- Understand complex text through close reading

Scaffolding for **WONDERS** Reading   Approaching Leveled Reader

Materials
- "Over the Top" Apprentice Leveled Reader: pp. 2–7
- Graphic Organizer: Theme

Go Digital
- Apprentice Leveled Reader eBook
- Downloadable Graphic Organizer
- Theme Digital Mini-Lesson

BEFORE READING

10–15 Minutes SL.5.1c SL.5.1d L.5.4a L.5.6 CCSS

Introduce "Over the Top"

- Read the Essential Question on the title page of "Over the Top" **Apprentice Leveled Reader**: *How can learning about nature be useful? We will read about students who used things from nature in a creative way to solve a problem.*

- Read the title of the main read. Have students look at the images. Ask: *What do you think this story will be about?* (A group of kids who have to escape from something.) *Why do you think that?* (the illustrations)

Expand Vocabulary

Display each word below. Say the words and have students repeat them. Then use the Define/Example/Ask routine to introduce each word.

1 barrier (page 3)

Define: something that stops people or other things from going past it

Example: The fallen tree made a *barrier* across the road.

Ask: Why might you see a *barrier* at a zoo?

2 commanded (page 6)

Define: ordered someone to do something

Example: The queen *commanded* the knights to return to the castle.

Ask: What tone of voice would you use to *command* your dog to stop barking?

3 miniature (page 3)

Define: much smaller than the usual size

Example: Ann needs *miniature* furniture for the doll house.

Ask: What other *miniature* things have you seen?

4 scurried (page 4)

Define: ran with short, quick steps

Example: The squirrels *scurried* through the forest.

Ask: When was the last time you *scurried*?

5 separate (page 6)

Define: different; away from others

Example: The spoons, knives, and forks are in *separate* parts of the drawer.

Ask: Why are some gyms in a *separate* part of the school?

DURING READING

20–30 Minutes RL.5.1 RL.5.2 SL.5.1b L.5.5a CCSS

Close Reading

Pages 2–3

Vocabulary Read the dialogue on page 2: "She can make a paintbrush speak." Explain that this is an example of personification. A human quality, speech, is given to an object. The idea is that Claudia's paintings are very expressive. Her paintbrush lets her tell a story.

Genre Read pages 2 and 3: *Where are Adam, Hania, and Mario?* (in the small world shown in the display) *Could this happen in real life?* (no) Remind students that a fiction story that could not happen in real life is a fantasy.

Theme Explain that often the theme, or message of a story, is related to how the characters solve a problem and what they learn as a result. Review the sequence of events on page 3 that lead the students to disappear into the display. Ask: *What happens to Adam at the top of page 3?* (His glasses fall into the display, and he goes in after them and disappears.) *What did Hania and Mario do?* (They went into the display after Adam.) *What is the problem?* (These three students have disappeared into the display.)

As they read the selection, have students record details in their Theme charts about what the characters say and do and what happens to them.

STOP AND CHECK *Read the question in the Stop and Check box on page 3.* (He could not figure out how the students could get smaller and smaller and disappear into the small world shown in the display.)

Pages 4–5

Vocabulary Have students find the word *unusual* at the top of page 4. Explain that the prefix un- means "not." Ask: *What does* unusual *mean? Use the prefix* un- *to figure it out.* (not usual, strange) *What might* unusual *animals be like?* (not usual, strange or weird)

Genre Have students read the first two paragraphs on page 4. Point out that Ms. Borek calls the animals "unusual" but Mr. Nizami calls them "dangerous." *How do you think Ms. Borek really feels about the animals?* (She thinks they are dangerous.) *How do you know?* (She turns pale when she learns the kids are in the display.) *Why does Claudia jump into the display?* (to rescue the students) *Can any of these things happen in real life?* (no)

Theme Ask: *What does Claudia do on page 4?* (climbs into the display) *Why does she do that?* (She wants to find Adam, Hania, and Mario.) *Why does she think she can help?* (She knows her way around the display.)

STOP AND CHECK Read the question in the Stop and Check box on page 4. (Adam's glasses fell into the display and he went in to get them.)

Pages 6–7

Genre Have students read the dialogue at the top of page 6. *What does Claudia say when the ground begins to shake?* (It's the linodocs!) *What are* linodocs? *(animals, like large, angry elephants)* Do linodocs *really exist? (No, they are imaginary creatures.)*

Vocabulary Have students find the word *realistic* in the third paragraph on page 6. Explain that it means something that seems real. Ask: *What would a very* realistic *display be like?* (It would seem very real.)

Problem and Solution Have students read the last three paragraphs on page 6. Ask: *What problem do the students and Claudia have?* (They are in a separate world and need to climb out of the display.)

Theme Point out that on pages 6 and 7, Claudia and Hania begin to come up with creative ideas for getting out of the display. Ask: *What is Claudia's idea?* (to make a ladder) *What does Hania add to Claudia's suggestion?* (She noticed wood by the lake and suggests they make a ladder out of it.) *What else does Claudia say?* (They can use plant fibers to make rope for the ladder.)

Genre *How will the group find food?* (Claudia says she painted some clams in the lake.) *Could this happen in real life?* (no)

STOP AND CHECK Read the question in the Stop and Check box on page 7. (The students are in a cave inside the display. They need rope to make a ladder so that they can climb out of the display.)

Have partners review their Theme charts for pages 2–7 and discuss what they learned.

 Quick Check **Do students understand weekly vocabulary in context? If not, review and reteach using the instruction on page 144.**

Can students use details about what the characters say and do to begin to identify the theme? If not, review and reteach using the instruction on page 144 and assign the Unit 3 Week 2 digital mini-lesson.

WEEK 2 LESSON 4

Objectives
- Understand and use new vocabulary words
- Read a fantasy
- Understand theme
- Understand complex text through close reading
- Respnd to the selection using text evidence to support ideas

Scaffolding for **Wonders** Approaching Leveled Reader

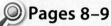

Materials
- "Over the Top" Apprentice Leveled Reader: pp. 8–20
- Graphic Organizer: Theme

☞ **Go Digital**
- Apprentice Leveled Reader eBook
- Downloadable Graphic Organizer
- Theme Digital Mini-Lesson

BEFORE READING

5–10 Minutes   SL.5.1c   SL.5.1d   L.5.4a   L.5.6

Expand Vocabulary

Display each word below. Say the words and have students repeat them. Then use the Define/Example/Ask routine to introduce each word.

1 pleaded (page 15)

Define: begged to do something

Example: As soon as Pat got off the roller coaster, he *pleaded* to ride again.

Ask: If you *pleaded* because you wanted something special, what would you say?

2 trembling (page 9)

Define: shaking from cold, fear, or excitement

Example: Hannah hoped that her voice wasn't *trembling* during her speech.

Ask: What would be hard to do with *trembling* hands?

3 ventured (page 8)

Define: went somewhere that is dangerous

Example: The team of explorers *ventured* out on their trip to the volcano.

Ask: Why might someone *venture* into a cave?

DURING READING

15–20 Minutes   RL.5.1   RL.5.2   SL.5.1b   L.5.5b

Close Reading

🔍 **Pages 8–9**

Vocabulary Have students identify the word *supplies* in the first paragraph on page 8. Ask: *What clues help you figure out its meaning?* (food and grass) Have students tell what *supplies* the group needed. (food, something to make a ladder, something to sleep on)

Theme Have students read paragraphs 2 through 5 on page 8. *How does the group decide whether the clams are safe to eat?* (They use what they know about clams.) *How do they get the clams open?* (Hania gives Mario a rock to use as a tool.)

Genre Ⓐ Ⓒ Ⓣ Explain that there may be realistic parts in a fantasy. Say: *On page 8, Adam says that his family gathers clams on the beach, so he knows how to eat clams. Could this really happen?* (yes)

Theme Have students read page 9. Then ask: *What problem does the group face at the end of Chapter 2?* (The plant fibers aren't strong enough to make a rope.)

STOP AND CHECK Read the question in the Stop and Check box on page 9. (They need a ladder to climb out of the display.)

🔍 **Pages 10–11**

Genre Ⓐ Ⓒ Ⓣ Have students read page 10. *When do the events on page 10 take place? How can you tell?* (next morning, was early morning and still dark outside)

Theme *What problem does Adam have when he wakes up the next morning?* (His head is stuck to the floor of the cave.) *How does Mario help him?* (He uses a rock and saws Adam's hair.)

Vocabulary Have students point to the word *run* in the first sentence on page 11. Explain that sap is a liquid found in some plants. Ask: *What does it mean when we say that sap runs?* (a liquid substance flows)

Theme *Read the first three paragraphs on page 11. What idea do the students get when they realize the sap made Adam's hair stick to the floor?* (They realize they can use it as glue.) *What will they use the glue for?* (the ladder) Have students add these details to their Theme charts.

Vocabulary *Read the fourth paragraph on page 11. What does the phrase "sleeping on a problem" mean?* (It is sometimes easier to solve a problem in the morning when you are rested.) Point out that in this case, Adam actually did sleep on top of the problem.

Pages 12–13

Genre **A C T** *Read page 13. What did Adam notice about the ladder once he climbed over the barrier?* (The ladder seemed tiny.) *What did he notice about his own size?* (He was as large as everyone else.) *Could this really happen?* (no)

Pages 14–15

Theme Have students read page 14. Ask: *What was happening to Claudia?* (A linodoc was charging the ladder. She didn't think she could hang on.) *How did Hania try to save Claudia?* (She threw sparkly rocks from the future into the display.) *Why was Claudia able to climb to safety?* (The linodoc stopped to look at the rocks.)

STOP AND CHECK Read the question in the Stop and Check box. (They made a ladder from plant fibers, wood, and glue made from sap. They used the ladder to climb out of the display.)

Theme Go over the details on their Theme charts together. Guide students to figure out the theme. Ask: *What lesson did the students learn?* (They used what they knew about nature to help them escape from the display.) *What message do you think the author is trying to communicate?* (We can use what we know and also be resourceful and work together to solve problems creatively.)

AFTER READING

10–15 Minutes **RL.5.1** **RL.5.2** **RL.5.9** **W.5.9a** **L.5.4a**

Respond to Reading

Compare Texts Have students compare how characters in "Survivaland" and "Over the Top" used what they learned about nature to solve problems. Then ask: *Have you ever had to solve a problem using what you know about nature?*

Summarize Have students turn to page 16 and summarize the selection. (should include details from the selection about how the characters used knowledge about nature and were resourceful problem solvers)

Text Evidence

Have partners work together to answer questions on page 16. Remind students to use their Theme charts.

Theme (Claudia knew how to make rope with plant fibers. She used the rope to make a ladder.)

Vocabulary (extremely awful or scary)

Write About Reading (The group was trapped in a display. They were resourceful and used what they knew about nature to escape. They ate clams from a lake and used grass for beds. They used plant fibers, sap, and wood to make a ladder to climb out of the display.)

Independent Reading

Encourage students to read the paired selection "Rain-Forest Treasures" on pages 17–19. Have them summarize the selection and compare it to "Over the Top." Have them work with a partner to answer the "Make Connections" questions on page 19.

Quick Check Can students identify the theme? If not, review and teach using the instruction on page 144 and assign the Unit 3 Week 2 digital mini-lesson.

Can students respond to the selection using text evidence? If not, provide, sentence frames to help them organize their ideas.

WEEK 2 LESSON 5

Objectives
- Review weekly vocabulary words
- Review theme
- Write an analysis about the most important plot events

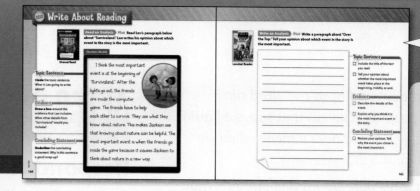

Materials
- Visual Vocabulary Cards: 85–92
- Interactive Worktext, pp. 164–165
- Assessment Book, pp. 32–33

☞ **Go** Digital
- Visual Vocabulary Cards
- Theme Mini-Lesson
- Interactive eWorktext

Scaffolding for **Wonders** Reading/Writing Workshop

REVIEW AND RETEACH

5–10 Minutes   RL.5.2   L.5.4a   L.5.6   **CCSS**

Weekly Vocabulary

Display one **Visual Vocabulary Card** at a time and ask students to use the vocabulary word in a sentence. If students have difficulty, have them find the word in "Survivaland" and use the context clues to define it.

Comprehension: Theme

I Do   Say: *I am going to look closely again at "Survivaland" to look for clues to the theme.* Read aloud the last three paragraphs of page 159 and the first paragraph of page 160 in the **Interactive Worktext.** Say: *I can tell Latrice knows a lot about nature. She knows which direction the sun rises and sets. This helps her know which direction to run. What happens to the characters? They escape the sandstorm. These details are clues to the theme: Learning about nature is useful.*

We Do   Display: *Pam found a necklace in the hall. She wanted to keep it at first. Then Pam thought, "That wouldn't be honest." She took it to the Lost and Found. A girl there was looking for a lost necklace. Pam held up the necklace. It was the girl's. The girl was happy. Pam was glad she had been honest.* Ask: *What does Pam want to do first?* (keep the necklace) *What does she think?* (That wouldn't be honest.) *What does she do?* (takes the necklace to the Lost and Found) *What happens to Pam?* (She returns the necklace. She is glad she was honest.) *What is the message?* (Be honest.)

You Do   Display: *Everyone but Jo was in the play. Jo was too shy, but she liked to make things. "People can help in different ways. Why don't you make the props?" her teachers said. Jo liked that idea.* Have partners look for what the characters say and do to identify the theme.

WRITE ABOUT READING

25–35 Minutes   W.5.1a   W.5.1d   W.5.4   W.5.5   W.5.9a   **CCSS**

Read an Analysis

Ask students to look back at "Survivaland" in the **Interactive Worktext**. Have volunteers review the events of the story. Ask: *Which event do you think is the most important?*

- Read aloud the directions on page 164. Then read aloud the student model. Say: *Leo's writing is not a summary. Leo is writing an analysis of the story's plot. He is writing his opinion about which event is the most important.*

- *An analysis starts with a topic sentence, then gives text evidence, and ends with a concluding statement.* Have students circle the topic sentence. *What information has Leo included?* (the title, his opinion of which story event is the most important) Ask: *Which words tell you this is Leo's opinion?* (I think)

- Review the purpose of text evidence. *In an analysis, it's important to include key details from the story that support your opinion. Underline the key details in Leo's paragraph.* (four sentences after the topic sentence) *Look back at "Survivaland." What other details might be included as text evidence? Think about which details support Leo's opinion that the events at the beginning are the most important.* (Possible answer: Jackson complained, "It's too hard to have to know all about nature to win.")

- *The final element is the concluding statement. Underline the concluding statement.* Ask: *How is the concluding sentence like the topic sentence?* (Both tell which event is the most important.) *How is it different?* (Possible answer: It sums up all the text evidence. It tells why it is the most important event.)

 Write an Analysis

Analytical Writing

Guided Writing Read the writing prompt on page 165 together. Have students write a paragraph about "Over the Top" or another story they read this week. Say: *Remember to use the checklist. It will help you include the right details in each section.* Guide students to ask "how" and "why" questions as they analyze text evidence.

Peer Conference Have students read their analysis to a partner. Listeners should identify the strongest text evidence that supports their opinion and discuss any sentences that are unclear.

Teacher Conference Check students' writing for complete sentences and text evidence that supports their opinion. Review the concluding statement. Ask: *Does this sentence tie all of the elements together?* If necessary, have students revise the concluding statement by restating the topic sentence.

Level Up

▲ Approaching Leveled Reader

▲ Reading/Writing Workshop

Apprentice Leveled Reader

▲ Interactive Worktext

IF students read the Apprentice Level Reader fluently and the **Interactive Worktext** Shared Read fluently and answer the Respond to Reading questions

THEN read together the Approaching Level Reader main selection and the **Reading/Writing Workshop** Shared Read from *Reading Wonders*. Have students take notes as they read, using self-stick notes. Then ask and answer questions about their notes.

Writing Rubric

	4	3	2	1
Topic Sentence	Topic sentence presents a clear opinion.	Topic sentence presents an opinion, somewhat clearly.	Topic is presented in short phrases; opinion is unclear	There is no topic sentence; no opinion is presented.
Text Evidence	Opinion is supported by two or more text details.	Opinion is only supported by one detail from the text.	Little to no evidence from the text supports opinion.	No text evidence is included; does not support opinion.
Concluding Statement	Clearly restates an opinion; wraps up all the details.	Restatement is less focused; attempts to wrap up the details.	Vaguely restates opinion. Doesn't correlate well to text evidence.	There is no conclusion.
Writing Style	Writes in complete sentences. Uses correct spelling and grammar.	Uses complete sentences and phrases. Writing has spelling and grammar errors.	Few or no complete sentences. There are many spelling and grammar errors.	Does not write accurately or in complete sentences.

ASSESSMENT

Weekly Assessment

Have students complete the Weekly Assessment using **Assessment** book pages 32–33.

WEEK 3 LESSON 1

Objectives
• Develop oral language
• Build background about patterns in nature
• Understand and use weekly vocabulary
• Read expository text

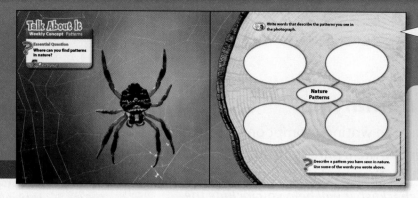

Materials
• Interactive Worktext, pp. 166–173
• Visual Vocabulary Cards: 93–100

☞ **Go** Digital
• Interactive eWorktext
• Visual Vocabulary Cards

Scaffolding for **Wonders** Reading/Writing Workshop

WEEKLY CONCEPT

5–10 Minutes SL.5.1b SL.5.1c

Talk About It

Essential Question Read aloud the Essential Question on page 166 of the **Interactive Worktext**: *Where can you find patterns in nature?* Explain that a pattern is the repetition of shapes, colors, lines, or actions. Say: *We can find many patterns in nature. When we look around, we can find patterns on land, in the sky, and in plants and animals,*

• Discuss the photograph on page 166. Say: *What kind of animal do you see?* (a spider) *What pattern of repeating colors do you see?* (red and black)

I Do Say: *I am going to think of a pattern I have seen in nature. I have seen butterflies that have a pattern of dots on their wings. I am going write "butterflies" as an example of nature patterns in the web on page 167.*

We Do Say: *Let's look closely at the photograph and discuss other patterns we can see in nature.* Point to the legs on the left side of the spider. *How many legs do you see on the left side of the spider?* (4) Point to the legs on the right side of the spider. *How many legs do you see on the right side of the spider?* (4) *Are all of the legs have the same colors?* (yes) *What pattern of colors do you see?* (red and black stripes) *What pattern do you see in the web?* (Possible answers: repeating lines, shapes) Guide students to add words to the web on page 167. Have them discuss other spiders or insects they know with patterns and add words to the web.

You Do Have partners describe another pattern they have seen in nature. Ask: *What patterns have you seen on land or up in the sky? What patterns have you seen on plants or animals? What did you see? What colors, shapes, or actions created a pattern?*

REVIEW VOCABULARY

10–15 Minutes L.5.1a L.5.4 L.5.5c L.5.6

Review Weekly Vocabulary Words

• Use the **Visual Vocabulary Cards** to review the weekly vocabulary.

• Read together the directions for the Vocabulary activity on page 168 of the **Interactive Worktext**. Then complete the activity.

1 visible Have students use the following sentence frame: _____ , _____ , and _____ are visible. (Possible answers: board, desk, clock, books, desks, plants, windows)

2 moisture *What is a lake? What is a desert? What is a rainforest?* Have partners discuss each question to help them decide which place has very little moisture. (a desert)

3 particles Say: *A grain of sand is a* particle. *Brainstorm with a partner other examples of* particles. (Possible answers: dirt, crumbs) Have partners complete the sentence starter to describe the size of a particle: *A particle is _____.* (Possible answers: very small, tiny, little)

4 erode Have partners ask each other questions about each option to figure out which phrase means the opposite of *erode.* (build up)

5 formation Point out the suffix *-ation.* Explain to students that *-ation* is added to the end of a word and means "the act or result of." *(form, -ation,* something that has been formed)

6 repetition Have students write their name to show repetition. Then have them use their name to complete the sentence frame: _____ , _____ ,

_____ *is an example of repetition.* (Students should write and say their name more than once.)

7 **contact** Have students use the sentence starter: *I am in* contact *with* _____. (Possible answers: a pencil, a book, the floor, a chair, a table) Ask: *What is another way to say you are in* contact *with something?* (Possible answer: I am touching it.)

8 **structure** Ask students to visualize a playground. Have them complete the sentence starter: _____ *is a* structure *at a playground.* (Possible answers: slide, swing set, jungle gym) After students complete their drawings have partners ask: *What* structure *did you draw?*

High-Utility Words

Explain that prepositions, such as *above, over,* and *into,* are connecting words that show a direction or a location of something. Have students turn to page 169 of the **Interactive Worktext.** Discuss the meaning of the circled word *toward.* Ask partners to circle the other prepositions in the passage. (near, through, over, from) Write the frame: *The cat walked* _____ *the house.* Have students use different prepositions in the sentence and tell how each changes the meaning of the sentence.

ELL ENGLISH LANGUAGE LEARNERS

Display the prepositions *near, inside, through,* and *over.* Point to and say each preposition. Have students repeat. Then have them show the meaning of the word by using their hands or other objects in the room, such as a desk or door.

READ COMPLEX TEXT

15–20 Minutes   RI.5.1   RF.5.4c

Read: "Patterns of Change"

- Have students turn to page 170 in the **Interactive Worktext** and read aloud the Essential Question. Explain that they will read an informational text about how different types of rocks are formed. Ask: *What is the title?* ("Patterns of Change") *What do you see in the photograph?* (rock) *What kinds of patterns do you see?* (Possible answer: stripes and swirling patterns) *What do you think you will learn about these patterns?* (Possible answer: how they were made)

- Read "Patterns of Change" together. Note that the weekly vocabulary words are highlighted in yellow. Expand vocabulary words are highlighted in blue.

- Have students use the "My Notes" section on page 170 to write questions they have, words they don't understand, and details they want to remember. Model how to use the "My Notes" section. *I can write notes about questions I have as I read. In the first paragraph on page 171, I see the word* forces, *and I'm not sure what it means here. I will write* forces *with a question mark beside it in the "My Notes" section. As I continue to read the paragraph, I don't understand how patterns can form in rocks. I will write a question in the "My Notes" section:* How do patterns in rocks form?

ELL ENGLISH LANGUAGE LEARNERS

As you read together, have students pause to mark anything about the text that they find confusing or unclear. Help them write questions in the "My Notes" section and guide them to locate answers.

 Quick Check Can students understand the weekly vocabulary in context? If not, review vocabulary using the **Visual Vocabulary Cards** before teaching Lesson 2.

Objectives

- Read expository text
- Understand complex text through close reading
- Recognize and understand main idea and key details
- Respond to the selection using text evidence to support ideas

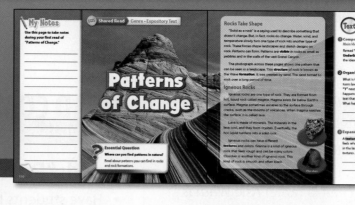

Materials

Interactive Worktext, pp. 170–175

☞ **Go** Digital

- Interactive eWorktext
- Main Idea and Key Details Mini-Lesson

REREAD COMPLEX TEXT

20–25 Minutes   RI.5.1   RI.5.2   RI.5.3   RI.5.4   **CCSS**

Close Reading: "Patterns of Change"

Reread "Patterns of Change" with students. As you read together, discuss important passages in the text. Have students respond to text-dependent questions, including those in the **Interactive Worktext**.

Page 171

Main Idea and Key Details Say: *Key details are the most important details. As you reread "Rocks Take Shape," think about which details are the most important. I read "Water, wind, and temperature slowly transform one type of rock into another type of rock." This detail tells me what causes rocks to change. Let's underline this key detail. Find another key detail in the first paragraph that also supports the idea that rocks change.* (These forces shape landscapes and sketch designs on rock.) *Now find a key detail in the second paragraph that supports the idea that rocks change.* (The sand turned to rock over a long period of time.)

Vocabulary Have students reread the second paragraph. *What is a pattern?* (repetition of shapes, colors, lines, or actions) Ask: What *pattern do you see in the photograph on the page?* (rows of wavy lines)

High-Utility Words Have student locate the prepositions *below, to,* and *through* in the third paragraph. Have students describe or point to demonstrate the meaning of each word.

Organization A C T Have students reread the second paragraph under "Igneous Rocks." Explain that in this section, the author describes the sequence of events that turns liquid lava into solid rock. *What first happens*

to the lava in this sequence of events? (minerals in the lava cool) *What happens next?* (crystals form) *What happens last?* (The hot liquid hardens into rock.)

Expand Vocabulary Have students point to the word *textures.* Read the definition of texture aloud. Ask: *What is the texture of granite? Look for words that describe what it feels like.* (rough) *What is the texture of obsidian?* (smooth)

Page 172

Connection of Ideas A C T Have students reread the first paragraph. *What causes igneous rocks to change?* (water and wind erode them) *What is the effect?* (bits of broken rock are carried to a beach, riverbank, or desert)

Expand Vocabulary Discuss the word *material.* Point to the words "kind of rock." Say: *Rock is a kind of* material. *Sedimentary rock can be made up of bits of rock, sand, bones, shells, and plants.* Reread the next paragraph. *What material is made up of bones and shells?* (limestone)

Main Idea and Key Details Have students reread the third paragraph. *Which sentences in this paragraph give key details?* (Sandstone is formed from sand. Limestone is made up of bones and shells.) *What do these details have in common?* (They both tell the names of different sedimentary rock. Both tell what the rock is made up.) *What is the main idea of this paragraph?* (Different sedimentary rocks can be made up of different things.)

Organization A C T Point to the headings and explain that the text is organized into sections. Ask: *Which section tells how sedimentary rocks are made?* (the section headed Sedimentary Rocks) *Which section tells what happens to sedimentary rock over time?* (Rock Formations)

Organization A C T Have students reread "Rock Formations." *The author describes the order of events that* forms layers of sedimentary rock, called strata. Reread the first two paragraphs in this section. What is the first thing that happens to sedimentary rock? (A layer of sedimentary rock can form.) What happens next? (A different layer of sedimentary rock can form on top of it.) What happens after the layers build up? (Each layer press down on the ones below it.)

Page 173

Main Idea and Key Details *Have partners reread the first paragraph and underline key details.* (The layers of rock below are pressed down. They are pushed deeper and deeper. They are heated by magma. The weight of the layers and the heat cause metamorphic rock to form.) *What do these details have in common?* (Each detail tells about a change that causes metamorphic rock to form.) *What is the main idea of this paragraph?* (Possible answer: Many changes cause metamorphic rock to form.)

Main Idea and Key Details *Have partners reread the second paragraph together and draw a box around key details.* (Liquid rock cools and becomes solid rock. Solid rock builds up from sand into cliffs. Solid rock changes back to liquid rock.) *What do these details have in common?* (Each detail tells about a change during the rock cycle.) *What is the main idea?* (Rocks go through a cycle of changes.)

Expand Vocabulary *Discuss the word process. What clues in the second paragraph help you understand the meaning of process?* (Possible answers: repetition, cycle, pattern, repeats again and again) **Have students complete the sentence starter:** *One step in the process of the rock cycle is _____.* (Possible answers: Liquid rock cools and becomes solid rock. Rock builds up. Solid rock changes back to liquid rock.)

Genre **A C T** *Read the caption and look at the diagram. Describe two ways a rock can change from one type of rock to another.* (Possible answers: cooling, eroding, squeezing, heating)

RESPOND TO READING

10–20 Minutes   RI.5.2   W.5.9b   SL.5.1a   **CCSS**

Respond to "Patterns of Change"

Have students summarize "Patterns of Change" orally to demonstrate comprehension. Then have partners answer the questions on page 174 of the **Interactive Worktext** using the discussion starters. Tell them to use text evidence to support their answers. Have students write the page number(s) on which they found the text evidence for each question.

1. *What pattern is found in the way sedimentary rock and strata are formed?* (Possible answer: Both form by building up and pressing down. Text Evidence: p. 172)

2. *What pattern can be seen in layers of sedimentary rock?* (Possible answer: Layers of sedimentary rock create patterns of thick lines. Text Evidence: p. 172)

3. *How is the rock cycle a pattern?* (Possible answer: The rock cycle is a pattern because it repeats over and over again. Liquid rock cools and becomes solid rock. Solid rock is pushed down and becomes liquid rock. Text Evidence: p. 173)

After students discuss the questions on page 174, have them write a response to the question on page 175. Tell them to use their partner discussions and notes about "Patterns of Change" to help them. Circulate and provide guidance.

 Quick Check **Do students understand vocabulary in context? If not, review and reteach using the instruction on page 154.**

Can students use key details to determine the main idea? If not, review and reteach using the instruction on page 154 and assign the Unit 3 Week 3 digital mini-lesson.

Can students write a response to "Patterns of Change"? If not, provide sentence frames to help them organize their ideas.

Objectives
- Understand and use new vocabulary words
- Read expository text
- Recognize and understand main idea and key details
- Understand complex text through close reading

Scaffolding for **Wonders** Approaching Leveled Reader

Materials
- "Weather Patterns" Apprentice Leveled Reader: pp. 2–7
- Graphic Organizer: Main Idea and Key Details

☞ **Go** Digital
- Apprentice Leveled Reader eBook
- Downloadable Graphic Organizer
- Main Idea and Key Details Digital Mini-Lesson

BEFORE READING

10–15 Minutes   SL.5.1c   SL.5.1d   L.5.4a   L.5.6

Introduce "Weather Patterns"

- Read the Essential Question on the title page of "Weather Patterns" **Apprentice Leveled Reader**: *Where can you find patterns in nature? We will read about weather patterns that we can and can't predict.*

- Read the title of the main read. Have students look at the table of contents and the images in the selection. *Is this expository text or fiction?* (expository text) *How do you know?* (gives information, includes photos, diagrams, maps) *What do the photographs mainly show?* (what the weather is like in different places)

Expand Vocabulary

Display each word below. Say the words and have students repeat them. Then use the Define/Example/Ask routine to introduce each word.

❶ conditions (page 7)

Define: the way something is

Example: Winter *conditions* can be cold and snowy.

Ask: What are the weather *conditions* today?

❷ occur (page 4)

Define: happen

Example: Wildfires can *occur* when it is hot and dry.

Ask: What would you do if a storm would *occur*?

❸ weird (page 3)

Define: strange, unusual

Example: The sky turned a *weird* shade of green.

Ask: What *weird* weather have you ever seen?

DURING READING

20–30 Minutes   RI.5.1   RI.5.2   SL.5.1b   SL.5.1d   L.5.6

Close Reading

🔍 **Pages 2–3**

Specific Vocabulary **A C T** This selection includes a great deal of domain-specific vocabulary relating to meteorology. As students read the selection, review the meaning of challenging words such as *meteorologists, precipitation, tropics, evaporates,* and *prevailing wind.*

Organization **A C T** Read the third paragraph on page 2. Point out the text structure of a sequence of causes and effects. Ask: *Do you see a signal word in the first sentence?* (causes) *What is the cause?* (The sun warms the air.) *What is the effect?* (Warm air rises.) *What happens after the warm air rises?* (Cold air moves in.) *How does this create wind?* (Movement of the hot and cold air causes wind.)

Main Idea and Key Details Have students read the last paragraph on page 2. Ask: *What are the key details?* (Scientists who study weather are called meteorologists. They study patterns in the weather. This helps them predict wind, rain, snow, and tornadoes.) *What do these details have in common?* (The details all tell about how meteorologists study weather patterns to predict the things that make up our weather.) *What is the main idea of this paragraph?* (By studying weather patterns, scientists can predict our everyday weather.)

Have students record these ideas in a Main Idea and Key Details Chart. Have them complete additional charts as they read the selection.

Pages 4–5

Organization ⒶⒸⓉ Have students read page 4. Ask: *Do you see signal words in the first paragraph?* (As a result) Say: *These words signal a cause-and-effect text structure. The cause is that the sun's rays are strongest at the equator. What effect does this have?* (The tropics are hot.) *Where are the sun's rays the weakest?* (North and South poles) *What effect does this have?* (The poles are cold.)

Genre ⒶⒸⓉ *Look at the diagram on page 4. Read the caption. What do the arrows in the diagram tell you about the sun's rays?* (They hit the equator more directly.) *What does the diagram explain?* (why the tropics are hot and the poles are cold) Have partners point to the tropics and the poles and discuss the effect of the sun's rays on these areas.

Main Idea and Key Details Have students read page 5. *What are some key details in the first paragraph?* (The sun causes water to evaporate. Then water vapor cools and falls back to earth. Then the cycle starts again.) *What are some key details in the second paragraph?* (The water cycle causes weather patterns.) *What do these details have in common?* (They are all about what causes the water cycle and how it affects weather.) *What is the main idea on page 5?* (The sun's heat causes the water cycle, which creates weather patterns.)

Genre ⒶⒸⓉ Have students review "The Water Cycle" diagram on page 5. *What do the arrows in the diagram show?* (the direction in which water is moving as it evaporates, forms clouds, and then falls back down to Earth) Have partners trace the movement of water through the water cycle, from ocean to sky and back again. Read the text in the yellow box aloud. Ask: *What additional information does this caption give us?* (where the water in our atmosphere comes from)

Pages 6–7

Vocabulary Read the first paragraph on page 6. *What is a prevailing wind?* (a wind that regularly blows) *What does a prevailing wind mean in the United States?* (the wind blows from the west)

Genre ⒶⒸⓉ *Read page 6. Look at the diagram, key, and compass. What does the circle represent?* (Earth) *What do the arrows on Earth show?* (the direction of prevailing winds) *What happens to the prevailing winds from the tropics as Earth rotates?* (The wind curves and creates prevailing westerly winds in temperate zones.) Have partners point out each of the elements listed in the key on the diagram.

Vocabulary In the diagram on page 6, what clues in the key help you understand what temperate means? (A *polar zone* is very cold, *the tropics* are hot, so *temperate* must mean mild.)

Main Idea and Key Details Have students review "Prevailing Wind." Say: *Name one key detail from each paragraph.* (The U.S. has a prevailing wind from the west. Earth's rotation causes temperate areas to have westerly winds. Prevailing winds also come from local conditions. A cool sea breeze in hot Australia is one local condition.) *What do each of these details have in common?* (They are all about prevailing winds, or the regular wind in an area.) *What is the main idea of this section?* (Prevailing winds are caused by Earth's rotation and local conditions, and they affect our weather.)

Stop and Check Read the question on page 7. (The heat makes warm air rise above cold air, and the cold air moves down and replaces the warm air. This pattern is repeated, and this movement causes wind.)

Have partners review their Main Idea and Details charts for pages 2-7 and discuss what they learned.

✔ *Quick Check* Do students understand weekly vocabulary in context? If not, review and reteach using the instruction on page 154.

Can students find main ideas and key details? If not, review and reteach using the instruction on page 154 and assign the Unit 3 Week 3 digital mini-lesson.

Objectives
- Understand and use new vocabulary words
- Read expository text
- Understand main idea and key details
- Understand complex text through close reading
- Respond to the selection using text evidence to support ideas

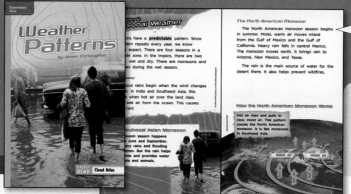

Materials
- "Weather Patterns" Apprentice Leveled Reader: pp. 8–24
- Graphic Organizer: Main Idea and Key Details

Go Digital
- Apprentice Leveled Reader eBook
- Downloadable Graphic Organizer
- Main Idea and Key Details Digital Mini-Lesson

Scaffolding for **WONDERS** Approaching Leveled Reader

BEFORE READING

5–10 Minutes   SL.5.1c SL.5.1d L.5.4a L.5.6 **CCSS**

Expand Vocabulary

Display each word below. Say the words and have students repeat them. Then use the Define/Example/Ask routine to introduce each word.

1 denser (page 12)

Define: heavier, packed closer together

Example: Our footsteps packed the snow and made it *denser*.

Ask: What is *denser*, a rock or a feather?

2 experience (page 15)

Define: have or feel the effects of a condition

Example: Our area may *experience* severe thunderstorms.

Ask: What weather do you *experience* during spring?

3 fierce (page 10)

Define: powerful and severe in force

Example: The *fierce* wind blew down a tree.

Ask: What kind of *fierce* weather have you seen?

4 predictable (page 8)

Define: expected because of known behavior

Example: My route home from school is *predictable*.

Ask: What things do you do every day that are *predictable*?

DURING READING

15–20 Minutes   RI.5.1 RI.5.2 SL.5.1b SL.5.1d L.5.6 **CCSS**

Close Reading

 Pages 8–9

Genre **ACT** *What text features do you see on page 8?* (chapter title: Seasonal Weather; heading: Monsoons; photograph and sidebar with heading: The Southeast Asian Monsoon) *What information can you get from these features?* (title: the chapter is about seasons; heading: the section is about monsoons; photo and sidebar: give more information about monsoon rains)

Organization **ACT** *Read about monsoons on pages 8 and 9. What causes monsoons?* (As hot air rises, it pulls wet air from oceans over land.) *What happens as the result of a monsoon?* (heavy rains in Mexico and U.S.)

Main Idea and Key Details *What are the key details in the first paragraph on page 8?* (There are four seasons in the temperate zones and two seasons in the tropics.) *What do these details have in common?* (Seasons repeat each year.) *What is the main idea of this paragraph?* (Seasons have predictable patterns.)

Vocabulary Have students point to the word *prevent* in the last line on page 9. *What clues in the paragraph tell you what* prevent *means?* (Rain could help stop wildfires from starting.)

 Pages 10–11

Organization **ACT** *Read "Hurricanes and Tornadoes" on pages 10 and 11. How are hurricanes and tornadoes similar?* (fierce storms, dangerous winds, regular seasons) *How are they different?* (Hurricanes form over water, and winds blow up to 150 miles per hour. Tornadoes occur over land, and winds blow up to 320 miles an hour.)

Vocabulary Have students point to the word *dangerous* in the first paragraph on page 10. *What clues in the paragraph tell you what* dangerous *means?* (damage)

Stop and Check *Read the question in the Stop and Check box on page 10.* (They provide water for people, plants, and animals and help prevent wildfires.)

Genre **ACT** *Look at the map on page 11. How does it provide more information about the text?* (It shows the location of Tornado Alley and which states are affected.)

Pages 12–13

Organization **ACT** *Read "Katabatic Winds" on pages 12 and 13. How are katabatic winds in Antarctica similar to those in California?* (Cool heavy air collects over high land, then falls downhill.) *How are they different?* (Antarctica wind is cold and wet, Santa Ana wind is dry and hot.)

Main Idea and Key Details *What are the key details on page 13?* (The Santa Ana wind is a warm katabatic wind; forms when cool air comes from the desert, then falls down the mountains.) *What do these details have in common?* (Details are all features of the Santa Ana wind.) *What is the main idea of Chapter 3?* (The Santa Ana wind has many features.)

Pages 14–15

Genre **ACT** *Look at the diagram on page 14. What do the colors orange and dark blue stand for in the diagram?* (Orange means warmer, and dark blue means cooler.)

Stop and Check *Read the question in the Stop and Check box on page 15.* (They don't follow usual weather patterns and are harder to predict.)

Vocabulary Have students point to the word *switch* at the top of page 15. *How do the patterns* switch? (Dry areas have floods and wet areas are dry.)

Pages 16–17

Connection of Ideas **ACT** *Read the first three paragraphs of the conclusion. What weather patterns did the author explain in this selection?* (winds; prevailing winds; water cycle; seasonal patterns such as monsoons, hurricanes, and tornadoes; katabatic winds; El Niño)

AFTER READING

10–15 Minutes   RI.5.1   RI.5.2   RI.5.9   W.5.9b   L.5.4a   CCSS

Respond to Reading

Compare Texts Have students compare how "Weather Patterns" and "Rock Formations" show patterns in nature. Then say: *What patterns have you observed in nature?*

Summarize Have students turn to page 18 and summarize one section of the selection. (Answers should include key details from the section.)

Text Evidence

Have partners work to answer questions on page 18. Ask them to use their Main Idea and Key Details charts.

Main Idea and Details (Key Details: Moist, warm air moves in from ocean and heavy rain falls in Mexico. Monsoon moves north and brings rain to Arizona, New Mexico, and Texas. Main Idea: The North American monsoon season brings rain to Mexico and the U.S.)

Vocabulary (The caption tells about water in the air. *Moisture* must mean water.)

Write About Reading (*El Niño changes normal weather patterns* is the main idea. It causes weather patterns to switch. Dry areas can flood. Wet areas are dry. Winters can be colder than usual.)

Independent Reading

Encourage students to read the paired selection "Cloud Atlas" on pages 19–21. Have them summarize the selection and compare it to "Weather Patterns." Have them work with a partner to answer the "Make Connections" questions on page 21.

 Quick Check Can students find main ideas and key details? If not, review and reteach using the instruction on page 154 and assign the Unit 3 Week 3 digital mini-lesson.

Can students respond to the selection using text evidence? If not, provide sentence frames to help them organize their ideas.

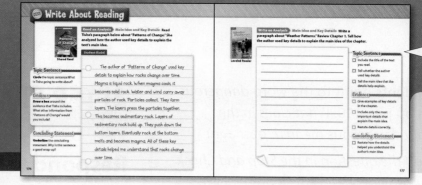

Objectives
- Review weekly vocabulary words
- Review main idea and key details
- Write an analysis about how an author uses key details

Materials
- Visual Vocabulary Cards: 93–100
- Interactive Worktext, pp. 176–177
- Assessment Book, pp. 34–35

☞ **Go** Digital
- Visual Vocabulary Cards
- Main Idea and Key Details Digital Mini-Lesson
- Interactive eWorktext

Scaffolding for **Wonders** Reading/Writing Workshop

REVIEW AND RETEACH

5–10 Minutes   RI.5.2   L.5.4a   L.5.6

Weekly Vocabulary

Display one **Visual Vocabulary Card** at a time and ask students to use the vocabulary word in a sentence. If students have difficulty, have them find the word in "Patterns of Change" and use the context clues to define it.

Comprehension: Main Idea/Details

I Do Display and read aloud: *Some storms can be dangerous. Heavy rain can cause floods. Lightning can strike trees. Wind can cause power lines to fall.* Underline the key details. Say: *These are the key details. I am going to look at what these key details have in common to figure out the main idea. All of these details tell dangerous effects of storms. I can tell that the main idea is: Storms can be dangerous.*

We Do Display: *Starting a rock collection is fun and easy. You can find lots of rocks in parks and streams. After washing them, you can use the Internet to help you identify the type of rock. There are many rock-collecting Web sites with photos of different rocks. Then you can label the rocks and display them for everyone to look at.* Ask: *Which sentences give key details?* (sentences 2–4) *What do these details have in common?* (They all tell how easy it is to start a rock collection.) *What is the main idea?* (Starting a rock collection is easy.)

You Do Display: *Dogs are great pets. Dogs are fun to play with. It is fun to pet them, too. They can do tricks. They are also loyal.* Have partners identify key details and look for what they have in common to figure out the main idea.

WRITE ABOUT READING

25–35 Minutes   W.5.2a   W.5.2d   W.5.4   W.5.5   W.5.9b

Read an Analysis

- Ask students to look back at "Patterns of Change" in the **Interactive Worktext**. Have volunteers review the key details they marked on page 171 that supported the idea that rocks change. Repeat with pages 172 and 173. *How did the key details help you understand the main ideas in the text?*

- Read aloud the directions on page 176. Read aloud the student model. *Tisha's writing is not a summary. She is writing an analysis of "Patterns of Change." It is a detailed description of how the author used key details explain the text's main idea.*

- Say: *When you write an analysis, you must include certain elements. Circle the topic sentence. What important information is included in that sentence?* (text's title, how the author used key details, the main idea of the text)

- *Another element of analysis is text evidence. The student supports the topic sentence with evidence from the text that shows how the author used key details to explain the main idea. Reread the model and draw a box around the text evidence.* (sentences 2 through 10) *Look back at your notes about "Patterns of Change." What other details could Tisha have included?* (Possible answer: the rock cycle repeats over and over)

- *The final element is the concluding statement.* Have students underline the concluding statement. *How is the concluding statement like the topic sentence?* (Both say that the author used key details. Both include the author's main idea.) *Which words wrap up all the details in the paragraph?* (All of these key details)

Write an Analysis
Analytical Writing

Guided Writing Read the writing prompt on page 177 together. Have students write about "Weather Patterns" or another text they read this week. Have them review their notes. *Use the checklist to help you figure out what information to include in each section.* If students have difficulty, guide them to ask "how" and "why" questions about the weather pattern explained in each paragraph.

Peer Conference Have students read their analysis to a partner. Listeners should identify the strongest text evidence that supports the topic sentence and discuss any sentences that are unclear.

Teacher Conference Check students' writing for complete sentences and text evidence that supports their topic. Review the concluding statement. Ask: *Does this sentence tie all of the elements together?* If necessary, have students revise the concluding statement by restating the topic sentence.

Level Up

▲ Apprentice Leveled Reader

▲ Approaching Leveled Reader

▲ Interactive Worktext

▲ Reading/Writing Workshop

IF students read the `Apprentice Level` Reader fluently and the **Interactive Worktext** Shared Read fluently and answer the Respond to Reading questions

THEN read together the `Approaching Level` Reader main selection and the **Reading/Writing Workshop** Shared Read from *Reading Wonders*. Have students take notes as they read, using self-stick notes. Then ask and answer questions about their notes.

Writing Rubric

	4	3	2	1
Topic Sentence	There is one clear, focused topic sentence.	Topic sentence is less focused, somewhat clear.	Topic is presented in short phrases.	There is no topic sentence.
Text Evidence	Topic is supported by two or more text details.	Evidence includes only one detail from the text.	Little to no evidence is cited from the text.	No text evidence is included.
Concluding Statement	Clearly restates the topic sentence; wraps up all the details.	Restatement is less focused; attempts to wrap up the details.	Vaguely restates the topic. Doesn't correlate well to text evidence.	There is no conclusion.
Writing Style	Writes in complete sentences. Uses correct spelling and grammar.	Uses complete sentences and phrases. Writing has spelling and grammar errors.	Few or no complete sentences. There are many spelling and grammar errors.	Does not write accurately or in complete sentences.

ASSESSMENT

Weekly Assessment

Have students complete the Weekly Assessment using **Assessment** book pages 34–35.

WEEK 3

▶ **Mid-Unit Assessment,** pages 88–95

▶ **Fluency Assessment,** pages 250–265

Unit 3 Mid-Unit Assessment

CCSS TESTED SKILLS

✔ COMPREHENSION	✔ VOCABULARY
• Theme RL.5.2	• Context Clues L.5.4a
• Theme RL.5.2	
• Main Idea and Key Details RI.5.2	

Using Assessment and Writing Scores

↺ RETEACH	IF ...	THEN ...
COMPREHENSION	Students answer 0–5 multiple-choice items correctly ...	... reteach tested skills using instruction on pages 364–371.
VOCABULARY	Students answer 0–2 multiple-choice items correctly ...	... reteach tested skills using instruction on page 364.
WRITING	Students score mostly 1–2 on weekly writing rubrics throughout the unit...	... reteach writing using instruction on pages 372–373.

Fluency Assessment

Conduct assessments individually using the differentiated fluency passages in Assessment. Students' expected fluency goal for this Unit is 117–137 WCPM with an accuracy rate of 95% or higher.

Weeks 4 and 5

Monitor students' progress on the following to inform how to adjust instruction for the remainder of the unit.

ADJUST INSTRUCTION	
ACCESS COMPLEX TEXT	If students need more support for accessing complex text, provide additional modeling of prompts in Lesson 2 of Week 4, pages 160–161, and Week 5, pages 170–171. After you model how to identify the text evidence, guide students to find text evidence in Lessons 3 and 4 in Week 4, pages 162–165, and Week 5, pages 172–175.
FLUENCY	For those students who need more support with Fluency, focus on the Fluency lessons in the Foundational Skills Kit.
WRITING	If students need more support incorporating text evidence in their writing, conduct the Write About Reading activities in Lessons 4 and 5 as group writing activities.
FOUNDATIONAL SKILLS	Review student's individualized progress in *PowerPAL for Reading* to determine which foundational skills to incorporate into your lessons for the remainder of the unit.

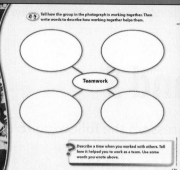

WEEK 4 LESSON 1

Objectives
- Develop oral language
- Build background about the benefits of people working as a group
- Understand and use weekly vocabulary
- Read expository text

Scaffolding for **Wonders** Reading/Writing Workshop

Materials
- Interactive Worktext, pp. 178–185
- Visual Vocabulary Cards: 101–108

☞ **Go** Digital
- Interactive eWorktext
- Visual Vocabulary Cards

WEEKLY CONCEPT

5–10 Minutes   SL.5.1b SL.5.1c CCSS

Talk About It

Essential Question Read aloud the Essential Question on page 178 of the **Interactive Worktext**: *What benefits come from people working as a group?* Explain that benefits are things that are helpful or useful. Say: *Sometimes it helps to work with others to do or make something.*

- Discuss the photograph on page 178. Say: *What do you see?* (a band) *How are the people in this photograph working together?* (they are playing music together)

  I Do Say: *One benefit about playing in a band is that you can learn how to get better at playing an instrument. Others can help you improve how you play or teach you new ways of doing things. I will write "learning from others" in the word web on page 179.*

  We Do Say: *Let's look at the photograph together and think about other benefits of playing in a band. How can you tell that these people are a group?* (Possible answers: They are wearing the same uniform. They all have instruments.) *What is a benefit of a band playing their instruments together? Think about how the instruments will sound when they play together.* (Possible answers: The music will be louder. The sounds will create music.) Guide students to add these words to the word web on page 179. Have them brainstorm other ways playing in a band has benefits and add words to the web.

  You Do Have partners describe a time when they worked with others. Ask: *What did you do? Who did you work with? What was helpful about working with others? What did you achieve?*

REVIEW VOCABULARY

10–15 Minutes   L.5.4a L.5.5c L.5.6 CCSS

Review Weekly Vocabulary Words

- Use the **Visual Vocabulary Cards** to review the weekly vocabulary.

- Read together the directions for the Vocabulary activity on page 180 of the **Interactive Worktext**. Then complete the activity.

1 **mimic** Have one partner *mimic* the sound of a farm animal and ask their partner: *What animal sound did I mimic?* Have the other partner guess the animal. (Possible answers: a cow mooing, a sheep baaing, a chicken clucking) Have partners switch roles.

2 **collaborate** Have students review the options and complete the following sentence frame: *People collaborate when they are _____ and _____.* (having a bake sale, playing in a band) Ask: *How are the activities you named alike?* (People work together to do them.)

3 **techniques** Have partners demonstrate their *technique*. (Students' actions will vary.) Ask: *Did you and your partner have the same* technique *or different* techniques? (Students' answers will vary.)

4 **function** Have students complete these sentence frames: *One object I see in this classroom is a _____. The* function *of a _____ is to _____.* (Possible answers: clock, tell time; stapler, hold papers together; pen, write)

5 **dedicated** Ask: *Have you ever* dedicated *your time to studying a school subject or playing a sport? Why did you* dedicate *your time?* (Possible answers: liked the subject, to get good grades; want to be an athlete, to improve, to compete) Have partners discuss why the girl might have *dedicated* her time to playing the piano. (Possible answers: She wanted to get better. She wanted to become a piano player.)

6 **artificial** Explain that an antonym is a word with the opposite meaning of another word. Have partners discuss the meaning of *artificial* and the meaning of each option. (real)

7 **obstacle** *Picture yourself walking on a path through the woods. Name something that might be an* obstacle. (Possible answers: stream, log, big rock) *Would you be able to continue on the path?* (no) *What would you have to do?* (I'd have to figure out a way around it.)

8 **flexible** Before drawing, have partners discuss athletes or types of sports they know about where players have to be *flexible*. Ask students to describe their drawings by using the sentence frame: *A _____ must be* flexible *because _____.*(Drawings may include a dancer, ice skater, gymnast, or wrestler.)

High-Utility Words

Explain that a possessive, such as *Tom's hat*, shows that the hat belongs to Tom. An *s'* at the end of a word shows that two or more people or things own something. Display and say examples: *girls' skirts, plants' leaves*. Have students turn to page 181 in the **Interactive Worktext**. Have partners circle possessives in the passage. (teams', flags', coaches', players', fans', teams') Write the sentence: *All of the _____ costumes were pretty.* Have students use a possessive to complete the sentence.

> **ELL** **ENGLISH LANGUAGE LEARNERS**
>
> Have students demonstrate plural possessives. Have students pick up their pencils. Write: *students' pencils*. Read the words together. Point out the *s'* in *students'.*

READ COMPLEX TEXT

15–20 Minutes   RI.5.1 RF.5.4c SL.5.1

Read: "Gulf Spill Superheroes"

- Have students turn to page 182 in the **Interactive Worktext** and read aloud the Essential Question. Explain that they will read about an oil spill in the Gulf of Mexico. Ask: *What is the title?* ("Gulf Spill Superheroes") *What does the photo on page 182 show?* (a group of people working together to lift something) *Use these clues. What do you think you will learn about in this selection?* (heroes who worked together to clean up after an oil spill)

- Read "Gulf Spill Superheroes" together. Note that the weekly vocabulary words are highlighted in yellow. Expand vocabulary words are highlighted in blue.

- Have students use the "My Notes" section on page 182 to write questions they have, words they don't understand, and details they want to remember. Model how to use the "My Notes" section. *On page 183 in the first paragraph, I don't know what an oil-drilling platform is. I will write* oil-drilling platform *with a question mark beside it in the "My Notes" section. I also don't understand where the broken pipeline was. I will write a question about that. When we reread the selection, I will ask my questions so I better understand what I am reading.*

> **ELL** **ENGLISH LANGUAGE LEARNERS**
>
> As you read together, have students highlight the parts of the text they have questions about. After reading, help them write their questions in the "My Notes" column.

 Quick Check Can students understand the weekly vocabulary in context? If not, review vocabulary using the **Visual Vocabulary Cards** before teaching Lesson 2

Teach and Model WORKTEXT

WEEK 4 LESSON 2

Objectives
- Read expository text
- Understand complex text through close reading
- Recognize and understand main idea and key details
- Respond to the selection using text evidence to support ideas

Scaffolding for **WONDERS** Reading/Writing Workshop

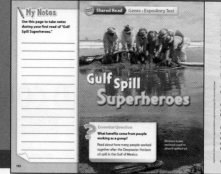

Materials
Interactive Worktext, pp. 182–187

Go Digital
- Interactive eWorktext
- Main Idea and Key Details Digital Mini-Lesson

REREAD COMPLEX TEXT

20–25 Minutes   RI.5.1   RI.5.2   RI.5.4   **CCSS**

Close Reading: "Gulf Spill Superheroes"

Reread "Gulf Spill Superheroes" with students. As you read together, discuss important passages in the text. Have students respond to text-dependent questions, including those in the **Interactive Worktext**.

Page 183

Prior Knowledge **A C T** Build background about oil and offshore drilling. *We use oil for fuel in our cars and for heating our homes. Oil also is used to make plastic. Oil is found deep below Earth's surface. A lot of oil is under the floor of the ocean. Oil rigs are equipment used to drill for oil in the ocean. A pipeline brings oil up from under the ocean floor.* Have students reread the first paragraph. *What happened to an oil-drilling rig?* (it exploded) *Where did this happen?* (in the Gulf of Mexico) *What happened to the pipe that carried the oil?* (it broke)

Expand Vocabulary Have students point to the word *disaster*. Read the definition aloud. *What clues in the first paragraph help you understand the meaning of* disaster? (exploded, massive fires raged, oil spewed from a broken pipeline) *What was damaged in the disaster? List two things.* (Possible answers: the oil-drilling rig, a pipeline)

Expand Vocabulary Have students reread "Helpers in the Water." Discuss the word *experts*. *What are some examples of experts?* (firefighters, U.S. Coast Guard, scientists, biologists, engineers) *Which type of expert worked to fix the broken pipeline?* (engineers)

Main Idea and Key Details Have students reread the fourth paragraph. Check that students have marked two important details. (Possible answers: Engineers

came up with different ways to fix the broken pipeline. They discussed techniques. Experts had to use robots. These devices had artificial arms and special tools to stop the spill. Many of the engineers' first efforts failed.) Discuss how these details fit together, or what they have in common. Then model identifying the main idea by putting the details together. *There are several key details in this paragraph about how the experts fixed the pipeline.* Reiterate them. *All these details show that engineers had to work hard to fix the pipeline. By figuring out what these details have in common, I figured out the main idea.* Work with students to identify key details in the last paragraph and use them to determine the main idea. (Key details: After nearly three months, workers fixed the damaged pipe. It would take many months to clean up the mess left behind. Main idea: Problems from the disaster took a long time to fix.)

Page 184

Expand Vocabulary Have students locate *tracked*. *What does* tracked *mean?* (watched closely) *What word in the first paragraph is a synonym for* tracked? (followed)

Connection of Ideas **A C T** Have students tell the details they marked about veterinarians in the third paragraph. (dedicated their efforts to helping animals, spent time capturing and treating animals, returned them to the wild) Ask: *What did naturalists and ecologists do?* (cleaned up the animals' habitats) *How were both groups alike? Complete the sentence frame: Both groups wanted to help _____.* (animals) *How were their jobs different?* (Veterinarians captured and treated the animals and returned them to the wild. Naturalists and ecologists cleaned the animals' habitats.)

High-Utility Words Have students identify a possessive in the third paragraph. (animals') *What belongs to them?* (habitats)

Main Idea and Key Details Have students reread the last paragraph. *I read that fishermen needed help. I read that "Government workers checked fishing areas." This important detail tells how people helped fishermen. Let's underline it. What other key details did you read in this paragraph?* (They told fishermen where it was safe to fish. Bankers and insurance companies helped fishermen find ways to make up for lose income.) Ask: *What do these details have in common?* (Each detail tells how a group of people helped fishermen.) *What is the main idea?* (Many different groups of people helped fishermen.)

Page 185

Main Idea and Key Details Have partners read the first paragraph. Ask: *What is the SWORD?* Have students point to text evidence. (Possible answers: Shallow-water Weathered Oil Recovery Device, a small type of boat) Check that students mark key details. (It had mesh bags that hung between two its two sides. The boat could mimic a pool skimmer. It picked up oil as it moved.) *What do the details have in common?* (They all tell how the SWORD cleaned up oil.) *What is the main idea?* (The SWORD cleaned up oil.)

Expand Vocabulary Have students locate *mission* in the last paragraph. Ask: *What clues help you understand the meaning of mission?* (efforts, jobs, goals and tasks)

Connection of Ideas Read this sentence in the last paragraph: "The success of such a huge mission depended on how well these heroes worked together." Ask: *What evidence in the first paragraph supports the author's opinion that the workers were heroes?* (Experts worked together to come up with new ways to clean up the oil in the water. They needed to trap floating globs of oil that could ruin beaches.) *What did these workers save?* (Possible answers: water; beaches)

RESPOND TO READING
10–20 Minutes   RI.5.1 W.5.9b SL.5.1d

Respond to "Gulf Spill Superheroes"

Have students summarize "Gulf Spill Superheroes" orally to demonstrate comprehension. Then have partners answer the questions on page 186 of the **Interactive Worktext** using the discussion starters. Tell them to use text evidence to support their answers. Have students write the page number(s) on which they found the text evidence for each question.

1. *How did people work together right after the explosion?* (Firefighters worked with the U.S. Coast Guard to put out the fire. Crews in boats and planes moved survivors from the rig. Text Evidence: p. 183)

2. *How did people work together to help animals after the spill?* (Veterinarians, naturalists, and ecologists worked together to help animals that had been harmed and return them to the wild. Text Evidence: p. 184)

3. *What groups of people worked together to help fishermen?* (Bankers, insurance companies, and government workers all helped fishermen. Text Evidence: p. 184)

After students discuss the questions on page 186, have them write a response to the question on page 187. Tell them to use their partner discussions and notes about "Gulf Spill Superheroes" to help them. Circulate and provide guidance.

Quick Check Do students understand vocabulary in context? If not, review and reteach using the instruction on page 166.

Can students use key details to determine main idea in the text? If not, review and reteach using the instruction on page 166 and assign the Unit 3 Week 4 digital mini-lesson.

Can students write a response to "Gulf Spill Superheroes"? If not, provide sentence frames to help them organize their ideas.

Objectives
- Understand and use new vocabulary words
- Read expository text
- Recognize and understand main idea and key details
- Understand complex text through close reading

Scaffolding for **Wonders** Approaching Leveled Reader

Materials
- "The Power of a Team" Apprentice Leveled Reader: pp. 2–8
- Graphic Organizer: Main Idea and Key Details

👉 **Go Digital**
- Apprentice Leveled Reader eBook
- Downloadable Graphic Organizer
- Main Idea and Key Details Digital Mini-Lesson

BEFORE READING

10–15 Minutes   SL.5.1c   SL.5.1d   L.5.4a   L.5.6   CCSS

Introduce "The Power of a Team"

- Read the Essential Question on the title page of "The Power of a Team" **Apprentice Leveled Reader**: *What benefits come from people working as a group? We will read about people working together to make discoveries.*

- Read the title of the main read. Have students look at the images throughout the selection. Ask: *Is this a fiction or a nonfiction selection?* (nonfiction) *What do you think it will be about?* (Possible answers: teams of scientists, robots, teams of doctors)

Expand Vocabulary

Display each word below. Say the words and have students repeat them. Then use the Define/Example/Ask routine to introduce each word.

1 analyzing (page 8)

Define: examining or studying carefully

Example: Scientists are *analyzing* the habits of honeybees.

Ask: How good are you at *analyzing* math problems?

2 results (page 3)

Define: the end product, out come

Example: The news showed the *results* of the storm.

Ask: What might be the *results* of studying for a test?

3 rove (page 4)

Define: travel or roam, wander

Example: The jeep will *rove* across the sand dunes.

Ask: Would you like to *rove* around a rain forest?

4 signals (page 7)

Define: messages or communications

Example: The football coach used hand *signals*.

Ask: What is the purpose of traffic *signals*?

5 substance (page 6)

Define: a material or matter

Example: Glue is a sticky *substance*.

Ask: Describe the *substance* your desk is made from.

DURING READING

20–30 Minutes   RI.5.1   RI.5.2   RI.5.3   RI.5.4   L.5.4.a   CCSS

Close Reading

🔍 **Pages 2–3**

Genre A C T *Read the sidebar at the bottom of page 3. What is the heading?* (A Team Effort) *What do you learn from this sidebar?* (Howard Florey was the first scientist to try working in a team. His team found better ways to treat infections and saved lives.)

Vocabulary *Find the word* infection *in the sidebar at the bottom of page 3. What clues help you understand the meaning of* infection? (treat, cure, illnesses) *How might an* infection *be treated?* (with penicillin) *What is an* infection? (illness, disease, sickness)

🔍 **Pages 4–5**

Vocabulary *Find the word* data *in the first paragraph on page 4. What does it mean? How do you know?* (information that is gathered and sent, such as information about rocks and soil) *What do you think the* data *the robots gather tells about Mars?* (what the rocks and soil are made of, what the land is like)

Main Idea and Key Details Ask: *What are key details in the first paragraph on page 4?* (A team of NASA scientists built and launched two robots. The robots travel across Mars and scan rocks and soil. They send data to Earth.) *What do these details have in common?* (They are about how scientists developed two robots to gather data on Mars.) *What is the main idea of the paragraph?* (Scientists sent two robots to explore Mars.) As students read the selection, have them record key details and main ideas for sections in their Main Idea and Key Details charts.

Organization (ACT) Have students read page 5. Point out the problem and solution structure. *What problem did the scientists face after* Spirit *landed on Mars?* (An air bag blocked the ramp *Spirit* needed to exit the lander.) *How did they solve the problem?* (A driver in the control room turned *Spirit* around and down a side ramp.)

Pages 6–7

Main Idea and Key Details *Read page 6. What are the key details in each paragraph?* (*Spirit*'s wheel burst and the team found ways to keep it going. *Spirit* got stuck in soil, the team used a model to find a way to free it. This led to the discovery of silica, which showed that Mars once had water.) *What do the details have in common?* (They tell about problems that *Spirit* had on Mars and what happened when the team solved its problems.) *What is the main idea of page 6?* (A team of scientists worked to solve *Spirit*'s problems and made a discovery.)

Connection of Ideas (ACT) *Read "A NASA Experience" on page 7. What are the key details?* (Thirteen teams of students and teachers worked with NASA scientists, helped during launches and landings of the rovers, woke up at 4:00 A.M. for meetings, and had jobs to do.) *How does "A NASA Experience" connect to the main ideas of Chapter 1?* (Students and teachers learned how teams of NASA scientists work together.)

Genre (ACT) Have students study the photos and read the captions on pages 6 and 7. Ask: *Where were the two photos taken? What do they show?* (The photo on page 6 was taken on Earth. It shows the model rover used to figure out how to get *Spirit* unstuck. The photo on page 7 was taken on Mars by *Opportunity*. It shows craters.)

Page 8

Connection of Ideas (ACT) *Read the two paragraphs on page 8. How is* Curiosity *similar to* Opportunity *and* Spirit? (It is a robot, roves Mars, gathers data about rocks and soil.) *What happened to* Opportunity *and* Spirit? (*Spirit* stopped sending signals. *Opportunity* is still roving on Mars.) *Why do you think NASA sent another robot to Mars?* (Scientists want to keep exploring Mars. *Curiosity* is a science lab. It has better tools and can find out even more.)

Vocabulary *Why do you think NASA named the third rover* Curiosity? (*Curiosity* means a desire to know about something. The rover was sent to Mars because we want to know about Mars.)

Genre (ACT) Have students study the photo and read the caption on page 8. *What additional information does the photo and caption provide?* (*Curiosity* uses a laser to vaporize rocks and then analyzes the rock dust.)

Stop and Check Read the question in the Stop and Check box on page 8. (They set up a sand trap to mimic *Spirit*'s problem and then used a model of *Spirit* to try out their ideas about how to free it.)

Have partners review their Main Idea and Key Details charts for pages 2–8 and discuss what they learned.

✓ *Quick Check* **Do students understand weekly vocabulary in context? If not, review and reteach using the instruction on page 166.**

Can students determine Main Idea and Key Details? If not, review and reteach using the instruction on page 166 and assign the Unit 3 Week 4 digital mini-lesson.

WEEK 4 LESSON 4

Objectives
- Understand and use new vocabulary
- Read expository text
- Recognize and understand main idea and key details
- Understand complex text through close reading
- Respond to the selection using text evidence to support ideas

Scaffolding for **Wonders** Approaching Leveled Reader

Materials
"The Power of a Team" Apprentice Leveled Reader: pp. 9–24
- Graphic Organizer: Main Idea and Key Details

Go Digital
- Apprentice Leveled Reader eBook
- Downloadable Graphic Organizer
- Main Idea and Key Details Digital Mini-Lesson

BEFORE READING

5–10 Minutes   SL.5.1c SL.5.1d L.4.a L.5.6 CCSS

Expand Vocabulary

Display each word below. Say the words and have students repeat them. Then use the Define/Example/Ask routine to introduce each word.

1 automatically (page 12)

Define: done without thought or attention

Example: Breathing is something that we do *automatically*.

Ask: What are some other things that you do *automatically*?

2 injury (page 14)

Define: damage or harm that is done

Example: I had a knee *injury* after falling off my bike.

Ask: What might cause an *injury* on the playground?

3 progress (page 17)

Define: improvement

Example: The coach saw some *progress* in the way the team played.

Ask: Where have you shown the most *progress* in school this year?

DURING READING

15–20 Minutes   RI.5.1 RI.5.2 SL.5.1b SL.5.1d L.5.6 CCSS

Close Reading

Page 9

Organization **ACT** Have students read page 9. *What problem did the two scientists at Bell Labs have?* (A hissing sound came through their antenna as they studied radio waves in space.) *What steps did the scientists take to solve the problem?* (pointed the antenna in other directions, cleaned bird droppings from the antenna) *Did their solutions work?* (No, the hissing sound was still there.)

Pages 10–11

Main Idea and Key Details Have students read page 11. *What are the key details of the text on page 11?* (Scientists at Bell Labs are looking for ways to communicate better. They are studying how the body works. A network and our nervous system work in a similar way.) *What do these details have in common?* (They tell about how the scientists are comparing the human body and communication networks.) *What is the main idea of page 11?* (Scientists at Bell Labs are studying how the human nervous system works to find ways to communicate better.) Have students record information on their Main Idea and Key Details charts as they continue reading the selection.

Pages 12–13

Vocabulary Have students find the word *jam* in the first paragraph on page 12. *What clue helps you understand the meaning of* jam *in this sentence?* (stop working)

STOP AND CHECK Read the question in the Stop and Check box on page 12. (The scientists at Bell Labs discovered cosmic microwave background radiation.)

Connection of Ideas Ⓐ Ⓒ Ⓣ Have students read page 13. *Read the sentences about Marc's injury in the second paragraph and the sidebar "Spinal Cord Injuries." How are they connected?* ("Spinal Cord Injuries" explains why Marc is paralyzed. His crushed spinal cord can't carry signals from his brain to his body.)

🔍 **Pages 14–15**
Main Idea and Key Details *What are the key details on page 15?* (Miami project scientists are trying to repair spinal tissue. They think injecting special cells into the damaged area might help. They tested their ideas on rats and plan to try it on humans.) *What is the main idea of the sidebar?* (Miami Project Scientists are developing a way to repair damaged spinal tissue.)

Genre Ⓐ Ⓒ Ⓣ Have students review the diagram on page 15. *How does the diagram help you understand the caption?* (It shows how by injecting Schwann cells, myelin is produced and surrounds the nerves.)

🔍 **Pages 16–17**
Main Idea and Key Details Have students read the sidebar "Robot Teams" on page 16. *What are the key details of the text in the sidebar?* (Dr. McClurkin wants to create groups of robots that work as a team. They might be able to explore on Mars. He got the idea from honeybees working as a team.) *What is the main idea of the sidebar?* (Dr. McClurkin wants to send teams of robots to Mars.)

STOP AND CHECK Have students read the question in the Stop and Check box on page 16. (Miami Project scientists discovered ways to prevent spinal cord damage, help patients recover, repair spinal tissue, and reduce patients' pain.)

Connection of Ideas Ⓐ Ⓒ Ⓣ How does the "Conclusion" on page 17 connect to the ideas in the "Introduction" on pages 2 and 3? (It took a team of scientists to discover evidence of the big bang theory. It took hundreds of scientists to put rovers on Mars. Through the efforts of teams of scientists, paralyzed people may be able to walk again.)

AFTER READING
10–15 Minutes   RI.5.1   RI.5.2   RI.5.9   W.5.9b   L.5.4a   Ⓒ Ⓒ Ⓢ Ⓢ

Respond to Reading
Compare Texts Have students compare how experts in "Gulf Spill Superheroes" and "The Power of a Team" worked together as a team to reach a goal. Then say: *Tell about a time when you were part of a successful team.*

Summarize Have students turn to page 18 and summarize the selection. (Include details from selection showing the benefits from working together as a team.)

🔍 **Text Evidence**
Have partners work to answer questions on page 18. Ask students to use their Main Idea and Key Details charts.

Main Idea and Key Details (Key Details: A team of scientists sent three rovers to Mars. *Spirit* and *Opportunity* helped make new discoveries. *Curiosity* has tools to discover more. Main Idea: Scientists work together to make important discoveries about Mars.)

Vocabulary (to get well again)

Write About Reading (Details: After a spinal cord injury, doctors cooled patients off and then warmed them up. This helped patients. Main Idea: Scientists worked together to help spinal cord patients recover.)

Independent Reading
Encourage students to read the paired selection "Hands on the Wheel" on pages 19–21. Have them summarize it and compare it to "The Power of a Team." Have partners answer the "Make Connections" questions on page 21.

✓ *Quick Check* Can students identify Main Idea and Key Details? If not, review and reteach using the instruction on page 166 and assign the Unit 3 Week 4 digital mini-lesson.

Can students respond to the selection using text evidence? If not, provide, sentence frames to help them organize their ideas.

WEEK 4 LESSON 5

Objectives
- Review weekly vocabulary words
- Review main idea and key details
- Write an analysis about how an author uses key details

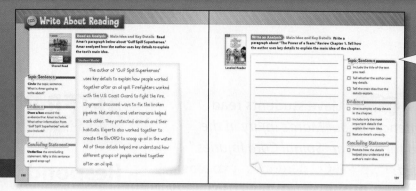

Scaffolding for **Wonders** Reading/Writing Workshop

Materials
- Visual Vocabulary Cards: 101–108
- Interactive Worktext, pp. 188–189
- Assessment Book, pp. 36–37

☞ **Go Digital**
- Visual Vocabulary Cards
- Main Idea and Key Details Digital Mini-Lesson
- Interactive eWorktext

REVIEW AND RETEACH

5–10 Minutes　　RI.5.2　L.5.4a　L.5.6 CCSS

Weekly Vocabulary

Display one **Visual Vocabulary Card** at a time and ask students to use the vocabulary word in a sentence. If students have difficulty, have them find the word in "Gulf Spill Superheroes" and use the context clues to define it.

Comprehension: Main Idea/Details

I Do Display and read: *The ostrich is the biggest of all birds. A male ostrich can weigh as much as 345 pounds. It can be as much as eight feet tall.* Say: *To figure out the main idea, I will look for the most important details. Underline the key details. I will figure out what these details have in common. Both tell how ostriches are very big. The main idea must be: Ostriches are very big birds.*

We Do Display: *We get many things from plants. Some foods we eat come from plants. Plants give us cloth for our clothing. They give us paper, too. The wood we use to build some homes comes from plants.* Ask: *What are the key details?* (Foods we eat come from plants. Plants give us cloth for our clothing. They give us paper. The wood we use to build homes comes from plants.) Ask: *What do these key details have in common?* (The details are about what plants give us.) *What is the main idea of this paragraph?* (We get many things from plants.)

You Do Display: *Art museums are great places to learn. You can see art up close at museums. There are tour guides who tell visitors about works of art. Many museums also have workshops that let visitors create their own art.* Have partners identify the key details and tell what they have in common. Then have students tell the main idea.

WRITE ABOUT READING

25–35 Minutes　　W.5.2a　W.5.2d　W.5.4　W.5.5　W.5.9b CCSS

Read an Analysis

- Ask students to look back at "Gulf Spill Superheroes" in the **Interactive Worktext**. Have volunteers review the main idea and key details in the selection.

- Read aloud the directions on page 188. Read aloud the student model. *Amar's writing is not a summary. It is an analysis, or detailed description, of how the author of "Gulf Spill Superheroes" uses details to explain a main idea. When you analyze, you ask yourself "how" and "why" questions to think about the way the text is developed and what readers learn from it.*

- Say: *An analysis includes certain parts. The first is the topic sentence.* Have students circle the topic sentence. *What information has Amar included in this sentence?* (the title of the text, author uses key details, the main idea of the text)

- Say: *Another part of analysis is text evidence. Amar supports the topic sentence with evidence from the text. He includes details from the text that show that different groups of people worked together after the oil spill.* Have students draw boxes around the text evidence. (sentences 2–5) Say: *Look back at the key details you marked in "Gulf Spill Superheroes." What other details could Amar have included?* (Possible answer: Weather experts tracked storms.)

- *The final part is a concluding statement. A good concluding statement restates the information in the topic sentence.* Have students underline the concluding statement. Ask: *How is this statement like the topic sentence?* (Both say the details show how different people worked together after an oil spill.) *Which words wrap up the details?* (All of these details)

Write an Analysis
Analytical Writing

Guided Writing Read the writing prompt on page 189 together. Have students write about "The Power of a Team" or another text they read this week. Say: *Use the checklist to help you figure out the information to include in each section.* Guide students to ask "how" and "why" questions, such as *How do details explain the main idea?*

Peer Conference Have students read their analysis to a partner. Listeners should identify the strongest text evidence that supports the topic sentence and discuss any sentences that are unclear.

Teacher Conference Check students' writing for complete sentences and text evidence that supports their topic. Review the concluding statement. Ask: *Does this sentence tie all of the elements together?* If necessary, have students revise the concluding statement by restating the topic sentence.

Level Up

▲ Approaching Leveled Reader

▲ Reading/Writing Workshop

▲ Apprentice Leveled Reader

▲ Interactive Worktext

IF students read the Apprentice Level Reader fluently and the **Interactive Worktext** Shared Read fluently and answer the Respond to Reading questions

THEN read together the Approaching Level Reader main selection and the **Reading/Writing Workshop** Shared Read from *Reading Wonders*. Have students take notes as they read, using self-stick notes. Then ask and answer questions about their notes.

Writing Rubric

	4	3	2	1
Topic Sentence	There is one clear, focused topic sentence.	Topic sentence is less focused, somewhat clear.	Topic is presented in short phrases.	There is no topic sentence.
Text Evidence	Topic is supported by two or more text details.	Evidence includes only one detail from the text.	Little to no evidence is cited from the text.	No text evidence is included.
Concluding Statement	Clearly restates the topic sentence; wraps up all the details.	Restatement is less focused; attempts to wrap up the details.	Vaguely restates the topic. Doesn't correlate well to text evidence.	There is no conclusion.
Writing Style	Writes in complete sentences. Uses correct spelling and grammar.	Uses complete sentences and phrases. Writing has spelling and grammar errors.	Few or no complete sentences. There are many spelling and grammar errors.	Does not write accurately or in complete sentences.

ASSESSMENT

Weekly Assessment

Have students complete the Weekly Assessment using **Assessment** book pages 36–37.

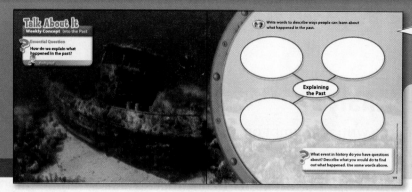

Objectives
- Develop oral language
- Build background about how we explain what happened in the past
- Understand and use weekly vocabulary
- Read persuasive text

Scaffolding for **Wonders** McGraw-Hill Reading Reading/Writing Workshop

Materials
- Interactive Worktext, pp. 190–197
- Visual Vocabulary Cards: 109–116

☞ **Go** Digital
- Interactive eWorktext
- Visual Vocabulary Cards

WEEKLY CONCEPT

5–10 Minutes   SL.5.1b   SL.5.1c   CCSS

Talk About It

Essential Question Read aloud the Essential Question on page 190 of the **Interactive Worktext**: *How do we explain what happened in the past?* Say: *Events that happened in the past can be a mystery. We can learn what happened by looking for clues in objects that remain.*

- Discuss the photograph on page 190. Ask: *What do you see in the photograph?* (a diver, a sunken boat) *Did the boat just sink or did it happen in the past? How can you tell?* (in the past; shells and algae cover the boat)

  I Do Say: *I wonder if the diver read about a boat that had sunk and went exploring to find it. I know some ways to learn what happened in the past is to "read" and "explore." I will write these words in the web on page 191.*

  We Do Say: *Let's look at the photo and look for other ways people can learn about the past. What is the diver in the photograph doing?* (looking at a sunken boat) *What questions do you think the diver has about the boat?* (Possible answers: What happened to the boat that caused it to sink? When did the boat sink?) *How can the diver answer these questions?* (look for clues around the boat; look for a hole) Then have them discuss other ways the diver can find out what happened to the boat and add words to the web on page 191.

  You Do Have partners name a historical event and share questions they have about it. Then have them answer the following questions, using some words they wrote in the web, as appropriate: *What would you do first to answer your questions? What would you look for? What would you study? Who would you talk to?*

REVIEW VOCABULARY

10–15 Minutes   L.5.4a   L.5.5c   L.5.6   CCSS

Review Weekly Vocabulary Words

- Use the **Visual Vocabulary Cards** to review the weekly vocabulary.

- Read together the directions for the Vocabulary activity on page 192 of the **Interactive Worktext**. Then complete the activity.

❶ preserved Ask: *Where would you put a photograph or a letter to preserve it?* (album, box) Have partners discuss which item has been *preserved* and explain their choice using the sentence frame: *A _____ is preserved because _____.* (photograph in an album; the album protects the photograph)

❷ archaeologist Have students discuss things that archaeologists look for. Then ask: *What do they do to look for these things?* Explain that there may be more than one correct answer. (dig to find remains of an ancient city; put together pieces of an ancient pot)

❸ historian Ask: *What does a historian know a lot about?* (history) Model asking questions about the topics: *Would a historian be the best person to ask about outer space?* (no) Have partners ask each other similar questions about the other topics.

❹ era Have students brainstorm important events and people from an early era in American history. Then have students complete the sentence frame: *_____ was president during an early era in American history.* (Answers will vary but should name a president from an earlier time in history.)

❺ remnants Ask students if they have ever been camping or been to a campground. Show pictures as necessary. Ask: *What have you seen or smelled at a campground that is a remnant of a campfire?* (<u>Possible answers</u>: ashes, burned wood, smoke)

6 **reconstruct** Point out the base word *construct* and discuss its meaning with students. (to build) Point out the prefix *re-* and remind students that it can mean "again." Help students put together word parts to figure out the meaning of *reconstruct*. (<u>Possible answers</u>: to build again; put something back together)

7 **fragments** Say: *A synonym is a word with the same or almost the same meaning as another word*. Have students discuss the meanings of the options to determine which words are synonyms for *fragments*. (bits, pieces)

8 **intact** After students complete their drawings, have them complete the sentence frame: *A vase that is intact is _____.* (<u>Possible answer</u>: whole, in one piece)

High-Utility Words

Explain that indefinite pronouns such as *someone, one, a few, all,* and *anything* do not name specific people, places, or things. Have students turn to page 193 of the **Interactive Worktext**. Have partners circle indefinite pronouns in the passage. (Many, Others, one, All, no one, Some, A few) Then have partners take turns looking around the room and using indefinite pronouns in sentences about the classroom. Provide an example: *Many students are sitting at their desks.*

ELL ENGLISH LANGUAGE LEARNERS

Help students identify indefinite pronouns in the passage. Then use indefinite pronouns in questions, for example: *Which one of the desks is yours? Are all of the students sitting at their desks? Are there many of us or a few?*

READ COMPLEX TEXT

15–20 Minutes   RI.5.1   RI.5.4c

Read: "What Was the Purpose of the Inca's Strange Strings?"

- Have students turn to page 194 in the **Interactive Worktext** and read aloud the Essential Question. Explain that they will read a text that gives two points of view about a mystery from the past. Ask: *What is the selection title?* ("What Was the Purpose of the Inca's Strange Strings?") *What do the photos show?* (ruins; object made of strings) *Why do you think the strings are a mystery?* (They were used long ago.)

- Read "What Was the Purpose of the Inca's Strange Strings?" together. Note that the weekly vocabulary words are highlighted in yellow. Expand Vocabulary words are in blue.

- Have students use the "My Notes" section on page 194 to write questions they have, words they don't understand, and details they want to remember. Model how to use the "My Notes" section. Say: *I can write notes about things I don't understand or words I don't know. On page 195, I see the word* quipu. *I'm not sure how to pronounce it, so I'll write the word with a question mark after it. As I continue to read, I am not sure what the knots stand for. I will write:* What do the knots in the quipu stand for? *in the "My Notes" section.*

ELL ENGLISH LANGUAGE LEARNERS

Have students highlight details or words that are unclear or confusing to them. After reading, help students write questions in "My Notes" about the text they highlighted.

 Quick Check Can students understand the weekly vocabulary in context? If not, review vocabulary using the **Visual Vocabulary Cards** before teaching Lesson 2.

WEEK 5 LESSON 2

Objectives
- Read persuasive text
- Understand complex text through close reading
- Recognize and understand author's point of view
- Respond to the selection using text evidence to support ideas

Scaffolding for Wonders McGraw-Hill Reading Reading/Writing Workshop

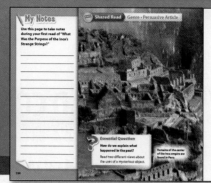

Materials
Interactive Worktext, pp. 194–199

☞ **Go** Digital
- Interactive eWorktext
- Author's Point of View Mini-Lesson

REREAD COMPLEX TEXT

20–25 Minutes   RI.5.3   RI.5.6   RI.5.8   L.5.4a   L.5.6   CCSS

Close Reading: "What Was the Purpose of the Inca's Strange Strings?"

Reread "What Was the Purpose of the Inca's Strange Strings?" with students. As you read together, discuss important passages in the text. Have students respond to text-dependent questions, including those in the **Interactive Worktext**.

🔍 Page 195

Sentence Structure Ⓐ Ⓒ Ⓣ Point to and read aloud the sentence "The Incas invented the quipu (pronounced KWEE-poo)." Have students underline the text in parentheses. Say: *Text in parentheses gives more detailed information about the text that came before. What word do you see just before the parentheses?* (quipu) *What does the text in parentheses tell you about this word?* (how to say it) Say the word with students.

Connection of Ideas Ⓐ Ⓒ Ⓣ Have students look at the photograph on page 195 and read the caption. Ask: *What does the photograph show?* (a quipu) Then point to the second paragraph. Say: *This paragraph describes what we see in the photograph.* Have students reread the second paragraph. Ask: *What are the strings tied to?* (a thick cord) *Which part of the quipu did Incas use to count?* (knots) Have students point to the strings, cord, and the knots in the photograph.

Expand Vocabulary Ask students to find the word *represent* in the second paragraph. Read the sentence. Ask: *What does represent mean?* (to stand for something) *What did the knots on the quipu represent?* Underline the text evidence. (numbers)

Author's Point of View Say: *The sentence below the heading "Strings of Numbers" states that the quipu was an ancient calculator. I think that must be the author's point of view. I'll look for details that support that position. The last paragraph says that experts believe knots on the strings represent numbers. That is one detail that supports the author's point of view. Let's draw a box around it. What other detail supports the author's point of view?* (Possible answers: They would tie knots on the quipu to record the numbers. They could add up the numbers.)

🔍 Page 196

Author's Point of View Read aloud the first two paragraphs. Say: *The author gives additional details to support his or her position that the quipu was a calculator. Which sentences tell about using the quipu to add numbers? Mark this text evidence.* (Incas could add up the knots to get the sum. They could also find the total of many strings or many quipus.)

Genre Ⓐ Ⓒ Ⓣ Say: *Authors often support their point of view by presenting information in diagrams or graphs.* Have students review the diagram and reread the caption. Ask: *What does the diagram explain?* (how to count with a quipu)

Expand Vocabulary Discuss the word *value*. Read the sentence. Then point to the diagram. Ask: *Do the knots at the top or the bottom of the string have a higher value?* (top) *What is the value of the first string? Circle this number.* (132) Point out that when the value of all the knots on this quipu are added together, the total is 552.

Organization Ⓐ Ⓒ Ⓣ Point to the title "Strings of Words." Say: *This selection includes two articles about the same topic. What did the author of the first article think quipu's were used to do?* (add up numbers) Read aloud the title of the second article and the sentence below it. *Does this author agree or disagree with the first author?*

(disagree) *How do you know?* (Possible answers: I see the word counterpoint. The sentence below the title says the quipu was an Incan language, not a calculator.)

Sentence Structure **ACT** Reread the first paragraph in "Strings of Words." Say: *Which sentence includes dashes?* (the second sentence) *What detailed information is given between the dashes?* (the exact years of the peak era of the empire)

Page 197

High-Utility Words Have students find the word *many* in the second paragraph. Read the sentence. Say: *The word* many *is an indefinite pronoun that does not name the specific researchers.* Ask partners to reread the paragraph and identify another indefinite pronoun. (Others)

Expand Vocabulary Read aloud the definition of *symbols.* Have students locate the word in the second paragraph. *Which nearby word or phrase is a clue to the meaning of* symbol? (a form of language)

Author's Point of View Review the author's point of view in "Strings of Words." Say: *An author uses facts to support a position. A fact can be proven. What did researchers find that support the author's position that quipus were used as a language?* (a three-knot pattern in the strings of seven different quipus) *What are some facts in the fourth paragraph that support the author's position?* (Handwritten pages were found in a box holding fragments of a quipu. The writing says the quipus were woven symbols. The text even includes a list of words matched to some symbols.)

Author's Point of View Have students compare information in the second paragraph on page 197 to information on page 195. Have partners identify details that are similar. (Quipus are made of strings that hang from a thick cord. On the strings are clusters of knots. Many researchers believe the clusters stand for numbers.) Have students use the sentence frame: *In "Strings of Words," the author thinks quipus are _____. In "Strings of Numbers," the author thinks quipus are _____.* (an Incan language; an ancient calculator)

RESPOND TO READING

10–20 Minutes   RI.5.1   RI.5.3   W.5.9b   SL.5.1d   CCSS

Respond to "What Was the Purpose of the Inca's Strange Strings?"

Have students summarize "Strings of Numbers" and "Strings of Words" orally to demonstrate comprehension. Then have partners answer the questions on page 198 of the **Interactive Worktext** using the discussion starters. Tell them to use text evidence to support their answers. Have students write the page number(s) on which they found the text evidence for each question.

1. *What do historians agree is true about the quipu?* (The quipu is ancient, used by the Incas, made of strings attached to a thick cord. Evidence: pp. 195, 196, 197)

2. *Why do some historians think the quipu was a calculator?* (Inca officials would count crops and people. They would tie knots in the quipu to record numbers. Incas could add up the knots to get the sum. Evidence: pp. 195, 196)

3. *Why do some historians think the quipu is a language?* (There is the same pattern in seven quipus. A 17th century text say quipus are woven symbols. The text matches some symbols to words. Evidence: p. 197)

After students discuss the questions on page 198, have them write a response to the question on page 199. Tell them to use their partner discussions and notes about the articles. Circulate and provide guidance.

 Quick Check **Do students understand vocabulary in context? If not, review and reteach using the instruction on page 176.**

Can students use key details to determine author's point of view? If not, review and reteach using the instruction on page 176 and assign the Unit 3 Week 5 digital mini-lesson.

Can students write a response to "What Was the Purpose of the Inca's Strange Strings?" If not, give sentence frames to help them organize their ideas.

WEEK 5 LESSON 3

Objectives
- Understand and use new vocabulary
- Read expository text
- Recognize and understand the author's point of view
- Understand complex text through close reading

Materials
- "The Anasazi" Below Approaching Leveled Reader: pp. 2–11
- Graphic Organizer: Author's Point of View

☞ **Go** Digital
- Apprentice Leveled Reader eBook
- Downloadable Graphic Organizer
- Author's Point of View Mini-Lesson

Scaffolding for **Wonders** McGraw-Hill Reading Approaching Leveled Reader

BEFORE READING

10–15 Minutes   SL.5.1c SL.5.1d L.5.4a L.5.6

Introduce "The Anasazi"

- Read the Essential Question on the title page of "The Anasazi" **Below Approaching Leveled Reader**: *How do we explain what happened in the past? We will read about the ancient civilization of the Anasazi.*

- Read the title of the main read. Have students look at the images. Read the chapter titles. *What will we learn about the Anasazi?* (who they were; how they lived, what happened to them)

Expand Vocabulary

Display each word below. Say the words and have students repeat them. Then use the Define/Example/Ask routine to introduce each word.

1 **abandoned** (page 3)

Define: left behind, given up completely

Example: The baby birds *abandoned* their nest when they could fly.

Ask: How can you tell when a house has been *abandoned?*

2 **dwellings** (page 7)

Define: homes; places where people live

Example: Many city *dwellings* are apartments.

Ask: In what kind of *dwelling* would you like to live?

3 **identify** (page 9)

Define: recognize, figure out

Example: My brother can *identify* any type of car.

Ask: Can you *identify* which knapsack is yours?

4 **original** (page 8)

Define: first version of something; complete object

Example: A stump is all that is left of the *original* tree.

Ask: What could you do to restore a broken cup to its *original* condition?

5 **socialized** (page 10)

Define: took part in activities with family and friends

Example: I *socialized* with my cousins at dinner.

Ask: What do you do when you *socialize* with friends?

DURING READING

20–30 Minutes   RI.5.1 RI.5.8 RI.6.6 SL.5.1b L.5.6

Close Reading

🔍 **Pages 2–3**

Vocabulary Help students to figure out challenging domain-specific words throughout the selection by using context clues, root words, the glossary, and other clues. For example, have students locate *ceremonies* on page 3. Explain that *ceremonies* are important social or religious events. Ask: *Where did the Anasazi hold their ceremonies?* (in large buildings called *kivas*)

Sentence Structure Ⓐ Ⓒ Ⓣ Read pages 2–3. Have students find the exclamation point in the first paragraph on page 3. Say: *Sentences that end with an exclamation point show surprise or strong feeling. This sentence says that the kiva roof weighed 95 tons. A ton is 2,000 pounds. Why do you think the author ends the sentence with an exclamation point?* (It's surprising the kiva had such a heavy roof.)

Author's Point of View Have students review the first paragraph on page 3. Ask: *How does the author describe the building skills of the Anasazi?* (They were amazing builders.) Discuss the details about the amazing skills of the Anasazi. Ask: *In paragraph 3, how does the author describe the farming methods of the Anasazi?* (advanced) *What point of view do you think the author will present in this selection?* (The Anasazi had an important/advanced/rich culture.) As students read, have them record information in their Author's Point of View charts.

Pages 4–5

Genre **A C T** Read pages 4–5. Say: *Expository texts often include maps and sidebars that support an author's point of view.* Ask: *What does the map on page 4 show?* (where the Anasazi lived) *What additional information does the sidebar on page 5 give you?* (how archaeologists use different ways to find out how a culture developed)

Vocabulary Have students find the word *artifacts* in the sidebar. Ask: *How are artifacts at a site layered?* (newer at the top; older farther down) *What might the artifacts include?* (things people once used such as pots or tools)

Pages 6–7

Sentence Structure **A C T** Read pages 6–7. Say: *In the first paragraph on page 7, I see a comma after the phrase* Around 750 to 900 C.E. *The commas help me understand where to pause when reading.* Ask: *What words are set off by commas in the next part of the sentence?* (*stone, mud,* and *brick*) *What do these words describe?* (different building materials the Anasazi used)

Author's Point of View Say: *On page 3, the author states that the Anasazi were skilled builders. Let's figure out how the author supports this point of view on pages 5 to 7. Where did early Anasazi people live?* (in caves) *How did Anasazi homes change over time?* (became larger, lasted longer; towns built near water; cliff dwellings like apartment blocks)

STOP AND CHECK Read the question in the Stop and Check box on page 7. (Archaeologists have found baskets, buildings, and evidence of dams and canals.)

Pages 8–9

Sentence Structure **A C T** Read pages 8–9. Say: *I notice that the author asks the question* Why? *on page 9. What does the author wonder about?* (why the Anasazi made pots with round bottoms) *Which sentence answers the question?* (next sentence: They did not have tables.)

Vocabulary Ask students to find the word *reservoir* in the sidebar. Have them complete the sentence frame: *A reservoir is made to collect and hold* _____. (water)

Pages 10–11

Author's Point of View Read pages 10–11. Say: *The author tells how archaeologists gather information and what their beliefs are about the Anasazi. How do you think the author feels about archaeologists?* Have partners discuss the author's viewpoint. (Archaeologists are skilled experts who base ideas on careful study.)

Genre **A C T** Ask: *What text features on these pages support the information in the text?* (photo, caption, diagram) *How does the diagram help you understand the information about Casa Rinconada Kiva?* (It shows how the structure was organized.)

Sentence Structure **A C T** Ask: *Which sentence on page 11 includes parentheses?* (last sentence in first paragraph) *What does the text within the parentheses tell you?* (how many kilometers are in 60 miles)

STOP AND CHECK Read the question in the Stop and Check box on page 11. (They use artifacts and designs of homes to figure out how people worked and socialized.)

Have partners review their Author's Point of View charts for pages 2–11 and discuss what they learned.

 Quick Check Do students understand weekly vocabulary in context? If not, review and reteach using the instruction on page 176.

Can students identify author's point of view? If not, review and reteach using the instruction on page 176 and assign the Unit 3 Week 5 digital mini-lesson.

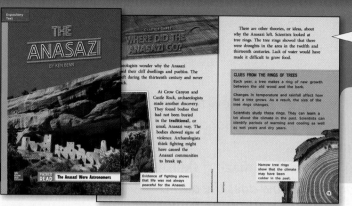

Objectives
- Understand and use new vocabulary
- Read expository text
- Recognize and understand the author's point of view
- Understand complex text through close reading
- Respond to the selection using text evidence to support ideas

Materials
"The Anasazi" Apprentice Leveled Reader: pp. 12–24
- Graphic Organizer: Author's Point of View

☞ **Go** Digital
- Apprentice Leveled Reader eBook
- Downloadable Graphic Organizer
- Author's Point of View Mini-Lesson

Scaffolding for **Wonders** Approaching Leveled Reader

BEFORE READING

5–10 Minutes   SL.5.1c SL.5.1d L.5.4a L.5.6 **CCSS**

Expand Vocabulary

Display each word below. Say the words and have students repeat them. Then use the Define/Example/Ask routine to introduce each word.

1 **descendants** (page 15)

Define: offspring of a certain family or group

Example: Many pioneer *descendents* live in our town.

Ask: Where do you think your *descendants* will live?

2 **merged** (page 14)

Define: combined to form one thing

Example: Three streams *merged* to form a river.

Ask: What happens when two roads *merge*?

3 **traditional** (page 12)

Define: usual; according to customs or beliefs

Example: Turkey is a *traditional* food at Thanksgiving.

Ask: What are some *traditional* ways to celebrate the Fourth of July?

DURING READING

15–20 Minutes   RI.5.1   RI.5.8   RI.6.6   SL.5.1b   L.5.6 **CCSS**

Close Reading

 Pages 12–13

Cause and Effect Read pages 12–13. Say: *The title of this chapter tells me I will learn some reasons the Anasazi left their dwellings and pueblos. One idea is that fighting caused their communities to break up. What is another possible cause?* (Lack of water made it hard to grow food.)

Vocabulary Read aloud the first sentence on page 13. Ask: *What word in the sentence helps you to understand the meaning of* theories? (ideas)

Vocabulary Ask students to locate the word *droughts* on page 13. Ask: *What showed archaeologists that there were droughts in the area where the Anasazi lived?* (tree rings) Have students complete the sentence frame: *Droughts occur when there is a lack of* _____. (water)

Connection of Ideas **A C T** Ask: *What information does the sidebar give?* (how the size of tree rings changes and what scientists can learn from tree rings) Have students turn to a partner and discuss why the author included this sidebar in Chapter Three. (The chapter gives reasons why the Anasazi left their homes. Scientists used tree rings to figure out that lack of water might have been one reason.)

 Pages 14–15

Sentence Structure **A C T** Read pages 14–15. Say: *The author uses a question and answer format on page 14. First the author asks where the Anasazi went. Then the author gives the answer: Evidence shows the Anasazi migrated south. What other question can you find on page 14?* (But what about the other Anasazi people?) Have students paraphrase what they read to answer the question. (Modern Pueblo people believe the Anasazi merged with other cultures.)

Author's Point of View Say: *On page 15, the author describes the descendants of the Anasazi. What words in the second and third sentences help you identify the author's point of view about the Anaszi?* (The modern people, like their ancestors, farm "skillfully," make "beautiful" baskets, and "lovely" pottery. These words show the author thinks highly of the Anasazi and their accomplishments.)

STOP AND CHECK Read the question in the Stop and Check box on page 15. (The Anasazi might have left because of violence or drought.)

Pages 16–17

Main Idea and Key Details Read pages 16–17. Say: *The author states that archaeologists have studied the Anasazi for nearly 200 years. What important facts have archaeologists learned about the Anasazi?* Have students turn to a partner and identify four key details. (Farming was important to their lives. Their building skills improved and they worked together to build large structures. They made beautiful baskets and pottery. They left the area in the thirteenth century.)

Sentence Structure ⒶⒸⓉ Say: *The first sentence in the last paragraph begins with the phrase "As a result." I'll have to reread the paragraph before this to figure out the sentence.* Have students complete the sentence frame: *As a result of _____, many people have concluded that the Anasazi did not vanish.* (the work of archaeologists)

Vocabulary Point out, at the top of page 17, the phrase *left the area.* Then have students find the word *vanish* in the last paragraph. Ask: *What is another way to say vanish?* (left the area, disappeared)

Author's Point of View Ask: Have students read the last paragraph on page 17. Ask: *What is the author's point of view about modern Pueblo people?* (The author believes that modern Pueblo people are proud to have the Anasazi as their ancestors.) *Do you think the author agrees with this point of view about the Anasazi? How can you tell?* (The author would agree. He has given a lot of evidence about how the Anasazi were skilled farmers, builders, and craftsmen.)

AFTER READING
10–15 Minutes   RI.5.1   RI.5.2   RI.5.9   W.5.9b   L.5.4a   CCSS

Respond to Reading

Compare Texts Have students compare the ancient cultures described in "What Was the Purpose of the Inca's Strange Strings?" and "The Anasazi." Ask: *Which culture is more interesting to you? Tell why.*

Summarize Have students turn to page 18 and summarize the selection. (Include details about who the Anasazi were, how they lived, why they left their homes.)

Text Evidence

Have partners work together to answer questions on page 18, using their Author's Point of View charts.

Author's Point of View (The author feels the ancient Anasazi civilization was rich, productive, and important.)

Vocabulary (*sophisticated:* highly developed, advanced. Clue: Houses were larger and lasted longer.)

Write About Reading (The author thinks that the Anasazi had a rich culture. They built "amazing" structures and "beautiful" structures. The author thinks that the modern Pueblo people are proud of their ancestors, and carry on their traditions.)

Independent Reading

Encourage students to read the paired selection "The Anasazi Were Astronomers" on pages 19–21. Have them summarize the selection and compare it to "The Anasazi." Have them work with a partner to answer the "Make Connections" questions on page 21.

 Quick Check Can students identify author's point of view? If not, review and teach using the instruction on page 176 and assign the Unit 3 Week 5 digital mini lesson.

Can students respond to the selection using text evidence? If not, provide sentence frames to help them organize their ideas.

Objectives
- Review weekly vocabulary words
- Review the author's point of view
- Write an analysis of how well an author supports a position

Materials
- Visual Vocabulary Cards: 109–116
- Interactive Worktext, pp. 200–201
- Assessment Book, pp. 38–39

☞ **Go Digital**
- Visual Vocabulary Cards
- Author's Point of View Mini-Lesson
- Interactive eWorktext

Scaffolding for **WONDERS** McGraw-Hill Reading Reading/Writing Workshop

---

REVIEW AND RETEACH

5–10 Minutes   RI.5.1 RI.6.6 L.5.4a L.5.6 CCSS

Weekly Vocabulary

Display one **Visual Vocabulary Card** at a time and ask students to use the vocabulary word in a sentence. If students have difficulty, have them find the word in "What Was the Purpose of the Inca's Strange Strings?" and use the context clues to define it.

Comprehension: Author's Point of View

I Do Write and say: *Historians have exciting jobs. They figure out mysteries. They search for important clues about our past.* Tell students that you will look for details that give clues to the author's point of view. Say: *The author uses* exciting *to describe studying history. The author also says historians look for important clues. I think the author's point of view is that historians do interesting and important work.*

We Do Write and say: *Music is a great subject to study. Some experts think that playing music improves kids' thinking skills. It also helps kids have better rhythm.* Ask: *What word does the author use to describe music?* (great) *What details does the author give about playing music?* (experts think that playing music improves kids' thinking skills; helps kids have better rhythm) *What is the author's point of view?* (Music is good for kids.)

You Do Display: *Studying the past is important. Studying the past helps us know what people were like. It helps us better understand changes in the environment.* Have partners tell opinion words, details that support the author's position, and the author's point of view.

WRITE ABOUT READING

25–35 Minutes   W.5.1a W.5.1b W.5.1d W.5.9b CCSS

Read an Analysis

- Ask students to look back at "What Was the Purpose of the Inca's Strange String?" in the **Interactive Worktext**. Have volunteers review their notes. *How well did the authors of the articles support their points of view?*

- Read aloud the directions on page 200. Read aloud the student model. *Alexa's writing is not a summary. Alexa writes her opinion about how well the author of the article "Strings of Words" supports his or her position.*

- *An analysis always includes certain elements. Circle the topic sentence. What important information is included in this sentence?* (text's title; Alexa's opinion that the author did a good job; the author's position on the topic)

- *Another element of an analysis is* text evidence. *Alexa supports the topic sentence with facts and details from the text. Reread the model and draw a box around the text evidence.* (sentences 2–5) *Look back at your notes about "Strings of Words." What other information might be included as text evidence in the model?* (Possible answer: The 17th century text was found in a box holding fragments of a quipu.)

- *The final element is the* concluding statement. *Underline the concluding statement. How is the concluding statement like the topic sentence?* (Both include the words "I think" and both tell the author's position that quipus were used as a language.) *Which words does Alexa use to wrap up the text evidence?* ("all of these details")

 Write an Analysis

Analytical Writing

Guided Writing Read the writing prompt on page 201 together. Have students write about "The Anasazi" or another nonfiction text they read this week. Have them review their notes. *Use the checklist to help you figure out the right information to include in each section.* Guide students to ask "how" and "why" questions to analyze text evidence, such as *Why are these details important?*

Peer Conference Have students read their analysis to a partner. Listeners should identify the strongest text evidence that supports the topic sentence and discuss any sentences that are unclear.

Teacher Conference Check students' writing for complete sentences and text evidence that supports their topic. Review the concluding statement. *Does this sentence tie all of the elements together?* If necessary, have students revise the concluding statement by restating the topic sentence.

Level Up

▲ Approaching Leveled Reader

▲ Reading/Writing Workshop

▲ Apprentice Leveled Reader

▲ Interactive Worktext

IF students read the **Apprentice Level** Reader fluently and the **Interactive Worktext** Shared Read fluently and answer the Respond to Reading questions

THEN read together the **Approaching Level** Reader main selection and the **Reading/Writing Workshop** Shared Read from *Reading Wonders*. Have students take notes as they read, using self-stick notes. Then ask and answer questions about their notes.

Writing Rubric

	4	3	2	1
Topic Sentence	Topic sentence presents a clear opinion.	Topic sentence presents an opinion, somewhat clearly.	Topic is presented in short phrases; opinion is unclear.	There is no topic sentence; no opinion is presented.
Text Evidence	Opinion is supported by two or more text details.	Opinion is only supported by one detail from the text.	Little to no evidence from the text supports opinion.	No text evidence is included; does not support opinion.
Concluding Statement	Clearly restates an opinion; wraps up all the details.	Restatement is less focused; attempts to wrap up the details.	Vaguely restates opinion. Doesn't correlate well to text evidence.	There is no conclusion.
Writing Style	Writes in complete sentences. Uses correct spelling and grammar.	Uses some complete sentences. Writing has spelling and grammar errors.	Few or no complete sentences. There are many spelling and grammar errors.	Does not write accurately or in complete sentences.

ASSESSMENT

Weekly Assessment

Have students complete the Weekly Assessment using **Assessment** book pages 38–39.

ASSESS and Differentiate

▶ **Unit Assessment,**
pages 140–148

▶ **Fluency Assessment,**
pages 250–265

▶ **Exit Test,**
pages 196–204

Unit 3 Assessment

CCSS TESTED SKILLS

✔ COMPREHENSION	✔ VOCABULARY
• Theme **RL.5.2** • Theme **RL.5.2** • Main Idea and Key Details **RI.5.2** • Main Idea and Key Details **RI.5.2** • Author's Point of View **RI.5.8, RI.6.6**	• Context Clues **L.5.4a**

Using Assessment and Writing Scores

RETEACH

	IF ...	THEN ...
COMPREHENSION	Students answer 0–7 multiple-choice items correctly ...	... reteach tested skills using instruction on pages 364–371.
VOCABULARY	Students answer 0–3 multiple-choice items correctly ...	... reteach tested skills using instruction on page 364.
WRITING	Students score mostly 1–2 on weekly Write About Reading rubrics throughout the unit...	... reteach writing using instruction on pages 372–373.

LEVEL UP

	IF ...	THEN ...
COMPREHENSION	Students answer 8–10 multiple-choice items correctly ...	... have students read the *Weather Patterns* Approaching Leveled Reader. Use the Level Up lesson on page 180.
WRITING	Students score mostly 3–4 on weekly Write About Reading rubrics throughout the unit...	... use the Level Up Write About Reading lesson on page 181 to have students compare two selections from the unit.

Fluency Assessment

Conduct assessments individually using the differentiated fluency passages in **Assessment**. Students' expected fluency goal for this Unit is 117–137 WCPM with an accuracy rate of 95% or higher.

Exit Test

If a student answers 13–15 multiple choice items correctly on the Unit Assessment, administer the Unit 3 Exit Test at the end of Week 6.

Time to Exit WonderWorks

Exit Test

If...
Students answer 13–15 multiple choice items correctly...

Fluency Assessment

If...
Students achieve their Fluency Assessment goal for the unit...

Level Up Lessons

If...
Students are successful applying close reading skills with the Approaching Leveled Reader in Week 6...

If...
Students score mostly 4–5 on the Level Up Write About Reading assignment...

Foundational Skills Kit

If...
Students have mastered the Unit 3 benchmark skills in the Foundational Skills Kit and *PowerPAL for Reading* adaptive learning system...

Then...
... consider exiting the student from *Reading WonderWorks* materials into the Approaching Level of *Reading Wonders*.

Approaching Leveled Reader

Apprentice Leveled Reader

Write About Reading

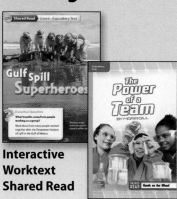

Interactive Worktext Shared Read

Apprentice Leveled Reader

Read Approaching Leveled Reader

RI.5.10

Weather Patterns

Before Reading

Preview Discuss what students remember about weather patterns and seasonal weather. Tell them that they will be reading a more challenging version of *Weather Patterns*.

Vocabulary Use routines in the **Visual Vocabulary Cards** to review the Weekly Vocabulary words. Use pages 150 and 152 to review the Expand Vocabulary words.

A C T During Reading

▶ **Vocabulary** Review the following weather-related words that are new to this level: *annually* (page 3), *expands* (page 4), *agriculture* (page 8), *locations* (page 10), and *plateau* (page 12). Point out that the word *drives* is used to mean "causes" on page 2 in paragraph 3.

▶ **Connection of Ideas** Students may need help connecting the captions with the information in the main text. Point out that captions usually provide additional, supporting information. See pages 3, 8, and 9. With students, summarize the information on each page. Then read the captions and discuss how they are connected.

▶ **Sentence Structure** Students may need help understanding the use of hyphens. Read aloud the following sentence on page 10: *These fierce storms can damage man-made structures.* Point out that the hyphen is connecting two words before a noun, and they now act as an adjective. Ask: *What kind of structures can be damaged?* (ones made by man, man-made ones) Then say: *Turn to page 11. Look at the first sentence under Tornadoes.* Read it aloud and ask: *What does a tornado cloud look like?* (twisting, funnel-shaped; shaped like a funnel)

After Reading

Ask students to complete the Respond to Reading questions on page 18 after they have finished reading. Provide additional support as needed to help students use the weekly vocabulary strategy to answer question 3.

Write About Reading

W.5.2   W.5.9b

Read an Analysis

- Distribute the Unit 3 Downloadable Model and Practice that compares two texts, the **Interactive Worktext** Shared Read "What Was the Purpose of the Inca's Strange Strings?" and the **Apprentice Leveled Reader** "The Anasazi." Read the paragraph aloud.

- Point out the signal word *both* in the topic sentence, which tells readers how the two texts are alike. Have students circle and reread the topic sentence. Ask: *What other information does Steve include in his topic sentence?* (titles of both texts; how they are alike)

- Have students mark text evidence. Ask: *What details does Steve include from "What Was the Purpose of the Inca's Strange Strings?" to show it is different from "The Anasazi"?* (sentences 2–4) *What details does Steve include from "The Anasazi" to show it is different from "What Was the Purpose of the Inca's Strange Strings?"?* (sentences 5–8) *Why is the concluding sentence a good wrap up?* (It restates how they are alike and different.)

Write an Analysis
Analytical Writing

Guided Practice Display this prompt: *Write a paragraph that compares how people worked together in "Gulf Spill Superheroes" and "The Power of a Team."*

- Alternatively, let students select two texts to compare.

- Use the Unit 3 Downloadable Model and Practice to guide students' writing.

- Tell students to include details from each text that shows how the people's work described in each text are alike and different.

- For the concluding statement, remind students to restate the topic sentence and wrap up the details.

Teacher Conference Check students' writing for complete sentences. Did they begin with a topic sentence? Did they cite text evidence? Did they restate the topic sentence in the last sentence?

Writing Rubric

	4	3	2	1
Topic Sentence	There is one clear, focused topic sentence.	Topic sentence is less focused, somewhat clear.	Topic is presented in short phrases.	There is no topic sentence.
Text Evidence	Topic is supported by two or more text details.	Evidence includes only one detail from the text.	Little to no evidence is cited from the text.	No text evidence is included.
Concluding Statement	Clearly restates the topic sentence; wraps up all the details.	Restatement is less focused, attempts to wrap up the details.	Vaguely restates the topic. Doesn't correlate well to text evidence.	There is no conclusion.
Writing Style	Writes in complete sentences. Uses correct spelling and grammar.	Uses complete sentences and phrases. Writing has spelling and grammar errors.	Has few or no complete sentences. There are many spelling and grammar errors.	Does not write accurately or in complete sentences.

UNIT 4 PLANNER
IT'S UP TO YOU

Week 1 Sharing Stories	Week 2 Discoveries	Week 3 Take Action

Week 1 — Sharing Stories

ESSENTIAL QUESTION
What kinds of stories do we tell? Why do we tell them?

Build Background

CCSS Vocabulary
L.5.4a *commenced, deeds, exaggeration, heroic, impress, posed, sauntered, wring*

Access Complex Text
Genre

CCSS Comprehension
RL.5.6 Skill: Point of View
Respond to Reading

CCSS Write About Reading *Analytical Writing*
W.5.9a Inform/Explain: Genre

Week 2 — Discoveries

ESSENTIAL QUESTION
What can you discover when you give things a second look?

Build Background

CCSS Vocabulary
L.5.4a *astounded, concealed, inquisitive, interpret, perplexed, precise, reconsider, suspicious*

Access Complex Text
Organization

CCSS Comprehension
RL.5.6 Skill: Point of View
Respond to Reading

CCSS Write About Reading *Analytical Writing*
W.5.9a Opinion: Point of View

Week 3 — Take Action

ESSENTIAL QUESTION
What can people do to bring about a positive change?

Build Background

CCSS Vocabulary
L.5.4a *anticipation, defy, entitled, neutral, outspoken, reserved, sought, unequal*

Access Complex Text
Sentence Structure

CCSS Comprehension
RI.5.8
RI.6.6 Skill: Author's Point of View
Respond to Reading

CCSS Write About Reading *Analytical Writing*
W.5.9b Inform/Explain: Author's Point of View

ASSESSMENT

Week 1
✓ **Quick Check**
Vocabulary, Comprehension

✓ **Weekly Assessment**
Assessment Book, pp. 40–41

Week 2
✓ **Quick Check**
Vocabulary, Comprehension

✓ **Weekly Assessment**
Assessment Book, pp. 42–43

Week 3
✓ **Quick Check**
Vocabulary, Comprehension

✓ **Weekly Assessment**
Assessment Book, pp. 44–45

✓ **MID-UNIT ASSESSMENT**
Assessment Book, pp. 96–103

✓ **Fluency Assessment**
Assessment Book, pp. 250–265

Use the Foundational Skills Kit for explicit instruction of phonics, structural analysis, fluency, and word recognition. Includes *PowerPAL for Reading* adaptive learning system.

Week 4
Consider Our Resources

ESSENTIAL QUESTION
Why are natural resources valuable?

Build Background

CCSS **Vocabulary**
L.5.4a absorb, affect, circulates, conserve, cycle, glaciers, necessity, seeps

Access Complex Text **A C T**
Organization

CCSS **Comprehension**
RI.5.8
RI.6.6 Skill: Author's Point of View
Respond to Reading

CCSS **Write About Reading** 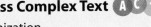 *Analytical Writing*
W.5.9b Inform/Explain: Author's Point of View

Week 5
Express Yourself

ESSENTIAL QUESTION
How do you express something that is important to you?

Build Background

CCSS **Vocabulary**
L.5.4a barren, expression, meaningful, plumes

Poetry Terms
alliteration, lyric, meter, stanza

Access Complex Text **A C T**
Connection of Ideas

CCSS **Comprehension**
RL.5.2 Skill: Theme
Respond to Reading

CCSS **Write About Reading** *Analytical Writing*
W.5.9a Inform/Explain: Genre

Week 6
ASSESS

RETEACH ↓   ↓ LEVEL UP

Reteach
Comprehension Skills

Vocabulary

Write About Reading

Level Up
Read Approaching Leveled Reader

Write About Reading:
Compare Texts

A S S E S S M E N T

 **Quick Check**
Vocabulary, Comprehension

✓ **Weekly Assessment**
Assessment Book, pp. 46–47

✓ **Quick Check**
Vocabulary, Comprehension

✓ **Weekly Assessment**
Assessment Book, pp. 48–49

✓ **Unit Assessment**
Assessment Book, pp. 149–157

✓ **Fluency Assessment**
Assessment Book, pp. 250–265

✓ **EXIT TEST**
Assessment Book, pp. 205–213

ABOUT UNIT 4

Unit 4

IT'S UP TO YOU

THE **BIG** IDEA

How do we decide what's important?

UNIT 4 OPENER,
pp. 202–203

The Big Idea

How do we decide what's important?

COLLABORATE

Talk About It

Read aloud the Big Idea on page 203 of the **Interactive Worktext:** *How do we decide what's important?* Have students think about something that is important to them. Say: *It's up to you to choose what is important. We each may choose something different. My pet dog is important to me. My dog is important to me because she's loyal, loving, and playing with her makes me happy. What is important to you? What helped you decide that it is important to you?* (Answers will vary, but students may name a friend, family member, pet, or activity and should give reasons to explain their choice.)

Discuss the photograph on pages 202–203. Ask: *What is the girl in the photograph painting a picture of?* (a person holding a world) Say: *Use the clues in this picture. What do you think is important to the girl?* (<u>Possible answer:</u> taking care of the earth) *Is this also important to you? Why or why not?* Have partners or small groups discuss this question and share their ideas with the class.

Tell students that deciding what's important to us affects our actions. Say: *In this unit, we will be reading ten selections about what people do when they decide what's important to them. In one of the selections, a girl rescues people during a terrible storm. In another selection, a man uses his skill as a speaker to persuade others to end slavery.*

Build Fluency

Each week, use the **Interactive Worktext** Shared Reads and **Apprentice Leveled Readers** for fluency instruction and practice. Keep in mind that reading rates vary with the type of text that students are reading as well as the purpose for reading. For example, comprehension of complex informational texts generally requires slower reading.

Explain/Model Use the Fluency lessons on pages 374–378 to explain the skill. Then model the skill by reading the first page of the week's Shared Read or Leveled Reader.

Practice/Apply Choose a page from the Shared Read or Leveled Reader. Have one group read the top half of the page one sentence at a time. Remind children to apply the skill. Have the second group echo-read the passage. Then have the groups switch roles for the second half of the page. Discuss how each group applied the skill.

> **Weekly Fluency Focus**
>
> **Week 1** Expression
> **Week 2** Rate and Accuracy
> **Week 3** Phrasing
> **Week 4** Accuracy and Expression
> **Week 5** Expression and Phrasing

Foundational Skills Kit You can also use the **Lesson Cards** and **Practice** pages from the **Foundational Skills Kit** for targeted Fluency instruction and practice.

A C T Access Complex Text

Qualitative Quantitative
Reader and Task
TEXT COMPLEXITY

Interactive Worktext

	Week 1	Week 2	Week 3	Week 4	Week 5
	"How Mighty Kate Stopped the Train"	"Where's Brownie?"	"Frederick Douglass: Freedom's Voice"	"Power from Nature"	"How Do I Hold the Summer?"
Quantitative	Lexile 710 TextEvaluator™ 34	Lexile N/A TextEvaluator™ N/A	Lexile 700 TextEvaluator™ 33	Lexile 710 TextEvaluator™ 35	Lexile N/A TextEvaluator™ N/A
Qualitative	• Genre • Connection of Ideas • Vocabulary	• Organization • Purpose • Sentence Structure • Genre • Connection of Ideas	• Sentence Structure • Vocabulary	• Organization • Connection of Ideas • Genre • Vocabulary	• Connection of Ideas • Genre • Vocabulary
Reader and Task	The Weekly Concept lessons will help determine the reader's knowledge and engagement in the weekly concept.				
	Weekly Concept: p. 186 Questions and tasks: pp. 188–189	Weekly Concept: p. 196 Questions and tasks: pp. 198–199	Weekly Concept: p. 206 Questions and tasks: pp. 208–209	Weekly Concept: p. 218 Questions and tasks: pp. 220–221	Weekly Concept: p. 228 Questions and tasks: pp. 230–231

Apprentice Leveled Reader

	Week 1	Week 2	Week 3	Week 4	Week 5
	"Paul Bunyan"	"The Mysterious Teacher"	"Jane Addams: A Woman of Action"	"The Delta"	"Tell Me the Old, Old Stories"
Quantitative	Lexile 680 TextEvaluator™ 16	Lexile N/A TextEvaluator™ N/A	Lexile 630 TextEvaluator™ 24	Lexile 690 TextEvaluator™ 22	Lexile 590 TextEvaluator™ 29
Qualitative	• Genre • Sentence Structure • Vocabulary	• Organization • Sentence Structure • Genre • Vocabulary	• Sentence Structure • Organization • Connection of Ideas • Genre • Vocabulary	• Organization • Connection of Ideas • Sentence Structure • Genre • Vocabulary	• Connection of Ideas • Sentence Structure • Genre • Vocabulary
Reader and Task	The Weekly Concept lessons will help determine the reader's knowledge and engagement in the weekly concept.				
	Weekly Concept: p. 186 Questions and tasks: pp. 190–193	Weekly Concept: p. 196 Questions and tasks: pp. 200–203	Weekly Concept: p. 206 Questions and tasks: pp. 210–213	Weekly Concept: p. 218 Questions and tasks: pp. 222–225	Weekly Concept: p. 228 Questions and tasks: pp. 232–234

See pages 379 for details about Text Complexity measures.

WEEK 1 LESSON 1

Objectives
- Develop oral language
- Build background about storytelling
- Understand and use weekly vocabulary
- Read a tall tale

Materials
- Interactive Worktext, pp. 204–211
- Visual Vocabulary Cards: 117–124

 Go Digital
- Interactive eWorktext
- Visual Vocabulary Cards

Scaffolding for **Wonders** Reading/Writing Workshop

WEEKLY CONCEPT

5–10 Minutes   SL.5.1b   SL.5.1c

Talk About It

Essential Question Read aloud the Essential Questions on page 204 of the **Interactive Worktext**: *What kinds of stories do we tell? Why do we tell them?* Say: *We read, write, and tell stories aloud. These stories can be made-up or tell about something that happened in real life. Telling stories is a way to share experiences and show what is important to us.*

- Discuss the photo on page 204. Ask: *What are the people doing with their bodies and faces? How are they sharing a story?* (Possible answers: dancing, singing, acting)

I Do Say: *I am going to look closely at the photograph to figure out how and why these people are telling a story. I see stage lights and a curtain. I can tell the people are putting on a play. This is one way to tell a story. I am going to write "putting on a play" in the web about sharing stories on page 205. I also notice that the performers are smiling. This is a clue that they are telling a story to entertain. I will add "to entertain" to the web.*

We Do Say: *Let's look at the photo together. What are the people wearing?* (costumes) *Do they look like clothes people wear today?* (no) *What do you see in the background?* (fake buildings) *Do they look like new buildings or old buildings?* (old) *Use these clues. Do you think the story takes place in the past or today?* (in the past) *Why do you think people share stories about the past?* (to teach people about the past) Guide students to add these words to the web.

You Do Have partners tell about their favorite story. Ask: *What is your favorite story? Who shared the story with you? What do you learn from the story? How does it make you feel?*

REVIEW VOCABULARY

10–15 Minutes   L.5.1   L.5.4a   L.5.5c   L.5.6

Review Weekly Vocabulary Words

- Use the **Visual Vocabulary Cards** to review the weekly vocabulary.

- Read together the directions for the Vocabulary activity on page 206 of the **Interactive Worktext**. Then complete the activity.

1 deeds Have partners discuss which options are good deeds and complete the sentence frame: _____ *and* _____ *are examples of good deeds.* (help someone carry a box; lend someone a pencil) Then have partners take turns telling an example of a good deed they have done.

2 impress Ask: *How do you look when something impresses you? Use your face to show me how you feel.* (Students may raise eyebrows.) Have students brainstorms movies or books that impressed them and use the sentence frame: *I was impressed by* _____ *because* _____*.* (Answers will vary.)

3 commenced Explain that a synonym is a word that has the same or almost the same meaning as another word. Point to the synonym *begin. What does* begin *mean?* (to start) *What is another synonym for* commence*?* (start, get going) Ask students to form the past tense of *commence.*

4 posed Pantomime holding a camera and ask: *How do you pose for a picture? Use your face and hands to show how you would pose.* (Actions will vary.) *What do you do with your body when you pose for a picture?* Have students complete the sentence frame: *When I pose, I* _____*.* (keep still; don't move)

5 exaggeration Ask: *Can a tree next to a house be very large?* (yes) *Can the branches of a tree reach into outer space?* (no) *Which description is an* exaggeration? *Why?* (The tree branches are in outer space. A tree can't grow that high in real life.)

6 sauntered Have students identify specific actions they are doing to demonstrate *saunter. How did you move when you sauntered?* (I walked in a slow way.)

7 wring Ask students if they have ever had to *wring* out a towel. Ask: *What did the towel feel like?* (wet) *What did you do? Show me with your hands.* (Students should show a twisting motion with their hands.) *Why did you wring it out?* (Possible answer: to get some of the water out)

8 heroic Have partners discuss movies they have seen or real events when a person did something *heroic.* Ask students to describe their drawing by using the sentence frame: _____ *is heroic because* _____. (Drawings may include a firefighter putting out a fire, a lifeguard helping a swimmer.)

High-Utility Words

Explain that words that end in the suffix *–ly,* such as *slowly,* are adverbs. *Adverbs describe actions: The boys walked* slowly. Have students look at the High-Utility Words activity on page 207 in the **Interactive Worktext.** Ask partners read the passage and circle words that end in *–ly.* (suddenly, quickly, bravely, wildly, calmly, boldly, neatly) Write the sentence: *I walked* _____ *through the hall.* Have students use different adverbs in the sentences and tell how each changes the meaning.

READ COMPLEX TEXT

15–20 Minutes   RL.5.1   RF.5.4c

Read "How Mighty Kate Stopped the Train"

- Have students turn to page 208 in the **Interactive Worktext** and read aloud the Essential Questions. Explain that they will read a tall tale about how one girl saves people. Ask: *What is the title?* ("How Mighty Kate Stopped the Train") *The word* mighty *means "strong." What does the illustration show?* (a girl holding a train in the air) *Put these clues together. What do you think Kate is like?* (Possible answers: strong, brave)

- Read "How Mighty Kate Stopped the Train" together. Note that weekly vocabulary words are highlighted in yellow. Expand Vocabulary words are in blue.

- Have students use the "My Notes" section on page 208 to write questions they have, words they don't understand, and details they want to remember. Model how to use this section. *I can write notes as I read. In the first sentences on page 209, I see words that I don't understand. I will write* y'all *in the "My Notes" section. I also read that the story takes place "back when railroads were still pretty new," but I don't know when that is. I will write:* When does this story take place? *As I continue to read, I'll ask my questions and write details I want to remember.*

 Quick Check Can students understand the weekly vocabulary in context? If not, review vocabulary using the **Visual Vocabulary Cards** before teaching Lesson 2.

Objectives
- Read a tall tale
- Understand complex text through close reading
- Recognize and understand point of view
- Respond to the selection using text evidence to support ideas

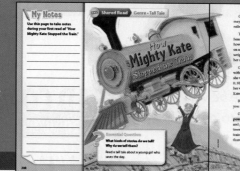

Materials
Interactive Worktext, pp. 208–213

☞ **Go** Digital
- Interactive eWorktext
- Point of View Mini-Lesson

Scaffolding for **Wonders** Reading/Writing Workshop

REREAD COMPLEX TEXT

20–25 Minutes   RL.5.1 RL.5.4 RL.5.6 L.5.4a CCSS

Close Reading: "How Mighty Kate Stopped the Train"

Reread "How Mighty Kate Stopped the Train" with students. As you read together, discuss important passages in the text. Have students respond to text-dependent questions, including those in the **Interactive Worktext**.

Page 209

Vocabulary Read aloud the first two sentences. *What does y'all mean?* (you all) *What clues helped you figure out the meaning of the word?* (Some of you) *Is the narrator speaking to another character?* (no) *Who does y'all refer to?* (Possible answers: us, readers)

Point of View Say: *The narrator tells what happens in a story. A narrator has a point of view, or way of telling the story.* Read aloud the second paragraph. Model using text evidence to identify determine the narrator's point of view. *I read "The star of this amazing tale is a young gal."* Circle the word *star*. *I know a sports star is someone who is very good. The word star is a clue that the narrator thinks the young gal is great.* Have students reread the next two sentences and circle other words and phrases that describe Kate. (unbelievably strong, mighty) *Use these clues. What does the narrator think of Mighty Kate?* (The narrator thinks Kate is very strong.)

Expand Vocabulary Have students locate the word *powerful*. Say: *The text says, "a powerful storm struck outside her home." Which sentence helps you understand how powerful the storm was?* (Rain poured down, and gusts of wind blew so hard that houses shook in fear and trees ran for their lives!)

Genre (A C T) Say: *A tall tale is a made-up story. It has characters that may be exaggerated and events that could not happen in real life. Read aloud: "The tiny babe picked up the doc." Could a tiny baby pick up a doctor?* (no) *Let's underline this event. Reread the third paragraph. What other things did Mighty Kate do that could not happen in real life?* (She just tossed the enormous rock aside; Kate stepped in and pulled them both out—with just one hand!)

Page 210

Connection of Ideas (A C T) Read the first three sentences aloud. *Why did Mighty Kate run outside? Go back to the last paragraph on page 209 to look for details.* (there was a thunderous crash) *What had Kate seen before she ran outside?* (a train carrying coal crossing Creek Bridge) *What happened to the bridge and train? Point to text evidence.* (The bridge, whipped by the storm, had fallen into the creek. So had the train!)

Genre (A C T) Remind students that in a tall tale the hero is stronger, braver, and more clever than other characters. Have students draw a box around *"She swept away the mess with one arm."* in the first paragraph. Ask: *What mess did Mighty Kate sweep away?* (a twisted pile of rails) *Would a young girl be able to do this in real life?* (no) *What does this tell about Mighty Kate?* (She is extra strong.) *What other details show that Kate is extra strong?* (yanked each man up with one hand; ascended the vine, with the other hand)

Expand Vocabulary Read aloud the definition of *ascended. What words in this sentence help you understand the meaning of* ascended? (get back up) *How did Mighty Kate ascend the vine to save the men?* (She ascended the vine with one hand.)

Point of View Have students paraphrase the events in the first paragraph. Ask: *Would it be safe or dangerous to do these things?* (dangerous) *Why does Mighty Kate do them?* (to save the workers) *What does this tell about Kate?* (She is helpful and brave.) Then have students reread the second paragraph. Ask: *What words does the narrator use to describe Mighty Kate and her actions?* (brave, heroic, smart) *Put all these clues together. What is the narrator's point of view?* (Mighty Kate is brave, helpful, and smart.)

Page 211

Genre (ACT) Ask: *What does Kate do when the log is about to strike?* (She grabs it.) *Could a real girl do this?* (no) *Draw a box around this detail.* Have partners read the rest of the paragraph and stop after each sentence to ask: *Could that happen in real life?* Then have them mark those details that are exaggerated. (She began to wring it with her bare hands; that wet log was nothing but a twisted twig!)

Expand Vocabulary Have students point to the word *warnings*. Ask: *What are warnings?* (messages that danger is coming) *What danger did Kate need to warn the driver about?* (the broken bridge) Have student reread the third and fourth paragraphs. Ask: *What warnings did Kate give to the train driver?* (She whistled loudly—so loudly that the train driver heard it and stopped the train; Kate ran up and told him that Creek Bridge was out.)

High-Utility Words Ask students to identify a word in the second paragraph that ends in *–ly.* (loudly) Ask: *What does the word* loudly *describe?* (Kate's whistling)

Point of View Have partners review the narrator's point of view so far in the story. (The narrator thinks Kate is brave, smart, and helpful.) Then have partners reread the next two paragraphs. Ask: *Which descriptive words and details show this point of view?* (Possible answers: Kate raced after it; she got a bright idea; the driver thanked the brave girl who had saved the day.) Then have students reread the last paragraph. *What does the narrator think of the way Mighty Kate stopped the train? Point to text evidence.* (The narrator thinks it was a good idea; "Mighty Kate's good idea")

RESPOND TO READING

10–20 Minutes   RL.5.1   W.5.9a   SL.5.1d

Respond to "How Mighty Kate Stopped the Train"

Have students summarize "How Mighty Kate Stopped the Train" orally to demonstrate comprehension. Then have partners answer the questions on page 212 of the **Interactive Worktext** using the discussion starters. Tell them to use text evidence to support their answers. Have students write the page number(s) on which they found the text evidence for each question.

1. *What events at the beginning of the story couldn't happen in real life?* (As a baby, Kate picked up a doctor. She tossed an enormous rock. She pulled a horse and buggy out of a ditch with one hand. Evidence: p. 209)

2. *What does Kate do that makes her a hero?* (Kate saved two men after a train crash. She also stopped a passenger train before it reached the broken bridge. Text Evidence: p. 210, 211)

3. *What does Mighty Kate do during the storm that is amazing?* (She pulled two workers up a vine. She grabbed a huge log. Text Evidence: p. 210, 211)

After students discuss the questions on page 212, have them write a response to the question on page 213. Tell them to use their partner discussions and notes about "How Mighty Kate Stopped the Train" to help them. Circulate and provide guidance.

 Quick Check Do students understand vocabulary in context? If not, review and reteach using the instruction on page 194.

Can students find details to determine the narrator's point of view? If not, review and reteach using the instruction on page 194 and assign the Unit 4 Week 1 digital mini-lesson.

Can students write a response to "How Mighty Kate Stopped the Train"? If not, provide sentence frames to help them organize their ideas.

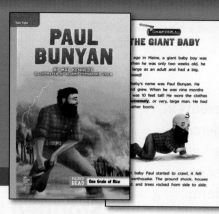

Objectives
- Understand and use new vocabulary
- Read a tall tale
- Recognize and understand point of view
- Understand complex text through close reading

Materials
- "Paul Bunyan" Apprentice Leveled Reader, pp. 2–9
- Graphic Organizer: Point of View

☞ **Go** Digital
- Apprentice Leveled Reader eBook
- Downloadable Graphic Organizer
- Point of View Mini-Lesson

Scaffolding for **Wonders** Approaching Leveled Reader

BEFORE READING

10–15 Minutes   SL.5.1c   SL.5.1d   L.5.4a   L.5.6   **CCSS**

Introduce "Paul Bunyan"

- Read the Essential Question on the title page of "Paul Bunyan" **Apprentice Leveled Reader**: *What kinds of stories do we tell? Why do we tell them? We will read an entertaining story about a great woodsman who helped many people.*

- Read the title. Have students look at the illustrations. *What do the pictures tell you about the story of Paul Bunyan?* (It is not a true story. Paul is not a real person.)

Expand Vocabulary

Display each word below. Say the words and have students repeat them. Then use the Define/Example/Ask routine to introduce each word.

1 **curious** (page 7)

Define: wanting to know about something

Example: The boy was *curious* about the grasshopper.

Ask: What was something that made you *curious*?

2 **extremely** (page 2)

Define: very much or greatly

Example: This is an *extremely* long line for a movie.

Ask: Why might a person feel *extremely* tired?

2 **gusts** (page 7)

Define: sudden bursts or rushes of air

Example: The trees swayed. The strong *gusts* of wind made the trees bend and sway.

Ask: What happens when you are in a *gust* of wind?

4 **thaw** (page 9)

Define: when something that is frozen warms up

Example: The frozen lake began to *thaw* when the weather got warmer.

Ask: What is one way to *thaw* a frozen dinner?

DURING READING

20–30 Minutes   RL.5.1   RL.5.6   SL.5.1b   L.5.4a   **CCSS**

Close Reading

🔍 **Pages 2–3**

Genre Have students read page 2. Ask: *Look at the first paragraph. Where does the story take place?* (Maine) *Who is this story about?* (a giant baby boy) *How do you know the story isn't true?* (The baby has a beard and is the size of an adult.)

Sentence Structure **A C T** Have students find the exclamation points on page 2. Point out that exclamation points are a way of showing surprise or excitement. *Why do you think the author used exclamation points in these sentences?* (The details described are amazing, for example, a huge baby with a beard.)

Point of View Remind students that a narrator is the person who tells a story. The narrator in "Paul Bunyan" is not a character in the story. Have them read the second and third paragraphs. *What details show that the narrator thinks Paul Bunyan is amazing?* (uses exclamation marks in the sentence: When he was nine months old, he was 10 feet tall!; When baby Paul started to crawl, it felt like an earthquake.)

Have students record details they identify on their Point of View charts as they read the selection.

Genre A C T *In the third paragraph, what happened when Paul crawled?* (it felt like an earthquake, houses wobbled, trees rocked) *What makes these details humorous?* (They are funny exaggerations.)

Problem and Solution *Read the first paragraph on page 3. How did the townspeople feel about the shaking ground?* (They felt frightened.) *What did Paul's parents do to solve the problem?* (put him in a floating cradle and pushed him out to sea) *What problem did this create?* (When Paul moved in his cradle, the movement made huge waves which flooded the towns.)

Point of View *Read the second paragraph on page 3. How does the narrator describe Paul's parents?* (Filled with sadness; His mother cried as she waved good-bye to her boy) *What do these details show about the narrator's opinion of the parents?* (Narrator feels that the parents don't want to hurt Paul.)

Genre A C T *Name two events on page 3 that would not happen in real life.* (Paul's parents put him out to sea. When Paul moved in the cradle, it made huge waves that flooded the towns.)

Pages 4–5

Genre A C T *Read the third paragraph on page 4. What does Paul do that could not happen in real life?* (He cries so much that his tears form a river.) *What does baby Paul do when he sees the fish?* (He caught the fish, cleaned it with his knife, chopped firewood with his ax, and started a fire with the flint rocks.) *How is Paul not like a real baby?* (A real baby cannot do these kinds of things.)

STOP AND CHECK Read the question in the Stop and Check box on page 4. (They had no choice because the villagers wanted to stop the shaking.)

Pages 6–7

Vocabulary *Read the sentence on page 6 with the word* harsh. *What is* harsh? (the seasons) *How can a season be harsh?* (bad weather) *What* harsh *conditions did Paul face?* (snowstorms, blizzards, floods, thunderstorms, forest fires, wild winds)

STOP AND CHECK Read the question in the Stop and Check box on page 6. (He had to survive alone in the woods and face storms and fires.)

Point of View *On page 7, what details does the narrator use to show that Paul is curious?* (He asked what made the snow blue; he dressed in warm clothes and boots, sauntered out of his cave, and walked across the blue land. The thunder and lightning did not bother him.)

Pages 8–9

Vocabulary *Read the first two sentences on page 8. What was very loud?* (wind, thunder) *What did the wind and thunder do to the quiet sound?* (drowned it out) *What does* drowned out *mean?* (covered up)

Point of View *Read the first two paragraphs on page 9. What details describe how Paul takes care of Babe?* (gently picked up, carefully placed, "Don't worry, you'll be safe here.") *Why did the narrator choose these words?* (The narrator thinks Paul is gentle and helpful.)

Prior Knowledge A C T Students may not be familiar with the landforms mentioned in this tall tale. If possible, display a globe or map of the U.S. and Canada. Point out the Great Lakes and help students understand their size.

Genre A C T Have students read the last paragraph on page 9. *How were the Great Lakes made, according to this tall tale?* (Paul dug huge ponds in the ground to make watering holes for Babe the Blue Ox.) *Could this happen in real life?* (no)

STOP AND CHECK Read the question in the Stop and Check box on page 9. (Paul heard Babe crying.)

Have partners review their Point of View charts for pages 2–9 and discuss what they learned.

 Quick Check Do students understand weekly vocabulary in context? If not, review and reteach using the instruction on page 194.

Can students identify point of view? If not, review and reteach using the instruction on page 194 and assign the Unit 4 Week 1 digital mini-lesson.

WEEK 1 LESSON 4

Objectives
- Understand and use new vocabulary
- Read a tall tale
- Recognize and understand point of view
- Understand complex text through close reading
- Respond to the selection using text evidence to support ideas

Scaffolding for **McGraw-Hill Reading Wonders** Approaching Leveled Reader

Materials
- "Paul Bunyan" Apprentice Leveled Reader, pp. 10–20
- Point of View Graphic Organizer

☞ **Go Digital**
- Apprentice Leveled Reader eBook
- Downloadable Graphic Organizer
- Point of View Mini-Lesson

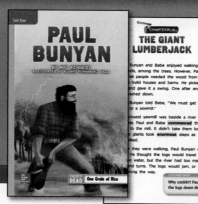

BEFORE READING

5–10 Minutes   SL.5.1c   SL.5.1d   L.5.4a   L.5.6

Expand Vocabulary

Display each word below. Say the words and have students repeat them. Then use the Define/Example/Ask routine to introduce each word.

❶ enormous (page 10)

Define: very large

Example: The *enormous* pile of snow would not melt.

Ask: What have you seen that is *enormous*?

❷ faithful (page 14)

Define: loyal and trusted

Example: Kim's brother was her most *faithful* friend.

Ask: Who is your most *faithful* friend? Why?

❸ frontier (page 15)

Define: a wild place where people are just beginning to live, or settle

Example: In the 1850s, many pioneers moved to the western *frontier*.

Ask: What would it be like to explore a new *frontier*?

❹ requirement (page 12)

Define: something that must be done because of a rule or a law

Example: A ticket is a *requirement* for getting into a concert.

Ask: What is a *requirement* for driving a car?

DURING READING

15–20 Minutes   RL.5.1   RL.5.6   SL.5.1b   L.5.4b

Close Reading

🔍 **Pages 10–11**

Problem and Solution *Read the first paragraph on page 10. What problem did Paul want to solve?* (People needed wood to build things.) *What was his solution?* (cut down trees so they could be turned into boards for building)

Vocabulary *What clue on page 10 helps you understand the word* sawmill? (Paul takes logs to the mill.) *What two words are in the compound word* sawmill? (*saw* and *mill*) *Use the meaning of the two words to tell what a* sawmill *is.* (A saw is a tool used for cutting wood; a mill is a building where things are made; a *sawmill* is a place to cut wood.)

STOP AND CHECK Read the question in the Stop and Check box on page 10. (The twists and turns of the river would cause the logs to get stuck and pile up.)

Genre Ⓐ Ⓒ Ⓣ Read page 11. Remind students that characters in tall tales do surprising and amazing things that real people cannot do. Ask: *What details about Paul and Babe on pages 10 and 11 show they are characters in a tall tale?* (Both are giants; Paul decided to make the river straight. He tied ropes to one side of the river and Babe's harness and Babe pulled the river straight.)

🔍 **Pages 12–13**

Vocabulary Ask students to find *amazingly* on page 12. *What is the root word? What clues tell you what it means?* (Amazing; more than a thousand giant workers met the requirement) Remind students that the suffix *-ly* is used to describe the way something happens. *What are some other words with the suffix* -ly? (*slowly, quickly, quietly*)

Genre **A** C **T** *Find a humorous exaggeration in the third paragraph on page 12.* (Workers needed to be more than 10 feet tall.) *Find other exaggerations in the first paragraph on page 13.* (bunkhouses a mile long)

STOP AND CHECK Read the question in the Stop and Check box on page 13. (He built a griddle the size of an ice rink.)

Point of View *On page 13, what happens when the cook asks how the pan will get greased?* (Paul had a hundred men tie bacon fat to their shoes and skate around the pan to grease it.) *What do you think the narrator wants us to think about Paul?* (He can solve any problem and do any task.) Have students record details they identify on their Point of View Chart as they read the selection.

Pages 14–15

Vocabulary Have students locate the word *frostbite* in the second sentence on page 14. *What are the two words in this compound word?* (*frost* and *bite*) *What does the story say helped solve the problem of* frostbite? (socks) *What might* frostbite *be?* (when feet get too cold and hurt)

Point of View *In the second paragraph on page 14, what are some of Paul's successes?* (started out alone in a cave, now has a logging camp; helped many people) *How does the narrator describe Paul?* (never tried to impress anyone, or show off his success; he and his faithful friend Babe stuck together) *What does the narrator think about Paul?* (The narrator admires Paul because he's a survivor, hardworking, modest, a good friend, and helps others.)

Genre **A** C **T** *What words and phrases in the third paragraph on page 14 explain why workers told stories about Paul Bunyan?* (heroic, always solving problems, good deeds he did for others)

STOP AND CHECK Read the question in the Stop and Check box on page 15. (He dragged an ax behind him as he walked across Arizona.)

AFTER READING

10–15 Minutes   RL.5.1   RL5.2   RL.5.9   W.5.9a   L.5.4a

Respond to Reading

Compare Texts Have students discuss how the tales of Mighty Kate and Paul Bunyan are similar and different. Then ask: *Why are tales like these entertaining?*

Summarize Have students turn to page 16 and summarize the selection. (Answers should include details that show that Paul performed amazing feats and helped people with his great strength and cleverness.)

Text Evidence

Have partners work together to answer questions on page 16. Have students use their Point of View Charts.

Point of View (The narrator admires Paul and shows this by telling about how Paul was kind to Babe and built a logging camp to help many people.)

Vocabulary (The word *peered* means looked at. Clues: looked around; saw)

Write About Reading (The narrator thinks Babe is a good friend for Paul. The narrator says, "At last Paul Bunyan had a friend." Babe and Paul do everything together and help many people. On the day Paul found Babe, his life "changed forever.")

Independent Reading

Encourage students to read the paired selection "One Grain of Rice" on pages 17–19. Have them summarize the selection and compare it to "Paul Bunyan." Have partners answer the "Make Connections" questions on page 19.

 Quick Check **Can students identify Point of View? If not, review and reteach using the instruction on page 194 and assign the Unit 4 Week 1 digital mini-lesson.**

Can students respond to the selection using text evidence? If not, provide, sentence frames to help them organize their ideas.

Objectives
- Review weekly vocabulary words
- Review point of view
- Write an analysis about how an author uses exaggeration in a tall tale

Scaffolding for **Wonders** McGraw-Hill Reading Reading/Writing Workshop

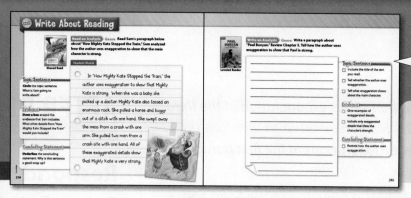

Materials
- Visual Vocabulary Cards: 117–124
- Interactive Worktext, pp. 214–215
- Assessment Book, pp. 40–41

☞ **Go** Digital
- Visual Vocabulary Cards
- Point of View Mini-Lesson
- Interactive eWorktext

REVIEW AND RETEACH

 5–10 Minutes   RL.5.1 RL.5.6 L.5.4a L.5.6

Weekly Vocabulary

Display one **Visual Vocabulary Card** at a time and ask students to use the vocabulary word in a sentence. If students have difficulty, have them find the word in "How Mighty Kate Stopped the Train" and use context clues to define it.

Comprehension: Point of View

I Do Display: *Sally runs fast. She runs so fast, she can go around the track in seconds! Everyone is amazed when they see Sally run.* Underline the second sentence: *This detail tells me that Sally is very fast.* Circle the word *amazed. This descriptive word shows that Sally is amazing. I can put these details together to figure out the narrator's point of view. I can tell the narrator thinks Sally is a very fast and amazing runner.*

We Do Display: *Bo is a huge dog. His bark is loud and scary. He shows his teeth and growls when neighbors walk by.* Ask: *What words describe Bo?* (huge, loud, scary) *What details describe what Bo does when neighbors walk by?* (He shows his teeth and growls.) *Put these details together. What does the narrator think about Bo?* (He is a big, scary dog.)

You Do Display: *Mike is so smart, he can solve any problem. One time, Mike's bike got a flat tire. He figured out how to fix it with only gum and tape. Mike is a brilliant problem solver.* Have partners circle descriptive words and underline details that describe Mike. Then have partners use these words and details to figure out the narrator's point of view.

WRITE ABOUT READING

 25–35 Minutes   W.5.4 W.5.5 W.5.9a

Read an Analysis

- Ask students to look back at "How Mighty Kate Stopped the Train" in the **Interactive Worktext**. Have volunteers review characters and story events. *How does the author use exaggeration to show that the main character is strong?*

- Read the directions on page 214. Read aloud the student model. Say: *Sam's paragraph is an analysis, or a detailed description, of how the author used exaggeration to show that Kate is strong.*

- *An analysis includes certain parts. The first is the* topic sentence. *Read the beginning of the paragraph and circle the topic sentence. What information has Sam included in this sentence?* (text's title; how the author uses exaggeration to show that Kate is strong)

- *Another part of an analysis is* text evidence. *Sam restates details from the text that show how the author uses exaggeration. He includes only those details that show that Kate is strong.* Have students draw a box around the text evidence. (sentences 2 through 5) *Look back at the details you marked in "How Mighty Kate Stopped the Train." What other details might be included as text evidence in the paragraph?* (Possible answer: Mighty Kate grabbed a log and wrung it until it was a twisted twig.)

- *The final part of an analysis is a* concluding statement. Have students underline the concluding statement. *How is this statement like the topic sentence?* (Both say exaggeration shows that Mighty Kate is very strong.) *What words wrap up the text evidence?* (all of these exaggerated details)

Write an Analysis

Guided Writing Read the writing prompt on page 215 together. Have students write about "Paul Bunyan" or another text they read this week. Have them review their notes. *Use the checklist to help you figure out the right information to include in each section.* Guide students to ask "how" and "why" questions, such as *How does exaggeration make the character seem extra strong?*

Peer Conference Have partners read their analyses to each other. Listeners should identify the strongest text evidence that supports the topic sentence and discuss any sentences that are unclear.

Teacher Conference Check students' writing for complete sentences and text evidence that supports the topic. Review the concluding statement. *Does the concluding statement tie all of the parts of the analysis together?* If necessary, have students revise the concluding statement by restating the topic sentence.

Level Up

▲ **Approaching Leveled Reader**

▲ **Reading/Writing Workshop**

▲ **Apprentice Leveled Reader**

▲ **Interactive Worktext**

IF students read the **Apprentice Level** Reader fluently and the **Interactive Worktext** Shared Read fluently and answer the Respond to Reading questions

THEN read together the **Approaching Level** Reader main selection and the **Reading/Writing Workshop** Shared Read from *Reading Wonders.* Have students take notes as they read, using self-stick notes. Then ask and answer questions about their notes.

Writing Rubric

	4	3	2	1
Topic Sentence	There is one clear, focused topic sentence.	Topic sentence is less focused, somewhat clear.	Topic is presented in short phrases.	There is no topic sentence.
Text Evidence	Topic is supported by two or more text details.	Evidence includes only one detail from the text.	Little to no evidence is cited from the text.	No text evidence is included.
Concluding Statement	Clearly restates the topic sentence; wraps up all the details.	Restatement is less focused; attempts to wrap up all the details.	Vaguely restates the topic. Doesn't correlate well to text evidence.	There is no conclusion.
Writing Style	Writes in complete sentences. Uses correct spelling and grammar.	Uses complete sentences and phrases. Writing has spelling and grammar errors.	Few or no complete sentences. There are many spelling and grammar errors.	Does not write accurately or in complete sentences.

ASSESSMENT

Weekly Assessment

Have students complete the Weekly Assessment using **Assessment** book pages 40–41.

WEEK 2 LESSON

1

Objectives
- Develop oral language
- Build background about taking a second look
- Understand and use weekly vocabulary
- Read a drama

Scaffolding for **Wonders** Reading/Writing Workshop

Materials
- Interactive Worktext, pp. 216–223
- Visual Vocabulary Cards: 125–132

☞ **Go** Digital
- Interactive eWorktext
- Visual Vocabulary Cards

WEEKLY CONCEPT

5–10 Minutes   SL.5.1b   SL.51c

Talk About It

Essential Question Read aloud the Essential Question on page 216 of the **Interactive Worktext**: *What can you discover when you give things a second look?* Say: *When you first look at something, you may not notice every detail. When you look again, you may discover things you didn't see at first.*

- Discuss the image on page 216. Ask: *What do you see?* (an illustration; people on a street)

I Do Say: *At first, I see an illustration of people on a street. When I look again, I notice that there is a real street at the bottom. I will write "I discovered that this picture is a photograph of a real mural" in the web on page 217.*

We Do Say: *Let's look for more details we may not have noticed at first. What other detail tells you this is a photograph of a real place?* (there is a real boy on the far left) *What do you notice when you look closely at the people's clothing?* (the man is wearing old-fashioned clothes; the others are wearing clothes people wear today) *What did you learn by taking a second look?* (Possible answers: this is a real mural; the mural shows people from different times)

You Do Have partners describe a time when they discovered something. Have them answer the questions: *What did you look at again? What did you discover when you took a second look? How did the discovery make you think differently about it?*

REVIEW VOCABULARY

10–15 Minutes   L.5.1   L.5.4a   L.5.5c   L.5.6

Review Weekly Vocabulary Words

- Use the **Visual Vocabulary Cards** to review the weekly vocabulary.

- Read together the directions for the Vocabulary activity on page 218 of the **Interactive Worktext**. Then complete the activity.

1 **concealed** Have students use the sentence starter: *I can conceal my book in _____ or _____.* (Possible answers: a desk, a backpack, behind a cabinet, under papers) Have students form the past tense of *conceal*.

2 **interpret** Pantomime yawning. Ask: *How would you interpret my action?* (Possible answers: You are tired; you are bored.)

3 **suspicious** Have partners discuss the options. Then have them complete the sentence frame: *I would feel suspicious if I heard _____.* (talking)

4 **precise** Have partners ask each other questions to help them decide which of the tools help them be *precise*. (a ruler, a scale) Have them complete the sentence frame to explain each of their choices: *A _____ tells me the precise _____.*

5 **perplexed** Ask: *What does* puzzled *mean? Which word is a synonym for* puzzled *and* perplexed? (confused) Then have partners review the other options and discuss which word has the opposite meaning of *perplexed*. (certain)

6 **reconsider** Point out the prefix *re-*. Explain to students that *re-* is added to the beginning of a word to say that something is done again. *What does the base word* consider *mean?* (to think about something)

What does reconsider *mean?* (to think about something again)

7 inquisitive Ask: *Would an inquisitive person ask a question?* (yes) *Would an inquisitive person tell a story?* (no) *Would an inquisitive person look up a word in the dictionary?* (yes) Ask students to name something else an inquisitive person might do.

8 astounded Offer an example of something that astounded you, such as an athlete's performance or a daring act. Have partners discuss things they have seen in movies, television, or in real life that have astounded them. Then have students complete the sentence frame: *I was astounded when I saw _____.* Have partners discuss and title their drawings. (Drawings will vary, but should show amazing things.)

High-Utility Words

Explain that writers use words such as *better* and *best* to make comparisons. The words *more, worse,* and *better* are used to compare two things. *Most, best,* and *worst* compare more than two things. Have students look at the High-Utility Words activity on page 219 of the **Interactive Worktext**. Have partners read the passage and circle words that compare. (better, best, worst, worse, more, most) Then have students partner read the passage and put a star next to those words that compare more than two things. (best, worst, most)

> **ELL ENGLISH LANGUAGE LEARNERS**
> Give students pencils of varying amounts. Display the words *more* and *most* and have students repeat. Point to two students and ask: *Who has more pencils?* Have students name their classmate. Repeat the activity pointing to more than two student and using the word *most.*

READ COMPLEX TEXT

15–20 Minutes   RL.5.1   RF.5.4c

Read: "Where's Brownie?"

- Have students turn to page 220 in the **Interactive Worktext** and read aloud the Essential Question. Explain that the characters in this play will use clues to find a lost pet. Ask: *What is the title?* ("Where's Brownie?") *What do the illustrations show?* (a reptile) Use these clues. *Who do you think Brownie is? Why might he be lost?* (a pet reptile; He is the same color as the curtain.)

- Read "Cast" and assign roles. Read aloud the stage directions as you read "Where's Brownie?" together. Weekly vocabulary words are highlighted in yellow. Expand Vocabulary words are highlighted in blue.

- Have students use "My Notes" on page 220 to write questions they have. Model: *I can write notes about questions I have as I read. When I read details about the setting on page 221, I wonder why the paper bag is wet and torn. In the "My Notes" section, I will write:* Why is there a wet, torn paper bag? *I will keep this question in mind as I continue to read. I also don't understand the Narrator's words,* "two heads are better than one." *I will write these words in the "My Notes" section. When we reread the drama, I will ask and answer these questions.*

> **ELL ENGLISH LANGUAGE LEARNERS**
> As you read together, have students highlight sections of text they have questions about. After reading, help students write their questions in the "My Notes" section.

 Quick Check Can students understand the weekly vocabulary in context? If not, review vocabulary using the **Visual Vocabulary Cards** before teaching Lesson 2.

WEEK 2 LESSON

2

Objectives
- Read a drama
- Understand complex text through close reading
- Recognize and understand point of view
- Respond to the selection using text evidence to support ideas

Scaffolding for **WONDERS** Reading/Writing Workshop

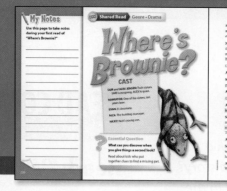

Materials
Interactive Worktext, pp. 220–225

☞ **Go** Digital
- Interactive eWorktext
- Point of View Mini-Lesson

REREAD COMPLEX TEXT

20–25 Minutes   RL.5.1   RL.5.3   RL.5.5   RL.5.6   L.5.4a   **CCSS**

Close Reading: "Where's Brownie?"

Reread "Where's Brownie?" with students. As you read together, discuss important sections of the text. Have students respond to text-dependent questions, including those in the **Interactive Worktext**.

🔍 Page 221

Genre **ACT** Explain that a drama, or play, is a story told through dialogue between characters. Point out that a play may also includes a narrator. Have students read the cast list on page 220. Ask: *Who are the characters in this play?* (Sam and Alex Jensen, Evan, Nick, and Nicky) *Who is the Narrator?* (one of the sisters)

Point of View Read aloud the Narrator's words. Ask: *Who is the Narrator's twin sister? Circle the text evidence.* (my twin sister, Sam) *If the Narrator's twin's sister is Sam, what is the name of the Narrator?* (Alex) *How do you know?* If students have difficulty, have them review the cast list on page 220. (The cast list says that Sam and Alex are twin sisters and the Narrator is one of the sisters.) Say: *The Narrator's point of view affects how people and events are described. Descriptive words and details are clues to the Narrator's point of view. Reread the Narrator's words. What detail does the Narrator tell about her sister?* (She makes problems worse rather than better.) *What does this detail tell about the Narrator's view of her sister?* (The Narrator thinks her sister causes trouble.)

High-Utility Words Point out the word *better* in the expression "two heads are better than one." Ask: *Does "better" compare two things or more than two things?* (two things) Have students look for other words that compare and discuss their meanings. (better, worse)

Sentence Structure **ACT** Say: *An ellipsis is a series of three dots that shows that a speaker pauses or trails off.* Have students locate a sentence that includes ellipses: (Like when we lost Brownie, our pet chameleon . . .) Ask: *Who is speaking?* (the Narrator) *What happens after this sentence?* (Alex enters.) *Do you think the ellipsis indicates that the Narrator pauses or trails off? How do you know?* (trails off; <u>Possible answer</u>: The action of the play begins; the Narrator doesn't speak again.)

Expand Vocabulary Have students reread the first lines of dialogue between Alex and Sam. Say: *Find the word* exhibit. *Where did Sam show her exhibit?* (the science fair) *What did Sam's exhibit show for others to see? Point to text evidence.* (Brownie; "Did everyone like Brownie?")

Organization **ACT** Explain that plays tell about characters' actions and feelings through stage directions. Have students reread the page. Ask: *What punctuation do you see around a stage direction?* (parentheses) *Which stage direction tells what Sam and Evan do when Alex enters the room?* (Alex enters. Sam and Evan quickly cover up their work.) *What "work" do Sam and Evan cover up? Look for clues in the Setting and stage directions.* (a "missing pet" poster) *Why do Sam and Evan cover this up when Alex enters the room?* (They don't want Alex to know Brownie is missing.)

Connection of Ideas **ACT** Have students reread the last three lines of dialogue. *What does Alex notice about the bag?* (The bottom is all wet; it has a rip.) *Where does Sam think the bag got wet?* (in the lobby) *Put these clues together. Where does Alex think Brownie is?* (the lobby)

🔍 Page 222

Organization **ACT** Explain that plays are organized into scenes and include setting details. Have students mark the text that describes the setting. Then have students review the setting description on page 221. Have them complete the sentence frames: *Scene One is set in _____.* (a bedroom in an apartment) *Scene Two is set in _____.* (the lobby)

Expand Vocabulary Have students locate the word *escaped*. Read the definition aloud. Ask: *What escaped?* (Brownie) *What did Brownie escape from?* (a bag) *What clues in the dialogue help you understand the meaning of escaped?* (from the bag; running around)

Point of View Say: *Speakers in a play can have different points of view. Where does Alex think Brownie is?* (in the lobby) *Why does Alex think Brownie is there? Point to text evidence.* (We think he escaped from the bag when Sam set it down near the fountain.) *Where does Nick think Brownie is?* (in the apartment) *Draw a box around text evidence.* (Maybe Brownie isn't down here. Try searching your apartment.)

Page 223

Purpose **A C T** Have students locate the word *GREEN* in Alex's dialogue. Have students reread the sentence with the word *GREEN* aloud. Ask: *What do you notice about this word* green *that is different than the other words in the sentence?* (All the letters are capitalized.) *Why do you think the author did this?* (so the speaker will say the words stronger or louder than the other words)

Organization **A C T** Have students locate the stage directions that tell about Sam's feelings. Ask: *How does Sam feel?* (confused) *Why is Sam confused?* (Brownie has always been brown, but is now green.) If students have difficulty, ask: *What is different about Brownie?*

Expand Vocabulary Have students locate *beloved*. Read aloud the Narrator's lines at the end of the play. Ask: *Which phrase helps you understand the meaning of beloved?* (favorite pet)

Point of View Have students draw a box around text that describes Brownie. (beloved, favorite pet) *Does the Narrator have a positive or negative point of view toward Brownie?* (positive) *How do you think the Narrator feels about Brownie?* (Possible answers: She loves Brownie; Brownie is important to her.)

RESPOND TO READING

10–20 Minutes   RL.5.1 W.5.9a SL.5.1d

Respond to "Where's Brownie?"

Have students summarize "Where's Brownie?" orally to demonstrate comprehension. Then have partners answer the questions on page 224 of the **Interactive Worktext** using the discussion starters. Tell them to use text evidence to support their answers. Have students write the page number(s) on which they found the text evidence for each question.

1. *What clues lead Alex, Sam, and Evan to look for Brownie in the lobby?* (Alex notices the bag is wet; Sam remembers Nicky playing in the fountain in the lobby; Alex spots a rip in the bag, so she thinks that Brownie is in the lobby. Text Evidence: p. 221, 222)

2. *What clues does Evan find each time he checks his device?* (He finds out that chameleons climb trees, love running water, and change colors to match their environment. Text Evidence: pp. 222, 223)

3. *Why does Alex tell Nicky to look in the tree again?* (She thinks Brownie has changed his colors to match the tree. Text Evidence: p. 223)

After students discuss the questions on page 224, have them write a response to the question on page 225. Tell them to use their partner discussions and notes about "Where's Brownie?" to help them. Circulate and provide guidance.

 Quick Check Do students understand vocabulary in context? If not, review and reteach using the instruction on page 204.

Can students use key details to determine point of view? If not, review and reteach using the instruction on page 204 and assign the Unit 4 Week 2 digital mini-lesson.

Can students write a response to "Where's Brownie?" If not, provide sentence frames to help them organize their ideas.

WEEK 2 LESSON

3

Objectives
- Understand and use new vocabulary
- Read drama
- Recognize and understand point of view
- Understand complex text through close reading

Scaffolding for **Wonders** Approaching Leveled Reader

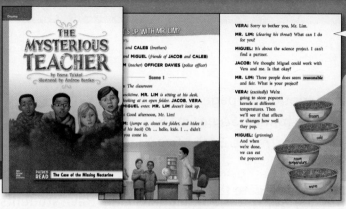

Materials
- "The Mysterious Teacher" Apprentice Leveled Reader, pp. 2–7
- Graphic Organizer: Point of View

☞ **Go** Digital
- Apprentice Leveled Reader eBook
- Downloadable Graphic Organizer
- Point of View Digital Mini-Lesson

BEFORE READING

10–15 Minutes   SL.5.1c   SL.5.1d   L.5.4a   L.5.6

Introduce "The Mysterious Teacher"

- Read the Essential Question on the title page of "The Mysterious Teacher" **Apprentice Leveled Reader**: *What can you discover when you give things a second look? We will read about a group of students who must give things a second look in order to solve a mystery.*

- Read the title. Have students look at the images on page 2. *What makes the teacher mysterious?* (He's hiding something behind his back.) *What mystery do you think the students will try to solve?* (They might find out what the teacher is hiding.)

Expand Vocabulary

Display each word below. Say the words and have students repeat them. Then use the Define/Example/Ask routine to introduce each word.

❶ concerned (page 4)

Define: worried about something

Example: I am *concerned* that it will rain on the day of our picnic.

Ask: How do people show they are *concerned*?

❷ reasonable (page 3)

Define: fair and sensible

Example: On a school night, I go to bed at the *reasonable* hour of nine o'clock.

Ask: What is a *reasonable* way to settle a disagreement with a friend?

❸ stubborn (page 7)

Define: not willing to accept change or give up

Example: The *stubborn* donkey would not go up the hill.

Ask: How does someone look when they are being *stubborn*?

DURING READING

20–30 Minutes   RL.5.1   RL.5.6   SL.5.1b   L.5.4a

Close Reading

🔍 **Pages 1–3**

Organization Ⓐ Ⓒ Ⓣ *Look at the table of contents on page 1. How is this play organized?* (It has three acts.) *What is the title of the Act 1?* (What's Up with Mr. Lim?)

Genre Ⓐ Ⓒ Ⓣ *Look at the list of names at the top of page 2. What is the purpose of this list?* (It names and describes the characters in the play.) *Read the Scene description. Which characters visit Mr. Lim in the classroom at lunchtime?* (Jacob, Vera, Miguel) *How do they know Mr. Lim?* (He is their teacher.)

Organization Ⓐ Ⓒ Ⓣ *Who speaks the first line of dialogue in Scene 1?* (Jacob) *Who does Jacob speak to?* (Mr. Lim) Point out the stage directions. *What do the stage directions tell you about Mr. Lim?* (He has a folder that he doesn't want the students to see.)

Sentence Structure Ⓐ Ⓒ Ⓣ Read the dialogue between Jacob and Mr. Lim on page 2. *How do we know that Mr. Lim's lines should be read with hesitation?* (Ellipses indicate pauses.)

Vocabulary Have students identify the word *affects* on page 3. *What clue help you understand the meaning of affects?* (changes)

Pages 4–5

Genre Have students read page 4. *What do you learn about the characters from the stage directions?* (Vera is worried about Mr. Lim and curious about the folder. Mr. Lim is keeping a secret.) *How do the stage directions help create the mystery?* (They show Mr. Lim's secretive behavior and that the students are suspicious that something is wrong.)

Organization Have students locate and read the description of Scene 2 at the top of page 5. *How is Scene 2 different from Scene 1?* (Scene 1 is inside a classroom. Scene 2 is on the school playground. Caleb is not in Scene 1 but is in Scene 2.) *How are Scene 1 and Scene 2 similar?* (It is lunchtime on the same day and Jacob, Miguel, and Vera are in both scenes.)

Point of View Read aloud page 5. Then model how to identify point of view. Say: *Each character has a point of view about Mr. Lim's actions. Vera says that Mr. Lim is acting weird, and she offers evidence to support her point of view. She says, "…he couldn't wait for us to leave." What else does Vera say about Mr. Lim's actions?* (She says that he was looking at a folder when they came in but he quickly concealed it behind his back.) *What is Vera's point of view about Mr. Lim?* (She thinks that he is acting strange.) Have students record the details that reveal Vera's point of view about Mr. Lim in their Point of View charts as they continue to read the selection.

Genre Have students read the stage direction at the bottom of page 5. *What do Jacob and Vera do?* (They both nod.) *What does this tell you about them?* (They agree with Miguel, who said that Mr. Lim seemed upset.)

Pages 6–7

Point of View Have students read page 7. *What does Miguel say about Mr. Lim?* (Mr. Lim was angry.) *Does Vera think Mr. Lim is angry?* (No, she thinks he's worried.) *Do any of the characters have the same point of view about Mr. Lim's behavior?* (no) *Why not?* (Vera thinks Mr. Lim is worried so he probably received bad news, Jacob thinks Mr. Lim is keeping secrets and could be a spy, Caleb thinks that Mr. Lim was keeping students' test papers secret.)

Problem and Solution *What mystery do the students want to solve?* (They want to find out why Mr. Lim is acting weird.) *What steps do they take to solve the mystery?* (They decide to follow him.)

STOP AND CHECK Read the question in the Stop and Check box on page 7. (Mr. Lim jumps up when the students come in the room and he hides a folder behind his back. Then he tells Vera that he is fine but he has a lot on his mind.)

Have partners review their Point of View charts for pages 2–7 and discuss what they learned.

Quick Check **Do students understand weekly vocabulary in context? If not, review and reteach using the instruction on page 204.**

Can students identify point of view? If not, review and reteach using the instruction on page 204 and assign the Unit 4 Week 2 digital mini-lesson.

Objectives
- Understand and use new vocabulary
- Read drama
- Recognize and understand point of view
- Understand complex text through close reading
- Respond to the selection using text evidence to support ideas

Materials
- "The Mysterious Teacher" Apprentice Leveled Reader, pp. 8–20
- Graphic Organizer: Point of View

☞ **Go Digital**
- Apprentice Leveled Reader eBook
- Downloadable Graphic Organizer
- Point of View Digital Mini-Lesson

Scaffolding for **Wonders** Approaching Leveled Reader

BEFORE READING

5–10 Minutes   SL.5.1c SL.5.1d L.5.4a L.5.6 CCSS

Expand Vocabulary

Display each word below. Say the words and have students repeat them. Then use the Define/Example/Ask routine to introduce each word.

1 **allowed** (page 14)

Define: given permission to do something

Example: Children were *allowed* to swim only when lifeguards. were there.

Ask: What would you like to be *allowed* to do?

2 **attention** (page 13)

Define: listen carefully or think about something

Example: The students paid *attention* to what the teacher said.

Ask: Why is it important to pay *attention* to directions?

3 **confusion** (page 9)

Define: a feeling when you don't understand what is happening

Example: In my *confusion,* I went to the wrong room.

Ask: What situation has caused you *confusion?*

4 **flustered** (page 11)

Define: feeling confused or slightly nervous

Example: Max was *flustered* because he arrived at the game late.

Ask: How would a person who is very *flustered* speak and act?

4 **identity** (page 12)

Define: who a person is

Example: Airlines allow people to use a driver's license to prove their *identity*.

Ask: What are some ways you can prove your *identity?*

DURING READING

15–20 Minutes   RL.5.1 RL.5.6 SL.5.1b L.5.4a CCSS

Close Reading

🔍 **Pages 8–9**

Organization ⒶⒸⓉ Read the title of Act 2 on page 8. *What do you think will happen in Act 2?* (The children will follow Mr. Lim.) *What did Caleb say at the end of Act 1 that gets you ready for Act 2?* ("Let's follow him after school. We'll see if he does anything suspicious.")

Point of View Ask students to read page 8. *Which characters express their ideas about Mr. Lim?* (Miguel, Caleb, Jacob) *What is Miguel's point of view?* (Mr. Lim isn't happy.) *What makes him think that?* (the way Mr. Lim looks) *Does Caleb agree with Miguel?* (no) *Why not?* (He thinks Officer Davies wouldn't make Mr. Lim unhappy because they are friends.) Have students identify Jacob's point of view. (Maybe Mr. Lim is in trouble.) Have students record details on their Point of View charts.

Organization ⒶⒸⓉ Have students read the stage direction at the top of page 9. What are the children doing? (hiding behind a bush) What does the stage direction in the middle of the page tell you about Mr. Lin? (He follows Officer Davies offstage.)

🔍 **Pages 10–11**

Organization ⒶⒸⓉ Have students read page 10. *Where does Scene 2 take place?* (outside police station) *Why are there two Scenes in Act 2?* (setting changed)

Point of View Have students read pages 10 and 11. *Each character presents a different point of view about Mr. Lim's visit to the police station. What does Jacob think?* (Mr. Lim's a spy. He's giving information to the police.) *What does Vera think?* (He's asking the police for help.) *What does Miguel think?* (He's paying parking tickets.) *What does Caleb think?* (He's visiting his friend, Officer Davies.) Have partners point out the evidence each speaker uses for his or her point of view.

Vocabulary Have students locate the word *imagination* on page 11. *Why does Caleb say, "You have too much imagination!"?* (He thinks his friends are making up stories about Mr. Lim. There is no proof in what they say.)

Pages 12–13

STOP AND CHECK Read the question in the Stop and Check box on page 12. (to find out the reason for his "suspicious" behavior)

Organization **A C T** Have students point to *Act 3*. Read aloud the title. *What part of the plot will happen in Act 3?* (The characters will solve the mystery.)

Point of View Have students read page 13. *What makes Vera think that Mr. Lim is worried about something?* (She sees him yawning and thinks he didn't sleep well because he was worrying.) *What does each character think Mr. Lim is worried about?* (Vera: his family; Miguel: paying parking tickets; Jacob: his cover has been blown) Have partners discuss how the characters' interpretations of this "clue" support their ideas about Mr. Lim.

Pages 14–15

Problem and Solution Review pages 14 and 15. *Why weren't the students able to solve the case of the mysterious teacher?* (Each student had a different point of view about Mr. Lim and interpreted his actions incorrectly.)

STOP AND CHECK Read the question in the Stop and Check box on page 15. (Mr. Lim was organizing a field trip to the old town jail. He kept it a secret in case he could not get permission for the tour.)

AFTER READING

10–15 Minutes RL.5.1 RL5.2 RL.5.9 W.5.9a L.5.4a **CCSS**

Respond to Reading

Compare Texts Have students discuss how taking a second look helps characters solve mysteries in "Where's Brownie?" and "The Mysterious Teacher." Ask: *When have you taken a second look in order to solve a problem?*

Summarize Have students turn to page 16 and summarize the events in "The Mysterious Teacher." (Answers should include details from the selection.)

Text Evidence

Have partners work together to answer questions on page 16. Have students use their Point of View Charts.

Point of View (Caleb does not see anything suspicious in Mr. Lim's actions. He says, "He was just grading tests.")

Vocabulary (The word *stress* means worry or difficulty. "It's the stress or worry from having a secret identity.")

Write About Reading (The stress of planning a field trip and keeping it secret makes Mr. Lim act differently. He hides the folder on page 2; goes to the police station on page 9; speaks in a sharp tone, on page 12.)

Independent Reading

Encourage students to read "The Case of the Missing Nectarine" on pages 17–19. Have them summarize the selection and compare it to "The Mysterious Teacher." Have them work with a partner to answer the "Make Connections" questions on page 19.

 Quick Check Can students identify point of view? If not, review and teach using instruction on page 204 and assign the Unit 4 Week 2 digital mini-lesson.

Can students respond to the selection using text evidence? If not, provide, sentence frames to help them organize their ideas.

WEEK 2 LESSON 5

Objectives
- Review weekly vocabulary words
- Review point of view
- Write an analysis to share an opinion about two characters

Scaffolding for **McGraw-Hill Reading Wonders** Reading/Writing Workshop

Materials
- Visual Vocabulary Cards: 125–132
- Interactive Worktext, pp. 226–227
- Assessment Book, pp. 42–43

☞ **Go Digital**
- Visual Vocabulary Cards
- Point of View Mini-Lesson
- Interactive eWorktext

REVIEW AND RETEACH

5–10 Minutes   RL.5.1   RL.5.6   L.5.4a   L.5.6   **CCSS**

Weekly Vocabulary

Display one **Visual Vocabulary Card** at a time and ask students to use the vocabulary word in a sentence. If students have difficulty, have them find the word in "Where's Brownie?" and use the context clues to define it.

Comprehension: Point of View

I Do Display and read aloud: *Tina and I went to a boring movie. When we left, Tina said, "It was funny! I laughed a lot!" But I didn't agree with her.* Say: *The narrator describes the movie as "boring." When Tina says she thought the movie was funny, the narrator "didn't agree." These descriptive words and details are clues to the narrator's point of view. I can tell the narrator thinks the movie was boring.*

We Do Display: *My brother Jack likes to play silly jokes. One time he hid behind the door. Then he jumped out and surprised me. We both laughed. "Behave," my mom told him.* Say: *We are going to find a point of view together. Who is the narrator's brother?* (Jack) *What words does the narrator use to describe his brother's jokes?* (silly) *What did the narrator do when his brother played a joke?* (laughed) *Use these clues. What does the narrator think of his brother?* (The narrator thinks Jack is funny.) *What did the narrator's mom say?* (Behave) *What does his mom think of Jack?* (He should behave.)

You Do Display another passage: *"Who wants to go fishing?" Dad asked. I frowned, but my sister Meg clapped her hands and grabbed her fishing pole. "Yes!" She was more excited than I was.* Have partners identify the narrator's point of view of the fishing trip. Then have them identify Meg's point of view.

WRITE ABOUT READING

25–35 Minutes   W.5.1a   W.5.1d   W.5.4   W.5.5   W.5.9a   **CCSS**

Read an Analysis

- Ask students to look back at "Where's Brownie?" in the **Interactive Worktext**. Have volunteers review their notes about the characters. *How did each character in "Where's Brownie?" try to solve the problem of the missing pet?*

- Read aloud the directions on page 226. Read aloud the student model. *Ava's paragraph is not a summary. It is an analysis of the characters in the story. Ava is giving her opinion about which character in "Where's Brownie?" is a better problem solver.*

- *An analysis always includes certain parts. The first is the* topic sentence. Have students circle the topic sentence. *What information has Ava included in this sentence?* (text's title; her opinion about the characters)

- *Another part of an analysis is* text evidence. *Ava supports her opinion with many details from the text. Each detail Ava includes shows why Alex is a better problem solver than Sam. Reread the model and draw a box around the text evidence. Look back at your notes about "Where's Brownie?" What other details might be included as text evidence in Ava's paragraph?* (The narrator says Sam makes problems worse rather than better.)

- *The final part is the* concluding statement. Have students underline the concluding statement. *How is the statement like the topic sentence?* (Both say that Alex is a better problem solver than Sam.) *Which words in the concluding statement wrap up the text evidence?* (For all these reasons)

Write an Analysis
Analytical Writing

Guided Writing Read the writing prompt on page 227 together. Have students write about "The Mysterious Teacher" or another text they read this week. Have them review their notes. *Use the checklist to help you figure out the right information to include in each section.* Guide students to ask "how" and "why" questions when they analyze text evidence.

Peer Conference Have students read their analysis to a partner. Listeners should identify the strongest text evidence that supports the topic sentence and discuss any sentences that are unclear.

Teacher Conference Check students' writing for complete sentences and text evidence that supports their opinion. Review the concluding statement. *Does this sentence tie all of the parts together?* If necessary, have students revise the concluding statement by restating their topic sentence.

Level Up

▲ Approaching Leveled Reader

▲ Reading/Writing Workshop

Apprentice Leveled Reader

▲ Interactive Worktext

IF students read the Apprentice Level Reader fluently and the **Interactive Worktext** Shared Read fluently and answer the Respond to Reading questions

THEN read together the Approaching Level Reader main selection and the **Reading/Writing Workshop** Shared Read from *Reading Wonders*. Have students take notes as they read, using self-stick notes. Then ask and answer questions about their notes.

Writing Rubric

	4	3	2	1
Topic Sentence	Topic sentence presents a clear opinion.	Topic sentence presents an opinion somewhat clearly.	Topic is presented in short phrases; opinion is unclear.	There is no topic sentence; no opinion is presented.
Text Evidence	Opinion is supported by two or more text details.	Opinion is supported by only one detail from the text.	Little to no evidence from the text supports opinion.	No text evidence is included; does not support opinion.
Concluding Statement	Clearly restates an opinion; wraps up the details.	Restatement is less focused; attempts to wrap up the details.	Vaguely restates opinion. Doesn't correlate well to text evidence.	There is no conclusion.
Writing Style	Writes in complete sentences. Uses correct spelling and grammar.	Uses complete sentences and phrases. Writing has spelling and grammar errors.	Few or no complete sentences. There are many spelling and grammar errors.	Does not write accurately or in complete sentences.

ASSESSMENT

Weekly Assessment

Have students complete the Weekly Assessment using **Assessment** book pages 42–43.

WEEK 3 LESSON 1

Objectives
- Develop oral language
- Build background about making a positive change
- Understand and use weekly vocabulary
- Read a biography

Scaffolding for **Wonders** Reading/Writing Workshop

Materials
Interactive Worktext, pp. 228–235
- Visual Vocabulary Cards: 133–140

☞ **Go** Digital
- Interactive eWorktext
- Visual Vocabulary Cards

WEEKLY CONCEPT

5–10 Minutes SL.5.1b SL.5.1c **CCSS**

Talk About It

Essential Question Read aloud the Essential Question on page 228 of the **Interactive Worktext**: *What can people do to bring about a positive change?* Explain that "to bring about a positive change" means to cause something good to happen. Say: *We can bring about a positive change when we work to help others.*

- Discuss the photograph on page 228. Ask: *How are these people taking action?* (Possible answers: marching, gathering, holding up signs) Explain the meanings of difficult words and phrases such as *segregated, decent,* and *first class citizenship.*

I Do Say: *I am going to look closely at the photograph and look for ways these people are working to make a change. I see signs that say "End segregated rules in public schools" and "Decent housing now!" These are all positive messages. Writing a message on a sign is one way to let others know about a change you want to make. I am going to write this in the web on page 229.*

We Do Say: *Let's look at the photograph together to look for other ways these people are working for a positive change. What are the people gathered to do?* (march) *What other signs do you see?* (We march for first class citizenship now! We march for jobs for all now!) Point to the buttons on the people's suits. *Ask: What is another way they are sharing a message?* (wearing buttons) Guide students to add their words to the web on page 229.

You Do Have partners brainstorm important people in history who have made a positive change. Ask: *What did he or she do? How did their actions help others?*

REVIEW VOCABULARY

10–15 Minutes L.5.1a L.5.4a L.5.5c L.5.6 **CCSS**

Review Weekly Vocabulary Words

- Use the **Visual Vocabulary Cards** to review the weekly vocabulary.

- Read together the directions for the Vocabulary activity on page 230 of the **Interactive Worktext**. Then complete the activity.

1 **defy** Have partners ask each other questions to help them decide which word is a synonym for *defy.* (disobey) Then have them discuss other words that have a similar meaning. (Possible answers: stand up to, challenge)

2 **entitled** Have students use this sentence starter: *On a bus, I am entitled to _____ and _____.* (talk to a friend; get off at a bus stop)

3 **sought** Ask partners to discuss the types of information that can be sought in dictionaries. Then, have students use the following sentence frame: *I sought _____ in a dictionary.* (Possible answers: a spelling; the meaning of a word; how to say a word)

4 **outspoken** Read aloud each sentence with expression and have students echo. Have students use this sentence frame: *_____ is outspoken because _____.* (Gina; she tells her opinion)

5 **anticipation** Ask: *Have you ever played or watched a sport and waited with anticipation? Why?* (Possible answer: Yes; I waited with anticipation for a player to pass a ball because the player was coming toward me.) Then have partners discuss why the baseball player waited with anticipation. (He knows the pitcher is going to throw the ball to him.)

6 **reserved** Have students point to an object that is *reserved* for a teacher and complete the sentence frame: *The _____ is reserved for _____.* (Possible answer: desk; my teacher)

7 **unequal** Point out the prefix *un-*. Explain that *un-* is added to the beginning of a word and often means "not." (equal; un; not the same)

8 **neutral** Have students brainstorm a list of people at a sports game. After each response, ask: *Is that person neutral? Why or why not?* After students complete their drawings, have them write a caption using this sentence frame: *During a sports game, a _____ must be neutral.* (referee)

High-Utility Words

Explain that linking words join two ideas. Some examples of linking words are *if, because, but, so,* and *when.* Have students look at the High-Utility Words activity on page 231 of the **Interactive Worktext**. Have partners circle linking words in the passage. (because, so, since, when, if) Display: *I am cold* and *I put on my coat.* Say: *I am going to join these two sentence parts using the linking word* when: *When I am cold, I put on my coat.* Have students use other linking words to join the two sentence parts. Then have them discuss how each linking word changes the meaning.

> **ELL ENGLISH LANGUAGE LEARNERS**
>
> Write the linking words *if, when,* and *so* on note cards. Then write *I am cold* and *I put on my coat* on separate cards. Help students use the linking words to join the two sentence parts. Then have them read their sentences aloud.

READ COMPLEX TEXT

15–20 Minutes   RI.5.1   RF.5.4c

Read: "Frederick Douglass"

- Have students turn to page 232 in the **Interactive Worktext** and read aloud the Essential Question. Explain that Frederick Douglass was a real person who escaped slavery and brought about a positive change for African Americans. Ask: *What is the title?* ("Frederick Douglass: Freedom's Voice") *Use the title as a clue. How do you think Frederick Douglass brought about change for African Americans?* (He spoke out against slavery.)

- Read "Frederick Douglass" together. Note that the weekly vocabulary words are highlighted in yellow. Expand Vocabulary words are highlighted in blue.

- Have students use the "My Notes" section on page 232 to write questions they have, words they don't understand, and details they want to remember. Model how to use the "My Notes" section. *I can write notes about questions I have as I read. In the first sentence on page 233, I am not certain what "lived in slavery" means. I will write these words with a question mark in the "My Notes" section. In the next paragraph, I wonder why Frederick escaped to the North. I will write the question:* Why did Frederick go to the North? *in the "My Notes" section. When we reread the story, I will ask my questions so I better understand what I am reading.*

> **ELL ENGLISH LANGUAGE LEARNERS**
>
> As you read together, have students highlight parts of the text they have questions about. After reading, help them write questions in the "My Notes" column.

 Quick Check Can students understand the weekly vocabulary in context? If not, review vocabulary using the **Visual Vocabulary Cards** before teaching Lesson 2.

Objectives
• Read a biography
• Understand complex text through close reading
• Recognize and understand author's point of view
• Respond to the selection using text evidence to support ideas

Scaffolding for **WONDERS** Reading/Writing Workshop

Materials
Interactive Worktext, pp. 232–237

☞ **Go** Digital
• Interactive eWorktext
• Author's Point of View Mini-Lesson

REREAD COMPLEX TEXT

20–25 Minutes | RI.5.1 | RI.6.6 | L.5.4a | L.5.5c | L.5.6 | CCSS

Close Reading: "Frederick Douglass"

Reread "Frederick Douglass" with students. As you read together, discuss important passages in the text. Have students respond to text-dependent questions, including those in the **Interactive Worktext**.

🔍 Page 233

Expand Vocabulary Discuss the definition of *dared*. Have students locate the word in the text. Ask: *What did Frederick dare to do?* (defy, or disobey, his "master") *What risk did Frederick dare take?* (being punished)

Author's Point of View Say: *An author's point of view is the author's attitude toward the person and events he or she is writing about.* Model using text evidence to find the author's point of view. *I read in the first sentence that Frederick "would become a great leader." Let's draw a box around this phrase. The word* great *is a positive word. I think this a clue to the author's point of view. Let's keep reading to find out.* Guide students to mark descriptive words and phrases. *Ask: What does the word* dared *tell you about Frederick Douglass?* (He was brave.) *What does "his love of words" tell you about Frederick?* (He was smart.) *What other words describe Frederick?* (courage) *Now review all the words you marked. Put these clues together. What does the author think abut Frederick Douglass?* (He was a great, smart, and courageous person.)

Sentence Structure 🅐🅒🆃 Point to and have students reread the sentence "He had read about their movement in William Lloyd Garrison's newspaper, *The Liberator.*" Point out the words in italics after the comma. Ask: *Sometimes a comma is used before a title of work.*

What is the title of the newspaper? (*The Liberator*) *How is this text different from the rest of the text?* (It is set in italics.) Explain that a *liberator* is someone who sets others free. Ask: *What did Frederick read about in this newspaper?* (the abolitionist movement) *Why do you think Frederick was inspired by this newspaper? Point to text evidence.* (He hoped to end slavery; "his hope of ending slavery")

High-Utility Words Have students reread the last paragraph. Ask: *Which sentence contains a linking word?* (Frederick read every issue because the ideas inspired him.) Have students read the sentence aloud and identify the linking word. (because)

🔍 Page 234

Expand Vocabulary Discuss the word *gathering*. Ask: *What word in the first paragraph has almost the same meaning as* gathering? (meeting) *Who was going to this gathering?* (Frederick, abolitionist speakers) *What was the reason for this gathering?* (to hear abolitionist speakers)

Sentence Structure 🅐🅒🆃 Say: *Punctuation affects the meaning of a sentence.* Have students underline the last sentence in the first paragraph. Ask: *What does an exclamation mark show?* (surprise or excitement) Have students draw a box around each sentence in the second paragraph that ends with an exclamation mark. (He felt nervous standing in front of so many people—especially white people! At the end of his speech, the audience immediately stood up and cheered!) *What feeling does the author express when Frederick begins his speech?* (surprise) *How do you know?* (There were many white people there.) *What feeling does the author express after Frederick's speech?* (excitement) *How do you know?* (The audience cheered.)

Connection of Ideas 🅐🅒🆃 Ask: *Who was in the audience cheering after Frederick's speech?* (William Lloyd

Garrison) *Who was this person? Look back at page 233 to help you.* (He published *The Liberator.*) *Do you think this person was important to Frederick Douglass?* (yes) *How do you know?* (The ideas in the newspaper inspired him.)

Author's Point of View Have students reread the last paragraph. Review the meaning of *captivated.* Ask: *What does this word tell you about Frederick's speeches?* (that people were interested in them) *Is it a positive or negative word?* (positive) *What other words and phrases describe Frederick's way of speaking?* (powerful words; strong presence; expressed his opinions clearly and with dignity; got others to support his ideas) *Put these details together. What does the author think of Frederick as a speaker?* (The author thinks Frederick was a powerful and persuasive speaker.)

Page 235

Sentence Structure **ACT** Have students reread the first paragraph. Ask: *What is the title of the book Frederick wrote?* (*Narrative of the Life of Frederick Douglass, an American Slave*) *How do you know?* (There is a comma before it and it is set in italics.) *What kind of book is it?* (an autobiography) *Have students mark the title of another work that Frederick published.* (*The North Star*) *Was this a book or a newspaper?* (a newspaper)

Expand Vocabulary Have students point to the word *status.* Ask: *What is a person's status?* (their position compared to others) *What word describes the status of women compared to men in Frederick's time?* (unequal)

Author's Point of View Have students reread the last paragraph. Explain the meaning of *causes.* Ask: *What did Frederick think about the way women were treated? Circle the text evidence.* (Frederick thought women should be treated as equals to men in society.) *What did Frederick think about the way African Americans were treated? Circle this sentence.* (He also thought African Americans should not be separated from others in schools.) *Does the author agree or disagree with Frederick's ideas?* (agrees) *How do you know? Draw a box around text evidence.* (the author describes Frederick's work as "these important causes.")

RESPOND TO READING

10–20 Minutes | RI.5.1 | RI.5.2 | RI.5.3 | W.5.9b | SL.5.1d | **CCSS**

Respond to "Frederick Douglass"

Have students summarize "Frederick Douglass" orally to demonstrate comprehension. Then have partners answer the questions on page 236 of the **Interactive Worktext** using the discussion starters. Tell them to use text evidence to support their answers. Have students write the page number(s) on which they found the text evidence for each question.

1. *What did Frederick do in 1841 to show he was against slavery?* (Possible answer: Frederick went to an abolitionist meeting; he gave a speech about the horrors of slavery. Text Evidence: p. 234)

2. *What did Frederick do to get others to support his ideas about slavery?* (Possible answer: He traveled and gave speeches; he expressed his opinions clearly and with dignity; he used powerful words and had a strong presence. Text Evidence: p. 234)

3. *What did Frederick publish about slavery?* (He published a book about his life as a slave and a newspaper with articles against slavery. Text Evidence: p. 235)

After students discuss the questions on page 236, have them write responses to the question on page 237. Tell them to use their partner discussions and notes about "Frederick Douglass" to help them. Circulate and provide guidance.

 Quick Check **Do students understand vocabulary in context? If not, review and reteach using the instruction on page 214.**

Can students use key details to determine author's point of view? If not, review and reteach using the instruction on page 214 and assign the Unit 4 Week 3 digital mini-lesson.

Can students write a response to "Frederick Douglass"? If not, provide sentence frames to help them organize their ideas.

WEEK 3 LESSON

3

Objectives
- Understand and use new vocabulary words
- Read a biography
- Recognize and understand author's point of view
- Understand complex text through close reading

Scaffolding for **Wonders** McGraw-Hill Reading Approaching Leveled Reader

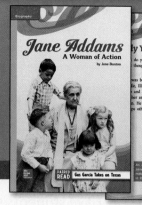
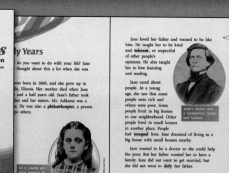

Materials
- "Jane Addams: A Woman of Action" Apprentice Leveled Reader: pp. 2–9
- Graphic Organizer: Point of View

👉 **Go** Digital
- Apprentice Leveled Reader eBook
- Downloadable Graphic Organizer
- Point of View Digital Mini-Lesson

BEFORE READING

10–15 Minutes | SL.5.1c SL.5.1d L.5.4a L.5.6 CCSS

Introduce "Jane Addams: A Woman of Action"

- Read the Essential Question on the title page of "Jane Addams: A Woman of Action" **Apprentice Leveled Reader**: *What can people do to bring about a positive change? We will read about how Jane Addams brought about positive changes in the lives of many people.*

- Read the title. Have students look at the photograph on page 1. *What are these women doing?* (protesting; showing that they want peace, not war) *What do you think it means to be a woman of action?* (a woman who does things to bring about change)

Expand Vocabulary

- Display each word below. Say the words and have students repeat them. Then use the Define/Example/Ask routine to introduce each word.

1 devasted (page 4)

Define: feeling very shocked and sad

Example: Emily was *devastated* when her best friend moved away.

Ask: How might someone who is *devastated* behave?

2 opportunities (page 7)

Define: chances to do something

Example: The teenagers were looking for *opportunities* to earn money during the summer.

Ask: What are some *opportunities* to have fun during the summer?

3 tolerant (page 3)

Define: letting people do, say, or believe what they want without criticizing them

Example: My parents are *tolerant* of the music I play.

Ask: Why is it important for people to be *tolerant*?

DURING READING

20–30 Minutes | RI.5.1 RI.5.8 RI.6.6 SL.5.1b L.5.6 CCSS

Close Reading

🔍 **Pages 2–3**

Genre Point out that biographies are often organized in chronological or time order. Read the second paragraph. *When was Jane born?* (1860) *How old was Jane when her mother died?* (two and a half years old) *What happened after her mother died?* (Her father took care of the children.) *How else do you know that the biography is organized in chronological order?* (title of Chapter 1, "Early Years")

Author's Point of View Read the last paragraph on page 2 and the first paragraph on page 3. *What does Jane want to be?* (like her father) *How does the author describe Jane's father on pages 2 and 3?* (a philanthropist, or person who helps people; taught her to be kind and tolerant; respectful of other people's opinions; taught her to love learning and reading) *What do these details tell you about the author's opinion, or point of view, toward Jane?* (Jane is kind, tolerant, loves learning, and wants to help others.) *What evidence does the author give in the last paragraph on page 3 to support that opinion?* (Jane wanted to be a doctor so she could help the poor.)

Have students add details about the author's point of view to their charts.

Connection of Ideas Ⓐ Ⓒ Ⓣ *Read the second paragraph on page 3. What did Jane notice about where rich people and poor people lived?* (They lived in different neighborhoods.) *How did this discovery connect to Jane's dream of living in a big house with small houses nearby?* (She thought rich people and poor people should live together.)

Pages 4–5

Sentence Structure Ⓐ Ⓒ Ⓣ Read the sentence in the second paragraph on page 4: *She went to school to become a doctor, but she was too sad to study.* Point out that the sentence has two ideas. Ask these questions to help students identify each separate idea: *What did Jane want to do?* (become a doctor) *Why didn't she become a doctor?* (She was too sad to study.) *Which word links these two ideas?* (but)

Organization Ⓐ Ⓒ Ⓣ Have students read page 5. *What happened after Jane Addams left college?* (She went overseas. In London, she saw people in poverty.) *When did Jane go back to London?* (a few years later) *What did she do after she visited Toynbee Hall?* (She decided to set up a settlement house like Toynbee House to help people back home.)

STOP AND CHECK Read the question in the Stop and Check box on page 5. (Jane's father inspired her to help others, and Toynbee Hall was an example of what she could do.)

Pages 6–7

Connection of Ideas Ⓐ Ⓒ Ⓣ Have students read the last paragraph on page 6 and the first paragraph on page 7. *What two purposes did Hull House have?* (Hull House would give wealthy people a chance to learn about poor people by helping them. It would also make the lives of working people better by giving them education and music lessons.)

Vocabulary Have students locate the word *local* on page 7. Point out that local means "the particular area where people live." *Why might local people come to clubs and classes at Hull House?* (It was near where they lived and would be easy for them to get to.)

STOP AND CHECK Read the question in the Stop and Check box on page 6. (Hull House was a big home in a poor neighborhood of smaller homes. Rich and poor people would live together.)

Sentence Structure Ⓐ Ⓒ Ⓣ Read the second paragraph on page 7. Point out the words *neither* and *nor*. Explain that some linking words work in pairs, such as *neither* and *nor*. *What two ideas about the neighbors do the words* neither *and* nor *connect?* (They are not rich. They are not educated.) *How are the people who live at Hull House different from the neighbors?* (They have more money and are educated.)

Pages 8–9

Author's Point of View *Read page 9. What evidence does the author use to support her view that Addams was "a kind person" who "inspired many people to help others"?* (Settlement houses were set up in other cities. She used money she earned to support her work.) Have students add details about the author's point of view to their charts.

STOP AND CHECK Read the question in the Stop and Check box on page 9. (take classes; get child care, help from doctors and lawyers; use gymnasium, theater, library, art gallery, museum; share knowledge and skills)

Have partners review their Author's Point of View charts for pages 2–9 and discuss what they learned.

✔ *Quick Check* Do students understand weekly vocabulary in context? If not, review and reteach using the instruction on page 214.

Can students identify an author's point of view? If not, review and reteach using the instruction on page 214 and assign the Unit 4 Week 3 digital mini-lesson.

Objectives
- Understand and use new vocabulary
- Read a biography
- Recognize and understand author's point of view
- Understand complex text through close reading
- Respond to the selection using text evidence to support ideas

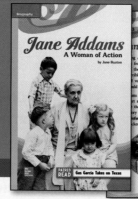
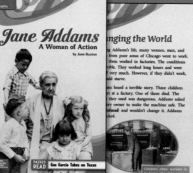

Scaffolding for **Wonders** Approaching Leveled Reader

Materials
- "Jane Addams: A Woman of Action" Apprentice Leveled Reader: pp. 10–20
- Graphic Organizer: Author's Point of View

☞ **Go Digital**
- Apprentice Leveled Reader eBook
- Downloadable Graphic Organizer
- Point of View Digital Mini-Lesson

BEFORE READING

5–10 Minutes   SL.5.1c   SL.5.1d   L.4.a   L.5.6

Expand Vocabulary

Display each word below. Say the words and have students repeat them. Then use the Define/Example/Ask routine to introduce each word.

1 courageous (page 14)

Define: brave

Example: The *courageous* fire fighter went into the burning building.

Ask: What other jobs require *courageous* people?

2 criticized (page 13)

Define: found fault with something

Example: The voters *criticized* the mayor's decision.

Ask: How do people often act when they are *criticized*?

3 recognition (page 14)

Define: public respect and thanks for good work or special achievements

Example: Several students received *recognition* for their good sportsmanship.

Ask: For what other skills or qualities might a student receive *recognition*?

4 refused (page 10)

Define: said no in a firm way

Example: The tired child was cranky and *refused* to pick up her toys.

Ask: Why would a person *refuse* to do something?

DURING READING

15–20 Minutes   RI.5.1   RI.5.8   RI.6.6   SL.5.1b   L.5.6

Close Reading

🔍 **Pages 10–11**

Author's Point of View *Read the first paragraph on page 10. What details show the author's point of view about the lives of workers in factories?* (from poor areas, terrible work conditions, long hours, not paid very much, work or starve) *What is the the author's opinion about the need for labor laws?* (Laws are needed to protect workers' safety, pay, and number of hours worked.) Have students record details and the author's point of view they support on their Author's Point of View chart as they read the selection.

Genre Ⓐ Ⓒ Ⓣ *Biographies often contain photographs that give information about the text. Look at the photograph on page 10 and read the caption. What does it show?* (children working in a factory) *Read the second paragraph. What details does it give about children working in a factory?* (Addams heard a terrible story. Three children were hurt in a factory; one died.) *How does the photograph help you understand the text?* (It helps readers see what working in a factory was like for children.)

Author's Point of View Ⓐ Ⓒ Ⓣ *Read "Children are Cheap" on page 11. What reasons did the factory owners give for not wanting child labor laws to change?* (hard work teaches children good values, families needed the money children earned) *Does the author believe that these were their reasons?* (No, she thinks child labor made it cheaper to run their businesses.) *What is the author's attitude toward the factory owners?* (They care more about money than the lives of their workers.)

Cause and Effect Read the first two paragraph on page 11. *Why did Jane talk to politicians to help the poor?* (She knew poverty would not stop unless the laws were changed.) *What kinds of laws did she want politicians to change?* (laws for safe work conditions, limit to number of hours worked in a day; free school for all children.)

Pages 12–13

Sentence Structure [ACT] Read the last sentence in "Everyone is Responsible" on page 12. Explain that quotation marks often show a person's exact words. *Whose exact words are in quotation marks?* (Addams's exact words) *How do you know?* (The sidebar is about Jane Addams. The sentence with the words in quotation marks begins with "Addams asked.")

Connection of Ideas [ACT] Have students read the first paragraph on page 12. *Why did Jane Adams help start the American Civil Liberties Union?* (to help people treated unfairly because of their race) Have students read the first two paragraphs on page 13. *What did Addams do to try to stop World War I?* (talked to people about peace and started groups for women to stop the war, including Women's Peace Party) Ask: *What was the purpose of starting these organizations?* (The organizations were started to change the world by changing people's attitudes.)

Page 14

Author's Point of View *What evidence on page 14 shows that the author admires Jane Addams?* (Addams is "one of America's best-loved leaders; she was courageous and brave; she never gave up her goal of helping others; Addams received the Nobel Peace Prize for her lifetime of work and the time line lists her accomplishments.)

STOP AND CHECK Read the question in the Stop and Check box on page 14. (She tried to help poor people, women, children, and people who were treated unfairly because of their race.)

AFTER READING

10–15 Minutes   RI.5.1   RI.5.2   RI.5.9   W.5.9b   L.5.4a   CCSS

Respond to Reading

Compare Texts Have students compare and contrast changes made by Frederick Douglass and Jane Addams. Then ask: *How can you help to make positive changes at school, or in your community?*

Summarize Have students turn to page 15 and summarize the selection. (Answers should include details from students' Author's Point of View charts.)

Text Evidence

Have partners work together to answer questions on page 15. Remind students to use their graphic organizer.

Author's Point of View (The author admires Addams. She describes Jane as kind and gives many examples of how she tried to help the poor.)

Vocabulary (*Wealthy* means "rich." The word *rich* comes after *wealthy*.)

Write About Reading (The author admires Addams for her work to stop child labor. Addams also "worked hard to make school free for all children." Things didn't change right away; child labor wasn't banned until 1938.)

Independent Reading

Encourage students to read the paired selection "Gus García Takes on Texas" on pages 16–18. Have them summarize the selection and compare it to "Jane Addams: A Woman of Action." Have them work with partners to answer the "Make Connections" questions on page 18.

 Quick Check Can students identify an author's point of view? If not, review and reteach using the instruction on page 214 and assign the Unit 4 Week 3 digital mini-lesson.

Can students respond to the selection using text evidence? If not, provide, sentence frames to help them organize their ideas.

Objectives
- Review weekly vocabulary words
- Review author's point of view
- Write an analysis about the author's point of view

Materials
- Visual Vocabulary Cards: 133–140
- Interactive Worktext, pp. 238–239
- Assessment Book, pp. 44–45

☞ **Go Digital**
- Visual Vocabulary Cards
- Author's Point of View Lesson
- Interactive eWorktext

Scaffolding for **Wonders** Reading/Writing Workshop

REVIEW AND RETEACH

5–10 Minutes   RI.5.1   RI.6.6   L.5.4a   L.5.6   CCSS

Weekly Vocabulary

Display one **Visual Vocabulary Card** at a time and ask students to use the vocabulary word in a sentence. If students have difficulty, have them find the word in "Frederick Douglass" and use context clues to define it.

Comprehension: Author's Point of View

I Do Display and say: *Lewis and Clark were two explorers. They bravely traveled across the West. No Americans had traveled that far before. It was a long and difficult trip, but they kept going.* Circle *bravely* and underline the last two sentences. Say: *The word* bravely *is a powerful word. The details also show me how brave and determined they were. I can use these clues to figure out the author's point of view:* Lewis and Clark were brave and determined explorers.

We Do Display: *Marie Curie was a brilliant scientist. Few women worked as scientists at the time. Her hard work led her to win many important scientific awards.* Ask: *What powerful words does the author use?* (brilliant, important) *What details does the author include?* (Few women worked as scientists at the time; her hard work led her to win awards.) *What does the author think about Marie Curie?* (The author thinks she was a very smart and important scientist.)

You Do Display: *Rosa Parks took a risk. She showed courage when she disobeyed a law she did not agree with. She inspired others to do what they think is right.* Have partners mark details and powerful words and then determine the author's point of view.

WRITE ABOUT READING

25–35 Minutes   W.5.4   W.5.5   W.5.9b   CCSS

Read an Analysis

- Ask students to look back at "Frederick Douglass" in the **Interactive Worktext**. Have volunteers review the details they marked about Frederick Douglass. *How did details in the text help you understand the author's point of view?*

- Read aloud the directions on page 238. Read aloud the student model. *Eli's writing is not a summary. It is an analysis, or a detailed description. Eli analyzed how details in "Frederick Douglass" show the author's point of view. When you analyze, you ask yourself "how" and "why" questions to think about how the text is developed and what readers learn from it.*

- *An analysis includes certain parts. The first is the* topic sentence. Have students circle the topic sentence. *What information has Eli included in this sentence?* (text's title; that details show the author's point of view)

- *Another part of an analysis is* text evidence. *Eli restates details from the text that show the author's point of view.* Have students draw boxes around the text evidence. (sentences 2-6) *Look back at the details you marked in "Frederick Douglass." What other details could Eli include as text evidence?* (Possible answer: he never imagined he would become a great leader)

- *The final part of an analysis is the* concluding statement. Have students underline the concluding statement. *How is the concluding statement like the topic sentence?* (Both say the author thinks Douglass was a great leader.) *What words does Eli use to wrap up all the details?* (All of these details)

![Analytical Writing] **Write an Analysis**

Guided Writing Read the writing prompt on page 239 together. Have students write about "Jane Addams" or another text they read this week. Have them review their Author's Point of View charts. *Use the checklist to help you figure out the information to include in each section.* Guide students to ask "how" and "why" questions, such as *Why does the author include these details?*

Peer Conference Have partners read their analyses to each other. Listeners should identify the strongest text evidence that supports the topic sentence and discuss any sentences that are unclear.

Teacher Conference Check students' writing for complete sentences and text evidence that supports their topic. Review the concluding statement. *Does the concluding statement tie all of the parts of the analysis together?* If necessary, have students revise the conclusion by restating the topic sentence.

Level Up

Apprentice Leveled Reader

▲ **Approaching Leveled Reader**

▲ **Interactive Worktext**

▲ **Reading/Writing Workshop**

IF students read the Apprentice Level Reader fluently and the **Interactive Worktext** Shared Read fluently and answer the Respond to Reading questions

THEN read together the Approaching Level Reader main selection and the **Reading/Writing Workshop** Shared Read from Reading Wonders. Have students take notes as they read, using self-stick notes. Then ask and answer questions about their notes.

Writing Rubric

	4	3	2	1
Topic Sentence	There is one clear, focused topic sentence.	Topic sentence is less focused, somewhat clear.	Topic is presented in short phrases.	There is no topic sentence.
Text Evidence	Topic is supported by two or more text details.	Evidence includes only one detail from the text.	Little to no evidence is cited from the text.	No text evidence is included.
Concluding Statement	Clearly restates the topic sentence; wraps up the details.	Restatement is less focused; attempts to wrap up the details.	Vaguely restates the topic. Doesn't correlate well to text evidence.	There is no conclusion.
Writing Style	Writes in complete sentences. Uses correct spelling and grammar.	Uses complete sentences and phrases. Writing has spelling and grammar errors.	Few or no complete sentences. There are many spelling and grammar errors.	Does not write accurately or in complete sentences.

ASSESSMENT

Weekly Assessment

Have students complete the Weekly Assessment using **Assessment** book pages 44–45.

WEEK 3

▶ **Mid-Unit Assessment,** pages 96–103

▶ **Fluency Assessment,** pages 250–265

Unit 4 Mid-Unit Assessment

CCSS TESTED SKILLS

✔ COMPREHENSION	✔ VOCABULARY:
• Point of View RL.5.1	• Context Clues L.5.4a
• Point of View RL.5.1	
• Author's Point of View RI.5.2, RI.6.6	

Using Assessment and Writing Scores

↻ RETEACH	IF ...	THEN ...
COMPREHENSION	Students answer 0–5 multiple-choice items correctly ...	... reteach tested skills using instruction on pages 364–371.
VOCABULARY	Students answer 0–2 multiple-choice items correctly ...	... reteach tested skills using instruction on page 364.
WRITING	Students score mostly 1–2 on weekly writing rubrics throughout the unit...	... reteach writing using instruction on pages 372–373.

Fluency Assessment

Conduct assessments individually using the differentiated fluency passages in Assessment. Students' expected fluency goal for this Unit is 117–137 WCPM with an accuracy rate of 95% or higher.

Weeks 4 and 5

Monitor students' progress on the following to inform how to adjust instruction for the remainder of the unit.

ADJUST INSTRUCTION	
ACCESS COMPLEX TEXT	If students need more support for accessing complex text, provide additional modeling of prompts in Lesson 2 of Week 4, pages 220–221, and Week 5, pages 230–231. After you model how to identify the text evidence, guide students to find text evidence in Lessons 3 and 4 in Week 4, pages 222–225, and Week 5, pages 232–235.
FLUENCY	For those students who need more support with Fluency, focus on the Fluency lessons in the Foundational Skills Kit.
WRITING	If students need more support incorporating text evidence in their writing, conduct the Write About Reading activities in Lessons 4 and 5 as group writing activities.
FOUNDATIONAL SKILLS	Review student's individualized progress in *PowerPAL for Reading* to determine which foundational skills to incorporate into your lessons for the remainder of the unit.

Objectives
- Develop oral language
- Build background about the value of natural resources
- Understand and use weekly vocabulary
- Read expository text

Materials
- Interactive Worktext, pp. 240–247
- Visual Vocabulary Cards: 141–148

☞ **Go** Digital
- Interactive eWorktext
- Visual Vocabulary Cards

Scaffolding for **Wonders** Reading/Writing Workshop

WEEKLY CONCEPT

Talk About It

Essential Question Read aloud the Essential Question on page 240 of the **Interactive Worktext:** *Why are natural resources valuable?* Say: *Natural resources are things in the world such as trees, water, air, rocks, soil, and minerals that we use. We use natural resources for food, to build homes, and to create energy to run machines.*

- Discuss the photograph on page 240. Ask: *What natural resources do you see in this photograph?* (water, trees, rocks, soil) Guide students to write each resource as headings on the web on page 241.

> **I Do** *In this photo I also see buildings, a dock, and a bridge. These look like they are made of wood. I know that wood comes from trees. I will write "make buildings and bridges" under "Trees" in the web on page 241.*

> **We Do** Say: *Let's look at the photograph for another way we use natural resources.* Point to the dam. Explain that a dam uses the energy from flowing water to create electricity. Point to the power lines in the photo. *These power lines bring electricity to buildings and houses. We use electricity to light our homes and to provide power for computers and other machines. What natural resource does a dam use?* (water) *Why is this natural resource important?* (It creates electricity.) Guide students to add these words to the web under "Water" on page 241. Have students discuss other ways that water is an important natural resource and add words to their web.

> **You Do** Have partners tell which natural resource is important to them and why it is important. Have them answer the questions: *Which natural resource is important to you? What does this natural resource provide?*

REVIEW VOCABULARY

Review Weekly Vocabulary Words

- Use the **Visual Vocabulary Cards** to review the weekly vocabulary.

- Read together the directions for the Vocabulary activity on page 242 of the **Interactive Worktext**. Then complete the activity.

1 **absorb** Have students use the following sentence starter: _____ *and* _____ *absorb water.* (Possible answers: sponge, paper towel, towel, cloth)

2 **affect** Have students discuss why they would put on a sweater. (Possible answers: I feel cold; I am going outside.) *How does putting on a sweater affect your body?* (Possible answer: I feel warmer.)

3 **circulates** Have students describe how they are moving when they circulate around their partner. (I moved around my partner in a circle.) Then have them complete the sentence frame using their partner's name: _____ *circulates around me.*

4 **cycle** Display a calendar. Have students point out things on the calendar that happen over and over in the *cycle* of the year. Have them complete the sentence frame: _____ *happen in a cycle.* (Possible answers: Days of the week, Months of the year)

5 **glaciers** Have partners ask each other questions to help them decide which of the words are related to glaciers. (ice, polar, frozen) Ask: *Are glaciers in places that are hot or cold?* (cold)

6 **conserve** Ask: *What happens when you start or turn on a sprinkler?* (Water comes out.) *What happens when you stop or turn off a garden hose?* (The water stops

---

dripping.) *Which action conserves water?* (turning off a dripping hose) *Why?* (Possible answers: It saves water; it keeps water from coming out.)

7 **seeps** Have students describe how water seeps using the synonyms. Then have students write another word that means almost the same as *seeps*. (Possible answers: drips, leaks, dribbles)

8 **necessity** Say this sentence using *necessity. Food is a necessity for people because our bodies need food to live.* Have students draw a necessity for a plant to grow and live. (Drawings will vary, but should show a plant and sun, water, or soil.) Have students use the sentence frame to write a caption: _____ *is a necessity for a plant to grow.*

High-Utility Words

Explain that an author sometimes use signal words to show how two people, things, or ideas are alike or different. Signal words that compare include *also, in addition, as well as,* and *too.* Signal words that contrast include *however, but, although, different than,* and *unlike.* Have students look at the High-Utility Words activity on page 243 of the **Interactive Worktext**. Have partners circle the compare and contrast words and phrases in the passage. (however, Although, In addition, as well as, Compared with) Have students take turns reading the sentences, identifying a signal word, and telling whether the word shows that two things are alike or different.

> **ELL ENGLISH LANGUAGE LEARNERS**
>
> Display a two-column chart with the heads *Compare* and *Contrast.* Then write the following compare and contrast words on note cards: *in addition, however, also, although.* Read each signal word aloud and have students repeat. Then have students tell which column to put the word.

READ COMPLEX TEXT

15–20 Minutes   RI.5.1   RF.5.4c   **CCSS**

Read: "Power from Nature"

- Have students turn to page 244 in the **Interactive Worktext** and read aloud the Essential Question. Explain that they will read about natural resources people use to create energy. Ask: *What is the title?* ("Power from Nature") *What does the picture show?* (Possible answers: windmills; wind turbines; wind farm) *Use these clues. What natural resource do these machines use?* (wind) *What do you think they help create?* (Possible answers: power, energy)

- Read "Power from Nature" together. Note that the weekly vocabulary words are highlighted in yellow. Expand Vocabulary words are highlighted in blue.

- Have students use the "My Notes" section on page 244 to write questions they have, words they don't understand, and details they want to remember. Model how to use the "My Notes" section. *I can write notes about questions I have as I read. In the first paragraph on page 245, I'm not sure what a power plant is. I will write* power plant *with a question mark in the "My Notes" section. In the second paragraph, I wonder why the author says that natural resources are "nature's gifts." I will write:* Why are natural resources nature's gifts? *When we reread the text, I will ask my questions so I better understand what I am reading.*

> **ELL ENGLISH LANGUAGE LEARNERS**
>
> As you read together, have students highlight the parts of the text they have questions about. After reading, help them write questions in the "My Notes" section.

 Quick Check Can students understand the weekly vocabulary in context? If not, review vocabulary using the **Visual Vocabulary Cards** before teaching Lesson 2.

Objectives
- Read expository text
- Understand complex text through close reading
- Recognize and understand author's point of view
- Respond to the selection using text evidence to support ideas

Materials
Interactive Worktext, pp. 244-249

☞ **Go** Digital
- Interactive eWorktext
- Author's Point of View Mini-Lesson

REREAD COMPLEX TEXT

20–25 Minutes   RI.5.1`   RI.5.8   RI.6.6   L.5.6   **CCSS**

Close Reading: "Power from Nature"

Reread "Power from Nature" with students. As you read together, discuss important passages in the text. Have students respond to text-dependent questions, including those in the **Interactive Worktext**.

🔍 Page 245

Expand Vocabulary Have students locate the word *resource* and read the sentence aloud. *Name a natural resource you read about.* (coal) *Why is coal useful? Complete the sentence: Coal is used to create _____.* (electricity)

Author's Point of View Say: *An author's point of view is his or her attitude or position on a topic. Powerful or strong words in a text are clues to the author's point of view.* Model using text evidence in the second paragraph to figure out an author's point of view. *I read that "Natural resources are nature's gifts." The word* gifts *is a powerful and positive word. Let's look for other powerful words in this paragraph. What are some other powerful words?* (riches, necessity for all life) *Review the words you underlined. Think about what these words have in common to help you figure out the author's point of view. Complete the sentence starter: The author thinks that natural resources are _____.* (Possible answer: The author thinks that natural resources are important and valuable.)

Vocabulary Explain the meanings of the domain-specific words *renewable* and *nonrenewable*. Ask: *What clues in the text help you understand the meanings of these words?* (*renewable:* do not run out; *nonrenewable:* can be used up)

Expand Vocabulary Read aloud the definition of *limited*. Have student point to the word. Ask: *What are some examples of energy sources that are* limited? (Possible answers: coal, gas, oil, uranium)

High-Utility Words Point out the signal word *in contrast* in the last paragraph. Ask: *Do these words show how two things are alike or different?* (different) Have students look for a signal word that shows how two things are alike. (also)

🔍 Page 246

Organization Ⓐ Ⓒ Ⓣ Explain that authors sometimes use headings to organize information in a text. Have students locate and reread the section "Challenges and Problems." Ask: *What are the key details of this section?* (Coal, natural gas, oil, and uranium have to be found and removed from the ground; they have to be processed; they can pollute the environment.) *Think about what these details have in common. What is the main idea of this section?* (There can be problems getting and using nonrenewable sources.)

Author's Point of View Have students reread the last two paragraphs. Ask: *What powerful words does the author use to tell about nonrenewable energy sources?* (problems; pollute, harm; ruin; dangerous) *What are some details the author includes in the last paragraph?* (Oil spills often seep into the ocean; Getting natural gas from the ground can also ruin an area; Nuclear energy creates dangerous waste.) *Are these words and details positive or negative?* (negative) *Put these clues together. What does the author think about using nonrenewable energy sources?* (Using nonrenewable resources is harmful.)

Expand Vocabulary Discuss the word *global*. Ask: *What words in the text are clues to the meaning of* global? (Possible answers: Earth's atmosphere, climate, sea levels)

Vocabulary Have students find the word *processed*. Explain that something that is *processed* is changed by going through machines or having chemicals added to it. *What is an example of something that is processed?* (oil) *What does oil become?* (gasoline)

Genre Ⓐ Ⓒ Ⓣ Direct students to the chart. Ask: *Does the U.S. use more renewable energy sources or nonrenewable energy sources?* (nonrenewable) *In 1949, what percentage of energy came from renewable sources?* (9%) *In 2010, what percentage of energy came from renewable sources?* (8%) *Between 1949 and 2010, has the percentage of energy that came from renewable energy sources increased or decreased?* (decreased)

🔍 **Page 247**

Author's Point of View *The reasons and evidence an author gives are clues to the author's position on a topic.* Have students reread "Solutions for the Future." *What does the author say we will have to do about getting energy from the sun?* (think of new ways we can get and store energy from the sun) *What reason does the author give that supports this point?* (the sun's energy is sometimes less available) *What fact or evidence supports this point.* (solar energy can only be gotten during the day) *Does the author think solar energy is the best solution for getting energy? Why or why not?* (no; the author thinks we have to find new ways to get energy from the sun)

Expand Vocabulary *Find the word* reducing. *What can the government and businesses work to* reduce? (pollution) *What can people work to* reduce? (energy use)

Organization Ⓐ Ⓒ Ⓣ Say: *An author can present information in a text in different ways. An author can present events in sequence or present information using causes and effects or problems and solutions.* Have students review the headings and their notes. Ask: *What is the first section about?* (natural resources and energy) *What is the next section about?* (challenges and problems of using nonrenewable sources of energy) *What is the last section about?* (solutions for solving energy problems) *How did the author organize information in the text? Did the author use sequence, causes and effects, or problems and solutions?* (problems and solutions)

RESPOND TO READING
10–20 Minutes   RI.5.1   RI.5.2   W.5.9b   SL.5.1d

Respond to "Power from Nature"

Have students summarize "Power from Nature" orally to demonstrate comprehension. Then have partners answer the questions on page 248 of the **Interactive Worktext** using the discussion starters. Tell them to use text evidence to support their answers. Have students write the page number(s) on which they found the text evidence for each question.

1. *Why are water, air, and sunlight important natural resources?* (They are a necessity for all life; they also can provide energy. Text Evidence: pp. 245, 247)

2. *How do people use natural resources?* (People use natural resources to get or make energy; to make things work, cook food, move ships, run machines. Text Evidence: pp. 245, 246)

3. *Why is the amount of natural resources we use important?* (Some natural resources are limited, or can run out; some can pollute the environment. Text Evidence: pp. 245, 246)

After students discuss the questions on page 248, have them write a response to the question on page 249. Tell them to use their partner discussions and notes about "Power from Nature" to help them. Circulate and provide guidance.

 Quick Check **Do students understand vocabulary in context? If not, review and reteach using the instruction on page 226.**

Can students use key details to determine the author's point of view? If not, review and reteach using the instruction on page 226 and assign the Unit 4 Week 4 digital mini-lesson.

Can students write a response to "Power from Nature"? If not, provide sentence frames to help them organize their ideas.

Objectives
- Understand and use new vocabulary words
- Read expository text
- Recognize and understand author's point of view
- Understand complex text through close reading

Scaffolding for **McGraw-Hill Reading WONDERS** Approaching Leveled Reader

Materials
"The Delta" Apprentice Leveled Reader: pp. 2–9
- Graphic Organizer: Author's Point of View

☞ **Go** Digital
- Apprentice Leveled Reader eBook
- Downloadable Graphic Organizer
- Point of View Digital Mini-Lesson

BEFORE READING

10–15 Minutes   SL.5.1c   SL.5.1d   L.5.4a   L.5.6   CCSS

Introduce "The Delta"

- Read the Essential Question on the title page of "The Delta" **Apprentice Leveled Reader**: *Why are natural resources so valuable? We will read about why the natural resources in the Delta region of the Mississippi River are valuable.*

- Read the title of the main read. Have students look at the images and read the chapter titles. *What features tell you this is a nonfiction book?* (photos, maps, diagrams, and factual headings) *Use what you see to predict what you will learn about the Delta.* (Possible answers: information about the Delta, where it is, how it was formed, why it is important)

Expand Vocabulary

Display each word below. Say the words and have students repeat them. Then use the Define/Example/Ask routine to introduce each word.

① behaves (page 5)

Define: acts or performs in a certain way

Example: Wind *behaves* in strange ways during a tornado.

Ask: How might a river *behave* when it rains a lot?

② depth (page 5)

Define: how deep something is

Example: The *depth* of the lake is 20 feet in the middle.

Ask: What is the *depth* of a bathtub?

③ economy (page 7)

Define: the way goods and services are made, sold, and bought in a country or region

Example: There are many jobs for people in a good *economy*.

Ask: Why are people happy when the *economy* is going well?

④ mild (page 4)

Define: not too hot or too cold

Example: The *mild* spring day felt pleasantly warm.

Ask: How would you dress for a *mild* spring day?

⑤ vast (page 2)

Define: very large

Example: The small house was surrounded by a *vast* lawn.

Ask: What *vast* area of land or water have you seen?

DURING READING

20–30 Minutes   RI.5.1   RI.5.8   RI.6.6   SL.5.1b   L.5.6   CCSS

Close Reading

 Pages 2–3

Genre Ⓐ Ⓒ Ⓣ Have students look at the map on page 2. Ask: *What does the map show?* (the states through which the Mississippi River runs) *What fact in the first paragraph does the map illustrate?* (It stretches across seven states.) Have students use the map to identify the seven states.

Vocabulary Have students find the word *goods* in the last paragraph on page 2. Explain that *goods* are things made to sell or use. Ask: *How does the Mississippi River help people with goods?* (The river is used to ship goods; it is like a highway.)

Author's Point of View To find an author's point of view about a topic, we can look at what he or she says about it. *What does the author say about the Mississippi Delta in the last paragraph on page 2?* (Food is grown in the Delta's fertile soil. Oil and gas fields provide energy. Goods are shipped on the Mississippi. It's like a highway for the area.) *What do these details show about the Delta?* (It is an important area that provides people with food, energy and a way to travel.) *What is the author's point of view about the Mississippi Delta?* (It's an important area in North America.)

Have students record evidence about the Delta and the author's point of view in the graphic organizer.

Specific Vocabulary (A C T) Have students read the sidebar at the bottom of page 3. Point out the domain-specific vocabulary words *alluvium, alluvial,* and *sediment* and go over the meanings.

Organization (A C T) *What does the sidebar "River Plains and Deltas" describe?* (how the Mississippi Delta formed) *What effect did the slower water at the river's mouth have?* (The slower water dropped more sediment, which built up and formed the Delta.)

Pages 4–5

Author's Point of View Have students read the last paragraph on page 4. *What does the author say about the Delta?* (Today the whole country benefits from the Delta.) *What does the author say about the Delta in the caption for the photograph?* (The Delta is important to the United States.) *What is the author's point of view about the Delta?* (It is important to the whole country.)

Sequence Have students study the diagram and text that goes with it on page 5. Explain that it shows how the water cycle works. Point out that in step 1 of the water cycle, water is stored in the ocean. *What happens in step 2?* (Water evaporates.) Have students look at steps 2, 3, and 4. *What happens after water condenses and then returns to the Earth as rain or snow?* (Water drains into the river.) *Where does the water go next?* (back into the ocean)

Pages 6–7

Connection of Ideas (A C T) Have students read page 6. *What details on page 6 explain why crops grow well in the Mississippi Delta region?* (The sediment carried by floods improves the soil. The soil helps the crops grow well. When plants die, the soil absorbs their nutrients. The region's warm climate helps agriculture because crops can be grown all year long.)

STOP AND CHECK Read the question on page 7. (Some of the natural resources of the Mississippi Delta are fertile soil, a mild climate, the Mississippi River, and forests.)

Pages 8–9

Vocabulary Have students find the word *stores* in the first paragraph on page 8. Explain that in this sentence, *stores* is a noun that means "a large amount of something." *What rich stores does the Mississippi Delta have?* (oil and natural gas)

Organization (A C T) Have students read page 9. *What problems have oil and gas caused in wetlands?* (Pipelines have harmed its ecosystems by upsetting water cycle; oil has seeped out from cracks in pipelines or spilled from oil rigs. The oil harmed plants and animals.)

Have partners review their Author's Point of View charts for pages 2–9 and discuss what they learned.

Quick Check Do students understand weekly vocabulary in context? If not, review and reteach using the instruction on page 226.

Can students determine the author's point of view? If not, review and reteach using the instruction on page 226 and assign the Unit 4 Week 4 digital mini-lesson.

Objectives
- Understand and use new vocabulary
- Read expository text
- Recognize and understand author's point of view
- Understand complex text through close reading
- Respond to the selection using text evidence to support ideas

Scaffolding for **Wonders** Approaching Leveled Reader

Materials
- "The Delta" Apprentice Leveled Reader: pp. 10–24
- Graphic Organizer: Author's Point of View

👉 **Go Digital**
- Apprentice Leveled Reader eBook
- Downloadable Graphic Organizer
- Point of View Digital Mini-Lesson

BEFORE READING

5–10 Minutes   SL.5.1c   SL.5.1d   L.5.4a   L.5.6

Expand Vocabulary

Display each word below. Say the words and have students repeat them. Then use the Define/Example/Ask routine to introduce each word.

1 activities (page 16)

Define: actions that people do together or alone

Example: There were many fun *activities* for children to do at the fair.

Ask: What kinds of *activities* would you plan for young children at a fair?

2 connect (page 10)

Define: to link two things

Example: These two streets *connect* to the main road.

Ask: *What are ways to* connect *two sides of a river?*

3 shallow (page 10)

Define: not deep

Example: We waded in *shallow* water that was just above our ankles.

Ask: How deep would you expect the water to be in a *shallow* pond?

DURING READING

15–20 Minutes   RI.5.1   RI.5.8   RI.6.6   SL.5.1b   L.5.6

Close Reading

🔍 **Pages 10–12**

Organization (A C T) Have students read page 10. *What is a profitable or money-making business in the Delta region?* (fishing) *What is the effect of pollution and lost habitats?* (fewer fish) *What might be the effect of fewer fish on business?* (Fishing may no longer be profitable.)

STOP AND CHECK *Read the Stop and Check box on page 10.* (Goods from the Delta region are carried on the river. The Mississippi River connects to other rivers and to the Gulf of Mexico.)

Organization (A C T) Have students read page 11. *What has happened to forested wetlands as a result of farming, forestry, and energy and water projects?* (The wetlands are smaller than they used to be.)

Author's Point of View *In the second paragraph on page 11, what does the author say the wetlands help to do?* (They keep sediment from washing out to sea. They help stop flooding and erosion. They clean water.) *What do these details tell you about how the author feels about wetlands?* (The author feels that wetlands are good and helpful.)

Remind students to record the details and author's point of view on their graphic organizer.

Genre (A C T) *What does the map on page 12 show?* (the Mississippi flyway) *What is a flyway?* (a pathway above the Mississippi River that birds fly above when they travel) *Why is the Mississippi River important for birds?* (Millions of birds breed in the Mississippi River wetlands.)

Pages 13–15

Author's Point of View Have students read page 13. *What is the effect of levees and dams on the Mississippi Delta?* (They upset the cycles that shape the region so little sediment is getting through to build up the land.) *What is the author's point of view about levees and dams?* (The author thinks that they are harmful.)

Organization Ⓐ Ⓒ Ⓣ *What is happening because sediment can't get through to build up the land?* (The coastline is shrinking and land could be lost.)

Connection of Ideas Ⓐ Ⓒ Ⓣ Have students read page 14. *What are scientists and engineers planning that would cause floods?* (build up the coastal areas and change the course of the river) *What will the floods do?* (Floods will build up sediment in shallow water and create new delta land.)

STOP AND CHECK Have students answer the question in the Stop and Check box on page 15. (People want to protect the Delta region to improve water quality so the many fish and animals have clean water. People also want to save the coastal areas.)

Pages 16–17

Compare and Contrast Reread the first two paragraphs on page 16. *How have people changed their ideas about the Mississippi Delta?* (In the past, people thought the resources would never run out. Today people know that the Delta is fragile and needs to be protected.)

Vocabulary Have students find the word *restore* in the third paragraph on page 16. Explain that *restore* means "to bring back to the way something once was." *What do we need to restore?* (the region of the Delta)

Author's Point of View *On page 17, what is the author's point of view about saving the Mississippi Delta?* (The author says it may be possible.) *How does the author say this can be done?* (People sharing ideas and learning about mistakes made in the past.)

AFTER READING
10–15 Minutes | RI.5.1 RI.5.2 RI.5.9 W.5.9b L.5.4a (CCSS)

Respond to Reading

Compare Texts Have students compare natural resources in "Power from Nature" with natural resources in "The Delta." Then say: *Why do we need to protect natural resources?*

Summarize Have students turn to page 18 and summarize the selection. (Answers should include details from the selection.)

Text Evidence

Have partners work together to answer questions on page 18. Remind students to use their graphic organizer.

Author's Point of View (It's important to protect the Delta from pollution and lack of sedimentation. Evidence: wetlands stop flooding; erosion; help water quality; levees and dams have upset natural cycles.)

Vocabulary (A clue to the meaning of *fragile* is the phrase "need to be protected.")

Write About Reading (The author thinks that the Delta's resources benefit the whole country. Students should include details that show the benefits.)

Independent Reading

Encourage students to read the paired selection "Get Rich with Compost" on pages 19–21. Have them summarize the selection and compare it to "The Delta." Have them work with a partner to answer the "Make Connections" questions on page 21.

 Quick Check Can students identify the author's point of view? If not, review and teach using the instruction on page 226 and assign the Unit 4 Week 4 digital mini lesson.

Can students respond to the selection using text evidence? If not, provide, sentence frames to help them organize their ideas.

**WEEK 4
LESSON
5**

Objectives
- Review weekly vocabulary words
- Review author's point of view
- Write an analysis about the author's point of view

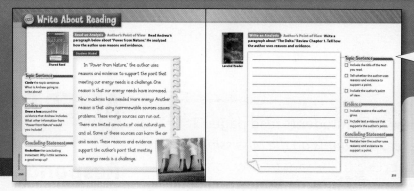

Materials
- Visual Vocabulary Cards: 141–148
- Interactive Worktext, pp. 250–251
- Assessment Book, pp. 46–47

☞ **Go** Digital
- Visual Vocabulary Cards
- Author's Point of View Lesson
- Interactive eWorktext

Scaffolding for **Wonders** Reading/Writing Workshop

REVIEW AND RETEACH

5–10 Minutes   RI.5.1   RI.6.6   L.5.4a   L.5.6

Weekly Vocabulary

Display one **Visual Vocabulary Card** at a time and ask students to use the vocabulary word in a sentence. If students have difficulty, have them find the word in "Power from Nature" and use context clues to define it.

Comprehension: Author's Point of View

I Do Display and read aloud: *Everyone must do their part to keep the environment clean. Small steps can cause a change. For example, when people recycle, there is less waste and pollution.* Say: Circle *must* and *save*. Say: *These are powerful words.* Underline the second and third sentences. Say: *These details both tell positive effects of keeping the environment clean. I can put these clues together to figure out the author's position. The author thinks people should clean up the environment.*

We Do Display: *Electric cars are the best cars for the future. Electric cars are good because they don't pollute the air as much as other types of cars. They give off smaller amounts of gases that pollute.* Ask: *What is the topic?* (electric cars) *Which words are powerful?* (best, good) *What details does the author include?* (they don't pollute as much as other cars; they give off a smaller amount of gases that pollute) *What is the author's point of view?* (Electric cars are better than other cars.)

You Do Display: *People need fresh water. People should fix leaky faucets to save fresh water. Fixing one leaky faucet can save 34 gallons of water each year.* Have partners identify powerful words and key details, and then determine the author's point of view.

WRITE ABOUT READING

25–35 Minutes   RI.5.8   W.5.4   W.5.5   W.5.9b

Read an Analysis

- Ask students to look back at "Power from Nature" in the **Interactive Worktext**. Have volunteers review text they marked that helped them determine the author's point of view. Ask: *How does the author use reasons and evidence to support a point of view?*

- Read aloud the directions on page 250. Read aloud the student model. *Andrew wrote an analysis, or a detailed description. He analyzed how the author uses reasons and evidence to support a point of view.*

- *When you write an analysis, you need to include certain elements. The first element is the topic sentence.* Have students circle the topic sentence. *What information has Andrew included in his topic sentence?* (the title of the text; that the author uses reasons and evidence to support a point; the author's point of view)

- *Another element of an analysis is text evidence. The student supports the topic sentence with reasons and evidence the author used. Reread the model and draw a box around the text evidence.* (sentences 2–6) *Look back at the text you marked in "Power from Nature." What other information would you include?* (Possible answers: Meeting our energy demands has not been easy; Nonrenewable energy sources have to be found, removed from the ground, and processed to be used.)

- *The final element of an analysis is the concluding statement. Underline the concluding statement. How is this sentence like the topic sentence?* (Both say that reasons and evidence support a point; both say that meeting our energy needs is a challenge.) *Which words wrap up the details?* (These reasons and evidence)

Write an Analysis

Analytical Writing

Guided Writing Read the writing prompt on page 251 together. Have students write about "The Delta" or another text they read this week. *Use the checklist to figure out what information to include in each section.* Guide students to ask "how" and "why" questions to analyze evidence, such as *Why is an author's point strong?*

Peer Conference Have students read their analysis to a partner. Listeners should identify the strongest text evidence that supports the topic sentence and discuss any sentences that are unclear.

Teacher Conference Check students' writing for complete sentences and text evidence that supports their topic. Review the concluding statement. *Does this sentence tie all of the elements together?* If necessary, have students revise the concluding statement by restating the topic sentence.

Level Up

▲ Approaching Leveled Reader

▲ Reading/Writing Workshop

▲ Apprentice Leveled Reader

▲ Interactive Worktext

IF students read the Apprentice Level Reader fluently and the **Interactive Worktext** Shared Read fluently and answer the Respond to Reading questions

THEN read together the Approaching Level Reader main selection and the **Reading/Writing Workshop** Shared Read from *Reading Wonders*. Have students take notes as they read, using self-stick notes. Then ask and answer questions about their notes.

Writing Rubric

	4	3	2	1
Topic Sentence	There is one clear, focused topic sentence.	Topic sentence is less focused, somewhat clear.	Topic is presented in short phrases.	There is no topic sentence.
Text Evidence	Topic is supported by two or more text details.	Evidence includes only one detail from the text.	Little to no evidence is cited from the text.	No text evidence is included.
Concluding Statement	Clearly restates the topic sentence; wraps up the details.	Restatement is less focused; attempts to wrap up the details.	Vaguely restates the topic. Doesn't correlate well to text evidence.	There is no conclusion.
Writing Style	Writes in complete sentences. Uses correct spelling and grammar.	Uses complete sentences and phrases. Writing has spelling and grammar errors.	Few or no complete sentences. There are many spelling and grammar errors.	Does not write accurately or in complete sentences.

ASSESSMENT

Weekly Assessment

Have students complete the Weekly Assessment using **Assessment** book pages 46–47.

WEEK 5 LESSON 1

Objectives
- Develop oral language
- Build background about expressing something that is important to you
- Understand and use weekly vocabulary
- Read poetry

Scaffolding for **McGraw-Hill Reading WONDERS** Reading/Writing Workshop

Materials
- Interactive Worktext, pp. 252–259
- Visual Vocabulary Cards: 149–152

☞ **Go Digital**
- Interactive eWorktext
- Visual Vocabulary Cards

WEEKLY CONCEPT

5–10 Minutes   SL.5.1b   SL.5.1c   (CCSS)

Talk About It

Essential Question Read aloud the Essential Question on page 252 of the **Interactive Worktext**: *How do you express something that is important to you?* Explain that *to express* means "to show or communicate." Say: *Family, friends, and culture may be important to you. We can express our feelings about them in different ways.*

- Discuss the photograph on page 252. Ask: *What are these people doing?* (singing, playing music) *Look at their faces. Do you think that the song is important to them? How do you know?* (yes; their faces show strong feeling)

I Do Say: *I am going to think of a time when I expressed what was important to me. My grandmother is special to me. To express that she is important to me, I made her a card. I drew a picture of the two of us on the card and sent it to her. The drawing showed my grandmother that she is important to me. I will write "draw a picture" in the word web on page 253.*

We Do Say: *Let's look at the photo and think about how these people are expressing something that is important to them. What are both of these people doing?* (singing) *What do you think might be important to them? Think about their actions as well as how the two people might know each other.* (Possible answers: music, friendship, family) Guide students to add words to the web on page 253 and brainstorm other ways people can express what is important.

You Do Have partners describe something that is important to them. Then have them answer the question: *What do you do that is an expression of what is important to you?*

REVIEW VOCABULARY

10–15 Minutes   RL.5.5   L.5.4a   L.5.5c   L.5.6   (CCSS)

Review Weekly Vocabulary Words

- Use the **Visual Vocabulary Cards** to review the weekly vocabulary.
- Read together the directions for the Vocabulary activity on page 254 of the **Interactive Worktext**. Then complete the activity.

1 **meaningful** Have students think about books they have read that are *meaningful* to them. Then have them use the sentence frame: *One book that is meaningful to me is _____.* (Answers will vary.)

2 **expression** Have partners act out reading, clapping, and whispering. Ask: *Which activity is an expression of excitement?* (clapping) *What is another expression of excitement?* Provide the sentence frame: *_____ is an expression of excitement.* (Possible answer: jumping up and down; shouting)

3 **barren** Have partners discuss the features of a desert and a rainforest. Then have them complete this sentence frame: *A _____ is barren because _____.* (desert; it doesn't have many plants)

4 **plumes** Have partners brainstorm animals that have *plumes*. Then have them use this sentence frame to write a caption: *A _____ has plumes.* (Possible answer: peacock, ostrich, bird)

Poetry Terms

Have students look at the Poetry Terms activity on page 255 of the **Interactive Worktext**. Read together the directions for the Poetry Terms activity. Read the poem aloud. Discuss the definitions of the poetry terms and give examples, as appropriate. Then have partners use the poem to complete each activity.

⑤ lyric Read aloud the definition. Say: *Reread the last two stanzas. Which line expresses a feeling?* (I feel free as I travel.)

⑥ alliteration Give examples of alliteration, such as *start and stop*. Reread the first stanza aloud, emphasizing the *p* sound in "push and pump." Ask: *Which two words are an example of alliteration?* (push; pump) Have partners find two more examples of alliteration in the poem. (Possible answers: pavement is my playmate; feel free; bumps can bother; turn and twist; leap and lift)

⑦ meter Say: *Let's listen for the poem's meter.* Read aloud the second line of "Free Time," emphasizing the stressed syllables (push, pump, ride). Ask: *How many stressed syllables do you hear?* (three)

⑧ stanza Have partners count the stanzas in "Free Time." Then have them complete this sentence frame: *The poem "Free Time" has _____ stanzas.* (four) Ask: *How many lines does each stanza have?* (two)

ELL ENGLISH LANGUAGE LEARNERS

For *lyric*, reread the definition and ask, *Does a lyric poem tell a story or describe a feeling?* For *alliteration*, have students echo examples. For *meter*, have students clap out the second line with you. For *stanza*, count the stanzas together.

READ COMPLEX TEXT
15–20 Minutes   RL.5.1   RF.5.4c

Read: "How Do I Hold the Summer?", "Catching a Fly," and "When I Dance"

- Have students turn to page 256 in the **Interactive Worktext** and read aloud the Essential Question. Explain that they will read three poems that show how people express things that are important to them. Ask: *What is the title of the first poem?* ("How Do I Hold the Summer?") *What do the photographs show?* (a boat on a lake, leaves turning color) *What do you think is important to the speaker of this poem?* (summer)

- Read "How Do I Hold the Summer?", "Catching a Fly," and "When I Dance" together. Note that the poems include some weekly vocabulary words but they are not highlighted.

- Have students use the "My Notes" section on page 256 to write questions they have, words they don't understand, and details they want to remember. Model how to use the section. *In the fourth line, I do not understand what "it" refers to. I will write a question about this in the "My Notes" section. I also do not know what the word* forbidding *means. I will write this word with a question mark by it in the "My Notes" section, too. When we reread the poems, I will ask my questions.*

ELL ENGLISH LANGUAGE LEARNERS

As you read together, have students highlight words they do not understand and lines they have questions about. After reading, help them write their questions in the "My Notes" column.

 Quick Check Can students understand the weekly vocabulary in context? If not, review vocabulary using the **Visual Vocabulary Cards** before teaching Lesson 2.

Objectives
- Read poetry
- Understand complex text through close reading
- Recognize and understand theme
- Respond to the selection using text evidence to support ideas

Materials
Interactive Worktext, pp. 256–261

☞ **Go** Digital
- Interactive eWorktext
- Theme Digital Mini-Lesson

REREAD COMPLEX TEXT

20–25 Minutes   RL.5.1   RL.5.2   RL.5.4   RL.5.5   RL.5.7   CCSS

Close Reading: "How Do I Hold the Summer?", "Catching a Fly," and "When I Dance"

Reread "How Do I Hold the Summer?", "Catching a Fly," and "When I Dance" with students. As you read together, discuss important passages in the text. Have students respond to text-dependent questions, including those in the **Interactive Worktext**.

Page 257

Stanza and Meter Ask: *How many stanzas are on page 256?* (two) *How many lines are in each stanza?* (four) *Now as I read aloud the first stanza, listen for the meter.* Reread the first stanza, exaggerating the stressed and unstressed syllables. Have students echo read and clap for each stressed syllable. Ask: *Which lines have the same meter?* (the second and fourth lines) *Now let's reread the stanzas and look for how the details in these stanzas are alike to help us understand the speaker's ideas. In the first stanza, I see the key details "the sun is setting sooner" and "my swimsuit's packed away." What do both of these details describe?* (things that happen when summer ends) *Reread the second stanza with a partner. What are some key details in the second stanza?* (the lake like cold, forbidding glass, last sailboat has crossed; green leaves gone gold, fall, float away; winter's veil of frost) *What do all these details describe?* (things that happen when summer ends) *How are the first and second stanza alike?* (both describe what happens when summer ends)

Connection of Ideas **A C T** Point out the words *cold, forbidding,* and *gone.* Ask: *Do these words express a negative or positive feeling about winter?* (negative)

Now reread the stanzas on page 257. What strong words and details describe summer? (Possible answers: light; green grass; soft plumes; pit of one ripe peach; cricket's chirp; bird's sweet call) *Think about the feelings these words express. Does the speaker have a positive or negative feeling about summer?* (positive)

Genre **A C T** Review features of *free verse* and *lyric* poetry. *Is this a lyric or a free verse poem?* (lyric) *How can you tell?* (It expresses a strong feeling; it has rhythm.)

Theme *On page 256, we read details about what happens when summer ends. Let's look for key details on page 257 that tell what the speaker does when summer ends to figure out the theme. I see the key details "I know I cannot ball up light, and green grass just won't keep." This tells me the speaker knows he or she can't make summer stay. Reread the next two stanzas. What will the speaker do first? Underline key details.* (I'll search for signs of summer, hold memories of each) *What will the speaker do next?* (store them up in a poem to read) *What does "them" refer to in the last stanza?* (memories of summer) *Review all the details you marked. What is the speaker's message about how to hold onto good memories?* (Possible answer: You can hold onto memories by writing a poem about them.)

Page 258

Connection of Ideas **A C T** Have students reread the title and review the photographs. Read aloud the first three stanzas. *What does the word "it" refer to in the first stanza?* (a fly) *What clues helped you?* (the title, the picture of the fly; upon the china plate next to the peas) *What does the speaker find in the second stanza?* (a lens) *What kind of lens do you think the speaker is referring to?* (a camera lens) *What clues in the text and images helped you?* (photograph of the camera; focused, zoomed in)

Alliteration Reread the second stanza, emphasizing the *f* sound in "finger flicked." Ask: *Which pair of words is*

an example of alliteration? (finger flicked) Have partners find other examples of alliteration in the poem. (<u>Possible answer</u>: framed, focused; plotting, planning; greedy goggle; webbed wings)

Metaphor Review that a metaphor compares two things without using *like* or *as*. Say: *Reread the fifth stanza. Which line in the fifth stanza contains a metaphor?* (the first line) Have partners complete the sentence frame: *The speaker compares _____ to _____.* (the fly's eyes; goggles) Ask: *How does the metaphor help you picture the fly? Tell a partner the size and shape of the fly's eyes.* (<u>Possible answer</u>: The fly's eyes are big and round.)

Theme *Let's reread the poem together and draw a box around key details. In the second stanza, what does the speaker do instead of raising a hand?* (found a lens) *What does the speaker notice about the fly after zooming in?* (<u>Possible answers</u>: it has hands; goggle eyes; webbed wings; it's like the speaker, invading) *What does the speaker do instead of swatting the fly?* (snapped) *What do you think the word "snapped" means here?* (take a photograph) *Let's puts these key details together. What is the poem's message about how to treat other living things?* (<u>Possible answer</u>: Be kind to other living things.)

Page 259

Alliteration Have partners reread the first three stanzas together and underline examples of alliteration. (dark, day, doesn't; get, groove, ground; feet feel)

Connection of Ideas **A C T** Have students reread the third, fourth, and fifth stanzas. Ask: *What does "That slap's/the only sound" refer to in the fourth stanza?* (the sound of the speaker's feet on the ground) *Point to text evidence.* (feet feel the ground) *What do details in the fourth stanza tell you about the speaker's way of dancing?* (The speaker makes noise when he or she dances.)

Theme Have a student reread the first and second stanzas. Ask: *Is a "dark day" a good day or a bad day?* (a bad day) *What does the speaker do on a "dark day"?* (dance) *What clues tell you this?* (I bust a move; get a groove; feet feel the ground; play my tracks) *Put these details together. What is the speaker's message about dancing?* (Dancing can make you feel better.)

RESPOND TO READING
10–20 Minutes   RL.5.1 W.5.9a SL.5.1d

Respond to "How Do I Hold the Summer?", "Catching a Fly," and "When I Dance"

Have students summarize the poems orally to demonstrate comprehension. Then have partners answer the questions on page 260 of the **Interactive Worktext** using the discussion starters. Tell them to use text evidence to support their answers. Have students write the page number(s) on which they found the text evidence for each question.

1. *In "How Do I Hold the Summer?" what does the speaker do to show that summer is important?* (searches for signs of summer; writes a poem; <u>Evidence</u>: p. 257)

2. *In "Catching a Fly," what does the speaker do to show that a fly can be important?* (takes a photograph of the fly rather than swatting it; <u>Evidence</u>: p. 258)

3. *In "When I Dance," what does the speaker do to show that feeling good is important?* (The speaker dances. <u>Evidence</u>: p. 259)

After students discuss the questions on page 260, have them write a response to the question on page 261. Tell them to use their discussions and notes about "How Do I Hold the Summer?", "Catching a Fly," and "When I Dance" to help them. Circulate and provide guidance.

✓ *Quick Check* **Do students understand vocabulary in context? If not, review and reteach using the instruction on page 236.**

Can students use key details to determine theme? If not, review and reteach using the instruction on page 236 and assign the Unit 4 Week 5 digital mini-lesson.

Can students write a response to the poems? If not, provide sentence frames to help them organize their ideas.

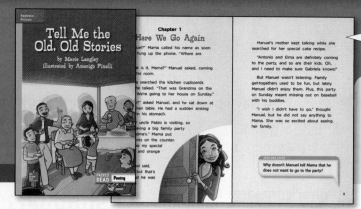

Objectives
- Understand and use new vocabulary
- Read realistic fiction
- Recognize and understand theme
- Understand complex text through close reading

Scaffolding for **Wonders** Approaching Leveled Reader

Materials
- "Tell Me the Old, Old Stories" Apprentice Leveled Reader: pp. 2–9
- Graphic Organizer: Theme

☞ **Go Digital**
- Apprentice Leveled Reader eBook
- Downloadable Graphic Organizer
- Theme Mini-Lesson

BEFORE READING

10–15 Minutes   SL.5.1c   SL.5.1d   L.5.4a   L.5.6   CCSS

Introduce "Tell Me the Old, Old Stories"

- Read the Essential Question on the title page of "Tell Me the Old, Old Stories" **Apprentice Leveled Reader:** *How do you express something that is important to you? We will read about how different members of a family express what is important to them.*

- Read the title of the main read. Have students look at the images. *What do you think this story will be about? is important to some of the characters?* (a boy and his family; food; a party)

Expand Vocabulary

Display each word below. Say the words and have students repeat them. Then use the Define/Example/Ask routine to introduce each word.

1 collapses (page 7)

Define: falls down or caves in

Example: The bookshelf is about to *collapse*.

Ask: How can you stop a bookshelf from *collapsing*?

2 conversation (page 7)

Define: two or more people talking to each other

Example: Mara enjoys *conversations* about books.

Ask: What is your favorite topic of *conversation*?

3 grip (page 6)

Define: a firm hold or grasp on something

Example: The player held the football in a strong *grip*.

Ask: When would you need a strong *grip* on your dog's leash?

4 sarcastic (page 5)

Define: said in a mean or joking way

Example: Your *sarcastic* answer hurt my feelings.

Ask: When have you made a *sarcastic* comment?

5 scoffed (page 5)

Define: made fun of or ridiculed

Example: People *scoffed* at the inventor's new ideas.

Ask: What would cause you to *scoff* at someone?

DURING READING

20–30 Minutes   RL.5.1   RL.5.2   SL.5.1b   L.5.4a   CCSS

Close Reading

🔍 **Pages 2–3**

Genre Ⓐ Ⓒ Ⓣ Read page 2. Review the features of realistic fiction. Ask: *Who are the characters?* (Manuel; his mother) *What is the setting?* (their home) *What are they doing?* (baking a cake; talking) *Could these characters, setting, and events happen in real life?* (yes)

Connection of Ideas Ⓐ Ⓒ Ⓣ On page 2, have students locate the phrase *a sinking feeling in his stomach*. Ask: *If you have a sinking feeling in your stomach, how do you feel?* (worried) *Why does Manuel feel this way?* (He is worried about what his mother will say.) *Where does Mama say they are going?* (to Grandma's house for a family party) *How does Manuel feel about this? How do you know?* (upset; He says "Cool" but he didn't mean it.)

Vocabulary On page 2, have students locate the word *ingredients*. Explain that it means foods you need to cook something. *What helps you understand what the word means?* (Mama is making an almond and orange cake.)

Theme Read page 3. Say: *The theme of a story is the main message or lesson about life that the author wants to share with readers. To figure out the theme, I pay close attention to what the characters do, say, and feel.* Model how to begin to identify the theme. Say: *Manuel wishes he didn't have to go to the family party. Why?* (They weren't fun anymore; he would rather play baseball.) As students read, have them record key details on their Theme chart.

STOP AND CHECK Read the question in the Stop and Check box on page 3. (He doesn't want to upset her. She is excited about the party.)

Pages 4–5

Connection of Ideas **A C T** Read page 4. Ask: *What is Mama thinking about when Manuel asks to use the phone?* (baking the cake) *Look back at page 2. Why is Mama baking the cake?* (to bring to the family party)

Theme Read page 5. Ask: *What does Vincent say about the family party?* (that it sounds cool) *What does Manuel think about what Vincent says at first?* (He thinks he's joking.) *What does he think after he hangs up the phone?* (He thinks maybe Vincent really meant it.)

STOP AND CHECK Read the question in the Stop and Check box on page 5. (because everyone tells the same old stories and also because he'll miss baseball)

Pages 6–7

Theme Have a student reread the last paragraph on page 6. Ask: *What do Manuel's family members to do show him that he is important to them?* (They kiss him. They tell him how much he has grown.)

Connection of Ideas **A C T** Say: *Look back again at the third paragraph on page 6. What does Grandma always say about making and sharing food?* (It is an expression of love.) Then have students read the second paragraph on page 7 and look at the illustration. Say: *The table is crowded with food. Everyone brought food to the party.*

Think about what Grandma says about food. What does this tell you about the family? (They love each other a lot.)

Pages 8–9

Connection of Ideas **A C T** Read the first paragraph on page 8 aloud. Ask: *Gabriela asks Pablo why he hasn't eaten the chicken she brought. Why does that make everyone laugh?* (Gabriela is making a joke about the time she played a trick on Pablo. She served him a live chicken in a stew pot. Everyone laughs because they know the story.) *Who retells the story?* (Pablo) *Look back at page 5. What is one of the reasons Manuel doesn't want to go to the party?* (Everyone retells the same old stories.)

Vocabulary In the fourth paragraph on page 8, have students locate the words *half listened*. Explain that it means listening without really paying attention. Ask: *Why is Manuel only half listening?* (He has heard the story many times before.)

Theme Have a student reread the fourth paragraph on page 8. Ask: *What does Manuel think about as he half listens to the story?* (He thinks Vincent may have been right. He realizes he doesn't know everything about the story.) *What does Manuel ask to show that he is interested in the story?* (He asks where the chicken came from.)

Have partners review their Theme charts for pages 2–9 and discuss what they learned.

 Quick Check **Do students understand weekly vocabulary in context? If not, review and reteach using the instruction on page 236.**

Can students determine theme from key details? If not, review and reteach using the instruction on page 236 and assign the Unit 4 Week 5 digital mini-lesson.

Objectives
- Understand and use new vocabulary
- Read realistic fiction
- Recognize and understand theme
- Understand complex text through close reading
- Respond to the selection using text evidence to support idea

Materials
- "Tell Me the Old, Old Stories" Apprentice Leveled Reader: pp. 10–20
- Graphic Organizer: Theme

☞ Go Digital
- Apprentice Leveled Reader eBook
- Downloadable Graphic Organizer
- Theme Mini-Lesson

Scaffolding for **Wonders** Approaching Leveled Reader

BEFORE READING

5–10 Minutes   SL.5.1c   SL.5.1d   L.5.4a   L.5.6   CCSS

Expand Vocabulary

Display each word below. Say the words and have students repeat them. Then use the Define/Example/Ask routine to introduce each word.

① introducing (page 13)

Define: making known, or having someone meet someone else

Example: The new student stood up while the teacher was *introducing* him to the class.

Ask: How would you *introduce* a new classmate to a friend?

② murmur (page 10)

Define: a low, soft sound or whisper

Example: In the library, I always speak in a *murmur*.

Ask: What would it sound like if you and your classmates spoke in a *murmur*?

③ remark (page 11)

Define: a comment, often an observation about something

Example: Andy was happy to hear his coach's *remark* that he was a fast runner.

Ask: What *remark* can you make about today's weather?

DURING READING

15–20 Minutes   RL.5.1   RL.5.2   SL.5.1b   L.5.4a   CCSS

Close Reading

🔍 **Pages 10–11**

Theme Read page 10. Ask: *What question does Manuel ask that shows he is interested in the family stories?* (He asks if Grandpa was still alive when the chicken flew out of the pot.) Have partners review the page and find another detail that shows Manuel is becoming more interested in his family. (He realized he would like to see the photos of his grandpa.)

STOP AND CHECK Read the question in the Stop and Check box on page 10. (Vincent has made him think about the party differently.)

Connection of Ideas **A C T** Read page 11. Discuss with students why Manuel thinks he's contacting his grandmother because of Vincent. Ask: *What did Vincent say about family gatherings that changed Manuel's attitude?* (They are cool.) *When did Vincent say that? Find Vincent's comment in chapter 1.* (At the top of page 5, VIncent said, "Wow, that sounds cool." He was talking about Manuel's family gathering.)

Theme Ask: *On page 11, why might Manuel want Vincent to see the photos, too?* (Vincent's comment made Manuel rethink his feelings about his family's parties and stories.)

Sentence Structure **A C T** Have students find the phrase *iHasta pronto!* on page 11. Explain that it means "See you soon!" in Spanish. Ask: *How can you tell these words are from another language?* (They are set in italics, the exclamation point is upside down at the beginning, and there is a second one at the end of the story.)

Pages 12–13

Connection of Ideas Ⓐ Ⓒ Ⓣ Read page 12. Ask: *What does Grandma say that she has ready for the boys?* (a snack) *Look back at page 6. How does Grandma feel about food?* (It is an expression of love.)

Theme Read page 13. Have partners look for details that show that sharing the photos with Manuel is important to Grandma. (She hesitates before opening the suitcase; she calls them special; she says it's like introducing his grandfather to him.)

Vocabulary Ask: *Why does Grandma say that she is introducing Manuel to his grandfather?* (He never met his grandfather, so looking at photos is how he can learn about him.)

Pages 14–15

Theme Ⓐ Ⓒ Ⓣ Have student read page 14. Ask: *How does Manuel feel about looking at the photos?* (He enjoys it.) Have partners find details that show that Manuel enjoys it. (He asks who is in the photos; He asks when they were taken.)

Vocabulary Ask: *On page 14, which words help you create a picture in your mind of the photo of the boy on the horse?* (barren Mexican landscape, hot and dry, feathery plumes, etc.)

Connection of Ideas Ⓐ Ⓒ Ⓣ Have a student read page 15. Ask: *Why does Vincent say Manuel is lucky?* (He has a grandma, lots of family, and old photos to look at.) *Does Vincent have a big family?* (no)

Theme Ⓐ Ⓒ Ⓣ Have students read the last paragraph on page 15. Ask: *What did Manuel learn from Vincent and by going to the family gathering and looking at the photos?* (He learned that family is important.) Say: *Think about what Manuel said, did, and felt in this story. What is the main message or lesson about life in this story?* (Time spent with family is special and worth sharing.)

STOP AND CHECK Read the question in the Stop and Check box on page 15. (Manuel invites Vincent because Vincent doesn't have a big family; he wants to share his family with Vincent.)

AFTER READING

10–15 Minutes   RL.5.1   RL5.2   RL.5.9   W.5.9a   L.5.4a   CCSS

Respond to Reading

Compare Texts Have students compare how one of the speakers in the poems "How Do I Hold the Summer?," "Catching a Fly," or "When I Dance" and one of the characters in "Tell Me the Old, Old Stories" expresses something that is important to them. Then ask: *How do you express something that is important to you?*

Summarize Have students turn to page 16 and summarize the selection. (Answers should show how the characters express things that are important to them.)

Text Evidence

Have partners work together to answer questions on page 16. Remind students to use their Theme charts.

Theme (Manuel wants to share family photos and events with Vincent. This shows that Manuel has learned that time with family is important and worth sharing.)

Vocabulary (to pause or wait for a moment)

Write About Reading (Family is important to Grandma. Sharing food is a way of sharing love. She also expresses it by showing Manuel the photographs of his grandpa. This shows that spending time with family is important.)

Independent Reading

Encourage students to read the paired selection "Family Ties" on pages 17–19. Have them identify literary elements in the poem, such as stanza and meter. Then ask them to summarize the poem. Have partners answer the "Make Connections" questions on page 19.

 Quick Check **Can students determine the theme from key details? If not, review and teach using the instruction on page 236 and assign the Unit 4 Week 5 digital mini-lesson.**

Can students respond to the selection using text evidence. If not, provide sentence frames to help them organize their ideas.

WEEK 5
LESSON

5

Objectives
- Review weekly vocabulary words
- Review theme
- Write an analysis about how a poet uses sensory language

Scaffolding for **Wonders** Reading/Writing Workshop

Materials
- Visual Vocabulary Cards: 149–152
- Interactive Worktext, pp. 262–263
- Assessment Book, pp. 48–49

☞ **Go Digital**
- Visual Vocabulary Cards
- Theme Mini-Lesson
- Interactive eWorktext

REVIEW AND RETEACH

5–10 Minutes   RL.5.1   RL.5.2   L.5.4   L.5.6

Weekly Vocabulary

Display one **Visual Vocabulary Card** at a time and ask students to use the vocabulary word in a sentence. If students have difficulty, have them find the word in "Tell Me the Old, Old Stories" and use the context clues to define it.

Comprehension: Theme

I Do   Write and read aloud these lines: *I ride because I love the Earth/And honor all it's truly worth./My bike and I, together we/Explore our planet, strong and free.* Circle the key details "I ride because I love the Earth" and "My bike and I, together we explore our planet." Underline the strong words *love, honor, strong,* and *free.* Say: *The details tell me riding a bike is important to the speaker. The strong words express a positive feeling. I can use these clues to figure out the poem's message: Riding a bike is a good way to explore the Earth.*

We Do   Write and read: *Dancers and gymnasts leap high,/Pilots can glide through the sky/But if I want to feel free/I go swimming at sea/And feel the waves passing by.* Ask: *What strong words do you see?* (leap, glide, free, passing by) *What feeling do these words express?* (feeling of freedom) *What are some key details?* (dancers and gymnasts leap high; pilots glide through the sky; I go swimming at sea) *What do all the details describe?* (ways to feel free) *Use these clues. What is the main message?* (There are many ways to feel free.)

You Do   Have students turn to page 255 of the **Interactive Worktext**. Have partners look for key details and determine the message or theme.

WRITE ABOUT READING

25–35 Minutes   W.5.2   W.5.4   W.5.5   W.5.9a

Read an Analysis

- Ask students to look back at "How Do I Hold the Summer?" in the **Interactive Worktext**. Have students review their notes and the poem, looking for sensory language. Ask: *How did the poet's use of sensory language help you imagine the change in seasons?*

- Read aloud the directions on page 262. *Ben's paragraph is an analysis, or detailed description, of how the poet uses sensory language. When you analyze a poem, you ask yourself "how" and "why" questions to help you understand how the poet shares the message of the poem.* Read aloud the student model.

- *An analysis always includes certain elements. Circle* the topic sentence. *What important information does Ben include in his topic sentence?* (poem's title; that the poet uses sensory language; what the sensory language shows)

- *Another part of an analysis is* text evidence. *Ben includes examples of sensory language from the poem and explains how the sensory language helped him imagine the seasons.* Have students draw boxes around the text evidence. (sentences 2–5) *Look back at your notes for "How Do I Hold the Summer?" What other example of sensory language could be included as text evidence in the model?* (<u>Possible answer</u>: winter's veil of frost)

- *The final part of an analysis is a* concluding statement. Have students underline the concluding statement. *Which words in the concluding statement wrap up the text evidence?* ("all of these details")

Write an Analysis

Analytical Writing

Guided Writing Read the writing prompt on page 263 together. Have students write about "Tell Me the Old, Old Stories" or another text they read this week. *Use the checklist to help you figure out the information to include in each section.* Guide students to ask "how" and "why" questions, such as *Why is this detail easy to imagine?* and *How do these details help me picture the characters?*

Peer Conference Have students read their analysis to a partner. Listeners should identify the strongest text evidence that supports the topic sentence and discuss any sentences that are unclear.

Teacher Conference Check students' writing for complete sentences and text evidence that supports their topic. Review the concluding statement. *Does this sentence tie all of the elements together?* If necessary, have students revise the concluding statement by restating the topic sentence.

Level Up

▲ Approaching Leveled Reader

▲ Reading/Writing Workshop

▲ Apprentice Leveled Reader

▲ Interactive Worktext

IF students read the Apprentice Level Reader fluently and the **Interactive Worktext** Shared Read fluently and answer the Respond to Reading questions

THEN read together the Approaching Level Reader main selection and the **Reading/Writing Workshop** Shared Read from *Reading Wonders*. Have students take notes as they read, using self-stick notes. Then ask and answer questions about their notes.

Writing Rubric

	4	3	2	1
Topic Sentence	There is one clear, focused topic sentence.	Topic sentence is less focused, somewhat clear.	Topic is presented in short phrases.	There is no topic sentence.
Text Evidence	Topic is supported by two or more text details.	Evidence includes only one detail from the text.	Little to no evidence is cited from the text.	No text evidence is included.
Concluding Statement	Clearly restates the topic sentence; wraps up all the details.	Restatement is less focused; attempts to wrap up the details.	Vaguely restates the topic. Doesn't correlate well to text evidence.	There is no conclusion.
Writing Style	Writes in complete sentences. Uses correct spelling and grammar.	Uses complete sentences and phrases. Writing has spelling and grammar errors.	Few or no complete sentences. There are many spelling and grammar errors.	Does not write accurately or in complete sentences.

ASSESSMENT

Weekly Assessment

Have students complete the Weekly Assessment using **Assessment** book pages 48–49.

WEEK 6

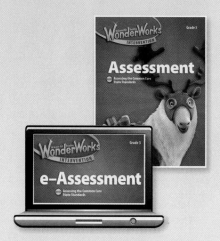

▶ **Unit Assessment,**
pages 149–157

▶ **Fluency Assessment,**
pages 250–265

▶ **Exit Test,**
pages 205–213

Unit 4 Assessment

CCSS TESTED SKILLS

✔ COMPREHENSION	✔ VOCABULARY
• Point of View RL.5.1	• Context Clues L.5.4a
• Point of View RL.5.1	
• Author's Point of View RI.5.2, RI.6.6	
• Author's Point of View RI.5.2, RI.6.6	
• Theme RL.5.2	

Using Assessment and Writing Scores

RETEACH

	IF ...	THEN ...
COMPREHENSION	Students answer 0–7 multiple-choice items correctly ...	... reteach tested skills using instruction on pages 364–371.
VOCABULARY	Students answer 0–3 multiple-choice items correctly ...	... reteach tested skills using instruction on page 364.
WRITING	Students score mostly 1–2 on weekly Write About Reading rubrics throughout the unit...	... reteach writing using instruction on pages 372–373.

LEVEL UP

	IF ...	THEN ...
COMPREHENSION	Students answer 8–10 multiple-choice items correctly ...	... have students read the *Ocean Threats* Approaching Leveled Reader. Use the Level Up lesson on page 240.
WRITING	Students score mostly 3–4 on weekly Write About Reading rubrics throughout the unit...	... use the Level Up Write About Reading lesson on page 241 to have students compare two selections from the unit.

Fluency Assessment

Conduct assessments individually using the differentiated fluency passages in **Assessment**. Students' expected fluency goal for this Unit is 117–137 WCPM with an accuracy rate of 95% or higher.

Exit Test

If a student answers 13–15 multiple-choice items correctly on the Unit Assessment, administer the Unit 4 Exit Test at the end of Week 6.

Time to Exit McGraw-Hill Reading WonderWorks

Exit Test

If...

Students answer 13–15 multiple choice items correctly...

Fluency Assessment

If...

Students achieve their Fluency Assessment goal for the unit...

Level Up Lessons

If...

Students are successful applying close reading skills with the Approaching Leveled Reader in Week 6...

If...

Students score mostly 4–5 on the Level Up Write About Reading assignment...

Foundational Skills Kit

If...

Students have mastered the Unit 4 benchmark skills in the Foundational Skills Kit and *PowerPAL for Reading* adaptive learning system...

Then...

... consider exiting the student from *Reading WonderWorks* materials into the Approaching Level of *Reading Wonders*.

WEEK 6

Read Approaching Leveled Reader

RI.5.10 CCSS

▶ **Read Approaching Leveled Reader**

Approaching Leveled Reader

Apprentice Leveled Reader

The Delta

Before Reading

Preview Discuss what students remember about the Mississippi Delta and the rich natural resources it provides. Tell them that they will be reading a more challenging version of *The Delta*.

Vocabulary Use routines on the **Visual Vocabulary Cards** to review the Weekly Vocabulary words. Use pages 222 and 224 to review the Expand Vocabulary words.

A C T During Reading

▶ **Vocabulary** Supply definitions for domain-specific social science words that are new to this level, such as: *acres* (page 2), *extends* (page 3), *topsoil* (page 6), and *extracting* (page 9). Provide a definition for *sustainable* (page 15) and point out how the suffix changes the word for *sustainability* (page 16).

▶ **Connection of Ideas** Students may need help grasping the idea that rivers provide more than just food, water, and transportation. Read aloud page 8, and explain the word *bounty* in the chapter title. Point out the bounties, or gifts, that the river's delta provides: oil and gas, or fossil fuels. Read page 9 and then ask: *What other bounties does the river's delta provide?* (iron, sand, clay, marble, and limestone) Explain that jobs and money are also types of bounties.

▶ **Sentence Structure** Students may need help understanding the use of dashes. Read aloud the following sentence on page 11: *Wetlands also affect water quality—they help to clean the water that passes through them.* Point out that a dash often comes before words that give more explanation. Ask: *What are the words before the dash about?* (water quality) *What do the words after the dash explain?* (how the wetlands help clean the water for good water quality)

After Reading

Ask students to complete the Respond to Reading on page 18 after they have finished reading. Provide additional support as needed to help students use the weekly vocabulary strategy to answer question 3.

▶ **Write About Reading**

Interactive Worktext Shared Read

Apprentice Leveled Reader

Write About Reading

W.5.1   W.5.9a

Read an Analysis

- Distribute the Unit 4 Downloadable Model and Practice that compares two related texts, the **Interactive Worktext** Shared Read "How Mighty Kate Stopped the Train" and the **Apprentice Leveled Reader** "Paul Bunyan." Read the paragraph aloud.

- Point out the signal word *both* in the topic sentence, which tells readers how the two texts are alike and the word *but* which signals a difference. Have students reread the topic sentence. Ask: *How do you know Toby is telling his opinion?* (he writes "I think") *What other information does Toby include in his topic sentence?* (titles of both texts)

- Ask: *What details does Toby include from "How Mighty Kate Stopped the Train" that support his opinion?* (sentences 2–5) *What details does Toby include from "Paul Bunyan" that support his opinion?* (the sixth sentence) *Why is the concluding statement a good wrap up?* (Toby restates his opinion.)*Which words wrap up the text evidence?* (for these reasons)

Analytical Writing Write an Analysis

Guided Practice Display: *Write a paragraph that compares the mysteries "Where's Brownie?" to the "The Mysterious Teacher." Give your opinion about which mystery was more suspenseful.*

- Alternatively, let students select two mysteries or adventure stories to compare.

- Use the Unit 4 Downloadable Model and Practice to guide students' writing.

- Tell them to begin with a topic sentence and include details from both texts to support their opinion..

- Remind students that the concluding statement should restate their opinion and wrap up the details.

Teacher Conference Check students' writing for complete sentences. Did they include a topic sentence that tells an opinion? Did they cite text evidence? Did they restate their opinion in the last sentence?

Writing Rubric

	4	3	2	1
Topic Sentence	Topic sentence presents a clear opinion.	Topic sentence presents an opinion, somewhat clearly.	Topic is presented in short phrases; opinion is unclear	There is no topic sentence; no opinion is presented.
Text Evidence	Opinion is supported by two or more text details.	Opinion is only supported by one detail from the text.	Little to no evidence from the text supports opinion.	No text evidence is included; does not support opinion.
Concluding Statement	Clearly restates an opinion; wraps up all the details.	Restatement is less focused, attempts to wrap up the details.	Vaguely restates opinion. Doesn't correlate well to text evidence.	There is no conclusion.
Writing Style	Writes in complete sentences. Uses correct spelling and grammar.	Uses complete sentences and phrases. Writing has spelling and grammar errors.	Has few or no complete sentences. There are many spelling and grammar errors.	Does not write accurately or in complete sentences.

UNIT 5 PLANNER
What's Next?

Week 1 New Perspectives	Week 2 Better Together	Week 3 Our Changing Earth

Week 1 — New Perspectives

ESSENTIAL QUESTION
What experiences can change the way you see yourself and the world around you?

Build Background

Vocabulary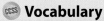
L.5.4a *disdain, focused, genius, perspective, prospect, stunned, superb, transition*

Access Complex Text **A C T**
Organization

Comprehension
RL.5.3 Skill: Character, Setting, Plot: Compare and Contrast
Respond to Reading

Write About Reading *Analytical Writing*
W.5.9a Opinion: Setting

Week 2 — Better Together

ESSENTIAL QUESTION
How do shared experiences help people adapt to change?

Build Background

Vocabulary
L.5.4a *assume, guarantee, nominate, obviously, rely, supportive, sympathy, weakling*

Access Complex Text **A C T**
Genre

Comprehension
RL.5.2 Skill: Character, Setting, Plot: Compare and Contrast
Respond to Reading

Write About Reading *Analytical Writing*
W.5.9a Inform/Explain: Setting

Week 3 — Our Changing Earth

ESSENTIAL QUESTION
What changes in the environment affect living things?

Build Background

Vocabulary
L.5.4a *atmosphere, decays, gradual, impact, noticeably, receding, stability, variations*

Access Complex Text **A C T**
Purpose

Comprehension
RI.5.3 Skill: Text Structure: Compare and Contrast
Respond to Reading

Write About Reading *Analytical Writing*
W.5.9b Inform/Explain: Compare and Contrast

A S S E S S M E N T

Week 1
✓ **Quick Check**
Vocabulary, Comprehension
✓ **Weekly Assessment**
Assessment Book, pp. 50–51

Week 2
✓ **Quick Check**
Vocabulary, Comprehension
✓ **Weekly Assessment**
Assessment Book, pp. 52–53

Week 3
✓ **Quick Check**
Vocabulary, Comprehension
✓ **Weekly Assessment**
Assessment Book, pp. 54–55

✓ **MID-UNIT ASSESSMENT**
Assessment Book, pp. 104–111

✓ **Fluency Assessment**
Assessment Book, pp. 266–281

Use the Foundational Skills Kit for explicit instruction of phonics, structural analysis, fluency, and word recognition. Includes *PowerPAL for Reading* adaptive learning system.

Week 4
Now We Know

ESSENTIAL QUESTION
How can scientific knowledge change over time?

Build Background

CCSS Vocabulary
L.5.4a approximately, astronomical, calculation, criteria, diameter, evaluate, orbit, spheres

Access Complex Text A C T
Connection of Ideas

CCSS Comprehension
RI.5.5 Skill: Text Structure: Cause and Effect
Respond to Reading

CCSS Write About Reading *Analytical Writing*
W.5.9b Inform/Explain: Cause and Effect

Week 5
Scientific Viewpoints

ESSENTIAL QUESTION
How do natural events and human activities affect the environment?

Build Background

CCSS Vocabulary
L.5.4a agricultural, declined, disorder, identify, probable, thrive, unexpected, widespread

Access Complex Text A C T
Purpose

CCSS Comprehension
RI.5.8 Skill: Author's Point of View
RI.6.6 Respond to Reading

CCSS Write About Reading *Analytical Writing*
W.5.9b Inform/Explain: Point of View

Week 6
ASSESS

RETEACH   LEVEL UP

Reteach
Comprehension Skills

Vocabulary

Write About Reading

Level Up
Read Approaching Leveled Reader

Write About Reading:
Compare Texts

A S S E S S M E N T

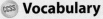 **Quick Check**
Vocabulary, Comprehension

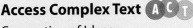 **Weekly Assessment**
Assessment Book, pp. 56–57

 Quick Check
Vocabulary, Comprehension

Weekly Assessment
Assessment Book, pp. 58–59

Unit Assessment
Assessment Book, pp. 158–166

Fluency Assessment
Assessment Book, pp. 266–281

 EXIT TEST
Assessment Book, pp. 214–222

Unit 5

What's Next?

The Big Idea

In what ways can things change?

UNIT 5 OPENER,
pp. 264–265

The Big Idea

In what ways can things change?

Talk About It

Read aloud the Big Idea on page 265 of the **Interactive Worktext:** *In what ways can things change?* Have students think about changes they have seen. Say: *The world around us changes. We change, too. Some changes happen over a long period of time. For example, a young tree takes many years to grow tall. Some changes happen quickly, such as changes in weather. In what ways have you changed since last year?* (Answers will vary.)

Discuss the photograph on pages 264–265. Point out the cocoon and explain how a caterpillar turns into a butterfly, as necessary. Say: *Look at the photograph. What change do you see happening?* (The butterfly is leaving its cocoon.) *What was the butterfly like before it was in the cocoon?* (It was a caterpillar.) *In what ways does a butterfly change?* (Possible answer: It changes from a caterpillar to a butterfly; it grows wings; it changes colors.) *What are some other changes in nature that you know about?* Have partners or small groups discuss this question and share their ideas with the class.

Tell students that changes are taking place all around us. Say: *In this unit, we will be reading ten selections about ways that things can change. In one of the selections, a boy faces changes when he starts middle school. In another selection, forests undergo changes caused by fire.*

Build Fluency

Each week, use the **Interactive Worktext** Shared Reads and **Apprentice Leveled Readers** for fluency instruction and practice. Keep in mind that reading rates vary with the type of text that students are reading as well as the purpose for reading. For example, comprehension of complex informational texts generally requires slower reading.

Explain/Model Use the Fluency lessons on pages 374–378 to explain the skill. Then model the skill by reading the first page of the week's Shared Read or Leveled Reader.

Practice/Apply Choose a page from the Shared Read or Leveled Reader. Have one group read the top half of the page one sentence at a time. Remind children to apply the skill. Have the second group echo-read the passage. Then have the groups switch roles for the second half of the page. Discuss how each group applied the skill.

> **Weekly Fluency Focus**
>
> **Week 1** Expression
> **Week 2** Expression and Phrasing
> **Week 3** Rate
> **Week 4** Accuracy
> **Week 5** Expression and Phrasing

You can also use the **Lesson Cards** and **Practice** pages from the **Foundational Skills Kit** for targeted Fluency instruction and practice.

Interactive Worktext

	Week 1	Week 2	Week 3	Week 4	Week 5
	"Miguel in the Middle"	"The Day the Rollets Got Their Moxie Back"	"Forests on Fire"	"Changing Views of Earth"	"Should Plants and Animals From Other Places Live Here?"
Quantitative	Lexile 800 TextEvaluator™ 43	Lexile 820 TextEvaluator™ 40	Lexile 850 TextEvaluator™ 36	Lexile 770 TextEvaluator™ 42	Lexile 800 TextEvaluator™ 48
Qualitative	• Organization • Vocabulary	• Genre • Vocabulary	• Purpose • Vocabulary	• Connection of Ideas • Vocabulary	• Purpose • Vocabulary
Reader and Task	The Weekly Concept lessons will help determine the reader's knowledge and engagement in the weekly concept.				
	Weekly Concept: p. 246 Questions and tasks: pp. 248–249	Weekly Concept: p. 256 Questions and tasks: pp. 258–259	Weekly Concept: p. 266 Questions and tasks: pp. 268–269	Weekly Concept: p. 278 Questions and tasks: pp. 280–281	Weekly Concept: p. 288 Questions and tasks: pp. 290–291

Apprentice Leveled Reader

	Week 1	Week 2	Week 3	Week 4	Week 5
	"King of the Board"	"The Picture Palace"	"Ocean Threats"	"Mars"	"The Great Plains"
Quantitative	Lexile 650 TextEvaluator™ 38	Lexile 640 TextEvaluator™ 31	Lexile 730 TextEvaluator™ 28	Lexile 680 TextEvaluator™ 24	Lexile 680 TextEvaluator™ 28
Qualitative	• Organization • Vocabulary	• Genre • Prior Knowledge • Vocabulary	• Purpose • Sentence Structure • Genre • Connection of Ideas • Vocabulary	• Connection of Ideas • Genre • Vocabulary	• Purpose • Connection of Ideas • Organization • Vocabulary
Reader and Task	The Weekly Concept lessons will help determine the reader's knowledge and engagement in the weekly concept.				
	Weekly Concept: p. 246 Questions and tasks: pp. 250–253	Weekly Concept: p. 256 Questions and tasks: pp. 260–263	Weekly Concept: p. 266 Questions and tasks: pp. 270–273	Weekly Concept: p. 278 Questions and tasks: pp. 282–285	Weekly Concept: p. 288 Questions and tasks: pp. 292–295

See pages 379 for details about Text Complexity measures.

Objectives
- Develop oral language
- Build background about experiences that can change your perspective
- Understand and use weekly vocabulary
- Read realistic fiction

Materials
- Interactive Worktext, pp. 266–273
- Visual Vocabulary Cards: 153–160

☞ **Go** Digital
- Interactive eWorktext
- Visual Vocabulary Cards

Scaffolding for **Wonders** Reading/Writing Workshop

WEEKLY CONCEPT

5–10 Minutes   SL.5.1b   SL.5.1c   CCSS

Talk About It

Essential Question Read aloud the Essential Question on page 266 of the **Interactive Worktext**: *What experiences can change the way you see yourself and the world around you?* Explain that your perspective is your view of the world and yourself. Say: *Going to new places, meeting new people, and trying new activities are some experiences that can change the way you see yourself and the world around you.*

- Discuss the photograph on page 266. Ask: *In what way is this girl experiencing the world in a new way?* (She's in an airplane looking down at the ground.)

I Do Say: *One time, I went swimming in the ocean. From the shore it looked calm. Underwater, I saw lots of fish moving everywhere. I felt surprised when I saw so many fish. I also felt weightless in the water. I will write "swimming in the ocean," "so many fish," and "felt weightless" in one oval of the web on page 267.*

We Do Say: *Let's look at the photo. Where is this girl?* (in a plane) *Does the ocean look close up or far away?* (far away) *Can she see more or less land than when she is on the ground?* (more) *What do you think it makes her think about the world?* (Possible answer: it's big, awesome) *How do you think this view makes her feel about herself?* (Possible answer: surprised, small) Guide students to add words to the web on page 267. have them tell how they would feel in the girl's place.

You Do Have partners describe an experience that made them see themselves or the world differently. Ask: *What did you do? How did it make you feel about yourself? What did it make you think about the world?*

REVIEW VOCABULARY

10–15 Minutes   L.5.1   L.5.4a   L.5.5c   L.5.6   CCSS

Review Weekly Vocabulary Words

- Use the **Visual Vocabulary Cards** to review the weekly vocabulary.

- Read together the directions for the Vocabulary activity on page 268 of the **Interactive Worktext**. Then complete the activity.

1 **genius** Have students complete the following sentence frame: *Two words that describe a genius are _____ and _____.* (smart, skilled)

2 **focused** Ask: *What things can make it hard to focus when you are studying?* (music, noise, TV, talking) Then have students discuss ways to stay focused when they are doing their homework. Have them use this sentence frame: *One way I stay focused when I do my homework is to _____.* (Possible answers: turn off my music; turn off TV; go to my room)

3 **stunned** Have partners ask each other questions to help them decide which of the words are synonyms for *shocked* and *stunned.* (amazed, surprised)

4 **superb** Ask: *Who at school is a superb athlete? Who in professional sports is a superb athlete? Write the name of one of these people.* (Answers will vary.) Then have partners explain their choices.

5 **disdain** Ask students to name a type of music or a sound they don't like to hear. Say: *Show me what you do when you hear this sound. How can you use your face and hands to show disdain?* (Students may cover their ears; facial expressions should show strong dislike.)

6 **prospect** Ask students if they have ever been to or seen a beach. Show pictures, as necessary. *How* *would you feel about the prospect of going to the beach? Have them use this sentence frame: I would feel _____ about the prospect of going to the beach because _____.* (Possible answers: excited, I love to swim; unhappy, I hate sand)

7 **perspective** Have students look to their right. Ask: *What do you see from your perspective?* Have students complete the sentence frame: *From my perspective I can see _____ and _____.* (Answers will vary.)

8 **transition** Ask students to name animals they've learned about that transition from one form to another during their life cycle. Have partners use the following sentence frame to describe their pictures: *Before the transition, the _____ has _____. After the transition, the _____ has _____.* (Drawings will vary, but may include a caterpillar/butterfly, tadpole/frog, baby chick/chicken.)

High-Utility Words

Remind students that pronouns such as *I, you, he, she,* and *it* take the place of the name of a person, place, or thing. Explain that some pronouns are indefinite, or do not tell the specific person, place, or thing they replace. Give examples, such as *someone, everybody, all, few, some,* and *none.* Have students look at the High-Utility Words activity on page 269 of the **Interactive Worktext**. Ask partners to circle the indefinite pronouns in the passage. (most, anybody, some, few, Everyone) Write the following sentence frame and have students complete it using indefinite pronouns: *_____ can come to the party.* Discuss how the pronouns change the meaning of the sentence

---

ELL ENGLISH LANGUAGE LEARNERS

Display the indefinite pronouns *all, some,* and *none.* Point to and say each example. Have students use their hands to show how many fingers each indefinite pronoun indicates.

READ COMPLEX TEXT

15–20 Minutes RL.5.1 RF.5.4c

Read: "Miguel in the Middle"

- Have students turn to page 270 in the **Interactive Worktext** and read aloud the Essential Question. Explain that they will read a story about a boy who is going through some changes in his life. Ask: *What does the illustration show?* (a boy at school) *Is the boy standing alone or with other students?* (alone) *Use these clues. What changes do you think the boy will face?* (Possible answers: going to a new school; making friends)

- Read "Miguel in the Middle" together. Note that the weekly vocabulary words are highlighted in yellow. Expand Vocabulary words are highlighted in blue.

- Have students use the "My Notes" section on page 270 to write questions they have, words they don't understand, and details they want to remember. Model how to use the "My Notes" section. *I can write notes about questions I have as I read. In the second paragraph on page 271, I see the word* district, *and I'm not sure what it means. I will write* district *with a question mark next to it in the "My Notes" section. I can look it up in a dictionary later. As I continue to read, I'll make notes about the different characters for when we talk about the story.*

ELL ENGLISH LANGUAGE LEARNERS

As you read together, have students pause to mark anything about the story that they find confusing or unclear. Guide them to write questions in the "My Notes" section.

 Quick Check **Can students understand the weekly vocabulary in context? If not, review vocabulary using the Visual Vocabulary Cards before teaching Lesson 2.**

WEEK 1 LESSON 2

Objectives
- Read realistic fiction
- Understand complex text through close reading
- Recognize and understand compare and contrast
- Respond to the selection using text evidence to support ideas

Scaffolding for McGraw-Hill Reading **Wonders** Reading/Writing Workshop

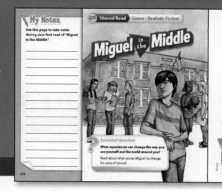

Materials
Interactive Worktext, pp. 270–275

Go Digital
- Interactive eWorktext
- Compare and Contrast Mini-Lesson

REREAD COMPLEX TEXT

20–25 Minutes — RL.5.1 RL.5.3 RL.5.4a L.5.5a L.5.6 **CCSS**

Close Reading: "Miguel in the Middle"

Reread "Miguel in the Middle" with students. As you read together, discuss important passages in the text. Have students respond to text-dependent questions, including those in the **Interactive Worktext**.

Page 271

Organization Ⓐ Ⓒ Ⓣ Read aloud the second paragraph on page 271. Say: *To understand the order of key events in a story, look for days, months, and other words that signal when events take place. I read the words "until now." This phrase is a clue that something has changed in the story. Let's figure out the key events. What happens to Miguel in September?* (he started middle school) *Where did Miguel go to school before this time?* (elementary school) *How did this event affect Miguel's life?* (he doesn't go to school with his closest friends)

Expand Vocabulary Discuss the meaning of *painful*. Read the sentence with *painful*. Ask: *What does Miguel say caused painful changes?* (the transition from elementary school) *What detail in the paragraph help you understand that Miguel's experience is painful?* (I've really missed my old friends.)

Compare and Contrast Say: *One way to understand how characters change in a story is to compare a character's feelings and actions in each setting.* Model using text evidence on page 271 to identify details about Miguel in each setting. *I read in the first paragraph that Miguel "always sat in the middle of the classroom." Is this in elementary or middle school?* (elementary) Have students draw a box around that sentence. *Where does*

Miguel sit in the classroom in middle school? Circle text evidence. (I'm in the front row.) *Who were most of Miguel's friends in elementary school? Draw a box around this detail.* (Most of them are classmates) *Does Miguel have the same friends in middle school? Circle text evidence.* (No. "All of my closest friends go to a different middle school") *What is another way Miguel's life in middle school is different than his life in elementary school?* (Circle: Also, my new teachers give us more homework.) Ask students to summarize how Miguel's life has changed. (he doesn't have as many friends in class; he sits in the front row; he has more homework)

Vocabulary Point out the figurative language *my heart wasn't dancing* in the last sentence. Ask: *Can a heart really dance?* (no) Ask: *What feeling does this phrase express?* (unhappiness) *What clues in the text helped you understand the meaning?* (Possible answers: painful changes; missed my old friends; more homework)

Page 272

Organization Ⓐ Ⓒ Ⓣ Say: *Sometimes events are told out of the order in which they happen.* Read the first two sentences. *The words "It happened because" tells me one event happened first and caused another event to happen. What caused Miguel and Jake to become good friends?* (Miguel was having trouble in math class.) *Let's write a "1" next to this sentence. Reread the rest of the paragraph. Which sentence tells what Miguel does because he was having trouble in math class?* (the last sentence of the paragraph) *Which sentence tells what happened as a result of these events?* (the first sentence of the paragraph)

Expand Vocabulary *What does* approach *mean?* (to walk up to someone) *What clues help you understand the meaning of* approached? *Look at the characters actions and dialogue.* (we were walking out of school; "Hey Jake," I began) *Who did Miguel approach?* (Jake)

Compare and Contrast *Have students reread the first paragraph. Ask: How is Miguel doing in math? Draw a box around text evidence.* (not well; I was having trouble with my math homework.) *What does Miguel decide to do?* (ask Jake for help) *Reread the last two paragraphs. Where do events in each paragraph take place?* (fifth paragraph: at Miguel's house; last paragraph: at school) *Does Miguel understand math at home? Circle text evidence.* (yes; I finally understood why eight-sixteenths is the same as one-half.) *Does Miguel understand math at school? Circle text evidence.* (yes; I was even able to answer a math problem) *How does Miguel change?* (he is better at math) *What causes Miguel to change?* (Jake helps him study)

Page 273

Expand Vocabulary Have students point to the word *realized. What does realize mean?* (to know or understand something) *What clues in the paragraph help you understand the meaning of* realized? (clever; knew)

Organization ⒶⒸⓉ Have students reread the page. *What events happen before winter vacation?* (Our teacher gave us a brainteaser; Jake and Miguel figure out the correct answer.) *What does Miguel plan to do next?* (Jake and I get to hang out during winter break. We're going to the Math Museum and all my new friends from middle school will come, too.)

High-Utility Words Point out the indefinite pronoun *most* in the third paragraph. Have students circle other indefinite pronouns in the paragraph. (some, everyone)

Compare and Contrast Have students review details about Miguel they had marked so far. *Reread the page and mark details that are clues to Miguel's feelings now.* (I feel sad that I'll be away from school; I'm glad Jake and I get to hang out together) *Then have students compare details about Miguel at the beginning and end of the story. How did Miguel feel about math at the beginning? How does he feel about math at the end?* (he doesn't like math at the beginning, he likes it at the end) *How does Miguel feel about his friends at the beginning?* (he misses his friends at the beginning; he has new friends at the end) *In what way is Miguel still the same?* (He is still in the middle of a large circle of friends.)

RESPOND TO READING

10–20 Minutes   RL.5.1   W.5.9a   SL.5.1d   CCSS

Respond to "Miguel in the Middle"

Have students summarize "Miguel in the Middle" orally to demonstrate comprehension. Then have partners answer the questions on page 274 of the **Interactive Worktext** using the discussion starters. Tell them to use text evidence to support their answers. Have students write the page number(s) on which they found the text evidence for each question.

1. *What does Miguel think about middle school at the beginning of the story?* (Miguel feels lonely; he misses his friends; he thinks middle school is hard because there is more homework. <u>Text Evidence</u>: p. 271)

2. *What does Miguel think about middle school at the end of the story?* (He feels better about middle school; he thinks middle school is fun because he has new friends, he likes doing math. <u>Text Evidence</u>: p. 273)

3. *What causes Miguel to change?* (Miguel changes because Jake helps him study math. Miguel gets better at math; he and Jake become friends. <u>Text Evidence</u>: pp. 272, 273)

After students discuss the questions on page 274, have them write a response to the questions on page 275. Tell them to use their partner discussions and notes about "Miguel in the Middle" to help them. Circulate and provide guidance.

 Quick Check Do students understand vocabulary in context? If not, review and reteach using the instruction on page 254.

Can students identify details to compare and contrast? If not, review and reteach using the instruction on page 254 and assign the Unit 5 Week 1 digital mini-lesson.

Can students write a response to "Miguel in the Middle"? If not, provide sentence frames to help them organize their ideas.

Objectives
- Understand and use new vocabulary
- Read realistic fiction
- Recognize and understand compare and contrast
- Understand complex text through close reading

Materials
- "King of the Board" Apprentice Leveled Reader: pp. 2–11
- Graphic Organizer: Compare and Contrast

☞ **Go** Digital
- Apprentice Leveled Reader eBook
- Downloadable Graphic Organizer
- Compare and Contrast Mini-Lesson

Scaffolding for **Wonders** Approaching Leveled Reader

BEFORE READING
10–15 Minutes   SL.5.1c   SL.5.1d   L.5.4a   L.5.6   CCSS

Introduce "King of the Board"

- Read the Essential Question on the title page of "King of the Board" **Apprentice Leveled Reader**: *What experiences can change the way you see yourself and the world around you? We will read about a boy who changes how he thinks of himself and his family when he finds a game he loves.*

- Read the title. Have students look at the images. *What do the title and the images tell you about the story?* (It's about a boy and the game of chess.)

Expand Vocabulary

Display each word below. Say the words and have students repeat them. Then use the Define/Example/Ask routine to introduce each word.

1 **chaos** (page 2)

Define: confusion and disorder

Example: The town was in *chaos* after the big storm.

Ask: What might cause *chaos* in a kitchen?

2 **invitation** (page 10)

Define: a request asking someone to attend something

Example: Tonya accepted the *invitation* to dinner.

Ask: What is your favorite kind of *invitation*?

3 **obsessed** (page 7)

Define: to be extremely absorbed by an interest

Example: My aunt is *obsessed* with reality shows.

Ask: Have you ever been *obsessed* with an interest?

4 **recreation** (page 4)

Define: activities people do for enjoyment

Example: Michael's family likes to hike at *recreation* areas such as forest preserves and national parks.

Ask: What is your favorite place for *recreation*?

5 **talented** (page 10)

Define: having a natural skill at something

Example: I love eating at the home of a *talented* cook.

Ask: Who do you know that is *talented* at something?

DURING READING
20–30 Minutes   RL.5.1   RL.5.3   SL.5.1b   L.5.4a   L.5.5b   CCSS

Close Reading
🔍 **Pages 2–3**

Organization Ⓐ Ⓒ Ⓣ   Read page 2. *What do the members of the narrator's family do on Saturday mornings?* (Dad searches for his baseball glove, Mom gets ready for tennis, Adam packs a bag for track, his cousins call, Grandpa drives Adam to the track on his way to play golf.) *What do you think the narrator does every Saturday morning? Why?* (He watches the action and feels left out. He says "I hate Saturday mornings" because he's not part of the family's activities.)

Compare and Contrast *On pages 2 and 3, I read that the narrator is different from his family. On page 2 he says, "I live in a family of sports stars." What examples does the narrator give?* (Dad's a baseball genius, Mom's a superb tennis player, Adam is the fastest runner at school.) *What statements on page 3 show how the narrator is different from his family?* ("I'm just not interested in sports...there is no sport that I really want to play...there is no sport that I really want to watch.")

Have students record details about characters, settings, and plot events on their Compare and Contrast chart as they read the selection.

STOP AND CHECK Read the question in the Stop and Check box on page 3. (Because everyone is getting ready to play a sport and he doesn't play a sport.)

Pages 4–6

Organization A C T Read page 4. *When and where does this part of the story take place?* (at breakfast one Saturday) *Who is Clinton?* (the narrator) *What do Mom and Dad want Clinton to do?* (meet them at the park after their games) Have a student read the first sentence on page 5. *Where is Clinton now?* (at the park) *What is happening?* (Clinton is waiting for his parents to arrive.) *What words helped you understand that the time and place changed?* (Later, while I waited…at the park)

Compare and Contrast Read pages 5 and 6. *How does Clinton feel when he watches the chess game?* (interested) *How do you know?* (completely focused; didn't want to miss the end of the game) Review the first paragraph on page 3. *What details tell how Clinton feels about watching sports?* (I get bored watching tennis or baseball; I get hot, tired, and sore from sitting and listening.) *How does Clinton behave differently in each setting?* (He is totally focused on the chess game, unlike baseball or tennis.)

VOCABULARY Have students find the phrase *bird's-eye view* on page 5. Explain that it means a view from above. Ask: What does Clinton climb up to get a *bird's-eye view* of? (two men playing chess on a giant board)

STOP AND CHECK Read the question in the Stop and Check box on page 6. (Clinton discovers a giant chess board game that captures his interest.)

Pages 7–8

Organization A C T *What phrase on page 7 tells you when Chapter 2 takes place?* (After our visit to the park) *What does Clinton do after he visits the park?* (starts learning about chess) *Why does Clinton become interested in chess?* (He liked the chess pieces and the way they moved.)

Compare and Contrast Read pages 7 and 8. *How does Clinton feel about chess?* (obsessed) *How does his dad feel about chess?* (not interested, it isn't his "thing.") *How does his grandpa feel about chess?* (the same; he'd rather play golf)

Organization A C T Read the second and third paragraphs on page 8. *What happened after Clinton couldn't find anyone to go with him to the park to watch chess?* (His mom agreed to meet him at the park after her game.) *When did that take place?* (the next Saturday)

Pages 9–11

Organization A C T Help students paraphrase the order of events on page 9. (The women see Clinton watching, they explain some rules, Clinton suggests moves, the game ends, and the women suggest he join a club.) *What words in each paragraph help you understand when each event happens?* (*When, After a while, After they finished*)

STOP AND CHECK Read the question in the Stop and Check box on page 9. (He becomes involved in the game and the chess players invite him to join a club.)

Connection of Ideas A C T *Read the title of Chapter 2 on page 7 and the last paragraph on page 10. How are these connected?* (Kings are chess pieces. Clinton understands that in chess a battle is fought for the King.)

STOP AND CHECK Read the question in the Stop and Check box on page 10. (He suggests some moves and shares his ideas.)

Have partners review their Compare and Contrast charts for pages 2–11 and discuss what they learned.

✓ *Quick Check* **Do students understand weekly vocabulary in context? If not, review and reteach using the instruction on page 254.**

Can students compare and contrast? If not, review and reteach using the instruction on page 254 and assign the Unit 5 Week 1 digital mini-lesson.

Objectives
- Understand and use new vocabulary
- Read realistic fiction
- Recognize and understand compare and contrast
- Understand complex text through close reading
- Respond to the selection using text evidence to support ideas

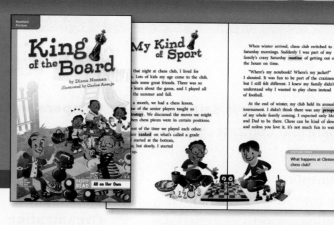

Scaffolding for **McGraw-Hill Reading WONDERS** Approaching Leveled Reader

Materials
- "King of the Board" Apprentice Leveled Reader: pp. 12–20
- Graphic Organizer: Compare and Contrast

☞ **Go Digital**
- Apprentice Leveled Reader eBook
- Downloadable Graphic Organizer
- Compare and Contrast Mini-Lesson

BEFORE READING

5–10 Minutes   SL.5.1c SL.5.1d L.5.4a L.5.6   CCSS

Expand Vocabulary

Display each word below. Say the words and have students repeat them. Then use the Define/Example/Ask routine to introduce each word.

❶ ranked (page 12)

Define: placed in an order, such as from best to worst

Example: The gym teacher *ranked* the runners by speed.

Ask: What can you do to be *ranked* more highly in your favorite sport or activity?

❷ routine (page 13)

Define: a usual way of doing something

Example: My daily *routine* includes preparing for class.

Ask: What is your daily *routine* in the morning?

❸ strategy (page 12)

Define: a planned course of action

Example: Tilly's *strategy* for passing the test is to study one chapter every night.

Ask: What is your *strategy* for doing well at school?

DURING READING

15–20 Minutes   RL.5.1 RL.5.3 SL.5.1b L.5.4a L.5.4b   CCSS

Close Reading

🔍 **Pages 12–13**

Organization Ⓐ Ⓒ Ⓣ Read page 12. Review with students the women's comments about the chess club on page 10. Point out that these details help readers understand how Chapter 3 begins. *What does Clinton do after he attends his first night of chess club?* (He continues to play every Tuesday night.) *How long does he continue to play on Tuesday nights?* (through the summer and fall) *When does a senior player give a chess lesson?* (once a month)

Organization Ⓐ Ⓒ Ⓣ Have students read page 13. *What happened at the beginning of winter?* (chess club switched to Saturday mornings) *Why is that important?* (Clinton is now part of his family's crazy routine.)

Compare and Contrast *Compare and contrast Clinton's life before he discovered chess on pages 2 and 3 with his life on page 13. What has changed?* (Clinton hated Saturday mornings; now he thinks they're fun. He used to watch his family play games; now they will watch him.) *What is the same?* (He doesn't like sports, feels he is different from his family, knows it's not fun to watch a game you don't love.)

Vocabulary Point out the word *annual* on page 13. Explain that *anno* is a Latin root word. It means "year." *How does this help you understand the meaning of* annual *tournament?* (happens once a year)

STOP AND CHECK Read the question in the Stop and Check box on page 13. (Kids who are Clinton's age attend. They have chess lessons and play each other. Players are ranked by how well they play.)

 **Pages 14–15**

Organization ACT Have students identify time order words on page 14 that tell about the day of the tournament. *How long did the games last?* (all day) *How long did Clinton's family stay at the tournament?* (the whole time) *When did some of Clinton's cousins play computer games?* (by the end of the day) *How long was Clinton's family stunned when he won the award?* (for a moment) *What word tells that the family stopped being stunned?* (then) *When did Dad give Clinton a chess set?* (after they got home)

Vocabulary Have students locate the multiple-meaning word *Promising* in the last paragraph on page 14. Explain that in this context it means "showing signs of being successful in the future." *How did Clinton's family react when he got an award for Most* Promising *Player?* (They were quiet at first and then they went wild with excitement.) *What does this award tell us about Clinton?* (Although he didn't win the trophy, he showed a lot of talent for chess. He might win the trophy the next time.)

Compare and Contrast Ask partners to discuss how Clinton's view of himself changes from the beginning to the end of the story. *How did Clinton feel at the beginning of the story on Saturday mornings?* (He did not feel part of his family of "sports stars.") *How does Clinton feel at the end of the story?* (Clinton finds his own sport—chess; his family supports him and he feels proud of himself and also accepted by the family.)

STOP AND CHECK Read the question in the Stop and Check box on page 15. (He didn't care about winning; it was more important feeling the support of his family.)

Theme Read the last paragraph on page 15. *How does Clinton's experience change the way he thinks of himself?* (Finding his sport helped him see that he has talents. He can be a chess star.) *How did it change his dad's view of him?* (He's proud that Clinton found his own way, even though it wasn't what he had dreamed for his son.)

AFTER READING

10–15 Minutes　　RL.5.1　RL5.2　RL.5.9　W.5.9a　L.5.4a　CCSS

Respond to Reading

Compare Texts Have students compare experiences that changed Clinton with those that changed Miguel. Then ask: *What experiences have you had that changed the way you see yourself or others?*

Summarize Have students turn to page 16 and summarize the selection. (Answers should include details about how Clinton changed after he found his sport.)

 Text Evidence

Have partners work together to answer questions on page 16. Remind them to use their graphic organizers.

Compare and Contrast (He was bored watching sports but completely focused watching chess.)

Vocabulary (Clinton didn't think they were rude because he got bored watching sports. *Blame* means to find fault or accuse someone of doing wrong.)

Write About Reading (Clinton's house is chaotic on Saturday mornings, but the chess club has organized activity. Clinton hated the Saturday morning rush, but loved chess club immediately because he liked chess.)

Independent Reading

Encourage students to read the paired selection "All on Her Own" on pages 17–19. Have them summarize the selection and compare it to "King of the Board." Have partners answer the "Make Connections" questions on page 19.

✓ *Quick Check* **Can students compare and contrast? If not, review and reteach using the instruction on page 254 and assign the Unit 5 Week 1 digital mini-lesson.**

Can students respond to the selection using text evidence? If not, provide sentence frames to help them organize their ideas.

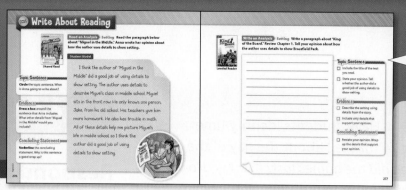

**WEEK 1
LESSON
5**

Objectives
• Review weekly vocabulary words
• Review compare and contrast
• Write an analysis about an author's use of details to show setting

Materials
• Visual Vocabulary Cards: 153–160
• Interactive Worktext, pp. 276–277
• Assessment Book, pp. 50–51

☞ **Go Digital**
• Visual Vocabulary Cards
• Compare/Contrast Mini-Lesson
• Interactive eWorktext

Scaffolding for **Wonders** Reading/Writing Workshop

REVIEW AND RETEACH

5–10 Minutes   RL.5.1   RL.5.3   L.5.4a   L.5.6   CCSS

Weekly Vocabulary

Display one **Visual Vocabulary Card** at a time and ask students to use the vocabulary word in a sentence. If students have difficulty, have them find the word in "Miguel in the Middle" and use context clues to define it.

Comprehension: Compare/Contrast

I Do Display and say: *Lisa used to live in the country. She played outdoors. She loved to take long hikes in the woods. Her family moved to a big city. Lisa still likes to play outdoors. But now she plays basketball at the city park.* Ask: *What did Lisa like to do in the country?* Underline *play outdoors* and *loved to take hikes.* Ask: *What does Lisa like to do now in the city?* Circle *play outdoors* and *play basketball in the city park. How is Lisa the same in both places? She likes to play outdoors. How is Lisa different now? She used to take long hikes, now she plays basketball in the park.*

We Do Display: *Devon loved to spend vacation at home playing video games. Then his mother suggested he visit his uncle, who was an artist. During his visit, Devon learned to draw characters. Now Devon wants to become a video game illustrator.* Ask: *What did Devon like to do at home during vacation?* (play video games) *What did Devon during his visit?* (learn to draw characters) *How is Devon different after visiting his uncle?* (He wants to become a video game illustrator.) *How did he stay the same?* (He still likes video games.)

You Do Have students reread the passage on page 269 of the **Interactive Worktext** and describe how Mia is the same and different in the hall and at lunch.

WRITE ABOUT READING

25–35 Minutes   W.5.1a   W.5.1b   W.5.4   W.5.5   W.5.9a   CCSS

Read an Analysis

• Ask students to look back at "Miguel in the Middle" in the **Interactive Worktext**. Have volunteers review their notes. *How well did the author use details to show the setting?*

• Read aloud the directions on page 276. Read aloud the student model. *Anna's writing is not a summary. The student is writing an* analysis, *or a detailed description, of how the author uses details to show setting. Anna is sharing her opinion about how the author used details to show setting.*

• Say: *When you write an analysis, you need to include certain elements. The first element is the topic sentence. Read the beginning of the paragraph and circle the topic sentence. What important information is included in this sentence?* (text's title; Anna's opinion about how the author uses details to show setting)

• *Another element of an analysis is* text evidence. *Anna supports her opinion with details from the text that show setting. Reread the model and draw a box around the text evidence.* (sentences 2–5) *Look back at your notes about "Miguel in the Middle." What other details might be included as text evidence in the model?* (Possible answer: the time of year, September)

• *The final element is the* concluding statement. *Have students underline the concluding statement. How is the concluding statement like the topic sentence?* (Both say the author did a good job of using details to show setting.) *Which part of the concluding statement wraps up the evidence?* ("All of these details help me picture Miguel's life in middle school")

Write an Analysis

Analytical Writing

Guided Writing Read the writing prompt on page 277 together. Have students write about "King of the Board" or another text they read this week. Have them review their notes. *Use the checklist to help you figure out the right information to include in each section.* Guide students to ask "how" and "why" questions, such as *How do details help me picture the setting?*

Peer Conference Have students read their analysis to a partner. Listeners should identify the strongest text evidence that supports the topic sentence and discuss any sentences that are unclear.

Teacher Conference Check students' writing for complete sentences and text evidence that supports their topic. Review the concluding statement. *Does this sentence tie all of the elements together?* If necessary, have students revise the concluding statement by restating the topic sentence.

Level Up

Apprentice Leveled Reader

Approaching Leveled Reader

Interactive Worktext

Reading/Writing Workshop

IF students read the Apprentice Level Reader fluently and the **Interactive Worktext** Shared Read fluently and answer the Respond to Reading questions

THEN read together the Approaching Level Reader main selection and the **Reading/Writing Workshop** Shared Read from *Reading Wonders*. Have students take notes as they read, using self-stick notes. Then ask and answer questions about their notes.

Writing Rubric

	4	3	2	1
Topic Sentence	Topic sentence presents a clear opinion.	Topic sentence presents an opinion, somewhat clearly.	Topic is presented in short phrases; opinion is unclear	There is no topic sentence; no opinion is presented.
Text Evidence	Opinion is supported by two or more text details.	Opinion is only supported by one detail from the text.	Little to no evidence from the text supports opinion.	No text evidence is included; does not support opinion.
Concluding Statement	Clearly restates an opinion; wraps up all the details.	Restatement is less focused; attempts to wrap up details.	Vaguely restates opinion. Doesn't correlate well to text evidence.	There is no conclusion.
Writing Style	Writes in complete sentences. Uses correct spelling and grammar.	Uses complete sentences and phrases. Writing has spelling and grammar errors.	Few or no complete sentences. There are many spelling and grammar errors.	Does not write accurately or in complete sentences.

ASSESSMENT

Weekly Assessment

Have students complete the Weekly Assessment using **Assessment** book pages 50–51.

WEEK 2 LESSON

1

Objectives
- Develop oral language
- Build background about adapting to change
- Understand and use weekly vocabulary
- Read historical fiction

Materials
Interactive Worktext, pp. 278–285
- Visual Vocabulary Cards: 161–168

☞ **Go** Digital
- Interactive eWorktext,
- Visual Vocabulary Cards

Scaffolding for **Wonders** Reading/Writing Workshop

WEEKLY CONCEPT

5–10 Minutes   SL.5.1b SL.5.1c CCSS

Talk About It

Essential Question Read aloud the Essential Question on page 278 of the **Interactive Worktext**: *How do shared experiences help people adapt to change?* Explain that to "adapt" to a change means to adjust or become used to something. Say: *Some changes can happen suddenly. They can affect a lot of people or a few. A big storm can damage a town. Your family may move to a new place. Sharing the experience can help people adjust to the change.*

- Discuss the photograph on page 278. Ask: *How are the people in the photograph sharing an experience?* (They are helping each other build a dam.)

  I Do Say: *One time a storm hit our neighborhood and all the power went out. Other people donated extra flashlights and batteries to help people get through the blackout. I will write "donating supplies" as one way people help others adapt to change on page 279.*

  We Do Say: *Let's look closely at the photo and think about ways these people are helping each other adapt to change. What are the people doing with the sandbags?* (building a dam) *What change do you think they are they preparing for?* (a flood) *What are they doing to help each other adapt to the change? Look at what they are doing and their expressions.* (They are working together; they are cheerful.) As students describe the people's actions and expressions, work with them to add words to their web on page 279.

  You Do Have partners tell about a change they have experienced, such as a move or change in schools. Ask: *What happened? Who did you share the experience with? How did others help you adapt to the change?*

REVIEW VOCABULARY

10–15 Minutes   L.5.4a L.5.6 CCSS

Review Weekly Vocabulary Words

- Use the **Visual Vocabulary Cards** to review the weekly vocabulary.

- Read together the directions for the Vocabulary activity on page 280 of the **Interactive Worktext**. Then complete the activity.

1 **weakling** Ask: *What word do you see in weakling?* (weak) *Do you think a weakling can lift heavy things? Why or why not?* (No; a weakling is not very strong.)

2 **nominate** Have students complete the sentence frame: *I would nominate _____ for class president because _____.* (Answers will vary.)

3 **assume** *What do you assume will happen when you see a dark sky and here thunder?* Have students complete this sentence frame: *I assume there will be a _____.* (thunderstorm)

4 **sympathy** Have partners read each sentence and talk about which person they would have sympathy for. (Kara lost a pet.) Have them explain their choices. (Possible answer: I would feel sorry for someone who lost a pet.)

5 **guarantee** Have students complete this sentence frame: *One thing I guarantee will happen during the school day is _____.* (Possible answers: the bell will ring; we'll go to lunch at noon; we'll read)

6 **supportive** Ask students if they have ever been to or seen a sports game on television. *Name people at a game who would be supportive of a team?* (Possible answers: coach, cheerleaders, fans) *What are some* *ways fans can show that they are supportive?* (Possible answers: clap, cheer, wear a team's colors)

7 rely Offer an example of a person players rely on: *Sports players rely on a coach to guide them.* Then have students complete the sentence frame: *Sports players rely on a goalie to _____.* (keep the other team from scoring a goal)

8 obviously Have partners list huge animals, such as an elephant, a rhino, and a gorilla. Then have them list small animals, such as a mouse, a chipmunk, and a canary. Ask students to describe their drawing by using a sentence frame: *The _____ is obviously bigger than the _____.* (Students should draw a picture of two animals, one much bigger than the other.)

High-Utility Words

Explain that a compound word is made up of two shorter words. Point out that sometimes knowing the meanings of the two shorter words can help you figure out the meaning of the compound word. Provide examples: *football, newspaper, mailbox.* Have students look at the High-Utility Words activity on page 281 of the **Interactive Worktext**. Have partners circle compound words in the passage. (sidewalk, inside, hallway, bookcase, bedroom, somewhere, downstairs, fireplace, upstairs) Then have partners discuss the meanings of the compound words.

> **ELL ENGLISH LANGUAGE LEARNERS**
>
> Write the following words on note cards: *bed, stairs, room, case, up, case, upstairs, bookcase,* and *bedroom.* Display and say the compound words *upstairs, downstairs,* and *bedroom.* Have students repeat. Then have students match each compound word with the two shorter words that make it up.

READ COMPLEX TEXT

15–20 Minutes   RL.5.1   RF.5.4c   CCSS

Read: "The Day the Rollets Got Their Moxie Back"

- Have students turn to page 282 in the **Interactive Worktext** and read aloud the Essential Question. Explain that they will read how members of a family help each other in a difficult time. Ask: *What is the title?* ("The Day the Rollets Got Their Moxie Back") Point out that the Rollets are a family. Explain the meaning of *moxie.* Ask: *What do you see in the picture?* (girls reading a letter) *Use these clues to make a prediction. Who do you think helps the family get their moxie back?* (Possible answer: the person who wrote the letter)

- Read together "The Day the Rollets Got Their Moxie Back." Note that weekly vocabulary words are highlighted in yellow. Expand Vocabulary words are in blue.

- Have students use the "My Notes" section on page 282 to write questions and notes as they read. Model how to use the section. *On page 283 in the last paragraph, I do not understand why Dad wants to catch the last rays of sunlight rather than turning a light on. I will add a question to the "My Notes" section. I am not sure what the word* fidgeted *means. I will write* fidgeted *with a question mark beside it. When we reread, I will ask my questions so I better understand what I am reading.*

> **ELL ENGLISH LANGUAGE LEARNERS**
>
> As you read together, have students highlight parts of the story they have questions about. After reading, help them write questions in the "My Notes" section.

 Quick Check Can students understand the weekly vocabulary in context? If not, review vocabulary using the **Visual Vocabulary Cards** before teaching Lesson 2.

Objectives
- Read historical fiction
- Understand complex text through close reading
- Recognize and understand compare and contrast
- Respond to the selection using text evidence to support ideas

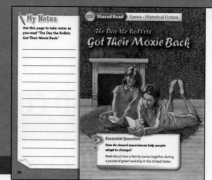

Materials
Interactive Worktext, pp. 282–287

☞ **Go** Digital
- Interactive eWorktext
- Compare and Contrast Mini-Lesson

REREAD COMPLEX TEXT

20–25 Minutes   RL.5.1 RL.5.3 RL.5.4 L.5.4 L.5.5b CCSS

Close Reading: "The Day the Rollets Got Their Moxie Back"

Reread "The Day the Rollets Got Their Moxie Back" with students. As you read together, discuss important passages in the text. Have students respond to text-dependent questions, including those in the **Interactive Worktext**.

🔍 **Page 283**

Vocabulary Reread the first sentence. Explain the idiom "like a lightning bolt from the blue". Then have students locate the phrase "hard times." Say: *This expression means a time when people have many problems. What details are clues that the family is having "hard times"?* (Ricky was at a work camp across the country, dad did not find work yet)

Genre Say: *Historical fiction stories are set at a real time in the past. These stories include characters that are made-up, but may include the names of real people that lived in the past and events that really happened.* Have students reread the first paragraph. *What year does the story take place?* (1937) *Is this in the past, present, or future?* (past) *What other details tell you the story takes place at a time in the past?* (President Roosevelt's employment program)

Expand Vocabulary Have students locate the word *imagined.* Ask: *Who did the narrator imagine?* (her brother, Ricky) *Where is Ricky?* (in Wyoming) *What did she imagine him doing? Underline the text evidence.* (looking up at snow-capped mountains, breathing in the smell of evergreens) *What caused the narrator to imagine Ricky?* (She got a letter from him.)

High-Utility Words Point to the word *meatloaf* in the third paragraph. Have students identify the two smaller words that make up the compound word. (meat, loaf) Ask: *What is a meatloaf?* (meat made in the shape of a loaf) Then have partners find other compound words on the page and discuss their meanings. (evergreen, sunlight, icebox)

Genre Say: *When you read historical fiction, you may see some unfamiliar words or expressions. Some words commonly used in the past may not be commonly used today.* Have students reread the last paragraph. Ask: *What items are in the kitchen? Draw a box around the description.* (a corner of the room with a stove, sink, and icebox) *Which word is unfamiliar?* (icebox) *What do you think the word means?* (a container that keeps things cold) *What do people call it today?* (refrigerator, fridge)

🔍 **Page 284**

Expand Vocabulary Discuss the meaning of the word *design.* Ask: *What detail helps you understand what Dad did to design the posters?* (Dad drew) *What other word or phrase in the paragraph is a clue to the meaning of the word?* (artist)

Compare and Contrast Say: *Characters in a story may be similar and different. Let's compare and contrast details about the characters to find out how they are alike and different.* Model comparing and contrasting details about the characters. Say: *I read that "Dad stayed where he was, looking gloomy." How does Dad feel?* (gloomy) *Let's underline this detail. Keep reading. What feeling does Mom express when she talks to Dad?* (sympathy) *What text evidence tells you this?* (her voice showing her sympathy) *How are Mom's and Dad's feelings alike?* (they both feel bad that there aren't any jobs for Dad) *Reread the second paragraph. Underline a detail that shows Mom's feelings when she serves dinner.* (she sang as she served) *How do* *you think Mom feels?* (happy, cheerful) *How are Mom and Dad's feelings different?* (Dad is gloomy, Mom is cheerful.)

Compare and Contrast *Have students reread the third paragraph. Ask: What did Ruth do at dinner?* (fidgeted) *How does Ruth feel?* (excited) *Does the narrator, Shirley, feel the same way? Circle text evidence.* (yes; "inside I wanted to get started on it, too") *Does Shirley act the same as Ruth? Circle text evidence* (no; "though calm on the outside") *How are the two alike?* (They are both excited about the talent show.) *How do they act differently?* (Ruth fidgets, Shirley acts calm.)

Page 285

Compare and Contrast Have students reread the first two paragraphs and paraphrase the events. Say: *Circle a detail in the first paragraph that is a clue to how Dad and other people feel as they wait in line. How do people feel?* (Like other men in line, Dad bowed his head in shame; ashamed) Point to the second paragraph. *Do people feel the same after Ruth starts to dance? Circle text evidence that supports your answer.* (No; people lifted their heads, frowns turned to smiles, folks began clapping along) *How do Ruth's actions affect people in line?* (She makes them feel better.)

Genre Have students reread the dialogue in the third, fourth, and fifth paragraphs. Ask: *What unfamiliar words or expressions do you see?* (moxie; oughta be in pictures) *What nearby clues help you understand the meaning of "moxie"?* (Ruth danced with spirit.) *Point to the fourth paragraph. What do you think "pictures" means in this sentence?* (movies) *What clues in the text helped you?* (nominate them for an Academy Award)

Compare and Contrast *How did Dad feel before they went to the soup kitchen? Review details you marked on page 284.* (gloomy) *How does Dad feel at the end of the story?* (pride; hopeful) *Underline text evidence.* ("Those are my girls," Dad said with pride; We were all filled with hope.) Say: *Compare details about Dad before and after Ruth dances. How is he still the same?* (He still does not have a job.) *How has he changed?* (Possible answers: He feels better, he shows pride and hope for the future.)

RESPOND TO READING

| 10–20 Minutes | RL.5.1 RL.5.3 W.5.9a SL.5.1d | |

Respond to "The Day the Rollets Got Their Moxie Back"

Have students summarize "The Day the Rollets Got Their Moxie Back" orally to demonstrate comprehension. Then have partners answer the questions on page 286 of the **Interactive Worktext** using the discussion starters. Tell them to use text evidence to support their answers. Have students write the page number(s) on which they found the text evidence for each question.

1. *How do Ricky's letters affect the family?* (Ruth and Shirley get excited when they read Ricky's letter. His letter gives Ruth and Shirley the idea to have a talent show. Text Evidence: p. 283)

2. *What do Ruth and Shirley do to help Dad keep working?* (They put on costumes; Dad draws show posters of them in costume. Text Evidence: p. 284)

3. *How do Ruth and Shirley make Dad feel better?* (Ruth and Shirley make Dad feel better by putting on a show for the people in line. Text Evidence: p. 285)

After students discuss the questions on page 286, have them write a response to the question on page 287. Tell them to use their partner discussions and notes about "The Day the Rollets Got Their Moxie Back" to help them. Circulate and provide guidance.

✓ *Quick Check* **Do students understand vocabulary in context? If not, review and reteach using the instruction on page 264.**

Can students use key details to compare and contrast. If not, review and reteach using the instruction on page 264 and assign the Unit 5 Week 2 digital mini-lesson.

Can students write a response to "The Day the Rollets Got Their Moxie Back"? If not, provide sentence frames to help them organize their ideas.

Objectives
- Understand and use new vocabulary
- Read historical fiction
- Recognize and understand compare and contrast
- Understand complex text through close reading

Materials
- "The Picture Palace" Apprentice Leveled Reader: pp. 2–7
- Graphic Organizer: Compare and Contrast

☞ **Go Digital**
- Apprentice Leveled Reader eBook
- Downloadable Graphic Organizer
- Compare and Contrast Mini-Lesson

BEFORE READING

10–15 Minutes   SL.5.1c SL.5.1d L.5.4a L.5.6 (CCSS)

Introduce "The Picture Palace"

- Read the Essential Question on the title page of "The Picture Palace." **Apprentice Leveled Reader:** *How do shared experiences help people adapt to change? We will read about two boys whose love of movies helped them reach a common goal during hard economic times.*

- Read the title of the main read. Have students look at the images. Ask: *Is the setting of this story now, or in the past? How do you know?* (The pictures show things like cars and games, characters' clothing, and places from a time in the past.)

Expand Vocabulary

Display each word below. Say the words and have students repeat them. Then use the Define/Example/Ask routine to introduce each word.

① hastily (page 6)

Define: *quickly*

Example: She *hastily* shut the door before her puppy ran out.

Ask: Why might you make a mistake when you do something *hastily?*

② heroine (page 6)

Define: a woman admired for great achievements

Example: Amelia Earhart is my *heroine* because she was the first woman to fly solo across the Atlantic Ocean.

Ask: What does it take to be someone's *heroine?*

③ slouched (page 5)

Define: sitting, standing, or walking with your shoulders and head drooping

Example: After the team lost, the players *slouched* into the locker room.

Ask: If you *slouched* in your chair, what would you look like?

④ sprinted (page 4)

Define: ran fast, raced

Example: The racer *sprinted* across the finish line.

Ask: Why might someone *sprint* to the train station?

DURING READING

20–30 Minutes   RL.5.1 RL.5.3 SL.5.1b L.5.4a L.5.5b (CCSS)

Close Reading

🔍 **Pages 2–3**

Prior Knowledge   Explain that the stock market crash of 1929 was an economic disaster which triggered the Great Depression, a time of financial hardship for the whole nation. Have students share what they may know about the Great Depression.

Genre (A C T) Read page 2 together and have students look at the illustration on page 3. Model using details to identify historical fiction. Say: *This story happens six years after the stock market crash of 1929. What year does the story take place?* (1935) Say: *In historical fiction, the story is made up but may include real people and events. I know that Frank and Joey are made-up characters, but Clark Gable was a real movie star. The characters in historical fiction speak the way people did at that time. Notice that Frank says, "We need moola to buy tickets." This tells us that back then people called money "moolah."*

Pages 4–5

Compare and Contrast Have students read the first paragraph on page 4. Model how to compare and contrast the impact the stock market crash had on Frank's and Joey's families. Say: *I read that the two families are different. Frank's dad had to sell their house and take a low-paying job. Still they had a place to live. Joey's family can't pay their rent sometimes and have been thrown out of their home. The families are alike, too. They both struggle to earn money and pay for things during the Great Depression.* Have students record details about how the Depression affected the characters' families on the compare and contrast graphic organizer.

Compare and Contrast Read the second, third, and fourth paragraphs on page 4. Ask: *How is Joey's plan different from Frank's?* (Frank wants to sell things. Joey wants to wash windows for people.) *How are the plans alike?* (Both are ways to make money.)

Vocabulary Point to the simile *as cute as a bug's ear* on page 4. Have students find text details to show that Frank thought that comparing Joey to a bug's ear was funny. (Frank grinned; laughing as he ran)

STOP AND CHECK Read the question in the Stop and Check box on page 4. (to buy tickets for the movie, *Call of the Wild*)

Genre Ⓐ Ⓒ Ⓣ Have students read page 5. Have them identify features of the setting that show this is historical fiction. Students may not recognize that Marie and Joey are playing jacks, a game that was more popular with girls in the past. Ask : *What game is Marie playing? Do children still play this game today?* (Possible answer: jacks; yes, but it is not as popular as it was in the past) Point out the small part of the stove that is visible. Note that it has legs. Ask: *When do you think people used stoves like the one in the illustration?* (in the 1930s)

Vocabulary Have students locate the phrase *absorbed in* at the bottom of page 5. Ask students to find clues that help them understand that it means "very interested in something." ("focused on" is a clue) *What kinds of things can you be* absorbed in? (a book, a movie, a video game, a conversation)

Compare and Contrast Have students compare and contrast Frank's reaction to playing jacks with Marie to Joey's reaction to playing the game with Marie. Ask: *How were their responses different?* (Frank said he was busy. Joey sat down and played with Marie.) *How were the responses the same?* (Both boys liked playing with Marie, but Frank didn't want Joey to think he was a weakling.)

Pages 6–7

Genre Ⓐ Ⓒ Ⓣ Have students read page 6. Ask: *Why is mom worried about Frank getting a job?* (She doesn't want him to quit school early.) Say: *During this time, many young people left school to get jobs to help earn money for their families.* Point out that Shirley Temple was a real movie star at this time. Say: *Shirley Temple had curly hair.* Ask students to use text details to explain why Marie had her hair "wound up in rags." (so that she could have curly hair, "curly like Shirley")

Compare and Contrast Ask: *On page 6, how does Mom react when Frank tells her he wants to earn money for a ticket to a movie?* (At first, she wants to make sure it is only a part-time job so Frank can stay in school. Then she is fine with the idea.) *On page 7, how does Dad react?* (He thinks it is fine because movies remind us dreams are still possible.) *How are their responses alike?* (Both support Frank earning money for a movie ticket.)

STOP AND CHECK Read the question in the Stop and Check box on page 7. (Frank thinks it might be wrong to spend money just for the movies when people have lost their jobs and homes.)

Have partners review their Compare and Contrast charts for pages 2–7 and discuss what they learned.

✓ *Quick Check* **Do students understand weekly vocabulary in context? If not, review and reteach using the instruction on page 264.**

Can students use details to compare and contrast characters? If not, review and reteach using the instruction on page 264 and assign the Unit 5 Week 2 digital mini-lesson.

Objectives
• Understand and use new vocabulary
• Read historical fiction
• Understand compare and contrast
• Understand complex text through close reading
• Respond to the selection using text evidence to support ideas

Scaffolding for Wonders Approaching Leveled Reader

Materials
◄ "The Picture Palace" Apprentice Leveled Reader: pp. 8–20
• Graphic Organizer: Compare and Contrast

 Go Digital
• Apprentice Leveled Reader eBook
• Downloadable Graphic Organizer
• Compare and Contrast Mini-Lesson

BEFORE READING

5–10 Minutes   SL.5.1c   SL.5.1d   L.5.4a   L.5.6   **CCSS**

Expand Vocabulary

Display each word below. Say the words and have students repeat them. Then use the Define/Example/Ask routine to introduce each word.

1 elaborate (page 11)

Define: having many parts or details

Example: The class made *elaborate* plans for the party.

Ask: What might an *elaborate* fountain look like?

2 glared (page 14)

Define: stared in a very angry way

Example: I *glared* at a person littering in the park.

Ask: How does it make a person feel to be *glared* at?

3 gruff (page 9)

Define: rough or rude

Example: The boss's *gruff* manner made the employees uncomfortable.

Ask: What does a *gruff* voice sound like?

4 throng (page 11)

Define: a large crowd of people

Example: A *throng* of people entered the football stadium for the big game.

Ask: Where might you see a *throng* of people?

DURING READING

15–20 Minutes   RL.5.1   RL.5.3   SL.5.1b   L.5.4a   L.5.5b   **CCSS**

Close Reading

🔍 **Pages 8–9**

Problem and Solution Have students read pages 8 and 9. Then have them use text details to answer questions about the boys' problem. Ask: *What problem do Frank and Joey have when they try to wash windows in their own neighborhood?* (Getting work was hard. They knocked on doors for an hour without success.) *What do Joey and Frank think they can do to solve their problem?* (They can walk across town to the big houses.) *Do they find a solution to their problem? Explain.* (No, because another person was already washing windows in that area.)

Compare and Contrast Ask: *On page 9, how does Joey react when the window washer yells at the boys?* (Joey yells back at the man. He runs away with Joey.) *How does Joey feel after this incident?* (sad; he thinks they will not be able to see the movie) Have students add these details to their Compare and Contrast charts.

Genre **A C T** Remind students that at this time people had trouble finding jobs. It was hard to earn money for basic things, such as housing and food. Have partners discuss what the window washer meant when he says, "I've got mouths to feed." (He has a family to support.) Have them talk about why the author might have included these words in this story.

Vocabulary Have students find the word *gloomily* in the last paragraph on page 9. Explain that words ending in *-ly* often describe how something is done. *What does the word* gloomily *describe?* (Joey's tone of voice as he says they will never see the movie.) *What is another word for* gloomily? (sadly)

Pages 10–11

Genre A C T Have students read page 10. Say: *During the Great Depression, competitive games with prize money for the winners were popular.* Ask: *What event like this did Frank and Joey want to participate in?* (Bank Night) *What do they have an opportunity to win? How does Joey answer?* (a five spot) *What words would we use today?* (five dollars)

STOP AND CHECK Have students read the question in the Stop and Check box. (He tells him about Bank Night, a contest at the Palace Theater with a five-dollar prize.)

Pages 12–13

Compare and Contrast Read the 4th through 6th paragraphs on page 13. Ask: *How do Frank and Joey respond when Joey's name is pulled? How are their reactions different?* (Joey gasped. Frank yelled "RUN!" Joey could not get through the crowd. Frank shouted "Go low.") *How does Frank's response affect the game?* (Frank helps Joey win the game.)

Vocabulary Have students identify the word *worm* in the last paragraph on page 13. Ask: *How did Joey look when he* wormed *his way to the stage?* (He dropped down low and crawled around people's legs.)

Pages 14–15

Problem and Solution Have students read page 14. Say: *Joey made it to the stage in 60 seconds. Now, what is his problem?* (The stage manager says the rules say, "No kids!") *How is the problem solved?* (The crowd boos and chants, "The kid gets the prize.")

STOP AND CHECK Read the question in the Stop and Check box. (The man with the briefcase offers Joey a job every week as a paper boy.)

Compare and Contrast Review that in the middle of the story, Joey feels sad. He thinks they will never see the movie. Ask: *What details tell how Joey feels at the end of the story?* (Five dollars and a new job! This might be the best day of my life!) Ask: *How has Joey changed?* (He feels great. He has money for the movie tickets and can earn more money for other things his family needs.)

AFTER READING

10–15 Minutes　　RL.5.1　RL.5.2　RL.5.9　W.5.9a　L.5.4a　CCSS

Respond to Reading

Compare Texts Have students compare and contrast the characters in "The Day the Rollets Got Their Moxie Back" with characters in "The Picture Palace" to show how their shared experiences helped them adapt to the Great Depression. *Tell about a shared experience that helped you.*

Summarize Have students turn to page 16 and summarize the selection. (Details should show how characters are changed by events.)

Text Evidence

Have partners work together to answer questions on page 16, using their Compare and Contrast charts.

Compare and Contrast (Joey's family was thrown out of their apartment because they didn't have money for rent. Frank's family had to leave their house. Frank's father lost his factory and took a low-paying job.)

Vocabulary (things you own)

Write About Reading (Frank and Joey are trying to get work washing windows. A man yells at them. Frank is scared but Joey yells back. Both boys are excited to learn about Bank Night.)

Independent Reading

Encourage students to read the paired selection "The Golden Age of Hollywood" on pages 17–19. Have them summarize the selection and compare it to "The Picture Palace." Have partners answer the "Make Connections" questions on page 19.

 Quick Check Can students compare and contrast characters? If not, review and teach using the instruction on page 264 and assign the Unit 5 Week 2 digital mini-lesson.

Can students respond to the selection using text evidence? If not, provide sentence frames to help them organize their ideas.

WEEK 2 LESSON 5

Objectives
- Review weekly vocabulary words
- Review compare and contrast
- Write an analysis about an author's use of details to show setting

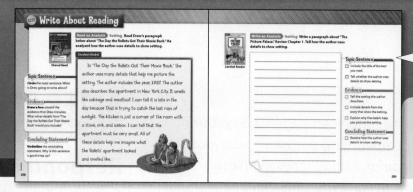

Materials
- Visual Vocabulary Cards: 161–168
- Interactive Worktext, pp. 288–289
- Assessment Book, pp. 52–53

☞ **Go** Digital
- Visual Vocabulary Cards
- Compare/Contrast Mini-Lesson
- Interactive eWorktext

Scaffolding for **Wonders** Reading/Writing Workshop

REVIEW AND RETEACH

5–10 Minutes   RL.5.3   L.5.4a   L.5.6

Weekly Vocabulary

Display one **Visual Vocabulary Card** at a time and ask students to use the vocabulary word in a sentence. If students have difficulty, have them find the word in "The Day the Rollets Got Their Moxie Back" and use the context clues to define it.

Comprehension: Compare/Contrast

I Do Display and read aloud: *Mom, Ben, and Alex get ready to go fishing. Ben does not like to fish, but he decides to go anyway to spend time with Mom and Alex. Alex loves to fish. He says, "I'm glad we'll be together all day."* Say: *The boys are going fishing with Mom. I read how they are different. Ben does not like to fish. Alex loves to fish.* Underline "he decides to go anyway to spend time with Mom and Alex" and what Alex says. *I can tell they both like to spend time with their family.*

We Do Display: *Sam and Jess like to play soccer. Sam scores a goal at the game. He jumps up and down. Jess frowns and walks off the field. He wanted to score the winning goal.* Ask: *What happens?* (Sam scores a goal.) *How does Sam feel?* (happy) *How do you know?* (He jumps up and down.) *How does Jess feel?* (He is upset.) *How do you know?* (He frowns and walks off the field.) *How are the two characters alike?* (Both like soccer.) *How are they different?* (Sam is happy; Jess is upset.)

You Do Display: *Jake and Miguel were in the same class. Miguel hated math. Jake was a math genius. Their teacher said there would be a math test on Friday. Miguel asked Jake to help him study.* Have partners compare and contrast characters, identifying which details show how the characters are alike or different.

WRITE ABOUT READING

25–35 Minutes   W.5.2a   W.5.2b   W.5.2e   W.5.5   W.5.9a

Read an Analysis

Ask students to look back at "The Day the Rollets Got Their Moxie Back" in the **Interactive Worktext**. Have volunteers review the setting of the story. Ask: *How did the author's use of details help you picture the setting?*

- Read aloud the introduction on page 288. Read aloud the student model. Say: *Drew's writing is not a summary. It is an analysis, or detailed description, of how the author uses details to show setting.*

- Say: *An analysis includes certain parts. The first is the topic sentence.* Have students circle the topic sentence. Ask: *What important information has Drew included in this sentence?* (the title of the selection; that the author uses many details to show setting)

- Say: *Another part of an analysis is text evidence. Drew includes details from the story that show the setting. He explains how each detail helps him picture the setting.* Have students draw a box around the text evidence. (sentences 2-6) Say: *Look back at your notes about "The Day the Rollets Got Their Moxie Back." What other details could Drew have included as text evidence?* (Possible answer: "Come set the table. Dinner's almost ready." They have a table in the apartment.)

- Say: *The final part of an analysis is the* concluding statement. *Underline the concluding statement* Ask: *How is the concluding statement like the topic sentence?* (In both, Drew says that the details helped him picture the setting.) *Which words in the concluding statement wrap up the evidence?* ("All of these details")

Write an Analysis

Analytical Writing

Guided Writing Read the writing prompt on page 289 together. Have students write about "The Picture Palace" or another text they read with a clear setting. Say: *Use the checklist to help you figure out the details to include in each section.* Guide students to ask "how" and "why" questions, such as *Why is the setting easy to picture?*

Peer Conference Have students read their analysis to a partner. Listeners should identify the strongest text evidence that supports the topic sentence and discuss any sentences that are unclear.

Teacher Conference Check students' writing for complete sentences and text evidence that supports their topic. Review the concluding statement. *Does this sentence tie all of the elements together?* If necessary, have students revise the concluding statement by restating the topic sentence.

Level Up

▲ Approaching Leveled Reader

▲ Reading/Writing Workshop

Apprentice Leveled Reader

▲ Interactive Worktext

IF students read the Apprentice Level Reader fluently and the **Interactive Worktext** Shared Read fluently and answer the Respond to Reading questions

THEN read together the Approaching Level Reader main selection and the **Reading/Writing Workshop** Shared Read from *Reading Wonders*. Have students take notes as they read, using self-stick notes. Then ask and answer questions about their notes.

Writing Rubric

	4	3	2	1
Topic Sentence	There is one clear, focused topic sentence.	Topic sentence is less focused, somewhat clear.	Topic is presented in short phrases.	There is no topic sentence.
Text Evidence	Topic is supported by two or more text details.	Evidence includes only one detail from the text.	Little to no evidence is cited from the text.	No text evidence is included.
Concluding Statement	Clearly restates the topic sentence; wraps up all the details.	Restatement is less focused; attempts to wrap up details.	Vaguely restates the topic. Doesn't correlate well to text evidence.	There is no conclusion.
Writing Style	Writes in complete sentences. Uses correct spelling and grammar.	Uses complete sentences and phrases. Writing has spelling and grammar errors.	Few or no complete sentences. There are many spelling and grammar errors.	Does not write accurately or in complete sentences.

ASSESSMENT

Weekly Assessment

Have students complete the Weekly Assessment using **Assessment** book pages 52–53.

WEEK 3
LESSON

1

Objectives
- Develop oral language
- Build background about changes in the environment that affect living things
- Understand and use weekly vocabulary
- Read expository text

Materials
- Interactive Worktext, pp. 290–297
- Visual Vocabulary Cards: 169–176

☞ **Go** Digital
- Interactive eWorktext
- Visual Vocabulary Cards

Scaffolding for **Wonders** McGraw-Hill Reading **Reading/Writing Workshop**

WEEKLY CONCEPT

5–10 Minutes SL.5.1c SL.5.1d

Talk About It

Essential Question Read aloud the Essential Question on page 290 of the **Interactive Worktext**: *What changes in the environment affect living things?* Explain that changes in the environment can be natural, such as a flood or hurricane, or can be caused by humans, such as making buildings or pollution. Say: *These changes cause plants, animals, and people to adjust or move to new places.*

- Discuss the photograph on page 290. Ask: *What kind of environment do you see?* (a city or town) *What living things do you see?* (a bird and chicks)

  I Do Say: *I am going to look closely at the photograph and think about one way a change in the environment has affected these birds. I see that the nest is made out of twigs, but I don't see trees around. The bird probably has to travel far to find twigs to make a nest. I am going to write this in the web on page 291 as an effect of a change in the environment.*

  We Do *Let's look at the photograph again together. What do you see around the nest?* (rooftops) *Where did the bird build its nest?* (on a roof) *Where do most birds build their nests in the wild?* (in trees) *What change do you think caused the bird to build its nest here?* (Trees were cut down; houses were built.) As students brainstorm changes and their effects on the birds, help them add their words to the web on page 291.

  You Do Have partners describe a change they have seen in the environment using some words they wrote. Give examples: floods, droughts, litter. Ask: *What change have you seen in the environment? What plants or animals were affected? How did they change?*

REVIEW VOCABULARY

10–15 Minutes L.5.4a L.5.5c L.5.6

Review Weekly Vocabulary Words

- Use the **Visual Vocabulary Cards** to review the weekly vocabulary.

- Read together the directions for the Vocabulary activity on page 292 of the **Interactive Worktext**. Then complete the activity.

1 **stability** Have partners describe each option. Ask: *Which do you think has more stability? Why?* (tricycle; <u>Possible answers:</u> It has more wheels; it doesn't fall over as easily.)

2 **decays** Ask: *What might cause a plant to decay?* (<u>Possible answers:</u> It doesn't get enough water, sun, or soil.) *What happens to a plant when it decays? Complete the sentence starter: When a plant decays, it _____.* (<u>Possible answers:</u> rots, breaks down, loses its leaves)

3 **impact** Have students use this sentence frame: *_____ would have the greatest impact on a player's performance because _____.* (Practicing every day; <u>Possible answers:</u> the more the player practices, the better the player will be)

4 **gradual** Have partners demonstrate stacking their books in a *gradual* way and describe what they did. (Add one at a time.)

5 **noticeably** Explain that a synonym is a word with the same or almost the same meaning as another word. Have partners discuss the meanings of each option. (clearly, obviously)

6 atmosphere Have students review the choices and tell where each animal lives. Then have them complete the sentence frame: *A _____ can live in Earth's atmosphere.* Have partners explain their choice.

7 receding Ask students if they have ever seen waves on a shore. Then have students describe the way waves move by using the sentence frame: *When a wave is receding, it goes _____.* (back out to the sea)

8 variations Have students discuss variations of cars they have seen. After students complete their drawings, have them write captions and title the drawing using the word *variations*. (Answers will vary, but should show two variations of a car.)

High-Utility Words

Explain that a suffix is added to the end of a word and changes its meaning. The suffix *-er* is added to an adjective to compare two things. The suffix *-est* is added to an adjective to compare more than two things. Have students look at the High-Utility Words activity on page 293 of the **Interactive Worktext**. Have partners circle words in the passage that end with the suffix *-er* and underline words that end with the suffix *-est*. (Circle: bigger, slower, greater; Underline: largest, fastest; longest) Then have partners reread the passage and discuss what is being compared in each sentence.

> **ELL ENGLISH LANGUAGE LEARNERS**
>
> Write the following words on note cards: *bigger, largest, greater, longest, slower,* and *fastest*. Say each word aloud and have students repeat. Then have students sort the words by the their suffixes.

READ COMPLEX TEXT

15–20 Minutes RI.5.1 RF.5.4c

Read: "Forests on Fire"

- Have students turn to page 294 in the **Interactive Worktext** and read aloud the Essential Question. Ask: *What is the title?* ("Forests on Fire") *What do the photographs show?* (burning trees and plants; firefighters; a cone, seedling, and tree) *Using these clues, what do you think this selection is about?* (what happens to trees and plants during a forest fire)

- Read "Forests on Fire" together. Note that the weekly vocabulary words are highlighted in yellow. Expand Vocabulary words are highlighted in blue.

- Have students use the "My Notes" section on page 294 to write questions they have, words they don't understand, and details they want to remember. Model how to use the "My Notes" section. *I can write notes about questions I have as I read. In the third paragraph on page 295, I am not sure what the word* prairie *means. I will write* prairie *with a question mark beside it in the "My Notes" section. In this same paragraph, I wonder what necessary changes come from fires. I will write a question in the "My Notes" section:* What necessary changes to the environment come from forest fires? *When we reread the text, I will ask my questions so I better understand what I am reading.*

> **ELL ENGLISH LANGUAGE LEARNERS**
>
> As you read together, have students highlight parts of the text they have questions about. After reading, help them write questions in the "My Notes" column.

 Quick Check Can students understand the weekly vocabulary in context? If not, review vocabulary using the **Visual Vocabulary Cards** before teaching Lesson 2.

WEEK 3 LESSON 2

Objectives
- Read expository text
- Understand complex text through close reading
- Recognize and understand compare and contrast text structure
- Respond to the selection using text evidence to support ideas

Materials
Interactive Worktext, pp. 294–299

☞ **Go Digital**
- Interactive eWorktext
- Compare and Contrast Mini-Lesson

Scaffolding for **WONDERS** Reading/Writing Workshop

REREAD COMPLEX TEXT

20–25 Minutes   RI.5.1   RI.5.3   RI.5.4   L.5.5c   L.5.6   **CCSS**

Close Reading: "Forests on Fire"

Reread "Forests on Fire" with students. As you read together, discuss important passages in the text. Have students respond to text-dependent questions, including those in the **Interactive Worktext**.

🔍 **Page 295**

Purpose Ⓐ Ⓒ Ⓣ Read aloud the first paragraph. Ask: *What does the author say we need to know about forest fires?* Provide the sentence frame: *The author wants people to know _____ and _____.* (how to put out forest fires; why forest fires happen)

Vocabulary Point out the words *destructive* and *productive* in the section heading. Ask: *What clues in the second paragraph help you understand the meaning of* destructive? (cause damage; take human lives and homes) Ask: *What clues in the third paragraph help you understand the meaning of* productive? (produce, or make, necessary changes) If students have difficulty, underline the root word parts before they look for clues.

Compare and Contrast *An author sometimes compares and contrasts ideas or information to explain a topic. Let's reread the section "Destructive and Productive" together. I read "Like rainstorms, wildfires are a force of nature." Rainstorms are compared to wildfires. Like is the signal word. Rainstorms and wildfires are a force of nature. Let's draw a box around that sentence.* Have students look for other sentences that tell how wildfires and rainstorms are alike. (Like big storms, wildfires are terrifying. Just as rain helps new plants grow, wildfires can also allow new life to grow.) Have them put a star next to signal words in the sentences they marked. (like; just as) *Now let's look*

for one way that wildfires are different from rainstorms. Reread the first paragraph. What words signal that rainstorms and wildfires are different? (however; unlike) *Underline the sentence.* (However, unlike rainstorms, wildfires are almost always destructive.)

Expand Vocabulary Have students point to the word *environments*. Read aloud the sentence. Ask: *What examples of environments does the author include?* (forests; prairies)

🔍 **Page 296**

Expand Vocabulary Read aloud the definition of *depend*. Then have students reread the second paragraph. Ask: *Which word in the second paragraph is a synonym for* depend? (need)

Compare and Contrast Have students reread the page. Ask: *Which paragraph tells about forests that have plants at different stages of growth? Draw a box around this paragraph. Let's find out how these forests are different than one another.* Point out that there are no signal words. Ask: *What will a forest recently struck by a fire have?* Provide the sentence frame: *A forest recently struck by fire will have _____.* (new seedlings) *What does a forest struck by fire twenty years ago have?* Provide the sentence frame: *A forest struck by fire twenty years ago may have _____.* (young trees) *What does a forest look like that has been untouched by fire for many years?* (It has mature trees.) *How are all of these forests alike?* (all have been struck by fire)

Expand Vocabulary Ask: *What does* provide *mean?* (to give something that is needed) Ask: *Reread the last paragraph. What two things do forests provide for insects and animals?* (food; habitats) *Give one example, using the sentence frame: A forest provides _____ for _____.* (Possible answer: A forest provides seeds for sparrows.)

Page 297

High-Utility Words Read aloud the last two sentences of the first paragraph. Ask: *Which word ends in the suffix -er?* *(fiercer)* *Why did wildfires become fiercer than they were before? Point to text evidence.* (buildup of decayed plant over many years provided more fuel)

Compare and Contrast Read aloud the first two paragraphs. Ask: *What is the author comparing?* (what the government did about wildfires in the past and what the government does today) *What did the government do about wildfires in the past? Underline text evidence.* (our government tried to totally stop wildfires) *Does the government do the same thing today? Underline text evidence that supports your answer.* (No; Today, the government has ways to manage wildfires; to limit fires before they burn out of control; to set small controlled fires) *How have the government's actions changed?* (Possible answer: Today, the government allows some fires to happen, but it limits them.)

Expand Vocabulary Have students point to the word *manage.* Ask: *What are examples of ways the government manages fires?* (limit fires before they burn out of control; set small controlled fires) *What is an effect of managing fires?* (It reduces the amount of vegetation that is fuel for a fire.)

Purpose   Have students reread the last paragraph. *Is the author's purpose to inform or entertain?* (inform) *An author may have more than one purpose for writing a text. An author may also include his or her opinion in an informational text. Reread the last paragraph. Circle opinion words and phrases.* Give examples, such as *must, should, good, bad,* and *harm.* (Possible answer: unfortunately, great harm, have to, always) *Use these clues. What does the author want people to do?* (be careful about how best to handle forest fires)

RESPOND TO READING

10–20 Minutes   RI.5.1   RI.5.2   RI.5.3   W.5.9b   SL.5.1d

Respond to "Forests on Fire"

Have students summarize "Forests on Fire" orally to demonstrate comprehension. Then have partners answer the questions on page 298 of the **Interactive Worktext** using the discussion starters. Tell them to use text evidence to support their answers. Have students write the page number(s) on which they found the text evidence for each question.

1. *How do wildfires affect plants?* (During a wildfire, plants can be destroyed. After a wildfire, plants can grow back. Plants that grow back may be adapted to fire. After a fire, forests can have different stages of growth. Text Evidence: pp. 295, 296)

2. *How do wildfires affect animals?* (During a wildfire, animals' homes can be destroyed. After a wildfire, some animals can find food and habitats. Text Evidence: pp. 295, 296)

3. *How do wildfires affect people?* (During a wildfire, people can feel terrified. Wildfires can take lives and homes. Text Evidence: pp. 295, 297)

After students discuss the questions on page 298, have them write a response to the question on page 299. Tell them to use their partner discussions and notes about "Forests on Fire" to help them. Circulate and provide guidance.

✓ **Quick Check** Do students understand vocabulary in context? If not, review and reteach using the instruction on page 274.

Can students use signal words and key details to identify compare and contrast text structure? If not, review and reteach using the instruction on page 274 and assign the Unit 5 Week 3 digital mini-lesson.

Can students write a response to "Forests on Fire"? If not, provide sentence frames to help them organize their ideas.

WEEK 3 LESSON 3

Objectives
- Understand and use new vocabulary
- Read expository text
- Recognize and understand compare and contrast
- Understand complex text through close reading

Scaffolding for **Wonders** Approaching Leveled Reader

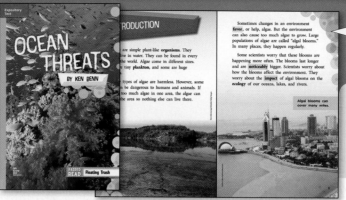

Materials
- "Ocean Threats" Apprentice Leveled Reader: pp. 2–11
- Graphic Organizer: Compare and Contrast

☞ **Go** Digital
- Apprentice Leveled Reader eBook
- Downloadable Graphic Organizer
- Compare and Contrast Mini-Lesson

BEFORE READING

10–15 Minutes   SL.5.1c   SL.5.1d   L.5.4a   L.5.6   CCSS

Introduce "Ocean Threats"

- Read the Essential Question on the title page of "Ocean Threats" **Apprentice Leveled Reader**: *What changes in the environment affect living things? We will read about how changes in the environment affect the growth of algae.*

- Read the title of the main read. Have students look at the images. *Is this a fiction or a nonfiction book?* (nonfiction) *How do you know?* (gives information; includes photos, captions, and a map) *What do most of the photographs show?* (algae, water)

Expand Vocabulary

Display each word below. Say the words and have students repeat them. Then use the Define/Example/Ask routine to introduce each word.

1 **evidence** (page 10)

Define: something giving proof or a reason to believe

Example: The overturned trash can was *evidence* that a raccoon had visited during the night.

Ask: What *evidence* would show that a pet dog had been in the mud?

2 **favor** (page 3)

Define: help something to happen or succeed

Example: The good weather *favored* our picnic plans.

Ask: What activities are *favored* by snowy weather?

3 **ideal** (page 9)

Define: having to do with being perfect

Example: The sunny, breezy weather was *ideal* for sailing.

Ask: What are the *ideal* conditions for a picnic?

DURING READING

20–30 Minutes   RI.5.1   RI.5.3   SL.5.1b   SL.5.1d   L.5.6   CCSS

Close Reading

🔍 **Pages 2–3**

Genre Ⓐ Ⓒ Ⓣ   Read the second paragraph on page 2. *In an expository text, an author includes facts, or statements that can be proven true. What facts does the author give about whether algae can harm humans?* (Many types of algae are harmless. However, some algae can be dangerous to humans and animals.)

Purpose Ⓐ Ⓒ Ⓣ   Explain that authors have a point of view about facts. Read the second paragraph on page 3. Point out the words *worry* and *worried*. These words show that the author is concerned about algal blooms. *Why are some scientists worried about algal blooms?* (the blooms could affect the ecology of oceans and rivers.)

🔍 **Pages 4–5**

Connection of Ideas Ⓐ Ⓒ Ⓣ   Read the title of Chapter 1, *What Are Algae?* Ask: *What do you think we will learn in chapter 1?* (what algae are) Point out that the title of each chapter is a question that the chapter answers.

Genre Ⓐ Ⓒ Ⓣ   Draw students' attention to the photos on pages 4 and 5. Read aloud the captions. *How do these photographs help you understand more about algae?* (Some algae are so tiny you need a microscope, some algae are red.)

Compare and Contrast Read aloud paragraphs 3 and 4 on page 4. *Do you see signal words?* (Like, Unlike) *Which sentence tells how algae are like plants?* (Like plants, algae can be simple or complex.) *Which sentences tell how they are different?* (Algae are not plants. Unlike plants, they lack roots, stems, and leaves.) Have students record comparisons in graphic organizers as they read.

Vocabulary Help students to understand the challenging domain-specific vocabulary in the selection by using context, word roots, and the glossary. At the bottom of page 5, students may know that the root *bio* means "life." Explain that *symbiosis* is a relationship where living things help each other. *What two things live together?* (algae and sea sponges)

Pages 6–7

Purpose A C T   *What happens to the water when there is an algal bloom? Use the photo on page 6 to help you answer.* (Algae can change the color of the water. The water looks more like plants than like water because there are so many algae.) Discuss with students how the author included this photo to help readers understand the harmful impact of algal blooms on ordinary people.

Cause and Effect Read aloud the fourth sentence in the first paragraph on page 6. Point out the signal word *cause.* Ask: *What two things cause algae to grow quickly?* (warm water temperatures and more gas in the water)

Genre A C T   Read aloud the last paragraph on page 7. *An expository text includes explanations and examples. What type of algal bloom does the author explain in this paragraph?* (super bloom) *From the name* super bloom, *what do you think a super bloom is?* (big algal bloom)

STOP AND CHECK Read the question in the Stop and Check box on page 7. (Algae mostly grow in water or in moist places like tree trunks on land.)

Pages 8–9

Compare and Contrast Read aloud the first paragraph on page 9. *How are land volcanoes and undersea volcanoes alike?* (Both release CO_2.) *How are they different?* (Land volcanoes release it into the atmosphere; undersea volcanoes release it into the ocean.)

Cause and Effect Read paragraph 3 on page 9. *What causes lakes, rivers, and oceans to become warmer?* (changes in the temperature of the atmosphere) *What happens to algae in warm water?* (It grows faster.)

Connection of Ideas A C T   Have students look at the photograph at the bottom of page 9 and read the caption. *How does this information relate to the first paragraph on page 8?* (Volcanoes are an example of something causing the environment to change quickly.)

Pages 10–11

Purpose A C T   Read page 10. *What do scientists think causes more algal blooms?* (Human activity changes the environment.) *What is one kind of human activity that might be causing changes in the environment?* (burning fossil fuels) Explain that this is the author's point of view.

Vocabulary Have students find the word *production* on page 10. Ask them what clues help them understand that the word means creation or development. *What is one kind of power that is produced?* (electricity)

Genre A C T   Have students look at the diagram on page 11. Have them use their fingers to trace energy paths on the diagram. *When some escaping energy is blocked by greenhouse gases and reflected back to Earth, the atmosphere becomes _____.* (warmer)

STOP AND CHECK Read the question in the Stop and Check box on page 11. (Humans do different things to cause algal blooms: burn fossil fuels, create pollution, cause the atmosphere to warm, and add nutrients to waterways from farms and sewers.)

✓ *Quick Check* Do students understand weekly vocabulary in context? If not, review and reteach using the instruction on page 274.

Can students identify compare and contrast text structure? If not, review and reteach using the instruction on page 274 and assign the Unit 5 Week 3 digital mini-lesson.

WEEK 3 LESSON 4

Objectives
- Understand and use new vocabulary
- Read expository text
- Recognize and understand compare and contrast
- Understand complex text through close reading
- Respond to the selection using text evidence to support ideas

Materials
- "Ocean Threats" Apprentice Leveled Reader: pp. 12–24
- Graphic Organizer: Compare and Contrast

☞ **Go Digital**
- Apprentice Leveled Reader eBook
- Downloadable Graphic Organizer
- Compare and Contrast Mini-Lesson

Scaffolding for **Wonders** Approaching Leveled Reader

BEFORE READING

5–10 Minutes SL.5.1c SL.5.1d L.5.4a L.5.6 CCSS

Expand Vocabulary

Display each word below. Say the words and have students repeat them. Then use the Define/Example/Ask routine to introduce each word.

❶ factor (page 16)

Define: a reason, feature, or influence

Example: Good study habits and organization are *factors* in getting good grades.

Ask: What *factors* do you consider when you make decisions about how to spend free time?

❷ irritation (page 13)

Define: condition of being sore, red, raw, or swollen

Example: Scratching your skin can cause *irritation*.

Ask: What *irritations* might someone get if they have a cold?

❸ oversupply (page 16)

Define: a stock in excess of need or demand

Example: When the store had an *oversupply* of jackets, the manager lowered prices to sell them quickly.

Ask: What would you do with an *oversupply* of pens?

DURING READING

15–20 Minutes RI.5.1 RI.5.3 SL.5.1b L.5.6 CCSS

Close Reading

🔍 **Pages 12–13**

Purpose Ⓐ Ⓒ Ⓣ Read the title of Chapter 3, *Why Should We Be Concerned?* Explain that the word *concerned* means "worried." *What do you think we will learn in chapter 3?* (why we should worry about algae) Point out that the use of the word *Concerned* shows the author's point of view about the facts he presents. The author thinks we should worry about algal blooms.

Compare and Contrast Have students read pages 12 and 13 and record the effects of algal booms on graphic organizers with the headings *Harmless and Harmful*. Read aloud the first sentence on page 12. *Which effects of algal blooms are harmless?* (changes to water color and effects on tourism) Point out the signal word *but* that introduces a different type of effect. (But) *Which effects are harmful?* (people getting sick) *What are two health threats linked to algal blooms?* (Vibrio bacteria; eye, throat, and nose irritation) *Under which heading do these effects belong?* (Harmful) *Record them under this heading.*

Vocabulary Have students find the word *encourages* in the first paragraph on page 13. Ask: *What clues help you understand this word's meaning? What is a synonym for encourages?* (Dust storms put iron into the sea and that causes algal blooms and helps bacteria to grow; helps.)

Sentence Structure Ⓐ Ⓒ Ⓣ Point out the word *Vibrio* on page 13. Ask: *How does this word look different from the other words?* (begins with a capital letter, italics) Explain that it is a scientific name for an organism. There is a convention to set scientific names which come from Latin in italics.

Pages 14–15

Compare and Contrast Read aloud page 14. Ask: *Are there signal words that show a contrast?* (Some; However) *What are different types of extreme dead zones?* (Some are smaller, but others are huge.) Have students record this information in a compare and contrast graphic organizer.

Vocabulary Have students find the word *extreme* in the second paragraph on page 14. Ask: *What clues help you understand this word's meaning?* (describes a very harmful algal bloom)

Genre **ACT** Draw students' attention to the map on page 14. Explain that an expository text may include a map to help students understand the impact of an effect, such as dead zones. Ask: *What do the yellow dots mean?* (dead zones in the ocean) *What two places have the most dead zones?* (North America and Europe) Have students discuss with partners where other dead zones are located around the world.

STOP AND CHECK Read the question in the Stop and Check box on page 15. (A dead zone is an area of a lake or ocean where all life has been killed off by a large algal bloom. However, not all algal blooms cause dead zones.)

Cause and Effect Read the last paragraph on page 15. *What do scientists think may happen as Earth warms up?* (There will be more algal blooms and dead zones in the ocean.)

Pages 16–17

Purpose **ACT** When a selection has a Conclusion, sometimes the author expresses an opinion. Read aloud the last paragraph on page 17. Ask: *What point of view or opinion does the author express?* (Protecting the environment may help limit harmful algal blooms.)

Connection of Ideas **ACT** Ask students to look back at pages 10 and 11. Ask: *How does this information relate to the second paragraph on page 17?* (The information there explains how businesses and farms help create algal blooms.)

AFTER READING

10–15 Minutes   RI.5.1   RI.5.2   RI.5.9   W.5.9b   L.5.4a   **CCSS**

Respond to Reading

Compare Texts Have students compare and contrast how changes to the environment brought about by fire or algae affect living things. Then, ask: *What responsibilities do humans have to limit such changes?*

Summarize Have students turn to page 18 and summarize the selection. (Answers should include details from the selection.)

Text Evidence

Have partners work together to answer questions on page 18 using their Compare and Contrast charts.

Compare and Contrast (Algae and plants both use photosynthesis to make their own food and both produce oxygen. Plants have stems, roots, and leaves. Algae do not.)

Vocabulary (*Sudden* means "fast or quick.")

Write About Reading (During an algal bloom, the water may change color or appear to have sludge. People who swim in the water can get sick. Seafood can become infected by a bacteria. Dead zones can result.)

Independent Reading

Encourage students to read the paired selection "Floating Trash" on pages 19–21. Have them summarize the selection and compare it to "Ocean Threats." Have them work with partners to answer the "Make Connections" questions on page 21.

 Quick Check **Can students identify compare-and-contrast text structure? If not, review and reteach using the instruction on page 274 and assign the Unit 5 Week 3 digital mini-lesson.**

Can students respond to the selection using text evidence? If not, provide sentence frames to help them organize their ideas.

WEEK 3 LESSON 5

Objectives
- Review weekly vocabulary words
- Review compare and contrast
- Write an analysis about how an author compares and contrasts to explain a topic

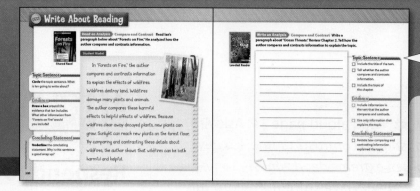

Materials
- Visual Vocabulary Cards: 169–176
- Interactive Worktext, pp. 300–301
- Assessment Book, pp. 54–55

☞ **Go** Digital
- **Visual Vocabulary Cards**
- **Compare/Contrast Mini-Lesson**
- **Interactive eWorktext**

Scaffolding for **Wonders** Reading/Writing Workshop

REVIEW AND RETEACH

5–10 Minutes   RI.5.3   L.5.4a   L.5.6   CCSS

Weekly Vocabulary

Display one **Visual Vocabulary Card** at a time and ask students to use the vocabulary word in a sentence. If students have difficulty, have them find the word in "Forests on Fire" and use the context clues to define it.

Comprehension: Compare/Contrast

I Do Write and say: *Like a river, a lake is a body of water. Both lakes and rivers have fish and other animals that live in water. A river is a moving body of water. However, water in a lake does not move from one area to another.* Say: *The author compares and contrasts rivers and lakes.* Underline the first two sentences. *These sentences tell me how they are alike.* Draw a box around the signal words *like* and *both*. Circle the last sentence. Draw a box around *however*. *The last sentence tells me how they are different.* Point out that the author uses signal words to compare and contrast.

We Do Display: *From far away, most volcanoes look like mountain peaks. But volcanoes have a crater or hole at the top of the peak. In contrast, mountains do not. Volcanoes can erupt, but mountains cannot erupt.* Ask: *What is being compared?* (mountains and volcanoes) *How are they alike?* (Both have peaks.) *How are they different?* (Volcanoes have a crater at the top and can erupt; mountains do not have craters and do not erupt.) *What signal words do you see?* (but, in contrast)

You Do Have students reread the last paragraph on page 245 in the **Interactive Worktext**. Have partners tell how renewable and nonrenewable energy sources are alike and different and identify signal words.

WRITE ABOUT READING

25–35 Minutes   W.5.2a   W.5.2e   W.5.4   W.5.5   W.5.9b   CCSS

Read an Analysis

- Ask students to look back at "Forests on Fire" in the **Interactive Worktext**. Have volunteers review their notes. *How did the author compare and contrast information to explain the effects of wildfires?*

- Read aloud the directions on page 300. Read aloud the student model. *Ian's writing is not a summary. The student is writing an analysis, or a detailed description, about how the author compares and contrasts information to explain the topic.*

- *An analysis always includes certain elements. Circle the* topic sentence. *What important information is included in this sentence?* (text's title; that the author compares and contrasts information to explain the effects of wildfires)

- *Another element of an analysis is* text evidence. *The student supports the topic sentence with details from the text that show the author compares and contrasts information about the topic. Reread the model and draw a box around the text evidence.* (sentences 2–5) *Look back at your notes about "Forests on Fire." What other information might be included as text evidence?* (Possible answer: Fire lets nutrients back into the soil.)

- *The final element is the* concluding statement. *Underline the concluding statement. How is the concluding statement like the topic sentence?* (Both say that the author compares and contrasts information or details.) *How is the concluding statement different?* (The concluding statement says "the author shows the effects can be both harmful and helpful.")

Write an Analysis
Analytical Writing

Guided Writing Read the writing prompt on page 301 together. Have students write about "Ocean Threats" or another text they read this week. Have them review their notes. *Use the checklist to help you figure out the right information to include in each section.* Guide students to ask "how" and "why" questions, such as *How does the author show that two things are alike?*

Peer Conference Have students read their analysis to a partner. Listeners should identify the strongest text evidence that supports the topic sentence and discuss any sentences that are unclear.

Teacher Conference Check students' writing for complete sentences and text evidence that supports their topic. Review the concluding statement. *Does this sentence tie all of the elements together?* If necessary, have students revise their concluding statement by restating their topic sentence.

Level Up

▲ Approaching Leveled Reader

▲ Reading/Writing Workshop

▲ Apprentice Leveled Reader

▲ Interactive Worktext

IF students read the `Apprentice Level` Reader fluently and the **Interactive Worktext** Shared Read fluently and answer the Respond to Reading questions

THEN read together the `Approaching Level` Reader main selection and the **Reading/Writing Workshop** Shared Read from *Reading Wonders*. Have students take notes as they read, using self-stick notes. Then ask and answer questions about their notes.

Writing Rubric

	4	3	2	1
Topic Sentence	There is one clear, focused topic sentence.	Topic sentence is less focused, but somewhat clear.	Topic is presented in short phrases.	There is no topic sentence.
Text Evidence	Topic is supported by two or more text details.	Evidence includes only one detail from the text.	Little to no evidence is cited from the text.	No text evidence is included.
Concluding Statement	Clearly restates the topic sentence; wraps up all the details.	Restatement is less focused; attempts to wrap up details.	Vaguely restates the topic. Doesn't correlate well to text evidence.	There is no conclusion.
Writing Style	Writes in complete sentences. Uses correct spelling and grammar.	Uses complete sentences and phrases. Writing has spelling and grammar errors.	Few or no complete sentences. There are many spelling and grammar errors.	Does not write accurately or in complete sentences.

ASSESSMENT

Weekly Assessment

Have students complete the Weekly Assessment using **Assessment** book pages 54–55.

▶ **Mid-Unit Assessment,** pages 104–111

▶ **Fluency Assessment,** pages 266–281

Unit 5 Mid-Unit Assessment

CCSS TESTED SKILLS

✔ COMPREHENSION	✔ VOCABULARY
• Character, Setting, Plot: Compare and Contrast **RL.5.3** • Character, Setting, Plot: Compare and Contrast **RL.5.3** • Compare and Contrast **RI.5.3**	• Context Clues **L.5.4a**

Using Assessment and Writing Scores

RETEACH	IF ...	THEN ...
COMPREHENSION	Students answer 0–5 multiple-choice items correctly ...	... reteach tested skills using instruction on pages 364–371.
VOCABULARY	Students answer 0–2 multiple-choice items correctly ...	... reteach tested skills using instruction on page 364.
WRITING	Students score mostly 1–2 on weekly writing rubrics throughout the unit...	... reteach writing using instruction on pages 372–373.

Fluency Assessment

Conduct assessments individually using the differentiated fluency passages in Assessment. Students' expected fluency goal for this Unit is 129–149 WCPM with an accuracy rate of 95% or higher.

Weeks 4 and 5

Monitor students' progress on the following to inform how to adjust instruction for the remainder of the unit.

ADJUST INSTRUCTION	
ACCESS COMPLEX TEXT	If students need more support for accessing complex text, provide additional modeling of prompts in Lesson 2 of Week 4, pages 280–281, and Week 5, pages 290–291. After you model how to identify the text evidence, guide students to find text evidence in Lessons 3 and 4 in Week 4, pages 282–285, and Week 5, pages 292–295.
FLUENCY	For those students who need more support with Fluency, focus on the Fluency lessons in the Foundational Skills Kit.
WRITING	If students need more support incorporating text evidence in their writing, conduct the Write About Reading activities in Lessons 3 and 4 as group writing activities.
FOUNDATIONAL SKILLS	Review student's individualized progress in *PowerPAL for Reading* to determine which foundational skills to incorporate into your lessons for the remainder of the unit.

WEEK 4 LESSON 1

Objectives
- Develop oral language
- Build background about how scientific knowledge changes over time
- Understand and use weekly vocabulary
- Read expository text

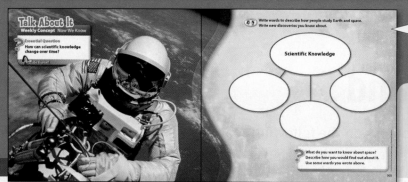

Materials
- Interactive Worktext, pp. 302–309
- Visual Vocabulary Cards: 177–184

☞ **Go** Digital
- Interactive eWorktext
- Visual Vocabulary Cards

Scaffolding for **Wonders** Reading/Writing Workshop

WEEKLY CONCEPT

5–10 Minutes   SL.5.1b   SL.5.1c

Talk About It

Essential Question Read aloud the Essential Question on page 302 of the **Interactive Worktext**: *How can scientific knowledge change over time?* Explain that over time, new tools and technologies are invented. Say: *These inventions help us know more about the universe.*

- Discuss the photograph on page 302. Ask: *What do you see?* (an astronaut) *What is the astronaut studying?* (Possible answers: Earth, space)

  I Do Say: *I am going to look closely at the photo and think about how people have been able to learn more about Earth and space. I see the astronaut is wearing a space suit. I know people were not always able to go out into space. This invention has helped people explore space and know more about it. I will write "the invention of the space suit" in the web on page 303.*

  We Do *Let's look closely at the photograph. Where is the astronaut?* (out in space) *What invention helped the astronaut get into space?* (rocket, shuttle) *What is the astronaut doing?* (Possible answers: exploring, using tools, taking pictures) *What do you see behind the astronaut?* (Earth) *What are some things the astronaut will be able to know more about?* (Possible answers: Earth, the moon, other planets) Then have students brainstorm new discoveries about space they know about. Help them add words to the web on page 303.

  You Do Have partners discuss what they would like to know about space and how they would find out about it. Have them use some words in the web to answer: *What do you want to know about space? What tools would you need to study it? Where would you explore?*

REVIEW VOCABULARY

10–15 Minutes   L.5.4a   L.5.4b   L.5.6

Review Weekly Vocabulary Words

- Use the **Visual Vocabulary Cards** to review the weekly vocabulary.

- Read together the directions for the Vocabulary activity on page 304 of the **Interactive Worktext**. Then complete the activity.

1 **evaluate** Have students use the sentence frame: *A doctor evaluates _____.* (Possible answers: patients, a person's health)

2 **astronomical** Point out the Greek root *astro-*. Explain that *astro-* means "star." Say: *Use this clue to help you figure out which things are astronomical.* (sun, star)

3 **spheres** Ask students to name items they have seen that are *spheres*. (Possible answers: orange, ball, bubble) Have students use the sentence starter: *The shape of a sphere is _____.* (round) Ask students to form the plural of *sphere*.

4 **calculation** Have students complete the sentence frame: *I do a calculation in _____ class.* (Possible answers: math, science)

5 **approximately** Have students tell what they can do with their hand to show the *approximate* height of their partner. Then have them compare their partner's height to an object or another student in the room and use the word *approximately*: *My partner is approximately as tall as _____.* (Answers will vary.)

6 **criteria** Have partners discuss *criteria* they use to choose a TV show or movie to watch before writing their answers. (Possible answers: how funny it is, the actors or actresses that are in it)

---

7 **orbit** Have students identify the specific actions they are using to demonstrate how to *orbit* around the desk. *What are you doing when you orbit the desk?* (circling the desk over and over again)

8 **diameter** Have students label the *diameter* of the circle on their drawings. (Drawings should show a circle with a line for the diameter and include a label.)

High-Utility Words

Explain that some words signal cause-and-effect relationships in a text. Give examples, such as *because, so, since,* and *as a result.* Explain that these words are clues that an author is describing a cause and an effect. Have students look at the High-Utility Words activity on page 305 of the **Interactive Worktext.** Ask partners to circle cause-and-effect signal words in the passage. (Because, so, Since, As a result, If) Write: _____ *it is raining,* _____. Ask students to use different cause-and-effect signal words to begin the sentence, and then complete the sentence. Have partners discuss how the signal word changes the meaning.

ELL ENGLISH LANGUAGE LEARNERS

Display the cause-and-effect signal words: *because, so, if.* Say each signal word and have students repeat. Then have partners choose from the words to complete the following sentence frame: *I need an umbrella* _____ *it is raining.* (Because, If)

READ COMPLEX TEXT

15–20 Minutes   RI.5.1   RF.5.4c

Read: "Changing Views of Earth"

- Have students turn to page 306 in the **Interactive Worktext** and read aloud the Essential Question. Explain that they will read an informational text about how we learned about Earth. Ask: *What is the title?* ("Changing Views of Earth") *What are the headings of each section?* (From the Ground, From the Sky, From Out in Space) *Use these clues. What do you think you will learn about in this selection?* (Possible answer: what we learn when we view Earth from the ground, from sky, and from space)

- Read "Changing Views of Earth" together. Note that weekly vocabulary words are highlighted in yellow. Expand vocabulary words are highlighted in blue.

- Have students use the "My Notes" section on page 306 to write questions they have, words they don't understand, and details they want to remember. Model how to use the "My Notes" section. *I can write notes about questions I have as I read. In the first paragraph on page 307, I see the word* innovation, *and I'm not sure what it means. I will write* innovation *with a question mark next to it in the "My Notes" section. When we reread, I will ask this question and other questions I have so I better understand what I am reading.*

ELL ENGLISH LANGUAGE LEARNERS

As you read together, have students pause to mark anything in the text that they find confusing or unclear. Guide them as they write related questions in the "My Notes" section.

 Quick Check Can students understand the weekly vocabulary in context? If not, review vocabulary using the **Visual Vocabulary Cards** before teaching Lesson 2.

WEEK 4 LESSON

2

Scaffolding for WONDERS **Reading/Writing Workshop**

Objectives
- Read expository text
- Understand complex text through close reading
- Recognize and understand cause and effect
- Respond to the selection, using text evidence to support ideas

Materials
Interactive Worktext, pp. 306–311

☞ **Go** Digital
- Interactive eWorktext
- Cause and Effect Mini-Lesson

REREAD COMPLEX TEXT

20–25 Minutes   RI.5.1   RI.5.3   RI.5.4   L.5.4a   L.5.6   CCSS

Close Reading: "Changing Views of Earth"

Reread "Changing Views of Earth" with students. As you read together, discuss important sections of the text. Have students respond to text-dependent questions, including those in the **Interactive Worktext**.

🔍 Page 307

Expand Vocabulary Discuss the word *vision*. *What words and phrases in the third paragraph are clues to the meaning of* vision? (he could see, observation) *What new tool changed Galileo's vision of the sky?* (a telescope)

Cause and Effect Say: *The author uses cause and effect to show what happened to Galileo and why it happened.* Model finding a cause and effect in the third paragraph. *I read, "Galileo pointed a telescope toward the night sky. This new tool heightened his vision. He could see stars, planets, and other spheres in the sky more clearly."* Pointing the new telescope toward the night sky is the cause. Seeing stars, planets, and other spheres more clearly is the effect. Point out that the author does not use signal words. Have students look for another cause and effect in the paragraph. Ask: *What caused Galileo to agree with Copernicus? Mark the cause and effect to support your answer.* (Cause: Each observation and calculation he made; Effect: led him to agree with another scientist's idea about the solar system.)

Connection of Ideas Ⓐ Ⓒ Ⓣ *Look at the two models of the solar system. Describe what the model on the left looks like looks like.* (an object at the center with circles around it) *Describe what the model on the right looks like looks like.* (an object at the center with circles around it) *How*

are these two models similar? (Both have an object at the center, with circles around it.) *Now look at the labels. How are the two models different?* (The one on the left shows the Earth at the center and the Sun going around it; the one on the right shows the Sun at the center and the Earth going around it.) *Which one is the Earth-centered model? Point to it.* (Students should point to the model on the left.) *Which one is the Sun-centered model? Point to it.* (Students should point to the model on the right.) *Which model did Galileo agree with?* (the Sun-centered model)

🔍 Page 308

Vocabulary Point out and explain the meaning of the Greek root "meter" in *thermometer* and *kilometer*. Have partners look for clues to the meaning of the words. (thermometer: weather; kilometer: heights) Then point to the domain-specific word *altitudes*. Have students look for clues to its meaning. (heights; airplanes; lift)

Expand Vocabulary Read aloud the definition and have students locate the word *transported*. *What nearby word is a synonym for* transported? (send) *What two things did scientists use hot-air balloons to transport?* (tools, scientists) *Where did they transport them to?* (the lower layers of the atmosphere)

Cause and Effect Reread the third paragraph aloud. *What did scientists want to do?* (go higher) *Why did they want to do this?* Have students mark the cause and its effect. (Cause: The more scientists learned; Effect: the higher they wanted to go.) Point out that there is no signal word in this cause and effect. *Now find a cause and effect in the last paragraph.* (Cause: Because airplanes had radio technology; Effect: data could be sent to scientists on the ground.) *What signal words do you see?* (Because)

Connection of Ideas Ⓐ Ⓒ Ⓣ *In the mid–1700s, what did scientists use to send tools into the sky?* (kites) *What did* *scientists use next to transport tools and scientists?* (hot-air balloons) *What was another way that scientists got information about the atmosphere?* (airplanes) *Which way do you think worked the best? Use text evidence.* Provide the sentence frame: *I think _____ were the best way to study the atmosphere because they could _____.* (Possible answers: go higher than kites and hot-air balloons; use radio technology to send data back to scientists)

Page 309

High-Utility Words Have partners identify cause-and-effect signal words in the first and second paragraphs. (so, because)

Cause and Effect Read aloud the first three sentences. *Circle a cause and underline its effect.* (Cause: Rockets could take satellites into orbit around Earth; Effect: Scientists could find out what the layers of the atmosphere were made up of.) *Read the rest of the paragraph. What else could scientists do as a result of sending satellites into orbit? Underline the effects.* (They could also measure the atmosphere's thinness. Scientists could make more accurate weather predictions) Have partners reread the second paragraph. Ask: *How did using satellites affect scientists' models of Earth's systems?* (They could make better models of Earth's systems.) *Underline another effect of using this technology.* (They could even come up with new ideas about how climate might change over time.)

Expand Vocabulary Have students locate and discuss the word *gathered.* Ask: *What word in the paragraph has almost the same meaning as* gathered? (collected)

Connection of Ideas **A C T** *Reread the page. What tools does NASA use to study Earth?* (Satellites; sensors; supercomputers) *Review details you marked on page 307. What tools did people first use to study Earth?* (telescope) *What do all these tools help scientists do?* (learn more about Earth and space) *How are they different?* (satellites view Earth from space; telescopes are used from the ground; sensors and supercomputers are better at measuring than telescopes.) If students have difficulty, ask: *What does each tool do? Where do scientists use each tool?* Guide them to locate answers in the text.

RESPOND TO READING

10–20 Minutes   RI.5.1 RI.5.3 W.5.9b SL.5.1d

Respond to "Changing Views of Earth"

Have students summarize "Changing Views of Earth" orally to demonstrate comprehension. Then have partners answer the questions on page 310 of the **Interactive Worktext** using the discussion starters. Tell them to use text evidence to support their answers. Have students write the page number(s) on which they found the text evidence for each question.

1. *How did kites and hot-air balloons change the way scientists study Earth?* (They could send tools and scientists up into the sky. Text Evidence: p. 308)

2. *How did airplanes change the way scientists study Earth?* (They could go higher than kites and hot-air balloons and send data using radio technology. Text Evidence: p. 308)

3. *How did rockets change the way scientists study Earth?* (Rockets could lift satellites into orbit; satellites could get information about Earth from space. Text Evidence: p. 309)

After students discuss the questions on page 310, have them write a response to the question on page 311. Tell them to use their partner discussions and notes about "Changing Views of Earth" to help them. Circulate and provide guidance.

 Quick Check Do students understand vocabulary in context? If not, review and reteach using the instruction on page 286.

Can students use signal words and key details to identify causes and effects? If not, review and reteach using the instruction on page 286 and assign the Unit 5 Week 4 digital mini-lesson.

Can students write a response to "Changing Views of Earth"? If not, provide sentence frames to help them organize their ideas.

WEEK 4 LESSON

3

Objectives
- Understand and use new vocabulary
- Read expository text
- Recognize and understand cause and effect
- Understand complex text through close reading

Materials
"Mars" Apprentice Leveled Reader: pp. 2–9
- Cause and Effect Graphic Organizer

☞ **Go Digital**
- Apprentice Leveled Reader eBook
- Downloadable Graphic Organizer
- Cause and Effect Mini-Lesson

Scaffolding for **Wonders** Approaching Leveled Reader

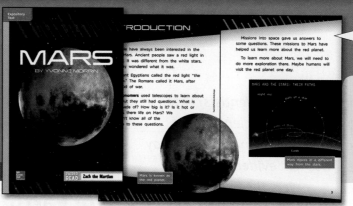

BEFORE READING

10–15 Minutes   SL.5.1c SL.5.1d L.5.4a L.5.6

Introduce "Mars"

- Read the Essential Question on the title page of "Mars" **Apprentice Leveled Reader**: *How can scientific knowledge change over time? We will read about how our understanding of Mars has changed as we develop new technologies.*

- Read the title of the main read. Have students read the chapter titles and look at the text features. *What do you think this book will be about?* (how Mars was discovered, how scientists have been exploring Mars)

Expand Vocabulary

Display each word below. Say the words and have students repeat them. Then use the Define/Example/Ask routine to introduce each word.

① details (page 7)

Define: all the separate facts or parts of the whole

Example: There are many *details* on Matt's new coat.

Ask: What is a *detail* on something you're wearing?

② discovered (page 9)

Define: became aware of, found out

Example: I *discovered* a shiny rock in my yard.

Ask: What is something you have *discovered*?

③ information (page 5)

Define: facts about someone or something

Example: I need more *information* before deciding.

Ask: What *information* do you have about the weather?

④ perfect (page 6)

Define: free of faults, exactly correct

Example: He can do a *perfect* back flip.

Ask: What is something *perfect* that you make or do?

DURING READING

20–30 Minutes   RI.5.1 RI.5.5 SL.5.1b L.5.6

Close Reading

🔍 **Pages 2–3**

Vocabulary *Read the first two paragraphs on page 2. What clues help you understand the word* ancient? (Romans called it Mars, after their god of war.)

Connection of Ideas Ⓐ Ⓒ Ⓣ *Read the text on pages 2 and 3. What is the color of the stars?* (white) *What is the color of Mars?* (red) *What do you learn about Mars from the diagram on page 3?* (Mars moves in a different way from the stars.) *Why were ancient people interested in Mars?* (They wanted to know why Mars was different.)

Cause and Effect *In the first paragraph on page 3, I read that missions into space have given us answers to some questions and helped us learn more about Mars.* Point out that this cause-and-effect text structure doesn't have signal words. Have students record the causes and effects they identify on their Cause and Effect chart as they continue reading the selection.

🔍 **Pages 4–5**

Genre Ⓐ Ⓒ Ⓣ Have students look at the chart on page 4. *Which planet is farther from the Sun, Earth or Mars? How do you know?* (Row 1 says that Mars is 142 million miles away from the Sun. Earth is 93 million miles away.) *How can you tell which planet is colder?* (Mars; line 5 of the chart gives average temperature.)

Connection of Ideas A C T *Read the text on page 4 and the chart "Mars Compared to Earth." What makes Mars a difficult place for us to visit?* (Mars is cold. The average temperature is minus 81°F compared with 57°F on Earth. It would be hard to breathe because the atmosphere is mostly carbon dioxide and we need oxygen. The difference in gravity would make it hard to walk. Mars is dry and seems to have no life.)

Connection of Ideas A C T *Read the first paragraph on page 5. Astronomers gathered a lot of information, or facts, about Mars. So why did they think that Mars was covered in forests and that people like us lived there?* (Astronomers made mistakes and came to the wrong conclusions.)

Cause and Effect Have students read the last paragraph on page 5 and identify a cause and its effect. (Cause: We learn something new. Effect: We change our ideas; old ideas are replaced with new ideas.)

Pages 6–7

Connection of Ideas A C T *Read the text on page 6 and study the diagram, "Orbits of Planets." How does the diagram show the ideas of Copernicus?* (The Sun is in the center and the planets orbit around the Sun.) *How does the diagram show the ideas of Kepler?* (The orbit of each planet is oval, not a perfect circle.) *Which planet is closest to Earth?* (Mars)

Cause and Effect Have students read page 7. *Are there any signal words in the first paragraph?* (As a result) *Why were astronomers able to see more details on Mars?* (Telescopes had gotten better over time.) *What happened when telescopes got better?* (Astronomers could see more details on Mars.) *What happened when the astronomer Herschel could see more details on Mars?* (He saw light patches near the poles on Mars.) *What did Herschel think about the light patches he saw on Mars?* (Herschel correctly thought that they might be polar ice caps.)

Pages 8–9

Connection of Ideas A C T Have students read the first paragraph on page 8. Then review the last paragraph on page 7. *What have you learned about Herschel on pages 7 and 8?* (He was right about Mars having polar ice caps; he figured out that Mars has an atmosphere.) Read aloud the sentence, *But Herschel made mistakes, too.* Ask: *What does this sentence tell you about Herschel?* (He made mistakes.) *What wrong ideas did Herschel have?* (The light and dark areas on Mars were land and oceans.) *What idea does the author want readers to understand?* (Astronomers have made discoveries, but they also made mistakes.)

Vocabulary Read the second paragraph on page 8. Point out the word *translator.* Ask: *What is the job of a translator?* (communicate words from one language into another language) *What mistake did the translator make?* (He translated *canali* to mean "canals" instead of "channels.") *What was the effect of this mistake?* (Canals are human-made, so people thought aliens had dug canals on Mars.)

STOP AND CHECK Read the question in the Stop and Check box on page 9. (Early astronomers learned that Mars has polar ice caps, an atmosphere, and two moons.)

Genre A C T *Read the time line on page 9. How does the time line support the ideas in Chapter 1?* (It summarizes important discoveries that astronomers made about Mars.) *What new information does the time line include?* (specific dates and information about Aristotle's discovery in 300 B.C.E.)

Have partners review their Cause and Effect charts for pages 2–9 and discuss what they learned.

✓ *Quick Check* Do students understand weekly vocabulary in context? If not, review and reteach using the instruction on page 286.

Can students determine causes and effects? If not, review and reteach using the instruction on page 286 and assign the Unit 5 Week 4 digital mini-lesson.

Objectives
- Understand and use new vocabulary
- Read expository text
- Recognize and understand cause and effect
- Understand complex text through close reading
- Respond to the selection using text evidence to support idea

Scaffolding for **McGraw-Hill Reading WONDERS** Approaching Leveled Reader

Materials

"Mars" Apprentice Leveled Reader: pp. 10–24
- Graphic Organizer: Cause and Effect

☞ **Go** Digital
- Apprentice Leveled Reader eBook
- Downloadable Graphic Organizer
- Cause and Effect Mini-Lesson

BEFORE READING

5–10 Minutes   SL.5.1c SL.5.1d L.5.4a L.5.6 **CCSS**

Expand Vocabulary

Display each word below. Say the words and have students repeat them. Then use the Define/Example/Ask routine to introduce each word.

1 communicate (page 12)

Define: share or send information

Example: Writing is one way to *communicate*.

Ask: What are some ways that you *communicate*?

2 contained (page 15)

Define: held

Example: The package *contained* a book and a note.

Ask: What is *contained* in your backpack or bag?

3 explore (page 16)

Define: study or research; learn through experiences

Example: Victor loves to *explore* caves.

Ask: Would you like to *explore* space someday?

DURING READING

15–20 Minutes   RI.5.1 RI.5.5 SL.5.1b L.5.6 **CCSS**

Close Reading

 Pages 10–11

Connection of Ideas A C T A C T Have students read the last paragraph on page 10. *What did the photos of Mariner 9 show us about Mars?* (dust storm, polar caps, volcanoes, canyons, and dry riverbeds) *Why did these photos make people think that Mars once had life?* (Riverbeds showed that there was once water.)

Connection of Ideas A C T *Look at the photos on pages 10 and 11 and read "Extreme Planet." How do these features connect to the text?* (They show amazing facts that we have learned about Mars from the space missions.)

 Pages 12–13

Cause and Effect Read the last paragraph on page 12. *Are there signal words?* (as a result) *Why will our knowledge of Mars keep growing?* (In the future, rovers and landers will use more advanced technology.) *The cause is: rovers and landers will use more advanced technology. The effect is: our knowledge of Mars will keep growing.*

Vocabulary *Find the word* advanced *on page 12. What is another word that means the same thing as* advanced? (better, improved)

Connection of Ideas A C T *Read "The Colors of Mars" and review page 12. Would astronomers today call Mars "the red one?" Why?* (No, because they do not know the true color of Mars.) *Why have ideas about the color of Mars changed since ancient times?* (We now know that colors can change for many reasons, including the weather. On Mars, the sky can look blue, tan, or pink.) *What is the effect of new knowledge?* (It can change ideas and raise more questions.)

STOP AND CHECK Read the question in the Stop and Check box on page 12. (We have used orbiters, landers, and rovers to take photos, test the soil, measure the weather, and do experiments.)

Cause and Effect *Read the text and features on page 13. Why is Earth the only planet in our solar system on which humans can live?* (Other planets don't have water, air we can breathe, or the right temperature.) *What is the cause?* (Earth has water and air and is not too cold or too hot.) *What is the effect?* (Humans can live on Earth.) Explain the reference to "Goldilocks and the Three Bears."

Pages 14–15

Connection of Ideas (A C T) *Read the first paragraph on page 14. In the past, how did scientists think all life on Earth got energy?* (from the sun) *What did scientists discover that changed their ideas?* (Some plants and animals get energy from chemicals or heat inside Earth.) *Why did this discovery lead some to believe there is life on Mars?* (Things that can live in extremely cold places could possibly live on Mars.)

Connection of Ideas (A C T) *Read the text on page 15. Explain the meaning of* fossilized. *Ask: What did some scientists think the meteorite contained?* (fossilized bacteria) *If the meteorite were from Mars, why would fossilized bacteria be an important discovery?* (Since bacteria is a life form, it proves life existed on Mars.)

Cause and Effect *Read the feature "Face on Mars" on page 15. Are there any signal words?* (As a result) *What did the earlier photos in 1976 show?* (They seemed to show a human face.) *What caused a change in our ideas about a face on Mars?* (Clearer and more detailed photographs showed there is no face on Mars.)

Pages 16–17

Connection of Ideas (A C T) *Read the first paragraph on page 16. What are scientists planning to study in future missions to Mars?* (atmosphere of Mars, under the surface of Mars, soil and rocks) *Review pages 14 and 15. What are scientists hoping to learn from those studies?* (Is there life on Mars and was there ever life on Mars?) *How will studying below the surface of Mars help scientists get answers to their questions?* (They could discover water, which is needed to support life.)

STOP AND CHECK Read the question in the Stop and Check box on page 16. (Earth is in just the right place to support life; it has water and air, it's not too hot or cold.)

Genre (A C T) Have students look at the image on pages 16 and 17 and read the caption. Explain that it is an illustration, not an actual photograph. *What does the image show?* (an artist's idea of the equipment that people would need to explore Mars in the future)

AFTER READING
10–15 Minutes   RI.5.1   RI.5.2   RI.5.9   W.5.9b   L.5.4a   CCSS

Respond to Reading

Compare Texts Have students compare how technology helped scientists learn more about Earth in "Changing Views of Earth" with how technology changed our ideas about Mars. Ask: *Has technology ever helped you discover something?*

Summarize Have students turn to page 18 and summarize the selection. (Answers should show how technology helped us learn more about Mars.)

Text Evidence

Have partners work together to answer questions on page 18 using their Cause and Effect charts.

Cause and Effect (A photograph taken of Mars in 1976 looked like a face. Better photos of Mars were taken in the 1990s and 2000s and showed there wasn't a face.)

Vocabulary (*Difficult* means "hard to do.")

Write About Reading (Using telescopes, astronomers could see dark and light areas on Mars. They thought these areas were land and oceans. Better telescopes showed that light areas were polar ice caps. Orbiters, landers, and rovers told us more about the surface, soil, and weather on Mars.)

Independent Reading

Encourage students to read the paired selection "Zach the Martian" on pages 19–21. Have them summarize the selection and compare it to "Mars." Have partners answer the "Make Connections" questions on page 21.

Quick Check Can students identify cause and effect? If not, review and reteach using the instruction on page 286 and assign the Unit 5 Week 4 digital mini-lesson.

Can students respond to the selection using text evidence? If not, provide sentence frames to help them organize their ideas.

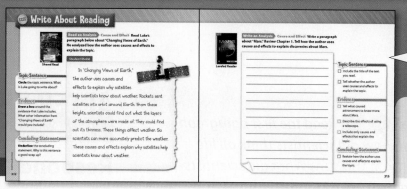

WEEK 4 LESSON 5

Objectives
- Review weekly vocabulary words
- Review cause and effect
- Write an analysis about how the author uses causes and effects to explain a topic

Materials
- Visual Vocabulary Cards: 177–184
- Interactive Worktext, pp. 312–313
- Assessment Book, pp. 56–57

☞ **Go Digital**
- Visual Vocabulary Cards
- Cause and Effect Mini-Lesson
- Interactive eWorktext

Scaffolding for **Wonders** Reading/Writing Workshop

REVIEW AND RETEACH

5–10 Minutes   RI.5.3   RI.5.4a   L.5.6   (CCSS)

Weekly Vocabulary

Display each **Visual Vocabulary Card** and ask students to use the vocabulary word in a sentence. If students have difficulty, have them find the word in "Changing Views of Earth" and use the context clues to define it.

Comprehension: Cause and Effect

I Do   Write and say: *Jackie ran a mile, so she felt tired.* Write *cause* above the first part of the sentence and *effect* above the second part. Circle the word *so.* Say: *This sentence shows a cause and its effect. Authors organize ideas using causes and effects. They often use signal words, such as* because, so, as a result, *or* therefore *to show a cause and its effect.* Display: *Jackie ran a mile. She felt tired.* Point out that in these sentences there is a cause, *Jackie ran a mile*, and an effect, *She felt tired*, without any signal words.

We Do   Display: *It started raining on Eric's walk home from school. As a result, he got soaked.* Say: *Let's find the cause and effect together. Are there any signal words?* (As a result) *What happened to Eric?* (he got soaked) *Why did Eric get soaked?* (It started raining on his walk home from school.) *What is the cause?* (It started raining.) *What is the effect?* (Eric got soaked.)

You Do   Display: *Mrs. Lee's dog went missing. So all of the neighbors decided to help. They searched the neighborhood and called out the dog's name. When that didn't work, they put up posters. As a result, someone found Mrs. Lee's dog.* Have partners identify the causes and effects and identify the signal words.

WRITE ABOUT READING

25–35 Minutes   W.5.2a   W.5.2e   W.5.4   W.5.5   W.5.9b   (CCSS)

Read an Analysis

- Ask students to look back at "Changing Views of Earth" in the **Interactive Worktext**. Have volunteers review their notes. *How did the author use causes and effects to explain the topic?*

- Read aloud the directions on page 312. Read aloud the student model. *Luke's writing is not a summary. The student is writing an* analysis, *or a detailed description, of how the author uses causes and effects to explain the topic.*

- Say: *When you write an analysis, you need to include certain elements. The first element is the* topic sentence. *Circle the topic sentence. What important information has Luke included in this sentence?* (text's title; that the author uses causes and effects to explain the topic)

- *Another element of an analysis is* text evidence. *Luke supports the topic sentence with details from the text. Reread the paragraph and draw a box around the text evidence.* (sentences 2–5) *Look back at your notes about "Changing Views of Earth." What other information could Luke have included as text evidence?* (Possible answers: Scientists were able to make better models of Earth's systems.)

- *The final element of an analysis is the* concluding statement. *Have students underline the concluding statement. How is the concluding statement like the* topic sentence? (Both say that causes and effects explain why satellites help scientists know about weather.) *Which words does Luke use to wrap up the text evidence?* ("These causes and effects")

![Analytical Writing] Write an Analysis

Guided Writing Read the writing prompt on page 313 together. Have students write about "Mars" or another text they read this week. Have them review their notes. *Use the checklist to help you figure out what information to include in each section.* Guide students to ask "how" and "why" questions as they analyze text evidence.

Peer Conference Have students read their analysis to a partner. Listeners should identify the strongest text evidence that supports the topic sentence and discuss any sentences that are unclear.

Teacher Conference Check students' writing for complete sentences and text evidence that supports their topic. Review the concluding statement. *Does this sentence tie all of the elements together?* If necessary, have students revise the concluding statement by restating the topic sentence.

Level Up

▲ Approaching Leveled Reader

▲ Reading/Writing Workshop

▲ Apprentice Leveled Reader

▲ Interactive Worktext

IF students read the Apprentice Level Reader fluently and the **Interactive Worktext** Shared Read fluently and answer the Respond to Reading questions

THEN read together the Approaching Level Reader main selection and the **Reading/Writing Workshop** Shared Read from *Reading Wonders*. Have students take notes as they read, using self-stick notes. Then ask and answer questions about their notes.

Writing Rubric

	4	3	2	1
Topic Sentence	There is one clear, focused topic sentence.	Topic sentence is less focused, somewhat clear.	Topic is presented in short phrases.	There is no topic sentence.
Text Evidence	Topic is supported by two or more text details.	Evidence includes only one detail from the text.	Little to no evidence is cited from the text.	No text evidence is included.
Concluding Statement	Clearly restates the topic sentence; wraps up all the details.	Restatement is less focused; attempts to wrap up details.	Vaguely restates the topic. Doesn't correlate well to text evidence.	There is no conclusion.
Writing Style	Writes in complete sentences. Uses correct spelling and grammar.	Uses complete sentences and phrases. Writing has spelling and grammar errors.	Few or no complete sentences. There are many spelling and grammar errors.	Does not write accurately or in complete sentences.

ASSESSMENT

Weekly Assessment

Have students complete the Weekly Assessment using **Assessment** book pages 56–57.

WEEK 5 LESSON 1

Objectives
- Develop oral language
- Build background about how natural events and human activities affect the environment
- Understand and use weekly vocabulary
- Read informational text

Scaffolding for **Wonders** McGraw-Hill Reading Reading/Writing Workshop

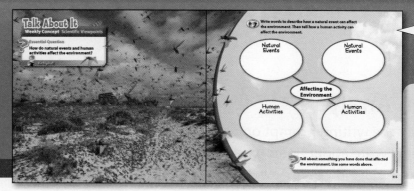

Materials
- Interactive Worktext, pp. 314–321
- Visual Vocabulary Cards: 185–192

☞ **Go** Digital
- Interactive eWorktext
- Visual Vocabulary Cards

WEEKLY CONCEPT

5–10 Minutes   SL.5.1b   SL.5.1c   CCSS

Talk About It

Essential Question Read aloud the Essential Question on page 314 of the **Interactive Worktext**: *How do natural events and human activities affect the environment?* Give examples of natural events (weather, earthquakes, and animal behaviors) and human activities (building houses, polluting, preserving land). Say: *Natural events and human activities can affect, or change, the environment.*

- Discuss the photograph on page 314. Ask: *How are the insects in the photograph affecting the environment?* (Possible answers: they are swarming, covering land)

I Do Say: *I am going to now look at the photograph and think of another way the environment has been affected by a human activity or a natural event. I see a sandy road with tire marks in it. Creating roads is a human activity that affects the environment. I am going to write "roads" under "Human Activities" on page 315.*

We Do Say: *Let's look at the photo and think about another way the environment has been affected. What do you notice about the land?* (It is covered with insects.) *What is causing this change?* (The insects are swarming.) *Is this a human activity or a natural event?* (natural event) Have students add words to the appropriate oval in the web on page 315. Then have them describe a human activity that has affected the environment and add words to the web on page 315.

You Do Have partners discuss how they have affected the environment (for example, picking up litter, planting trees). Have students answer the questions, using key words from the web as appropriate: *What did you do? In what way did the environment change?*

REVIEW VOCABULARY

10–15 Minutes   L.5.4a   L.5.5c   L.5.6   CCSS

Review Weekly Vocabulary Words

- Use the **Visual Vocabulary Cards** to review the weekly vocabulary.

- Read together the directions for the Vocabulary activity on page 316 of the **Interactive Worktext**. Then complete the activity.

1 **probable** Have students discuss the meaning of *likely* and the meanings of the options. *Which of the words shown is a synonym for* probable? (possible)

2 **declined** Have students review the options and then complete the sentence frame: *A town that has declined looks _____.* (empty)

3 **identify** Have partners describe their backpack. Then have them complete this sentence frame: *I can identify my backpack by its _____ and because it has _____.* (Possible answers: color; my notebook inside)

4 **disorder** Have partners brainstorm words or phrases to describe an animal that has a *disorder*. (Possible answers: not well, sick, unhealthy) Then have students choose one of these words to complete the sentence.

5 **thrive** Ask: *Where does a fish live?* (Possible answers: in a lake, ocean, river) *What does it need to thrive there?* Have students complete the sentence frame: *A fish needs _____ and _____ to thrive.* (Possible answers: water; food)

6 **widespread** Discuss each animal's habitat, asking questions such as, *Where does a polar bear live?* Then model asking questions to help students decide which animal is the most *widespread*: *Is a polar bear more widespread than a bird?* Then have partners

decide which of the three animals would be the most *widespread*. (bird)

7 **unexpected** Point out the prefix *un-* and review that it means "not." Have students use these word parts to determine a meaning. (not expected) *How do you feel when something unexpected happens?* (<u>Possible</u> <u>answer</u>: surprised)

8 **agricultural** Ask students if they have ever seen agricultural tools. Show pictures as necessary. Ask them to describe what agricultural tools are used to do. Have students describe their drawings by using the sentence frame: *A _____ is an agricultural tool that is used to _____.* (Drawings will vary, but may include a spade, wheelbarrow, hose, tractor.)

High-Utility Words

Explain that a suffix is a word part added to the end of a word that changes the word's meaning. Have students look at the High-Utility Words activity on page 317 in the **Interactive Worktext**. Discuss the meaning of the suffix *-ful*. Have partners circle words that end in *-ful* in the passage. (powerful, playful, fearful, careful, skillful) Have students use the meaning of the suffix to suggest meanings for each word. Then have partners read the passage.

> **ELL ENGLISH LANGUAGE LEARNERS**
>
> Display the words *powerful, fearful,* and *careful.* Point to and say each word. Have students repeat and use their hands, face, and body to demonstrate the meaning of each word.

READ COMPLEX TEXT
15–20 Minutes   RI.5.1   RI.5.4c **CCSS**

Read: "Should Plants and Animals from Other Places Live Here?"

- Have students turn to page 318 in the **Interactive Worktext** and read aloud the Essential Question. Explain that they will read a selection that includes two different articles about new species of plants and animals that are brought to our country. *Review the titles of each article. Which article do you think is for bringing new species into the country?* ("New Arrivals Welcome") *Which do you think is against bringing new species into the country?* ("A Growing Problem")

- Read "Should Plants and Animals from Other Places Live Here?" together. Note that the weekly vocabulary words are highlighted in yellow. Expand Vocabulary words are in blue.

- Have students use the "My Notes" section on page 318 to write questions they have, words they don't understand, and details they want to remember. Model how to use this section. *I can use the "My Notes section to write questions and notes. In the third paragraph, I'm not sure what a "natural enemy" is, so I'll write a question about this in the "My Notes" section. I'm also not sure about the meaning of the word "pesticides," so I'll write it under "My Notes" with a question mark.*

> **ELL ENGLISH LANGUAGE LEARNERS**
>
> As you read together, have students mark or highlight words and parts of the text they find confusing. After reading, help them write questions in the "My Notes" section.

 Quick Check Can students understand the weekly vocabulary in context? If not, review vocabulary using the **Visual Vocabulary Cards** before teaching Lesson 2.

WEEK 5 LESSON 2

Objectives
- Read persuasive text
- Understand complex text through close reading
- Recognize and understand author's point of view
- Respond to the selection using text evidence to support ideas

Scaffolding for McGraw-Hill Reading **Wonders** Reading/Writing Workshop

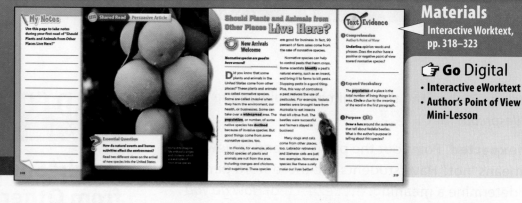

Materials
Interactive Worktext, pp. 318–323

☞ **Go** Digital
- Interactive eWorktext
- Author's Point of View Mini-Lesson

REREAD COMPLEX TEXT

20–25 Minutes   RI.5.1   RI.5.4   RI.5.8   RI.6.6   L.5.4a   CCSS

Close Reading: "Should Plants and Animals from Other Places Live Here?"

Reread "Should Plants and Animals from Other Places Live Here?" with students. As you read together, discuss important passages in the text. Have students respond to text-dependent questions, including those in the **Interactive Worktext**.

🔍 Page 319

Vocabulary Point out the domain-specific words *nonnative*, *invasive*, and *pests* in the first and third paragraphs. Have partners discuss any meanings they know and then look for clues in that will help them understand the meaning of the words in the text. (<u>nonnative</u>: from other places; <u>invasive</u>: harm the environment, our health, or businesses; take over a widespread area; <u>pests</u>: harm crops)

Author's Point of View Explain that the selection includes two articles. Say: *The author of each article has a different point of view, or position. To figure out each author's point of view, look for opinion words, reasons, and evidence such as details and facts. The title of the first article is "New Arrivals Welcome." Which word expresses a strong feeling?* (welcome) *Let's underline this word.* Have students read the sentence below the title and tell an opinion word. (good) *Does the author have a positive or negative point of view towards nonnative species?* (positive) *Let's keep reading to look for other opinion words, reasons, and evidence that support this point of view.* Have partners reread the rest of the page and underline other opinion words. (help; good; plus;

successful; surely; better) Offer an example of a reason (these species are good for business) and evidence (90 percent of farm sales come from the sale of nonnative species). Then have partners point to and discuss other reasons and evidence the author includes. (help to control pests; the beetles were successful; farmers stayed in business; dogs and cats come from other places; nonnative species like these surely make our lives better)

Expand Vocabulary Have students find the word *population. What word in the sentence helps you understand the meaning of* population? (number)

Purpose Ⓐ Ⓒ Ⓣ Have students reread the third paragraph and mark sentences that tell about Vedalia beetles. Ask: *Where did Vedalia beetles come from?* (Australia) *Why were they brought here?* (to eat insects that kill citrus fruit) *Were Vedalia beetles good or bad for businesses? How do you know?* (good; farmers stayed in business) *What is the author's purpose in telling us that Vedalia beetles were successful?* (to show that nonnative species can be helpful)

🔍 Page 320

Author's Point of View Read the title of the article aloud. Ask: *What word in the title of this article expresses a feeling?* (Problem) *Does this word express a positive or a negative feeling?* (negative) *Read the sentence below and the first paragraph. Which words express strong feelings?* (threaten, problem, threatening) *Does the author have a positive or negative point of view towards nonnative species?* (negative) Have partners keep reading and mark other opinion words that express this point of view. (harmful, damage, problems, danger, problem)

Expand Vocabulary Read aloud the definition. Have students locate and read aloud the sentence. Ask: *What are pythons threatening to do?* (reduce the population of native species)

High-Utility Words Point to *harmful* in the second paragraph. *What is the base word?* (harm) *What is the suffix?* (-ful) Have students use the meaning of the suffix to figure out the meaning of the word. (full of harm)

Purpose Ⓐ Ⓒ Ⓣ Have students reread the second paragraph. *How much does it cost to fix the damage from nonnative species? Mark text evidence.* ($137 billion) *Do you think the cost is a lot or a little?* (a lot) *Do you think spending so much is good or bad for the country?* (bad) *What is the author's purpose in telling us the cost of the damage caused by nonnative species?* (to show that nonnative species are harmful to the country)

Vocabulary Point out the domain-specific word *endangered* in the fourth paragraph. *What does it mean when a plant is endangered? What clues helped you figure out the meaning?* (Possible answer: it is in danger of not surviving; crowd out)

🔍 Page 321

Purpose Ⓐ Ⓒ Ⓣ Have students read the chart title and text. *What is the author's purpose in including this chart? Mark the text evidence.* (The chart shows the helpful and harmful effects of four nonnative species.)

Author's Point of View Review with students the second paragraph under "New Arrivals Welcome." *What is one reason the author gives that supports the point that nonnative species are helpful?* (They are good for business.) *Now look at the column "Helpful Effects" on this chart. Which detail tells about a helpful effect on businesses?* (important to California businesses) *Which species on the chart is good for businesses?* (olives)

Author's Point of View Review with students the author's point of view in "A Growing Problem." *Have students review the column "Harmful Effects." Which details tells about a harmful effect on plants?* (crowds out native plants; Destroys 400 species of plants, including citrus and vegetable crops) *Which species on the chart are harmful to native plants?* (kudzu; Mediterranean fruit fly) Have partners review the chart, photo, and caption on the page. *What other details support the point that nonnative species threaten native plants?* (the caption)

RESPOND TO READING

10–20 Minutes   RI.5.1   RI.5.3   W.5.9b   SL.5.1d

Respond to "Should Plants and Animals from Other Places Live Here?"

Have students summarize "New Arrivals Welcome" and "A Growing Problem" orally to demonstrate comprehension. Then have partners answer the questions on page 322 of the **Interactive Worktext** using the discussion starters. Tell them to use text evidence to support their answers. Have students write the page number(s) on which they found the text evidence for each question.

1. *How did bringing Vedalia beetles to the U.S. affect other living things?* (They eat insects that kill citrus fruit; farmers stayed in business. Evidence: p. 319)

2. *How did bringing Asian carp to the U.S. affect the environment?* (The fish thrive in the Mississippi River; the fish is a danger to the Great Lakes; it caused numbers of native fish to go down. Evidence: p. 320)

3. *How did bringing kudzu to the U.S. affect the environment?* (Kudzu stops soil erosion; it crowds out native plants. Evidence: p. 321)

After students discuss the questions on page 322, have them write a response to the question on page 323. Tell them to use partner discussions and notes about the selection to help them. Circulate and provide guidance.

 Quick Check Do students understand vocabulary in context? If not, review and reteach using the instruction on page 296.

Can students use opinion words and key details to determine author's point of view? If not, review and reteach using the instruction on page 296 and assign the Unit 5 Week 5 digital mini-lesson.

Can students write a response to "Should Plants and Animals from Other Places Live Here?" If not, provide sentence frames to help them organize their ideas.

WEEK 5 LESSON 3

Objectives
- Understand and use new vocabulary
- Read persuasive text
- Recognize and understand author's point of view
- Understand complex text through close reading

Scaffolding for WONDERS Approaching Leveled Reader

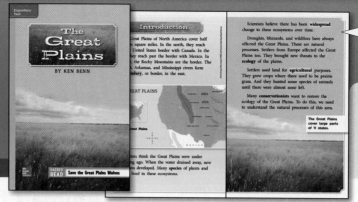

Materials
- "The Great Plains" Below Approaching Leveled Reader: pp. 2–7
- Graphic Organizer: Author's Point of View

☞ **Go** Digital
- Apprentice Leveled Reader eBook
- Downloadable Graphic Organizer
- Author's Point of View Mini-Lesson

BEFORE READING

10–15 Minutes   SL.5.1c   SL.5.1d   L.5.4a   L.5.6

Introduce "The Great Plains"

- Read the Essential Question on the title page of "The Great Plains" **Apprentice Leveled Reader:** *How do natural events and human activities affect the environment? We will read about an area called the Great Plains and how animals and people have shaped and been shaped by the environment.*

- Read the title of the main read. Have students look at the images. *Is this book fiction or nonfiction?* (nonfiction) *How do you know?* (photos, captions, maps, sidebars that give information) *What do you think you will learn about in this book?* (where the Great Plains area is located, what the area is like)

Expand Vocabulary

Display each word below. Say the words and have students repeat them. Then use the Define/Example/Ask routine to introduce each word.

1 **boundary** (page 2)

Define: line that separates two areas of land
Example: A river is the *boundary* between the states.

Ask: How would you research the *boundary* between United States and Canada?

2 **difference** (page 6)

Define: a way of being unlike or different

Example: We felt a *difference* in temperature at night.

Ask: What is the *difference* between winter weather and spring weather?

3 **entire** (page 7)

Define: as a whole, everything

Example: The *entire* audience stood up and cheered.

Ask: Why is it good for the *entire* class to agree on rules?

DURING READING

20–30 Minutes   RI.5.1   RI.5.8   RI.6.6   SL.5.1b   L.5.6

Close Reading

🔍 **Pages 2–3**

Purpose Ⓐ Ⓒ Ⓣ *How does the map on page 2 help to support the facts the author states in the text?* (It shows how big the Plains are, so it's easier to understand "half a million square miles." It shows the boundaries.)

Main Idea and Details *In the first paragraph on page 2, what details support the main idea that the Great Plains of North America cover a wide area?* (half a million square miles; borders with Canada and Mexico, etc.)

Vocabulary Help students figure out challenging domain-specific vocabulary in the selection. For example, point out that on page 2, *species* appears in bold type, which means that students can find its definition in the glossary at the back of the book.

Author's Point of View Explain that an author of an article may have a point of view or opinion. To identify the author's point of view, look at details such as word choice, and the reasons and evidence the author gives. *On page 3, what does the author say about the settlers from Europe?* (They brought new threats to the ecology of the plains.) *Is the author's point of view toward settlers positive or negative?* (negative) *What word supports your answer?* (threats)

Have students record details in their Author's Point of View charts as they read the selection.

Vocabulary Have students point out the word *processes* in the last paragraph on page 3. Explain that *processes* means "a series of events that happen naturally and cause changes." *What natural processes have affected the Great Plains?* (droughts, blizzards, wildfires)

Pages 4–5

Purpose **ACT** Have students read pages 4 and 5. Point out that the author describes a sequence of events from long ago until today. This is how scientists think the area we now call the Great Plains has changed over time. Ask: *What forces have shaped the land in the Great Plains?* (Streams carried rocks and soil from the Rocky Mountains. Water cut into the rock and wore down hills.)

Connection of Ideas **ACT** Review with students that in the Introduction on page 3, the author said we need to understand the natural processes of the Great Plains. *What natural processes does the author describe on pages 4 and 5?* (how water shaped the land; that the kinds of animals on the plains have changed; how the Black Hills were formed)

Vocabulary Have students point to the word *tower* in the sidebar on page 5. Explain that it is used in a verb meaning "to rise up high." Ask: *What other meanings do you know for* tower? (a tall structure) *Why do the Black Hills* tower *above the plains?* (The hills are high and the plains are flat.)

Pages 6–7

Organization **ACT** Have students read page 6. Point out that the author uses a cause and effect text structure to describe how the climate of the Great Plains changed. *Do you see a signal word in the first paragraph?* (Because) *The author says that it rained more during the Ice Age. What effect did this have on the Great Plains?* (They were covered with forests.) *How did the climate change after the Ice Age?* (The climate got drier.) *What effects did this have on the Great Plains?* (Forests changed to grasslands. The mammoths died out, but bison thrived.)

Author's Point of View *On page 7, what negative words does the author use to describe droughts on the plains?* (harmful, hard, die, must leave the area) *What do these words tell you about the author's point of view toward droughts?* (The author views droughts as damaging, but as something that has happened naturally many times on the plains.)

Purpose **ACT** Have students read the sidebar on page 7, and review the image and caption. Ask: *Why are mussels important?* (They are an important part of the food web. They give protein for animals.) *Why do you think the author includes these text features about mussels?* (The sidebar and caption show how animals on the plains are connected. The information also shows how important water is to the Great Plains.)

STOP AND CHECK Have students answer the Stop and Check question on page 7. (Long ago the area was covered by sea. Then the area was lifted up. It was covered in forest. It rained a lot. After the Ice Age, the climate got drier. The forests turned into grasslands, and many large animals became extinct.)

✓ *Quick Check* Do students understand weekly vocabulary in context? If not, review and reteach using the instruction on page 296.

Can students identify the author's point of view? If not, review and reteach using the instruction on page 296 and assign the Unit 5 Week 5 digital mini-lesson.

WEEK 5 LESSON 4

Objectives
- Understand and use new vocabulary
- Read persuasive text
- Recognize and understand author's point of view
- Understand complex text through close reading
- Respond to the selection using text evidence to support ideas

Scaffolding for **Wonders** Approaching Leveled Reader

Materials
- "The Great Plains" Apprentice Leveled Reader: pp. 8–24
- Graphic Organizer: Author's Point of View

☞ **Go** Digital
- Apprentice Leveled Reader eBook
- Downloadable Graphic Organizer
- Author's Point of View Mini-Lesson

BEFORE READING

5–10 Minutes   SL.5.1c   SL.5.1d   L.5.4a   L.5.6

Expand Vocabulary

Display each word below. Say the words and have students repeat them. Then use the Define/Example/Ask routine to introduce each word.

1 exchange (page 9)

Define: give something to get something; trade

Example: The Native Americans gave the settlers food in *exchange* for tools.

Ask: Why would you *exchange* a gift for another item?

2 graze (page 11)

Define: to use land for feeding animals

Example: The farmer thought the field would be a good place to *graze* his hungry cows.

Ask: Would you put animals to *graze* in a field of grass or a field of rocks? Why?

3 regarded (page 13)

Define: thought of; had an opinion about something

Example: People in the Midwest have always *regarded* tornadoes as a common threat.

Ask: What do you *regard* as a good movie?

4 roamed (page 15)

Define: to move around in a large area

Example: Wolves once *roamed* around our country.

Ask: What are some animals that might *roam* around a forest?

DURING READING

15–20 Minutes   RI.5.1   RI.5.8   RI.6.6   SL.5.1b   L.5.6

Close Reading

🔍 **Pages 8–9**

Author's Point of View *On page 8, what sentence tells you the author's point of view about how Native Americans lived on the plains?* (But they did not harm the environment very much.)

Cause and Effect *On page 9, what effect did horses have on the way Native Americans hunted?* (They could move faster and kill more bison.)

Purpose Ⓐ Ⓒ Ⓣ Have students read the last paragraph on page 9. *Why did fur trappers come to the Great Plains?* (to get furs from beavers and other animals) *What was the effect?* (the numbers of many animals went down)

🔍 **Pages 10–11**

Purpose Ⓐ Ⓒ Ⓣ Have students read the sidebar on page 10. Ask: *What does the author see as a problem with the Ogallala Aquifer?* (people taking water faster than it can flow back in) *Based on the photo and caption, what group is part of the problem?* (farmers who use a lot of water to grow crops)

Author's Point of View Have students read pages 10 and 11. Ask: *On page 11, what does the author think of farming practices on the plains?* (They were harmful.) *What words are a clue to the author's point of view?* (used up, toxic, killed helpful insects)

Cause and Effect *Why did the soil on the plains blow away during the drought in the 1930s?* (After the crops died, there was nothing left to hold the soil in place.)

Vocabulary *On page 11, what was the Dust Bowl?* (It was a time when the air was full of soil blowing away.)

Page 12

Purpose Ⓐ🄲Ⓣ *What does the chart on page 12 show? Why do you think the author included it?* (It summarizes how humans have affected the Great Plains. It shows how their impact got worse over time.)

STOP AND CHECK Have students answer the question in the Stop and Check box on page 12. (Farmers used fertilizers and sprays, used up soil nutrients, eroded topsoil, and killed good insects. A drought killed the crops and the soil blew away.)

Pages 13–15

Purpose Ⓐ🄲Ⓣ *What information on page 13 shows that people have changed how they feel about prairie fires?* (Research shows that fires help the ecology. They clear away old growth and add nutrients to the soil.)

Author's Point of View *In the box on page 14, how does the author present a balanced point of view?* (The author tells why prairie dogs are important and why many people dislike prairie dogs.)

Connection of Ideas Ⓐ🄲Ⓣ *In the chapter's first paragraph on page 13, the author mentions food webs. What food webs does the author mention on pages 14 and 15?* (Bison eat prairie grass so the grass is kept short. They also spread prairie grass seeds. Prairie dogs eat only short grass. Black-footed ferrets eat prairie dogs.)

STOP AND CHECK Have students answer the Stop and Check question on page 15. (They are working to restore prairie grasses, understand the role of fire on the prairies, and increase native animal populations.)

Pages 16–17

Cause and Effect *What are some of the reasons the Great Plains' ecosystems have changed over time?* (climate change, droughts, fires, storms, and human activity)

Author's Point of View *How does the author view restoring the grasslands?* (The author is in favor of it, but says it will be a big job.) *What more does the author say we need to understand before trying to restore the grasslands?* (biodiversity and the issues)

AFTER READING
10–15 Minutes   RI.5.1   RI.5.2   RI.5.9   W.5.9b   L.5.4a   CCSS

Respond to Reading

Compare Texts Have students compare "Should Plants and Animals from Other Places Live Here?" with "The Great Plains." Then say: *How do natural events and human activities affect the environment?*

Summarize Have students turn to page 18 and summarize the selection. (Also include details about present efforts and challenges to restoring the prairie.)

Text Evidence

Have partners work together to answer questions on page 18 using their Author's Point of View charts.

Author's Point of View (The author wants people to understand the Great Plains and to restore the region.)

Vocabulary ("killed insects" helps to explain *toxic*)

Write About Reading (Students may identify the author's point of view as being concerned about how trappers, pioneers, and farmers have all harmed the ecology of the area. The author also presents details to balance this out on page 12: farmers now know the problems and try crops that are better for the Plains.)

Independent Reading

Encourage students to read the paired selection "Save the Great Plains Wolves" on pages 19–21. Have them summarize the selection and compare it to "The Great Plains." Have them work with a partner to answer the "Make Connections" questions on page 21.

✔ *Quick Check* **Can students identify the author's point of view? If not, review and teach using the instruction on page 296 and assign the Unit 5 Week 5 digital mini-lesson.**

Can students respond to the selection using text evidence? If not, provide sentence frames to help them organize their ideas.

WEEK 5
LESSON

5

Objectives
• Review weekly vocabulary words
• Review author's point of view
• Write an analysis about an author's use of reasons and evidence to support a position

Scaffolding for **Wonders** Reading/Writing Workshop

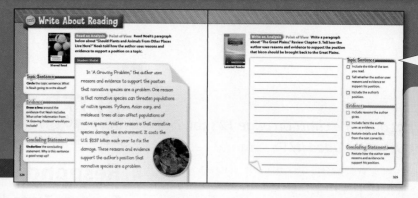

Materials
• Visual Vocabulary Cards: 185–192
• Interactive Worktext, pp. 324–325
• Assessment Book, pp. 58–59

☞ **Go** Digital
• Visual Vocabulary Cards
• Author's Point of View Mini-Lesson
• Interactive eWorktext

REVIEW AND RETEACH

5–10 Minutes   RI.5.1   RI.6.6   L.5.4a   L.5.6

Weekly Vocabulary

Display one **Visual Vocabulary Card** at a time and ask students to use the vocabulary word in a sentence. If students have difficulty, have them find the word in "Should Plants and Animals from Other Places Live Here?" and use the context clues to define it.

Comprehension: Author's Point of View

I Do Write and say: *Gypsy moth caterpillars are pests. They damage trees. They eat and harm the leaves. Then the tree is not as strong and can become sick.* Say: *To determine the author's point of view, I look for reasons and evidence, and the author's choice of words.* Underline *pest, damage, harm. These words express a negative feeling.* Circle the last three sentences. *These reasons and facts support the author's point of view that gypsy moth caterpillars are harmful.*

We Do Display: *Kudzu is a terrible problem. The vines block sunlight and kill native plants. This harmful plant is difficult to stop. It now covers millions of acres in the United States.* Ask: *What opinion words do you see?* (terrible problem, kill, harmful) *What reasons and evidence does the author include?* (block sunlight and kill native plants, it is difficult to stop. It now covers millions of acres in the United States.) *Use these clues. What is the author's point of view?* (Kudzu is harmful.)

You Do Display: *Horses are helpful. They help move things. They easily herd animals. They are friendly.* Have partners tell opinion words, details that support the author's position, and the author's point of view.

WRITE ABOUT READING

25–35 Minutes   W.5.2   W.5.4   W.5.5   W.5.9b

Read an Analysis

• Ask students to look back at "Should Plants and Animals from Other Places Live Here?" in the **Interactive Worktext**. Have volunteers review their notes. *How did the authors of the articles support their positions?*

• Read aloud the directions on page 324. *In his paragraph, Noah does not summarize. He writes an analysis, or a detailed description about how the author of "A Growing Problem" supported his or her position on the topic.* Read aloud the student model.

• Say: *When you write to analyze a text, you need to start with a* topic sentence. Have students read the beginning of the student model and circle the topic sentence. *What important information is included in this sentence?* (the title of the text; that the author used reasons and evidence; the author's position)

• *The next part is* text evidence. *Noah supports his topic sentence by citing two reasons and related evidence from the text. Draw a box around the text evidence.* (sentences 2–5) *Look at your notes about "Should Plants and Animals from Other Places Live Here?" What other reasons might be included in the model as evidence?* (Possible answer: A flu virus came to the U.S. carried by birds.)

• *The last part is the* concluding statement. *Underline the concluding statement. How is this sentence like the topic sentence?* (Both sentences say that reasons and evidence support the author's position; both tell the author's position.) *Which words does Noah use to wrap up the paragraph?* ("These reasons and evidence")

Analytical Writing — Write an Analysis

Guided Writing Read the writing prompt on page 325 together. Have students write about "The Great Plains" or another text they read this week. Have them review their notes. *Use the checklist to help you figure out the right information to include.* Guide students to ask questions to analyze text evidence, such as *Why is the author's position strong?*

Peer Conference Have students read their analysis to a partner. Listeners should identify the strongest text evidence that supports the topic sentence and discuss any sentences that are unclear.

Teacher Conference Check students' writing for complete sentences and text evidence that supports their topic. Review the concluding statement. *Does this sentence tie all of the elements together?* If necessary, have students revise the concluding statement by restating the topic sentence.

Level Up

▲ Approaching Leveled Reader

▲ Reading/Writing Workshop

▲ Apprentice Leveled Reader

▲ Interactive Worktext

IF students read the Apprentice Level Reader fluently and the **Interactive Worktext** Shared Read fluently and answer the Respond to Reading questions

THEN read together the Approaching Level Reader main selection and the **Reading/Writing Workshop** Shared Read from *Reading Wonders*. Have students take notes as they read, using self-stick notes. Then ask and answer questions about their notes.

Writing Rubric

	4	3	2	1
Topic Sentence	There is one clear, focused topic sentence.	Topic sentence is less focused, somewhat clear.	Topic is presented in short phrases.	There is no topic sentence.
Text Evidence	Topic is supported by two or more text details.	Evidence includes only one detail from the text.	Little to no evidence is cited from the text.	No text evidence is included.
Concluding Statement	Clearly restates the topic sentence; wraps up all the details.	Restatement is less focused; attempts to wrap up the details.	Vaguely restates the topic sentence.	There is no conclusion.
Writing Style	Writes in complete sentences. Uses correct spelling and grammar.	Uses some complete sentences. Writing has some spelling and grammar errors.	Few or no complete sentences. There are many spelling and grammar errors.	Does not write accurately or in complete sentences.

ASSESSMENT

Weekly Assessment

Have students complete the Weekly Assessment using **Assessment** book pages 58–59.

WEEK 6

▶ **Unit Assessment,**
pages 158–166

▶ **Fluency Assessment,**
pages 266–281

▶ **Exit Test,**
pages 214–222

Unit 5 Assessment

CCSS TESTED SKILLS

✔ COMPREHENSION	✔ VOCABULARY
• Character, Setting, Plot: Compare and Contrast RL.5.3	• Context Clues L.5.4a
• Character, Setting, Plot: Compare and Contrast RL.5.3	
• Compare and Contrast RI.5.3	
• Cause and Effect RI.5.5	
• Author's Point of View RI.5.5 , RI.6.6	

Using Assessment and Writing Scores

RETEACH	IF ...	THEN ...
COMPREHENSION	Students answer 0–7 multiple-choice items correctly ...	... reteach tested skills using instruction on pages 364–371.
VOCABULARY	Students answer 0–3 multiple-choice items correctly ...	... reteach tested skills using instruction on page 364.
WRITING	Students score mostly 1–2 on weekly Write About Reading rubrics throughout the unit...	... reteach writing using instruction on pages 372–373.

LEVEL UP	IF ...	THEN ...
COMPREHENSION	Students answer 8–10 multiple-choice items correctly ...	... have students read the *Ocean Threats* Approaching Leveled Reader. Use the Level Up lesson on page 300.
WRITING	Students score mostly 3–4 on weekly Write About Reading rubrics throughout the unit...	... use the Level Up Write About Reading lesson on page 301 to have students compare two selections from the unit.

Fluency Assessment

Conduct assessments individually using the differentiated fluency passages in **Assessment**. Students' expected fluency goal for this Unit is 129–149 WCPM with an accuracy rate of 95% or higher.

Exit Test

If a student answers 13–15 multiple-choice items correctly on the Unit Assessment, administer the Unit 5 Exit Test at the end of Week 6.

Time to Exit WonderWorks

Exit Test

If...

Students answer 13–15 multiple choice items correctly...

Fluency Assessment

If...

Students achieve their Fluency Assessment goal for the unit...

Level Up Lessons

If...

Students are successful applying close reading skills with the Approaching Leveled Reader in Week 6...

If...

Students score mostly 4–5 on the Level Up Write About Reading assignment...

Foundational Skills Kit

If...

Students have mastered the Unit 5 benchmark skills in the Foundational Skills Kit and *PowerPAL for Reading* adaptive learning system...

Then...

... consider exiting the student from *Reading WonderWorks* materials into the Approaching Level of *Reading Wonders*.

Read Approaching Leveled Reader

RI.5.10

▶ **Read Approaching Leveled Reader**

Approaching Leveled Reader

Apprentice Leveled Reader

Ocean Threats

Before Reading

Preview Discuss what students remember about algae and algal blooms. Tell them that they will be reading a more challenging version of *Ocean Threats*.

Vocabulary Use routines on the **Visual Vocabulary Cards** to review the Weekly Vocabulary words. Use pages 270 and 272 to review the Expand Vocabulary words.

A C T During Reading

▶ **Vocabulary** Provide definitions for the following science words and phrases that are new to this level: *discolored* (page 7), *probable* (page 10), and *agricultural runoff* (page 11).

▶ **Organization** Students may need help understanding the cause-and-effect relationships described in greater detail in the Approaching Leveled Reader. the idea of a food web with how the algae can harm people. Read aloud page 12. Ask: *Where do the algae start?* (in the water) *Where do shellfish, like shrimp and lobsters, live?* (in the water) *If a human eats seafood that lived in algae-infested water, what can happen as a result?* (They can become infected with harmful bacteria.)

▶ **Sentence Structure** Students may need help understanding complex sentences. Read aloud the second sentence of the second paragraph on page 9. Point out that this page contains several phrases after commas. These phrases give readers more information. Ask: *What phrases come after* Sun storms *and* energy? (or solar flares, or heat) *What do these phrases do?* (explain or define the words) *What raises the temperature of the atmosphere?* (the energy from a Sun storm)

▶ **Write About Reading**

Interactive Worktext Shared Read

Apprentice Leveled Reader

After Reading

Ask students to complete the Respond to Reading questions on page 18 after they have finished reading. Provide additional support as needed to help students use the weekly vocabulary strategy to answer question 3.

Write About Reading

W.5.2 W.5.9b

Read an Analysis

- Distribute the Unit 5 Downloadable Model and Practice that compares two related texts, the **Interactive Worktext** Shared Read "Changing Views of Earth" and the **Apprentice Leveled Reader** "Mars." Read the paragraph aloud to students.

- Point out the signal words *similar* and *both* in the topic sentence, which tells readers how the two texts are alike. Have students circle and reread the topic sentence. Ask: *What other information does Roberta include in her topic sentence?* (titles of both texts; how they are alike)

- Have students mark text evidence. Ask: *What details does Roberta include from "Changing Views of Earth" to show it is different from "Mars"?* (sentences 2–3) *What details does she include from "Mars" to show it is different from "Changing Views of Earth"?* (sentences 4–5) *Why is the concluding sentence a good wrap up?* (It restates how they are alike and different.)

Write an Analysis
Analytical Writing

Guided Practice Display: *Write a paragraph that compares "Should Plants and Animals from Other Places Live Here?" to "The Great Plains." Tell how the topics are alike and different.*

- Alternatively, let students select two texts themselves to compare.

- Remind students that their topic sentence should tell how the texts are alike.

- Tell students to include details from each text that shows how the topics are alike and different.

- For the concluding statement, remind students to restate the topic sentence and wrap up the details.

Teacher Conference Check students' writing for complete sentences. Did they begin with a topic sentence? Did they cite text evidence? Did they restate the topic sentence in the last sentence?

Writing Rubric

	4	3	2	1
Topic Sentence	There is one clear, focused topic sentence.	Topic sentence is less focused, somewhat clear.	Topic is presented in short phrases.	There is no topic sentence.
Text Evidence	Topic is supported by two or more text details.	Evidence includes only one detail from the text.	Little to no evidence is cited from the text.	No text evidence is included.
Concluding Statement	Clearly restates the topic sentence; wraps up all the details.	Restatement is less focused; attempts to wrap up the details.	Vaguely restates the topic. Doesn't correlate well to text evidence.	There is no conclusion.
Writing Style	Writes in complete sentences. Uses correct spelling and grammar.	Uses complete sentences and phrases. Writing has spelling and grammar errors.	Has few or no complete sentences. There are many spelling and grammar errors.	Does not write accurately or in complete sentences.

UNIT 6 PLANNER
Linked In

Week 1 Joining Forces	Week 2 Getting Along	Week 3 Adaptations

ESSENTIAL QUESTION *How do different groups contribute to a cause?*	**ESSENTIAL QUESTION** *What actions can we take to get along with others?*	**ESSENTIAL QUESTION** *How are living things adapted to their environment?*
Build Background	**Build Background**	**Build Background**
Vocabulary L.5.4a *bulletin, contributions, diversity, enlisted, intercept, operations, recruits, survival*	**Vocabulary** L.5.4a *abruptly, ally, collided, confident, conflict, intervene, protective, taunting*	**Vocabulary** L.5.4a *adaptation, agile, cache, dormant, forage, frigid, hibernate, insulates*
Access Complex Text Organization	**Access Complex Text** Connection of Ideas	**Access Complex Text** Genre
Comprehension RL.5.2 Skill: Theme Respond to Reading	**Comprehension** RL.5.2 Skill: Theme Respond to Reading	**Comprehension** RI.5.3 Skill: Text Structure: Cause and Effect Respond to Reading
Write About Reading *Analytical Writing* W.5.9a Inform/Explain: Theme	**Write About Reading** *Analytical Writing* W.5.9a Opinion: Genre	**Write About Reading** *Analytical Writing* W.5.9b Opinion: Cause and Effect

A S S E S S M E N T

✓ **Quick Check** Vocabulary, Comprehension ✓ **Weekly Assessment** Assessment Book, pp. 60–61	✓ **Quick Check** Vocabulary, Comprehension ✓ **Weekly Assessment** Assessment Book, pp. 62–63	✓ **Quick Check** Vocabulary, Comprehension ✓ **Weekly Assessment** Assessment Book, pp. 64–65

✓ **MID-UNIT ASSESSMENT**
Assessment Book, pp. 112–119

✓ **Fluency Assessment**
Assessment Book, pp. 266–281

Use the Foundational Skills Kit for explicit instruction of phonics, structural analysis, fluency, and word recognition. Includes *PowerPAL for Reading* adaptive learning system.

Week 4
Making a Difference

ESSENTIAL QUESTION
What impact do our actions have on our world?

Build Background

CCSS Vocabulary
L.5.4a *export, glistening, influence, landscape, native, plantations, restore, urged*

Access Complex Text
Connection of Ideas

CCSS Comprehension
RI.5.5 Skill: Text Structure: Problem and Solution
Respond to Reading

CCSS Write About Reading *Analytical Writing*
W.5.9b Inform/Explain: Problem and Solution

Week 5
Out in the World

ESSENTIAL QUESTION
What can our connections to the world teach us?

Build Background

CCSS Vocabulary
L.5.4a *blares, connection, errand, exchange*

Poetic Terms
assonance, consonance, imagery, personification

Access Complex Text
Genre

CCSS Comprehension
RL.5.6 Skill: Point of View
Respond to Reading

CCSS Write About Reading *Analytical Writing*
W.5.9a Opinion: Genre

Week 6
ASSESS

RETEACH   **LEVEL UP**

Reteach
Comprehension Skills

Vocabulary

Write About Reading

Level Up
Read Approaching Leveled Reader

Write About Reading:
Compare Texts

A S S E S S M E N T

✓ *Quick Check*
Vocabulary, Comprehension

✓ Weekly Assessment
Assessment Book, pp. 66–67

✓ *Quick Check*
Vocabulary, Comprehension

✓ Weekly Assessment
Assessment Book, pp. 68–69

✓ Unit Assessment
Assessment Book, pp. 167–175

✓ Fluency Assessment
Assessment Book, pp. 266–281

✓ EXIT TEST
Assessment Book, pp. 223–231

Unit
6

Linked In

Big Idea
How are we all connected?

UNIT 6 OPENER,
pp. 326–327

The Big Idea

How are we all connected?

Talk About It

Read aloud the Big Idea on page 327 of the **Interactive Worktext:** *How are we all connected?* Have students think about people or places they are connected to. Say: *We can be connected to others by having similar goals or doing similar activities. We can also be connected to special places that are important to us. I am connected to other teachers, because we all teach. I am connected to all of you because we work together on the same activities. I am connected to the place where I grew up because I remember all of the things I used to do there. What people or places are you connected to?* (Answers will vary.)

Discuss the photo on pages 326–327. Ask: *How are the people in the group similar?* (they are all marching in the parade, wearing red, helping to carry a flag) *How do you think the people in the group are connected?* (Possible answers: They are American; they are patriotic; they work together.) *How does living in the same place make you feel connected to others?* Have partners or small groups discuss this question and share their ideas with the class.

Tell students that we can be connected to others in many ways. Say: *In this unit, we will be reading ten selections about ways people and other living things are connected. In one selection, a young girl connects with others by helping a cause. In another selection, we'll find out how living things are connected to their environment.*

Build Fluency

Each week, use the **Interactive Worktext** Shared Reads and **Apprentice Leveled Readers** for fluency instruction and practice. Keep in mind that reading rates vary with the type of text that students are reading as well as the purpose for reading. For example, comprehension of complex informational texts generally requires slower reading.

Explain/Model Use the Fluency lessons on pages 374–378 to explain the skill. Then model the skill by reading the first page of the week's Shared Read or Leveled Reader.

Practice/Apply Choose a page from the Shared Read or Leveled Reader. Have one group read the top half of the page one sentence at a time. Remind children to apply the skill. Have the second group echo-read the passage. Then have the groups switch roles for the second half of the page. Discuss how each group applied the skill.

Weekly Fluency Focus

Week 1 Expression and Phrasing
Week 2 Intonation
Week 3 Rate and Accuracy
Week 4 Expression and Phrasing
Week 5 Expression and Phrasing

Foundational Skills Kit You can also use the **Lesson Cards** and **Practice** pages from the **Foundational Skills Kit** for targeted Fluency instruction and practice.

Access Complex Text

Qualitative / Quantitative
Reader and Task

TEXT COMPLEXITY

Interactive Worktext

	Week 1	Week 2	Week 3	Week 4	Week 5
	"Shipped Out"	"The Bully"	"Mysterious Oceans"	"Words to Save the World: The Work of Rachel Carson"	"To Travel!"
Quantitative	Lexile 730 TextEvaluator™ 42	Lexile 760 TextEvaluator™ 28	Lexile 920 TextEvaluator™ 40	Lexile 870 TextEvaluator™ 46	Lexile N/A TextEvaluator™ N/A
Qualitative	• Organization • Sentence Structure • Vocabulary	• Connection of Ideas • Sentence Structure • Vocabulary	• Genre • Vocabulary	• Connection of Ideas • Genre • Vocabulary	• Genre • Connection of Ideas • Vocabulary
Reader and Task	The Weekly Concept lessons will help determine the reader's knowledge and engagement in the weekly concept.				
	Weekly Concept: p. 306 Questions and tasks: pp. 308–309	Weekly Concept: p. 316 Questions and tasks: pp. 318–319	Weekly Concept: p. 326 Questions and tasks: pp. 328–329	Weekly Concept: p. 338 Questions and tasks: pp. 340–341	Weekly Concept: p. 348 Questions and tasks: pp. 350–351

Apprentice Leveled Reader

	Week 1	Week 2	Week 3	Week 4	Week 5
	"Mrs. Gleeson's Records"	"Winning Friends"	"Cave Creatures"	"Marjory Stoneman Douglas: Guardian of the Everglades"	"Your World, My World"
Quantitative	Lexile 660 TextEvaluator™ 29	Lexile 650 TextEvaluator™ 33	Lexile 710 TextEvaluator™ 23	Lexile 700 TextEvaluator™ 29	Lexile 680 TextEvaluator™ 36
Qualitative	• Organization • Prior Knowledge • Connection of Ideas • Vocabulary	• Connection of Ideas • Genre • Sentence Structure • Vocabulary	• Genre • Sentence Structure • Connection of Ideas • Vocabulary	• Connection of Ideas • Genre • Vocabulary	• Genre • Sentence Structure • Vocabulary
Reader and Task	The Weekly Concept lessons will help determine the reader's knowledge and engagement in the weekly concept.				
	Weekly Concept: p. 306 Questions and tasks: pp. 310–313	Weekly Concept: p. 316 Questions and tasks: pp. 320–323	Weekly Concept: p. 326 Questions and tasks: pp. 330–333	Weekly Concept: p. 338 Questions and tasks: pp. 342–345	Weekly Concept: p. 348 Questions and tasks: pp. 352–355

See pages 379 for details about Text Complexity measures.

WEEK 1 LESSON 1

Objectives
- Develop oral language
- Build background about how different groups contribute to a cause
- Understand and use weekly vocabulary
- Read historical fiction

Scaffolding for **Wonders** Reading/Writing Workshop

Materials
- Interactive Worktext, pp. 328–335
- Visual Vocabulary Cards: 193–200

👉 **Go** Digital
- Interactive eWorktext
- Visual Vocabulary Cards

WEEKLY CONCEPT

5–10 Minutes   SL.5.1b   SL.5.1c CCSS

Talk About It

Essential Question Read aloud the Essential Question on page 328 of the **Interactive Worktext**: *How do different groups contribute to a cause?* Review the meaning of *contribute.* Explain that the meaning of *cause* in this question means "a goal." Say: *People can contribute to a cause in many ways. When people with different skills work together, they can better achieve a goal or help a cause.*

- Discuss the photograph on page 328. Ask: *What cause do you think these groups are helping?* (a rescue at sea)

> **I Do** Say: *I am going to look closely at the photograph to look for ways each group is contributing to the cause. I see a helicopter. The helicopter is able to rescue the people faster than the boat. The helicopter pilot and crew are contributing their ability to fly a helicopter to the rescue effort. I will write this in the web on page 329.*

> **We Do** Say: *Now let's look at the photo together to look for another way a group is contributing to the cause. How are the people driving the boats contributing to the rescue effort?* (Possible answer: they got the people out of the water; they are able to move the people by boat) *How are their skills different from the skills of the helicopter crew?* (they can drive boats) As students describe what they see, work with them to add words to the web on page 329. Then have them tell another way a group could contribute to this cause.

> **You Do** Have partners describe a time when they worked with others for a cause or to achieve a goal. Ask: *What cause or goal did you work to help? What did you do to help? Who did you work with? How did others help the cause? Why was working with others helpful?*

REVIEW VOCABULARY

10–15 Minutes   L.5.1   L.5.4a   L.5.5c   L.5.6 CCSS

Review Weekly Vocabulary Words

- Use the **Visual Vocabulary Cards** to review the weekly vocabulary.
- Read together the directions for the Vocabulary activity on page 330 of the **Interactive Worktext**. Then complete the activity.

1 **survival** Have students use the sentence frame: *Two things that a plant needs for survival are _____ and _____.* (Possible answers: sun, water, soil)

2 **intercept** Ask students if they have ever been to or seen a football, basketball, or soccer game. Show pictures of players intercepting a ball, as necessary. Ask students to use the following sentence frame: *When a player intercepts a ball in a game, the player _____.* (catches it before another player gets it)

3 **contributions** Discuss with students things that an animal shelter might need. Then have them use the sentence starter: *Two contributions a person could make to an animal shelter are _____.* (Possible answers: give money, volunteer time, give food)

4 **operations** Give one example of a computer operation you know how to do, such as logging in. Then ask: *What computer operations can you do?* Have them use the sentence starters: *Two computer operations I know how to do are _____ and _____.* (Possible answers: opening a document, accessing the internet)

5 **diversity** Have partners ask each other questions to help them decide which of the options mean the same as *diversity.* (variety, many kinds)

6 recruits Discuss what it takes to be a great soccer team member. Then have students complete the sentence frame: _____ and _____ would be good recruits for a soccer team because _____. (Answers will vary; reasons may include that they are good athletes, run fast, or work well with others.)

7 enlisted Have students complete this sentence starter: *I would get people to enlist in a clean-up project by _____.* (Possible answers: talking to people about it; putting up posters to let people know about the project; posting a sign-up sheet) Ask students to form the past tense of *enlist*.

8 bulletin Discuss what happens at a school carnival. Ask: *What information would you include on a bulletin for a carnival?* (a heading, the date and time, the location, what kinds of activities there will be; Drawings and information will vary.)

High-Utility Words

Remind students that a pronoun takes the place of a noun. Have students look at the High-Utility Words activity on page 331 of the **Interactive Worktext**. Discuss the definition and examples of indefinite pronouns. Then have partners circle indefinite pronouns in the passage. (everyone, someone, others, no one, anywhere, something) Then have students look around the room and complete the sentence frames: *I see that everyone is wearing _____. I see that someone has a _____. No one is wearing _____.*

ELL ENGLISH LANGUAGE LEARNERS

Help students complete their sentence frames. Then ask questions with indefinite pronouns. *What is everyone wearing? Is someone wearing a sweater or a tee-shirt? Is anyone wearing a coat or boots?*

READ COMPLEX TEXT
15–20 Minutes   RL.5.1 RF.5.4c

Read: "Shipped Out"

- Have students turn to page 332 in the **Interactive Worktext** and read aloud the Essential Question. Explain that they will read about a young girl's way of contributing to the war effort during World War II. Ask: *Look at the illustrations. What do you think the girl will do to contribute to the war effort?* (make cupcakes)

- Read "Shipped Out" together. Note that the weekly vocabulary words are highlighted in yellow. Expand Vocabulary words are highlighted in blue.

- Have students use the "My Notes" section on page 332 to write questions they have, words they don't understand, and details they want to remember. Model how to use the "My Notes" section. *I can write questions and notes about the story as I read. When I read the first paragraph on page 333, I wonder what Libby means when she says "Like my dad, I've packed my things and shipped out." I don't understand what "shipped out" means, so I will write "shipped out" with a question mark in the "My Notes" section. I am also not sure why Libby feels "like a prisoner of war." I will write Why does Libby feel like a prisoner? I will ask myself these questions when I reread to better understand what I am reading.*

ELL ENGLISH LANGUAGE LEARNERS

As you read together, have students highlight parts of the story they think are confusing or have questions about. After reading, help them write questions and notes in the "My Notes" section about the parts they highlighted.

 Quick Check Can students understand the weekly vocabulary in context? If not, review vocabulary using the **Visual Vocabulary Cards** before teaching Lesson 2.

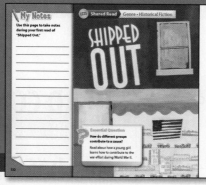

WEEK 1 LESSON 2

Objectives
- Read historical fiction
- Understand complex text through close reading
- Recognize and understand theme
- Respond to the selection using text evidence to support ideas

Materials
Interactive Worktext, pp. 332–337

👉 **Go Digital**
- Interactive eWorktext
- Theme Mini-Lesson

Scaffolding for **McGraw-Hill Reading Wonders** Reading/Writing Workshop

REREAD COMPLEX TEXT

20–25 Minutes   RL.5.1   RL.5.2   RL.5.3   L.5.4a   L.5.6   CCSS

Close Reading: "Shipped Out"

Reread "Shipped Out" with students. As you read together, discuss important passages in the text. Have students respond to text-dependent questions, including those in the **Interactive Worktext**.

🔍 Page 333

Prior Knowledge Ⓐ Ⓒ Ⓣ Read the first two paragraphs. Ask students what they know about World War II. Explain the main events and the meaning of *Allies*, if necessary.

Organization Ⓐ Ⓒ Ⓣ *In the first paragraph Libby says, "I've packed my things and shipped out, away from home." Reread the second paragraph. Where did Libby go? Let's circle this detail.* (I'm stuck in my aunt's apartment above her bakery.) *What events happened before this that caused Lucy to move there?* Guide students to answer the question by using the sentence frame: *Libby moved to _____ because _____ and _____.* (her aunt's apartment; her Dad went to work on a battleship; Mom work is working double shifts at the clothing factory)

Theme Model using text evidence to find details about the theme. Say: *In the first paragraph, Libby thinks "I'm trapped, not able to do much while the war goes on." I also read "nothing I do will help the Allies win World War II." The words "not able to do much" and "nothing I do will help" show what Libby thinks about her contributions to the war effort.* Have students underline these details. Ask: *What does Libby think of herself?* (She isn't doing anything to help.) Have students reread the next two paragraphs. Ask: *What does Libby ask her mother?* (if she snuck things like poems for the soldiers into the pockets) *Does her*

mother think this is a helpful contribution? Underline text evidence. (No; She said the pockets were to hold tools for war survival, not silly things like poetry. No one appreciates my creative contributions) *Who thinks Libby's contributions are helpful? Underline text evidence.* (Aunt Lucia; Aunt Lucia says my help is important.) *What does Libby do that is helpful?* (She helps her aunt in the bakery.)

High-Utility Words Have students point to the indefinite pronoun *no one* in the third paragraph. Then have partners reread the last paragraph and identify any indefinite pronouns they see. (some, others, any)

Expand Vocabulary *Which words and phrases in the last paragraph help you understand the meaning of* translate? (listen; immigrants; several languages) *What does Aunt Lucia and others help translate?* (the news about the war) *Point to text evidence.* (news; bulletin about fighting in the Pacific)

🔍 Page 334

Organization Ⓐ Ⓒ Ⓣ Say: *Sometimes a narrator describes events that happened before the main action of the story. Have students paraphrase important details and events from the previous page.* (Libby works with her aunt in the bakery; her dad is in the Pacific Ocean; her mom works shifts at a factory) Then have them reread page 334 and paraphrase the events described in each paragraph. Say: *Compare these events to the events on the previous page. Which events happen before Libby helps her aunt in the bakery?* (Libby's parents listen to the radio; Dad joins the navy; Libby gets mad and goes to her room) *Mark these paragraphs.* (the first three) *Which words tell you that Libby is remembering past events?* (I remember; Looking back)

Expand Vocabulary Point to the word *ashamed*. Which sentence helps you understand what it means to feel ashamed? (I wished I hadn't acted so selfishly.)

Theme Reread the second and third paragraphs. *What does Libby do right after her father tells her he is going to join the navy? Mark the text evidence.* ("You can't just leave," I said. I stomped on the floor for emphasis and stormed off to my bedroom.) If necessary, explain the meaning of *stomped* and *stormed off*. Ask: *What can you tell about her feelings from the way she acts?* (She is upset and angry.) *Does she feel the same now? Point to text evidence.* (no; Looking back, I feel ashamed.) *How does Libby change?* (She isn't angry anymore, she is ashamed.) *What does Libby learn about her dad's work in the navy?* (It is important and needed.)

🔍 Page 335

Expand Vocabulary Discuss the word *supplies*. Have students locate *supplies* in the first paragraph and read aloud the sentence. *Which word helps you understand the meaning of* supplies*?* (needs)

Organization Ⓐ Ⓒ Ⓣ Have students reread the page. Ask: *Which paragraph describes events that happened before Libby's dad leaves?* (the third paragraph) *What does Libby remember?* (what her dad said to her, her promise, and the poem she gave to him) *What does Libby decide to do after she remembers these events?* (draw a picture of the cupcakes and send it with a letter to her dad)

Sentence Structure Ⓐ Ⓒ Ⓣ Have students reread the last two sentences in the third paragraph. *What does* it *refer to in the last sentence?* (Libby's poem) *What do the quotation marks show?* (the words of Libby's poem)

Theme Have students review their notes about Libby at the beginning and middle of the story. *What did Libby think about her contributions to the war effort at the beginning of the story?* (She doesn't think she can help.) Then have partners look for details on page 335 that show Libby's thoughts and feelings about her work. (At last, I feel like I've done something right. I think about the money we might make and how it may buy supplies my dad needs.) *What does Libby think about her contributions now?* (She thinks her contributions are helpful.) *What lesson does Libby learn about helping a cause?* (There are many different ways to contribute to a cause.)

RESPOND TO READING

10–20 Minutes   RL.5.1   RL.5.3   W.5.9a   SL.5.1d CCSS

Respond to "Shipped Out"

Have students summarize "Shipped Out" orally to demonstrate comprehension. Then have partners answer the questions on page 336 of the **Interactive Worktext** using the discussion starters. Tell them to use text evidence to support their answers. Have students write the page number(s) on which they found the text evidence for each question.

1. *What does Libby's dad do to help the military during the war?* (He joins the navy and works as a mechanic on battleships. Text Evidence: p. 333, 334)

2. *What does Libby's mom do to help soldiers?* (She makes uniforms for soldiers. She works double shifts to make the uniforms. Text Evidence: p. 333)

3. *What does Libby do to help during the war?* (She helps her aunt in the bakery because her workers joined the army. She makes cupcakes for a military fundraiser. She sends a picture and letter for her dad to share with others. Text Evidence: p. 333, 334, 335)

After students discuss the questions on page 336, have them write a response to the question on page 337. Tell them to use their partner discussions and notes about "Shipped Out" to help them. Circulate and provide guidance.

 Quick Check Do students understand vocabulary in context? If not, review and reteach using the instruction on page 314.

Can students use key details to determine the story's theme? If not, review and reteach using the instruction on page 314 and assign the Unit 6 Week 1 digital mini-lesson.

Can students write a response to "Shipped Out"? If not, provide sentence frames to help them organize their ideas.

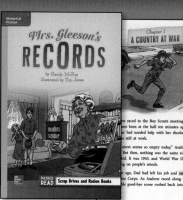

**WEEK 1
LESSON**

3

Scaffolding for **Wonders** Approaching Leveled Reader

Objectives
- Understand and use new vocabulary words
- Read historical fiction
- Recognize and understand theme
- Understand complex text through close reading

Materials
- "Mrs. Gleeson's Records" Apprentice Leveled Reader: pp. 2–8
- Graphic Organizer: Theme

☞ **Go Digital**
- Apprentice Leveled Reader eBook
- Downloadable Graphic Organizer
- Theme Mini-Lesson

BEFORE READING

10–15 Minutes SL.5.1c SL.5.1d L.5.4a L.5.6 **CCSS**

Introduce "Mrs. Gleeson's Records"

- Read the Essential Question on the title page of "Mrs. Gleeson's Records" **Apprentice Leveled Reader**: *How do different groups contribute to a cause? We will read about a boy who learns that the most important contributions are the ones that are hardest to make.*

- Read the title. Have students look at the illustrations. *When do you think this story takes place?* (in the past) *What clues tell you that?* (old-fashioned cars, clothes)

Expand Vocabulary

Display each word below. Say the words and have students repeat them. Then use the Define/Example/Ask routine to introduce each word.

① **adored** (page 6)

Define: loved very much

Example: Kevin *adored* chocolate-covered raisins.

Ask: How would you act if someone gave you a present that you *adored*?

② **demand** (page 5)

Define: a need or a want

Example: Water was in *demand* during the drought.

Ask: What might be in *demand* during hot weather?

③ **flourish** (page 7)

Define: a gesture that attracts the attention of others

Example: My dad presented dinner with a *flourish*.

Ask: Show me how you would give a book to your neighbor with a *flourish*.

④ **permanent** (page 4)

Define: always present, unchanged for a long time

Example: Sue knew her sister was a *permanent* friend.

Ask: Do you think buildings are *permanent*? Why?

DURING READING

20–25 Minutes RL.5.1 RL.5.2 SL.5.1b L.5.5a **CCSS**

Close Reading

🔍 **Pages 2–3**

Prior Knowledge **A C T** Discuss with students what they have learned about World War II and the effect of this global conflict on the United States.

Theme Say: *To identify a story's theme, or overall message, I must pay attention to details about the main character and important events in the story. I need to think about how characters change. On page 2, I see the main character is Andrew. He's a Boy Scout. What important event affects Andrew?* (World War II; his dad enlisted in the Marine Corps a year ago) *I read that the empty streets remind Andrew how life has changed since the war, and it makes him think about his dad. These details will help me identify the theme as I continue to read the story.* Have students record what characters do and say and how events affect them on their Theme chart as they read on.

Organization **A C T** Tell students that a flashback is an event that took place earlier and is inserted into the main action of the story. *Read the last paragraph on page 2. What event on page 3 is told in flashback?* (last time Andrew saw his dad) *What is Andrew remembering?* (what he and his dad said to each other just before Dad left) *How does the author help you know when Andrew's flashback ends?* (The text changes back to regular type.)

Organization (A C T) Ask: *How can you tell that the text at the bottom of page 3 is a letter?* (It starts, "Dear Dad, and it ends "Your son, Andrew".) *When did Andrew write this letter?* (A year ago; this is the first letter Andrew wrote to his dad after he went off to boot camp.)

STOP AND CHECK *Read the question in the Stop and Check box on page 3.* (Andrew's dad left to fight in WWII. Andrew promised to write to him.)

Pages 4–5

Organization (A C T) *When did the events on page 3 take place?* (a year before the main action of the story) *What time period does the next part of the story describe?* (the year after Dad left for war) *What details on page 4 help you understand the time order?* (The Carson household was quieter these days, This year)

Theme *Which characters do you learn about on page 4?* (Andrew's mom, Granddad, a neighbor) *What are the activities of these characters?* (Mom works in a car plant, Granddad grows vegetables, a neighbor preserves tomatoes to raise money) *What do these characters' actions have in common?* (contributing to the war effort)

Vocabulary Read the second sentence in paragraph 2 on page 4. *To what does the author compare Granddad's plants?* (soldiers) *How are the plants similar to soldiers?* (lined up in straight rows) *Which words signal a comparison?* (as straight as) *Why does the author compare plants to soldiers?* (the war is on people's minds)

Organization (A C T) Read the first paragraph on page 5. *How does this part of the story connect to the beginning of the story?* (The story begins with Andrew racing to the Boy Scouts meeting because he is late, and now he has arrived at the meeting.)

Vocabulary *Read the fourth paragraph on page 5. What clues help you understand* scarce? (Things that are *scarce* are being *recycled* and *reused*; they are *badly needed*.) *What does* scarce *mean?* (hard to get, short supply)

Theme *On page 5, what will the Boy Scouts be doing?* (collecting scrap) *Why?* (raise money, provide materials for war) *Who will be contributing?* (the community)

STOP AND CHECK *Read the question in the Stop and Check box on page 5.* (Dad is away at war, Mom works in a car assembly plant, Granddad is always working in the garden, everyone wants to contribute to the war effort.)

Pages 6–7

Genre (A C T) *What story elements on pages 6 and 7 are typical of the time period, 1943?* (wagon, scrap drive, the ladies dressed up like soldiers, record player and records, Mrs. Gleeson's furniture, characters' clothing)

Theme *How does Mrs. Gleeson feel about her new record? How can you tell?* (She is excited. She plays the record for Emily and Andrew and starts dancing to the music.)

Page 8

Vocabulary Read the first paragraph on page 8. *What clues help you understand the meaning of the expression, "kick up your heels"?* (Mrs. Gleeson is happy and dramatic; she and Emily start to dance to the music.)

Organization (A C T) *Read the third paragraph. Is Mrs. Gleeson talking about the past, present, or future?* (future) *Why does Mrs. Gleeson think the record will be important in the future?* (It proves how people kept going during the war, shows how music helped them survive hard times.)

Theme *How does Mrs. Gleeson react when Andrew tells her about the scrap drive?* ("It's important that we all make a contribution.")

STOP AND CHECK *Read the question in the Stop and Check box on page 8.* (They brought tomatoes from Granddad's garden so Mrs. Gleeson could make her stewed tomatoes. They told her about the scrap drive.)

Have partners review their Theme charts for pages 2–8 and discuss what they learned.

✓ Quick Check Do students understand weekly vocabulary in context? If not, review and reteach using the instruction on page 314.

Can students find the elements of theme? If not, review and reteach using the instruction on page 314 and assign the Unit 6 Week 1 digital mini-lesson.

Objectives
- Understand and use new vocabulary words
- Read historical fiction
- Understand theme
- Understand complex text through close reading
- Respond to the selection using text evidence to support ideas

Materials
- "Mrs. Gleeson's Records" Apprentice Leveled Reader: pp. 9–20
- Graphic Organizer: Theme

 Go Digital
- Apprentice Leveled Reader eBook
- Downloadable Graphic Organizer
- Theme Mini-Lesson

Scaffolding for **Wonders** Approaching Leveled Reader

BEFORE READING

5–10 Minutes   SL.5.1c   SL.5.1d   L.5.4a   L.5.6   CCSS

Expand Vocabulary

Display each word below. Say the words and have students repeat them. Then use the Define/Example/Ask routine to introduce each word.

1 donated (page 10)

Define: gave something to help a cause

Example: Many employees *donated* their time and money to set up a tutoring center in the neighborhood.

Ask: What have you *donated* that helped someone?

2 glorious (page 13)

Define: fantastic, very great

Example: Ice cream on a hot day tastes *glorious*.

Ask: What have you seen or done lately that was *glorious*?

3 startled (page 12)

Define: surprised, jolted

Example: The cat *startled* Jeffrey when she jumped in his lap.

Ask: When was the last time you were *startled*?

4 treasured (page 11)

Define: highly valued

Example: Her grandmother's necklace was a *treasured* heirloom.

Ask: What is your most *treasured* possession?

DURING READING

15–20 Minutes   RL.5.1   RL.5.2   SL.5.1b   L.5.5b   CCSS

Close Reading

Page 9

Organization A C T *Read the first sentence on page 9. How long has it been since Mr. Dalwinkle announced the scrap drive?* (about one week) *What happened at the end of Chapter 2 that helps you understand when Chapter 3 takes place?* (Andrew told Mrs. Gleeson that the scrap drive would be next Saturday.)

Theme Review how to identify a story's theme. Have students tell what the characters are doing and saying on page 9. (Everyone is doing something for the scrap drive. Boy Scouts and volunteers are collecting donations from neighbors who feel, "Every little bit helps.") Have students continue to record details in their Theme charts as they read.

Connection of Ideas A C T Have students read the last paragraph on page 9. Paraphrase the proverb, *Waste not, want not*: "If we don't waste what we have, we won't be wanting in the future." *How does this motto connect to the Boy Scouts' scrap drive?* (Nothing is being wasted. Everything is being reused and made into other things that are needed for the war effort.)

Pages 10–11

Theme *Review pages 10 and 11. Why does Mrs. Gleeson want to donate her records?* (They contain shellac that can be reused.) *Does Mrs. Gleeson have anything else to donate?* (no) *Why doesn't Andrew accept her donation?* (He knows how much she loves her records.) *How is Mrs. Gleeson's donation different from the other donations?* (Her treasured music is not junk that could be thrown away.)

STOP AND CHECK *Read the question in the Stop and Check box on page 11.* (He wants Mrs. Gleeson to keep the music she loves so much.)

Pages 12–13

Theme *What happens to Andrew the next time he visits Mrs. Gleeson with Ernie?* (he is caught in a lie, his scoutmaster scolds him, his face burns and he can only say, "well, um…") *What does Andrew learn about Mrs. Gleeson from her actions?* (She is determined to do her part for the war effort and is willing to sacrifice something she loves.)

Organization **A C T** Remind students that the scrap drive took place soon after the story began (page 2). *Find the date on page 13.* (August 1945) *In what year did the story begin?* (1943) *How much time passes from when Andrew misses the sound of music coming from Mrs. Gleeson's house to when the war ends?* (two years) *What details on page 13 help you understand that time is passing?* (sometimes he heard her whistling; the war went on and on; Andrew wrote to his father whenever he could; there were fewer donations now; one glorious day in August 1945; the war was finally over; after three years away, Dad was coming home)

Vocabulary Have students find the word *gruff* at the top of page 12. Explain that it means "rough or harsh." *What clues help you understand the meaning of* gruff? (It describes Mr. Dalwinkle's voice when he yells at Andrew.)

Pages 14–15

Theme Review page 14. *Who are Mrs. Gleeson's "old friends"?* (the Andrews Sisters' music) *What do you think Andrew learned from his experiences supporting the war effort?* (People feel good about being able to contribute to a cause, even when it requires a sacrifice.)

STOP AND CHECK *Read the question in the Stop and Check box on page 14.* (The music is lively and upbeat, the war is over and life has returned to normal, Mrs. Gleeson has gotten back her treasured records.)

AFTER READING

10–15 Minutes   RL.5.1   RL5.2   RL.5.9   W.5.9a   L.5.4a

Respond to Reading

Compare Texts Have students compare what Libby and Andrew learn about contributions to the war effort Ask: *Have you ever made a contribution to a group effort?*

Summarize Have students turn to page 16 and summarize the selection. (Answers should show different ways people contributed to the war effort and what Andrew learned from Mrs. Gleeson's contribution.)

Text Evidence

Have partners work together to answer questions on page 16. Remind students to use their Theme charts.

Theme (Mrs. Gleeson's contribution is especially important because she gives up something dear to her.)

Vocabulary (*Scrap* is any kind of material that can be reused for another purpose.)

Write About Reading (Scrap was used to make military equipment and ammunition. Many people had family fighting in the war. Everyone wanted the U.S. to win the war and wanted to do what they could to help.)

Independent Reading

Encourage students to read the paired selection "Scrap Drives and Ration Books" on pages 17–19. Have them summarize the selection and compare it to "Mrs. Gleeson's Records." Have them work with a partner to answer the "Make Connections" questions on page 19.

✔ *Quick Check* **Can students determine the theme in a story? If not, review and reteach using the instruction on page 314 and assign the Unit 6 Week 1 digital mini-lesson.**

Can students respond to the selection using text evidence? If not, provide sentence frames to help them organize their ideas.

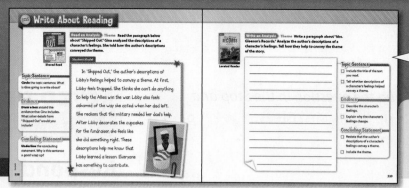

WEEK 1 LESSON 5

Objectives
- Review weekly vocabulary words
- Review theme
- Write an analysis about how an author conveys a theme

Materials
- Visual Vocabulary Cards: 193–200
- Interactive Worktext, pp. 338–339
- Assessment Book, pp. 60–61

☞ **Go Digital**
- Visual Vocabulary Cards
- Theme Mini-Lesson
- Interactive eWorktext

Scaffolding for **Wonders** Reading/Writing Workshop

REVIEW AND RETEACH

5–10 Minutes   RL.5.2 L.5.4a L.5.6 **CCSS**

Weekly Vocabulary

Display one **Visual Vocabulary Card** at a time and ask students to use the vocabulary word in a sentence. If students have difficulty, have them find the word in "Shipped Out" and use context clues to define it.

Comprehension: Theme

I Do Read aloud the last paragraph of page 334 and the first paragraph on page 335 of the **Interactive Worktext**. Say: *I am going to look closely again at what the characters say and do to help me figure out the theme.* Underline: "At first, I'm not interested" and "Then I realize I can make flags with the frosting and berries." Circle: "'Wonderful!' Aunt Lucia says." *Libby's thoughts tell me she changes. Aunt Lucia's response tells me Libby's work is appreciated. These are clues to the story's theme: "People can help in many different ways."*

We Do Display: *Seth wanted to run for class president, but he wasn't sure he would win. "Have confidence," his mom said. "You'll never know if you don't try." Seth was surprised when many classmates voted for him. He won!* Say: *Let's find the theme together. How does Seth feel?* (not sure) *What does his mom say?* ("Have confidence. You'll never know if you don't try.") *What happens to Seth?* (He wins.) *Put these details together. What lesson does Seth learn?* (Be confident in trying new things.)

You Do Display: *Jamal dropped his bag and his papers went everywhere. Some students laughed. Brad turned to them and asked, "How would you feel if that were you?" He helped Jamal.* Have partners identify what the characters do and say to figure out the theme.

WRITE ABOUT READING

25–35 Minutes   W.5.4 W.5.5 W.5.9a **CCSS**

Read an Analysis

- Ask students to look back at "Shipped Out" in the **Interactive Worktext**. Have volunteers review their notes. *How did the author convey the theme, or overall message, of the story?*

- Read aloud the directions on page 338. Read aloud the student model. *Gina's paragraph is not a summary. It's an analysis of how the author's descriptions of a character's feelings conveyed, or showed, a theme or lesson. In an analysis, you ask yourself "how" and "why" questions to think about how the story is told and what readers can learn from it.*

- Review that an analysis includes a topic sentence, text evidence, and a concluding statement. Have students circle the topic sentence in Gina's paragraph. *What information did Gina include in her topic sentence?* (the title; how the author conveyed a theme)

- *The next part of an analysis is* text evidence. *Gina gives details from the story to support what she thinks is the story's theme. Reread Gina's paragraph and draw a box around the text evidence.* (sentences 2–5) *Look back at your notes about "Shipped Out." What other details could be included as text evidence in Gina's analysis?* (Possible answers: Libby thinks no one appreciates her creative contributions to the war effort.)

- *The last part of an analysis is the* concluding statement. *Underline the concluding statement. How is Gina's concluding statement like the topic sentence?* (Both say that the descriptions of Libby's feelings conveyed a theme or lesson.) *How is it different?* (It includes the story's lesson.)

Write an Analysis

Analytical Writing

Guided Writing Read the writing prompt on page 339 together. Have students write about "Mrs. Gleeson's Records" or another text that they read this week. Have them review their notes and Theme charts. *Use the checklist to help you figure out what information to include in each section.* Guide students to ask "how" and "why" questions to analyze text evidence.

Peer Conference Have students read their analysis to a partner. Listeners should identify the strongest text evidence that supports the topic sentence and discuss any sentences that are unclear.

Teacher Conference Check students' writing for complete sentences and text evidence that supports their topic. Review the concluding statement. *Does this sentence tie all of the elements together?* If necessary, have students revise the concluding statement by restating the topic sentence.

Level Up

▲ Approaching Leveled Reader

▲ Reading/Writing Workshop

▲ Apprentice Leveled Reader

▲ Interactive Worktext

IF students read the Apprentice Level Reader fluently and the **Interactive Worktext** Shared Read fluently and answer the Respond to Reading questions

THEN read together the Approaching Level Reader main selection and the **Reading/Writing Workshop** Shared Read from *Reading Wonders*. Have students take notes as they read, using self-stick notes. Then ask and answer questions about their notes.

Writing Rubric

	4	3	2	1
Topic Sentence	There is one clear, focused topic sentence.	Topic sentence is less focused, somewhat clear.	Topic is presented in short phrases.	There is no topic sentence.
Text Evidence	Topic is supported by two or more text details.	Evidence includes only one detail from the text.	Little to no evidence is cited from the text.	No text evidence is included.
Concluding Statement	Clearly restates the topic sentence; wraps up all the details.	Restatement is less focused; attempts to wrap up the details.	Vaguely restates the topic. Doesn't correlate well to text evidence.	There is no conclusion.
Writing Style	Writes in complete sentences. Uses correct spelling and grammar.	Uses complete sentences and phrases. Writing has spelling and grammar errors.	Few or no complete sentences. There are many spelling and grammar errors.	Does not write accurately or in complete sentences.

ASSESSMENT

Weekly Assessment

Have students complete the Weekly Assessment using **Assessment** book pages 60–61.

WEEK 2 LESSON 1

Objectives
- Develop oral language
- Build background about how people can get along
- Understand and use weekly vocabulary
- Read realistic fiction

Materials
- Interactive Worktext, pp. 340–347
- Visual Vocabulary Cards: 201–208

☞ **Go** Digital
- Interactive eWorktext
- Visual Vocabulary Cards

Scaffolding for **WONDERS** Reading/Writing Workshop

WEEKLY CONCEPT

5–10 Minutes   SL.5.1b SL.5.1c CCSS

Talk About It

Essential Question Read aloud the Essential Question on page 340 of the **Interactive Worktext**: *What actions can people take to get along with others?* Explain that to "get along" means to be friendly. Say: *Sometimes people have problems with others. When this happens, people have to work to get along.*

- Discuss the photograph on page 340. Ask: *What two groups of people do you see in the photograph?* (two teams) *Do you think they are friendly when they are playing? Why or why not?* (no; their on different teams)

I Do Say: *One time, when I was watching a soccer game, I saw two players not getting along. Then I saw a referee step between them and talk to both players. The referee calmed them down and made them shake hands. Sometimes a person can step in to help people get along. I will write this in the web on page 341.*

We Do Say: *Now let's look at the photo together to look for another way people can get along. What are the players doing?* (high-fiving, shaking hands) *Is this something that friends or enemies do?* (friends) As students describe the players and their actions, work with them to add words to the web on page 341. Then have them tell how they would get along with a player from another team.

You Do Have partners describe a time when they had a problem with someone and what they did that helped them get along. Have them use some of the words they wrote. Ask: *What problem did you have? What did you do to get along? Did you ask for help from others or solve the problem on your own?*

REVIEW VOCABULARY

10–15 Minutes   L.5.4a L.5.5c L.5.6 CCSS

Review Weekly Vocabulary Words

- Use the **Visual Vocabulary Cards** to review the weekly vocabulary.

- Read together the directions for the Vocabulary activity on page 342 of the **Interactive Worktext**. Then complete the activity.

1 taunting *What does* kind *mean? Does a kind person taunt another person?* (No, a *kind* person is nice.) Have partners ask each other similar questions to help them decide which of the options describe someone who taunts another person. (mean)

2 abruptly Point out the suffix *-ly*. Explain that *-ly* is added to the end of a word and means "in a certain way." (abrupt; ly; in a sudden or unexpected way)

3 ally To help students craft their responses, have them use the sentence starter: *A teammate is an ally because _____.* (Possible answers: a teammate is on the same side as other players; a teammate helps others on the team)

4 conflict Have partners ask each other questions to help them decide which of the words are synonyms for *conflict.* (disagreement, argument)

5 intervene Read the sentence aloud. Then provide the sentence frame: *The girl could intervene between a cat and a bird by _____.* (Possible answers: picking up the cat; bringing the cat inside; standing between them)

6 confident Have students identify the specific actions they are taking to show they are confident. Ask: *How does a confident person stand?* (Possible actions:

standing straight and tall, shoulders back, chin up, head held high)

7 **collided** Ask: *How can you use your hands to show what happens when two things collide?* (Possible actions: clapping hands together, hitting two fists together, hitting a fist against the palm of the other hand)

8 **protective** Have students describe their drawing by using this sentence frame: *A _____ wears protective clothing to work.* (Possible answers: firefighter, police officer, construction worker, football player) Have students describe the protective clothing in their drawing to a partner and tell why the person wears it.

High-Utility Words

Explain that the prefix *un-* means "not" in words such as *unsafe*, *unclear*, or *unkind*. Discuss the meaning of each word. Then have students look at the High-Utility Words passage on page 343 of the **Interactive Worktext**. Have partners circle words with the prefix *un-* in the passage. (unusual, unhappy, unfriendly, unexpected, unsure) Then have students take turns reading the sentences, identifying the words they circled, and discussing the meaning of each word.

> **ELL ENGLISH LANGUAGE LEARNERS**
>
> Write on note cards: *happy, friendly, sure.* Have students say the words aloud and discuss their meanings. Then write *un* on a note card. Have students add the prefix to each word and say the word aloud. Have students use their face and hands to show the meaning of the new word.

READ COMPLEX TEXT

15–20 Minutes RL.5.1 RF.5.4c **CCSS**

Read: "The Bully"

- Have students turn to page 344 in the **Interactive Worktext** and read aloud the Essential Question. Explain that they will read about how one student handles a problem with a bully. Ask: *What is the title?* ("The Bully") *What do the pictures show on the first two pages?* (One boy is angrily staring at another boy who looks scared. A different boy is helping the scared boy pick up his books.) *Use these clues. What do you think will happen to the boy in the blue shirt?* (Possible answer: a bully will pick on him, a friend will help him)

- Read "The Bully" together. Note that the weekly vocabulary words are highlighted in yellow. Expand Vocabulary words are highlighted in blue.

- Have students use the "My Notes" section on page 344 to write questions they have, words they don't understand, and details they want to remember. Model how to use the "My Notes" section. Say: *In the first paragraph, I see the word* victims, *and I am not sure what it means. I will write* victims *with a question mark next to it in the "My Notes" section. On page 346, I wonder why Michael can't believe that Ramon stopped to help him. I will write this question in the "My Notes" section. When we reread the story, I will ask my questions so I better understand what I am reading.*

> **ELL ENGLISH LANGUAGE LEARNERS**
>
> As you read together, have students highlight parts of the story they find confusing or unclear. After reading, help them write questions in the "My Notes" section.

 Quick Check **Can students understand the weekly vocabulary in context? If not, review vocabulary using the Visual Vocabulary Cards before teaching Lesson 2.**

WEEK 2 LESSON

2

Objectives
- Read realistic fiction
- Understand complex text through close reading
- Recognize and understand theme
- Respond to the selection using text evidence to support ideas

Materials
Interactive Worktext, pp. 344–349

☞ **Go** Digital
- Interactive eWorktext
- Theme Mini-Lesson

Scaffolding for McGraw-Hill Reading **Wonders** Reading/Writing Workshop

REREAD COMPLEX TEXT

20–25 Minutes   RL.5.1   RL.5.2   RL.5.4   L.5.5b   L.5.6   **CCSS**

Close Reading: "The Bully"

Reread "The Bully" with students. As you read together, discuss important passages in the text. Have students respond to text-dependent questions, including those in the **Interactive Worktext**.

 Page 345

Theme Say: *As I read, I will pay close attention to details about the characters and what happens to them. When I am done reading, I can put these details together to figure out the theme. Let's look for details about Michael in the first paragraph. Who does Michael think is "trouble" in the first sentence?* (J.T.) *Point to other details in the paragraph that tell you about J.T.* (the school bully; he seemed to enjoy taunting anyone he felt like; he was tall and strong) *What does Michael do when J.T. picks on him? Underline text evidence.* (he usually just took it quietly) *What does Michael's response to J.T. tell you about him?* (Possible answers: He is afraid to stand up to J.T.; he is not as strong as J.T.) *Why is Michael afraid of J.T.?* (J.T. is the school bully. He is tall and strong.)

Expand Vocabulary Have students locate the word *nervous* in the second paragraph and read the sentence aloud. Ask: *What does* nervous *mean?* (afraid, worried) *What clues help you understand the meaning of* nervous? (trying not to tremble) *What did J.T. do and say that made Michael nervous?* (He walked up to him. He snapped at him. He said, "Hey, let me see those books!")

Sentence Structure **ACT** Read the first sentence in the third paragraph. Point out that the first two commas separate J.T.'s actions. Ask: *What did J.T. do first?* (grabbed a math book) *What did he do next?* (looked inside) *What*

did he do last? (shoved it at Michael) *What does the text after the last comma tell you?* (what Michael does after J.T. shoves the book at him)

Connection of Ideas **ACT** Ask a student to reread the first sentence in the fourth paragraph. Ask: *What detail describes what Michael looks like after he drops his books?* (his cheeks turning red) *What does this tell you about the way Michael feels?* (He is embarrassed or angry.) *What detail describes what Michael does after he drops his books?* (half kicked the fallen books) *Why would Michael kick the books? Think about the feeling this action expresses.* (He is angry.) *Why does Michael feel embarrassed and angry?* Have students look for text evidence in the story. (Possible answers: Michael hated the idea that he let J.T. get away with bullying others; a group of students watched as Michael held out the books; he walked away, laughing loudly)

 Page 346

Theme Have students reread the dialogue between Michael and Ramon. *What is Michael's problem?* (J.T. picks on him) *What does Michael want Ramon to do to help him solve the problem? Circle the text evidence.* (What if you just intervene and tell J.T. to stop picking on me?) *Does Ramon think this is a good or bad idea?* (bad) *What does Ramon do and say that tells you this?* (Ramon laughs and walks away. He tells Michael, "Try honey instead.") *Why do you think Ramon responds this way?* (Possible answer: He wants Michael to deal with the bully on his own by getting along rather than by fighting.)

Connection of Ideas **ACT** Ask: *What did Ramon's grandmother say when Ramon had a problem with someone? Circle this saying.* (You can catch more flies with honey than with vinegar.) *What does the saying mean? Circle text evidence.* (Being kind to your enemies may work better than being angry at them.) *What* is Ramon referring to when he says "That's vinegar"? (Michael's idea that Ramon should threaten J.T.) *What does Ramon say Michael should do instead?* (try honey) *Think about the meaning of Ramon's grandmother's saying. What does Ramon mean when he says "Try honey instead"?* (Try being kind instead.)

Expand Vocabulary Have students locate the word *advice* and read the paragraph. Ask: *What word in the paragraph has almost the same meaning as* advice? (suggestion) *Who gave Michael* advice? (Ramon) *What does Michael think about Ramon's advice? Point to text evidence.* (It's good advice; "It sounded like a good plan")

🔍 Page 347

High-Utility Words *Which word in the first paragraph has a prefix?* (unexpected) *What is the prefix?* (un-) *What does the prefix mean?* (not) *What does* unexpected *mean?* (not expected)

Expand Vocabulary Discuss the meaning of *mutter.* Read aloud the fourth paragraph. Ask: *Who muttered?* (J.T.) *Why did he mutter?* (He was speechless because of Michael's kindness.)

Theme *What does Michael do right after J.T. trips? Mark the text evidence.* (He bent down and helped J.T. pick up his books.) *What do you think gave Michael the idea to do this?* (Ramon's advice) *What does J.T. say next?* (He thanks Michael.) *What does J.T. do?* (He took his books and walked away.) *Think about what Michael does and what happens to him. What message about life does the author want to share with readers?* (Possible answer: Being kind is a better way to solve a problem with someone than by fighting back.)

Connection of Ideas Ⓐ Ⓒ Ⓣ Have students reread the fifth paragraph and mark what Ramon says to Michael. (My grandmother would be proud of you.) *Review Ramon's grandmother's advice and Michael's actions. What did Michael do that would make Ramon's grandmother proud?* (He followed her advice and was kind to his enemy.)

RESPOND TO READING

10–20 Minutes RL.5.1 RL.5.3 W.5.9a SL.5.1d

Respond to "The Bully"

Have students summarize "The Bully" orally to demonstrate comprehension. Then have partners answer the questions on page 348 of the **Interactive Worktext** using the discussion starters. Tell them to use text evidence to support their answers. Have students write the page number(s) on which they found the text evidence for each question.

1. *What does Michael usually do when J.T. bullies him?* (Michael takes it quietly. He doesn't stand up to J.T. <u>Text Evidence</u>, p. 345)

2. *How does Ramon help Michael solve his problem with J.T.?* (Ramon gives Michael advice. He tells Michael that being kind would work better than being angry. <u>Text Evidence</u>, p. 346)

3. *What does Michael do at the end of the story to solve his problem with J. T.?* (Michael helps J.T. when J.T. trips and drops his books. J.T. thanks Michael and walks away without bullying him. <u>Text Evidence</u>, p. 347)

After students discuss the questions on page 348, have them write a response to the question on page 349. Tell them to use their partner discussions and notes about "The Bully" to help them. Circulate and provide guidance.

 Quick Check **Do students understand vocabulary in context? If not, review and reteach using the instruction on page 324.**

Can students use key details to determine the theme? If not, review and reteach using the instruction on page 324 and assign the Unit 6 Week 2 digital mini-lesson.

Can students write a response to "The Bully"? If not, provide sentence frames to help them organize their ideas.

WEEK 2 LESSON 3

Objectives
- Understand and use new vocabulary words
- Read realistic fiction
- Recognize and understand theme
- Understand complex text through close reading

Materials
- "Winning Friends" Apprentice Leveled Reader: pp. 2–9
- Graphic Organizer: Theme

☞ **Go** Digital
- Apprentice Leveled Reader eBook
- Downloadable Graphic Organizer
- Theme Mini-Lesson

Scaffolding for **WONDERS** Approaching Leveled Reader

BEFORE READING

10–15 Minutes   SL.5.1c   SL.5.1d   L.5.4a   L.5.6

Introduce "Winning Friends"

- Read the Essential Question on the title page of "Winning Friends" **Apprentice Leveled Reader**: *What actions can we take to get along with others? We will read about how a girl tries to save a friendship.*

- Read the title. Have students look at the images. *Who do you think are the main characters in this story?* (Possible answer: two girls at school)

Expand Vocabulary

Display each word below. Say the words and have students repeat them. Then use the Define/Example/Ask routine to introduce each word.

❶ auditions (page 2)

Define: an interview or try out where people show their skills to be chosen for a role or a job

Example: Jamal was nervous about the *auditions* because he was the youngest drummer trying out.

Ask: Why are there *auditions* to choose performers?

❷ dismissed (page 7)

Define: allowed to leave

Example: The teacher *dismissed* the class for lunch.

Ask: When have you been *dismissed* early from class?

❸ rehearsal (page 3)

Define: a trial performance to prepare for a public appearance

Example: The band played the song at the *rehearsal*.

Ask: What might happen at a *rehearsal* for a play?

DURING READING

20–25 Minutes   RL.5.1   RL.5.2   SL.5.1b   L.5.5b

Close Reading

🔍 **Pages 2–3**

Vocabulary Read the expression *"I made it!"* on page 2. Ask: *What clues in the first paragraph help you understand what "I made it" means?* ("I'm in the school musical!")

Theme Say: *I look for what characters do and say and what happens to them. How do they change from the beginning to the end of the story? These details may be clues to the theme, or message of the story. On page 2, I read that Ella and Jalissa are best friends and they do everything together. Now Jalissa is in a play but Ella is not. I wonder if this will affect their friendship.* As students read, have them record details about what the characters do and say and what happens on their Theme chart.

Genre Ⓐ Ⓒ Ⓣ Have students find the idiom "shoot some baskets" in the fifth paragraph on page 3. Say: *This expression means Ella wants to play basketball with Jalissa. How does Jalissa respond to Ella's invitation?* (Jalissa apologizes and says she has to go practice her lines for the musical.) *Is this dialogue something that real people might say to each other?* (yes)

Connection of Ideas Ⓐ Ⓒ Ⓣ Have students read the last paragraph on page 3. *What happened earlier that causes Ella to have these thoughts?* (Ella felt left out when the girls talked about the musical. Then Jalissa turned down Ella's invitation to shoot baskets and hurried off to read lines with them.) *What does Ella hope doesn't last much longer?* (Jalissa talking only about the musical; the musical taking up all of Jalissa's time)

⊚ Pages 4–5

Connection of Ideas Ⓐ Ⓒ Ⓣ Have students read the first paragraph on page 4. *Why does Ella feel that Jalissa wants her to feel left out?* (All Jalissa talked about was the musical.) *What does Ella do to find out how Jalissa really feels?* (She asks her, "Don't you want to hang out with me anymore?") *How do Ella's feelings change?* (She thinks if she gets to know Jalissa's friends she won't feel left out.)

Vocabulary Have students find the word *hesitantly* in paragraph 4 on page 4. Explain that it means "uncertainly." *Why is Ella speaking* hesitantly*?* (She is afraid that Jalissa doesn't like her anymore.)

STOP AND CHECK Read the question in the Stop and Check box on page 4. (Ella hopes she and Jalissa can spend time together like they used to.)

Theme *What does Ella do on page 4 that shows how she feels about her friendship with Jalissa?* (She asks Jalissa to come to the lake, she asks Jalissa if she wants to be friends, she agrees to go to the rehearsal) *Why does Ella do these things?* (She doesn't want to lose her friendship.) *Does Jalissa feel the same way? Why?* (No. She's busy with her new friends, not thinking about Ella.)

⊚ Pages 6–7

Theme Have students read page 6 and the first paragraph on page 7. *How does Jalissa act toward Ella?* (Jalissa ignores Ella and only talks to her new friends.) *What does Jalissa and her friends do that affects Ella?* (They didn't invite Ella to the slumber party. They leave the rehearsal together and leave Ella behind.)

Connection of Ideas Ⓐ Ⓒ Ⓣ Have students read the last two paragraphs on page 7. *Why is Ella close to tears?* (She was hoping to spend time with Jalissa, but Jalissa tells her to go away.) *What has Jalissa been doing since she got into the play? Give examples from pages 2 to 6.* (talking about the musical, practicing lines, slumber party with girls in the play, rehearsals) *Why do you think Jalissa tells Ella to go away?* (Ella's not in the musical. Jalissa only thinks about the musical.)

Genre Ⓐ Ⓒ Ⓣ *Read the dialogue on page 7. How are the characters like people in real life?* (They use language that sounds real: *What are you guys up to now? Cool. I'll catch you tomorrow.* They have feelings like real people.)

⊚ Pages 8–9

Vocabulary *What expression on page 8 means that Ella has an idea?* (as if a light switched on in Ella's head)

Connection of Ideas Ⓐ Ⓒ Ⓣ Have students review page 8. *What reason does Ella give her mother for wanting to enter the contest with Jalissa?* ("If we play a violin duet, we might win!") *What is the most important reason Ella wants to enter the contest?* (Playing the violin together would remind Jalissa that they were best friends.) *Reread the first paragraph on page 2. Do you think Ella's reasons for entering the contest are reasons that Jalissa might share? Why?* (No. Jalissa won the audition to be in the musical and might not be interested in entering another contest. All she thinks about is the musical and doesn't seem to worry about Ella being her best friend.)

Theme Have students review page 9. *What does Ella say to convince Jalissa to play a duet with her?* ("The prize is a trip to Wonderworld!" "Come on. We can practice when you don't have rehearsals." "Please? We can play a piece we already know.")

STOP AND CHECK Read the question in the Stop and Check box on page 9. (Jalissa doesn't want anything to get in the way of the musical so she wants to think about being in the talent show with Ella.)

Have partners review their Theme charts for pages 2–9 and discuss what they learned.

✔️ *Quick Check* Do students understand weekly vocabulary in context? If not, review and reteach using the instruction on page 324.

Can students use details to determine the theme? If not, review and reteach using the instruction on page 324 and assign the Unit 6 Week 2 digital mini-lesson.

Objectives
- Understand and use new vocabulary words
- Read realistic fiction
- Recognize and understand theme
- Understand complex text through close reading
- Respond to the selection using text evidence to support ideas

Scaffolding for **McGraw-Hill Reading Wonders** Approaching Leveled Reader

Materials
- "Winning Friends" Apprentice Leveled Reader: pp. 10–20
- Graphic Organizer: Theme

☞ **Go Digital**
- Apprentice Leveled Reader eBook
- Downloadable Graphic Organizer
- Theme Mini-Lesson

BEFORE READING

5–10 Minutes SL.5.1c SL.5.1d L.5.4a L.5.6

Expand Vocabulary

Display each word below. Say the words and have students repeat them. Then use the Define/Example/Ask routine to introduce each word.

① announcement (page 14)

Define: a communication or statement

Example: The mayor made an *announcement* about the Thanksgiving holiday parade.

Ask: Who makes *announcements* at school?

② half-heartedly (page 10)

Define: without any real interest or enthusiasm

Example: He *half-heartedly* accepted the second-place trophy.

Ask: Why might someone enter a contest *half-heartedly*?

③ politely (page 15)

Define: with good manners

Example: Our class listened *politely* to the speaker.

Ask: How would you behave *politely* at a party?

④ struggle (page 11)

Define: a battle or difficult effort

Example: It was a *struggle* for the climber to reach base camp before nightfall.

Ask: What can a *struggle* teach you about life?

DURING READING

15–20 Minutes RL.5.1 RL.5.2 SL.5.1b L.5.5b

Close Reading

🔍 **Pages 10–11**

Theme Ⓐ Ⓒ Ⓣ Review with students how to identify the theme of a story. *Read page 10. How does Jalissa act as she talks with Ella about the contest?* (isn't enthusiastic, half-heartedly agrees to meet to practice, seems bored) *What reason does Jalissa give for having those feelings?* (She doesn't know if it's a good idea, the musical is a lot of work.) *How does Jalissa act toward Ella the next day? Why?* (She criticizes Ella's selection of a Bach concerto. She's not interested in doing anything but the play.) Have students record details about the characters in their Theme charts as they read the selection.

Connection of Ideas Ⓐ Ⓒ Ⓣ *What did Ella want to say to Jalissa, but didn't?* (Ella felt like telling her to forget it. She also felt like saying, "And you bring a better mood.") *Reread the third and fifth paragraphs. What thoughts stoppe d Ella from expressing her feelings?* (Jalissa had agreed to enter the contest. Maybe her attitude would change once they got started.) *Reread the last paragraph on page 9.* Have students discuss the connection between Ella's thoughts on page 9 with her behavior on page 10. (Ella remains upbeat because the contest is her plan for saving their friendship.)

Vocabulary Have students read the fifth paragraph on page 11. *What does the expression* in ages *mean in the first sentence?* (for a long time) *What did Ella feel for the first time in ages?* (they were friends again) *Had it been a long time?* (no, a little over a week) *Why does Ella feel that it had been a long time?* (They used to be together every day; she misses their friendship a lot.)

Theme *What happens to Ella when the girls begin playing their violins?* (The music makes Ella forget their conflict.) *Read the last paragraph on page 11. What is Ella determined to do?* (work to keep their friendship alive)

Pages 12–13

Vocabulary Have students find *cast* in the second paragraph of page 12. Explain that it means the people in a play. *What other meanings do you know for* cast? (something that holds a broken limb; throw)

STOP AND CHECK Have students read page 12. *Read the question in the Stop and Check box on page 12.* (She had a meeting but Ella insisted on practicing more.)

Connection of Ideas (A)(C)(T) Have students read the first three paragraphs on page 13. *How does Jalissa realize that she hasn't been a good friend to Ella?* (Playing the violin with Ella made her remember how they used to hang out together.) *What does Jalissa do?* (She apologizes.) *Why hasn't Jalissa been a good friend?* (She was excited to be in the play; she forgot about Ella.)

Theme *Reread the fourth paragraph. What does Jalissa ask Ella?* (Do you think you can forgive me?) *How does Ella respond?* (Of course! You're my best friend.) *What do the characters learn?* (Being patient and admitting to mistakes helped them get along and stay friends.)

Pages 14–15

Sentence Structure (A)(C)(T) Have students read the second paragraph on page 14. *When did Ella and Jalissa walk across the stage?* (after the announcer introduced them)*What did they do after they walked across the stage?* (stopped in the center, lifted their violins, began playing)

Connection of Ideas (A)(C)(T) *Read the third and fourth paragraphs on page 15. How is Ella feeling? Why?* (unsure, she wanted to win first prize) *How is Jalissa feeling? Why?* (happy; restoring her friendship with Ella was more important to her than winning first prize)

STOP AND CHECK Read the question in the Stop and Check box on page 15. (After Jalissa told Ella she was sorry, and Ella forgave Jalissa, the girls spent time together practicing for the contest.)

AFTER READING

10–15 Minutes   RL.5.1   RL5.2   RL.5.9   W.5.9a   L.5.4a   **CCSS**

Respond to Reading

Compare Texts Have students compare what the characters in "Winning Friends" and "The Bully" do to get along with others. Then say: *Tell about some things you do to get along with others.*

Summarize Have students turn to page 16 and summarize the selection. (Answers should show what Ella does to save her friendship with Jalissa.)

Text Evidence

Have partners work together to answer questions on page 16. Remind students to use their Theme charts.

Theme (Ella doesn't give up on her friend. She keeps trying, even when Jalissa makes it hard. She asks Jalissa to enter a talent contest with her.)

Vocabulary (*attitude* means "mood")

Write About Reading (The contest is how Ella fought for their friendship. It made Jalissa realize she'd been a bad friend. Making an effort and admitting mistakes won back their friendship. Getting along is more important than winning a contest.)

Independent Reading

Encourage students to read the paired selection "Empathy: The Answer to Bullying" on pages 17–19. Have them summarize the selection and compare it to "Winning Friends." Have them work with a partner to answer the "Make Connections" questions on page 19.

✓ *Quick Check* **Can students identify the theme of a story? If not, review and reteach using the instruction on page 324 and assign the Unit 6 Week 2 digital mini-lesson.**

Can students respond to the selection using text evidence? If not, provide sentence frames to help them organize their ideas.

WEEK 2 LESSON 5

Objectives
- Review weekly vocabulary words
- Review theme
- Write an analysis about how well an author developed a realistic story

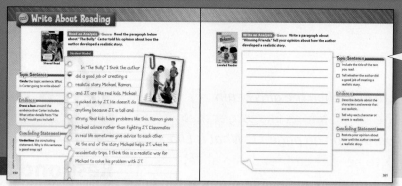

Materials
- Visual Vocabulary Cards: 201–208
- Interactive Worktext, pp. 350–351
- Assessment Book, pp. 62–63

☞ **Go Digital**
- Visual Vocabulary Cards
- Theme Mini-Lesson
- Interactive eWorktext

Scaffolding for **WONDERS** Reading/Writing Workshop

REVIEW AND RETEACH

5–10 Minutes   RL.5.2 L.5.4a L.5.6

Weekly Vocabulary

Display one **Visual Vocabulary Card** at a time and ask students to use the vocabulary word in a sentence. If students have difficulty, have them find the word in "The Bully" and use the context clues to define it.

Comprehension: Theme

I Do Display: *Maria wanted to be in the school play. She didn't think she would get the part so she wasn't going to try out. Her friend Teresa knew how much Maria wanted to be in the play. "You'll never know if you could get a part if you don't try." Maria tried out and got the part she wanted.* Say: *I am going to look for clues to the theme.* Underline the first two sentences. Say: *These details tell what Maria thinks. Theresa says,"You'll never know if you don't try." What happens to Maria as a result? She tries and gets a part. These are clues to the theme: Try and you may succeed.*

We Do Display: *Paul didn't like playing soccer, but he felt left out because his friends were on a team. The coach said, "There's another way to be a part of a team. You can cheer us on!" Paul was happy to cheer on his friends.* Ask: *What details tell about Paul?* (He didn't like playing soccer, but he felt left out.) *What does the coach say?* (There's another way to be a part of a team.) *What does Paul do as a result?* (cheers on the team) *What happens to him?* (He is happy.) *What is the theme?* (There are many ways to be a part of a team.)

You Do Have partners reread the passage on page 343 of the **Interactive Worktext** and use clues about the characters and what happens to figure out the theme.

WRITE ABOUT READING

25–35 Minutes   W.5.1a W.5.1d W.5.4 W.5.5 W.5.9a

Read an Analysis

- Ask students to look back at "The Bully" in the **Interactive Worktext**. Have volunteers review their notes about what the characters do and say. Ask: *How did the author develop a realistic story?*

- Read aloud the directions and student model on page 350. Say: *Carter is writing an analysis, or a detailed description, of how the author develops realistic characters and events in "The Bully." He is giving his opinion about how the author made the story realistic .*

- Say: *An analysis always includes certain elements. Circle the topic sentence. Ask: What important information has Carter included in this sentence?* (text's title; his opinion of how the author created a realistic story)

- Say: *Another part of an analysis is text evidence. Carter describes details about the characters and events that are realistic. He tells why each character or event is realistic. Reread the model and draw a box around the text evidence.* (sentences 2–6) Say: *Look back at "The Bully." What other details might be included as text evidence?* (When J.T. made Michael drop his books, Michael's face turned red and he half-kicked the books. A real kid would be embarrassed and angry in this situation, too.)

- Say: *The final part of an analysis is the concluding statement. Underline the concluding statement. Ask: How is the concluding statement like the topic sentence?* (Both include "I think" and say that the story is realistic.) *Which words does Carter use to wrap up all the text evidence?* ("this is a realistic way for Michael to solve his problem with J.T.")

Write an Analysis

Analytical Writing

Guided Writing Read the writing prompt on page 351 together. Have students write about "Winning Friends" or another realistic fiction text they read this week. Say: *Use the checklist. It will help you figure out the right information to include in each section.* Remind students to use examples from the story that support their opinion. Guide students to ask "how" and "why" questions.

Peer Conference Have students read their analysis to a partner. Listeners should identify the strongest text evidence that supports the topic sentence and discuss any sentences that are unclear.

Teacher Conference Check students' writing for complete sentences and how well they cited text evidence to support their opinion. Review the concluding statement. *Does this sentence tie all of the elements together?* If necessary, have students revise the concluding statement by restating the topic sentence.

Level Up

▲ Approaching Leveled Reader

▲ Reading/Writing Workshop

▲ Apprentice Leveled Reader

▲ Interactive Worktext

IF students read the Apprentice Level Reader fluently and the **Interactive Worktext** Shared Read fluently and answer the Respond to Reading questions

THEN read together the Approaching Level Reader main selection and the **Reading/Writing Workshop** Shared Read from *Reading Wonders*. Have students take notes as they read, using self-stick notes. Then ask and answer questions about their notes.

Writing Rubric

	4	3	2	1
Topic Sentence	Topic sentence presents a clear opinion.	Topic sentence presents an opinion, somewhat clearly.	Topic is presented in short phrases; opinion is unclear.	There is no topic sentence; no opinion is presented.
Text Evidence	Opinion is supported by two or more text details.	Opinion is only supported by one detail from the text.	Little to no evidence from the text supports opinion.	No text evidence is included; does not support opinion.
Concluding Statement	Clearly restates an opinion; wraps up all the details.	Restatement is less focused; attempts to wrap up the details.	Vaguely restates opinion. Doesn't correlate well to text evidence.	There is no conclusion.
Writing Style	Writes in complete sentences. Uses correct spelling and grammar.	Uses complete sentences and phrases. Writing has spelling and grammar errors.	Few or no complete sentences. There are many spelling and grammar errors.	Does not write accurately or in complete sentences.

ASSESSMENT

Weekly Assessment

Have students complete the Weekly Assessment using **Assessment** book pages 62–63.

WEEK 3 LESSON 1

Objectives
- Develop oral language
- Build background about how living things are adapted to their environment
- Understand and use weekly vocabulary
- Read expository text

Materials
- Interactive Worktext, pp. 352–359
- Visual Vocabulary Cards: 209–216

☞ **Go** Digital
- Interactive eWorktext
- Visual Vocabulary Cards

Scaffolding for **WONDERS** Reading/Writing Workshop

WEEKLY CONCEPT

5–10 Minutes   SL.5.1b SL.5.1c

Talk About It

Essential Question Read aloud the Essential Question on page 352 of the **Interactive Worktext**: *How are living things adapted to their environment?* Explain that when something is adapted to an environment, it fits with the environment. Say: *Sometimes we can learn how an animal is adapted to its environment by looking at the animal closely.*

- Discuss the photograph on page 352. Ask: *What kind of animal do you see in the photograph?* (an insect) *What kind of environment do you see around the animal?* (plants, leaves)

  I Do Say: *I am going to look closely at the photograph and think of words I can use to describe the insect and its environment. I see that the insect is green. I see that leaves around the insect are green, too. I will write "green insect" and "green leaves" in the web on page 353.*

  We Do Say: *Now let's look at the photo together and think of other words we can use to describe the insect and the environment. What do you notice about the shape of the insect?* (It is long and pointed at one end; it looks like a leaf.) *How does the insect fit with its environment?* (It looks like the leaves around it.) As students brainstorm words, work with them to add words to the web on page 353.

  You Do Have partners talk about how the insect's color, shape, and body parts keep it safe from animals that would want to catch it. Have them use some of the words they wrote. Ask: *How do you think the insect's color helps it hide? How do you think the insect's shape helps it hide? How do you think its legs help it get away from other animals?*

REVIEW VOCABULARY

10–15 Minutes   L.5.4a L.5.4b L.5.6

Review Weekly Vocabulary Words

- Use the **Visual Vocabulary Cards** to review the weekly vocabulary.

- Read together the directions for the Vocabulary activity on page 354 of the **Interactive Worktext**. Then complete the activity.

1 **dormant** Ask: *What does dormant mean?* (at rest or not active) Explain that antonyms are words with opposite meanings. Have partners discuss the meanings of the options to decide which word is an antonym. (active)

2 **cache** *Look around the room and choose a good place to cache a book.* Then have students write their choice using the sentence starter: *I would cache my favorite book _____.* (<u>Possible answers</u>: inside my desk, inside my backpack)

3 **hibernate** Ask: *Does an animal hunt when it hibernates?* (no) Have partners ask each other similar questions to determine which words tell what an animal does when it hibernates. (rest)

4 **insulates** Ask: *Which piece of clothing better insulates against the cold: a coat or a sweater?* (coat) *a visor or a hat?* (hat) *shoes or boots?* (boots) *Why?* (<u>Possible answer</u>: They are thicker and warmer.) Have partners compare how a blanket and a sheet insulates against the cold. Ask: *Which is better?* (A blanket is better.) *Why?* (It is thicker and warmer than a sheet.)

5 **forage** Ask students if they have ever seen a squirrel or similar animal forage for food. Provide pictures as necessary. Have students use the sentence starter:

When squirrels forage for food, they _____. (Possible answer: dig under leaves and twigs to look for seeds and nuts)

6 **frigid** Have students identify the specific actions they are using to demonstrate how they would feel on a *frigid* day. Ask: *What happens to your face, hands, and body when you are outside on a frigid day?* (Possible answer: My teeth chatter. My body shivers. I wrap my arms around my chest.)

7 **adaptation** Point out the suffix *-ation*. Explain that *-ation* is added to the end of a word to mean "act or a process." Help students put together the word parts to figure out the meaning of *adaptation*. (the act of adapting or changing)

8 **agile** Have partners brainstorm types of athletes and performers who must be agile. Have students use the following sentence frame to describe their drawings: *A _____ is agile because _____.* (Drawings will vary; responses may include: a basketball player, a gymnast, a tightrope walker.) Have students compare their drawings and decide which ones show the most agile performers or athletes.

High-Utility Words

Explain that a suffix is a word part that is added to the end of a word and changes its meaning. Have students look at the High-Utility Words activity on page 355 of the **Interactive Worktext**. Read aloud the definition and examples. Have partners circle words with the suffixes *-ion* and *-ation* in the passage. (celebration, decorations, directions, transportation, relaxation, conversation) Ask students to add *-ion* to the word *correct* and tell its meaning. Repeat with *-ation* and the word *present*.

> **ELL ENGLISH LANGUAGE LEARNERS**
>
> Have students raise their hands and repeat after you when they hear you say a word with the suffix *-ion* or *-ation*. Use the following words: *correction, decorate, direction, presentation, transport*.

READ COMPLEX TEXT

15–20 Minutes | RI.5.1 RF.5.4c **CCSS**

Read: "Mysterious Oceans"

- Have students turn to page 356 in the **Interactive Worktext** and read aloud the Essential Question. Explain that they will read about sea creatures that live in deep oceans. Ask: *What is the title?* (Mysterious Oceans) *What does the photograph on page 356 show?* (a fish) *Where do you think this photograph was taken?* (deep in the ocean)

- Read "Mysterious Oceans" together. Note that the weekly vocabulary words are highlighted in yellow. Expand Vocabulary words are highlighted in blue.

- Have students use the "My Notes" section on page 356 to write questions they have, words they don't understand, and details they want to remember. Model how to use the "My Notes" section. Say: *I can write notes about questions I have as I read. In the first paragraph on page 357, I am not sure what the word* enclosed *means. I will write* enclosed *with a question mark beside it in the "My Notes" section. As I continue to read this page, I am not sure how there can be mountains on the ocean floor. I'll write a question:* What do underwater mountains look like? *When we reread the story, I will ask my questions so I better understand what I am reading.*

> **ELL ENGLISH LANGUAGE LEARNERS**
>
> As you read together, have students highlight parts of the text they have questions about. After reading, help them write questions in the "My Notes" section.

 Quick Check Can students understand the weekly vocabulary in context? If not, review vocabulary using the **Visual Vocabulary Cards** before teaching Lesson 2.

WEEK 3 LESSON 2

Objectives
- Read expository text
- Understand complex text through close reading
- Recognize and understand cause and effect
- Respond to the selection using text evidence to support ideas

Materials
Interactive Worktext, pp. 356–361

Go Digital
- Interactive eWorktext
- Cause and Effect Mini-Lesson

Scaffolding for **Wonders** Reading/Writing Workshop

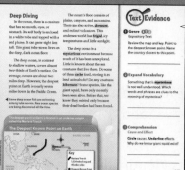

REREAD COMPLEX TEXT

20–25 Minutes   RI.5.1   RI.5.3   RI.5.4   L.5.4a   L.5.6   **CCSS**

Close Reading: "Mysterious Oceans"

Reread "Mysterious Oceans" with students. As you read together, discuss important passages in the text. Have students respond to text-dependent questions, including those in the **Interactive Worktext**.

Page 357

Genre Ⓐ Ⓒ Ⓣ Have students reread the last sentence in the second paragraph. Say: *The author included a map to help readers understand this text.* Have students draw a box around the title of the map. Ask: *What does the title tell you about the map?* (The map shows the deepest known point on Earth.) Point to the labels on the map. Ask: *What important places do the labels show?* (countries and oceans) Say: *Read the caption and the key. Then turn to a partner and take turns asking questions about the map key.* Then have partners match the key symbol to the deepest known point on Earth. Have students locate the label that names the country closest to this point. (Philippines)

Expand Vocabulary Have students locate the word *mysterious*. Discuss its meaning. Ask: *What clues in this paragraph help you understand the meaning of mysterious?* (much of it has been unexplored; little is known)

Cause and Effect Reread the last paragraph. Say: *The author used cause and effect to show what happened and why it happened.* Model using text evidence to find a cause and effect in the paragraph. Say: *I read, "The deep ocean is a mysterious environment because much of it has been unexplored."* Because much of it has been

unexplored *is the cause.* The deep ocean is a mysterious environment *is the effect.* Because *is the signal word.* Give other examples of signal words: *as a result, since, when,* and *so.* Help students find another cause and effect in the paragraph. Have them circle the cause, underline the effect, and draw a box around any signal words. (Cause: Because their dead bodies had been found. Effect: we knew they existed; signal word: because) Ask: *Why do we know that giant squid exist? Give two reasons.* (they have been seen alive; dead bodies have been found)

Page 358

Vocabulary Explain the meanings of domain-specific words, such as *submersible, pincers, bioluminous, lure,* and *prey.* Then have partners look for clues to the meanings in the text. (submersible: submarine; pincers: catch; bioluminous: naturally glowing; lure: attract; prey: grab)

Genre Ⓐ Ⓒ Ⓣ Have students reread the captions under each photograph. Ask: *Which caption describes an adaptation? Draw a box around this caption.* (A striated frogfish (left) lures its prey. Its nose is an adaptation to life in the deep ocean.) *Which part of the creature is an adaptation to life in the deep ocean?* (its nose) *How does it help the animal survive? Use clues from the caption and photograph.* (It helps it lure its prey.)

High-Utility Words Have students locate a word in the first paragraph that has the suffix *-ation.* (exploration) Ask: *What does this word mean?* (the act of exploring)

Cause and Effect Have students reread the first sentence. *What was invented?* (the submarine) *What happened because the submarine was invented?* (Scientists could then reach the deep ocean floor.) Point out the cause and help students mark the effect. Have students reread the next sentence and mark a cause and effect. Ask: *How much of the underwater world have scientists seen?* (only five percent of the underwater world) *Why* *have they only seen five percent of the underwater world? What is the cause?* (exploration has been difficult)

Expand Vocabulary Have students locate the word *anticipate* and reread the sentence. Ask: *What did scientists anticipate about life in the deep ocean?* (few sea creatures survive in the deep ocean) *What did scientists know that caused them to anticipate this? Circle text evidence.* (Scientists knew that food sources rarely drift down from the ocean's surface.)

Page 359

Vocabulary Have students find the word *vents* in the first paragraph. Ask: *What is a vent? What clue helped you understand the meaning of the word?* (cracks)

Expand Vocabulary Have students find the word *bursts* in the first paragraph. Ask: *What is a word in this sentence that means almost the same thing as* bursts? (gushes)

Genre ⒶⒸⓉ Have students mark a heading. (Heated Habitats) *What does a heading tell you?* (what the section will be about) *What heated habitat did you learn about in this section?* (areas around vents in the ocean floor)

Vocabulary Help students find and pronounce the word *chemosynthesis.* Have partners look for clues in the paragraph to understand its meaning. (transform the chemicals from the vents into food)

Cause and Effect Have students reread the second paragraph and find an example of a cause and effect. Point out that there is no signal word. If students have difficulty ask: *What effect do bacteria have on the Pompeii worm? What causes the Pompeii worm to be insulated?* (Cause: the Pompeii worm has a coat of bacteria on its back; Effect: this coat insulates it from heat) Next, have students reread the next two paragraphs to find other examples. Have them identify any signal words. (Cause: Because of chemosynthesis; Effect: animals are able to flourish in these habitats. Signal word: *Because;* Cause: scientists keep exploring; Effect: they are sure to discover many more ocean species; Signal word: *If*) *Review the causes and effects you marked. Why are animals able to flourish near vents?* (because of chemosynthesis)

RESPOND TO READING

10–20 Minutes   RI.5.1   RI.5.2   RI.5.3   W.5.9b   SL.5.1d   ⒸⒸⓈⓈ

Respond to "Mysterious Oceans"

Have students summarize "Mysterious Oceans" orally to demonstrate comprehension. Then have partners answer the questions on page 360 of the **Interactive Worktext** using the discussion starters. Tell them to use text evidence to support their answers. Have students write the page number(s) on which they found the text evidence for each question.

1. *How is a deep-sea starfish different than a starfish that lives in shallow water?* (It grows larger and is more aggressive; Text Evidence: page 358)

2. *How do anglerfish get food in the deep ocean?* (An anglerfish gets food by using a bioluminous lure on its head to attract fish; it uses huge jaws to quickly grab prey; Text Evidence: page 358)

3. *How do creatures that live near ocean vents get food?* (Many creatures transform the chemicals from the vents into food; creatures that don't transform the chemicals into food, eat the ones that do; Text Evidence: page 359)

After students discuss the questions on page 360, have them write a response to the question on page 361. Tell them to use their partner discussions and notes about "Mysterious Oceans" to help them. Circulate and provide guidance.

 Quick Check Do students understand vocabulary in context? If not, review and reteach using the instruction on page 334.

Can students use signal words and key details to determine a cause and an effect? If not, review and reteach using the instruction on page 334 and assign the Unit 6 Week 3 digital mini-lesson.

Can students write a response to "Mysterious Oceans"? If not, provide sentence frames to help them organize their ideas.

WEEK 3 LESSON

3

Objectives
- Understand and use new vocabulary words
- Read expository text
- Recognize and understand cause and effect
- Understand complex text through close reading

Materials
- "Cave Creatures" Apprentice Leveled Reader: pp. 2–9
- Graphic Organizer: Cause and Effect

☞ **Go** Digital
- Apprentice Leveled Reader eBook
- Downloadable Graphic Organizer
- Cause and Effect Mini-Lesson

Scaffolding for **McGraw-Hill Reading Wonders** Approaching Leveled Reader

BEFORE READING

10–15 Minutes   SL.5.1c   SL.5.1d   L.5.4a   L.5.6   CCSS

Introduce "Cave Creatures"

- Read the Essential Question on the title page of "Cave Creatures" **Apprentice Leveled Reader**: *How are living things adapted to their environment? We will read facts about how adaptations help animals live in a special environment.*

- Read the title of the main read. Have students look at the images. Ask: *How do you know that this is expository text?* (gives information, includes photos, captions, a map, diagrams) *What do you think it will be about?* (caves and animals living in caves)

Expand Vocabulary

Display each word below. Say the words and have students repeat them. Then use the Define/Example/Ask routine to introduce each word.

① **attract** (page 6)

Define: pull toward; make something move towards

Example: Magnets *attract* some metals.

Ask: What colors *attract* your attention?

② **echo** (page 5)

Define: a repeated sound

Example: The songs of birds *echo* through the forest.

Ask: How can you make your voice *echo*?

③ **particular** (page 3)

Define: the one place or thing you are talking about

Example: Let's pick a *particular* place to meet.

Ask: Why might you need a *particular* book?

④ **shelter** (page 4)

Define: something that covers or protects

Example: When it began to rain, we moved our picnic under the *shelter*.

Ask: What would you do if you needed *shelter* from a rainstorm?

DURING READING

20–25 Minutes   RI.5.1   RI.5.3   SL.5.1b   L.5.6   CCSS

Close Reading

Pages 2–3

Vocabulary Read page 2. Have students locate the word *formations* in the third paragraph and read the caption. Explain that *formations* has the root word *form*, and it means shapes. *What words in the caption help you figure out the meaning of* formations? (rock shapes)

Connection of Ideas Ⓐ Ⓒ Ⓣ Say: *Look at the text feature and map on page 3. Read the map title. What does the map show?* (where Mammoth Cave and Krubera Cave are located in the world) *Read the first two sentences of page 2. How do the map and text feature relate to the beginning of the Introduction?* (They give more information about where caves are found in the world, and how large and deep they can be.)

Cause and Effect Read the first paragraph on page 3. Say: *There is no signal word, but I notice a cause and its effect. The text says:* Other animals live in caves all the time. *This is a cause. The effect is that these animals have developed adaptations that help them survive in a cave.* Have students record the causes and effects they identify on their charts as they read the selection.

Pages 4–5

Vocabulary Help students figure out the meaning of challenging domain-specific vocabulary words by using context, word roots, or the glossary. For example, in the first paragraph on page 4, the difficult word *trogloxenes* is followed by its definition: *which means cave visitors.*

Genre ACT Say: *Look at the photos and read the captions on page 5.* Explain that *hibernation* is a form of deep sleep. Ask: *How do caves help the Virginia big-eared bat in the winter?* (Caves give them a place to hibernate.)

Cause and Effect Read the last paragraph on page 5. Say: *There is no signal word, but I notice a cause and its effect. The text says:* Air inside the cave is warmer than the air outside. *This is a cause.* Ask: *What happens because the air inside a cave is warmer than the air outside? What is the effect?* (A cave helps insulate animals from the cold, so animals such as bears spend the winter in a cave.)

Pages 6–7

Cause and Effect Have students read the second paragraph on page 6. Ask: *Are there any signal words?* (as a result) Ask: *Why do animals living in the twilight zone have adaptations to help them survive?* (There isn't a lot of food or light in the twilight zone.) *What happens to animals because there isn't a lot of food or light in the twilight zone?* (They have adaptations to help them survive.) *What is the cause and effect?* (Cause: There isn't a lot of food or light in the twilight zone; Effect: Animals living here have adaptations to help them survive.)

Vocabulary Have students find the word *prey* in the last paragraph on page 6. Ask: *What clues in the sentences can help you understand the meaning of* prey? (make it come close, tiny insects, stuck in the web until it is hungry)

Cause and Effect Have students read the last paragraph on page 6. Ask: *What signal word do you see?* (when) *What is the cause and effect?* (Cause: tiny insects get close to the light; Effect: they get stuck in the web.)

Genre ACT Have students look at the photo and read the text at the bottom of page 7. Explain that crickets usually make chirping sounds. Ask: *How has this cricket adapted to life in a cave?* (it's quiet; uses air puffs to communicate) *Why?* (to avoid being eaten)

Pages 8–9

Cause and Effect Have students read the second paragraph on page 8. Ask: *What is the cause and effect in this paragraph?* (Cause: Molds, fungi, and bacteria break down the material. Effect: Microscopic animals can eat it.) *What signal word helped you to find the cause and effect relationship?* (After)

STOP AND CHECK Read the question in the Stop and Check box on page 8. (Animals must adapt because it is cool and damp in caves, and caves lack food and light.)

Main Idea and Key Details Have partners use key details to paraphrase what they have read about how creatures adapt to living in caves. (Bats use echolocation to find their way around. Glowworms light up their stomachs to attract insects to eat. Cave weta use long antennae to move around and find food.)

Genre ACT Say: *Look at the diagram on page 9. What does it show?* (how cave creatures get food) Say: *Trace the arrows from tiny insects and mites.* Ask: *What cave creatures eat tiny insects and mites?* (beetles, centipedes, spiders) Ask: *Why are small insects important to bats and frogs?* (The small insects are food for bats and frogs.) Have partners trace relationships on the cave food diagram and discuss them.

Have partners review their Cause and Effect charts for pages 2–9 and discuss what they learned.

Quick Check Do students understand weekly vocabulary in context? If not, review and reteach using the instruction on page 334.

Can students use details to determine a cause and its effect? If not, review and reteach using the instruction on page 334 and assign the Unit 6 Week 3 digital mini-lesson.

WEEK 3 LESSON 4

Objectives
- Understand and use new vocabulary
- Read expository text
- Recognize and understand cause and effect
- Understand complex text through close reading
- Respond to the selection using text evidence to support ideas

Scaffolding for **Wonders** Approaching Leveled Reader

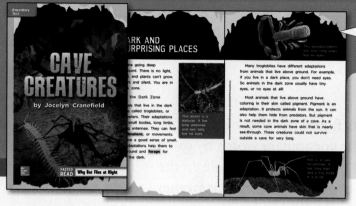

Materials
- "Cave Creatures" Apprentice Leveled Reader: pp. 10–24
- Cause and Effect Graphic Organizer

☞ **Go** Digital
- Apprentice Leveled Reader eBook
- Downloadable Graphic Organizer
- Cause and Effect Mini-Lesson

BEFORE READING

5–10 Minutes   SL.5.1c SL.5.1d L.5.4a L.5.6

Expand Vocabulary

Display each word below. Say the words and have students repeat them. Then use the Define/Example/Ask routine to introduce each word.

1 fumes (page 15)

Define: unpleasant or harmful gases

Example: The *fumes* from the truck exhaust made me choke.

Ask: What would you do if you smelled *fumes* inside a garage?

2 hostile (page 14)

Define: unfavorable, harmful, or difficult

Example: Very cold places are *hostile* environments for most animals.

Ask: How might you prepare for *hostile* weather conditions?

3 vibrations (page 10)

Define: rapid back and forth movements; shaking

Example: The strong *vibrations* shook our house during the earthquake.

Ask: Show me how you would cause the strings of a guitar to *vibrate*.

DURING READING

15–20 Minutes   RI.5.1 RI.5.3 SL.5.1b L.5.6

Close Reading

🔍 **Pages 10–11**

Genre Ⓐ Ⓒ Ⓣ Have students read the second paragraph on page 10 and look at the photo on this page. Ask: *Why do you think the author included this photo?* (help readers understand animals' adaptations)

Cause and Effect Have students read the first paragraph on page 11. Point out the signal word, *if*. Ask: *What happens if animals live in a dark place?* (They don't need eyes.) Say: *The cause is* you live in a dark place. *The effect is* you don't need eyes. Point out the signal word, *so*. Ask: *What happens to animals that live in a dark zone and don't need eyes?* (They have tiny eyes or no eyes at all.) *What is the cause?* (They live in a dark zone.) *What is the effect?* (They have tiny eyes or no eyes.) Have students add this to their Cause and Effect charts.

Vocabulary Have students locate the word *pigment* in the second paragraph on page 11. Ask: *What word helps you understand the meaning of* pigment? (coloring)

Cause and Effect Have students read the last paragraph on page 11. Ask: *What signal words are included in this paragraph?* (as a result) *What is the cause?* (pigment is not needed in the dark zone of a cave) *What is the effect?* (some cave animals have adapted to have see-through skin)

🔍 **Pages 12–13**

Connection of Ideas Ⓐ Ⓒ Ⓣ Say: *Look at the chart on page 12. Read the title. What does the chart show?* (zones of a cave) *Name the three zones.* (entrance, twilight, dark) Have partners review chapter 1 and discuss the types of animals that live in each zone.

Vocabulary Have students find the word *aquatic* in the first paragraph on page 13. Explain that it means living in water, and contains the Latin root *aqua*. Ask: *What clues help you understand the meaning of* aquatic? (streams and ponds)

Cause and Effect Have students read page 13. Point out that although there are no signal words, there are cause and effect relationships. *In paragraph one, the cause is that many caves have underground streams and ponds. What happens because there is water in caves? What is the effect?* (Aquatic animals can live in caves.)

Pages 14–15

Cause and Effect Have students read the first paragraph on page 15. Ask: *Why have microscopic creatures been found in ice caves?* (They can survive temperatures below zero degrees.) Say: *Tell the cause and effect.* (Cause: They can survive temperatures below zero; Effect: Microscopic creatures have been found in ice caves.) Ask: *Is there a signal word in this cause and effect relationship?* (no)

STOP AND CHECK Read the question in the Stop and Check box on page 15. (Cave creatures have different adaptations from animals living above ground. Cave creatures might have tiny eyes and be colorless as an adaptation to dark caves.)

Pages 16–17

Cause and Effect Have students read the first two sentences on page 17. Ask: *Why have scientists found some rare species living in caves?* (These animals can't leave the caves very easily.) *What signal word did you notice?* (so) *What is the cause?* (Animals that live deep inside caves can't leave very easily.) *What is the result?* (Scientists have found some rare species living there.)

Main Idea and Key Details Say: *I read that scientists go deep underground to learn about cave creatures. They bring creatures out of the caves. They study the creatures in their laboratories.* Ask: *What do these details have in common? What is the main idea?* (Scientists found ways to learn about cave animals and their adaptations.)

AFTER READING

10–15 Minutes   RI.5.1 RI.5.2 RI.5.9 W.5.9b L.5.4a

Respond to Reading

Compare Texts Have students compare how creatures adapt to living in the deep ocean with how creatures adapt to living in caves. Then say: *What is one way in which a deep ocean environment is similar to a dark zone environment?* (There is no or little light in both.)

Summarize Have students turn to page 18 and summarize the selection. (Answers should include details from the selection about adaptations to life in a cave.)

Text Evidence

Have partners work together to answer questions on page 18 using their Cause and Effect charts.

Cause and Effect (some creatures have tiny eyes and no pigment because they have adapted to living in a dark cave; signal words: *if, so, as a result*)

Vocabulary (live with; *found there, survive*)

Write About Reading (Troglobites' adaptations include small bodies, long limbs, and long antennae. Extremophiles adapted to temperatures in ice caves.)

Independent Reading

Encourage students to read the paired selection "Why Bat Flies at Night" on pages 19–21. Have them summarize the selection and compare it to "Cave Creatures." Have them work with a partner to answer the "Make Connections" questions on page 21.

✓ *Quick Check* **Can students identify cause and effect relationships in an article? If not, review and teach using the instruction on page 334 and assign the Unit 6 Week 3 digital mini-lesson.**

Can students respond to the selection using text evidence? If not, provide sentence frames to help them organize their ideas.

WEEK 3 LESSON 5

Objectives
- Review weekly vocabulary words
- Review cause and effect
- Write an analysis about how well an author uses causes and effects to explain a topic

Scaffolding for **Wonders** Reading/Writing Workshop

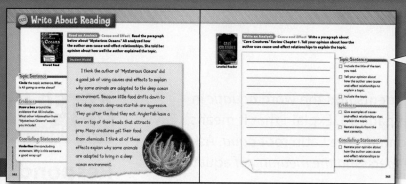

Materials
- **Visual Vocabulary Cards:** 209–216
- **Interactive Worktext,** pp. 362–363
- **Assessment Book,** pp. 64–65

☞ **Go** Digital
- **Visual Vocabulary Cards**
- **Cause and Effect Mini-Lesson**
- **Interactive eWorktext**

REVIEW AND RETEACH

5–10 Minutes   RI.5.3   L.5.4a   L.5.6

Weekly Vocabulary

Display one **Visual Vocabulary Card** at a time and ask students to use the vocabulary word in a sentence. If students have difficulty, have them find the word in "Mysterious Oceans" and use context clues to define it.

Comprehension: Cause and Effect

I Do Display and read aloud: *A gecko's feet have ridges. So a gecko can stick to smooth surfaces.* Ask: *Why can a gecko stick to smooth surfaces?* A gecko's feet have ridges. Write *cause* above the first sentence and *effect* above the second sentence. Circle the word *so. Authors may organize ideas using causes and effects. They often use signal words, such as* because, so, *and* since. Point out that sometimes there are no signal words. Display: *A gecko's feet have ridges. This adaptation helps it stick to smooth surfaces.* Point out that there is still a cause (gecko's feet have ridges) and effect (it sticks to smooth surfaces) but no signal words.

We Do Display: *Spider monkeys have long arms. As a result, they can swing through the trees quickly.* Ask: *What do spider monkeys have?* (long arms) *What can they do because they have long arms?* (swing through the trees quickly) *What is the cause?* (spider monkeys have long arms) *What is the effect?* (they can swing through the trees quickly) *What is the signal word or phrase?* (as a result)

You Do Have partners reread the passage on page 355 of the **Interactive Worktext**. Have partners identify causes and effects, and point out any signal words.

WRITE ABOUT READING

25–35 Minutes   W.5.1a   W.5.1d   W.5.4   W.5.5   W.5.9b

Read an Analysis

- Ask students to look back at "Mysterious Oceans" in the **Interactive Worktext**. Have volunteers review the causes and effects in the selection. Ask: *How did the author's use of cause-and-effect relationships help you understand the topic of the text?*

- Read aloud the introduction on page 362. Read aloud the student model. Say: *Ali is writing an analysis, or a detailed description, of how the author uses cause-and-effect relationships. Ali's analysis supports her opinion about how well the author uses causes and effects to explain the topic.*

- Say: *An analysis always includes certain elements. Circle the topic sentence. What information has Ali included in this sentence?* (text's title; her opinion about how the author uses causes and effects; the topic)

- Say: *Another part of an analysis is* text evidence. *Ali gives examples of causes and effects in the text that support her opinion.* Have students reread the model and draw a box around the text evidence. (sentences 2–4) Say: *Look back at your notes about "Mysterious Oceans." What other causes or effects could Ali have included as text evidence?* (Possible answer: With their huge jaws, anglerfish can quickly and easily grab their prey.)

- Say: *The final part of an analysis is the* concluding statement. *Underline the concluding statement.* Ask: *How is the concluding statement like the topic sentence?* (Both include "I think" and restate the topic.) *Which words does Ali use to wrap up all the examples from the text?* ("all of these effects")

Write an Analysis

Guided Writing Read the writing prompt on page 363 together. Have students write about "Cave Creatures" or another nonfiction selection they read this week. Have them review their Cause and Effect charts. Say: *Use the checklist to help you figure out the information to include in each section.* Guide students to ask "how" and why" questions as they analyze text evidence.

Peer Conference Have students read their analysis to a partner. Listeners should identify the strongest text evidence that supports the topic sentence and discuss any sentences that are unclear.

Teacher Conference Check students' writing for complete sentences and text evidence that supports their opinion. Review the concluding statement. *Does this sentence tie all of the elements together?* If necessary, have students revise the concluding statement by restating the topic sentence.

Level Up

▲ Approaching Leveled Reader

▲ Reading/Writing Workshop

Apprentice Leveled Reader

▲ Interactive Worktext

IF students read the Apprentice Level Reader fluently and the **Interactive Worktext** Shared Read fluently and answer the Respond to Reading questions

THEN read together the Approaching Level Reader main selection and the **Reading/Writing Workshop** Shared Read from *Reading Wonders*. Have students take notes as they read, using self-stick notes. Then ask and answer questions about their notes.

Writing Rubric

	4	3	2	1
Topic Sentence	Topic sentence presents a clear opinion.	Topic sentence presents an opinion, somewhat clearly.	Topic is presented in short phrases; opinion is unclear.	There is no topic sentence; no opinion is presented.
Text Evidence	Opinion is supported by two or more text details.	Opinion is only supported by one detail from the text.	Little to no evidence from the text supports opinion.	No text evidence is included; does not support opinion.
Concluding Statement	Clearly restates an opinion; wraps up all the details.	Restatement is less focused; attempts to wrap up the details.	Vaguely restates opinion. Doesn't correlate well to text evidence.	There is no conclusion.
Writing Style	Writes in complete sentences. Uses correct spelling and grammar.	Uses complete sentences and phrases. Writing has spelling and grammar errors.	Few or no complete sentences. There are many spelling and grammar errors.	Does not write accurately or in complete sentences.

ASSESSMENT

Weekly Assessment

Have students complete the Weekly Assessment using **Assessment** book pages 64–65.

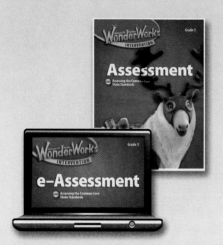

▶ **Mid-Unit Assessment,** pages 112–119

▶ **Fluency Assessment,** pages 266–281

Unit 6 Mid-Unit Assessment

CCSS TESTED SKILLS

✔ COMPREHENSION	✔ VOCABULARY
• Theme RL.5.2	• Context Clues L.5.4a
• Theme RL.5.2	
• Cause and Effect RI.5.3	

Using Assessment and Writing Scores

⟲ RETEACH	IF …	THEN …
COMPREHENSION	Students answer 0–5 multiple-choice items correctly …	… reteach tested skills using instruction on pages 364–371.
VOCABULARY	Students answer 0–2 multiple-choice items correctly …	… reteach tested skills using instruction on page 364.
WRITING	Students score mostly 1–2 on weekly writing rubrics throughout the unit…	… reteach writing using instruction on pages 372–373.

Fluency Assessment

Conduct assessments individually using the differentiated fluency passages in Assessment. Students' expected fluency goal for this Unit is 129–149 WCPM with an accuracy rate of 95% or higher.

Weeks 4 and 5

Monitor students' progress on the following to inform how to adjust instruction for the remainder of the unit.

ADJUST INSTRUCTION	
ACCESS COMPLEX TEXT	If students need more support for accessing complex text, provide additional modeling of prompts in Lesson 2 of Week 4, pages 340–341, and Week 5, pages 350–351. After you model how to identify the text evidence, guide students to find text evidence in Lessons 3 and 4 in Week 4, pages 342–345, and Week 5, pages 352–355.
FLUENCY	For those students who need more support with Fluency, focus on the Fluency lessons in the Foundational Skills Kit.
WRITING	If students need more support incorporating text evidence in their writing, conduct the Write About Reading activities in Lessons 3 and 4 as group writing activities.
FOUNDATIONAL SKILLS	Review student's individualized progress in *PowerPAL for Reading* to determine which foundational skills to incorporate into your lessons for the remainder of the unit.

Teach and Model WORKTEXT

Objectives
- Develop oral language
- Build background about how our actions impact the world
- Understand and use weekly vocabulary
- Read a biography

Scaffolding for **Wonders** McGraw-Hill Reading Reading/Writing Workshop

Materials
- Interactive Worktext, pp. 364–371
- Visual Vocabulary Cards: 217–224

☞ **Go** Digital
- Interactive eWorktext
- Visual Vocabulary Cards

WEEKLY CONCEPT

5–10 Minutes   SL.5.1b SL.5.1c   CCSS

Talk About It

Essential Question Read aloud the Essential Question on page 364 of the **Interactive Worktext**: *What impact do our actions have on our world?* Explain that when you have an impact on the world, you cause it to change. Say: *Our actions can have positive and negative impacts on the world.*

- Discuss the photograph on page 364. Ask: *What are these people picking up?* (bottles) *What are they putting the bottles into?* (recycling bins)

I Do   Say: *I am going to look closely at the photograph and think about another way people's actions impact the world. I wonder why the people have to pick up the bottles from the ground. Other people must have littered, or thrown their bottles on the ground, rather than throwing them away. Littering is an action that has a negative impact on the world. I will write "pick up litter" in the web on page 365.*

We Do   Say: *Now let's look at the photo and think of words to describe what the people in the photograph are doing and how their actions are making a difference. What are the people doing?* (recycling; picking up bottles) *How are their actions making a difference in the world around them?* (They are cleaning up the world around them.) *Will their actions have a positive or negative impact?* (positive) Guide students to add these words to the web on page 365.

You Do   Have partners talk about something they have done that has caused a change in the world around them. Have them use some of the words they wrote. Ask: *What did you do? Why did you do it? Did your actions have a positive or negative impact on the world?*

REVIEW VOCABULARY

10–15 Minutes   L.5.4a L.5.4b L.5.6   CCSS

Review Weekly Vocabulary Words

- Use the **Visual Vocabulary Cards** to review the weekly vocabulary.

- Read together the directions for the Vocabulary activity on page 366 of the **Interactive Worktext**. Then complete the activity.

1 **restore**   Have students use the sentence starter: *To restore a broken plate, I would _____.* (glue the pieces back together)

2 **glistening**   *Does the word* dull *have the same meaning as* glistening? (no) *Does the word* dull *have the opposite meaning of* glistening? (yes) Have partners ask each other questions to help them decide which of the words mean *glistening* and which of the words mean the opposite of *glistening.* (Circle: shining; Underline: dull)

3 **native**   Have partners explain their choice using the sentence starter: *_____ is native to California because _____.* (Amy; she was born there)

4 **plantations**   *Can a banana come from a plantation?* (yes) Have partners ask each other questions to help them decide which items might come from a plantation. (banana, cotton)

5 **urged**   Have students use the following sentence frame: *To urge his players, a coach might say, "_____."* (Possible answers: You can do it! You'll get better! You'll be a winning team!) *Now say these words aloud. Use your hands, face, and voice to show how a coach would urge players.* Then have students form the past tense.

6 **influence** Have partners discuss the options to help them decide which of the activities might influence them to see a movie. (seeing an ad for the movie, reading a good review) Then have students tell their partner which option would have the strongest influence.

7 **export** Have students use the following sentence frame: *A company can export goods by _____ or by _____.* (Possible answers: cargo plane, cargo ship, freighter, truck, freight train)

8 **landscape** Ask students to describe the landscape of the region in which they live. Show pictures or maps as necessary. Give examples of landforms, such as mountains, deserts, valleys, forests, swamps, coasts. Have students compare their drawings and label any landforms. (Drawings will vary, but should include a drawing of a landscape with labels.)

High-Utility Words

Have students look at the High-Utility Words activity on page 367 of the **Interactive Worktext**. Read the definition and example. Give other examples, such as *excitement* and *placement* and discuss their meanings. Then have partners circle words in the passage that have the suffix -*ment*. (improvement, accomplishment, arrangement, involvement, achievement) Write the following sentence frames. Have students complete each sentence by adding the suffix –*ment* to the underlined word: *When I announce the time, I make an _____. When I encourage my friend to practice, I give him _____.* (announcement, encouragement). Have students read their sentences.

ELL ENGLISH LANGUAGE LEARNERS

Write base words such as *improve, involve,* and *place* and the suffix *ment* on index cards. Display *improve* and *ment* together and say *improvement*. Have students repeat. Then have them add the suffix to the other base words and say each word aloud.

READ COMPLEX TEXT

15–20 Minutes   RI.5.1   RF.5.4c **CCSS**

Read: "Words to Save the World"

- Have students turn to page 368 in the **Interactive Worktext** and read aloud the Essential Question. Explain that they will read about a woman who worked to save the environment. Ask: *What is the title?* ("Words to Save the World: The Work of Rachel Carson") *What do the photographs show?* (a woman using binoculars and a microscope) *Use these clues. What do you think Rachel Carson was interested in?* (science, writing)

- Read "Words to Save the World" together. Note that the weekly vocabulary words are highlighted in yellow. Expand Vocabulary words are in blue.

- Have students use the "My Notes" section on page 368 to write questions they have, words they don't understand, and details they want to remember. Model how to use the "My Notes" section. *I can write notes about questions I have as I read. In the first paragraph on page 369, I read that Rachel Carson "raised awareness about environmental issues." I wonder what "raised awareness" means. I will write this phrase with a question mark next to it in the "My Notes" section: As I read, I will write notes about Rachel Carson that I want to remember when we talk about the biography.*

ELL ENGLISH LANGUAGE LEARNERS

Have students highlight text they have questions about as you read together. After reading, help them write notes and questions in the "My Notes" column.

 Quick Check Can students understand the weekly vocabulary in context? If not, review vocabulary using the **Visual Vocabulary Cards** before teaching Lesson 2.

WEEK 4 LESSON 2

Objectives
- Read a biography
- Understand complex text through close reading
- Recognize and understand problem and solution text structure
- Respond to the selection using text evidence to support ideas

Scaffolding for **WONDERS** Reading/Writing Workshop

Materials
Interactive Worktext, pp. 368–373

👉 **Go** Digital
- Interactive eWorktext
- Problem and Solution Mini-Lesson

REREAD COMPLEX TEXT

20–25 Minutes   RI.5.1   RI.5.3   RI.5.4   L.5.4a   L.5.6   **CCSS**

Close Reading: "Words to Save the World: The Work of Rachel Carson"

Reread "Words to Save the World: The Work of Rachel Carson" with students. As you read together, discuss important passages in the text. Have students respond to text-dependent questions, including those in the **Interactive Worktext**.

🔍 Page 369

Genre **ACT** Read the first paragraph aloud. Explain the meaning of domain-specific words and phrases such as *raised awareness* and *environmental movement*. Then ask: *Who is Rachel Carson?* (a writer) *What did she write?* (*Silent Spring*) *Why is her book important today?* (It began an environmental movement that continues today.)

Problem and Solution Say: *The author tells about Rachel Carson's work by describing problems she faced and the steps she took to solve the problems.* Model using text evidence to identify problems and solutions in the text. *In the first paragraph, I read: "Rachel Carson raised awareness about environmental issues." So, a problem Rachel encountered was a problem in the environment. Raising awareness, or informing others, was one way Rachel tried to solve the problem. What did the government do to try to solve the problem?* (The U.S. government passed laws to protect the environment.)

High-Utility Words *Point to the word* government *in the first paragraph. What does* govern *mean?* (rule) *What is the suffix?* (-ment) *What does it mean?* ("the act of") *Put the meanings of the word parts together to figure out the meaning of the word. What does* government *mean?* (the act of being governed or ruled)

Expand Vocabulary Discuss the word *encourage*. Have students locate *encouraged* and read the sentence. *What was Rachel encouraged to do?* (explore the landscape surrounding the family's farm) *What effect did this have on Rachel?* (Rachel's love of nature grew.)

Connection of Ideas **ACT** Discuss with students the meaning of the heading, "Early Influences." Then have students reread the second paragraph. Ask: *What did Rachel's interests as a child lead her to study in school?* (writing and biology) *Draw a box around the paragraph that describes Rachel's career.* (last paragraph) *Give examples of jobs Rachel did.* (Possible answers: created radio programs for the U.S. Bureau of Fisheries; editor; wrote articles about nature; wrote three books about the ocean) *From her work, what do you think she was still interested in as an adult?* (writing, nature)

Genre **ACT** *Review the photo and captions on page 368 and 369. What do the photos and captions tell you about Rachel Carson?* (Possible answers: She gathered information, she worked alone; she used tools such as microscopes and binoculars to gather facts.)

🔍 Page 370

Problem and Solution *Reread the first paragraph. Who were Olga and Stuart Huckins?* (Rachel's friends) *What did they own?* (land reserved for wildlife) *What was the problem with using DDT on their land?* (DDT seemed to harm birds.) *What caused the problem?* (the spraying of DDT on their land) *What did the Huckins do to try to solve the problem?* (wrote a letter to Rachel)

Problem and Solution Read the first sentence in the second paragraph. Explain that *In response* means to take action. *What was the first thing Rachel did to begin solving the problem?* (hired people to study the Huckins's claim) *Did this help to solve the problem?* (no) *Why not?* (the study was taking a long time) *What did Rachel decide* *to do next?* (study the problem alone and publish her findings) *Circle two more steps Rachel took to solve the problem.* (encouraged readers to speak out against the chemical companies; Rachel spoke at the committee's meetings and gave facts to influence its decisions)

Connection of Ideas **A C T** *Review the second and third paragraphs. In* Silent Spring, *what did Rachel urge readers to imagine?* (a world without songbirds) *Why did Rachel have readers do this?* (because chemicals were harming birds) *What effect did* Silent Spring *have on readers? Look for details in the third paragraph.* (They spoke out against chemical corporations. They demanded an investigation. They asked the government to control pesticide use.)

Page 371
Connection of Ideas **A C T** *Review page 370. What did Rachel claim about DDT and other pesticides?* (DDT caused damage to birds and eggs; pesticides were dangerous) *What did chemical companies do after Rachel made these claims? Give two examples.* (Possible answers: They tried to speak out against Rachel's claims; published reports that put down her ideas; they created television commercials that told people their products were safe.) *How did these actions affect people's opinions about pesticide use?* (They did not change many people's opinions.)

Expand Vocabulary Help students paraphrase Rachel Carson's quote in the second paragraph. Discuss the meaning of *alter. Which word in this quote describes one way a pesticide can alter nature?* (destroy)

Problem and Solution Have students reread the second paragraph. *What problem did Rachel worry about?* (that once pesticides poisoned an area, it might be impossible to restore it back to the way it had been before) *How did Rachel's words and efforts help solve the problem?* (They led the government to control the use of some pesticides.) If students have difficulty, ask: *What did Rachel's words and efforts lead the government to do?*

RESPOND TO READING

10–20 Minutes   RI.5.1   RI.5.3   W.5.9b   SL.5.1d

Respond to "Words to Save the World: The Work of Rachel Carson"

Have students summarize the biography orally to demonstrate comprehension. Then have partners answer the questions on page 372 of the **Interactive Worktext** using the discussion starters. Tell them to use text evidence to support their answers. Have students write the page number(s) on which they found the text evidence for each question.

1. *What did Rachel do when she learned about the Huckins's problem with pesticide?* (She hired people to study the problem; she studied the problem alone, and published her findings. Text Evidence: p. 370)

2. *What effect did* Silent Spring *have on readers' opinions of pesticides?* (Readers asked the government to control pesticide use. Text Evidence: p. 370)

3. *How did Rachel's words affect the government's actions on pesticide use?* (Her book led the president to create a committee to study the problem. Her words led the government to control the use of some pesticides. Text Evidence: pp. 369, 370, 371)

After students discuss the questions on page 372, have them write a response to the question on page 373. Tell them to use their partner discussions and notes on the selection to help them. Circulate and provide guidance.

 Quick Check Do students understand vocabulary in context? If not, review and reteach using the instruction on page 346.

Can students use key details to determine a problem and a solution? If not, review and reteach using the instruction on page 346 and assign the Unit 6 Week 4 digital mini-lesson.

Can students write a response to "Words to Save the World"? If not, provide sentence frames to help them organize their ideas.

WEEK 4 LESSON 3

Objectives
- Understand and use new vocabulary words
- Read a biography
- Recognize and understand problem and solution
- Understand complex text through close reading

Scaffolding for **Wonders** Approaching Leveled Reader

Materials
"Marjory Stoneman Douglas: Guardian of the Everglades" Apprentice Leveled Reader: pp. 2–6
- Graphic Organizer: Problem/Solution

☞ **Go** Digital
- Apprentice Leveled Reader eBook
- Downloadable Graphic Organizer
- Problem and Solution Mini-Lesson

BEFORE READING

10–15 Minutes   SL.5.1c SL.5.1d L.5.4a L.5.6

Introduce "Marjory Stoneman Douglas: Guardian of the Everglades"

- Read the Essential Question on the title page of "Marjory Stoneman Douglas: Guardian of the Everglades" **Apprentice Leveled Reader**: *What impact do our actions have on our world? We will read about a woman who worked to save a wilderness area.*

- Read the title. Have students look at the images. *What type of wilderness area do you think this will be about?* (grassy, swampy)

Expand Vocabulary

Display each word below. Say the words and have students repeat them. Then use the Define/Example/Ask routine to introduce each word.

① **issues** (page 6)

Define: things to be concerned about

Example: We discussed *issues,* such as pollution.

Ask: What *issues* are important to you?

② **orator** (page 4)

Define: speaker

Example: The politician was a brilliant *orator.*

Ask: What makes someone a good *orator*?

③ **plight** (page 5)

Define: a dangerous or difficult situation

Example: The *plight* of the lost dog worried Steven.

Ask: Why should we care about the *plight* of lost pets?

④ **useless** (page 2)

Define: not able to be used

Example: The ripped balloon is now *useless.*

Ask: Why is a balloon with a hole in it *useless*?

DURING READING

20–25 Minutes   RI.5.1 RI.5.5 SL.5.1b L.5.6

Close Reading

🔍 Pages 2–3

Connection of Ideas Ⓐ Ⓒ Ⓣ *Read page 2. What details in the first paragraph describe how some people viewed the Everglades?* (useless swamp, too wet for growing crops or building houses) *What details in the second paragraph describe how Marjory Stoneman Douglas viewed the Everglades?* (special, beauty, miracle, expanse, shining and slow-moving) *How might these different views cause a conflict?* (People like Douglas would want to preserve the Everglades and others wouldn't care.)

Vocabulary Read Douglas's quote and point out the word *expanse*. Explain that an *expanse* is a wide, open area. *What details and features in the text help you understand what the Everglades look like?* (the glades seemed to go on forever, water flowed all across the area; photo shows grass and water)

Problem and Solution Explain that when we read a biography, we should try to identify the problems the person faced, and how she solved them. Say: *As I review page 2, I think that figuring out how to protect the Everglades is a problem that Marjory will want to solve, but I'll continue to read to check for more evidence.*

Have students record evidence of problems and solutions on their Problem and Solution charts as they read the selection.

Genre Ⓐ Ⓒ Ⓣ *Review page 3. How can you tell this selection is a biography?* (Douglas is a real person, there are facts about her life, a photo shows Marjory as a child) *What part of Marjory's life will be the focus of this biography?* (her involvement with the Everglades)

Connection of Ideas Ⓐ Ⓒ Ⓣ *On page 3, what interests did Marjory have during her childhood?* (the library, learning new things from books) *What did those interests teach her to do?* (research) *How did Marjory's childhood interests influence her life as an adult?* (She used her research skills to become a writer.)

🔍 Pages 4–5

Connection of Ideas Ⓐ Ⓒ Ⓣ Have students read page 4. *What two roles did Marjory have in college?* (editor, orator) *What did she do at the department store?* (taught) *What skills did Marjory use in those roles?* (speaking, she gave speeches; writing and editing; teaching) *Why do you think the author chose to include these experiences in the biography?* (Marjory will use these skills later to communicate her ideas.)

Problem and Solution *On page 4, what problem did Marjory face after she graduated from college in 1912?* (She didn't know what to do next.) *What made it difficult for her to decide what to do?* (Back then women were not encouraged to have careers.) *How did Marjory find a way to use her education?* (She worked in a department store, but used her skills to teach grammar and math to the sales clerks.)

Connection of Ideas Ⓐ Ⓒ Ⓣ Have students review the first two sentences on page 3 and then read the information about Frank Stoneman on page 5. Ask: *In what ways was Marjory's father an early influence on her becoming the "Guardian of the Everglades"?* (Marjory moved to Miami because her father lived there. He was the editor of *The Miami Herald* and hired her to write. She learned that he wanted to save the Everglades.)

Cause and Effect Have students read the second paragraph on page 5. *What effect did World War I have on Marjory?* (She joined the Red Cross.) *What experience did she have in the Red Cross that had a lasting effect?* (She saw the terrible conditions that refugees faced during the war.) *How did these experiences change Douglas?* (Douglas was always sympathetic to people in trouble.)

🔍 Page 6

Problem and Solution Have students read page 6. *What problem did the city of Miami have after World War I?* (population increased, so it needed more land) *How did land developers decide to solve that problem?* (drain the wetlands of the Everglades) *What did Douglas do to try to protect the Everglades?* (She wrote a column in *The Miami Herald* urging that the Everglades be made into a national park.)

Connection of Ideas Ⓐ Ⓒ Ⓣ *What work did Douglas do as the assistant editor of* The Miami Herald? (wrote a column about important issues) *What work did Douglas do for the Red Cross?* (wrote about the work of the Red Cross and urged people to support their efforts) *How were both jobs similar?* (She wrote to inform people of issues and encourage them to support efforts to improve the lives of others.)

STOP AND CHECK *Read the question in the Stop and Check box on page 6.* (She wrote about living conditions, women's rights, and protecting the Everglades.)

Have partners review their Problem and Solution charts for pages 2–6 and discuss what they learned.

✅ ***Quick Check*** **Do students understand weekly vocabulary in context? If not, review and reteach using the instruction on page 346.**

Can students find problems and solutions? If not, review and reteach using the instruction on page 346 and assign the Unit 6 Week 4 digital mini-lesson.

Objectives
- Understand and use new vocabulary
- Read a biography
- Recognize and understand problem and solution
- Understand complex text through close reading
- Respond to the selection using text evidence to support ideas

Materials
- "Marjory Stoneman Douglas: Guardian of the Everglades" Apprentice Leveled Reader: pp. 7–20
- Graphic Organizer: Problem/Solution

☞ **Go** Digital
- Apprentice Leveled Reader eBook
- Downloadable Graphic Organizer
- Problem and Solution Mini-Lesson

Scaffolding for **Wonders** Approaching Leveled Reader

BEFORE READING

5–10 Minutes   SL.5.1c   SL.5.1d   L.5.4a   L.5.6

Expand Vocabulary

Display each word below. Say the words and have students repeat them. Then use the Define/Example/Ask routine to introduce each word.

1 enhanced (page 13)

Define: made better or greater in value

Example: Leo's new glasses *enhanced* his vision.

Ask: In what way have computers *enhanced* our lives?

2 founded (page 14)

Define: started or established

Example: The town *founded* a shelter for stray animals.

Ask: When was the United States *founded*?

3 remote (page 8)

Define: far away from other things or people

Example: The *remote* village did not have electricity.

Ask: How do you use the *remote* control for a TV?

4 unique (page 8)

Define: unlike anything else, the only one of its kind

Example: Each person's fingerprints are *unique*.

Ask: What else is special or *unique* about you?

DURING READING

15–20 Minutes   RI.5.1   RI.5.5   SL.5.1b   L.5.6

Close Reading

🔍 **Pages 7–9**

Connection of Ideas Ⓐ Ⓒ Ⓣ *On page 7, what did Douglas do between 1924 and 1941?* (wrote short stories for magazines) *What happened in 1941?* (a friend asked her to write about the Miami River) *What effect did this request have on Douglas?* (It inspired her to suggest she write a book about the Everglades instead.)

Vocabulary Read the quote on page 8 aloud. Help students to understand the challenging vocabulary. Point out that many of the words describe something very large or powerful, for example, *vast, enormous,* and *massive.* Then ask: *What clue in the quotation helps you understand what* unique *means?* (Nothing anywhere else is like them.)

Connection of Ideas Ⓐ Ⓒ Ⓣ Ask students to look at the map on page 9. *What does the map show?* (how water flows through the Everglades) Ask students to point to the Everglades on the map. *How does this map help you understand the first text on page 9?* (The map shows the lake and the way its water flows through the Everglades. It shows why the Everglades are a river of grass.)

Connection of Ideas Ⓐ Ⓒ Ⓣ Ask students to read "The Ecosystem" on page 9. Then have them look back at the photographs on pages 6 and 7 and review the captions. Ask: *How do these photographs and captions connect with the text in "The Ecosystem" on page 9?* (They show living things that are part of the Everglades ecosystem.)

STOP AND CHECK *Read the question in the Stop and Check box on page 9.* (She called the area a glistening "river of grass" and described its beauty.)

Pages 10–11

Connection of Ideas **A C T** *Read page 10. What problem did Douglas write about in* The Everglades: River of Grass? (how the Everglades provided water for everyone) *Look back at page 6. What did she write about in her newspaper column?* (protecting the Everglades) *What happened in 1947?* (The president made one-third of the Everglades a national park.)

STOP AND CHECK *Read the question in the Stop and Check box on page 11.* (It doesn't have beautiful or amazing features, and has a difficult landscape.)

Problem and Solution *After the creation of Everglades National Park, why did Douglas continue to speak about her book?* (Areas not protected by the national park were still at risk.) *What was happening that caused Douglas concern?* (Owners of sugar plantations and land developers dug canals and drained water from marshes.)

Pages 12–13

Problem and Solution *Review page 12. Why did Douglas want to stop an airport project in the Everglades?* (draining the water would damage the environment) *How did Douglas stop the airport?* (She started a group and spoke out.) *What signal word indicates that there was still a problem?* (However) *What was the next problem?* (to restore the water by making polluters clean it up and getting rid of canals that carried away water)

Genre **A C T** *Why do you think the author included the feature "Protecting Other Wetlands" on page 12 and the photo on page 13?* (to show the effects of Douglas's work and the awards she received for her efforts)

STOP AND CHECK *Read the question in the Stop and Check box on page 13.* (pollution, threats from sugarcane farms, developers wanted to build housing, an airport)

Page 14

Problem and Solution *Read page 14. How is the Everglades Forever Act a result of Douglas's work?* (The purpose of the act is to preserve the water in the Everglades, which Douglas fought for all her life.)

AFTER READING

10–15 Minutes   RI.5.1   RI.5.2   RI.5.9   W.5.9b   L.5.4a   **CCSS**

Respond to Reading

Compare Texts Have students compare the impact Marjory Stoneman Douglas had on her world with the impact Rachel Carson had on her world. Then say: *What impact would you like to have on our world?*

Summarize Have students turn to page 15 and summarize the selection. (Answers should include details that show how Marjory worked to save the Everglades.)

Text Evidence

Have partners work together to answer questions on page 15 using their Problem and Solution Charts.

Problem and Solution (If the wetlands were drained, water wouldn't flow into the aquifers and southern Florida would become a desert. She wanted the Everglades to be protected as a national park.)

Vocabulary (caring deeply about someone's problems)

Write About Reading (She respected the environment and saw it was at risk; wrote a book about the Everglades to raise awareness and worked to have it made a national park; formed groups to fight developers.)

Independent Reading

Encourage students to read the paired selection "The Story of the Tree Musketeers" on pages 16–18. Have them summarize the selection and compare it to Marjory Stoneman Douglas's biography. Have partners answer the "Make Connections" questions on page 18.

 Quick Check Can students identify problems and solutions? If not, review and reteach using the instruction on page 346 and assign the Unit 6 Week 4 digital mini-lesson.

Can students respond to the selection using text evidence? If not, provide sentence frames to help them organize their ideas.

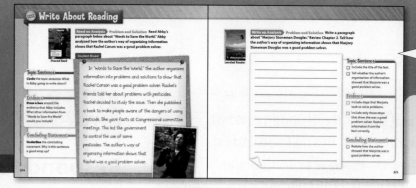

WEEK 4 LESSON 5

Objectives
- Review weekly vocabulary words
- Review problem and solution
- Write an analysis about how an author organizes information in a biography

Materials
- Visual Vocabulary Cards: 217–224
- Interactive Worktext, pp. 374–375
- Assessment Book, pp. 66–67

☞ **Go Digital**
- Visual Vocabulary Cards
- Problem/Solution Mini-Lesson
- Interactive eWorktext

Scaffolding for **Wonders** Reading/Writing Workshop

REVIEW AND RETEACH

5–10 Minutes   RI.5.1   RI.5.3   L.5.4a   L.5.6

Weekly Vocabulary

Display one **Visual Vocabulary Card** at a time and ask students to use the vocabulary word in a sentence. If students have difficulty, have them find the word in "Words to Save the World: The Work of Rachel Carson" and use context clues to define it.

Comprehension: Problem/Solution

I Do Display: *Norman Borlaug saw that people needed more food. He studied wheat. He experimented with ways to make it grow faster. Because of his work, farmers were able to grow more wheat and people had more food.* Underline the first sentence. Say: *This is the problem.* Circle the next two sentences. Say: *These are the steps to solve the problem.* Draw a box around the last sentence. Say: *This is the solution that resulted.*

We Do Display: *Wangari Maathai saw a problem. People were cutting down too many trees in her country. It was hurting the land. She taught people to replant trees. Because of her work, her country's environment improved.* Say: *Let's find the problem and solution together. What did Wangari see as a problem?* (People were cutting down too many trees.) *What did she do to try to solve the problem?* (taught people to replant trees) *What was the solution that resulted?* (Her country's environment improved.)

You Do Have partners reread the passage on page 367 of the **Interactive Worktext**. Have partners ask each other questions to determine problems, steps to solve the problems, and the solution.

WRITE ABOUT READING

25–35 Minutes   W.5.2   W.5.4   W.5.5   W.5.9b

Read an Analysis

- Ask students to look back at "Words to Save the World: The Work of Rachel Carson" in the **Interactive Worktext**. Have volunteers review their notes. *How did the author's way of organizing information show that Rachel was a good problem solver?*

- Read aloud the directions on page 374. Read aloud the student model. *Abby's writing is not a summary. She is writing an* analysis, *or a detailed description, of "Words to Save the World." She tells how the author organized information to show that Rachel was a good problem solver.*

- Say: *When you write an analysis, you need to include certain elements. The first element is the* topic sentence. *Circle the topic sentence. What information is included in that sentence?* (text's title; that the author's way of organizing information shows that Rachel was a good problem solver)

- *Another element of an analysis is* text evidence. *Abby supports the topic sentence with problems and solutions from the text that show that Rachel was a good problem solver. Reread the paragraph and draw a box around the text evidence.* (sentences 2–5) *Look back at your notes about "Words to Save the World." What other information could be included?* (Rachel hired people to study the Huckins's claims.)

- *The final element is the* concluding statement. *Have students underline the concluding statement. How is the concluding statement like the topic sentence?* (Both say that Rachel was a good problem solver.) *Why is it a good wrap up?* (It restates the topic sentence.)

Analytical Writing · **Write an Analysis**

Guided Writing Read the writing prompt on page 375 together. Have students write about "Marjory Stoneman Douglas" or another text they read this week. Have them review their notes. *Use the checklist to help you figure out what information to include in each section.* Guide students to ask "how" and "why" questions as they analyze text evidence.

Peer Conference Have students read their analysis to a partner. Listeners should identify the strongest text evidence that supports the topic sentence and discuss any sentences that are unclear.

Teacher Conference Check students' writing for complete sentences and text evidence that supports their topic. Review the concluding statement. *Does this sentence tie all of the elements together?* If necessary, have students revise the concluding statement by restating the topic sentence.

Level Up

▲ Approaching Leveled Reader

▲ Reading/Writing Workshop

▲ Apprentice Leveled Reader

▲ Interactive Worktext

IF students read the Apprentice Level Reader fluently and the **Interactive Worktext** Shared Read fluently and answer the Respond to Reading questions

THEN read together the Approaching Level Reader main selection and the **Reading/Writing Workshop** Shared Read from *Reading Wonders*. Have students take notes as they read, using self-stick notes. Then ask and answer questions about their notes.

Writing Rubric

	4	3	2	1
Topic Sentence	There is one clear, focused topic sentence.	Topic sentence is less focused, somewhat clear.	Topic is presented in short phrases.	There is no topic sentence.
Text Evidence	Topic is supported by two or more text details.	Evidence includes only one detail from the text.	Little to no evidence is cited from the text.	No text evidence is included.
Concluding Statement	Clearly restates the topic sentence; wraps up all the details.	Restatement is less focused; attempts to wrap up the details.	Vaguely restates topic. Doesn't correlate well to text evidence.	There is no conclusion.
Writing Style	Writes in complete sentences. Uses correct spelling and grammar.	Uses complete sentences and phrases. Writing has spelling and grammar errors.	Few or no complete sentences. There are many spelling and grammar errors.	Does not write accurately or in complete sentences.

ASSESSMENT

Weekly Assessment

Have students complete the Weekly Assessment using **Assessment** book pages 66–67.

WEEK 5
LESSON

1

Objectives
- Develop oral language
- Build background about our connections to the world
- Understand and use weekly vocabulary
- Read poetry

Materials
Interactive Worktext, pp. 376–383
- Visual Vocabulary Cards: 225–228

☞ **Go Digital**
- Interactive eWorktext
- Visual Vocabulary Cards

Scaffolding for **Wonders** Reading/Writing Workshop

WEEKLY CONCEPT

5–10 Minutes   SL.5.1b   SL.5.1c   CCSS

Talk About It

Essential Question Read aloud the Essential Question on page 376 of the **Interactive Worktext**: *What can our connections to the world teach us?* Explain that "connections to the world" include friendships and relationships with others as well as experiences. Say: *We can learn about the world, others, and ourselves when we make connections.*

- Discuss the photo on page 376. Ask: *How are these people connecting to the world?* (they are out in nature; they are using a smart phone)

I Do Say: *I see that the people are in nature together. Taking a walk together in the woods is one way people can connect with others and the world around them. They can learn about the world by looking around and asking each other questions. I will write these connections in the web on page 377.*

We Do Say: *Let's look at the photo together. What is the woman in the middle holding?* (a smart phone) *How does this device help people connect with the world?* (people can take photos and send them to others; they can connect to the internet) *How can the people in the photo learn about the world by using this device?* (Possible answers: They can take a photo and then study it later; they can use the internet to look up information about what they see.) *Have students add words to the web on page 377 and brainstorm other ways peoples can connect with and learn from the world.*

You Do Have partners describe a connection they have made with a person or place. Ask: *Who or what did you connect with? What did you learn from this connection?*

REVIEW VOCABULARY

10–15 Minutes   RL.5.4   L.5.4a   L.5.5a   L.5.5c   L.5.6   CCSS

Review Weekly Vocabulary Words

- Use the **Visual Vocabulary Cards** to review the weekly vocabulary.

- Read together the directions for the Vocabulary activity on page 378 of the **Interactive Worktext**. Then complete the activity.

1 **connection** Have students use the following sentence frame: *I have a strong connection with _____ because _____.* (Answers will vary.)

2 **exchange** Say: *A synonym is a word with the same or almost the same meaning as another word.* Have partners discuss which option is a synonym for *exchange.* (trade)

3 **blares** Ask students to imitate the sounds of a siren, a fire alarm, and a breeze. Explain that more than one of these things *blares.* Have students identify which *blares.* (siren, fire alarm) Ask: *What is something else that blares?* Have partners brainstorm examples, if necessary.

4 **errand** Offer an example of an errand and ask students to give examples of other errands they do at school or errands their family members do. Then have students draw their picture and write a caption using the sentence starter: *On this errand, _____.* (Drawings may include picking up books, getting groceries.)

Poetry Terms

Have students look at the Poetry Terms activity on page 379 of the **Interactive Worktext**. Read together the directions for the Poetry Terms activity. Read the poem aloud. Discuss the definitions of the poetry terms and give examples, as appropriate. Then have partners use the poem to complete each activity.

5 **personification** Ask: *What word do you see in the word personification?* (person) Read aloud the definition. Then read aloud the first five lines of the poem. Ask: *Which description of the raindrops is an example of personification?* (Drops of silver/bounced and danced) If students have difficulty, ask: *Which words describe something only a human would do?* Ask: *What do you picture when you read these words?* (rain drops bouncing in rhythm) Then have partners reread the last five lines and identify another example of personification. (rain still clung to me)

6 **assonance** Read aloud the first line of the poem, emphasizing the vowel sound in *gray* and *day*. Say: *These words have the same long* a *vowel sound. This pair of words is an example of assonance.* Have students reread the next line. Ask: *Which pair of words is another example of assonance?* (rain, came)

7 **consonance** Read aloud lines 3–5 in the first stanza, emphasizing the final consonant sounds in *bounced* and *danced.* Ask: *Which pair of words is an example of consonance?* (bounced, danced) Repeat for lines 6–8, emphasizing the middle consonant sounds in *written* and *letters.* Ask: *Which pair of words is another example of consonance?* (written, letters)

8 **imagery** Have students close their eyes as you read aloud the last five lines. Say: *Which words create imagery?* (Possible answers: far-off, sunny beach; cold rain still clung to me) If students have difficulty, ask: *Which details can you picture clearly?*

> **ELL ENGLISH LANGUAGE LEARNERS**
>
> Point out examples of *personification* and *imagery* in the poem and have students draw pictures to illustrate them. For *assonance* and *consonance*, provide examples and have students echo them.

READ COMPLEX TEXT

15–20 Minutes   RL.5.1   RF.5.4c

Read: "To Travel!" and "Wild Blossoms"

- Have students turn to page 380 in the **Interactive Worktext** and read aloud the Essential Question. Explain that they will read two poems about making connections. Ask: *What is the title of the first poem?* ("To Travel!") *What does the photograph show?* (a landscape, a house) *What do you think the speaker of this poem has a connection with?* (a place)

- Read "To Travel!" and "Wild Blossoms" together. Note that the poems include the weekly vocabulary words but that they are not highlighted.

- Have students use the "My Notes" section on page 380 to write questions they have, words they don't understand, and details they want to remember. Model how to use the "My Notes" section: *In the second stanza of "To Travel!" I don't understand the meaning of "a novel waves her arms to me." I'll write a question about this in "My Notes." I'm also confused about the meaning of the word* customs *in the second stanza on page 381, so I'll write the word with a question mark after it in the "My Notes" section.*

> **ELL ENGLISH LANGUAGE LEARNERS**
>
> As you read the poems together, have students highlight words or phrases that are confusing to them. After reading, help students write questions in "My Notes" section.

 Quick Check Can students understand the weekly vocabulary in context? If not, review vocabulary using the **Visual Vocabulary Cards** before teaching Lesson 2.

Objectives
• Read poetry
• Understand complex text through close reading
• Recognize and understand point of view
• Respond to poetry using text evidence to support ideas

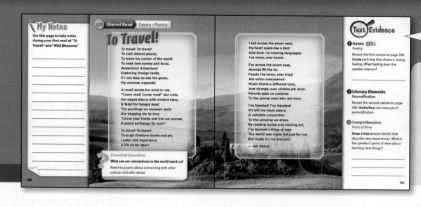

Materials
Interactive Worktext, pp. 380–385

☞ **Go** Digital
• Interactive eWorktext
• Point of View Mini-Lesson

REREAD COMPLEX TEXT

20–25 Minutes   RL.5.2   RL.5.4   RL.5.6   RF.5.4b   L.5.5a   **CCSS**

Close Reading: "To Travel!" and "Wild Blossoms"

Reread "To Travel!" and "Wild Blossoms" with students. As you read together, discuss important elements of the poems. Have students respond to text-dependent questions, including those in the **Interactive Worktext**.

🔍 **Page 381**

Genre **A C T** Say: *In lyric poems such as "To Travel!" a poet often uses rhythm and punctuation to express a strong feeling.* Read aloud the first four lines on page 380. Ask: *What punctuation marks do you see in the first line of the poem?* (exclamation marks) *What feelings can an exclamation mark show?* (excitement or surprise) *Let's circle this line.* Then have students reread the rest of the stanza and look for other exclamation marks. (Adventure! Adventure!; My universe expands!) *Now let's listen to the rhythm of the stanza. Reread the first stanza, having students join you in tapping out the rhythm. Think about the feeling the rhythm expresses. What feeling does the speaker express?* (excitement)

Personification Read aloud the second stanza. Circle and read aloud "A novel waves her arms to me./'Come read! Come Read!' she cries." Point out that *her* and *she* refers to the novel. Say: *I know that a novel does not have arms and cannot wave or cry out. This is an example of personification. These actions are things a person does when he or she is excited, so I can tell that the book must be exciting.* Have students mark another example of personification in the stanza. (Possible answers: pages: "Her pages dance"; eyes: "hungry eyes"; paintings: "paintings on museum walls/Are begging me to tour") If

students have difficulty, ask: *What objects do things that only humans can do?*

Connection of Ideas **A C T** Have students reread the first and the third stanza. Ask: *Does the speaker actually travel to other places?* (no) *How does the speaker experience what life is like in another place? Point to text evidence.* (through timeless books and art)

Point of View Say: *To find the speaker's point of view I will look for key details and clues to the speaker's feelings. In the first stanza on page 380, I read "To seek new names and faces./Adventure! Adventure!" These details describe having new experiences. I know an adventure is a new experience that is exciting. I also see exclamation marks, which express excitement. I think these are clues to the speaker's point of view. Let's keep reading and look for more clues. What details on page 381 tell about new experiences?* (Possible answers: And soon I'm hearing languages/I've never, ever heard; Foods I've never ever tried/Are eaten everywhere!/Music blares a different tune,/And strange new clothes are worn.; I've traveled! I've traveled! It's left me more aware.) *Use these clues. What do you think is the speaker's point of view about learning new things?* (Learning new things is exciting.)

Connection of Ideas **A C T** Have partners reread the first stanza on page 380 and the last stanza of the poem. *What does the speaker do to explore other places?* (reads books and looks at art) *What lesson does the speaker learn? Point to text evidence.* (The world was made not just for me,/But made for me and you!)

🔍 **Page 382**

Assonance Give examples of assonance, as necessary, such as *home* and *grow*. Read aloud together the first three lines of the poem. Ask: *Which line includes an example of assonance?* (third line) *Circle the words.* (wheels, weaving, between, sunbeams)

Genre A C T Read aloud the first stanza. Ask: *Who are the characters in this narrative poem?* (Grandmother and the speaker) *What does the speaker do first?* (pedal her bike downtown to get seeds) *What important event happens when the speaker returns to Grandmother's house?* (Grandmother tears off the top of the seed packets and shakes them around the backyard.)

Point of View Have students reread the last sentence. *How does the speaker feel as she watches Grandmother?* (surprised) *Which words describe the way Grandmother shook out the seeds?* (willy-nilly) Say: *The word* willy-nilly *can mean "carelessly." Use these clues. How do you think the speaker feels about Grandmother's actions?* Provide the sentence starter to guide students: *The speaker thinks Grandmother's actions are _____.* (careless)

Page 383

Consonance Read aloud the fourth line. Have partners identify words that are examples of consonance. (bees buzzed) Have them repeat the words and discuss what the /z/ sound makes them think of. (bees buzzing)

Genre A C T Have students reread the sixth line. Explain that *swifts* and *sparrows* are birds. Have partners identify imagery that helps them picture the birds. (quick, happy, dipped, dove, darted) *In your own words, what do you picture these birds doing?* (flying quickly)

Point of View Have students reread the page and mark words that describe the speaker's and Grandmother's actions. (danced, arms outstretched, letting seeds loose, joyfully dreaming) Ask: *Review the words you marked. What do these words tell you about the speaker's feelings about planting seeds with Grandmother?* (Possible answers: she is excited; joyful; free)

Connection of Ideas A C T Think about the speaker's point of view at the beginning of the poem and at the end. *How has the speaker's point of view changed?* (At first, the speaker thought her grandmother was careless. Now she sees that her grandmother is carefree.) If students have difficulty, ask: *What did the speaker think about Grandmother's actions at the beginning? What does the speaker do at the end of the poem?*

RESPOND TO READING

10–20 Minutes   RL.5.1   W.5.9a   SL.5.1d   CCSS

Respond to "To Travel!" and "Wild Blossoms"

Have students summarize "To Travel!" and "Wild Blossoms" orally to demonstrate comprehension. Then have partners answer the questions on pages 384 of the **Interactive Worktext** using the discussion starters. Tell them to use text evidence to support their answers. Have students write the page number(s) on which they found the text evidence for each question.

1. *What does the speaker of "To Travel!" learn about other people through books and art?* (People around the world have different languages, food, music, clothes, and customs. Text Evidence: p. 381)

2. *What does the speaker of "To Travel!" learn about himself through books and art?* (He shares the world with everyone. Text Evidence: p. 381)

3. *What does the speaker of "Wild Blossoms" learn by helping her grandmother?* (Possible answers: She learns how to plant seeds and how to be more carefree. Text Evidence: pp. 382, 383)

After students discuss the questions on page 384, have them write a response to the question on page 385. Tell them to use their partner discussions and notes about "To Travel!" and "Wild Blossoms" to help them. Circulate and provide guidance.

✓ *Quick Check* Do students understand vocabulary in context? If not, review and reteach using the instruction on page 356.

Can students use key details to determine point of view? If not, review and reteach using the instruction on page 356 and assign the Unit 6 Week 5 digital mini-lesson.

Can students write a response to "To Travel!" and "Wild Blossoms"? If not, provide sentence frames to help them organize their ideas.

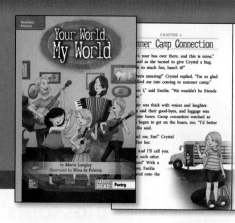

**WEEK 5
LESSON**

3

Objectives
- Understand and use new vocabulary
- Read realistic fiction
- Recognize and understand point of view
- Understand complex text through close reading

Materials
"Your World, My World" Apprentice Leveled Reader: pp. 2–10
- Graphic Organizer: Point of View

🖝 **Go** Digital
- Apprentice Leveled Reader eBook
- Downloadable Graphic Organizer
- Point of View Mini-Lesson

Scaffolding for **Wonders** Approaching Leveled Reader

BEFORE READING

10–15 Minutes   SL.5.1c   SL.5.1d   L.5.4a   L.5.6   CCSS

Introduce "Your World, My World"

- Read the Essential Question on the title page of "Your World, My World" **Apprentice Leveled Reader**: *What can our connections to the world teach us? We will read how two girls from different backgrounds make connections with each other and the world.*

- Read the title and table of contents of the main read. Have students look at the images. *What do you think this selection will be about?* (a musical family; girls at summer camp) *Why do you think that?* (cover art; chapter titles)

Expand Vocabulary

Display each word below. Say the words and have students repeat them. Then use the Define/Example/Ask routine to introduce each word.

1 immersed (page 8)

Define: completely involved

Example: Time goes by quickly when you are *immersed* in a good book.

Ask: What activities have you been *immersed* in this week?

2 melodies (page 5)

Define: tunes; pleasing music

Example: Jason played soft *melodies* on the piano.

Ask: What are some of your favorite *melodies*?

3 sudden (page 7)

Define: quick; not expected

Example: A *sudden* storm caught me without an umbrella.

Ask: What *sudden* changes in the weather have you observed?

DURING READING

20–30 Minutes   RL.5.1   RL.5.6   SL.5.1b   L.5.4b   CCSS

Close Reading

🔍 Pages 2–3

Genre A C T   Read pages 2–3. Ask: *What did the girls do when they said good-bye?* (They promised to e-mail, call, and see each other again soon.) *Is this something that real friends might do when camp ends?* (yes)

Point of View Say: *Thinking about the words a character uses, the thoughts they express, and their actions can help a reader understand the character's point of view.* Read the first two paragraphs on page 2 aloud. Ask: *What was Crystal's point of view about camp? How do you know?* (She enjoyed camp. She said it was "amazing." She was glad her mother convinced her to go because she met Emilia as a result.) As students read, have them record information about Crystal's point of view in their Point of View chart.

Vocabulary Have students locate *disaster* on page 3. Explain that a *disaster* is something that is very bad or disappointing. Ask: *How did Crystal feel and act when she thought camp would be a* disaster? (She felt like going home. She kept her head down.) *What made Crystal realize that camp might not be a* disaster? (A girl [Emilia] asked about Crystal's mandolin. Crystal liked her.)

Pages 4–5

Vocabulary Read pages 4–5. Have students find the word *immigrated* on page 4. Explain that *immigrate* means to come into a country to live. Ask: *What clues on page 4 help you figure out what* immigrated *means?* ("lived in New York City; "from Italy")

Genre ⒶⒸⓉ Say: *Characters in realistic fiction speak like people from real life.* Reread the dialogue at the bottom of page 4. Ask: *Who is speaking? How do you know?* (Emilia and Crystal; They are identified by name; *Emilia explained; Crystal said*)

Point of View Read the text of the phone call on page 5. Ask: *How does Emilia feel in this part of the story? How can you tell how Emilia feels?* (happy and excited; she says "Oh, wow!" and squeals.) *What is Emilia excited about?* (Crystal invited Emilia to visit her in Roanoke.) *What is Crystal's point of view about Emilia's visit?* (She is looking forward to showing Emilia around.)

STOP AND CHECK Read the question in the Stop and Check box on page 5. (Emilia is going to Roanoke, Virginia to visit her friend Crystal.)

Pages 6–7

Point of View Read the first three paragraphs on page 6. Ask: *What was Emilia's point of view about flying?* (Emilia was calm about flying because she had flown before.) *Was Crystal's point of view about flying the same or different? How do you know?* (different; Crystal asks Emilia, "Weren't you scared?" She isn't sure she would be as calm.) *What does Crystal's mom think about Crystal's attitude?* (She knows that Crystal would be nervous to fly alone.)

Vocabulary Have students locate the word *glanced* in the third paragraph on page 6. Explains that it means looked quickly at something. Ask: *Which word in the sentence helps you understand* glanced? (quickly)

Genre ⒶⒸⓉ Say: *Realistic fiction takes place in settings that are real or that seem real.* Ask: *In what real place did the girls hike on page 7?* Have students complete the sentence frame: *The girls hiked in _____.* (the Blue Ridge Mountains near Roanoke, Virginia)

Vocabulary Have students find the word *reassured* on page 7. Ask: *What clues in the paragraph help you figure out what* reassured *means?* ("Don't worry.")

STOP AND CHECK Read the question in the Stop and Check box on page 7. (Emilia is worried about bears.)

Pages 8–10

Point of View Read pages 8–10. Ask: *What was Emilia's point of view about the food and music she shared with Crystal's family? How do you know?* (Emilia thinks they were wonderful. She called the meal amazing, and was delighted that the family played music with her.)

Vocabulary Read the last paragraph on page 8. Explain that sometimes authors use figurative language to help readers understand an experience. Ask: *What do you think the phrase "the mandolin came to life in her hands" means?* (Emilia played the mandolin very easily and well, so that it seemed to be alive.)

Point of View Ask: *On page 10, where does Crystal take Emilia on her last day in Virginia?* (the Roanoke Wildlife Rescue Center) *What happens there?* (Injured and orphaned wild mammals are helped.) *How does Crystal feel about the Center?* (She thinks it is a special place. She helps out there sometimes.)

STOP AND CHECK Read the question in the Stop and Check box on page 10. (Emilia learned what traditional Appalachian music is like. She learned about the joy of playing music with others.)

Have partners review their Point of View charts for pages 2–10 and discuss what they learned.

✅ *Quick Check* **Do students understand weekly vocabulary in context? If not, review and reteach using the instruction on page 356.**

Can students use key details to determine point of view? If not, review and reteach using the instruction on page 356 and assign the Unit 6 Week 5 digital mini-lesson.

WEEK 5 LESSON 4

Objectives
- Understand and use new vocabulary
- Read realistic fiction
- Recognize and understand point of view
- Understand complex text through close reading
- Respond to the selection using text evidence to support ideas

Materials

"Your World, My World" Apprentice Leveled Reader: pp. 11–20
- Graphic Organizer: Point of View

☞ **Go Digital**
- Apprentice Leveled Reader eBook
- Downloadable Graphic Organizer
- Point of View Mini-Lesson

Scaffolding for **Wonders** Approaching Leveled Reader

BEFORE READING

5–10 Minutes   SL.5.1c   SL.5.1d   L.5.4a   L.5.6

Expand Vocabulary

Display each word below. Say the words and have students repeat them. Then use the Define/Example/Ask routine to introduce each word.

1   challenge (page 12)

Define: a contest to find the best

Example: Our team played well and won the *challenge*.

Ask: What is a *challenge* you can win?

2   flash (page 15)

Define: very short time

Example: The work was easy, and I finished it in a *flash*.

Ask: What can you do in a *flash*?

3   plucked (page 14)

Define: pulled strings on a musical instrument

Example: Margie *plucked* a string on her violin.

Ask: What other musical instruments can be *plucked*?

4   reduction (page 12)

Define: the act of cutting back or making less of something

Example: A *reduction* in my allowance means I have less money to spend.

Ask: How can we cause a *reduction* in the amount of electricity we waste?

DURING READING

15–20 Minutes   RL.5.1   RL.5.6   SL.5.1b   L.5.4b

Close Reading

🔍 **Page 11**

Vocabulary   Read page 11. Say: *Emilia learned a lot about wildlife and the environment in Virginia.* Have students find *environment* in the second to last paragraph on page 11. Ask: *What words on page 11 give you a clue about the meaning of* environment? (world around my home)

Point of View   *What point of view did Emilia and Poppa share about the environment?* (We should care for the environment wherever we are.)

🔍 **Pages 12–13**

Genre   Read pages 12–13. Say: *People in realistic fiction communicate with each other just like real people do. In this chapter, Emilia and Crystal e-mail each other.* Ask: *What did Emilia say to Crystal in her first e-mail?* (Emilia said she wanted to show that she cared about nature. She had to figure out what she could do.) *How can you tell which text is Emilia's e-mail?* (The words are in quotes; the words "Emilia wrote.")

Key Details   Ask: *On page 12, how did Emilia help care for the environment near her home?* Have students complete the sentence frame: *Emilia volunteered to help with _____.* (the Green Schools program)

Vocabulary   Have students find the word *reusing* on page 12. Say: *The prefix* re- *means again. How can that help you understand the meaning of* reusing? (reusing means using again) Point out that the letters *re* at the beginning of a word do not always stand for the prefix *re-*. For example, the letters *re* in *reducing* are not a prefix meaning "again."

Point of View Ask: *On page 13, what was Crystal's point of view about visiting New York?* (Crystal was afraid to visit New York and didn't want to go.) **Have partners find text evidence that shows that this is Crystal's point of view.** (She was also scared; Going to summer camp was Crystal's first big trip away from home; Crystal told her mom she didn't want to go.)

Pages 14–15

Genre A C T Read pages 14–15. Say: *Like real people, the characters in realistic fiction often make important changes in their lives. In this chapter, Emilia decided to care more about nature. What new direction did Crystal take with her life?* (Crystal decided to learn more about the world.)

Cause and Effect Ask: *What helped Crystal make the decision to go to New York?* Have students turn to a partner and discuss the answer. (<u>Possible answer:</u> Crystal remembered that she helped Emilia when Emilia was scared of bears. Crystal realized that Emilia could help her not be scared in New York.)

Point of View *How did Crystal's point of view about visiting New York change?* (At first Crystal was afraid of New York and didn't want to go. At the end of the story, Crystal was excited and couldn't wait to visit Emilia.)

Genre A C T Have students read the sentence in quotation marks in the second to last paragraph on page 15. Ask: *Who is saying these words? How do you know?* (These words are in Emilia's e-mail. She is responding to Crystal's e-mail saying she will come to New York; "Emilia's reply")

Sentence Structure A C T Have students read the last paragraph on page 14. Explain that this long sentence shows Crystal's excitement as she thinks out loud. *Why do you think the sentence end in a dash?* (Crystal ran out of ideas; she is speaking quickly, trying to talk herself into going to New York.)

STOP AND CHECK Read the question in the Stop and Check box on page 15. (Emilia decided to care more about the world around her home and looked for ways to help the environment.)

AFTER READING

10–15 Minutes RL.5.1 RL5.2 RL.5.9 W.5.9a L.5.4a CCSS

Respond to Reading

Compare Texts Have students compare the point of view of speakers in "To Travel!" and "Wild Blossoms" to the point of view held by the characters in "Your World, My World." Then say: *What have you learned about making connections to the world?*

Summarize Have students turn to page 16 and summarize the selection. (Answers should include details that show both Crystal's and Emilia's points of view.)

Text Evidence

Have partners work together to answer questions on page 16 using their Point of View charts.

Point of View (Crystal realizes that Emilia will help her overcome her fear of the city.)

Vocabulary (*Management* is the process of handling or controlling something.)

Write About Reading (Crystal doesn't like camp at first and is scared of going to New York. Emilia doesn't mind going away from home and is not scared of flying.)

Independent Reading

Encourage students to read the paired poetry selection "Do I Know You?" on pages 17–19. Have them summarize the poem and compare the speakers to the characters in "Your World, My World." Ask students to identify rhymes in the poem. Have partners answer the "Make Connections" questions on page 19.

 Quick Check **Can students use key details to determine point of view? If not, review and reteach using the instruction on page 356 and assign the Unit 6 Week 5 digital mini-lesson.**

Can students respond to the selection using text evidence. If not, provide sentence frames to help them organize their ideas.

WEEK 5 LESSON 5

Objectives
- Review weekly vocabulary words
- Review point of view
- Write an analysis about how an author uses imagery to show setting

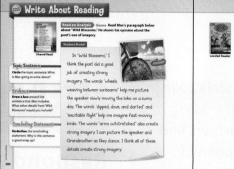

Materials
- Visual Vocabulary Cards: 225–228
- Interactive Worktext, pp. 386–387
- Assessment Book, pp. 68–69

☞ **Go** Digital
- Visual Vocabulary Cards
- Point of View Mini-Lesson
- Interactive eWorktext

Scaffolding for **Wonders** McGraw-Hill Reading Reading/Writing Workshop

REVIEW AND RETEACH

5–10 Minutes   RL.5.1   RL.5.6   L.5.4a   L.5.6

Weekly Vocabulary

Display one **Visual Vocabulary Card** at a time and ask students to use the vocabulary word in a sentence. If students have difficulty, have them find the word in "To Travel!" or "Wild Blossoms" and use context clues to define it.

Comprehension: Point of View

I Do Write and read aloud these lines: *When Maria fingers dance,/On the piano keys,/A flutter of sounds,/ Tickle my ears,/And awaken my feet.* Tell students that you will look for details and strong words that give clues to the speaker's point of view. Circle *dance, flutter, tickle my ears,* and *awaken my feet.* Say: *These strong words and details are clues that the speaker feels excitement when he or she hears Maria play the piano.*

We Do Write and read aloud these lines: *When I run,/ the pavement becomes a long runway,/And I race to take off,/and my heart lifts and soars, free.* Ask: *What strong words do you see?* (race, lifts, soars, free) *What key details does the speaker use to describe the experience of running?* (the pavement becomes a runway; I race to take off; my heart lifts and soars) *What feeling do all of these words and details express?* (Possible answers: excitement, feeling free) *What is the speaker's point of view about running?* (It's exciting and freeing.)

You Do Have students turn to page 379 of the **Interactive Worktext**. Have partners identify strong words and details that describe Grandpa's letter. Then have them use these clues to tell the speaker's point of view.

WRITE ABOUT READING

25–35 Minutes   W.5.1a   W.5.1b   W.5.1d   W.5.9a

Read an Analysis

- Ask students to look back at "Wild Blossoms" in the **Interactive Worktext**. Have volunteers review their notes. Ask: *How did the poet's use of imagery help you picture the speaker and the setting?*

- Read aloud the directions on page 386. Say: *Max's paragraph is an analysis, or detailed description, of the poem "Wild Blossoms." In his analysis, Max gives his opinion about how well the poet created imagery in the poem.* Read aloud the student model.

- Say: *An analysis includes certain elements. The first element is the* topic sentence. Have students circle the topic sentence in the student model. Ask: *What information does Max include in his topic sentence?* (poem's title; his opinion that the poet did a good job of creating strong imagery)

- *Another element of an analysis is* text evidence. *Max supports his opinion with details from the poem.* Reread the model and have students draw a box around the text evidence. (sentences 2–4) *What other details from the poem would support Max's opinion?* (Possible answer: tore off the tops of the seed packet and shook them willy-nilly around the backyard)

- *The final element of an analysis is the* concluding statement. Reread the concluding statement in the student model and have students underline it. Ask: *How is Max's concluding statement like his topic sentence?* (Both include the words "I think" and both say that the poet created strong imagery.) *Which words in this sentence wrap up the text evidence?* (all of these details)

Analytical Writing — Write an Analysis

Guided Writing Read the writing prompt on page 387 together. Have students write about "Your World, My World" or another realistic fiction selection. Say: *Use the checklist to help you figure out the right information to include in each section of your analysis.* If students have difficulty, help them look for the use of strong imagery in one setting rather than multiple settings.

Peer Conference Have students read their analysis to a partner. Listeners should identify the strongest text evidence that supports the topic sentence and discuss any sentences that are unclear.

Teacher Conference Check students' writing for complete sentences and text evidence that supports their opinion. Review the concluding statement. *Does this sentence tie all of the elements together?* If necessary, have students revise the concluding statement by restating the topic sentence.

Level Up

▲ Approaching Leveled Reader

▲ Reading/Writing Workshop

▲ Apprentice Leveled Reader

▲ Interactive Worktext

IF students read the **Apprentice Level** Reader fluently and the **Interactive Worktext** Shared Read fluently and answer the Respond to Reading questions

THEN read together the **Approaching Level** Reader main selection and the **Reading/Writing Workshop** Shared Read from *Reading Wonders*. Have students take notes as they read, using self-stick notes. Then ask and answer questions about their notes.

Writing Rubric

	4	3	2	1
Topic Sentence	Topic sentence presents a clear opinion.	Topic sentence presents an opinion, somewhat clearly.	Topic is presented in short phrases; opinion is unclear.	There is no topic sentence; no opinion is presented.
Text Evidence	Opinion is supported by two or more text details.	Opinion is only supported by one detail from the text.	Little to no evidence from the text supports opinion.	No text evidence is included; does not support opinion.
Concluding Statement	Clearly restates an opinion; wraps up all the details.	Restatement is less focused; attempts to wrap up the details.	Vaguely restates opinion. Doesn't correlate well to text evidence.	There is no conclusion.
Writing Style	Writes in complete sentences. Uses correct spelling and grammar.	Uses complete sentences and phrases. Writing has spelling and grammar errors.	Few or no complete sentences. There are many spelling and grammar errors.	Does not write accurately or in complete sentences.

ASSESSMENT

Weekly Assessment

Have students complete the Weekly Assessment using **Assessment** book pages 68–69.

WEEK 6

▶ **Unit Assessment,**
pages 167–175

▶ **Fluency Assessment,**
pages 266–281

▶ **Exit Test,**
pages 223–231

Unit 6 Assessment

CCSS TESTED SKILLS

✔ COMPREHENSION	✔ VOCABULARY:
• Theme **RL.5.2**	• Context Clues **L.5.4a**
• Theme **RL.5.2**	
• Cause and Effect **RI.5.3**	
• Problem and Solution **RI.5.5**	
• Point of View **RL.5.6**	

Using Assessment and Writing Scores

↺ RETEACH	IF ...	THEN ...
COMPREHENSION	Students answer 0–7 multiple-choice items correctly ...	... reteach tested skills using instruction on pages 364–371.
VOCABULARY	Students answer 0–3 multiple-choice items correctly ...	... reteach tested skills using instruction on page 364.
WRITING	Students score mostly 1–2 on weekly Write About Reading rubrics throughout the unit...	... reteach writing using instruction on pages 372–373.

↥ LEVEL UP	IF ...	THEN ...
COMPREHENSION	Students answer 8–10 multiple-choice items correctly ...	... have students read the *Marjory Stoneman Douglas: Guardian of the Everglades* Approaching Leveled Reader. Use the Level Up lesson on page 360.
WRITING	Students score mostly 3–4 on weekly Write About Reading rubrics throughout the unit...	... use the Level Up Write About Reading lesson on pages 361 to have students compare two selections from the unit.

Fluency Assessment

Conduct assessments individually using the differentiated fluency passages in **Assessment**. Students' expected fluency goal for this Unit is 129–149 WCPM with an accuracy rate of 95% or higher.

Exit Test

If a student answers 13–15 multiple-choice items correctly on the Unit Assessment, administer the Unit 6 Exit Test at the end of Week 6.

Time to Exit

Exit Test

If...
Students answer 13–15 multiple choice items correctly...

Fluency Assessment

If...
Students achieve their Fluency Assessment goal for the unit...

Level Up Lessons

If...
Students are successful applying close reading skills with the Approaching Leveled Reader in Week 6...

If...
Students score mostly 4–5 on the Level Up Write About Reading assignment...

Foundational Skills Kit

If...
Students have mastered the Unit 6 benchmark skills in the Foundational Skills Kit and *PowerPAL for Reading* adaptive learning system...

Then...
... consider exiting the student from *Reading WonderWorks* materials into the Approaching Level of *Reading Wonders*.

WEEK 6

▶ **Read Approaching Leveled Reader**

Approaching Leveled Reader

Apprentice Leveled Reader

▶ **Write About Reading**

Interactive Worktext Shared Read

Apprentice Leveled Reader

Read Approaching Leveled Reader

RI.5.10

Marjory Stoneman Douglas: Guardian of the Everglades

Before Reading

Preview Discuss what students remember about Marjory Stoneman Douglas and her work to protect the Everglades. Tell them that they will be reading a more challenging version of *Marjory Stoneman Douglas: Guardian of the Everglades*.

Vocabulary Use routines on the **Visual Vocabulary Cards** to review the Weekly Vocabulary words. Use pages 342 and 344 to review the Expand Vocabulary words.

A C T During Reading

▷ **Vocabulary** Review new words. Provide the meanings of challenging words, such as *variety* (page 2), *basic* (page 4), *thrilled* (page 5), *stunning* (page 10), and *hostile* (page 13).

▷ **Genre** Students may need help understanding the additional quotations from and about Marjory Stoneman Douglas throughout the selection. Read aloud the second paragraph on page 13. Ask: *What does Sam Poole think about Marjory Stoneman Douglas?* (He is impressed by her.) *How can you tell?* (He says that she was a small person who made a big difference.)

▷ **Sentence Structure** Students may need help understanding the use of a colon in a sentence. Point to the first sentence in the second paragraph on page 9. Model reading it aloud, pausing at the colon. Then ask: *What comes before the colon?* (Douglas was right) *What comes after the colon?* (more information about the subject) *What information is given after the colon?* (The Everglades are a river of grass.)

After Reading

Ask students to complete the Respond to Reading questions on page 18 after they have finished reading. Provide additional support as needed to help students use the weekly vocabulary strategy in question 3.

Write About Reading

W.5.1 W.5.9a

Read an Analysis

- Distribute the Unit 6 Downloadable Model and Practice that compares two related texts, the **Interactive Worktext** Shared Read "Shipped Out" and the **Apprentice Leveled Reader** "Mrs. Gleeson's Records." Read the paragraph aloud.

- Point out the signal word *alike* in the topic sentence, which tells readers how the two texts are alike, and the word *but* which signals a difference. Have students reread the topic sentence. Ask: *How do you know Victoria is telling her opinion?* (she writes "I think") *What other information does Victoria include in her topic sentence?* (titles of both texts)

- Ask: *What details does Victoria include from "Mrs. Gleeson's Records" that support her opinion?* (sentences 2–4) *What details does Victoria include from "Shipped Out" that support her opinion?* (the fifth sentence) *Why is the concluding statement a good wrap up?* (Victoria restates her opinion.)

Analytical Writing Write an Analysis

Guided Practice Display the prompt: *Write a paragraph that compares "The Bully" to "Winning Friends." Tell your opinion about which author did a better job of developing realistic characters.*

- Alternatively, let students select two texts to compare.

- Use the Unit 6 Downloadable Model and Practice to guide students' writing.

- Tell them to begin with a topic sentence and include details from both texts to support their opinion.

- Remind students that the concluding statement should restate their opinion and wrap up all the details.

Teacher Conference Check students' writing for complete sentences. Did they include a topic sentence that tells an opinion? Did they cite text evidence? Did they restate their opinion in the last sentence?

Writing Rubric

	4	3	2	1
Topic Sentence	Topic sentence presents a clear opinion.	Topic sentence presents an opinion, somewhat clearly.	Topic is presented in short phrases; opinion is unclear	There is no topic sentence; no opinion is presented.
Text Evidence	Opinion is supported by two or more text details.	Opinion is only supported by one detail from the text.	Little to no evidence from the text supports opinion.	No text evidence is included; does not support opinion.
Concluding Statement	Clearly restates an opinion; wraps up all the details.	Restatement is less focused; attempts to wrap up the details.	Vaguely restates opinion. Doesn't correlate well to text evidence.	There is no conclusion.
Writing Style	Writes in complete sentences. Uses correct spelling and grammar.	Uses complete sentences and phrases. Writing has spelling and grammar errors.	Has few or no complete sentences. There are many spelling and grammar errors.	Does not write accurately or in complete sentences.

Additional Resources

Reteach

Model Lessons

English Language Learner Strategies

Program Information

WEEKLY VOCABULARY

L.5.4a L.5.6 CCSS

- Use the **Visual Vocabulary Cards** to reteach Weekly Vocabulary words. Focus on any words that students found difficult. Display the card and have students read the word. Show the image. Explain the word's meaning and have them repeat the meaning and use the word in a sentence. Provide sentence starters as needed. For example, say: *Something that is simple to do is _____*. For more practice, have students use the Partner Talk activities on the **Visual Vocabulary Cards**.

- Have students write the words on a sheet of paper or index cards. Say the meaning of a word. Have students hold up the card and say the word. Then have them repeat the meaning and use the word in a sentence orally.

- Have students write a sentence using each word. Then ask them to draw a picture to illustrate their sentence.

- For any vocabulary words that students continue to find troublesome, reinforce the meanings using the Define/Example/Ask routine. Describe the routine in detail to students.

   Define Tell students the meaning of the word using student-friendly language, or words they already know. For example, say: *The word* enormous *means "very big."* Try restating the definition or using it differently from the way it was first presented.

   Example Give students an example of how the word is used, using their own common experiences. For example, say: *Our school has an* enormous *gym. It is bigger than any other room in the school.*

   Ask Use a question to help students connect the word to known words and use the word in speaking. For example, ask: *What have you seen that is* enormous? *What words mean the same, or nearly the same, as* enormous? *What words mean the opposite of* enormous? Through questions, you can observe if students understand a word's meaning. If they don't, try using a series of Yes/No questions such as these: *Would an ant that is 10 feet tall be* enormous? *Is 20 feet an* enormous *distance for you to walk?*

- Always have students pronounce the words multiple times. Ask them to discuss meanings with a partner, which will give them opportunities to use the words in speaking and listening.

- If students confuse words that look or sound the same, such as *carnival* and *carnivore*, write the words on the board, one above the other. Say each word slowly. Have students repeat it. Then help students compare the spellings. Ask: *What's the same in both words? What's different*

AUTHOR'S POINT OF VIEW

RI.5.8 RI.6.6 CCSS

Informational

Unit and Week	Pages
Unit 1, Week 5	50–57
Unit 3, Week 5	170–177
Unit 4, Week 3	208–215
Unit 4, Week 4	220–227
Unit 5, Week 5	290–297

I Do Display and read aloud: *Littering is a terrible way of getting rid of garbage. When people leave garbage on the ground, they ruin the environment. Animals' habitats become covered with trash. Animals may even eat the garbage and get sick.* Model identifying the author's point of view. Say: *Author's choose words that express a point of view or opinion about the topic. The words* terrible *and* ruin *are powerful opinion words. Both words express a strong negative feeling.* Point out the last three sentences. *The author also includes reasons to support his or her point of view or opinion. I think the author's point of view is: People should not litter.*

We Do Display: *Wind power is amazing. Energy from the force of the wind can be used to make electricity. Unlike using oil, wind power does not give off harmful pollution. Wind power is also available everywhere.* Say: *Let's figure out the author's point of* view. Ask: *What powerful opinion word do you see in the first sentence?* (amazing) *What reasons and evidence does the author include?* (energy from the force of the wind can be used to make electricity; wind power does not give off harmful pollution; wind power is available everywhere) *Use these clues. What is the author's point of view?* (We should use wind power.)

You Do Display this short passage: *Scientists who study space know a lot about astronomy and math. These scientists are so smart that they can identify stars and planets from far away. They can figure out distances between objects in space. These clever scientists can even tell if a planet is mostly made of gas without ever visiting it!*

Have partners identify strong opinion words, and reasons and evidence. Then have them use these clues to tell the author's point of view in their own words. (Opinion words: smart, clever; Evidence: They can identify stars and planets from far away. They can figure out distances between objects in space; scientists can even tell if a planet is made of gas without visiting it. Author's point of view: Scientists who study space are very smart.)

For more practice, have students use the digital mini-lesson or use the **Interactive Worktext** Shared Read or **Apprentice Leveled Reader** from one of the weeks in the chart above.

CAUSE AND EFFECT

RI.5.3 **CCSS**

Informational

Unit and Week	Pages
Unit 1, Week 3	28–35
Unit 5, Week 4	280–287
Unit 6, Week 3	328–335

I Do Display and read aloud: *The rainstorm lasted two days. It caused the river to flood.* Say: *Why did the river flood? The reason is: The rainstorm lasted two*

days. Write *Cause* over the first sentence and *Effect* over the second. Circle the word *caused*. Say: *This text shows a cause and effect. The first sentence tells why something happened. The second sentence tells what happened as a result. Authors often use signal words such as* because, caused, as a result, so, *and* therefore *to show a cause and effect.* Display these variations with different signal words: *Because the rainstorm lasted two days, the river flooded. The rainstorm lasted two days. So the river flooded.*

Display: *The thunder was loud. I covered my ears.* Point out that in these sentences there is a cause (the thunder was loud) and an effect (I covered my ears) but no signal words.

We Do Display: *Michael missed the bus. As a result, he was late for school.* Say: *Let's find a cause and its effect together. What did Michael do?* (missed the bus) *What happened because Michael missed the bus?* (He was late for school.) *What is the cause?* (Michael missed the bus) *What is the effect?* (Michael was late for school.) *What are the signal words?* (as a result)

You Do Display this short passage: *Peter felt sick, so he stayed home from school. Peter got a lot of sleep during the day. As a result, he feels much better now.*

Have partners identify causes and effects, and identify the signal words. (Cause: Peter felt sick; Effect: He stayed home from school; Cause: Peter got a lot of sleep; Effect: He feels much better now. Signal words: so, as a result)

For more practice, have students use the digital mini-lesson or use the **Interactive Worktext** Shared Read or **Apprentice Leveled Reader** from one of the weeks in the chart above.

COMPARE AND CONTRAST

RL.5.3 CCSS

Literature

Units and Weeks	Pages
Unit 2, Week 2	78–85
Unit 5, Week 1	248–255
Unit 5, Week 2	258–265

I Do Display and read aloud: *Miranda was unhappy when she first arrived at summer camp. Miranda had lots of friends at school, but here she didn't know anyone. Later that day, Miranda met two girls in her cabin. They invited her to sit with them at lunch. Miranda liked her new camp friends.* Say: *Characters, settings, and events change in a story. We can compare and contrast characters, settings, and events to help us identify these changes and how they affect the plot. How does Miranda feel when she gets to summer camp? She is unhappy. Does Miranda feel the same or different later that day? I read that Miranda liked her new camp friends. I can tell she feels differently after they invited her to lunch. She is happier than when she first arrived.*

We Do Display: *Miranda's new friends, Leah and Dana, have been to camp before. "My favorite part of going to camp is when we have campfires and tell scary stories," Leah tells Miranda at lunch. Dana whispers to Miranda that she doesn't like scary stories. Miranda is unsure if she'll like them, but she looks forward to hearing the stories at the campfire tonight.* Ask: *How are Dana and Leah alike?* (They have both been to camp before.) *How are they different?* (Leah likes scary stories; Dana does not.) *How is Miranda like the other girls?* (She is at camp) *How is she different?* (She is not sure if she will like the stories.)

You Do Display this short passage: *Later that night, everyone gathers around the campfire. Miranda sits with Leah and Dana again. When the camp counselor announces story hour, Leah claps her hands in excitement. As the storyteller begins, Dana covers her ears and whispers to Miranda, "Tell me when the scary part is over!" Miranda nods to Dana, but leans in to better hear the exciting story.*

Have partners tell how the setting, characters, and events are alike and different at night compared to earlier that day. (Alike: Dana, Miranda, and Leah sit together. Leah wants to hear the story; Dana doesn't. Dana whispers to Miranda. Different: They are sitting around a campfire. They are listening to a story. Miranda likes the story.)

For more practice, have students use the digital mini-lesson or use the **Interactive Worktext** Shared Read or **Apprentice Leveled Reader** from one of the weeks in the chart above.

COMPARE AND CONTRAST

RI.5.3 CCSS

Informational Text

Unit and Week	Pages
Unit 5, Week 3	268–275

I Do Display and read aloud: *Both leopards and cheetahs are large, spotted cats. Cheetahs hunt during the day, but leopards hunt at night. Unlike cheetahs, leopards often hunt from trees.* Say: *Authors may organize informational texts by comparing and contrasting people, things, or ideas. Signal words, such as* like *and* both *tell me that an author is making a comparison, or showing that two things are alike. Words such as* but, however, *and* unlike, *signal a contrast. In the first sentence, I see the word* Both. *This word signals that the author is telling how leopards and cheetahs are alike. In the next two sentences, I see the words* but *and* Unlike. *These words signal that the author is telling how cheetahs and leopards are different.*

Display: *Cheetahs hunt during the day. Leopards hunt at night.* Point out that in these sentences there are no signal words. But the author is still showing a contrast.

We Do Display: *Earth and Mars are both planets. Like Earth, Mars has canyons and volcanoes. However, Earth is mostly covered by water and Mars is mostly rock.* Say: *Let's find out how the information is alike and different. What is being compared?* (Mars and Earth) *How are they different?* (Earth is mostly covered by water; Mars is mostly rock.) *What signal word tells you that they are different?* (However) *How are Earth and Mars alike?* (Both are planets; both have canyons and volcanoes.) *What signal words tell you they are alike?* (both; like)

You Do Display this short passage: *George Washington and Abraham Lincoln were both great presidents. Unlike George Washington, Abraham Lincoln was a lawyer before he became president. Both were good speakers, but Lincoln is better known for his great speeches.*

Have partners identify how George Washington and Abraham Lincoln are alike and different. (Alike: Both were great presidents; both were good speakers. Different: Abraham Lincoln was a lawyer; George Washington was not. Lincoln is better known for his great speeches.) Then have them identify the signal words. (both, unlike, but)

For more practice, have students use the digital mini-lesson or use the **Interactive Worktext** Shared Read or **Apprentice Leveled Reader** from the week in the chart above.

MAIN IDEA AND KEY DETAILS

RI.5.2 **CCSS**

Informational

Units and Weeks	Pages
Unit 3, Week 3	148–155
Unit 3, Week 4	160–167

I Do Display and read aloud: *Park rangers work to protect parks. Some park rangers give hikes and tell people about the importance of the park. Some park rangers help clean up areas. There are also park rangers that fight wildfires.* Underline sentences 2, 3, and 4. Say: *These are the key details. They tell about the topic of the text: park rangers. Now I will figure out what these details have in common. Each detail tells about something park rangers do. I can tell that the main idea is: Park rangers do many kinds of work to protect parks.*

We Do Display: *Cell phones today are used to do more than just make phone calls. People can use cell phones to store phone numbers. People can also use cell phones to type and send messages. Some people even use these devices to play games and watch movies.* Work with students to identify the main idea. Ask: *What is the topic of the passage?* (cell phones) *What are the key details?* (People can store phone numbers; people can use cell phones to type and send messages; people use these devices to play games and watch movies.) *What do these details have in common?* (They are all about things people can do with cell phones.) *What is the main idea?* (People can use cell phones to do many things.)

You Do Display this short passage: *Everyone should have a computer at home. With a computer, you can look up facts and write a paper without leaving your desk. Computers let you go shopping from home. They even play music and movies.*

Have partners identify the topic and key details. Then have them determine what the key details have in common in order to identify the main idea. (Topic: computers; Key details: look up facts and write a paper without leaving your desk; shop from home; play music and movies; Main idea: Computers help people do many things.)

For more practice, have students use the digital mini-lesson or use the **Interactive Worktext** Shared Read or **Apprentice Leveled Reader** from one of the weeks in the chart above.

POINT OF VIEW

RL.5.6 CCSS

Literature

Unit and Week	Pages
Unit 4, Week 1	188–195
Unit 4, Week 2	198–205
Unit 6, Week 5	350–357

I Do Display and read aloud: *Scott grabbed the ball from Mark and ran to the end of the court. He slammed the ball through the net. "I am the best!" Scott shouted, rudely.* Model identifying the point of view. Say: *A narrator or speaker's point of view refers to the way a story is told. You can figure out a narrator's or speaker's point of view by looking for key details and descriptive words. I read that Scott "grabbed the ball from Mark." I also read that Scott shouted "rudely." I can tell from these descriptions that the narrator thinks Scott is not playing nicely.*

We Do Display: *Jen and I were walking past Ms. Lee's house. When I saw that her big, scary dog was outside, I quickly ran ahead. But Jen just stopped and gazed at the dog over the fence. "He's so cute! He's licking his paws just like a little puppy!" Jen said.* Point out that a narrator can have a different point of view from the characters. *How does the narrator describe Ms. Lee's dog?* (big, scary) *What does the narrator do?* (runs ahead) *What do these details tell you about the narrator's point of view?* (The narrator thinks Ms. Lee's dog is scary.) *What does Jen think about Ms. Lee's dog?* (Jen thinks Ms. Lee's dog is cute) *What details tell you this?* (she stopped and gazed at the dog; He's so cute! He's licking his paws just like a little puppy!)

You Do Display this short passage: *I stepped on something sticky. When I raised my foot to see what it was, I frowned. "Gross!" I said. Some thoughtless person had thrown a piece of chewing gum on the sidewalk. Now my shoes were completely ruined.*

Have partners identify details and descriptive words that are clues to the narrator's point of view and then determine the point of view about the events. (Details and descriptive words: frowned; "Gross!"; thoughtless; ruined. Point of view: The narrator is upset and angry about stepping in gum.)

For more practice, have students use the digital mini-lesson or use the **Interactive Worktext** Shared Read or **Apprentice Leveled Reader** from one of the weeks in the chart above.

PROBLEM AND SOLUTION

RL.5.3 CCSS

Literature

Unit and Week	Pages
Unit 1, Week 2	18–25

I Do Display and read aloud: *Nathan's printer won't work. He needs to print out his report for school. Nathan asks Dan if he can print his report at Dan's house. Dan helps Nathan print his report.* Remind students that characters in a story often have a problem. Say: *Nathan has a problem.* Write *Problem* above the first two sentences. Then explain that the way a character fixes or solves the problem is the solution. *What does Nathan do next to try to solve his problem? He asks Dan if he can print his report at Dan's house. What solves his problem? Dan helps Nathan print his report.* Write *Solution* above this sentence.

We Do Display: *Beth ran over a nail while riding her bike. Her tire was completely flat. Beth walked her bike home. She used special tape to patch the hole. Then she filled the tire with air.* Say: *Let's find the problem and solution together.* Ask: *What is Beth's problem?* (Her bike tire got a hole.) *What is the first step she took to solve the problem?* (She walked her bike home.) *What was the solution to fixing the bike?* (She used special tape to patch the hole. She filled the tire with air.)

You Do Display this short passage: *Deb borrowed her brother's mitt for her baseball game. She accidentally left it at the field. When Deb went back to get it, she couldn't find it. She looked on the bleachers. She asked people if they had seen it. Finally, she went to the lost and found. The mitt was in the box.*

Have partners identify the problem, the steps Deb takes to solve the problem, and the solution. (Problem: Deb lost her brother's mitt. Steps to solve the problem: Deb goes back to the field. She looked on the bleachers. She asked people if they had seen it. Solution: Deb goes to the lost and found and finds the mitt there.)

For more practice, have students use the digital mini-lesson or use the **Interactive Worktext** Shared Read or **Apprentice Leveled Reader** from the week in the chart above.

PROBLEM AND SOLUTION

RI.5.3 **CCSS**

Informational

Unit and Week	Pages
Unit 2, Week 1	68–75
Unit 6, Week 4	340–347

I Do Display and read aloud: *In the 1870s, photographers had to use a lot of equipment. A photographer named George Eastman decided to experiment with chemicals and materials. As a result, he came up with an easier way to take photographs by using a paper coated with chemicals.* Remind students that authors sometimes use a problem and solution structure in informational texts. Write *Problem* above the first sentence and *Solution* above the third sentence. Say: *This text shows a problem and solution. The first sentence tells the problem. The second sentence tells the steps to solve the problem. The last sentence tells the solution.* Circle the signal words *as a result. Authors use signal words such as* as a result *and* therefore *to show a solution*

to a problem.

Display: *The first cameras could only take pictures when there was lots of light. The flashbulb was invented to help people take photographs when there was little light.* Point out that in these sentences there is a problem (The first cameras could only take pictures when there was lots of light) and a solution (The flashbulb was invented to help people take photographs when there was little light) but no signal words.

We Do Display: *In the 1800s, women were not allowed to vote. So many women made speeches about voting rights. They held parades. They talked to people in government to get them to change the law. After many years, the government changed the law to let women vote.* Say: *Let's find the problem and solution together.* Ask: *What problem did women have in the 1800s?* (they were not allowed to vote) *What did women do to try to solve the problem?* (They made speeches about voting rights; they held parades; they talked to people in government to get them to change the law.) *What was the solution?* (The government changed the law to let women vote.)

You Do Display: *The first cars had problems. When it was raining or snowing, a car driver had to get out of the car to wipe the window. Mary Anderson came up with an idea for a tool that could attach to a car and wipe the window. Later, the tool was made and added to many cars. As a result, drivers could safely wipe their windows without getting out of their cars.*

Have partners identify the problem, the steps to solve the problem, the solution, and any signal words. (Problem: a driver had to get out of the car to wipe the window. Steps to solve the problem: Mary Anderson came up with an idea for a tool that could attach to a car and wipe the window. Later, the tool was made and added to many cars. Solution: Drivers could wipe the window without getting out their cars. Signal words: as a result)

For more practice, have students use the digital mini-lesson or use the **Interactive Worktext** Shared Read or **Apprentice Leveled Reader** from one of the weeks in the chart above.

SEQUENCE

RL.3.3

Literature

Unit and Week	Pages
Unit 1, Week 1	8–15

I Do Display and read aloud: *Nicky and his class went to the zoo. First, a guide showed them the bird exhibit. Then, the class had lunch. After lunch, the class walked to the reptile exhibit. They waited for the alligator to come out. Finally the alligator appeared!* Underline *first, then, after* and *finally.* Say: *These are sequence words that help me figure out in what order the events took place.* Number the sentences as you model figuring out the order of events: *What happened first? The guide showed them the bird exhibit. What happened next? The class had lunch. What happened after? The class walked to the reptile exhibit and waited for the alligator to come out. The alligator appeared last.*

Display: *The class walked to the reptile exhibit. They waited for the alligator to come out.* Point out that there are no sequence words. But there is still a sequence of events.

We Do Display: *Pat went to Grandma's house. At first, Pat was bored because she wasn't around her friends. Then Grandma took her to a park. They canoed across a river. After that, they had a picnic. They had a fun day!* Say: *Let's figure out the sequence of events together. What happened first?* (Pat went to Grandma's house.) *What happened next?* (Pat was bored) *What happened then?* (Grandma took her to the park. They canoed across a river.) *What happened after?* (They had a picnic.) *What are the sequence words?* (At first, Then, After that)

You Do Display this short passage: *Dad and I arrived at camp late last night. After feeding the horses, we found some wood. Next, Dad made a fire. We put up our tents. Then we warmed up some dinner. Soon we crawled into our tents and went to bed.*

Have partners identify the sequence of events and the sequence words that help them follow the order of events. (<u>Sequence of events:</u> They arrived at camp, fed the horses, found wood, made a fire, put up tents, warmed up dinner, crawled into tents, went to bed. <u>Sequence words:</u> late last night, After, Next, Then, Soon)

For more practice, have students use the digital mini-lesson or use the **Interactive Worktext** Shared Read or **Apprentice Leveled Reader** from the week in the chart above.

SEQUENCE

RI.5.3

Informational

Unit and Week	Pages
Unit 1, Week 4	40–47
Unit 2, Week 3	88–95

I Do Display and read aloud: *Marie Curie was born in Poland in 1867. As a child, she became interested in math and science. In 1891, she went to college in France. Later, she became a teacher.* Model identifying the sequence of events. Say: *Authors often tell about events in the order, or sequence, in which they happened.* Underline *1867, as a child, 1891, later.* Say: *These words tell me when the events in Marie Curie's life took place.* Give other examples of signal words such as *first, after, later,* and *then.*

Display: *Marie's sister went to Paris. Marie followed her there.* Point out there is also a sequence of events in these sentences, but no signal words.

We Do Display: *Making butter is easy. First, pour some heavy cream into a small jar. Then add a little bit of salt. Next, shake the jar. Keep shaking. After a while, you'll have butter.* Say: *Let's figure out the sequence of events together. Which sentence tells what happens first?* (second sentence) *Let's write "1" next to this sentence. What happens next? Write a "2" next to this sentence.* (Add a little bit of salt.) Continue to guide students to number the rest of the sentences in order. Ask: *What are the signal words?* (First, Then, Next, After a while)

You Do Display this short passage: *On the morning of July 16, 1969, the Apollo 11 spacecraft left the earth on its way to the moon. First, the shuttle circled the earth. Then it headed for the moon. The shuttle circled the moon for 24 hours. Finally, on July 20th, the astronauts landed on the moon.*

Have partners number the events in order and identify signal words. (Sequence of events: 1. Apollo 11 spacecraft left the earth. 2. The shuttle circled the earth. 3. It headed for the moon. 4. The shuttle circled the moon for 24 hours. 5. the Astronauts landed on the moon. Signal words: July 16, 1969, First, Then, Finally, On July 20th)

For more practice, have students use the digital mini-lesson or use the **Interactive Worktext** Shared Read or **Apprentice Leveled Reader** from one of the weeks in the chart above.

THEME

RL.5.2 CCSS

Literature

Unit and Week	Pages
Unit 2, Week 4	100–107
Unit 2, Week 5	110–117
Unit 3, Week 1	128–135
Unit 3, Week 2	138–145
Unit 4, Week 5	230–237
Unit 6, Week 1	308–315
Unit 6, Week 2	318–325

I Do Remind students that a story's theme is the message or lesson the author wants to communicate. Display and read aloud: *Ben was the shortest boy in school. But he wanted to try out for the basketball team, anyway. "I know I'm not as tall*

as other kids," Ben told the coach. "But I can still help the team." Ben practiced. At his tryout, he moved so fast, the tall boys couldn't get the ball from him. Ben made the team! Say: *I will look at what the characters do, say, and feel to figure out the theme. I read that Ben decided to try out for basketball, even though he knows he is not as tall as the other kids. He says he can help the team in other ways. He practices before he tries out. The result of all Ben's work is that he makes the team. I think the theme is that you can do anything if you believe in yourself and work hard.*

We Do Display: *Justine borrowed her sister's sweater. At lunch, she got ketchup on it. The sweater was ruined. Justine worried that her sister would be mad. She wanted to hide the sweater. Justine told her friend Jean. "Be honest." Jean said. "She'll understand." Justine told her sister when she got home. Her sister told her to be more careful next time. Justine was glad she told the truth.* Say: *Let's figure out the theme together. What does Justine do?* (gets ketchup on her sister's sweater) *What does her friend say?* (Be honest.) *What happens to Justine?* (She tells her sister about the sweater and her sister tells her to be careful.) *What message do you think the author wants to share?* (Honesty is the best policy.)

You Do Display this short passage: *Jay was new on the soccer team. He didn't talk to anyone, so Gus thought Jay was stuck up. One day, Gus saw Jay staring at him while he was kicking the soccer ball. Gus went up to him. Jay blushed. "Sorry," he said quietly. "I was just watching you kick. You're very good." Gus asked if he wanted to play. "You bet!" Jay said. Gus realized he had judged Jay too quickly. Jay wasn't stuck up. He was just shy.*

Have partners discuss what the characters do and say and then determine the theme of the story. (Possible answer: Don't be quick to judge people.)

For more practice, have students use the digital mini-lesson or use the **Interactive Worktext** Shared Read or **Apprentice Leveled Reader** from one of the weeks in the chart above.

INFORM/EXPLAIN

W.5.2a W.5.2b W.5.2e W.5.5

Review an Analysis

- Have students turn to a student model of an analysis that informs and explains in the **Interactive Worktext.** Read aloud the student model while students follow along.

- Explain to students that in this analysis the student informs and explains how an author developed the text. Point out the topic sentence includes the text's title and tells what the paragraph is about. Have students point out facts, details, quotations, and other text evidence that support the topic.

- Read aloud the last sentence. Have students turn to a partner and answer the questions: *Which words wrap up the paragraph? What does this student explain about the text?*

Revise an Analysis

Revise Writing Work with students to select a writing product that they completed in Weeks 1–5 that would benefit from revision. Review with students the writing you selected and the related **Interactive Worktext** lesson. Discuss the writing selection and the checklist of items that the selection should include.

Guide students to check that their writing begins with a topic sentence and that it includes the title of the selection. Have students identify whether or not the writing includes details from the text that support the topic. Remind students to check for a strong conclusion.

Guide students to determine how best to revise their writing. Work with them to add or improve the elements that they found were missing or in need of work. Have students revise the writing based on their review.

Teacher Conference Compare students' revision to their original writing. Check students' writing for complete sentences. Did they begin with a topic sentence? Did they cite text evidence to support their topic? Did the concluding sentence restate the topic sentence and tie the evidence together?

OPINION

W.5.1a W.5.1b W.5.1d W.5.5

Review an Analysis

- Have students turn to a student model of an analysis that shares an opinion in the **Interactive Worktext.** Read aloud the student model while students follow along.

- Explain to students that in this analysis the student gives an opinion about the text. Point out that the topic sentence includes the text's title and tells an opinion. Point out any opinion words, such as *I think, good/bad,* and *exciting.* Have students point out facts, details, quotations, and other text evidence that support the student's opinion.

- Read aloud the last sentence. Have students turn to a partner and answer the questions: *Which words wrap up the paragraph? What is the student's opinion about the text?*

Revise an Analysis

Revise Writing Work with students to select a writing product that they completed in Weeks 1–5 that would benefit from revision. Review with students the writing you selected and the related **Interactive Worktext** lesson. Discuss the writing selection and the checklist of items that the selection should include.

Guide students to check that their writing begins with a topic sentence and that it includes the selection title. Have students identify whether or not the writing includes details from the text that support their opinion. Tell students to check for a strong conclusion.

Guide students to determine how best to revise the writing. Guide them to add elements that they found were missing or improve elements in need of work. Have them revise the writing based on their review.

Teacher Conference Compare students' revision to their original writing. Check students' writing for complete sentences. Did they begin with a topic sentence that tells an opinion? Did they cite text evidence to support their opinion? Did the concluding sentence restate their opinion and tie the evidence together?

Inform/Explain

Writing Rubric

	4	3	2	1
Topic Sentence	There is one clear, focused topic sentence.	Topic sentence is less focused, somewhat clear.	Topic is presented in short phrases.	There is no topic sentence.
Text Evidence	Topic is supported by two or more text details.	Evidence includes only one detail from the text.	Little to no evidence is cited from the text.	No text evidence was included.
Concluding Statement	Clearly restates the topic sentence; wraps up all the details.	Restatement is less focused; attempts wrap up the details.	Vaguely restates the topic. Doesn't correlate well to text evidence.	There is no conclusion.
Writing Style	Writes in complete sentences. Uses correct spelling and grammar.	Uses complete sentences and phrases. Writing has spelling and grammar errors.	Few or no complete sentences. There are many spelling and grammar errors.	Does not write accurately or in complete sentences.

Opinion

Writing Rubric

	4	3	2	1
Topic Sentence	Topic sentence presents a clear opinion.	Topic sentences presents an opinion somewhat clearly.	Topic is presented in short phrases; opinion is unclear.	There is no topic sentence; no opinion is presented.
Text Evidence	Opinion is supported by two or more text details.	Opinion is only supported by one detail from the text.	Little to no text evidence supports opinion.	No text evidence was included; does not support opinion.
Concluding Statement	Clearly restates an opinion; wraps up all the details.	Restatement is less focused; attempts to wrap up the details.	Vaguely restates opinion. Doesn't correlate well to text evidence.	There is no conclusion.
Writing Style	Writes in complete sentences. Uses correct spelling and grammar.	Uses complete sentences and phrases. Writing has spelling and grammar errors.	Few or no complete sentences. There are many spelling and grammar errors.	Does not write accurately or in complete sentences.

Intonation

CCSS
RF.5.4a,
RF.5.4b **Objective** Read statements, questions, and exclamations with proper intonation in connected text

I Do Explain that good readers change their voices to show what sentences mean. Tell students that they should read different types of sentences differently. Write these sentences on the board.

We go to the park. Where is the park? We love the park! Read them in a flat monotone.

Then model reading each sentence with proper intonation. Explain how you decided to read each sentence differently Model circling the punctuation in each sentence. Remind students that a sentence that ends with a period is read in a steady way. In a sentence that ends in a question mark, you raise your voice at the end. A sentence that ends with an exclamation point is read with strong feeling or excitement.

We Do Have students turn to the Interactive Worktext or Apprentice Level Reader for the week and choose a section to read fluently. As a group, circle and name the punctuation mark at the end of each sentence. Have the students tell how each sentence should be read. Provide corrective feedback.

Read aloud the passage and create a summary with the group. Point out how reading different types of sentences with proper expression helps readers understand the passage. Read aloud the passage again.

Model echo reading a few sentences from the passage with a volunteer. Then have students echo read the passage. Have students lead while you respond. Ask students to say how they read each phrase or sentence before you repeat it. Prompt them with this question each time it is your turn: How should I change my voice when I read this sentence?

Corrective Feedback Have partners practice reading the passage aloud to each other, focusing on reading sentences with correct intonation.

Have partners discuss the comprehension questions at the end of the passage. Then discuss the questions as a group.

Corrective Feedback Provide corrective feedback for errors in intonation, as well as errors in pronunciation. Point out the student's error and model reading the sentence or word correctly. Then have the student read the sentence or word again.

Expression

RF.5.4a,
RF.5.4b

Objective Understand how to read dialogue with expression

I Do Explain to students that a conversation that is written down is called *dialogue*. Say: When dialogue is read aloud, good readers use their voices to sound like the character who is speaking. They express the same feeling as the character. Ask students to listen as you pretend to be helping someone in a store:

"Can I help you? The greeting cards are against the wall. Let me know if you need anything else."

Explain that if the words you just said were written down, they would be called dialogue. Tell students that there are special ways of writing dialogue so readers know who said which part of the conversation and how they sounded when they said those words. Write the sentences below. Model reading each sentence aloud.

"Sarah, did you practice for the game?" John asked.

"Yes, I practiced kicking!" Sarah said.

Circle all the quotation marks. Quotation marks show where someone's exact words begin and end. Reread just the spoken words.

Underline words that aren't enclosed in quotation marks. These words tell who is speaking. They may also tell how the speaker says the words.

Circle the punctuation marks inside the quotation marks. These marks help you know whether to ask a question, make a statement, or show strong feeling. Reread the spoken words, using your voice to indicate sentence changes.

We Do Have students turn to an Interactive Worktext selection or Apprentice Level Reader that has dialogue and choose a section to read fluently. Guide students in circling the dialogue. Then have them underline the words that tell who is speaking. Next, have students echo read the passage with you.

You Do Have students partner-read the passage, reviewing the circled dialogue and underlined words. Remind students to read the dialogue as if they are the characters in the story. Have them alternate reading the other sentences.

Corrective Feedback Provide corrective feedback about reading dialogue with expression. Point out the student's error and model reading the sentence correctly. Have students read the sentence again.

Phrasing

CCSS

RF.5.4a,
RF.5.4b

Objective **Pause at commas and at end punctuation, using appropriate phrasing**

Explain that fluent readers pause after commas and after the punctuation at the end of a sentence as they read aloud. The punctuation marks show them how to use phrasing, or putting in pauses, to make the text more understandable.

Write a **period (.)** on the board: A period tells readers to pause at the end of a sentence. Display these sentences: *The goat kicked the can. Then it began to talk.* Model reading the sentences aloud, pausing at the end of each sentence. Point to each period as you pause.

Write a **question mark (?)** on the board. A question mark tells readers to raise their voice at the end of the question and then pause. Write the sentences as questions. *Did the goat kick the can? Did it begin to talk?* Then model reading each sentence aloud, raising your voice and then pausing. Point to each question mark as you do so.

Write an **exclamation point (!)** on the board. An exclamation point tells readers to read the sentence with strong feeling and then pause. Display these sentences: *The goat kicked the can! Then it began to talk!* Then model reading each sentence aloud, showing strong feeling and then pausing. Point to each exclamation mark.

Write a **comma (,)** on the board. A comma tells readers to pause for a short amount of time. A comma can separate two parts of a sentence. It separates items in a list. It is also used in dialogue. Display: *My cat has a gray coat, but she has white paws. She has a long tail, short ears, and a pink nose. "She's cute!" said Mom.* Circle the commas. Model reading the sentences aloud, pausing at the commas and pointing to them.

We Do Have students turn to the Interactive Worktext or Apprentice Level Reader for the week and choose a section to read fluently. Guide students in circling end punctuation and underlining any commas. Then model reading one sentence at a time as students echo read after you, focusing on phrasing. Repeat lines as needed. Then read the passage chorally with students.

You Do Have students practice partner reading the passage. Have them take turns reading the passage aloud, pausing at commas and at the end of each sentence. Remind them to pause for a short amount of time after commas and a slightly longer time after end punctuation. Remind them to use the appropriate expression and intonation for a period, an exclamation point, or a question mark.

Corrective Feedback Provide corrective feedback for appropriate phrasing by pausing for the appropriate amount of time at commas and at end punctuation. Point out the student's error and model reading the sentence with correct phrasing. Have the students reread the sentence.

Rate

RF.5.4a, RF.5.4b

Objective **Identify and demonstrate when to slow down reading**

I Do Explain to students that good readers slow down their pace of reading when the content is difficult. It is easier to think carefully about what you read when you read more slowly. It is helpful to slow down when reading nonfiction books or articles about science or social studies. When you slow down, you can pay attention to difficult vocabulary and complicated ideas.

Explain that a good reader must decide how and when to slow down reading.

- Is the text nonfiction? Is it about a social studies or science topic?
- Does the text have long words or unfamiliar vocabulary?
- Does the text have new ideas that you want to understand?

Read the following passage aloud. Guide students in recognizing that this is a nonfiction passage with technical words. Read it slowly and clearly. Think aloud as you encounter technical vocabulary by saying: I wonder what that means. I'm going to keep reading to find out.

A shooting star is a meteor. A meteor is a space rock. If the meteor lands on Earth, it is called a meteorite. *The bright streak of a shooting star is hot glowing air. It is made from the heat of a meteor as it speeds through Earth's atmosphere.*

We Do Have students turn to a nonfiction Interactive Worktext or Apprentice Level Reader and choose a section to read fluently.. Tell students that this is a nonfiction passage, so they should look for unfamiliar words. Model read the passage aloud at a slow pace. Help students understand that reading slowly will help them remember facts. Then do a choral reading with students.

You Do Have students partner-read the passage. Ask them to take turns reading the passage aloud. Then provide students a couple of comprehension questions about the text. Have partners discuss the questions. Then discuss the questions as a group.

Corrective Feedback Provide corrective feedback on student's reading rate. Explain that it is important to slow down in order to understand new words and complex text. Point out the student's error and model reading the sentence correctly. Have students repeat reading the sentence.

CCSS

RF.5.4a,
RF.5.4b

Accuracy

Objective Read words with accuracy and fluency

I Do Explain to students that when reading aloud, good readers pronounce each word clearly and correctly so their readers will not be confused.

Tell students to listen for a mistake as you say this sentence: *My mother said, "I am making (mumble, mumble).* Say: The way I read this sentence was confusing because you couldn't hear all the words.

Write and read aloud this sentence, mispronouncing the word *weather*: *The weather is cold today.* Say: The way I read this sentence was confusing because I didn't pronounce all the words correctly. **Point to the word** *weather*. I should have pronounced that word /WETHer/, not
/WEETHer/. Then you would have understood me.

Write the sentence below and model reading it two or three times, each time with clearer and more correct pronunciation of the words *wind* and *sky*. Then ask students to read the sentence, pronouncing each word clearly and correctly.

The wind blew the kite across the sky.

We Do Have students turn to a nonfiction Interactive Worktext or Apprentice Level Reader and choose a section to read fluently. Model reading the passage aloud. Point out how you are reading every word clearly and correctly.

Model how to echo read the passage with a volunteer. Then echo read with the class, Read one sentence at a time and have students echo read it. Remind them to pronounce words clearly and correctly.

You Do Have partners echo read the passage aloud to each other. Tell students to let their partners know if they did not understand a word that was read.

Give students one or two comprehension questions about the passage. Have partners discuss the questions. Then discuss the questions as a group.

Corrective Feedback Provide corrective feedback for errors in pronunciation, or accuracy. Point out the student's error and model reading the sentence correctly. Have students read the sentences again.

Text Complexity

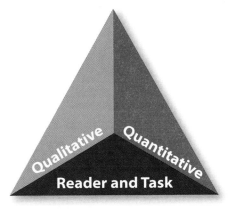

Qualitative | Quantitative

Reader and Task

Quantitative Measures

Two tools have been used to determine the quantitative dimension of text complexity for texts in *Reading WonderWorks*.

- **Lexile**
- **ETS** *Text Evaluator*™ measures more explicit feature of text
  —Connection of Ideas
  —Vocabulary
  —Sentence Structure
  —Organization

Reading WonderWorks provides complex texts for Grade 5 intervention students at their level. Students begin in the Grades 2–3 text complexity band (as defined by the Common Core State Standards) and accelerate into the Grades 4–5 text complexity band by the middle of the year. This allows them to exit into the *Reading Wonders* Approaching group by the end of Grade 5.

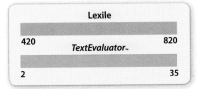

Text Complexity Range for Grades 2–3

Lexile	
420	820

TextEvaluator™	
2	35

Text Complexity Range for Grades 4–5

Lexile	
740	1010

TextEvaluator™	
23	51

Qualitative Measures

Specific aspects of the qualitative dimensions of text complexity are identified. Scaffolded instruction is provided to help students access these features of the text.

- Structure
  - **Organization**
  - **Genre**
- Language Conventionality and Clarity
  - **Vocabulary**
  - **Sentence Structure**
- Knowledge Demands
  - **Prior Knowledge**
- Levels of Meaning/Purpose
  - **Purpose**
  - **Connection of Ideas**

Reader and Tasks

Readers' engagement and knowledge of the concept will influence the complexity of a text. In addition, the questions and tasks applied to a text will affect the complexity.

READING Complex Text

Use Your Own Text

Choose your own text

Get Ready

- Use this lesson with a text of your choice.
- Assign reading of the text. You may wish to do this by section or chapters.
- Chunk the text into shorter important passages for rereading.
- Present an Essential Question.

Read the Text *What does the author tell us?*

Assign the Reading

Ask students to read the assigned sections of the text independently. For sections that are more difficult for students, you may wish to read the text aloud or ask students to read with a partner.

Take Notes

As students read, ask them to take notes on difficult parts of the text. Model how to take notes on

- identifying details or parts that are unclear
- words they do not know
- information they feel is important
- ways in which information or events are connected
- the genre of the text

You may wish to have students complete a graphic organizer, chosen from within the unit, to take notes on important information as they read. The graphic organizer can help them summarize the text.

Help students access the complex features of the text. Scaffold instruction on the following features as necessary:

- Purpose
- Genre
- Vocabulary
- Sentence Structure

- Connection of Ideas
- Organization
- Prior Knowledge

Reread the Text *What does the text mean?*

Ask Text-Dependent Questions/Generate Questions

 Ask students to reread the shorter passages from the text, focusing on how the author provides information or develops the characters, setting, and plot. Focus questions on the following:

Literature Selections	**Informational Text**
Character, Setting, and Plot Development	Main Idea and Supporting Key Details
Word Choice	Word Choice
Genre	Text Structure
Point of View	Text Features
	Genre
	Author's Point of View

Have students discuss questions they generated. As each student shares a question, ask all students to go back into the text to find text evidence to answer the question. Encourage students to

- point out the exact place within the text they found the evidence
- reread and paraphrase the section of the text that they think supports their answer
- discuss how well the cited evidence answers the question
- identify when an answer to a question cannot be found in the text

Write About the Text *Think about what the author wrote.*

Essential Question

Have students respond in writing to the Essential Question, considering the complete text. Students can work with a partner and use their notes and graphic organizers to locate evidence that can be used to answer the question.

COLLABORATE

Making the Most of Collaborative Conversations

The Common Core State Standards state that students must have ample opportunities to take part in a variety of rich, structured conversations—as part of a whole class, in small groups, and with a partner.

Students should practice using the prompt and response frames below for collaborative conversations with partners until the frames become routine.

Core Skills	Prompt Frames	Response Frames
Elaborate and Ask Questions to Request Clarification	Can you tell me more about it? Can you give some details on…? Can you be more specific? What do you mean by…? How/Why is that important?	I think it means that… In other words… It's important because… It's similar to when…
Support Ideas with Text Evidence	What do you think of the idea that…? Can we add to this idea? Do you agree? What are other ideas /points of view? What else do we need to think about? How does that connect to the idea…?	The text says that… An example from another text is… According to… Some evidence that supports that is…
Build On and/or Challenge Partner's Idea	What do we know so far? To recap, I think that… I'm not sure that was clear. How can we relate what I said to the topic/ question?	I would add that… I want to follow up on your idea… Another way to look at it is… What you said made me think of….
Paraphrase	What have we discussed so far? How can we summarize what we talked about? What can we agree upon? What are the main points or ideas we can share? What relevant details support the main points or ideas? What key ideas can we take away?	So, you are saying that… Let me see if I understand you… Do you mean that…? In other words… It sounds like you are saying that…
Determine the Main Idea and Supporting Details	What have we discussed so far? How can we summarize what we talked about? What can we agree upon? What are the main points or ideas we can share? What relevant details support the main points or ideas? What key ideas can we take away?	We can say that… The main idea seems to be… As a result of this conversation, we think that we should… The evidence suggests that…

Understanding English Language Learner Levels

The **English Language Learners** in your classroom have a variety of backgrounds. Each student has differences in ethnic background, first language, socioeconomic status, quality of prior schooling, and levels of language proficiency. In addition, English language learners bring diverse sets of academic knowledge and cultural perspectives that should be respected and leveraged to enrich learning.

Many English language learners bring oral language proficiency, literacy knowledge, and skills in their first languages that can be used to facilitate language and literacy development in English. It is important to note that students may be at different levels in each language domain (listening, speaking, reading, and writing). Systematic, explicit, and appropriately-scaffolded instruction help English Language Learners attain English proficiency and meet the high expectations defined in the Common Core State Standards.

Beginning

This level of language proficiency is often referred to as the "silent" stage, in which students' receptive skills are engaged. It is important that teachers and peers respect a language learner's initial silence or allow the student to respond in his or her native language. It is often difficult for teachers to identify the level of cognitive development at this stage, due to the limited proficiency in the second language.

Beginning students require significant language support in their early stages of language development. As they gain experience with English, support may become moderate or light for familiar tasks and topics.

The Beginning Student...

- recognizes English phonemes that correspond to phonemes produced in primary language;
- initially demonstrates more receptive than productive English skills;
- communicates basic needs and information in social and academic settings using gestures, learned words or phrases, and/or short sentences;
- follows one- or two-step oral directions;
- answers *wh-* questions (who, what, when, where, why, which);
- comprehends words, phrases, and basic information about familiar topics as presented through stories and conversations
- identifies concepts about print and text features;
- reads short grade-appropriate text with familiar vocabulary and simple sentences, supported by graphics or pictures;
- draws pictures and writes labels;
- expresses ideas using visuals and short responses;
- uses familiar vocabulary related to everyday and academic topics.

Intermediate

Students at this level begin to tailor their English language skills to meet communication and learning demands with increasing accuracy. They possess knowledge of vocabulary and grammatical structures that allow them to more fully participate in classroom activities and discussions. They are generally more comfortable producing both spoken and written language.

Intermediate students require moderate support for cognitively demanding activities and light support for familiar tasks and topics.

The Intermediate Student...

- pronounces most English phonemes correctly while reading aloud;
- communicates more complex personal needs, ideas, and opinions using increasingly complex vocabulary and sentences;
- follows multi-step oral directions;
- initiates and participates in collaborative conversations about social and academic topics, with support as needed;
- asks questions, retells stories or events, and comprehends basic content-area concepts;
- comprehends information on familiar and unfamiliar topics with contextual clues;
- reads increasingly complex grade-level text supported by graphics, pictures, and context clues;
- increases correct usage of written and oral language conventions;
- uses vocabulary learned, including academic language, to provide information and extended responses in contextualized oral and written prompts.

Advanced

Students at this level possess vocabulary and grammar structures that approach those of an English-proficient speaker. Advanced students demonstrate consistent general comprehension of grade-level content. They engage in complex social and academic activities.

While the English language proficiency of these students is advanced, some language support for accessing content is still necessary.

The Advanced Student...

- applies knowledge of common English morphemes in oral and silent reading;
- communicates complex feelings, needs, ideas, and opinions using increasingly complex vocabulary and sentences;
- understands more nonliteral social and academic language about concrete and abstract topics;
- initiates and sustains collaborative conversations about grade-level academic and social topics;
- reads and comprehends a wide range of complex literature and informational texts at grade level;
- writes using more standard forms of English on various academic topics;
- communicates orally and in writing with fewer grammatical errors;
- tailors language, orally and in writing, to specific purposes and audiences.

Facilitating Language Growth

Beginning

Student's Behaviors	Teacher's Behaviors	Questioning Techniques
• Points to or provides other nonverbal responses • Actively listens and responds to one- or two-step oral directions, especially commands • Initially, understands more than he or she can produce • Begins speaking in one- or two-word utterances, expanding to short phrases and simple sentences • Reads short grade-appropriate text with scaffolds • Draws pictures and writes labels	• Gestures • Focuses on conveying meanings and vocabulary development • Does not force students to speak right away (allows silent period) • Shows visuals and real objects • Writes words for students to see • Pairs students with more proficient learners • Provides speaking and writing frames and models • Asks *yes/no* and *either/or* questions	• Point to the _____. • Find the _____. • Put the _____ next to the _____. • Do you have the _____? • Is this the _____? • Who wants the _____? • Yes/no (Did you like the story?) • Either/or (Is this fiction or nonfiction?) • Short response *wh-* questions (Why did the dog hide?)

Intermediate

Student's Behaviors	Teacher's Behaviors	Questioning Techniques
• Produces increasingly complex sentences • Listens with greater understanding • Asks questions and retells stories or events • Reads increasingly complex grade-level text with scaffolds • Produces short written responses, including academic language	• Asks higher-order questions with one-word answers • Models correct responses • Ensures supportive, low-anxiety environment • Does not overtly call attention to grammar errors • Asks short *wh-* questions • Asks open-ended questions that stimulate language production	• General questions that encourage lists of words (What words describe the main character?) • Tell me about _____. • Talk about _____. • Describe _____. • How do you know? • Why? Why not?

Advanced

Student's Behaviors	Teacher's Behaviors	Questioning Techniques
• Participates in complex reading and writing activities • Demonstrates increased levels of accuracy and is able to produce language with varied grammatical structures and academic language • May need support in abstract, cognitively demanding subjects	• Fosters conceptual development and expanded literacy through content • Continues to make lessons comprehensible and interactive • Teaches critical thinking skills • Continues to be alert to individual differences in language and culture	• What is this selection about? • What does this character think? How do you know? • Compare/contrast _____. How are these similar/different? • Why do you think that _____? Yes, tell me more about _____. • Do you agree with the author's point of view? Why/why not?

(ELL) Collaborative Conversations

Strategies for English Language Learners

One of the most effective ways in which to increase the oral language proficiency of your English Language Learners is to give students many opportunities to do a lot of talking in the classroom. Providing the opportunities and welcoming all levels of participation will motivate students to take part in the class discussions. You can employ a few basic teaching strategies that will encourage the participation of all language proficiency levels of English Language Learners in whole class and small group discussions.

☑ Wait/Different Responses

- Be sure to give students enough time to answer the question.
- Let students know that they can respond in different ways depending on their levels of proficiency. Students can
  - answer in their native language;
  - ask a more proficient ELL speaker to repeat the answer in English;
  - answer with nonverbal cues (pointing to related objects, drawing, or acting out).

> **Teacher:** Where is Charlotte?
>
> **ELL Response:** (Student points to the web in the corner of the barn.)
>
> **Teacher:** Yes. Charlotte is sitting in her web. Let's all point to Charlotte.

☑ Repeat

- Give positive confirmation to the answers that each English Language Learner offers. If the response is correct, repeat what the student has said in a clear voice and at a slower pace. This validation will motivate other ELLs to participate.

> **Teacher:** How would you describe the faces of the bobcats?
>
> **ELL Response:** They look scared.
>
> **Teacher:** That's right, Silvia. They are scared. Everyone show me your scared face.

☑ Revise for Form

- Repeating an answer allows you to model the proper form for a response. You can model how to answer in full sentences and use academic language.
- When you repeat the answer, correct any grammar or pronunciation errors.

> **Teacher:** Who are the main characters in the story *Zathura*?
>
> **ELL Response:** Danny and Walter is.
>
> **Teacher:** Yes. Danny and Walter <u>are</u> the main characters. Remember to use the verb <u>are</u> when you are telling about more than one person. Let's repeat the sentence.
>
> **All:** Danny and Walter <u>are</u> the main characters.

☑ Clarify for Meaning

- Repeating an answer offers an opportunity to clarify the meaning of a response.

> **Teacher:** Where did the golden feather come from?
>
> **ELL Response:** The bird.
>
> **Teacher:** That's right. The golden feather came from the Firebird.

☑ Elaborate

- If students give a one-word answer or a nonverbal cue, elaborate on the answer to encourage multiple exchanges and model fluent speaking and grammatical patterns.

- Provide more examples or repeat the answer using proper academic language.

> **Teacher:** Why is the girls' mother standing with her hands on her hips?
>
> **ELL Response:** She is mad.
>
> **Teacher:** Can you tell me more? Why is she mad?
>
> **ELL Response:** Because the girls are late.
>
> **Teacher:** Ok. What do you think the girls will do?
>
> **ELL Response:** They will promise not to be late again.
>
> **Teacher:** Anyone else have an idea?

☑ Ask Questions about Key Details

- Prompt students to give a more comprehensive response by asking additional questions or guiding them to get to an answer.

> **Teacher:** Listen as I read the caption under the photograph. What information does the caption tell us?
>
> **ELL Response:** It tells about the butterfly.
>
> **Teacher:** What did you find out about the butterfly?
>
> **ELL Response:** It drinks nectar.
>
> **Teacher:** Yes. The butterfly drinks nectar from the flower.

Making the Most of Collaborative Conversations

Use all the speaking and listening opportunities in your classroom to observe students' oral language proficiency.

- Response to oral presentations
- Responding to text aloud
- Following directions
- Small group work
- Informal, social peer discussions
- One-on-one conferences

Scope & Sequence

	K	1	2	3	4	5	6
READING PROCESS							
Concepts About Print/Print Awareness							
Understand directionality (top to bottom; tracking print from left to right; return sweep, page by page)	✔						
Locate printed word on page	✔						
Develop print awareness (concept of letter, word, sentence)	✔						
Identify separate sounds in a spoken sentence	✔						
Understand that written words are represented in written language by a specific sequence of letters	✔						
Distinguish between letters, words, and sentences	✔						
Identify and distinguish paragraphs							
Match print to speech (one-to-one correspondence)							
Name uppercase and lowercase letters	✔						
Phonological Awareness							
Recognize and understand alliteration							
Segment sentences into correct number of words							
Identify, blend, segment syllables in words		✔					
Recognize and generate rhyming words	✔	✔					
Identify, blend, segment onset and rime	✔	✔					
Phonemic Awareness							
Count phonemes	✔	✔					
Isolate initial, medial, and final sounds	✔	✔					
Blend spoken phonemes to form words	✔	✔					
Segment spoken words into phonemes	✔	✔					
Distinguish between long- and short-vowel sounds	✔	✔					
Manipulate phonemes (addition, deletion, substitution)	✔	✔					
Phonics and Decoding /Word Recognition							
Understand the alphabetic principle	✔	✔					
Sound/letter correspondence	✔	✔	✔	✔			
Blend sounds into words, including VC, CVC, CVCe, CVVC words	✔	✔	✔	✔	✔	✔	✔
Blend common word families	✔	✔	✔	✔			
Initial consonant blends		✔	✔	✔	✔	✔	✔
Final consonant blends		✔	✔	✔	✔	✔	✔
Initial and medial short vowels	✔	✔	✔	✔	✔	✔	✔

KEY	✔ = Assessed Skill Tinted panels show skills, strategies, and other teaching opportunities.

	K	1	2	3	4	5	6
Decode one-syllable words in isolation and in context	✔	✔	✔	✔	✔	✔	✔
Decode multisyllabic words in isolation and in context using common syllabication patterns		✔	✔	✔	✔	✔	✔
Monitor accuracy of decoding							
Identify and read common high-frequency words, irregularly spelled words	✔	✔	✔	✔	✔	✔	✔
Identify and read compound words, contractions		✔	✔	✔	✔	✔	✔
Use knowledge of spelling patterns to identify syllables		✔	✔	✔	✔	✔	✔
Regular plurals		✔	✔	✔	✔	✔	✔
Long vowels (silent *e*, vowel teams)	✔	✔	✔	✔	✔	✔	✔
Vowel digraphs (variant vowels)		✔	✔	✔	✔	✔	✔
r-Controlled vowels		✔	✔	✔	✔	✔	✔
Hard/soft consonants		✔	✔	✔	✔	✔	✔
Initial consonant digraphs		✔	✔	✔	✔	✔	✔
Medial and final consonant digraphs		✔	✔	✔	✔	✔	✔
Vowel diphthongs		✔	✔	✔	✔	✔	✔
Identify and distinguish phonemes (initial, medial, final)	✔	✔	✔				
Silent letters		✔	✔	✔	✔	✔	✔
Schwa words				✔	✔	✔	✔
Inflectional endings		✔	✔	✔	✔	✔	✔
Triple-consonant clusters		✔	✔	✔	✔	✔	✔
Unfamiliar and complex word families				✔	✔	✔	✔
Structural Analysis/Word Analysis							
Common spelling patterns (word families)			✔	✔	✔	✔	✔
Common syllable patterns			✔	✔	✔	✔	✔
Inflectional endings			✔	✔	✔	✔	✔
Contractions			✔	✔	✔	✔	✔
Compound words			✔	✔	✔	✔	✔
Prefixes and suffixes			✔	✔	✔	✔	✔
Root or base words			✔	✔	✔	✔	✔
Comparatives and superlatives			✔	✔	✔	✔	✔
Greek and Latin roots			✔	✔	✔	✔	✔
Fluency							
Apply letter/sound knowledge to decode phonetically regular words accurately	✔	✔	✔	✔	✔	✔	✔
Recognize high-frequency and familiar words	✔	✔	✔	✔	✔	✔	✔
Read regularly on independent and instructional levels							
Read orally with fluency from familiar texts (choral, echo, partner)							
Use appropriate rate, expression, intonation, and phrasing		✔	✔	✔	✔	✔	✔
Read with automaticity (accurately and effortlessly)		✔	✔	✔	✔	✔	✔
Use punctuation cues in reading		✔	✔	✔	✔	✔	✔
Adjust reading rate to purpose, text difficulty, form, and style							

	K	1	2	3	4	5	6
Repeated readings							
Timed readings		✔	✔	✔	✔	✔	✔
Read with purpose and understanding		✔	✔	✔	✔	✔	✔
Read orally with accuracy		✔	✔	✔	✔	✔	✔
Use context to confirm or self-correct word recognition		✔	✔	✔	✔	✔	✔

READING LITERATURE

Comprehension Strategies and Skills

	K	1	2	3	4	5	6
Read literature from a broad range of genres, cultures, and periods			✔	✔	✔	✔	✔
Access complex text			✔	✔	✔	✔	✔
Build background							
Preview and predict							
Establish and adjust purpose for reading							
Evaluate citing evidence from the text							
Ask and answer questions			✔	✔	✔	✔	✔
Inferences and conclusions, citing evidence from the text			✔	✔	✔	✔	✔
Monitor/adjust comprehension including reread, reading rate, paraphrase							
Recount/Retell							
Summarize			✔	✔	✔	✔	✔
Story structure (beginning, middle, end)			✔	✔	✔	✔	✔
Make connections between and across texts				✔	✔	✔	✔
Point of view			✔	✔	✔	✔	✔
Author's purpose							
Cause and effect			✔	✔	✔	✔	✔
Compare and contrast (including character, setting, plot, topics)			✔	✔	✔	✔	✔
Classify and categorize			✔				
Literature vs informational text			✔				
Illustrations, using			✔	✔			
Theme, central message, moral, lesson			✔	✔	✔	✔	✔
Problem and solution (problem/resolution)			✔	✔	✔	✔	✔
Sequence of events			✔	✔	✔	✔	✔

Literary Elements

	K	1	2	3	4	5	6
Character			✔	✔	✔	✔	✔
Plot development/Events			✔	✔	✔	✔	✔
Setting			✔	✔	✔	✔	✔
Stanza				✔	✔	✔	✔
Alliteration						✔	✔
Assonance						✔	✔
Dialogue							
Foreshadowing						✔	✔

	K	1	2	3	4	5	6
Flashback						✔	✔
Descriptive and figurative language			✔	✔	✔	✔	✔
Imagery					✔	✔	✔
Meter					✔	✔	✔
Onomatopoeia							
Repetition			✔	✔	✔	✔	✔
Rhyme/rhyme schemes			✔	✔	✔	✔	✔
Rhythm			✔				
Sensory language							
Symbolism							
Write About Reading/Literary Response Discussions							
Reflect and respond to text citing text evidence			✔	✔	✔	✔	✔
Connect literary texts to other curriculum areas							
Identify cultural and historical elements of text							
Evaluate author's techniques, craft							
Analytical writing							
Interpret text ideas through writing, discussion, media, research							
Book report or review							
Locate, use, explain information from text features			✔	✔	✔	✔	✔
Organize information to show understanding of main idea through charts, mapping							
Cite text evidence			✔	✔	✔	✔	✔
Author's purpose/ Illustrator's purpose							

READING INFORMATIONAL TEXT

Comprehension Strategies and Skills

	K	1	2	3	4	5	6
Read informational text from a broad range of topics and cultures			✔	✔	✔	✔	✔
Access complex text			✔	✔	✔	✔	✔
Build background							
Preview and predict			✔				
Establish and adjust purpose for reading							
Evaluate citing evidence from the text							
Ask and answer questions			✔	✔	✔	✔	✔
Inferences and conclusions, citing evidence from the text			✔	✔	✔	✔	✔
Monitor and adjust comprehension including reread, adjust reading rate, paraphrase							
Recount/Retell							
Summarize			✔	✔	✔	✔	✔
Text structure			✔	✔	✔	✔	✔
Identify text features			✔	✔	✔	✔	✔
Make connections between and across texts			✔	✔	✔	✔	✔

	K	1	2	3	4	5	6
Author's point of view				✔	✔	✔	✔
Author's purpose			✔				
Cause and effect			✔	✔	✔	✔	✔
Compare and contrast			✔	✔	✔	✔	✔
Classify and categorize			✔				
Illustrations and photographs, using			✔	✔	✔	✔	✔
Instructions/directions (written and oral)			✔	✔	✔	✔	✔
Main idea and key details			✔	✔	✔	✔	✔
Persuasion, reasons and evidence to support points/persuasive techniques						✔	✔
Predictions, making/confirming							
Problem and solution			✔	✔	✔	✔	✔
Sequence, chronological order of events, time order, steps in a process			✔	✔	✔	✔	✔

Writing About Reading/Expository Critique Discussions

	K	1	2	3	4	5	6
Reflect and respond to text citing text evidence		✔	✔	✔	✔	✔	✔
Analytical writing							
Interpret text ideas through writing, discussion, media, research							
Locate, use, explain information from text features			✔	✔	✔	✔	✔
Organize information to show understanding of main idea through charts, mapping							
Cite text evidence			✔	✔	✔	✔	✔
Author's purpose/Illustrator's purpose							

Text Features

	K	1	2	3	4	5	6
Recognize and identify text and organizational features of nonfiction texts			✔	✔	✔	✔	✔
Captions and labels, headings, subheadings, endnotes, key words, bold print			✔	✔	✔	✔	✔
Graphics, including photographs, illustrations, maps, charts, diagrams, graphs, time lines			✔	✔	✔	✔	✔

WRITING

Writer's Craft

	K	1	2	3	4	5	6
Relevant supporting evidence			✔	✔	✔	✔	✔
Strong opening, strong conclusion			✔	✔	✔	✔	✔
Beginning, middle, end; sequence			✔	✔	✔	✔	✔
Precise words, strong words, vary words							
Transition words				✔	✔	✔	✔
Select focus and organization			✔	✔	✔	✔	✔
Points and counterpoints/Opposing claims and counterarguments							
Use reference materials (online and print dictionary, thesaurus, encyclopedia)							

Writing Applications

	K	1	2	3	4	5	6
Writing about text			✔	✔	✔	✔	✔
Analytical writing			✔	✔	✔	✔	✔

	K	1	2	3	4	5	6

Penmanship/Handwriting

	K	1	2	3	4	5	6
Write legibly in manuscript using correct formation, directionality, and spacing							

SPEAKING AND LISTENING

Speaking

	K	1	2	3	4	5	6
Participate in classroom activities and discussions							
Build on others' talk in conversation, adding new ideas							
Come to discussion prepared							
Paraphrase portions of text read alone or information presented							
Stay on topic when speaking							
Use language appropriate to situation, purpose, and audience							
Use verbal communication in effective ways and improve expression in conventional language							
Retell a story, presentation, or spoken message by summarizing							
Use complete, coherent sentences							
Deliver presentations (narrative, summaries, research, persuasive); add visuals							
Speak audibly (accuracy, expression, volume, pitch, rate, phrasing, modulation, enunciation)							

Listening

	K	1	2	3	4	5	6
Determine the purpose for listening							
Give oral directions							
Develop oral language and concepts							
Listen openly, responsively, attentively, and critically							
Listen to identify the points a speaker makes							
Listen responsively to oral presentations (determine main idea and key details)							
Ask and answer relevant questions (for clarification to follow-up on ideas)							
Identify reasons and evidence presented by speaker							
Recall and interpret speakers' verbal/nonverbal messages, purposes, perspectives							

LANGUAGE

Vocabulary Acquisition and Use

	K	1	2	3	4	5	6
Develop oral vocabulary and choose words for effect							
Use academic language			✔	✔	✔	✔	✔
Identify persons, places, things, actions			✔	✔			
Determine or clarify the meaning of unknown words			✔	✔	✔	✔	✔
Synonyms, antonyms, and opposites			✔	✔	✔	✔	✔
Use context clues such as word, sentence, paragraph, definition, example, restatement, description, comparison, cause and effect			✔	✔	✔	✔	✔
Use word identification strategies			✔	✔	✔	✔	✔
Unfamiliar words			✔	✔	✔	✔	✔

	K	1	2	3	4	5	6
Multiple-meaning words			✔	✔	✔	✔	✔
Compound words			✔	✔	✔	✔	✔
Words ending in -er and -est			✔	✔	✔	✔	✔
Root words (base words)			✔	✔	✔	✔	✔
Prefixes and suffixes			✔	✔	✔	✔	✔
Greek and Latin affixes and roots			✔	✔	✔	✔	✔
Inflectional endings			✔	✔	✔	✔	✔
Use print and online reference sources for word meaning (dictionary, glossaries)			✔	✔	✔	✔	✔
Homographs				✔	✔	✔	✔
Homophones			✔	✔	✔	✔	✔
Contractions			✔	✔	✔	✔	✔
Figurative language such as metaphors, similes, personification			✔	✔	✔	✔	✔
Idioms, adages, proverbs, literal and nonliteral language			✔	✔	✔	✔	✔
Listen to, read, discuss familiar and unfamiliar challenging text							
Identify real-life connections between words and their use							
Use acquired words and phrases to convey precise ideas							
Use vocabulary to express spatial and temporal relationships							
Identify shades of meaning in related words							
Morphology				✔	✔	✔	✔
Conventions of Standard English/Grammar, Mechanics, and Usage							
Sentence concepts: statements, questions, exclamations, commands							
Pronouns							
Contractions							
Conjunctions							
Commas							
Question words							
Quotation marks							
Prepositions							
Spelling							
Write irregular, high-frequency words	✔	✔	✔	✔	✔	✔	✔
ABC order	✔	✔					
Write letters	✔	✔					
Words with short vowels	✔	✔	✔	✔	✔	✔	✔
Words with long vowels	✔	✔	✔	✔	✔	✔	✔
Words with digraphs, blends, consonant clusters, double consonants			✔	✔	✔	✔	✔
Words with vowel digraphs and ambiguous vowels			✔	✔	✔	✔	✔
Words with diphthongs			✔	✔	✔	✔	✔
Words with r-controlled vowels			✔	✔	✔	✔	✔
Use conventional spelling		✔	✔	✔	✔	✔	✔

	K	1	2	3	4	5	6
Words with silent letters			✔	✔	✔	✔	✔
Words with hard and soft letters			✔	✔	✔	✔	✔
Inflectional endings including plural, past tense, drop final e and double consonant when adding -ed and -ing, changing y to i			✔	✔	✔	✔	✔
Compound words			✔	✔	✔	✔	
Homonyms/homophones			✔	✔	✔	✔	✔
Prefixes and suffixes			✔	✔	✔	✔	✔
Root and base words				✔	✔	✔	✔
Syllables: patterns, rules, closed, open				✔	✔	✔	✔
Words with Greek and Latin roots						✔	✔
Words with spelling patterns, word families		✔	✔	✔	✔	✔	✔

RESEARCH AND INQUIRY

Study Skills

	K	1	2	3	4	5	6
Directions: read, write, give, follow (includes technical directions)			✔	✔	✔	✔	✔
Evaluate directions for sequence and completeness							
Use parts of a book to locate information							
Interpret information from graphic aids			✔	✔	✔	✔	✔
Use graphic organizers to organize information and comprehend text			✔	✔	✔	✔	✔

Research Process

	K	1	2	3	4	5	6
Generate and revise topics and questions for research							
Narrow focus of research, set research goals							
Find and locate information using print and digital resources			✔	✔	✔	✔	✔
Record information systematically (note-taking, outlining, using technology)							
Evaluate reliability, credibility, usefulness of sources and information							
Use primary sources to obtain information							
Organize, synthesize, evaluate, and draw conclusions from information							
Participate in and present shared research							

Technology

	K	1	2	3	4	5	6
Use computer, Internet, and other technology resources to access information							

College and Career Readiness Anchor Standards for READING

The K–5 standards on the following pages define what students should understand and be able to do by the end of each grade. They correspond to the College and Career Readiness (CCR) anchor standards below by number. The CCR and grade-specific standards are necessary complements—the former providing broad standards, the latter providing additional specificity—that together define the skills and understandings that all students must demonstrate.

Key Ideas and Details

1. Read closely to determine what the text says explicitly and to make logical inferences from it; cite specific textual evidence when writing or speaking to support conclusions drawn from the text.

2. Determine central ideas or themes of a text and analyze their development; summarize the key supporting details and ideas.

3. Analyze how and why individuals, events, and ideas develop and interact over the course of a text.

Craft and Structure

4. Interpret words and phrases as they are used in a text, including determining technical, connotative, and figurative meanings, and analyze how specific word choices shape meaning or tone.

5. Analyze the structure of texts, including how specific sentences, paragraphs, and larger portions of the text (e.g., a section, chapter, scene, or stanza) relate to each other and the whole.

6. Assess how point of view or purpose shapes the content and style of a text.

Integration of Knowledge and Ideas

7. Integrate and evaluate content presented in diverse media and formats, including visually and quantitatively, as well as in words. *

8. Delineate and evaluate the argument and specific claims in a text, including the validity of the reasoning as well as the relevance and sufficiency of the evidence.

9. Analyze how two or more texts address similar themes or topics in order to build knowledge or to compare the approaches the authors take.

Range of Reading and Level of Text Complexity

10. Read and comprehend complex literary and informational texts independently and proficiently.

English Language Arts

Grade 5

Each standard is coded in the following manner:

Strand	Grade Level	Standard
RL	5	1

Reading Standards for Literature

Key Ideas and Details

RL.5.1	Quote accurately from a text when explaining what the text says explicitly and when drawing inferences from the text.
RL.5.2	Determine a theme of a story, drama, or poem from details in the text, including how characters in a story or drama respond to challenges or how the speaker in a poem reflects upon a topic; summarize the text.
RL.5.3	Compare and contrast two or more characters, settings, or events in a story or drama, drawing on specific details in the text (e.g., how characters interact).

Craft and Structure

RL.5.4	Determine the meaning of words and phrases as they are used in a text, including figurative language such as metaphors and similes.
RL.5.5	Explain how a series of chapters, scenes, or stanzas fits together to provide the overall structure of a particular story, drama, or poem.
RL.5.6	Describe how a narrator's or speaker's point of view influences how events are described.

Integration of Knowledge and Ideas

RL.5.7	Analyze how visual and multimedia elements contribute to the meaning, tone, or beauty of a text (e.g., graphic novel, multimedia presentation of fiction, folktale, myth, poem).
RL.5.8	(Not applicable to Literature)
RL.5.9	Compare and contrast stories in the same genre (e.g., mysteries and adventure stories) on their approaches to similar themes and topics.

Range of Reading and Level of Text Complexity

RL.5.10	By the end of the year, read and comprehend literature, including stories, dramas, and poetry, at the high end of the grades 4–5 text complexity band independently and proficiently.

Reading Standards for Informational Text

Key Ideas and Details

RI.5.1	Quote accurately from a text when explaining what the text says explicitly and when drawing inferences from the text.
RI.5.2	Determine two or more main ideas of a text and explain how they are supported by key details; summarize the text.
RI.5.3	Explain the relationships or interactions between two or more individuals, events, ideas, or concepts in a historical, scientific, or technical text based on specific information in the text.

Craft and Structure

RI.5.4	Determine the meaning of general academic and domain-specific words and phrases in a text relevant to a *grade 5 topic or subject area.*
RI.5.5	Compare and contrast the overall structure (e.g., chronology, comparison, cause/effect, problem/solution) of events, ideas, concepts, or information in two or more texts.
RI.5.6	Analyze multiple accounts of the same event or topic, noting important similarities and differences in the point of view they represent.

Integration of Knowledge and Ideas

RI.5.7	Draw on information from multiple print or digital sources, demonstrating the ability to locate an answer to a question quickly or to solve a problem efficiently.
RI.5.8	Explain how an author uses reasons and evidence to support particular points in a text, identifying which reasons and evidence support which point(s).
RI.5.9	Integrate information from several texts on the same topic in order to write or speak about the subject knowledgeably.

Range of Reading and Level of Text Complexity

RI.5.10	By the end of the year, read and comprehend informational texts, including history/social studies, science, and technical texts, at the high end of the grades 4–5 text complexity band independently and proficiently.

Reading Standards: Foundational Skills

There are no standards for Print Concepts (1) or Phonological Awareness (2) in Foundational Skills for Grade 5.

Phonics and Word Recognition

RF.5.3	Know and apply grade-level phonics and word analysis skills in decoding words.
RF.5.3a	Use combined knowledge of all letter-sound correspondences, syllabication patterns, and morphology (e.g., roots and affixes) to read accurately unfamiliar multisyllabic words in context and out of context.

Fluency

RF.5.4	Read with sufficient accuracy and fluency to support comprehension.
RF.5.4a	Read grade-level text with purpose and understanding.
RF.5.4b	Read grade-level prose and poetry orally with accuracy, appropriate rate, and expression on successive readings.
RF.5.4c	Use context to confirm or self-correct word recognition and understanding, rereading as necessary.

College and Career Readiness Anchor Standards for WRITING

The K–5 standards on the following pages define what students should understand and be able to do by the end of each grade. They correspond to the College and Career Readiness (CCR) anchor standards below by number. The CCR and grade-specific standards are necessary complements—the former providing broad standards, the latter providing additional specificity—that together define the skills and understandings that all students must demonstrate.

Text Types and Purposes

1. Write arguments to support claims in an analysis of substantive topics or texts, using valid reasoning and relevant and sufficient evidence.

2. Write informative/explanatory texts to examine and convey complex ideas and information clearly and accurately through the effective selection, organization, and analysis of content.

3. Write narratives to develop real or imagined experiences or events using effective technique, well-chosen details, and well-structured event sequences.

Production and Distribution of Writing

4. Produce clear and coherent writing in which the development, organization, and style are appropriate to task, purpose, and audience.

5. Develop and strengthen writing as needed by planning, revising, editing, rewriting, or trying a new approach.

6. Use technology, including the Internet, to produce and publish writing and to interact and collaborate with others.

Research to Build and Present Knowledge

7. Conduct short as well as more sustained research projects based on focused questions, demonstrating understanding of the subject under investigation.

8. Gather relevant information from multiple print and digital sources, assess the credibility and accuracy of each source, and integrate the information while avoiding plagiarism.

9. Draw evidence from literary or informational texts to support analysis, reflection, and research.

Range of Writing

10. Write routinely over extended time frames (time for research, reflection, and revision) and shorter time frames (a single sitting or a day or two) for a range of tasks, purposes, and audiences.

English Language Arts

Grade 5

Each standard is coded in the following manner:

Strand	Grade Level	Standard
W	5	1

Writing Standards

Text Types and Purposes

W.5.1	Write opinion pieces on topics or texts, supporting a point of view with reasons and information.
W.5.1a	Introduce a topic or text clearly, state an opinion, and create an organizational structure in which ideas are logically grouped to support the writer's purpose.
W.5.1b	Provide logically ordered reasons that are supported by facts and details.
W.5.1c	Link opinion and reasons using words, phrases, and clauses (e.g., *consequently*, *specifically*).
W.5.1d	Provide a concluding statement or section related to the opinion presented.
W.5.2	Write informative/explanatory texts to examine a topic and convey ideas and information clearly.
W.5.2a	Introduce a topic clearly, provide a general observation and focus, and group related information logically; include formatting (e.g., headings), illustrations, and multimedia when useful to aiding comprehension.
W.5.2b	Develop the topic with facts, definitions, concrete details, quotations, or other information and examples related to the topic.
W.5.2c	Link ideas within and across categories of information using words, phrases, and clauses (e.g., *in contrast*, *especially*).
W.5.2d	Use precise language and domain-specific vocabulary to inform about or explain the topic.
W.5.2e	Provide a concluding statement or section related to the information or explanation presented.
W.5.3	Write narratives to develop real or imagined experiences or events using effective technique, descriptive details, and clear event sequences.
W.5.3a	Orient the reader by establishing a situation and introducing a narrator and/or characters; organize an event sequence that unfolds naturally.

W.5.3b	Use narrative techniques, such as dialogue, description, and pacing, to develop experiences and events or show the responses of characters to situations.
W.5.3c	Use a variety of transitional words, phrases, and clauses to manage the sequence of events.
W.5.3d	Use concrete words and phrases and sensory details to convey experiences and events precisely.
W.5.3e	Provide a conclusion that follows from the narrated experiences or events.

Production and Distribution of Writing

W.5.4	Produce clear and coherent writing in which the development and organization are appropriate to task, purpose, and audience.
W.5.5	With guidance and support from peers and adults, develop and strengthen writing as needed by planning, revising, editing, rewriting, or trying a new approach. (Editing for conventions should demonstrate command of Language standards 1–3 up to and including grade 5.)
W.5.6	With some guidance and support from adults, use technology, including the Internet, to produce and publish writing as well as to interact and collaborate with others; demonstrate sufficient command of keyboarding skills to type a minimum of two pages in a single sitting.

Research to Build and Present Knowledge

W.5.7	Conduct short research projects that use several sources to build knowledge through investigation of different aspects of a topic.
W.5.8	Recall relevant information from experiences or gather relevant information from print and digital sources; summarize or paraphrase information in notes and finished work, and provide a list of sources.
W.5.9	Draw evidence from literary or informational texts to support analysis, reflection, and research.
W.5.9a	Apply *grade 5 Reading standards* to literature (e.g., "Compare and contrast two or more characters, settings, or events in a story or a drama, drawing on specific details in the text [e.g., how characters interact]").
W.5.9b	Apply *grade 5 Reading standards* to informational texts (e.g., "Explain how an author uses reasons and evidence to support particular points in a text, identifying which reasons and evidence support which point[s]).

Range of Writing

W.5.10	Write routinely over extended time frames (time for research, reflection, and revision) and shorter time frames (a single sitting or a day or two) for a range of discipline-specific tasks, purposes, and audiences.

College and Career Readiness Anchor Standards for
SPEAKING AND LISTENING

The K–5 standards on the following pages define what students should understand and be able to do by the end of each grade. They correspond to the College and Career Readiness (CCR) anchor standards below by number. The CCR and grade-specific standards are necessary complements—the former providing broad standards, the latter providing additional specificity—that together define the skills and understandings that all students must demonstrate.

Comprehension and Collaboration

1. Prepare for and participate effectively in a range of conversations and collaborations with diverse partners, building on others' ideas and expressing their own clearly and persuasively.

2. Integrate and evaluate information presented in diverse media and formats, including visually, quantitatively, and orally.

3. Evaluate a speaker's point of view, reasoning, and use of evidence and rhetoric.

Presentation of Knowledge and Ideas

4. Present information, findings, and supporting evidence such that listeners can follow the line of reasoning and the organization, development, and style are appropriate to task, purpose, and audience.

5. Make strategic use of digital media and visual displays of data to express information and enhance understanding of presentations.

6. Adapt speech to a variety of contexts and communicative tasks, demonstrating command of formal English when indicated or appropriate.

 CCSS Common Core State Standards

English Language Arts

Grade 5

Each standard is coded in the following manner:

Strand	Grade Level	Standard
SL	5	1

Speaking and Listening Standards

Comprehension and Collaboration

SL.5.1	Engage effectively in a range of collaborative discussions (one-on-one, in groups, and teacher-led) with diverse partners on *grade 5 topics and texts*, building on others' ideas and expressing their own clearly.
SL.5.1a	Come to discussions prepared, having read or studied required material; explicitly draw on that preparation and other information known about the topic to explore ideas under discussion.
SL.5.1b	Follow agreed-upon rules for discussions and carry out assigned roles.
SL.5.1c	Pose and respond to specific questions by making comments that contribute to the discussion and elaborate on the remarks of others.
SL.5.1d	Review the key ideas expressed and draw conclusions in light of information and knowledge gained from the discussions.
SL.5.2	Summarize a written text read aloud or information presented in diverse media and formats, including visually, quantitatively, and orally.
SL.5.3	Summarize the points a speaker makes and explain how each claim is supported by reasons and evidence.

Presentation of Knowledge and Ideas

SL.5.4	Report on a topic or text or present an opinion, sequencing ideas logically and using appropriate facts and relevant, descriptive details to support main ideas or themes; speak clearly at an understandable pace.
SL.5.5	Include multimedia components (e.g., graphics, sound) and visual displays in presentations when appropriate to enhance the development of main ideas or themes.
SL.5.6	Adapt speech to a variety of contexts and tasks, using formal English when appropriate to task and situation. (See grade 5 Language standards 1 and 3 for specific expectations.)

College and Career Readiness Anchor Standards for
LANGUAGE

The K–5 standards on the following pages define what students should understand and be able to do by the end of each grade. They correspond to the College and Career Readiness (CCR) anchor standards below by number. The CCR and grade-specific standards are necessary complements—the former providing broad standards, the latter providing additional specificity—that together define the skills and understandings that all students must demonstrate.

Conventions of Standard English

1. Demonstrate command of the conventions of standard English grammar and usage when writing or speaking.

2. Demonstrate command of the conventions of standard English capitalization, punctuation, and spelling when writing.

Knowledge of Language

3. Apply knowledge of language to understand how language functions in different contexts, to make effective choices for meaning or style, and to comprehend more fully when reading or listening.

Vocabulary Acquisition and Use

4. Determine or clarify the meaning of unknown and multiple-meaning words and phrases by using context clues, analyzing meaningful word parts, and consulting general and specialized reference materials, as appropriate.

5. Demonstrate understanding of figurative language, word relationships, and nuances in word meanings.

6. Acquire and use accurately a range of general academic and domain-specific words and phrases sufficient for reading, writing, speaking, and listening at the college and career readiness level; demonstrate independence in gathering vocabulary knowledge when encountering an unknown term important to comprehension or expression.

English Language Arts

Grade 5

Each standard is coded in the following manner:

Strand	Grade Level	Standard
L	5	1

Language Standards

Conventions of Standard English

L.5.1	Demonstrate command of the conventions of standard English grammar and usage when writing or speaking.
L.5.1a	Explain the function of conjunctions, prepositions, and interjections in general and their function in particular sentences.
L.5.1b	Form and use the perfect (e.g., *I had walked; I have walked; I will have walked*) verb tenses.
L.5.1c	Use verb tense to convey various times, sequences, states, and conditions.
L.5.1d	Recognize and correct inappropriate shifts in verb tense.
L.5.1e	Use correlative conjunctions (e.g., *either/or, neither/nor*).
L.5.2	Demonstrate command of the conventions of standard English capitalization, punctuation, and spelling when writing.
L.5.2a	Use punctuation to separate items in a series.
L.5.2b	Use a comma to separate an introductory element from the rest of the sentence.
L.5.2c	Use a comma to set off the words *yes* and *no* (e.g., *Yes, thank you*), to set off a tag question from the rest of the sentence (e.g., *It's true, isn't it?*), and to indicate direct addresses (e.g., *Is that you, Steve?*).
L.5.2d	Use underlining, quotation marks, or italics to indicate titles of works.
L.5.2e	Spell grade-appropriate words correctly, consulting references as needed.

Knowledge of Language

L.5.3	Use knowledge of language and its conventions when writing, speaking, reading, or listening.
L.5.3a	Expand, combine, and reduce sentences for meaning, reader/listener interest, and style.
L.5.3b	Compare and contrast the varieties of English (e.g., dialects, registers) used in stories, dramas, or poems.

Vocabulary Acquisition and Use	
L.5.4	Determine or clarify the meaning of unknown and multiple-meaning words and phrases based on *grade 5 reading and content,* choosing flexibly from a range of strategies.
L.5.4a	Use context (e.g., cause/effect relationships and comparisons in text) as a clue to the meaning of a word or phrase.
L.5.4b	Use common, grade-appropriate Greek and Latin affixes and roots as clues to the meaning of a word (e.g., *photograph, photosynthesis*).
L.5.4c	Consult reference materials (e.g., dictionaries, glossaries, thesauruses), both print and digital, to find the pronunciation and determine or clarify the precise meaning of key words and phrases.
L.5.5	Demonstrate understanding of figurative language, word relationships, and nuances in word meanings.
L.5.5a	Interpret figurative language, including similes and metaphors, in context.
L.5.5b	Recognize and explain the meaning of common idioms, adages, and proverbs.
L.5.5c	Use the relationship between particular words (e.g., synonyms, antonyms, homographs) to better understand each of the words.
L.5.6	Acquire and use accurately grade-appropriate general academic and domain-specific words and phrases, including those that signal contrast, addition, and other logical relationships (e.g., *however, although, nevertheless, similarly, moreover, in addition*).

Language Progressive Skills

Below are the grades 3 and 4 Language standards indicated by CCSS to be particularly likely to require continued attention in grade 5 as they are applied to increasingly sophisticated writing and speaking.

L.3.1f	Ensure subject-verb and pronoun-antecedent agreement.
L.3.3a	Choose words and phrases for effect.
L.4.1f	Produce complete sentences, recognizing and correcting inappropriate fragments and run-ons.
L.4.1g	Correctly use frequently confused words (e.g., *to, too, two; there, their*).
L.4.3a	Choose words and phrases to convey ideas precisely.
L.4.3b	Choose punctuation for effect.

Index

A

Academic language, *See also,* Access Complex Text: vocabulary; Vocabulary.

Access complex text. 380–381

connection of ideas, **1:** 8–9, 30–31, 40–41, 50–51, **2:** 68–69, 78–79, 80–81, 82–83, 88–89, 90–91, 104–105, 110–111, 114–115, **3:** 130–131, 132–133, 148–149, 160–161, **4:** 188–189, 198–199, 208–209, 210–211, 212–213, 222–223, 224–225, 230–231, **5:** 250–251, 270–271, 272–273, 292–293, **6:** 312–313, 318–319, 330–331, 332–333, 340–341, 350–351

genre, **1:** 10–11, 12–13, 18–19, 20–21, 22–23, 31–32, 42–43, 52–53, **2:** 68–69, 70–71, 72–73, 80–81, 82–83, 92–93, 100–101, 102–103, 104–105, 110–111, **3:** 130–131, 138–139, 148–149, 170–171, 172–173, 150–151, 152–153, 162–163, **4:** 188–189, 198–199, 200–201, 220–221, 222–223, 224–225, 230–231, **5:** 258–259, 270–271, 272–273, 280–281, 282–283, 284–285, **6:** 310–311, 328–329, 340–341, 342–343, 344–345, 350–351

organization, **1:** 18–19, **2:** 72–73, 100–101, 104–105, **3:** 130–131, 148–149, 162–163, 170–171, 174–175, **4:** 198–199, 200–201, 202–203, 210–211, 220–221, **5:** 248–249, 292–293, **6:** 308–309, 320–321

prior knowledge, **3:** 160–161, **4:** 190–191, **5:** 260–261, **6:** 308–309, 310–311

purpose, **2:** 88–89, **4:** 198–199, **5:** 268–269, 290–291

sentence structure, **1:** 18–19, 28–29, 42–43, **2:** 72–73, 78–79, 80–81, 82–83, 102–103, 104–105, **3:** 128–129, 132–133, 170–171, **4:** 190–191, 198–199, 200–201, 208–209, 234–234, **5:** 272–273, **6:** 308–309, 316–317, 322–323, 354–355

vocabulary **1:** 8–9, 10–11, 12–13, 18–19, 20–21, 22–23, 28–29, 30–31, 32–33, 40–41, 42–43, 44–45, 50–51, 52–53, 54–55, **2:** 68–69, 70–71, 72–73, 78–79, 80–81, 82–83, 88–89, 90–91, 92–93, 100–101, 102–103, 104–105, **3:** 128–129, 130–131, 132–133, 138–139, 140–141, 142–143, 148–149, 150–151, 152–153, 160–161, 162–163, 164–165, 170–171, 172–173, 174–175, **4:** 188–189, 190–191, 192–193, 198–199, 200–201, 202–203, 208–209, 210–211, 212–213, 220–221, 222–223, 224–225, **5:** 248–249, 250–251, 252–253, 258–259, 260–261, 262–263, 268–269, 270–271, 272–273, 280–281, 282–283, 284–285, 290–291, 292–293, 294–295, **6:** 308–309, 310–311, 312–313, 318–319, 320–321, 322–323, 328–329, 330–331, 332–333, 340–341, 342–343, 344–345, 352–353, 354–355. *See also* **Vocabulary.**

Alliteration. *See* Literary Elements.

Apprentice Leveled Reader, 1: 10–11, 12–13, 20–21, 22–23, 30–31, 32–33, 42–43, 44–45, 52–53, 54–55, **2:** 70–71, 72–73, 80–81, 82–83, 90–91, 92–93, 102–103, 104–105, **3:** 130–131, 132–133, 140–141, 142–143, 150–151, 152–153, 162–163, 164–165, 172–173, 174–175, **4:** 190–191, 192–193, 200–201, 202–203, 210–211, 212–213, 222–223, 224–225, **5:** 250–251, 252–253, 260–261, 262–263, 270–271, 272–273, 282–283, 284–285, 292–293, 294–295, **6:** 310–311, 312–313, 320–321, 322–323, 330–331, 332–333, 342–343, 344–345, 352–353, 354–355

Assessment

end-of-week, **1:** 15, 25, 35, 47, 57, **2:** 75, 85, 95, 107, 117, **3:** 135, 145, 155, 167, 177, **4:** 195, 205, 215, 227, 237, **5:** 255, 265, 275, 287, 297, **6:** 315, 325, 335, 347, 357

exit, **1:** 58–59, **2:** 118–119, **3:** 178–179, **4:** 238–239, **5:** 298–299, **6:** 358–359

fluency, **1:** 36–37, 58–59, **2:** 96–97, 118–119, **3:** 156–157, 178–179, **4:** 216–217, 238–239, **5:** 276–277, 298–299, **6:** 336–337, 358–359

progress monitoring, **1:** 36–37, 58–59, **2:** 96–97, 118–119, **3:** 156–157, 178–179, **4:** 216–217, 238–239, **5:** 276–277, 298–299, **6:** 336–337, 358–359

Quick Check and observational assessments. *See individual skills listings for* **Comprehension; Vocabulary; Writing. 1:** 7, 9, 11, 13, 17, 19, 21, 23, 27, 29, 31, 33, 35, 39, 41, 43, 45, 49, 51, 53, 55, **2:** 67, 69, 71, 73, 77, 79, 81, 83, 87, 89, 91, 93, 99, 101, 103, 105, 109, 111, 113, 115, **3:** 127, 129, 131, 133, 137, 139, 141, 143, 147, 149, 151, 153, 159, 161, 163, 165, 169, 171, 173, 175, 177, **4:** 187, 189, 191, 193, 197, 199, 201, 203, 207, 209, 211, 213, 219, 221, 223, 225, 229, 231, 233, 235, **5:** 247, 249, 251, 253, 257, 259, 261, 263, 267, 269, 271, 273, 279, 281, 283, 285, 289, 291, 293, 295, **6:** 307, 309, 311, 313, 317, 319, 321, 323, 327, 329, 331, 333, 339, 341, 343, 345, 349, 351, 353, 355

scoring rubrics, **1:** 15, 25, 35, 47, 57, 58–59, **2:** 75, 85, 95, 107, 117, 118–119, **3:** 135, 145, 155, 167, 177, 178–179, **4:** 195, 205, 215, 227, 237, 238–239, **5:** 255, 265, 275, 287, 297, 298–299, **6:** 315, 325, 335, 347, 357, 358–359

unit, **1:** 58–59, **2:** 118–119, **3:** 178–179, **4:** 238–239, **5:** 298–299, **6:** 358–359

Assonance. *See* Literary Elements.

Author's point of view. *See* Comprehension: author's point of view; Graphic Organizer.

B

Big Idea, Essential Question, **1:** 4–5, **2:** 64–65, **3:** 124–125, **4:** 184–185, **5:** 244–245, **6:** 304–305

Biographies. *See* Genre.

Build background, **1:** 4–5, 6, 10, 16, 20, 26, 30, 38, 42, 48, 52, **2:** 64–65, 66, 70, 76, 80, 86, 90, 98, 102, 108, 112, **3:** 124–125, 126, 130, 136, 140, 146, 150, 158, 162, 168, 172, **4:** 184–185, 186, 190, 196, 200, 206, 210, 218, 222, 228, 232, **5:** 244–245, 246, 250, 256, 260, 266, 270, 278, 282, 288, 292, **6:** 304–305, 306, 310, 316, 320, 326, 330, 338, 342, 348, 352

C

Captions, 3: 148–149, 150–151, 162–163, 170–171, 172–173, **4:** 212–213, **5:** 250–251, 284–285, **6:** 340–341, 342–343, 344–345

E

D

F

Key **3** = Unit 3

Free verse. *See* Poetry.

Folktale. *See* Genre.

G

Genre. *See* Access Complex Text.

    biography, 1: 40–41, **2:** 88–89, **4:** 208–209, **6:** 340–341

    drama, 4: 198–199

    expository text, 2: 68–69, **3:** 148–149, 160–161, **4:** 224–225, **5:** 268–269, 280–281, **6:** 328–329

    fairy tale, 2: 78–79

    fantasy, 3: 138–139

    folktale, 2: 92–93

    historical fiction, 5: 268–269, **6:** 308–309

    informational text, 2: 68–69, **3:** 148–149, 160–161, **4:** 224–225, **5:** 268–269, 280–281, **6:** 328–329

    magazine article, 1: 50–51, **3:** 170–171, **5:** 290–291

    narrative nonfiction, 1: 28–29

    poetry, 2: 110–111, **4:** 230–231, **6:** 350–351

    realistic fiction, 1: 8–9, 18–19, **3:** 128–129, **5:** 258–259, **6:** 318–319

    tall tale: 4: 188–189

Graphic aids. *See* Graphic Organizers.

Graphic Organizers

charts

    Author's Point of View, 1: 52–53, 54–55 **3:** 172–173, 174–175, **4:** 210–211, 212–213, 220–221, 222–223, **5:** 292–293, 294–295

    Cause and Effect, 1: 30–31, 32–33, **5:** 282–283, 284–285, **6:** 330–331, 332–333

    Compare and Contrast, 2: 80–81, 82–83, **5:** 250–251, 252–253, 260–261, 262–263, 270–271, 272–273

    Main Ideas/Key Details, 3: 150–151, 152–153, 162–163, 164–165

    Point of View, 4: 190–191, 192–193, 200–201, 202–203, **6:** 352–353, 354–355

    Problem and Solution, 1: 20–21, 22–23, **2:** 70–71, 72–73, **6:** 342–343, 344–345

    Sequence, 1: 10–11, 12–13, 42–43, 44–45, **2:** 90–91, 92–93

    Theme, 2: 102–103, 104–105, 112–113, 114–115, **3:** 130–131, 132–133, 140–141, 142–143, **4:** 230–231, 232–233, **6:** 310–311, 312–313

Graphs, 1: 42–43, 52–53

H

Historical fiction. *See* Genre.

I

Illustrations/photographs, 1: 10–11, 12–13, 20–21, 22–23, **2:** 70–71, 72–73, 80–81, **3:** 162–163, **4:** 212–213, **5:** 250–251, 284–285, **6:** 342–343, 344–345

Imagery, 4: 104–105

Independent reading. *See* Reading independently.

Informational text. *See* Genre: expository text/informational text.

K

Key details. *See* Comprehension: main idea and key details.

L

Legend, 2: 114–115 **3:** 150–151, 152–153

Lesson plans, *See* Unit Planners.

Leveled Reader Lessons, *See* Apprentice Leveled Reader.

Level Up, 1: 15, 25, 35, 47, 57, 60–61, **2:** 75, 85, 95, 107, 117 120–121, **3:** 135, 145, 155, 167, 177, 180–181, **4:** 195, 205, 215, 227, 237, 240–241, **5:** 255, 265, 275, 287, 297, 300–301, **6:** 315, 325, 335, 347, 357, 360–361

Listening. *See* Oral Language: Talk About it.

Literary Elements. *See* Comprehension.

Literary elements

    alliteration, 4: 230–231

    assonance, 6: 350–351

    consonance, 6: 350–351

    metaphor, 4: 230–231

    meter, 4: 230–231

    personification, 6: 350–351

    rhyme, **2:** 110–111

    repetition, **2:** 110–111

    stanza, **2:** 230–231

Literary response. *See also* Text connections.

M

Magazine article. *See* Genre.

Main ideas and key details. *See* Comprehension: main idea and key details; Graphic Organizer.

Maps

    See also Text features.

    1: 30–31, **3:** 172–173, **4:** 220–221, 222–223, **5:** 272–273

Metaphor. *See* Literary Elements.

Meter. *See* Literary Elements.

Modeling. *See* Comprehension.

N

Narrative. *See* Poetry.

Narrative Nonfiction. *See* Genre.

Narrator, 4: 198–199 *See also* Comprehension: point of view.

Nonfiction. *See* Genre: informational text.

Note-taking, 1: 7, 9, 17, 19, 27, 29, 39, 41, 49, 51, **2:** 67, 69, 77, 79, 87, 89, 99, 101, 109, 111, **3:** 127, 129, 137, 139, 147, 149, 159, 161, 169, 171, **4:** 187, 189, 197, 199, 207, 209, 219, 221, 229, 231, **5:** 247, 249, 255, 257, 267, 269, 279, 281, 289, 291, **6:** 307, 309, 317, 319, 327, 329, 339, 341, 349, 351

O

Organization. *See* Access Complex Text.

Oral language,

    Talk About It, 1: 6, 16, 26, 38, 48, **2:** 6, 76, 86, 98, 108, **3:** 126, 136, 146, 158, 168, **4:** 186, 196, 206, 218, 227, **5:** 246, 256, 266, 278, 288, **6:** 306, 316, 326, 338, 348

W